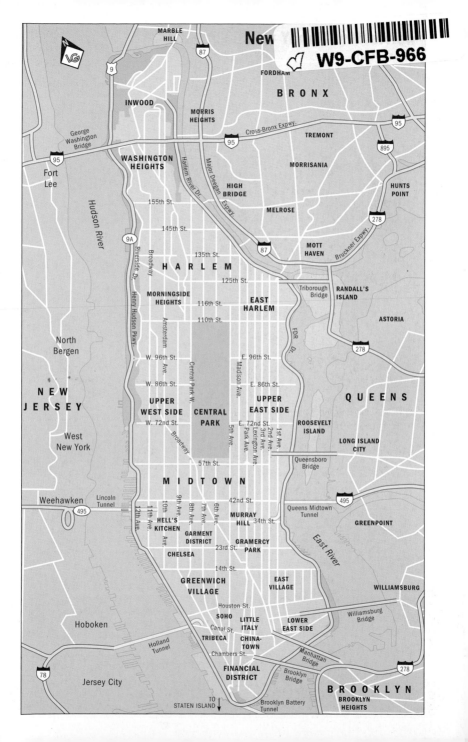

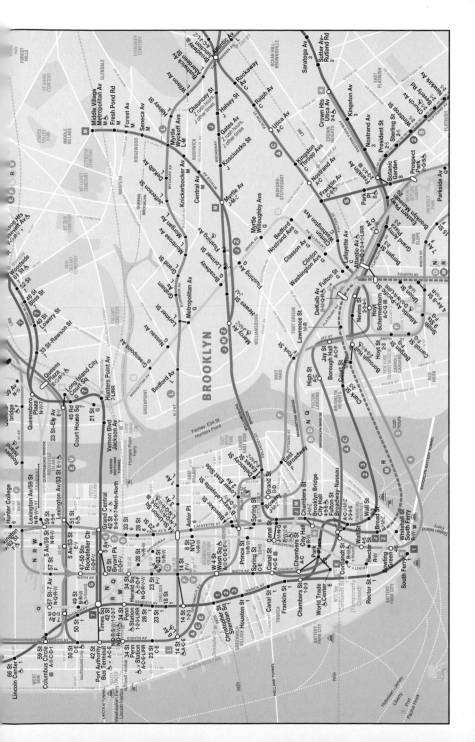

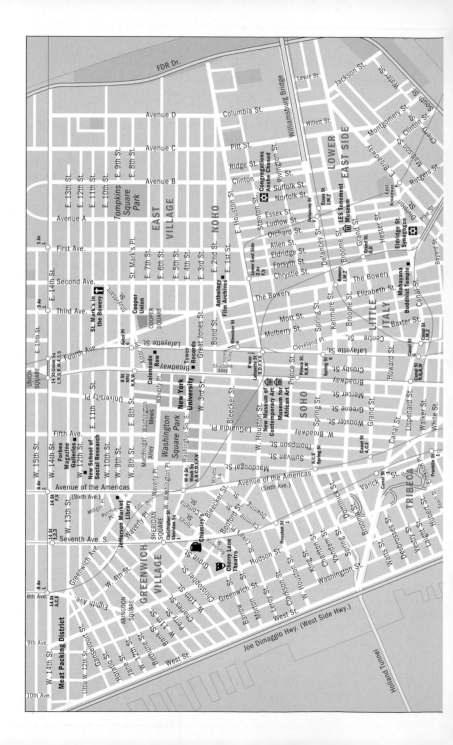

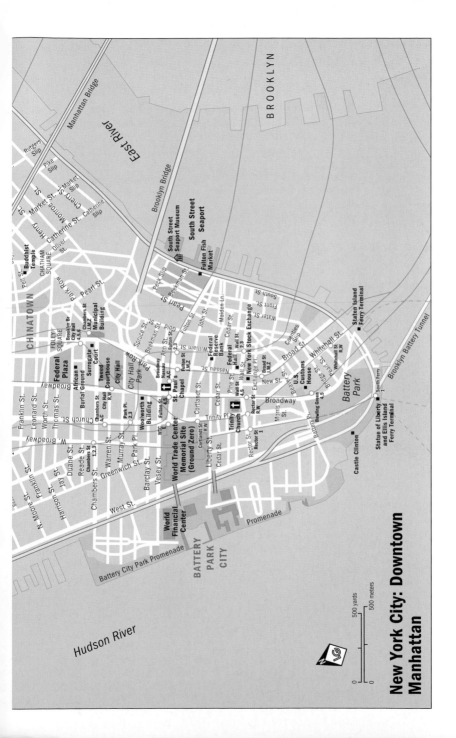

New York City: Downtown Manhattan

New York City: Midtown Manhattan

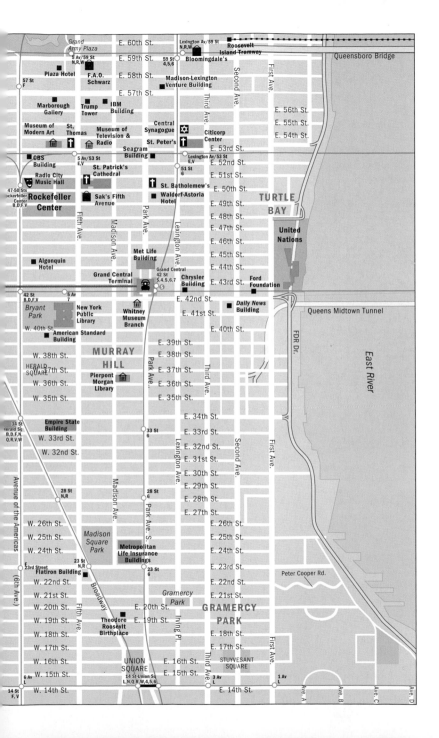

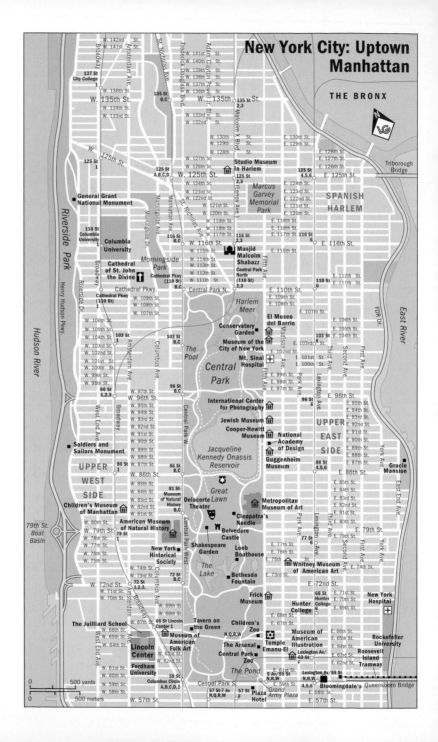

LET'S GO

■ PAGES PACKED WITH ESSENTIAL INFORMATION

"Value-packed, unbeatable, accurate, and comprehensive."

—The Los Angeles Times

"The guides are aimed not only at young budget travelers but at the independent traveler; a sort of streetwise cookbook for traveling alone."

—The New York Times

"Unbeatable; good sight-seeing advice; up-to-date info on restaurants, hotels, and inns; a commitment to money-saving travel; and a wry style that brightens nearly every page."

—The Washington Post

■ THE BEST TRAVEL BARGAINS IN YOUR BUDGET

"All the dirt, dirt cheap."

—People

"Let's Go follows the creed that you don't have to toss your life's savings to the wind to travel—unless you want to."

—The Salt Lake Tribune

■ REAL ADVICE FOR REAL EXPERIENCES

"The writers seem to have experienced every rooster-packed bus and lunar-surfaced mattress about which they write."

—The New York Times

"[Let's Go's] devoted updaters really walk the walk (and thumb the ride, and trek the trail). Learn how to fish, haggle, find work—anywhere."

—Food & Wine

"A world-wise traveling companion—always ready with friendly advice and helpful hints, all sprinkled with a bit of wit."

—The Philadelphia Inquirer

■ A GUIDE WITH A SPIRIT AND A SOCIAL CONSCIENCE

"Lighthearted and sophisticated, informative and fun to read. [Let's Go] helps the novice traveler navigate like a knowledgeable old hand."

—Atlanta Journal-Constitution

"The serious mission at the book's core reveals itself in exhortations to respect the culture and the environment—and, if possible, to visit as a volunteer, a student, or a teacher rather than a tourist."

—San Francisco Chronicle

LET'S GO PUBLICATIONS

TRAVEL GUIDES

Australia 9th edition
Austria & Switzerland 12th edition
Brazil 1st edition
Britain 2007
California 10th edition
Central America 9th edition
Chile 2nd edition
China 5th edition
Costa Rica 3rd edition
Eastern Europe 12th edition
Ecuador 1st edition
Egypt 2nd edition
Europe 2007
France 2007
Germany 13th edition
Greece 8th edition
Hawaii 4th edition
India & Nepal 8th edition
Ireland 12th edition
Israel 4th edition
Italy 2007
Japan 1st edition
Mexico 21st edition
Middle East 4th edition
New Zealand 7th edition
Peru 1st edition
Puerto Rico 2nd edition
South Africa 5th edition
Southeast Asia 9th edition
Spain & Portugal 2007
Thailand 3rd edition
Turkey 5th edition
USA 23rd edition
Vietnam 2nd edition
Western Europe 2007

ROADTRIP GUIDE

Roadtripping USA 2nd edition

ADVENTURE GUIDES

Alaska 1st edition
Pacific Northwest 1st edition
Southwest USA 3rd edition

CITY GUIDES

Amsterdam 4th edition
Barcelona 3rd edition
Boston 4th edition
London 15th edition
New York City 16th edition
Paris 14th edition
Rome 12th edition
San Francisco 4th edition
Washington, D.C. 13th edition

POCKET CITY GUIDES

Amsterdam
Berlin
Boston
Chicago
London
New York City
Paris
San Francisco
Venice
Washington, D.C.

LET'S GO

NEW YORK
CITY

CARL HUGHES EDITOR

RESEARCHER-WRITERS
AMBER JOHNSON
KATE PENNER

CLIFFORD S. EMMANUEL MAP EDITOR
LAURA E. MARTIN MANAGING EDITOR

ST. MARTIN'S PRESS ✖ NEW YORK

HELPING LET'S GO. If you want to share your discoveries, suggestions, or corrections, please drop us a line. We read every piece of correspondence, whether a postcard, a 10-page email, or a coconut. **Address mail to:**

> **Let's Go: New York City**
> **67 Mount Auburn St.**
> **Cambridge, MA 02138**
> **USA**

Visit Let's Go at **http://www.letsgo.com,** or send email to:

> **feedback@letsgo.com**
> **Subject: "Let's Go: New York City"**

In addition to the invaluable travel advice our readers share with us, many are kind enough to offer their services as researchers or editors. Unfortunately, our charter enables us to employ only currently enrolled Harvard students.

HOW TO USE THIS BOOK

ORGANIZATION. *Let's Go: New York City* divides this fast-paced city by neighborhood. The Discover chapter is organized by borough, with more detailed descriptions of the neighborhoods within each borough. Chapters are organized by activity or necessity: **Accommodations, Food, Sights, Museums, Entertainment, Shopping, Nightlife,** and **Daytrips.** The Accommodations, Food, Sights, Museums, Shopping, and Nightlife chapters are broken down into neighborhood groupings. The Entertainment chapter is organized according to establishment type. Thumbnail maps throughout the book provide helpful location reminders.

TRANSPORTATION INFO. *Let's Go* mentions the nearest **subway** station to most establishments. When there is no subway icon ([S]) it means that no subway station is close to the listing. Check the **Essentials** chapter for more information on transportation and the **Appendix** for maps.

PRICE DIVERSITY. Our favorite places are denoted by the Let's Go thumbs-up (👍). These selections offer the best combination of price and quality, but are not necessarily the cheapest listings. Listings are ranked first in order of quality, then alphabetically. Each listing is followed by a price icon, from ❶ to ❺. See the page on Price Ranges (p. ix) for a more detailed explanation.

SCHOLARLY ARTICLES. This year's guide contains three articles, written by contributing writers with special insight into their topics. Each opens a window onto a side of the city you probably haven't seen before. Madeleine Elfenbein writes about the issue of prisons and drug laws (p. 69), based on her own experience as a volunteer. Chef Rick Moonen writes about a day in the life of a professional chef, and the inspiration New York City provides (p. 123). Henry J. Stern, former Parks Commissioner, points out the parks that give New York its greenery (p. 187). If you're looking for trees, that's the one to read.

FEATURES. The best way to see this city that never sleeps is by foot—check out our new walking tours of Harlem, Greenwich Village, and SoHo.

COVERING THE BASICS. The first chapter, **Discover NYC,** contains neighborhood overviews, complete with new **Suggested Itinerary maps.** The **Essentials** chapter contains practical information on planning a budget, making reservations, and other useful tips for traveling in The Big Apple. The **Practical Information** chapter lists local services, from hospitals to fitness facilities to post offices. Take some time to peruse the **Life and Times** chapter, which briefly sums up the history, culture, and customs of the city. For study abroad, volunteer, and work options in New York, **Beyond Tourism** is all you need.

A NOTE TO OUR READERS. The information for this book was gathered by *Let's Go* researchers from May through August of 2006. Each listing is based on one researcher's opinion, formed during his or her visit at a particular time. Those traveling at other times may have different experiences since prices, dates, hours, and conditions are always subject to change. You are urged to check the facts presented in this book beforehand to avoid inconvenience and surprises.

CONTENTS

①②③④⑤
PRICE RANGES>>NEW YORK CITY

Our researchers list establishments in order of value from best to worst; our favorites are denoted by the Let's Go thumbs-up (☜). Since the best value is not always the cheapest price, we have incorporated a system of price ranges for quick reference. Our price ranges are based on a rough expectation of what you will spend. For **accommodations,** we base our price range off the cheapest price for which a single traveler can stay for one night. For **restaurants** and other dining establishments, we estimate the average amount that you will spend in that restaurant. The table below tells you what you will *typically* find in New York at the corresponding price range; keep in mind that a particularly expensive ice cream stand may still only be marked a ❷, depending on what you will spend.

ACCOMMODATIONS	RANGE	WHAT YOU'RE *LIKELY* TO FIND
❶	under $55	Dorm rooms or dorm-style rooms. Expect bunk beds and a communal bath; you may have to provide or rent towels and sheets.
❷	$55-80	Upper-end hostels or small hotels. You may have a private bathroom, or there may be a sink in your room and communal shower in the hall.
❸	$81-110	A small room with a private bath. Should have decent amenities, such as phone and TV. Breakfast may be included in the price of the room.
❹	$111-130	Similar to 3, but may have more amenities or be in a more touristed area.
❺	$131+	Large hotels or upscale chains. If it's a 5 and it doesn't have the perks you want, you've paid too much.
FOOD		
❶	under $7	Mostly street-corner stands, pizza places, or fast-food joints. Rarely ever a sit-down meal.
❷	$7-12	Some sandwiches and take-out options, but also quite a few ethnic restaurants or options outside of Manhattan.
❸	$13-20	Entrees are more expensive, but chances are, you're paying for decor and ambience.
❹	$21-34	As in 3, the higher prices are probably related to better service, but in these restaurants, the food will tend to be a little fancier or more elaborate.
❺	$35+	If you're not getting delicious food with great service in a well-appointed space, you're paying for nothing more than hype.

Manhattan: Neighborhoods

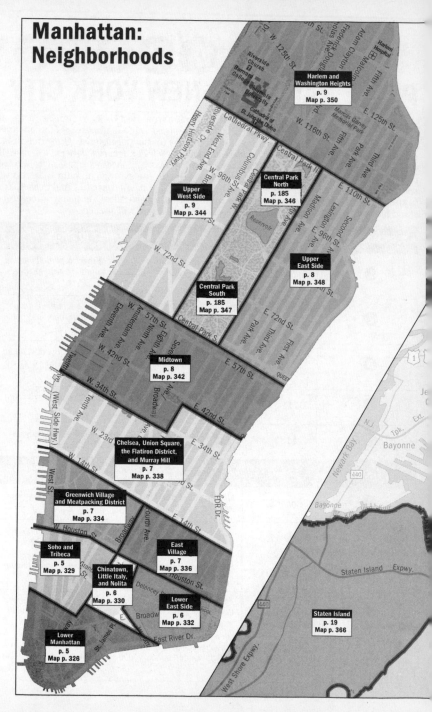

Harlem and Washington Heights
p. 9
Map p. 350

Upper West Side
p. 9
Map p. 344

Central Park North
p. 185
Map p. 346

Upper East Side
p. 8
Map p. 348

Central Park South
p. 185
Map p. 347

Midtown
p. 8
Map p. 342

Chelsea, Union Square, the Flatiron District, and Murray Hill
p. 7
Map p. 338

Greenwich Village and Meatpacking District
p. 7
Map p. 334

Soho and Tribeca
p. 5
Map p. 329

East Village
p. 7
Map p. 336

Chinatown, Little Italy, and Nolita
p. 6
Map p. 330

Lower East Side
p. 6
Map p. 332

Lower Manhattan
p. 5
Map p. 326

Staten Island
p. 19
Map p. 366

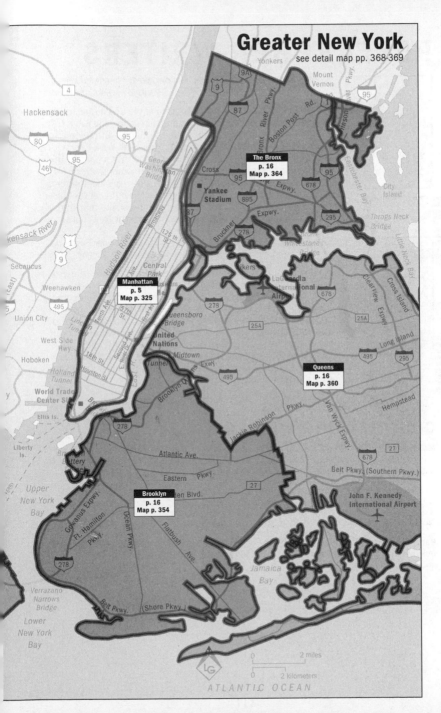

Greater New York

see detail map pp. 368-369

Hackensack

Yonkers

Mount Vernon

Bronx River Pkwy.

Boston Post Rd.

Hutchinson River Pkwy.

City Island

The Bronx
p. 16
Map p. 364

Cross

Yankee Stadium

Throgs Neck Bridge

Little Neck Bay

Secaucus

kensack River (East)

Weehawken

Union City

West Side Hwy.

Hoboken

Holland Tunnel

World Trade Center Site

Ellis Is.

Liberty Is.

Upper New York Bay

Hudson River

George Washington Bridge

Broadway

125th St.

Central Park

Tenth Ave.

Fifth Ave.

Second Ave.

Manhattan
p. 5
Map p. 325

Queensboro Bridge

United Nations

Midtown Tunnel

14th St.

Houston St.

Battery

Expwy.

Bruckner

Whitestone Bridge

Rikers

LaGuardia International Airport

Clearview Expwy.

Cross Island Pkwy.

Long Island

Hempstead

Queens
p. 16
Map p. 360

Van Wyck Expwy.

Jackie Robinson Pkwy.

Atlantic Ave.

Eastern Pkwy.

Linden Blvd.

Brooklyn
p. 16
Map p. 354

Gowanus Expwy.

Ft. Hamilton Pkwy.

Ocean Pkwy.

Flatbush Ave.

Belt Pkwy. (Southern Pkwy.)

John F. Kennedy International Airport

Verrazano Narrows Bridge

Lower New York Bay

Belt Pkwy. (Shore Pkwy.)

Jamaica Bay

0   2 miles
0   2 kilometers

ATLANTIC OCEAN

RESEARCHER-WRITERS

Amber Johnson *Upper West Side, Midtown West, Greenwich Village, Lower East Side, East Village, Brooklyn, Harlem, the Bronx*

Blessed with both a sunny California smile and a discerning cosmopolitan eye (honed last summer researching *Let's Go: London*), Amber put off putting her Public Health degree to use for a few more months by exploring New York City with gusto. Part history buff, she brought the city's past to life with a pair of well-designed walking tours and always-lively prose. Part romantic, she sought out the city's best sunset views, loveliest park strolls, and coolest pseudo-secret bars. Above all else a food critic, Amber should strike fear in the hearts of mediocre restauranteurs throughout New York.

Kate Penner *Chinatown, Little Italy and Nolita, Upper East Side, Chelsea, Brooklyn, Midtown East, Queens, SoHo*

A Government concentrator and a talented ballet dancer, Kate turned down an internship with the CIA to work for *Let's Go: New York City.* Her investigative spirit and versatile adaptability certainly served us well. Whether she was clubbing in Chelsea, riding the Cyclone on Coney Island, gawking at baby turtles in Chinatown, or dreaming about the purses she saw at Barneys, Kate brought wit and unflagging energy to her work. We can't promise that New York's fashion economy will survive her departure, but we're pretty sure she'll be back in SoHo soon.

CONTRIBUTING WRITERS

Madeleine Elfenbein, an editor and contributing writer for the *Harvard Advocate*, was the youngest member of the 2001 living wage sit-in at Harvard University. Having graduated in 2004, she continues to explore both writing and activism.

Rick Moonen graduated first in his class from the Culinary Institute of America in 1978. He has worked in the restaurant business for over 29 years, including eight as chef at the famed Oceana. His restaurant RM received a coveted three-star review from *The New York Times.* He is currently at work on a cookbook.

Henry Stern has served the City of New York as a member of City Council and as Commissioner of Parks and Recreation. He held the latter position under Mayors Ed Koch and Rudolph Guiliani.

ACKNOWLEDGMENTS

LET'S GO

CARL THANKS: Amber and Kate for allowing themselves to be mercilessly overworked and still bringing enthusiasm and creative vision to their jobs. Laura, for insightful edits and invaluable support. Mal, for City pride and (I think) forgiving me for J-J. Cliff for cartographic brilliance. Richard for expert production support and endless patience. Jenny for the octopi in Under Da Sea. Sam for the gossip, the sprinkles, and most of all the squalor. Chad, Jonathan, Jen, Kate, Sean, and Shauna, for making HDS more fun. Branden, Jeff, and Nicole, for understanding about the passports. Emily for Spanish lessons and trying oysters. Asher and Esther: when are we going to Espérance? Andy and Marquis: when are we going to Siberia? Dad, Mom, and John: when are we all going to New York? Aunt Lou Ann—you come too.

CLIFFORD THANKS: Thanks Kate and Amber for your fabulous maps. Thanks Carl for celebrating my hometown with finely polished prose. Thanks to my map editors, Kevin, Mariah, Shiyang, and Tom. You guys impressed me with your energy and hard work and made working in Mapland a blast. Thanks Richard for putting up with my endless questions, providing entertaining tidbits from the World Wide Web, and being generally awesome. Thank you Long John, Long Johnson, and Don Piano. You guys rock. Finally, thanks to my path-integrating, chininha-language partner. The office was not the same without you.

Publishing Director
Alexandra C. Stanek
Editor-in-Chief
Laura E. Martin
Production Manager
Richard Chohaney Lonsdorf
Cartography Manager
Clifford S. Emmanuel
Editorial Managers
August Dietrich, Samantha Gelfand, Silvia Gonzalez Killingsworth
Financial Manager
Jenny Qiu Wong
Publicity Manager
Anna A. Mattson-DiCecca
Personnel Manager
Sergio Ibarra
Production Associate
Chase Mohney
IT Director
Patrick Carroll
Director of E-Commerce
Jana Lepon
Office Coordinators
Adrienne Taylor Gerken, Sarah Goodin

Director of Advertising Sales
Mohammed J. Herzallah
Senior Advertising Associates
Kedamai Fisseha, Roumiana Ivanova

Editor
Carl Hughes
Managing Editor
Laura Martin
Map Editor
Clifford S. Emmanuel
Typesetter
Ariel Fox

President
Brian Feinstein
General Manager
Robert B. Rombauer

DISCOVER NYC

Even if you're visiting New York for the first time, you've seen some version of this city before. Images of it are everywhere—in movies and on television, in novels high- and low-brow, in songs, in classic photographs, and on the nightly news. You've probably watched enough Times Square ball drops and late-show lead-ins to anticipate its blaring horns, mega-watt neon lights, and skyscraper canyons—and, to be sure, New York will deliver them all. Perhaps you first fell in love with New York through Woody Allen movies—and imagine it to be full of neurotic writers and fledgling actors, who have affairs in Bohemian appartments and somehow can afford to eat out every night. While few live a lifestyle that glamorous, artists, intellectuals, and pseudo-intellectuals of every stripe do seem to gravitate here. Does your family tell stories of immigrant ancestors arriving at Ellis Island, penniless but hopeful? The 300 languages spoken on the city's streets and its incomparable array of ethnic cuisines prove that New York is still a melting pot today. Perhaps you were raised on *Eloise* stories at bedtime, and you dream of luxuriating in plushly decorated hotel suites. New York certainly has no shortage of those on offer, though unless you're here on an expense account, you'll likely have to content yourself with a drink in a chic hotel bar. If, with some trepidation, you're expecting the Gotham City of crime novels and the tabloid press—grimy and congested, dangerous and macabre—the extent to which New York has cleaned itself up in recent decades may surprise you, though a host of urban problems persist. On the other hand, if you're expecting New York's sidewalks to be as celebrity-packed as the pages of *Us Weekly*, you'll probably be let down—but who knows who you might spot parading in SoHo? The truth is, each of these facets of New York life contains an element of truth, but what makes the city so intense is that it's beyond any single cliché—and more than all of them put together. Happily, you could spend your whole life exploring New York and never exhaust its riches.

FACTS AND FIGURES

MAYOR: Michael Bloomberg, re-elected to a second four-year term in 2005.

POPULATION: 8.1 million, 18.7 million in the surrounding metropolitan area.

LAND AREA: 321 sq. mi.—the most densely populated region in North America.

MOST POPULATED BOROUGH: Brooklyn, with 2.5 million residents (Manhattan has 1.5 million).

RACIAL MIX: 45% white, 27% African American, 27% Latino, 10% Asian.

TOURISTS: 44.4 million visitors in 2006—83% domestic, 17% foreign.

SUBWAY: 468 stations, 660 mi. of track, and 1.4 billion annual riders.

LICENSED YELLOW CABS: 12,778.

HOTEL ROOMS: 71,000, with 85% occupancy on an average night.

NEW RESTAURANTS OPENED YEARLY: About 250.

ACRES OF PARKLAND: 28,000, 843 in Central Park.

MONEY EXCHANGED ANNUALLY ON THE NYSE: $5.5 trillion.

GOLD STORED AT THE FEDERAL RESERVE BANK: $600 billion's worth—in 27 lb. bars, locked 80 ft. underground by a 90-ton steel door.

TALLEST BUILDINGS: Empire State Building (1250 ft.), Chrysler Building (1046 ft.), American International Building (952 ft.).

TALLEST STRUCTURE IN 1664: A two-story windmill.

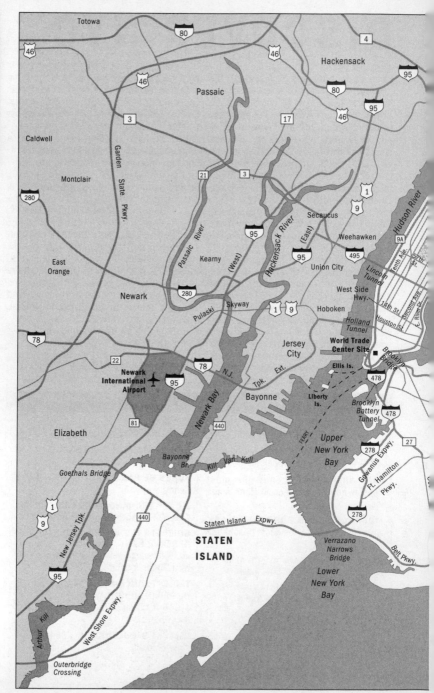

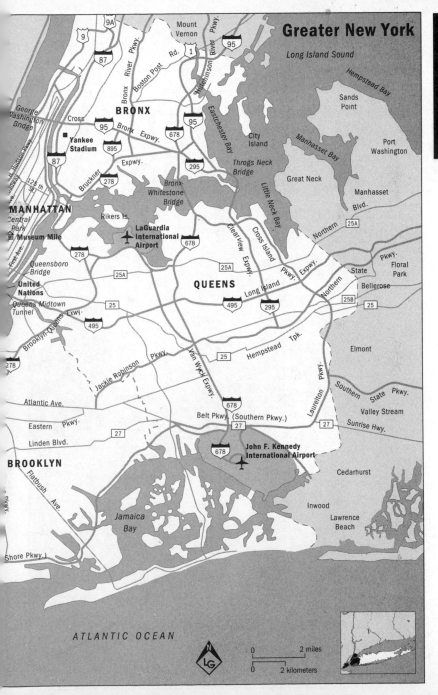

Greater New York

Long Island Sound

Hempstead Bay

Sands Point

Manhasset Bay

Port Washington

Great Neck

Manhasset

Blvd.

Mount Vernon

Hutchinson River Pkwy.

City Island

Throgs Neck Bridge

Little Neck Bay

Northern

State

Floral Park

Bellerose

BRONX

Bronx River Pkwy.

Boston Post Rd.

Eastchester Bay

Cross Bronx Expwy.

Bronx-Whitestone Bridge

Clearview Expwy.

Cross Island Pkwy.

Long Island

Northern

George Washington Bridge

Yankee Stadium

Bruckner Expwy.

Rikers Is.

LaGuardia International Airport

QUEENS

MANHATTAN

Central Park

Museum Mile

United Nations

Queensboro Bridge

Queens Midtown Tunnel

Queens Midtown Exwy.

Brooklyn-Queens

Jackie Robinson Pkwy.

Van Wyck Expwy.

Hempstead Tpk.

Elmont

Laurelton Pkwy.

Southern State Pkwy.

Valley Stream

Atlantic Ave.

Eastern Pkwy.

Linden Blvd.

Belt Pkwy. (Southern Pkwy.)

Sunrise Hwy.

BROOKLYN

Flatbush Ave.

John F. Kennedy International Airport

Cedarhurst

Inwood

Lawrence Beach

Jamaica Bay

Shore Pkwy.

ATLANTIC OCEAN

0 ———— 2 miles
0 ———— 2 kilometers

N

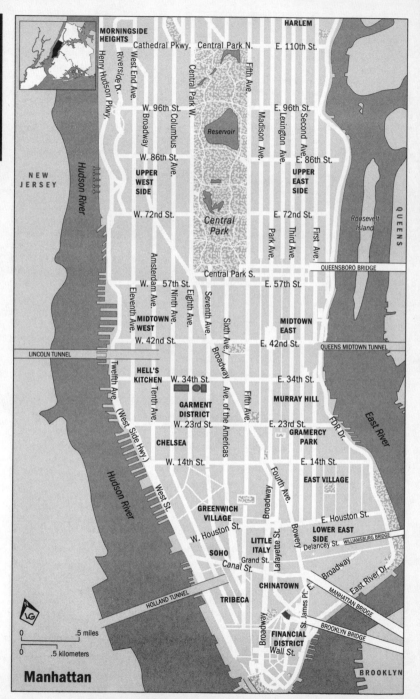

MORNINGSIDE
HEIGHTS
HARLEM

Cathedral Pkwy.   Central Park N.   E. 110th St.

Central Park W.

Fifth Ave.

West End Ave.

Riverside Dr.

Henry Hudson Pkwy.

W. 96th St.   E. 96th St.

Columbus Ave.

Broadway

Reservoir

Madison Ave.

Lexington Ave.

Second Ave.

W. 86th St.   E. 86th St.

NEW
JERSEY

Hudson River

UPPER
WEST
SIDE

UPPER
EAST
SIDE

W. 72nd St.   E. 72nd St.

*Central
Park*

Roosevelt
Island

QUEENS

Park Ave.

Third Ave.

First Ave.

Amsterdam Ave.

Central Park S.

QUEENSBORO BRIDGE

W. 57th St.   E. 57th St.

Ninth Ave.

Eighth Ave.

Eleventh Ave.

MIDTOWN
WEST

Seventh Ave.

Sixth Ave./

MIDTOWN
EAST

W. 42nd St.   E. 42nd St.

QUEENS MIDTOWN TUNNEL

LINCOLN TUNNEL

Broadway

HELL'S
KITCHEN   W. 34th St.   E. 34th St.

Tenth Ave.

Twelfth Ave. (West Side Hwy.)

GARMENT
DISTRICT

MURRAY HILL

Ave. of the Americas

Fifth Ave.

W. 23rd St.   E. 23rd St.   GRAMERCY
PARK

CHELSEA

FDR Dr.

East River

Hudson River

West St.

W. 14th St.   E. 14th St.

EAST VILLAGE

Fourth Ave.

GREENWICH
VILLAGE

Broadway

W. Houston St.   E. Houston St.

LOWER EAST
SIDE

LITTLE
ITALY   Delancey St.   WILLIAMSBURG BRIDGE

SOHO

Bowery

Lafayette St.

Grand St.

Broadway

Canal St.

East River Dr.

CHINATOWN

MANHATTAN BRIDGE

HOLLAND TUNNEL

TRIBECA

James Pl.

St. James Pl.

BROOKLYN BRIDGE

Broadway

FINANCIAL
DISTRICT
Wall St.

0   .5 miles

0   .5 kilometers

Manhattan

BROOKLYN

WHEN TO GO

A visit to New York is worthwhile at any time of the year, though the time you choose will undoubtedly color your visit. Spring and fall are the most temperate seasons during which to visit; the city can experience hot and muggy summers and cold and snowy winters. On the other hand, New York in the winter abounds with lavish holiday decorations and public celebrations, while in the summer it hosts an array of fun (and often free) outdoor festivals. As a general (but not always reliable) rule, hotel prices are cheapest during the summer, and most expensive during the holiday season and when major events and conventions are in town. If you're trolling the Internet for hotel deals, bear in mind that hotels catering primarily to business travelers often reduce their rates substantially on weekends.

NEIGHBORHOOD OVERVIEWS

MANHATTAN

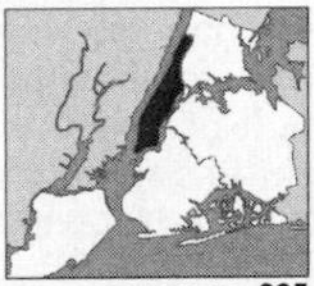

see map pp. 325

For many tourists, Manhattan *is* New York, and, while parts of the outer boroughs are definitely worth exploring, Manhattan is the city's undisputed heart. The lower portion of the island is a tangle of narrow streets, dating from the city's early years before urban planners arrived. Above 14th St., Manhattan is an organized grid. Avenues run north-south, their numbers increasing as you go west; streets run east-west, with their numbers increasing as you go north. The one exception is Broadway, which cuts diagonally across the island.

LOWER MANHATTAN

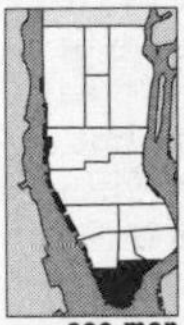

see map pp. 326-327

Lower Manhattan, the tip of the island south of Chambers St., is where New York gets to work making the money spent lavishly around the rest of the city. The **Financial District,** with **Wall Street** at its heart, is a supply-side economist's vision of heaven. The epicenter of the financial universe, this is where fortunes are made in minutes, and sometimes lost just as quickly. Sights in the neighborhood include historic **Trinity Church,** the **New York Stock Exchange,** and **Ground Zero,** the site of the future World Trade Center Memorial. Just north of the Financial District is the **Civic Center,** which clusters around **City Hall.** The area contains some of the best-preserved 19th-century architecture in the city. The **Brooklyn Bridge,** a marvel of industrial-age architecture, lies east of City Hall Park. The **South Street Seaport,** once filled with flop houses, seedy bars, and brothels servicing sailors in port, is now an open-air mall filled with chain restaurants catering to white-collar workers at happy hour. *(FINANCIAL DISTRICT: [S] 2, 3 to Wall St./William St.; 4, 5 to Bowling Green, Wall St./Broadway; R, W to Rector St., Whitehall St.; 2, 3, 4, 5, A, C, J, M, Z to Fulton St./Broadway/Nassau St.; J, M, Z to Broad St.; 1 to Rector St., South Ferry. THE CIVIC CENTER: [S] 2, 3 to Park Pl.; R, W to City Hall; 4, 5, 6 to Brooklyn Bridge/City Hall; J, M, Z to Chambers St./Centre St. SOUTH STREET SEAPORT: [S] 2, 3, 4, 5, A, C, J, M, Z to Fulton St./Broadway/Nassau St.)*

SOHO AND TRIBECA

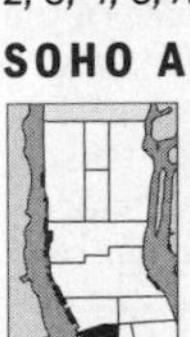

see map pp. 329

SoHo, the fashionable and pricey district "South of Houston" (say "HOW-ston") St., has gone in the last 50 years from a gritty industrial zone, to a hotbed of avant-garde artists and galleries, to a chic destination for high-end restaurants, shopping, and nightlife. Many galleries remain, though the most innovative ones have opted for the cheaper rents of Chelsea and DUMBO. TriBeCa, short for "Triangle Below Canal Street," has undergone a similar metamorphosis from industrial wasteland to gentrified hipness. *(SOHO: [S] C, E to Spring St./Ave. of the Americas*

TOP 10 WAYS TO SPEND A SUNNY DAY

1. Hunt for fresh, local produce at the Union Square Greenmarket (p. 132). Spoil your appetite with a burger at Madison Sq. Park's Shake Shack (p. 132).

2. Enjoy a Bring-Your-Own-Meat backyard barbecue at Moonshine (p. 309).

3. Read a book and munch on gelato at the Museum of Modern Art's sculpture garden (p. 225). Or, dodge the admission fee and head to Central Park's Conservatory Garden (p. 185) instead.

4. Grab an authentic New York pizza at Grimaldi's (p. 146). Work off the calories with a walk back to Manhattan across the Brooklyn Bridge (p. 202).

5. Wander in and out of Williamsburg's cutting-edge galleries (p. 243). Enjoy a delicious dinner in the garden of DuMont (p. 145).

6. Catch an afternoon game at Yankee Stadium. Afterward, enjoy dinner at Dominick's (p. 152).

7. Take in a Shakespeare play in Central Park's Delacorte Theater (p. 185). Follow it with a drink at Tavern on the Green (p. 186).

8. Enjoy a pilates, art, or kayaking class in Riverside Park (p. 193). Finish with a drink at the W 79th St. Boat Basin (p. 306).

9. Wander around Fort Tryon Park (p. 200), and stop in at The Cloisters (p. 234). Grab lunch at the New Leaf Cafe (p. 143).

10. Ride the LIRR to Jones Beach (p. 313). Catch an outdoor concert (p. 255), or just lounge on the sand.

(6th Ave.); 6 to Spring St./Lafayette St.; N, R, W to Prince St.; 1 to W Houston St.; B, D, F, V to Broadway/Lafayette St. TRIBECA: Ⓢ 1 to Canal St./Varick St.; A, C, E to Canal St./Ave. of the Americas (6th Ave.); 1 to Franklin St.; 1, 2, 3 to Chambers St./W Broadway; A, C to Chambers St./Church St.)

CHINATOWN, LITTLE ITALY, AND NOLITA

see map
pp. 330-331

It's not really accurate to say that a trip to Chinatown is like a trip to Asia—the area's bizarre combination of vibrant cultural authenticity with crass American capitalism somehow could only exist in New York. With over 300,000 Chinese residents (the second-largest Chinese-American community after San Francisco's), Chinatown is, despite the inevitable crush of tourists on the weekends, much more than a tourist trap. The area is home to seven Chinese newspapers, over 300 garment factories, and innumerable food shops and restaurants. Every available inch of space is used to hawk everything from dried ginseng roots, to baby turtles, to cheap cell phones, to fake Rolexes, to bubble tea.

While Chinatown thrives, historic Little Italy has shrunk in recent years. What remains of the neighborhood's sometimes kitschy embrace of Italian-American stereotypes is located along the three blocks of Mulberry St. from Canal to Broome St. A stroll through the area, still pleasant in the early evening, gives a sense of the old atmosphere, but the food is neither budget-friendly nor particularly extraordinary. Just to the north, the so-called Nolita ("North of Little Italy") district has grown into a trendy shopping and restaurant destination, its hip acronym now secured. (CHINATOWN: Ⓢ J, M, Z to Canal St./Centre St.; N, Q, R, W to Canal St./Broadway; 6 to Canal St./Lafayette St. Walk east on Canal St. to get to Mott St. Follow the curved street to get to the Bowery, Confucius Plaza, and E Broadway. LITTLE ITALY: Ⓢ 6 to Spring St./Lafayette St.; J, M, Z to Canal St./Centre St.; N, Q, R, W to Canal St./Broadway; 6 to Canal St./Lafayette St.; F to E Broadway; B, D, F, V to Broadway/Lafayette St.)

LOWER EAST SIDE

see map
p. 332

Down below East Houston and east of the Bowery lurks the Lower East Side, which in recent decades has gone from grimly poor to hiply gritty. Long home to densely populated tenements housing the successive waves of New York's immigrant population, the impact of the area's ethnic heritages is still visible. Buddhist prayer centers neighbor Jewish religious supply stores, well-established delis sell pastrami, pickles, and pierogi alongside Asian fusion bistros, and fashionable dive bars and after-hours clubs exploit the bohemian vibe. For many New Yorkers, the Lower East Side is home to some of the city's best nightlife. (Ⓢ *F, V to Lower East Side/2nd Ave.; F to E Broadway; F, J, M, Z to Delancey St./Essex St.*)

GREENWICH VILLAGE

In this counter-culture capital of the East Coast, located west of Broadway between Houston and 14th St., transgressions are a way of life, and no amount of hair dye, body piercings, or confused soapbox ranting is enough to faze the weathered "Villagers." The list of artists and intellectuals who have lived and worked here is impressive: Herman Melville and James Fenimore Cooper wrote American masterworks here; Mark Twain and Willa Cather depicted the American heartland

see map
pp. 334-335

from their adopted homes near Washington Sq.; John Reed, John Dos Passos, and e.e. cummings all began their writing careers here in relative obscurity; and the Beats dreamed of the open road from here in the 50s. One of the city's historic centers of GLBT life, the Village was the site of the Stonewall Riots of 1969, a crucial early step in the gay-rights movement. The **Meatpacking District,** filled with trendy bars, restaurants, and clubs, lies to the northwest. (Ⓢ *A, B, C, D, E, F, V to W 4th St.; A, C, E to 14th St./8th Ave.; 1, 2, 3 to 14th St./7th Ave.; F, V to 14th St./Ave. of the Americas (6th Ave.); L to 8th Ave./Ave. of the Americas (6th Ave.); 4, 5, 6, L, N, Q, R, W to 14th St./Union Sq.; 1 to Houston St., Christopher St.; N, R, W to 8th St./NYU; L to 6th Ave., 8th Ave.; 6 to Bleecker St.*)

EAST VILLAGE

The East Village was carved out of the Bowery and the Lower East Side in the early 1960s, as artists and writers drifted east of Greenwich Village in hopes of escaping its high rents. The area today is one of the city's most diverse districts, with punks, hippies, yuppies, goths, and ravers existing side-by-side. The area is a center for used book and clothing stores, underground rock shows, and Off-Off Broadway theater. The vibrancy and volatility of the neighborhood inspired the hit

see map
p. 336

musical *Rent*. East Sixth St. is called **"Little India"** for its door-to-door South Asian eateries. **Alphabet City,** east of First Ave., south of 14th St., and north of Houston St., is home to letter-named streets and great nightlife. (Ⓢ *6 to Astor Pl., Bleecker St.; L to 2nd Ave., 3rd Ave.; F, V to Lower East Side/2nd Ave.*)

CHELSEA

Chelsea hosts scores of the city's best art galleries and many of its most fashionable bars and clubs. It has also supplanted Greenwich Village as the undisputed capital of GLBT life in New York. Awesome gay bars, lounges, and clubs line the streets. (CHELSEA Ⓢ *1, 2, 3 to 14th St./7th Ave.; A, C, E, L to 14th St./8th Ave.; C, E to 23rd St./8th Ave.; 1 to 23rd St./7th Ave., 28th St./7th Ave.*)

UNION SQUARE, THE FLATIRON DISTRICT, AND MURRAY HILL

Though close to the heart of Midtown, these three primarily residential neighborhoods are surprisingly peaceful, filled with leafy trees and picturesque brownstones. Union Square is home to a burgeoning population of well-to-do and fun-loving professionals and a **farmers' market** four days a week. The townhouses surrounding **Gramercy Park,** a private park so exclusive you need a key to pass beyond its wrought-iron gates, have housed many of the city's most blue-blooded residents. Murray Hill, in the 30s on the East Side, is another tony residential area that makes a great spot for an afternoon stroll. The area is home to the **Morgan Library and Museum,** which recently completed a spectacular renovation and expansion of its complex. (Ⓢ *4, 5, 6, L, N, Q, R, W to 14th St./Union Sq.; 6 to 23rd St./Park Ave. S; N, R, W to 23rd St./Broadway; 6 to 28th St., 33rd St./Park Ave. S.*)

> **TAXIS 101.** A cab is available for business when the yellow light on its roof is illuminated. Drivers who are headed home turn on their "off duty" lights, though if you're going in the same direction as they are, they may still pick you up. Shift changes around 6pm can make hailing a taxi difficult; wait 30min. or so and available cabs will likely appear.

MIDTOWN WEST

Midtown West is neon-lit, hot-and-sweaty, brake-screeching Manhattan at its most intense. **Times Square,** its throbbing heart, is a constant sensory overload and perhaps the district that New Yorkers love to hate the most. In the 70s and 80s, the neighborhood became decidedly seedy—filled with peep shows, shady bars, and pickpockets. Time Square is well beyond such reproach now; indeed, some worry that its new family-friendly persona has supplanted its authentic urban grit.

see map pp. 342-343 The **Theater District,** centered along Broadway to the northwest, puts on more than 100 shows each night. To the northeast, you'll find **Rockefeller Center** and the recently renovated and expanded **Museum of Modern Art.**

To the south, **Herald Square,** so-named because it once housed the now-defunct *New York Herald,* is a hotspot of commercial bustle, home to giant complexes like **Macy's, Madison Square Garden, Penn Station,** and the **General Post Office.** Just to the east is the **Empire State Building,** the tallest skyscraper in New York. To the south, the **Garment District** is a center for textiles shopping, providing fashion lovers with the raw materials they need, without any marketing hype. **Hell's Kitchen,** west of the Garment District, was once one of the most dangerous neighborhoods in America. It got its portentous appellation when a police officer commented after a particularly brutal night, "We truly are in hell's kitchen." The area has gentrified substantially, and it is now one of Manhattan's best spots for inexpensive ethnic food. *(TIMES SQUARE AND THEATER DISTRICT:* S *1, 2, 3, 7, N, Q, R, S, W to 42nd St./ Times Square; A, C, E to 42nd St./Port Authority; B, D, F, V, 7 to 42nd St./Bryant Park. HELL'S KITCHEN:* S *1, 2, 3, to 34th St./Penn Station/7th Ave.; A, C, E to 34th St./Penn Station/8th Ave. HERALD SQUARE AND THE GARMENT DISTRICT:* S *B, D, F, N, Q, R, V, W to Herald Sq.*

MIDTOWN EAST

Mammoth office buildings and posh hotels dominate the skies on the East Side from about 42nd to 59th St. Here, conservatively dressed matrons browse astronomically priced stores, and harried business titans thread their way through packs of camera-toting, wide-eyed tourists. It's on the East Side where you'll find **Fifth Avenue, Madison Avenue,** and **Park Avenue,** boulevards whose names, synonymous with luxury, have entered American lore. The **Turtle Bay** neighborhood in the east 40s is home to the **United**

see map pp. 342-343 **Nations.** *(*S *4, 5, 6, 7, S to 42nd St./Grand Central; 6 to 51st St.; E, V to Lexington Ave./53rd St.; 4, 5, 6, N, R, W to 59th St./Lexington Ave.; F to Lexington Ave./63rd St.; B, D, F, V, 7 to 42nd St./Bryant Park; B, D, F, V to 47th St./50th St./Rockefeller Center.)*

UPPER EAST SIDE

The immaculately clean streets of the Upper East Side stretch east of Central Park from 59th St. to 96th St., where they harbor exclusive preschools, well-dressed nannies walking well-mannered children, and the city's highest concentration of uniformed doormen per square foot. **Museum Mile,** along Fifth Ave on Central Park, includes world-class giants like the **Metropolitan Museum of Art, the Frick, the Guggenheim,** and the **Museum of the City of New York,** as well as more specialized gems like the **International Center of Photography** and the **Jewish Museum.** If you love to shop, the Upper East

see map pp. 348-349

Side will be either your dream-come-true or your most dangerous nightmare, depending on the size of your bank account and your willingness to be satisfied with window shopping alone. ($\boxed{S}$ N, R, W to Fifth Ave./59th St.; 4, 5, 6, N, R, W to 59th St./Lexington Ave.; F to Lexington Ave./63rd St.; 6 to 68th St., 77th St., 96th St.; 4, 5, 6 to 86th St.)

 PLAN YOUR PUBLIC-TRANSIT ITINERARY ONLINE. While most of the country has become reliant on websites like Mapquest and Google Maps for driving directions, New York, where public transportation is key, has special needs. New websites like **www.hopstop.com, www.trips123,** and **www.publi-croutes.com** provide a similar service to that offered by driving-directions sites, but focus exclusively on car-free, public-transit options. They're especially useful for planning the most efficient route for journeys requiring multiple transfers.

UPPER WEST SIDE

see map pp. 344-345

Likely Manhattan's friendliest and most community-oriented neighborhood, the Upper West Side boasts residential quietude along Central Park West and Riverside Dr. and commercial buzz along **Columbus Avenue, Amsterdam Avenue,** and **Broadway.** Its residents may value a prep school education nearly as much as their blue-blooded neighbors across the park, but they're of a slightly crunchier bent. You'll find lots of organic fruit and maybe even some young moms participating in a "Strollercize" class—waving their arms in unison as they push their little ones. The neighborhood's biggest tourist attractions are **Lincoln Center** and the **American Museum of Natural History.** As you proceed farther north, the area becomes more diverse and colorful, though also less safe. The Upper West Side is home to New York's highest concentration of budget accommodations. ($\boxed{S}$ 1, A, B, C, D to 59th St./Columbus Circle; 1 to 66th St., 79th St., 86th St./Broadway; 1, 2, 3 to 72nd St./Broadway; B, C to 72nd St., 81st St., 86th St., 96th St./Central Park W; 1, 2, 3 to 96th St./Broadway.)

MORNINGSIDE HEIGHTS

see map pp. 350-351

Centering around the beautiful campus of **Columbia University,** Morningside Heights is full of bookstores, coffee shops, and affordable restaurants. The Episcopal **Cathedral of St. John the Divine** has been under construction since 1892 and still is not quite finished. Its windows and chapels memorialize the victims of the 20th century's worst tragedies. The nearby **Riverside Church,** housed in a soaring Gothic Revival edifice, has been at the forefront of progressive Christian social activism for most of the last century. ($\boxed{S}$ 1 to Cathedral Pkwy. (110th St.), 116th St./Columbia University, 125th St./Broadway.)

HARLEM

Harlem, the largest neighborhood in Manhattan, extends from 110th St. to the 150s, between the Hudson and East Rivers. The dangerous Harlem you've heard about refers largely to the area south of 125th St. in the Manhattan Valley, particularly along Frederick Douglass and Adam Clayton Powell Blvd; avoid this area at night. Though poorer than the rest of Manhattan, the area possesses great cultural vibrancy as America's historic capital of African-American culture, and this legacy is evident in the neighborhood's many nightclubs, churches, and restaurants. **Spanish Harlem** (El Barrio) is between 96th and 125th St. on the East Side. Though the neighborhood is quite poor (and best avoided at night), its main artery, E 116th St., overflows with colorful fruit stands, Puerto Rican eateries, and crushed ice vendors. **Washington Heights,** a largely Dominican neighborhood, occupies the hilly ground north of 155th St. (HARLEM: $\boxed{S}$ 6 to 103rd St., 110th St./Central Park N., 116th St. at Lexington Ave.; 4, 5, 6 to 125th St./

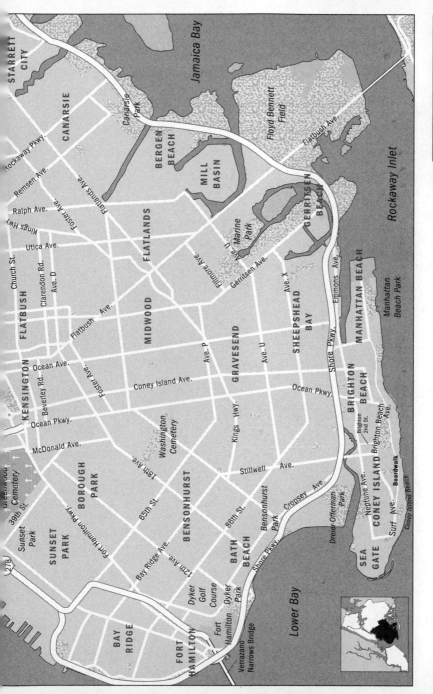

STARRETT CITY

CANARSIE

Jamaica Bay

Canarsie Park

Floyd Bennett Field

Rockaway Pkwy.

Remsen Ave.

BERGEN BEACH

Flatbush Ave.

Ralph Ave.

Foster Ave.

Flatlands Ave.

MILL BASIN

Rockaway Inlet

Kings Hwy.

Church St.

Utica Ave.

FLATLANDS

Marine Park

GERRITSEN BEACH

Clarendon Rd.

Ave. D

Fillmore Ave.

Gerritsen Ave.

FLATBUSH

Flatbush Ave.

MIDWOOD

Ave. X

MANHATTAN BEACH

KENSINGTON

Ocean Ave.

Beverley Rd.

Foster Ave.

GRAVESEND

Ave. P

SHEEPSHEAD BAY

Emmons Ave.

Manhattan Beach Park

Ocean Pkwy.

Coney Island Ave.

Ave. U

Shore Pkwy.

McDonald Ave.

Washington Cemetery

Ocean Pkwy.

BRIGHTON BEACH

Kings Hwy.

18th Ave.

BENSONHURST

Stillwell Ave.

Brighton 2nd St.

Brighton Beach Ave.

Greenwood Cemetery

BOROUGH PARK

Fort Hamilton Pkwy.

65th St.

Bensonhurst Park

Cropsey Ave.

Boardwalk

39th St.

CONEY ISLAND

Neptune Ave.

Sunset Park

86th St.

Dreier-Offerman Park

Surf Ave.

Coney Island Beach

SUNSET PARK

BATH BEACH

Shore Pkwy.

SEA GATE

278

12th Ave.

Bay Ridge Ave.

Lower Bay

BAY RIDGE

Dyker Golf Course

Dyker Park

FORT HAMILTON

Fort Hamilton

Verrazano Narrows Bridge

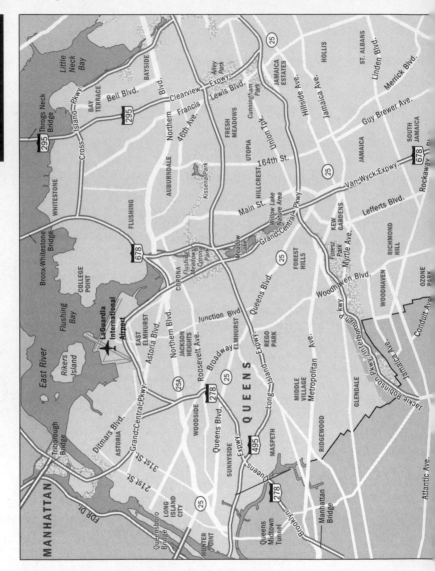

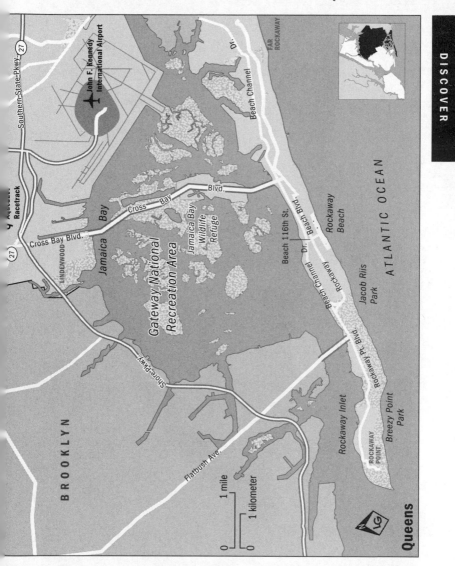

Southern State Pkwy. 27

27

Aqueduct Racetrack

John F. Kennedy International Airport

Cross Bay Blvd.

LINDENWOOD

Jamaica Bay

Cross Bay Blvd.

Gateway National Recreation Area

Jamaica Bay Wildlife Refuge

Beach Channel Dr.

FAR ROCKAWAY

Beach 116th St.

Beach Blvd.

Rockaway Beach

Beach Channel Dr.

Rockaway

Jacob Riis Park

ATLANTIC OCEAN

Shore Pkwy.

BROOKLYN

Flatbush Ave.

Rockaway Inlet

ROCKAWAY POINT

Rockaway Pt. Blvd.

Breezy Point Park

1 mile

1 kilometer

0

0

Queens

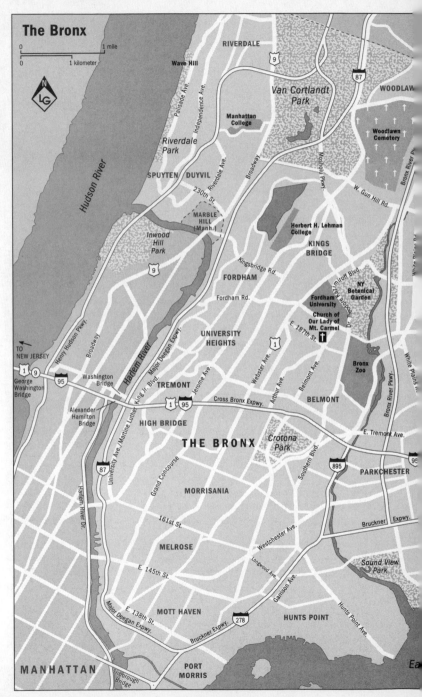

DISCOVER

The Bronx

0 _____ 1 mile
0 _____ 1 kilometer

N

RIVERDALE

Wave Hill

Van Cortlandt Park

WOODLAWN

Woodlawn Cemetery

Manhattan College

Riverdale Park

Hudson River

SPUYTEN DUYVIL

230th St.

MARBLE HILL (Manh.)

Inwood Hill Park

Palisade Ave.

Independence Ave.

Riverdale Ave.

Broadway

Mosholu Pkwy.

W. Gun Hill Rd.

Bronx River Pkwy.

White Plains Rd.

Herbert H. Lehman College

KINGS BRIDGE

Kingsbridge Rd.

FORDHAM

Fordham Rd.

Fordham University

NY Botanical Garden

Church of Our Lady of Mt. Carmel

E. 187th St.

Bronx Zoo

TO NEW JERSEY

George Washington Bridge

Henry Hudson Pkwy.

Broadway

Washington Bridge

Harlem River

Major Deegan Expwy.

University Ave./Martine Luther King Jr. Blvd.

UNIVERSITY HEIGHTS

Jerome Ave.

Webster Ave.

Arthur Ave.

Belmont Ave.

BELMONT

Bronx River Pkwy.

White Plains Rd.

Alexander Hamilton Bridge

TREMONT

Cross Bronx Expwy.

HIGH BRIDGE

THE BRONX

Crotona Park

E. Tremont Ave.

PARKCHESTER

Grand Concourse

MORRISANIA

Southern Blvd.

Harlem River Dr.

161st St.

MELROSE

E. 145th St.

Westchester Ave.

Longwood Ave.

Garrison Ave.

Sound View Park

Hunts Point Ave.

E. 138th St.

Major Deegan Expwy.

MOTT HAVEN

Bruckner Expwy.

HUNTS POINT

Bruckner Expwy.

MANHATTAN

Triborough Bridge

PORT MORRIS

Ea

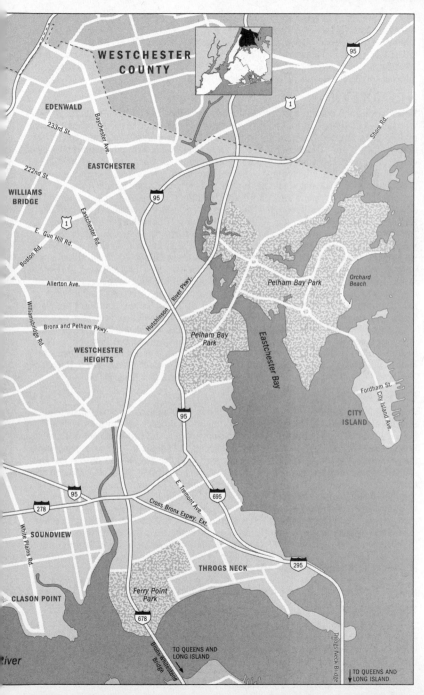

WESTCHESTER
COUNTY

EDENWALD

233rd St.

Barychester Ave.

EASTCHESTER

222nd St.

WILLIAMS
BRIDGE

1

E. Gun Hill Rd.

Eastchester Rd.

Boston Rd.

Allerton Ave.

Williamsbridge Rd.

Bronx and Pelham Pkwy.

WESTCHESTER
HEIGHTS

95

Hutchinson River Pkwy.

Shore Rd.

1

Pelham Bay Park

Orchard
Beach

Pelham Bay
Park

Eastchester Bay

95

Fordham St.

City Island Ave.

CITY
ISLAND

95

278

E. Tremont Ave.

695

Cross Bronx Expwy. Ext.

White Plains Rd.

SOUNDVIEW

THROGS NECK

295

CLASON POINT

Ferry Point
Park

678

Throgs Neck Bridge

River

Bronx-Whitestone Bridge

TO QUEENS AND
LONG ISLAND

TO QUEENS AND
LONG ISLAND

Lexington Ave.; 2, 3 to Central Park N (110th St.), 116th St., 125th St., 135th St./Lenox (6th) Ave.; 3 to 145th St./Lenox (6th) Ave., 148th St.; B, C to Cathedral Pkwy. (110th St.), 116th St., 135th St./Central Park W; A, B, C, D to 125th St./Central Park W, 145th St./St. Nicholas Ave.; 1 to 137th St., 145th St./Broadway. WASHINGTON HEIGHTS: [S] *C to 155th St./St. Nicholas Ave., 163rd St.; 1, A, C to 168th St./Broadway; A to 175th St., 181st St., 190th St.; 1 to 181st St./St. Nicholas Ave., 191st St.)*

BROOKLYN

Heir to a long and colorful history and the legacies of the numerous immigrant groups who have settled here, Brooklyn has undergone a renaissance in recent years as a hip address for young urbanites. Many young New Yorkers will tell you that, even if they could afford it, they'd rather live here than in Manhattan. Friendly, community-oriented, and green, Brooklyn is home to a host of galleries, restaurants, and nightlife—without the airs often affected in Manhattan. Brooklyn is New York's most populated borough, and on its own it would be the fourth-most populated city in the US.

Each of Brooklyn's many neighborhoods is distinct, but Brooklynites are united in a heartfelt pride in their borough. While large portions are quiet and residential, several neighborhoods make great tourist destinations. **Williamsburg,** centering around the cafes and shops of Beford and Berry St., is a formerly industrial district with a wonderfully funky feel to it—and some of the best nightlife in all of New York. **Brooklyn Heights** boasts rows of well-preserved 19th-century Greek Revival and Italianate houses and a cute main drag lined with cafes, bookstores, and mid-priced restaurants. Arthur Miller and W.H. Auden called this neighborhood home in the 1940s and 50s. The nearby **DUMBO** ("Down Under Manhattan Bridge Overpass") neighborhood is home to an active community of artists and galleries. To the southeast lies **Park Slope,** a picturesque neighborhood of brownstones, great dining, and scores of fun young residents. The area is also home to **Prospect Park,** which was designed by Olmsted and Vaux of Central Park fame; supposedly, they considered Prospect Park to be their superior effort. The excellent **Brooklyn Museum** and the **Brooklyn Botanic Garden** are also nearby. *(*[S] *F south of York St.; B, D, N, Q, W south of DeKalb Ave.; A, C south of High St.; 2, 3 south of Clark St.; M, R south of Court St.; 4, 5 south of Borough Hall.)*

QUEENS

Geographically the largest of New York's boroughs, Queens is a primarily residential area home to an astonishing diversity of ethnic populations. In addition to being the home of landmarks like the Mets' **Shea Stadium** and **JFK** and **LaGuardia Airports,** it also hosts several often-overlooked museums, such as the **American Museum of the Moving Image,** devoted to the art of film and television, and the **Museum for African Art.** But more than anything else, Queens is a true melting pot; about 50% of its residents are foreign-born. Chinese, German, Greek, Hindi, Italian, Korean, and Spanish are just some of the languages you'll hear on the streets. **Astoria,** known as "Little Athens" for its many Greek residents, is a great place to come if you're in the mood for heaps of garlicky lamb and fluffy pastries. New Yorkers head to Chinese- and Korean-populated **Flushing** for a more authentic Asian experience than that offered by Manhattan's tourist-filled Chinatown. As rents in Manhattan soar farther and farther out of reach, young professionals are increasingly relocating to western Queens neighborhoods like **Long Island City** (just 10min. from Midtown by train)—the once-industrial area is sometimes said to be "the new Brooklyn." *(*[S] *F east of 21st St.; N, W east of Queensboro Plaza; E, V east of 23rd St.; 7 east of Vernon Blvd.)*

THE BRONX

To many New Yorkers, the Bronx, the only New York borough on the mainland, epitomizes the poverty, street violence, and racial inequality, that often manages to lurk below the surface of New York life. Conditions in the borough have improved since the 1970s, when over 30 torched buildings burned unchecked every night, but it's

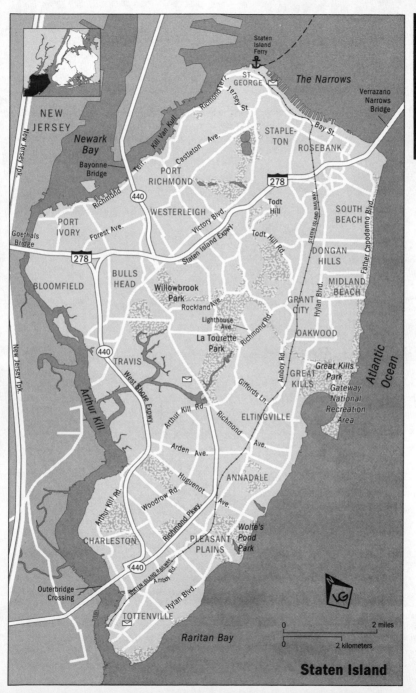

Staten Island Ferry

The Narrows

ST. GEORGE

Verrazano Narrows Bridge

NEW JERSEY

Newark Bay

STAPLETON

ROSEBANK

Bay St.

New Jersey Tpk.

Richmond Terr.

Jersey St.

Kill Van Kull

Castleton Ave.

Bayonne Bridge

PORT RICHMOND

278

Todt Hill

SOUTH BEACH

Terr.

Richmond

440

WESTERLEIGH

Victory Blvd.

Todt Hill Rd.

Staten Island Railway

DONGAN HILLS

Father Capodanno Blvd.

PORT IVORY

Forest Ave.

Staten Island Expwy.

Goethals Bridge

MIDLAND BEACH

BLOOMFIELD

BULLS HEAD

278

Willowbrook Park

Rockland Ave.

GRANT CITY

Hylan Blvd.

Lighthouse Ave.

La Tourette Park

Richmond Rd.

OAKWOOD

New Jersey Tpk.

440

TRAVIS

West Shore Expwy.

Amboy Rd.

Great Kills Park

Atlantic Ocean

Arthur Kill

Giffords Ln.

GREAT KILLS

Gateway National Recreation Area

Arthur Kill Rd.

Richmond

ELTINGVILLE

Ave.

Arden Ave.

Huguenot

ANNADALE

Woodrow Rd.

Ave.

Richmond Pkwy.

Wolfe's Pond Park

Arthur Kill Rd.

CHARLESTON

PLEASANT PLAINS

440

STATEN ISLAND RAILWAY

Amboy Rd.

Outerbridge Crossing

Hylan Blvd.

TOTTENVILLE

Raritan Bay

0   2 miles

0   2 kilometers

Staten Island

WWW.LETSGO.COM
HERE TODAY, WHEREVER YOU'RE HEADED TOMORROW.

Whether you're planning your next adventure or are already far afield, letsgo.com will play companion to your wanderlust.

LET'S GO
COSTA RICA

NEXT 96 km

LET'S GO
AUSTRALIA

Peruse our articles and descriptions as you select the spots you're off to next. If we're making your decision harder, consult fellow travelers on our written and photo forums or search for anecdotal advice in our researchers blogs.

If you're itching to leave, there's no need to shake that pesky travel bug. From embassy locations to passport laws, we keep track of all the essentials, so find out what you need to know fast, book that high-season hostel bed, and hit the road.

LET'S GO
THAILAND

READY. SET. LET'S GO

still best to know where you're going when you're here and to avoid the area alto-gether at night. The South Bronx remains one of the most unsafe areas of the city. That is not to say, however, that the Bronx has nothing to offer the tourist. The "Bronx Bombers" have made their home at **Yankee Stadium** since 1923. The **Bronx Zoo** and the nearby **New York Botanical Garden** are both world-class, and the borough's own **Little Italy** puts the Manhattan tourist trap to shame. The Bronx's historic central boulevard, the turn-of-the-century **Grand Concourse,** once home to the borough's wealthiest residents, is slowly being revitalized to capture some of the European-style elegance its designers intended. **City Island,** to the northeast of the borough on Long Island Sound, has the feel, surprisingly, of a maritime village in the midst of the Bronx. (**S** *4, 5, 6 above 138th St.; B, D above 161st St.; 1 above 231st St.)*

STATEN ISLAND

Sometimes referred to as New York's "forgotten borough," quiet and surprisingly rural Staten Island is decidedly unlike the rest of New York City. Indeed, its local pol-iticians periodically declare their intention to secede from New York City altogether, and many New Yorkers retort that they don't know why the island belongs to the city in the first place. Perhaps distaste for the borough derives from the fact that for much of the last century it was home to the **Fresh Kills Landfill,** which processed most of the city's trash and was the largest landfill in the US (and the tallest manmade hill on the East Coast). With the landfill closed since 2001, the area is slowly being trans-formed into a scenic wetland estuary, and the city has plans to turn it into a mixed-use public park three times the size of Central Park. For now, in addition to a couple of quirky museums, the borough boasts one highly worthwhile tourist destination—the scenic (and free) **Staten Island Ferry.**

▨ LET'S GO PICKS

BEST BAR IN WHICH TO ORDER A MANHATTAN: The Flatiron Lounge (p. 305), whose classic decor will make you feel like you're in a black-and-white film.

BEST STORE FOR A SPOILED BRAT: Dylan's Candy Shop (p. 138), selling every kind of candy imaginable.

BEST FULL MEAL AT 4AM: At Big Nick's Burger and Pizza Joint (p. 139), where the thick-as-a-phonebook menu is served 24hr.

BEST PLACE TO FEEL SMALL: Beneath the dinosaur skeletons at the Museum of Natural History (p. 232).

BEST MARGARITA AND MANHATTAN SKYLINE COMBO: On the rooftop deck of Alma (p. 148), in Brooklyn's Red Hook neighborhood.

QUAINTEST SKYLINE VIEW: From the bright red cable cars of the Roosevelt Island tram (p. 200), which loft you high above the East River.

BEST ALTERNATIVE TO MOM'S CHICKEN SOUP: A grilled-cheese sand-wich with tomato soup at Say Cheese!, in Hell's Kitchen (p. 134).

BEST PLACE TO GET MEDIEVAL: The Cloisters (p. 234), a tranquil setting for beautiful and fascinating medieval art.

BEST PLACE TO TOAST THE OLD COUNTRY: Beer Garden at Bohemian Hall (p. 309), a rowdy Czech restaurant operated by the Bohemian Citizens' Benevolent Society.

BEST PLACE TO RELIVE ELEMENTARY SCHOOL: With a cupcake at Buttercup Bake Shop (p. 141), devoted exclusively to chocolate and vanilla cupcakes with buttercream frosting.

BEST BAR TO IMPRESS YOUR DATE: The rooftop bar of the swanky Hotel Gan-sevoort (p. 300), where you can watch the sun set over the Hudson by candle-light.

BEST CHEAP THRILL: A ride on Coney Island's Cyclone roller coaster (p. 207), a Brooklyn standby since 1927.

BEST PLACE TO LINDY HOP: Under the stars at Lincoln Center, with Midsum-mer Night Swing (p. 247).

BEST PLACE TO EXPERIENCE PEDESTRIAN GRIDLOCK: Times Square at rush hour (p. 179).

BEST OF MANHATTAN (3 DAYS)

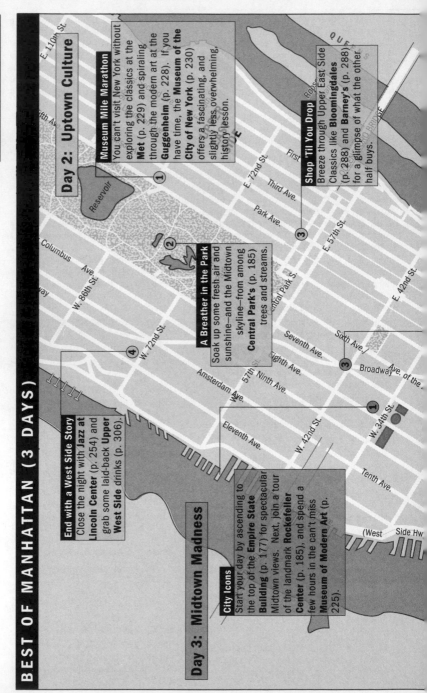

Day 2: Uptown Culture

Museum Mile Marathon
You can't visit New York without exploring the classics at the **Met** (p. 229) and spiraling through the modern art at the **Guggenheim** (p. 228). If you have time, the **Museum of the City of New York** (p. 230) offers a fascinating, and slightly less overwhelming, history lesson.

Shop 'Til You Drop
Breeze through Upper East Side Classics like **Bloomingdales** (p. 288) and **Barney's** (p. 288) for a glimpse of what the other half buys.

A Breather in the Park
Soak up some fresh air and sunshine—and the Midtown skyline—from among **Central Park's** (p. 185) trees and streams.

End with a West Side Story
Close the night with **Jazz at Lincoln Center** (p. 254) and grab some laid-back **Upper West Side** drinks (p. 306).

Day 3: Midtown Madness

City Icons
Start your day by ascending to the top of the **Empire State Building** (p. 177) for spectacular Midtown views. Next, join a tour of the landmark **Rockefeller Center** (p. 185), and spend a few hours in the can't miss **Museum of Modern Art** (p. 225).

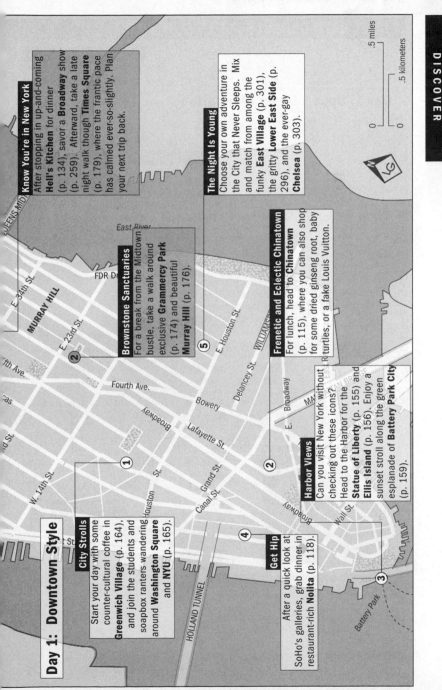

Know You're in New York

After stopping in up-and-coming **Hell's Kitchen** for dinner (p. 134), savor a **Broadway** show (p. 259). Afterward, take a late night walk though **Times Square** (p. 179), where the frantic pace has calmed ever-so-slightly. Plan your next trip back.

The Night Is Young

Choose your own adventure in the City that Never Sleeps. Mix and match from among the funky **East Village** (p. 301), the gritty **Lower East Side** (p. 296), and the ever-gay **Chelsea** (p. 303).

Brownstone Sanctuaries

For a break from the Midtown bustle, take a walk around exclusive **Grammercy Park** (p. 174) and beautiful **Murray Hill** (p. 176).

Frenetic and Eclectic Chinatown

For lunch, head to **Chinatown** (p. 115), where you can also shop for some dried ginseng root, baby R turtles, or a fake Louis Vuitton.

Harbor Views

Can you visit New York without checking out these icons? Head to the Harbor for the **Statue of Liberty** (p. 155) and **Ellis Island** (p. 156). Enjoy a sunset stroll along the green esplanade of **Battery Park City** (p. 159).

Get Hip

After a quick look at SoHo's galleries, grab dinner in restaurant-rich **Nolita** (p. 118).

Day 1: Downtown Style

City Strolls

Start your day with some counter-cultural coffee in **Greenwich Village** (p. 164), and join the students and soapbox ranters wandering around **Washington Square** and **NYU** (p. 165).

East River

MURRAY HILL

E. 34th St.

E. 23rd St.

FDR Dr

Fifth Ave.

Fourth Ave.

Broadway

Bowery

Lafayette St.

E. Houston St.

Delancey St.

Grand St.

Canal St.

Houston St.

St.

W. 14th St.

Broadway

E. Broadway

Wall St.

Battery Park

HOLLAND TUNNEL

QUEENS-MID.

.5 miles

.5 kilometers

0

0

N

DISCOVER

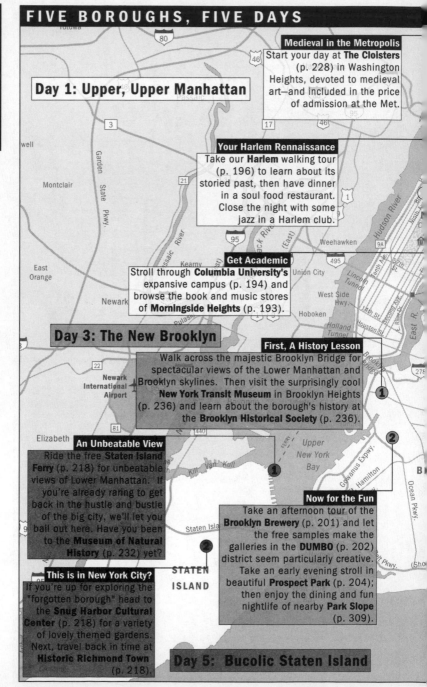

FIVE BOROUGHS, FIVE DAYS

Day 1: Upper, Upper Manhattan

Medieval in the Metropolis

Start your day at **The Cloisters** (p. 228) in Washington Heights, devoted to medieval art—and included in the price of admission at the Met.

Your Harlem Rennaissance

Take our **Harlem** walking tour (p. 196) to learn about its storied past, then have dinner in a soul food restaurant. Close the night with some jazz in a Harlem club.

Get Academic

Stroll through **Columbia University's** expansive campus (p. 194) and browse the book and music stores of **Morningside Heights** (p. 193).

Day 3: The New Brooklyn

First, A History Lesson

Walk across the majestic Brooklyn Bridge for spectacular views of the Lower Manhattan and Brooklyn skylines. Then visit the surprisingly cool **New York Transit Museum** in Brooklyn Heights (p. 236) and learn about the borough's history at the **Brooklyn Historical Society** (p. 236).

An Unbeatable View

Ride the free **Staten Island Ferry** (p. 218) for unbeatable views of Lower Manhattan. If you're already raring to get back in the hustle and bustle of the big city, we'll let you bail out here. Have you been to the **Museum of Natural History** (p. 232) yet?

This is in New York City?

If you're up for exploring the "forgotten borough" head to the **Snug Harbor Cultural Center** (p. 218) for a variety of lovely themed gardens. Next, travel back in time at **Historic Richmond Town** (p. 218).

Now for the Fun

Take an afternoon tour of the **Brooklyn Brewery** (p. 201) and let the free samples make the galleries in the **DUMBO** (p. 202) district seem particularly creative. Take an early evening stroll in beautiful **Prospect Park** (p. 204); then enjoy the dining and fun nightlife of nearby **Park Slope** (p. 309).

Day 5: Bucolic Staten Island

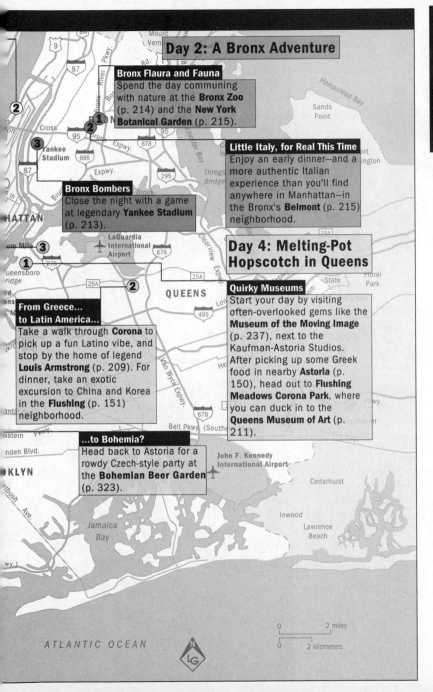

Day 2: A Bronx Adventure

Bronx Flaura and Fauna
Spend the day communing with nature at the **Bronx Zoo** (p. 214) and the **New York Botanical Garden** (p. 215).

Little Italy, for Real This Time
Enjoy an early dinner—and a more authentic Italian experience than you'll find anywhere in Manhattan—in the Bronx's **Belmont** (p. 215) neighborhood.

Bronx Bombers
Close the night with a game at legendary **Yankee Stadium** (p. 213).

Day 4: Melting-Pot Hopscotch in Queens

Quirky Museums
Start your day by visiting often-overlooked gems like the **Museum of the Moving Image** (p. 237), next to the Kaufman-Astoria Studios. After picking up some Greek food in nearby **Astoria** (p. 150), head out to **Flushing Meadows Corona Park**, where you can duck in to the **Queens Museum of Art** (p. 211).

From Greece... to Latin America...
Take a walk through **Corona** to pick up a fun Latino vibe, and stop by the home of legend **Louis Armstrong** (p. 209). For dinner, take an exotic excursion to China and Korea in the **Flushing** (p. 151) neighborhood.

...to Bohemia?
Head back to Astoria for a rowdy Czech-style party at the **Bohemian Beer Garden** (p. 323).

ESSENTIALS

PLANNING YOUR TRIP

ENTRANCE REQUIREMENTS
Passport (p. 26). Required of citizens of all foreign countries except Canada.
Visa (p. 27).
Work Permit (p. 27). Required for all foreigners planning to work in the US.

EMBASSIES AND CONSULATES

US CONSULAR SERVICES ABROAD

Australia: Moonah Pl., Yarralumla, Canberra, ACT 2600 (☎02 6214 5600; http://usembassy-australia.state.gov/consular). **Consulates:** MLC Centre, Level 59, 19-29 Martin Pl., **Sydney,** NSW 2000 (☎02 9373 9200; http://sydney.usconsulate.gov/sydney); 553 St. Kilda Rd., **Melbourne,** VIC 3004 (☎03 9526 5900; http://Melbourne.usconsulate.gov/Melbourne/index.html); 16 St. George's Terr., 13th fl., **Perth,** WA 6000 (☎08 9202 1224; http://perth.usconsulate.gov/perth/index.html).

Canada: Consular Section, 490 Sussex Dr., Ottawa, P.O. Box 866, Station B, Ottowa, Ontario K1P 5T1 (☎613-238-5335; www.usembassycanada.gov). **Consulates** (☎900-451-2778; www.amcits.com): 615 Macleod Trail SE, Room 1000, **Calgary,** AB T2G 4T8 (☎403-266-8962); 1969 Upper Water St., Purdy's Wharf Tower II, Ste. 904, **Halifax,** NS B3J 3R7 (☎902-429-2480); 1155 St-Alexandre, **Montréal,** QC H3B 1Z1 (mailing address: P.O. Box 65, Postal Station Desjardins, Montréal, QC H5B 1G1; ☎514-398-9695); 2 Pl. Terrasse Dufferin, behind Château Frontenac, **Québec City** (mailing address B.P. 939, Québec, QC G1R 4T9); 360 University Ave., **Toronto,** ON M5G 1S4 (☎418-692-2095); 1095 W Pender St., **Vancouver,** B.C. V6E 2M6 Canada.

Ireland: 42 Elgin Rd., Ballsbridge, Dublin 4 (☎01 668 8777; http://dublin.usembassy.gov).

New Zealand: 29 Fitzherbert Terr., Thorndon, Wellington (mailing address: P.O. Box 1190, Wellington; ☎04 462 6000; http://usembassy.org.nz). **Consulate:** 23 Customs St., Citibank Building, 3rd fl., Auckland (mailing address: Private Bag 92022, Auckland; ☎09 303 2724).

UK: 24 Grosvenor Sq., **London** W1A 1AE (☎020 7499 9000; www.usembassy.org.uk). **Consulates:** Queen's House, 14 Queen St., **Belfast,** N. Ireland BT1 6EQ (☎028 9032 8239); 3 Regent Terr., **Edinburgh,** Scotland EH7 5BW (☎0131 556 8315).

CONSULAR SERVICES IN THE US

Consulates in New York are listed at the Commission for the UN Consular Corps and Protocol, under Consular Affairs, at www.nyc.gov./html/unccp/html/consular/nyc_list.shtml.

Australia: 1601 Massachusetts Ave. NW, Washington, D.C, 20036-2273 (☎202-797-3000; www.austemb.org). **Consulate:** 150 E 42nd St., 34th fl., New York, NY 10017-5612 (☎212-351-6500; www.australianyc.org).

Canada: 501 Pennsylvania Ave. NW, Washington, D.C., 20001 (☎202-682-1740; www.canadianembassy.org). **Consulate:** 1251 Ave. of the Americas, New York, NY 10020-1175 (☎212-596-1628; www.dfait-maeci.gc.ca/new_york/).

Ireland: 2234 Massachusetts Ave. NW, Washington, D.C. 20008 (☎202-462-3939; www.irelandemb.org). **Consulate:** 345 Park Ave., New York, NY 10154-0004 (☎212-319-2555).

New Zealand: 37 Observatory Circle NW, Washington, D.C. 20008 (☎202-328-4800; www.nzembassy.com).

UK: 3100 Massachusetts Ave., Washington, D.C. 20008 (☎202-588-7800; www.britainusa.com/consular/embassy). **Consulate:** 845 3rd Ave., New York, NY 10022 (☎212-745-0200; www.britainusa.com/ny).

TOURIST OFFICES

Big Apple Greeter, 1 Centre St., Ste. 2035, New York, NY, 10007 (☎212-669-8159; www.bigapplegreeter.org).

The Bronx Tourism Council, 198 E 161 St., Ste. 201, Bronx, NY, 10451 (☎718-590-2766; www.ilovethebronx.com).

Brooklyn Information and Culture, 647 Fulton St., Brooklyn, NY 11217 (☎718-855-7882; www.brooklynx.org).

Harlem Visitors and Convention Association, 1 W 125th St., New York, NY 10027 (☎212-427-3317).

New York State Division of Tourism, P.O. Box 2603, Albany, NY 12220-0603 (☎518-474-4116 or 800-CALL-NYS; www.iloveny.com).

Times Square Information Center, 1580 Broadway, Ste. 800, New York, NY 10036 (☎212-768-1560; www.timessquarebid.org/visitor.html).

DOCUMENTS AND FORMALITIES

PASSPORTS

REQUIREMENTS

Citizens of Australia, Ireland, New Zealand, and the UK need valid passports to enter the US and to re-enter their home countries. The US does not allow entrance if the holder's passport expires in under six months; returning home with an expired passport is illegal, and may result in a fine.

NEW PASSPORTS

Citizens of Australia, Canada, Ireland, New Zealand, the UK, and the US can apply for a passport at any post office, passport office, or court of law. Any new passport or renewal applications must be filed well in advance of the departure date, although most passport offices offer rush services for a very steep fee.

PASSPORT MAINTENANCE

Photocopy the page of your passport with your photo. Carry one copy in a safe place apart from the original, and leave the other at home. Consulates also recommend that you carry an expired passport or an official copy of your birth certificate.

If you lose your passport, immediately notify the local police and the nearest embassy or consulate of your home government. To speed up its replacement, you will need to show ID and proof of citizenship. In some cases, a replacement may take weeks to process, and it may be valid only for a limited time. Any visas in your old passport will be lost. In an emergency, ask for temporary traveling papers that will permit you to re-enter your home country.

VISAS AND WORK PERMITS

Citizens of most countries need a visa—a stamp, sticker, or insert in your passport specifying the purpose of your travel and the permitted duration of your stay—for entrance to the US. See **www.unitedstatesvisas.gov** for more information. To obtain a visa, contact a US embassy or consulate. Recent security measures have made the visa application process more rigorous. Apply well in advance of your travel date.

Canadian citizens do not need to obtain a visa for admission to the US. Citizens of **Australia, New Zealand,** and most **European countries** can waive US visas through the **Visa Waiver Program.** Visitors qualify if they are traveling only for business or pleasure (*not* work or study), are staying for fewer than **90 days,** have proof of intent to leave (e.g., a return plane ticket), possess an I-94 form, and possess a machine-readable passport from a nation of which they are a citizen. See http://travel.state.gov/vwp.html for more information.

If you lose your I-94 form, you can replace it by filling out form I-102, although it's very unlikely that the form will be replaced within the time of your stay. The form is available at the nearest **Bureau of Citizenship and Immigration Services (BSIC)** office (www.bcis.gov), through the forms request line (☎800-870-3676), or online (www.bcis.gov/graphics/formsfee/forms/i-102.htm). **Visa extensions** are sometimes granted with a completed I-539 form; call the forms request line or get it online at www.immigration.gov/graphics/formsfee/forms/i-539.htm.

WORK PERMITS

Admission as a visitor does not include the right to work, which is authorized only by a **work permit.** Entering the US to study requires a special visa. For more information, see **Beyond Tourism,** p. 72.

IDENTIFICATION

When you travel, always have at least two forms of identification on you, including at least one photo ID. A passport and driver's license or birth certificate are usually adequate. Carry your IDs separately in case of theft or loss, and keep photocopies of all of them in your luggage and at home.

STUDENT, TEACHER, AND YOUTH IDENTIFICATION

The **International Student Identity Card (ISIC),** the most widely accepted form of student ID, provides discounts, access to a 24hr. emergency helpline, and insurance benefits for US cardholders (see **Insurance,** p. 33). Applicants must be full-time students at least 12 years of age. Because of the proliferation of fake ISICs, some services (particularly airlines) require additional proof of student identity.

The **International Teacher Identity Card (ITIC)** offers teachers the same insurance coverage as the ISIC, and similar but limited discounts. For travelers who are 25 years old or under but are not students, the **International Youth Travel Card (IYTC)** also offers many of the same benefits. Each of these identity cards costs US$22 or equivalent. ISICs and ITICs are valid for roughly one and a half academic years; IYTCs cards are valid for one year from the date of issue. Many student travel agencies (see p. 35) issue the cards. For a list of issuing agencies or more information, see the **International Student Travel Confederation (ISTC)** website (www.istc.org). A final alternative is the **International Student Exchange Card (ISE),** for students, faculty, and youth aged 12 to 26. The card provides discounts, medical benefits, access to a 24hr. emergency helpline, and the ability to purchase student airfares. The card costs US$25; call ☎800-255-8000 for more info, or visit www.isecard.com.

CUSTOMS

Upon entering the US, you must declare certain items from abroad and pay a duty on the value of those articles that exceeds the US customs allowance. Note that goods and gifts purchased at duty-free shops abroad are not exempt from duty or sales tax and thus must be declared as well; **duty-free** merely means that you need not pay a tax in the country of purchase.

MONEY

CURRENCY AND EXCHANGE

The currency chart below is based on August 2006 exchange rates between US dollars (US$) and Australian dollars (AUS$), Canadian dollars (CDN$), the European Union euros (EUR€), New Zealand dollars (NZ$), and British pounds (UK£). Check the currency converter on websites like **www.xe.com** or **www.oanda.com** or a large newspaper for the latest exchange rates.

CURRENCY	
AUS$1 = US$0.73	US$1 = AUS$1.37
CDN$1 = US$0.89	US$1 = CDN$1.12
EUR€1 = US$1.25	US$1 = EUR€0.80
NZ$1 = US$0.61	US$1 = NZ$1.65
UK£1 = US$1.82	US$1 = UK£0.55

As a general rule, it's cheaper to convert money in the US. Avoid airport exchanges, and bring enough dollars to last for the first 24-72 hours of your trip. When changing money, try to go only to banks that have at most a 5% margin between their buy and sell prices. Since you lose money with every transaction, **convert large sums** (unless the currency is depreciating rapidly), **but no more than you'll need.**

If you use traveler's checks or bills, carry some in small denominations (the equivalent of US$50 or less) for times when you are forced to exchange money at disadvantageous rates, but bring a range of denominations since charges may be levied per check cashed. Store your money in a variety of forms; ideally, at any given time you will be carrying some cash, traveler's checks, and an ATM and/or credit card.

TRAVELER'S CHECKS

Traveler's checks are one of the safest means of carrying funds. American Express and Visa are the most recognized brands. Many banks and agencies sell them for a small commission. Check issuers provide refunds if the checks are lost or stolen. Many provide extra services, such as stolen credit card help. Traveler's checks are readily accepted in New York, though the prevalence of ATMs has made them less common than they once were. Ask about toll-free hotlines and the location of refund centers when purchasing checks. Always carry emergency cash.

American Express: Checks available with commission at select banks, at all AmEx offices, and online (www.americanexpress.com; US residents only). American Express cardholders can also purchase checks by phone (☎888-269-6669). AAA (see p. 44) offers commission-free checks to its members. Checks available in Australian, Canadian, European, Japanese, British, and US currencies. For purchase locations or more information contact AmEx's service centers: in Australia ☎800 688 022, in New Zealand 050 855 5358, in the UK 0800 587 6023, in the US and Canada 800-221-7282; elsewhere, call the US collect at 801-964-6665.

Travelex: Thomas Cook MasterCard and Interpayment Visa traveler's checks available. For information about Thomas Cook MasterCard in Canada and the US call ☎800-223-

7373, in the UK 0800 622 101; elsewhere call the UK collect at +44 1733 318 950. For information about Interpayment Visa in the US and Canada call ☎800-732-1322, in the UK 0800 515 884; elsewhere call the UK collect at +44 1733 318 949. For more information, visit www.travelex.com.

Visa: Checks available (generally with commission) at banks worldwide. For the location of the nearest office, call the Visa Travelers Cheque Global Refund and Assistance Center: in the UK ☎0800 895 078, in the US 800-227-6811; elsewhere, call the UK collect at +44 2079 378 091. Checks available in British, Canadian, European, Japanese, and US currencies, among others. Visa also offers TravelMoney, a prepaid debit card that can be reloaded online or by phone. For more information on Visa travel services, see http://usa.visa.com/personal/using_visa/travel_with_visa.html.

CREDIT, DEBIT, AND ATM CARDS

Where they are accepted, credit cards often offer superior exchange rates—up to 5% better than the retail rate used by banks and other currency exchange establishments. Credit cards may also offer services such as insurance or emergency help, and are sometimes required to reserve hotel rooms or rental cars. **MasterCard** and **Visa** are the most frequently accepted; **American Express** cards work at some ATMs and at AmEx offices and major airports.

The use of ATM cards is widespread in New York. Depending on the system that your home bank uses, you can most likely access your personal bank account. ATMs get the same wholesale exchange rate as credit cards, but there is often a limit on the amount of money you can withdraw per day (usually around US$500). There is typically also a surcharge of US$1-5 per withdrawal.

Debit cards are as convenient as credit cards but have a more immediate impact on your funds. A debit card can be used wherever its associated credit card company (usually MasterCard or Visa) is accepted, yet the money is withdrawn directly from the holder's checking account. Debit cards often also function as ATM cards and can be used at associated banks and ATMs throughout New York.

The two major international money networks are **MasterCard/Maestro/Cirrus** (for ATM locations ☎800-424-7787 or www.mastercard.com) and **Visa/PLUS** (for ATM locations ☎800-847-2911 or www.visa.com). Most ATMs charge a transaction fee that is paid to the bank that owns the ATM.

GETTING MONEY FROM HOME

If you run out of money while traveling, the easiest and cheapest solution is to have someone back home make a deposit to your bank account. Failing that, consider one of the following options.

WIRING MONEY

It is possible to arrange a **bank money transfer,** which means asking a bank back home to wire money to a bank in New York. This is the cheapest way to transfer cash, but it's also the slowest, usually taking several days or more. Note that some banks may only release your funds in local currency, potentially sticking you with a poor exchange rate; inquire about this in advance. Money transfer services like **Western Union** are faster and more convenient than bank transfers—but also much pricier. Western Union has many locations worldwide. To find one, visit www.westernunion.com, or call in Australia ☎1800 173 833, in Canada and the US 800-325-6000, in the UK 0800 833 833, or in New York 800-225-5227. To wire money using a credit card (Discover, MasterCard, Visa), call in Canada and the US ☎800-225-5227, in the UK 0800 833 833. Money transfer services are also available to **American Express** cardholders and at select **Thomas Cook** offices.

TOP 10 WAYS TO SAVE IN NEW YORK CITY

Let's face it: New York is expensive, rivaled only by San Francisco as the most expensive US city. But armed with these tips, even the most cash-strapped traveler can have a great time here.
1. Walk and take the subway as much as possible. Consider investing in an unlimited-ride MetroCard (p. 41).
2. Shop for food at outdoor markets, like Union Square's Greenmarket (p. 132).
3. Watch for days or hours when museum admission is "pay what you wish" (p. 231).
4. Take advantage of flyers and coupons that allow you to bypass the cover charges at clubs—look for them in weekly papers, from promoters on the street, and on the Internet.
5. Seek out free Internet in libraries, open-air parks, and even Apple Stores (p. 287).
6. Consider outer-borough accommodations options (p. 106), where you'll get more amenities for less.
7. Take advantage of gourmet fixed-price lunches, like the one at Nougatine (p. 139).
8. Window shop to your heart's content; then check out the almost-real-looking knockoffs on Canal St. (p. 281).
9. Pay half-price for theater tickets at the TKTS booth (p. 258), or try for standing-room or student-rush tickets.
10. Shop at sample sales (p. 287), and get more style for less.

COSTS

No matter how frugal a traveler you are, New York is an expensive city to visit. Before you go, spend some time calculating a reasonable daily **budget.** Aside from the cost of your transportation to the city, your single largest expense will almost certainly be lodging, as New York hotels charge often astronomical rates for sometimes uninspiring digs.

TIPS FOR SAVING MONEY

Some simpler ways include searching out opportunities for free entertainment, splitting accommodation and food costs with trustworthy fellow travelers, and buying food in supermarkets rather than eating out. Museums often have certain days once a month or once a week when admission is free; plan accordingly. If you are eligible, consider getting an ISIC or an IYTC; many sights and museums offer reduced admission to students and youths. Walk everywhere you can in New York; you'll learn the most about the city by exploring it by foot. Drinking at bars and clubs quickly becomes expensive. It's cheaper to buy alcohol at a supermarket and imbibe before going out.

TIPPING

Tipping is more or less compulsory in the US. Remember that service is never included on a New York bill, unless you're in a large party at a restaurant (six or more people) and the tip is noted on the bill. As a general rule, tip cab drivers and waiters 15-20%, coat-checkers $1, bellhops around $1 per bag, hotel maids $1 per day, and bartenders $1 per drink.

TAXES

Quoted prices in *Let's Go* do not include New York's **8.625% sales tax,** which applies to hotel rooms (in addition to a **5% hotel tax** and a **$2 room fee per night**).

PACKING

Pack lightly. Lay out only what you absolutely need, then take half the clothes and twice the money. The Travelite FAQ (www.travelite.org) is a good resource for tips on traveling light. The online **Universal Packing List** (http://upl.codeq.info) will generate a customized list of suggested items based on your trip length, the expected climate, your planned activities, and other factors.

Converters and Adapters: In New York, electricity is **110V,** and 220V appliances don't like 110V current. Visit a hardware store for an adapter (which will allow your plug to fit in US outlets) and a converter (which will change the voltage your appliance receives). Don't make the mistake of using only an adapter unless appliance instructions say otherwise. For more information on all things adaptable, see http://kropla.com/electric.htm.

Toiletries: Condoms, deodorant, razors, tampons, and toothbrushes are, of course, readily available in New York, but it may be difficult to find the brand you're used to at home; bring extras if this might be an issue. Bring enough contact lenses and solution for your trip, and be sure to carry a copy of your glasses prescription in case you need an emergency replacement.

First-Aid Kit: For a basic first-aid kit, pack bandages, a pain reliever, antibiotic cream, a thermometer, a multifunction pocketknife, tweezers, moleskin, decongestant, motion-sickness remedy, and diarrhea or upset-stomach medication.

Film: Film and developing services are widespread and relatively inexpensive in New York, but if you don't want to bother with film, consider using a digital camera. Although it requires a steep initial investment, a digital camera means you never have to buy film again. Just be sure to bring along a large enough memory card and extra (or recharge-able) batteries. For more info on digital cameras, visit www.shortcourses.com/choosing/contents.htm. Less serious photographers may want to bring a disposable camera or two. Despite disclaimers, airport security X-rays can fog film, so buy a lead-lined pouch at a camera store or ask security to hand-inspect it. Always pack film in your carry-on luggage, since higher-intensity X-rays are used on checked luggage.

Other Useful Items: For safety purposes, you should bring a **money belt** and a small **padlock.** If you want to do laundry by hand, bring detergent, a small rubber ball to stop up the sink, and string for a makeshift clothes line. Other things you're liable to forget include: an umbrella, sealable **plastic bags** (for damp clothes, soap, food, shampoo, and other spillables), an **alarm clock,** safety pins, rubber bands, a flashlight, earplugs, garbage bags, and a small calculator. A **cell phone** can be a lifesaver (literally); see p. 45 for information on acquiring one that will work in New York.

Important Documents: Don't forget your passport, traveler's checks, ATM and/or credit cards, adequate ID, and photocopies of all of the aforementioned in case these documents are lost or stolen (p. 26). Also check that you have any of the following that might apply to you: a hosteling membership card (p. 89); driver's license (p. 27); travel insurance forms (p. 33); or ISIC (p. 27).

SAFETY AND HEALTH

GENERAL ADVICE

In an emergency, **dial ☎ 911.** In any type of crisis situation, the most important thing to do is to **stay calm.** Your country's embassy (p. 25) is usually your best resource when things go wrong. The government offices listed in the **Travel Advisories** box on p. 32 can provide information on the services they offer their citizens in case of emergencies abroad.

DRUGS AND ALCOHOL

You must be 21 years old to legally purchase alcoholic beverages in New York State. Most drinking spots and liquor stores do card. Be aware that using a fake ID can result in serious consequences, including an offense on your record and suspension of your real driver's license.

Possession of marijuana, cocaine, crack, heroin, methamphetamine, MDMA ("ecstasy"), hallucinogens, and most opiate derivatives (among many other chemicals) is punishable by stiff fines and imprisonment. Attempting to purchase illegal drugs of any sort is a **bad idea.** Out-of-towners seeking (or on) a high are walking targets—not just for cops, but for thieves as well.

If you carry **prescription drugs** when you travel, it is vital to have a copy of the prescriptions themselves readily accessible at US Customs. Check with the US Customs Service for more information before you head out.

SPECIFIC CONCERNS

TERRORISM

The September 11th attacks of 2001 revealed the vulnerability of large American cities to terrorist attacks and resulted in the enforcement of stringent safety measures at airports and major tourist sights throughout New York. Allow extra time for airport security and do not pack sharp objects in your carry-on luggage, as these will be confiscated. Check your home country's foreign affairs office for travel information and advisories, and be sure to follow the local news while in New York.

> ⚠ **TRAVEL ADVISORIES.** The following government offices provide travel information and advisories by telephone or via the web:
>
> **Australian Department of Foreign Affairs and Trade:** ☎612 6261 1111; www.dfat.gov.au.
>
> **Canadian Department of Foreign Affairs and International Trade (DFAIT):** Call ☎800-267-8376; www.dfait-maeci.gc.ca. Call for their free booklet, *Bon Voyage...But.*
>
> **New Zealand Ministry of Foreign Affairs:** ☎044 398 000; www.mfat.govt.nz.
>
> **United Kingdom Foreign and Commonwealth Office:** ☎020 7008 1500; www.fco.gov.uk.
>
> **US Department of State:** ☎888-407-4747; http://travel.state.gov. Visit the website for the booklet *A Safe Trip Abroad.*

PERSONAL SAFETY

EXPLORING AND TRAVELING

To avoid unwanted attention, try to blend in as much as possible when you're walking around New York. Familiarize yourself with your surroundings before setting out, and carry yourself with confidence. Check maps in shops and restaurants rather than on the street. If you are traveling alone, be sure someone at home knows your itinerary, and never admit that you're by yourself. When walking at night, stick to busy, well-lit streets and avoid dark alleyways. If you ever feel uncomfortable, leave the area as quickly and directly as you can, or duck into one of New York's many 24hr. convenience stores.

A good resource to be aware of is the Westside Crime Prevention Program's **Safe Haven** Program. Founded in 1984, the Safe Haven Program spans from W 59th St. to W 125th St., and to some locations in Harlem, the Upper East Side, and the Lower East Side. Participating merchants display a bright yellow Safe Haven decal on their door indicating that they are willing and able to provide shelter or contact the police. Though the program is intended for the protection of children, it can be reassuring for the lone traveler as well. See www.wcppny.org/program_tamar.html for more details.

There is no sure-fire way to avoid all the threatening situations you might encounter while traveling in New York, but a good **self-defense course** will give you concrete ways to react to unwanted advances. **Impact, Prepare, and Model Mugging** can refer you to local self-defense courses in Australia, Canada, Switzerland, and the US. Visit the website www.impactsafety.org for a list of chapters. Workshops (2-4hr.) start at US$50; full courses (20hr.) run US$350-500.

POSSESSIONS AND VALUABLES

There are a few steps you can take to minimize the financial risk associated with traveling. First, **bring as little with you as possible.** Second, bring a **combination lock** to secure your belongings at your hotel or hostel if it does not have a safe. Third, **bring as little cash as possible.** Keep your traveler's checks and ATM/credit cards in a **money belt**—not a "fanny pack"—along with your passport and ID cards. Fourth, **keep a small cash reserve separate from your primary stash.** This should be about US$50, along with your traveler's check numbers and photocopies of your passport, your birth certificate, and other important documents.

In large cities like New York, **con artists** often work in groups and may involve children. Beware of certain classics: sob stories that require money, rolls of bills "found" on the street, mustard spilled (or saliva spit) onto your shoulder to distract you while they snatch your bag. **Never let your passport and your bags out of your sight.** Beware of **pickpockets** in city crowds, especially on public transportation.

If you will be traveling with electronic devices, such as a laptop computer or a PDA, check whether your homeowner's insurance covers loss, theft, or damage when you travel. If not, you might consider purchasing a low-cost separate insurance policy. **Safeware** (☎ 800-800-1492; www.safeware.com) specializes in covering computers and charges $90 for 90-day comprehensive international travel coverage up to $4000.

PRE-DEPARTURE HEALTH

In your **passport** or your **wallet,** write the names of any people you wish to be contacted in case of a medical emergency, and a list of any allergies or medical conditions. If you take prescription drugs, consider carrying prescriptions or a statement from your doctor stating the medication's trade name, manufacturer, chemical name, and dosage. Be sure to keep all medication with you in your carry-on luggage. You can also pack a basic **first aid kit,** with band-aids, ointment, and other essentials.

INSURANCE

Travel insurance covers four basic areas: medical/health problems, property loss, trip cancellation/interruption, and emergency evacuation. Though regular insurance policies may well extend to travel-related accidents, you may consider purchasing separate travel insurance if the cost of potential trip cancellation, interruption, or emergency medical evacuation is greater than you can absorb. Prices for travel insurance purchased separately generally run about US$50 per week for full coverage, while trip cancellation/interruption may be purchased separately at a rate of US$3-5 per day depending on length of stay.

Medical insurance (especially university policies) often covers costs incurred abroad; check with your provider. **Canadian** provincial health insurance plans increasingly do not cover foreign travel; check with the provincial Ministry of Health or Health Plan Headquarters for details. **Homeowners' insurance** (or your family's coverage) often covers theft during travel and loss of travel documents (passport, plane ticket, railpass, etc.) up to US$500.

ISIC and **ITIC** (p. 27) provide basic insurance benefits to US cardholders, including US$100 per day of in-hospital sickness for up to 100 days and US$10,000 of accident-related medical reimbursement (see www.isicus.com for details). Cardholders have access to a toll-free 24hr. helpline for medical, legal, and financial emergencies overseas. **American Express** (☎800-338-1670) grants most cardholders automatic collision and theft car rental insurance on rentals made with the card.

USEFUL ORGANIZATIONS AND PUBLICATIONS

The American **Centers for Disease Control and Prevention** (**CDC;** ☎877-FYI-TRIP; www.cdc.gov/travel) maintains an international travelers' hotline and an informative website. Consult the appropriate government agency of your home country for consular information sheets on health, entry requirements, and other issues for various countries (see the listings in the box on **Travel Advisories,** p. 32). For general health info, contact the **American Red Cross** (☎202-303-4498; www.redcross.org).

STAYING HEALTHY

Common sense is the simplest prescription for good health while you travel. Drink lots of fluids, and wear sturdy, broken-in shoes and clean socks.

INFECTIOUS DISEASES

For detailed information on **Acquired Immune Deficiency Syndrome (AIDS),** call ☎866-644-KNOW, or visit www.knowhivaids.org. Within the state of New York, you can also call ☎800-541-2437 for information or ☎800-872-2777 for individual counseling. For a list of testing and counseling centers in New York city, visit www.nyaidsline.org; www.ppnyc.org/services/aids.html; or www.gmhc.org. **Sexually transmitted diseases (STDs)** such as Gonorrhea, genital warts, syphilis, and others are more common than HIV and can be just as serious. **Hepatitis B and C** can also be transmitted sexually. Though condoms may protect you from some STDs, oral or even tactile contact can lead to transmission. If you think you may have an STD, see a doctor immediately.

WOMEN'S HEALTH

Tampons, pads, and **contraceptive devices** are widely available. **Abortion** is legal in the US. For support and information, contact **Planned Parenthood,** located at Margaret Sanger Sq., 26 Bleecker St., New York, NY 10021 (☎212-965-7000; www.ppnyc.org/homepage.html).

GETTING TO NEW YORK CITY

BY PLANE

Four major airports serve the New York metropolitan region. The largest, **John F. Kennedy Airport** (JFK; ☎718-244-4444) is 15 mi. from midtown Manhattan in southern Queens and handles mostly international flights. **LaGuardia Airport** (LGA; ☎718-533-3400) is 9 mi. from midtown in Queens and the second largest, offering domestic flights as well as hourly shuttles to and from Boston and Washington, D.C. **Newark Liberty International Airport** (EWR; ☎973-961-6000), 16 mi. from midtown in Newark, NJ, offers both domestic and international flights at budget fares often not available at the other airports (though getting to and from Newark is pricey).

ESSENTIALS

AIRFARES

Fares for round-trip flights to New York City start around US$1000 from Australia; around US$300 from the Canadian east coast; around US$400 from the Canadian west coast; around US$600 from the UK; and around US$1300 from New Zealand.

BUDGET AND STUDENT TRAVEL AGENCIES

While knowledgeable agents can make your life easy and help you save, they may not spend the time to find you the lowest possible fare. Travelers holding **ISICs** and **IYTCs** (p. 27) qualify for big discounts from student travel agencies. Most flights from budget agencies are on major airlines, but in peak season some may sell seats on less reliable chartered aircraft.

STA Travel, 5900 Wilshire Blvd., Ste. 900, Los Angeles, CA 90036, USA (24hr. reservations and info ☎800-781-4040; www.statravel.com). A student and youth travel organization with over 150 offices worldwide (check their website for a listing of all their offices), including US offices in Boston, Chicago, L.A., New York, San Francisco, Seattle, and Washington, D.C. Ticket booking, travel insurance, railpasses, and more. Walk-in offices are located throughout Australia (☎03 9207 5900), New Zealand (☎09 309 9723), and the UK (☎08701 630 026).

Travel CUTS (Canadian Universities Travel Services Limited), 187 College St., Toronto, ON M5T 1P7, Canada (☎866-246-9762; www.travelcuts.com). Offices across Canada and the US including Los Angeles, New York, San Francisco, and Seattle.

USIT, 19-21 Aston Quay, Dublin 2, Ireland (☎01 602 1904; www.usit.ie), Ireland's leading student/budget travel agency has 20 offices throughout Northern Ireland and the Republic of Ireland. Offers programs to work, study, and volunteer worldwide.

> ✈ **FLIGHT PLANNING ON THE INTERNET.** The Internet may be a budget traveler's dream when it comes to finding and booking bargain fares, but the array of options can be overwhelming. Many airline sites offer last-minute deals online. **STA** (www.statravel.com) and **StudentUniverse** (www.studentuniverse.com) provide quotes on student tickets, while **Orbitz** (www.orbitz.com), **Expedia** (www.expedia.com), and **Travelocity** (www.travelocity.com) offer full travel services. **Priceline** (www.priceline.com) lets you specify a price, and obligates you to buy any ticket that meets it; **Hotwire** (www.hotwire.com) offers bargain fares, but won't reveal the airline or flight times until you buy. Other sites that compile deals include www.bestfares.com, www.flights.com, www.lowestfare.com, www.onetravel.com, and www.travelzoo.com.
>
> Increasingly, there are online tools available to help sift through multiple offers; **SideStep** (www.sidestep.com) and **Booking Buddy** (www.bookingbuddy.com) let you enter your trip information once and search multiple sites.
>
> An indispensable resource on the Internet is the **Air Traveler's Handbook** (www.faqs.org/faqs/travel/air/handbook), a comprehensive listing of links to everything you need to know before you board a plane.

COMMERCIAL AIRLINES

The commercial airlines' lowest regular offer is the **APEX** (Advance Purchase Excursion) fare, which provides confirmed reservations and allows "open-jaw" tickets. Generally, reservations must be made seven to 21 days ahead of departure, with seven- to 14-day minimum-stay and up to 90-day maximum-stay restrictions. These fares carry hefty cancellation and change penalties (fees rise in summer). Book peak-season APEX fares early. Use **Expedia** (www.expedia.com) or **Traveloc-**

A KILLER DEAL?

Forget flying, taking the train, or even riding Greyhound. For travel between New York and other cities on the East Coast, there's one unbeatably cheap deal: the Chinatown bus. Scores of budget travelers swear by these buses, but if you're considering riding for the first time, it's best to weigh the risks.

The many competing bus services, which pick up on the streets of New York's Chinatown and drop off somewhere in that of their destination, began as a service to Chinese laborers who needed to get to work opportunities cheaply. But as a wider range of travelers, Chinese and non-Chinese alike, began to hear of the cut-rate deal, the services grew into a lucrative cottage industry.

The industry's early days were rife with scandal and mob-like intrigue. In 2002, according to *The Boston Globe,* Farewell Bus Company owner De Jiang Chen intentionally smashed his bus into a New Century bus, crushing the rival owner's pelvis. A year later, Chen was found shot and killed. About the same time, several other Chinatown buses were torched, and a New Century employee was found stabbed to death. The situation became truly macabre when New York City police discovered a headless torso in a suitcase near a bus company office in Chinatown. The circumstances surrounding the murder remain uncertain, but many assume it to have been yet

ity (www.travelocity.com) to get an idea of the lowest published fares, then use the resources outlined here to try and beat those fares.

TICKET CONSOLIDATORS

Ticket consolidators, or **"bucket shops,"** buy unsold tickets in bulk from commercial airlines and sell them at discounted rates. The best place to look is in the Sunday travel section of any major newspaper (such as *The New York Times*), where many bucket shops place tiny ads. Call quickly, as availability is typically extremely limited. Not all bucket shops are reliable, so insist on a receipt that gives full details, and pay by credit card (in spite of the 2-5% fee) so you can stop payment if you never receive your tickets. For more info, see www.travel-library.com/air-travel/consolidators.html.

TRAVELING WITHIN THE US AND FROM CANADA

Some consolidators worth trying are **Rebel** (☎800-732-3588; www.rebeltours.com), **Cheap Tickets** (www.cheaptickets.com), **Flights.com** (www.flights.com), and **TravelHUB** (www.travelhub.com). But these are just suggestions to get you started in your research. Let's Go does not endorse any of these agencies. As always, be cautious, and research companies before you hand over your credit card number.

BY TRAIN

Though getting in or out of New York by train isn't necessarily cheaper than flying, it is certainly more scenic, and it delivers you directly to the heart of Midtown. You can save money by purchasing tickets in advance, so plan ahead. **Amtrak** (☎800-USA-RAIL/872-7245; www.amtrak.com) is the major provider of intercity passenger train service in the US. The website lists up-to-date schedules, fares, and arrival and departure info. Many qualify for discounts: senior citizens (10-15% off); students (15% off) with a Student Advantage Card or ISIC (see **By Bus,** p. 37, for how to purchase); travelers with disabilities (15% off); children ages 2 to 15 accompanied by a parent (50% off, 2-child max); children under age two (free with each adult ticket purchased); active-duty US military personnel, their spouses and dependents (10% off); Veterans Advantage members (15% off); and AAA members (10% off). To be eligible for most discounts, tickets must be purchased at least three days in advance. Some restrictions do apply, and can be found on the Amtrak website. Weekly specials listed online offer discounts of up to 90%.

  Amtrak's trains connect NYC to most other parts of the country through **Penn Station**, 33rd St. and Eighth Ave. (**S** 1, 2, 3 to 34th St./Penn Station/7th Ave.; A, C, E to 34th St.-Penn Station/8th Ave.) Routes run from Boston (4-5hr., one way from $54), Philadelphia (1½hr., one way from $42), and Washington, D.C. (3-4hr., one way from $63). The **Long Island Rail Road** and **New Jersey Transit** (p. 311) both run out of Penn Station. The local **MTA Metro-North Railroad** runs to upstate New York and parts of New Jersey out of **Grand Central Terminal**, 42nd St. and Park Ave. (www.grandcentralterminal.com; **S** 4, 5, 6, 7, S.)

BY BUS

The hub of the Northeast bus network, New York's **Port Authority Terminal**, 41st St. and Eighth Ave., is a huge modern facility with labyrinthine bus terminals. (☎212-564-8484. **S** A, C, E to 42nd St./Port Authority.) Port Authority has good information and security services, but the surrounding neighborhood is somewhat deserted at night, and it pays to call a cab.

  Greyhound (☎800-231-2222; www.greyhound.com) operates the largest number of lines, departing from **Boston** (4-6hr.; one way $35), **Montreal** (8-9hr.; one way $76.50), **Philadelphia** (2-3hr.; one way $21), and **Washington, D.C.** (4½-6hr.; one way $37). The fares listed require no advance purchase, but you can save by purchasing tickets in advance. A number of **discounts** are available on Greyhound's standard-fare tickets: students ride for 15% off with the Student Advantage Card (☎800-333-2920; www.studentadvantage.com; $20), senior citizens ride for 10% off, active-duty military personnel ride for 10% off, Veterans Advantage members ride for 15% off, children under 11 ride for 40% off when accompanied by an adult, and children under two ride for free in the lap of an adult (one per adult). A traveler with a physical disability may bring along a companion who may ride for 50% off after clearing them by calling ☎800-752-4841.

  The latest phenomenon in budget travel between cities on the east coast is the emergence of so-called Chinatown buses. Transporting travelers from one city's Chinatown to the next, these buses attract hordes of budget-minded travelers, Chinese and non-Chinese alike. Though the reliability and safety of these services can be spotty (see **A Killer Deal**, p. 36), they offer frequent departures at unbeatable prices (often half the price of Greyhound and a tiny fraction of the cost of a train or plane). The exact names and

another casualty of the bus wars.

  Today, the wild-west environment that once prevailed among Chinatown bus companies seems to have settled into a more peaceful stasis. Nonetheless, risks for passengers persist. In the summer of 2005, during a Fung Wah trip from Boston to New York, flames suddenly began licking from the bus's underside as it throttled down the highway. According to *The Boston Globe*, the 45 passengers on board only barely escaped before fire engulfed the vehicle. "I'm looking at the back of the bus where we were sitting," one passenger told the *Globe*, "and it's not even there anymore." "Every seat is burned," another said. "All the little TVs are cracked and melted."

  Their checkered past notwithstanding, Chinatown bus companies deliver hundreds of customers safely to their destinations every day, and many customers ride frequently. So long as you've got a sense of adventure, and can afford the buses' sporadic approach to punctuality, the services are a great no-frills way to get around the East Coast. If you need more peace of mind, however, there's always Greyhound. On the opposite end of the spectrum, a company called LimoLiner runs daily trips between New York and Boston for $79 one-way. The bus boasts wireless Internet, wide leather seats, personal video screens, beverage service, and fresh flowers in the bathroom (www.limoliner.com).

routes of Chinatown bus companies change frequently, but some of the major players include: to Boston, **Fung Wah** (www.fungwahbus.com; one-way $15); to Philadelphia, **Apex Bus** (www.apexbus.com; one-way $15); and to Washington D.C., **Washington Deluxe** (www.washny.com; one-way $20). Other possible destinations include Baltimore, Norfolk, VA, and even Atlanta. For bus departure locations, check the bus company's website. Advance purchase is possible online, but it is not always necessary. For a fuller list of Chinatown bus companies and their destinations, visit www.staticleap.com or www.chinatown-bus.com.

BY CAR

There are several major paths leading to Manhattan from outside of the city. From New Jersey there are three choices, each costing $6. The **Holland Tunnel** connects to lower Manhattan, the **Lincoln Tunnel** exits to Midtown in the West 40s and the **George Washington Bridge** crosses the Hudson River into northern Manhattan, offering access to either Harlem River Dr. or the West Side Hwy. From New England, take **I-95** and connect to the **Bruckner Expressway (I-287)**; if you are driving outbound, follow the I-95 signs because the Bruckner is not marked as I-287 until after its intersection with the **Cross Bronx Expressway**. Take the Bruckner to either the **Triborough Bridge** (toll $4.50) or the **Cross Bronx Expressway**, which crosses upper Manhattan to the upper west side of Manhattan, near the George Washington Bridge at Broadway and 175th St. Discounted tolls are often available for those with a prepaid E-ZPass (www.ezpass.com). The **speed limit** in New York State, as in most other states, is most often 55 mi. per hr. on highways (30 mi. per hr. on streets). As in other states, wearing a **seat belt** is required by law. For information on renting a car, see the **Practical Information** chapter (p. 80).

GETTING INTO NEW YORK CITY

THE AIRPORTS

You get what you pay for when it comes to airport transportation. A **taxi** is the most comfortable and convenient way of getting to the city, but it is also the most expensive. A cheaper shuttle service may be available through your **hotel**. If you make reservations ahead of time, be sure to ask about **limousine services**—some hostels offer transportation from the airports for a reasonable price. **Private shuttle companies** are a reliable and affordable choice if you don't mind group transportation and the lack of door-to-door service. Most take you from the airport to a number of central Manhattan destinations, such as Grand Central Terminal (42nd St. and Park Ave.), the Port Authority Bus Terminal (41st St. and Eighth Ave.), and some prominent hotels. Plan ahead: most private services peter out or vanish entirely between midnight and 6am.

Unfortunately, the cheapest way to travel is also the most inconvenient. **Public transportation** from New York's airports can be cumbersome and time-consuming, usually requiring multiple transfers between buses and subways. The best resource detailing ground transportation to the airports is the website of the Port Authority of New York and New Jersey (www.panynj.gov).

JOHN F. KENNEDY AIRPORT (JFK)

Located about 15 miles from Manhattan in Queens, JFK is a 40-60min. drive from Midtown; taxi fare is a flat rate of $45 plus tolls and tip.

BY SUBWAY. The **AirTrain** runs from JFK to two subway stops leading into the city. From **Howard Beach Station,** you can connect to the **A subway train.** From **Jamaica Station,** you can connect to the **E, J,** or **Z trains.** (Entire trip 60min.; AirTrain departs every 4-8min. 6am-11pm, every 15min. 11pm-6am; $5 plus subway fare on MetroCard.) Or connect from Jamaica Station to the **Long Island Rail Road (LIRR),** which goes direct to **Penn Station** (35min.; $12). All AirTrain rides within the airport are free. When coming to JFK from Manhattan, be sure you take the A train in the direction of Far Rockaway.

BY BUS. The local **Green Line Q10 Lefferts Boulevard bus** stops at the airport and connects to the A, E, F, J, and Z subway lines, which go into Manhattan. Tell the driver what line you want, and ask him to tell you where to get off. (60-75min.; every 15min., 24hr.; $2 cash or MetroCard for bus with subway transfer.) Although these routes are safe during the day, nighttime travelers should check with the information desk to find the safest way into the city.

BY SHUTTLE. The **SuperShuttle** (☎ 212-258-3826) will drop you anywhere in Manhattan between Battery Park and 227th St. (45-60min., 24hr., $17-19). The **New York Airport Service** express bus (☎ 718-875-8200; www.nyairportservice.com) is a private line that runs between JFK and Grand Central Terminal, Penn Station, the Port Authority, and Midtown hotels between 31st and 60th St. (1hr., departs JFK every 20-30min. 6:15am-11:10pm, $13-15). When you're leaving New York, discounted student tickets can be purchased at Grand Central Terminal. Inquire about all shuttles at JFK's Ground Transportation Center. Shuttles run between LGA and Grand Central Terminal, Penn Station, and Port Authority. (30-45min.; departs LGA for Grand Central, the Port Authority, and Penn Station, via a transfer at Grand Central, every 20-30min. 7:20am-11pm; $12-13.) If you are traveling out of New York, round-trip tickets ($27) can be purchased at Grand Central Terminal.

NEWARK AIRPORT (EWR)

New Jersey's Newark Airport is a 40-50min. drive from Midtown, with taxi fare running $40-55, plus tolls and tip. Taxis from the city are not required to go to Newark, but if they do, the fare will be an (expensive) established flat rate with a surcharge for baggage and round-trip tolls.

BY BUS. The New Jersey Transit Authority's Bus #107 goes from Newark International Airport (North Terminal) to Port Authority (NJTA; ☎ 800-772-2222 or 973-762-5100). Be sure to board the bus in the New York City direction. (20min., every 30-45min. 5:20am-1am, $3.60 exact fare.)

BY TRAIN. The **AirTrain** provides direct service between EWR's Newark International Airport Rail Link Station and Penn Station (20min. 5am-2am; $2.05). Look for "Monorail/AirTrain Link" signs (do not follow signs for "Ground Transportation"). The airport's Rail Link Station is accessible by Amtrak, NJTA, and PATH subway.

BY SHUTTLE. Olympia Airport Express (☎ 212-964-6233 or 908-354-3330) runs from the airport to locations in Lower and Midtown Manhattan, including the Port Authority and Grand Central Terminal (30-50min.; departs from terminals A, B, and C every 15min. 4:15am-11:45pm; $14). **SuperShuttle** (☎ 800-258-3826) runs from EWR to anywhere between Battery Park and 227th St. (30-60min., 24hr., $15-19).

LAGUARDIA AIRPORT (LGA)

LaGuardia is by far the closest airport to Manhattan, only a 20-25min. drive from Midtown. A taxi ride will likely run $21-30, plus tolls and tip.

BY BUS AND SUBWAY. The **M60 bus** connects to Manhattan subway line 1 at 110th St./Broadway; A, C, and D at 125th St./St. Nicholas Ave.; 2 and 3 at 125th St./Lenox (6th) Ave.; 4, 5, 6 at 125th St./Lexington Ave. In Queens, catch the N or W at Astoria Blvd./31st St. For 24hr. bus service between LGA and Queens subways, look for **Q33** and **Q48** stops in front of each terminal. The Q33 bus goes to Jackson Heights/Roosevelt Ave. in Queens for E, F, G, R, V, and 7; the Q48 bus goes to 74th St.-Broadway in Queens for E, F, G, R, V, 7. (Allow at least 90min. for all routes. M60 runs daily 4:50am-1am, Q33 and Q488. 24hr; $2.) Be careful traveling these routes at night.

BY SHUTTLE. The **SuperShuttle** (☎212-258-3826) will drop you anywhere in Manhattan between Battery Park and 227th St. (20-25min.; on demand 7am-11:30pm; $15-22). The **New York Airport Service** express bus (☎718-875-8200) runs between LGA and Grand Central Terminal (with an option to transfer to Penn Station), and the Port Authority (30-45min., departures ever 20-30min., $12-13). It services Midtown hotels between 31st and 60th St. If you are traveling out of New York, round-trip tickets ($21) can be purchased at Grand Central Terminal.

ISLIP LONG ISLAND MACARTHUR AIRPORT

The Long Island Airport caters primarily to small regional flights and private jets. While ultra-convenient to the Hamptons, it's hardly a convenient portal to Manhattan. Midtown is more than a two-hour drive away. There is no taxi service; a private towncar will run $140-210.

BY TRAIN. Take the shuttle van service or the **S-57 bus** to the **Ronkonkoma** train station. A shuttle ($5) departs from the baggage claim on the hour every 30min., 6am-10:30pm. The bus ($1.50) departs every hr., with no service Sundays. From Ronkonkoma, the **Long Island Rail Road (LIRR)** runs to **Penn Station.** (1½hr.; departs about every 30 min. on-peak, every hr. off-peak; $6.50.)

BY SHUTTLE. The **Hampton Jitney** (☎631-283-4600; www.hamptonjitney.com) offers non-stop service to 39th Street and 3rd Ave., with several additional drop-offs on 3rd Ave. up to 86th St. (1½hr.; departs almost every hr. 9:15am-9:30pm; $25.) The Jitney recommends taking a taxi (☎631-589-7878) between the stop and the airport.

GETTING AROUND NEW YORK CITY

⬛ BY FOOT

If you really want to fall in love with New York, you have to experience the city on foot. The sheer variety of neighborhoods, food, shops, and people becomes most vibrant when packed into a walk. Indian restaurants border designer boutiques; Park Ave. matrons march past Williamsburg punks. Plus, the turnover in the city is so great that you never know what undiscovered shop or snack spot lies just around the corner or down the next block.

Although having a destination is totally optional, you can often get around faster on foot than in traffic or by subway. Finding your way around mid- and uptown Manhattan is relatively easy. The city is built on a simple grid, with street numbers increasing to the north and avenue numbers increasing to the west. The grid breaks down below 14th St. Bring a map, and don't be turned off by the geography. Some of the best walking in the city is downtown, through tangled narrow streets that look like old Europe. In general, one mile equals about 20 avenue (north-south) or 10 street (east-west) blocks.

BY SUBWAY

The subway, which celebrated its centennial in 2004, is the transportation lifeline of New York. Each day, some 4.5 million people move through the city's 468 stations, riding the air-conditioned cars of the largest subway car fleet in the world. The subway covers its 660 miles of tracks 24hr. per day, 365 days per year, with only minor service changes and the exception of a few night and weekend lines.

On the whole, the subway remains one of the most reliable and cost-effective methods of transportation in New York. The fare is less than the starting price of a taxi. The subway is the best way to travel long distances north-south, especially when the city above is crowded by traffic. Once inside, a passenger may transfer onto other trains without restrictions. Free subway maps are available at station booths; additional copies are posted in all stations and cars.

In Manhattan, the biggest **subway hubs** are 42nd St./Grand Central on the East Side and 42nd St./Times Square on the West Side; these two stops are connected by the 7 and S trains. **The subway is much more useful for traveling north-south than east-west,** but crosstown shuttle buses run on several streets, including 14th, 23rd, 34th, 42nd, 57th, 79th, and 86th St. **Express trains** stop only at certain major stations; **locals** stop everywhere. Be sure to **check the letter or number and the destination of each train,** since trains with different destinations often use the same track.

Subway entrances are indicated by clearly labeled signs and stairs. Often, downtown and uptown lines will have entrances on opposite sides of the street. There are lit glass globes outside some entrances. Green means that the entrance is staffed 24hr., while red indicates that the entrance is closed or restricted in some way, usually during nighttime hours.

> **TIP** **WATCH OUT ON THE WEEKEND.** Don't let the subway foil your next weekend getaway. The B, V, W, and Z subway trains run only on the weekdays.

FARES

In 2003, the City of New York bid farewell to the subway token. Although some buses continue to accept exact change, you won't be able to get on the subway without a **MetroCard.** The magnetic-strip card, first introduced in 1995, is sold in all subway stations and at newsstands, pharmacies, and grocery stores with Metro-Card stickers in the storefront windows. Subway and bus fare is $2 per ride with the MetroCard, but the **Pay-Per-Ride MetroCard** gets you 20% credit automatically added after you spend $10—such as 12 rides for the price of 10. MetroCards can conveniently be used for subway-bus, bus-subway, subway-subway, and bus-bus transfers. When you swipe the card on the initial ride, a free transfer is electronically stored on your MetroCard and is good for up to 2hr. **Without the MetroCard, bus-subway and subway-bus transfers are not free.**

UNLIMITED METROCARDS

"Unlimited Rides" MetroCards (as opposed to "Pay-Per-Ride" cards) are sold in one-day **Fun Pass** ($7), **7-Day Unlimited Ride** ($24), and **30-Day Unlimited Ride** ($76) denominations, and are good for unlimited use of the subway and bus systems during a specified period. Unlimited Ride cards are a good deal for tourists who plan on visiting many sights. Riders who are over 65 or disabled qualify for a Reduced Fare card; visit www.mta.nyc.ny.us/nyct/fare/rfindex.htm for details.

ESSENTIALS

⚡TIP **PAY UP-FRONT TO SAVE.** Many tourists are turned off by the high cost of Unlimited-Ride MetroCards, and assume that they're not a good value in most cases. Before you jump to any conclusions, however, remember that the subway in New York isn't cheap, however you pay for it. Each individual trip costs $2. If you'll be making more than four trips in a day (which many tourists do), you'll save by buying the one-day pass. Your saving will be more substantial if you buy an Unlimited Ride MetroCard that covers a longer period.

SAFETY

The subway has become safer in recent years. Even so, it is not without its frustrations and occasional dangers. Cars can be rerouted for servicing, leaving you stranded, so keep an eye on service advisories posted throughout stations. Since trains and riders decrease at night, it's advisable—and often quicker—to take a cab after 11pm. On more remote routes, certain stations can be dangerous, especially after dark. If the neighborhood you are heading toward is safe, however, there is a better chance that the subway station will be safe as well. Central Manhattan is generally considered safe at all hours.

In general, stay away from the platform's edge, and board the train during non-rush hours from the off-peak waiting area, marked at the center of every platform. This area is monitored by cameras, and the conductor's car stops here. Once you board, stay near the middle to be close to the conductor. During rush hour, hold your bag with the opening facing you to discourage pickpockets.

BY BUS

Buses can take almost twice as long as subways, due to traffic. They will, however, get you closer to your destination, since most buses stop every two blocks or so and run crosstown (east-west) as well as uptown and downtown (north-south). They can be a nightmare for long-distance travel over north-south blocks, but for shorter and **especially crosstown trips,** they can be more convenient than trains.

The MTA transfer system provides north-south travelers with a paper slip valid for a free ride east-west, or vice versa, but you must ask the driver for a transfer when you board. Ring when you want to get off. If you use a MetroCard, you get a free transfer (within 2hr.) from bus to subway or from bus to bus.

Bus stops are indicated by a **blue sign post** announcing the bus number, or a shelter displaying a map and an unreliable schedule of arrival times. You can request any stop along the bus's route 10pm-5am. A flat fare ($2) is charged when you board. Dollar bills are not accepted; use either exact change or a MetroCard (p. 41). Ask for outer borough bus maps at any outer borough subway station—different restrictions apply to them, as many are operated by private companies.

BY TAXI

Only government-licensed **yellow taxis** are permitted by law to pick up passengers without previous arrangement. *Let's Go* does not recommend hiring a non-yellow **gypsy cab.** A cab is on duty if the light on the roof is lit; if it is dark, the cab is already taken. If you can't find taxis on the street, call a radio-dispatched cab (see **Practical Information,** p. 81, for phone numbers). Keep in mind that taxis allow a strict maximum of four passengers per car.

The **meter starts at $2.50** and clicks 40¢ for each one-fifth of a mile, or 20¢ per minute when the cab is not moving. A 50¢ night surcharge is in effect between 8pm and 6am. Bridge or tunnel tolls will be added to the total charge, and drivers might ask that you pay the tolls as you go through them. Cabbies also expect a 15-20% tip. Some drivers may illegally try to show the visitor the "scenic route"; glance at a street map before embarking to avoid being taken for a ride. Furthermore, an on-duty cab driver **must take you to any destination within the five boroughs of New York City,** no matter how far afield it might be.

Before you leave the cab, ask for a receipt, which will have the taxi's identification number (either its meter number or its medallion). You need this number to trace lost articles or to make a complaint to the **Taxi Commission** (from New York ☎ 311, from outside 212-NEW-YORK; www.nyc.gov).

BY CAR

If you can, avoid driving in the city. Aggressive taxis, careless pedestrians, and lunatic bicycle couriers crowd the streets. Vehicles routinely jump lanes without signaling.

CAR RENTALS

RENTAL AGENCIES

Agencies maintain varying minimum-age requirements and require proof of age as well as a security deposit. Agencies in Queens and Yonkers are often less expensive than their Manhattan counterparts, especially for one-day rentals. Most auto insurance policies will cover rented cars, and some credit cards take care of your rental insurance costs if you've charged the vehicle to their card (but be sure to ask about all the particulars from the companies themselves). Major car-rental agencies operating in New York include: **Avis** (☎ 800-230-4898; www.avis.com), **Dollar** (☎ 800-800-4000; www.dollar.com), **Enterprise** (☎ 800-736-8222; www.enterprise.com), **Hertz** (☎ 800-654-3131 or 800-831-2847; www.hertz.com), and **National** (☎ 800-227-7368; www.nationalcar.com).

You might also consider getting a membership at **Zipcar** (www.zipcar.com). The company, launched in 2002, provides members with temporary cars for about $10 per hour. The cars are located throughout the city, can be reserved online, and are available for use by members for any length of time. The service pays for gas, insurance, maintenance, and parking.

COSTS AND INSURANCE

Rental car prices start at around $100 per day from national companies. Expect to pay more for larger cars and for 4WD. Return the car with a full tank of gas (petrol) to avoid high fuel charges at the end. Be sure to ask whether the price includes **insurance** against theft and collision. Beware that cars rented on an **American Express** or **Visa/Mastercard Gold** or **Platinum** credit cards in the US might *not* carry automatic insurance; check with your credit card company. Insurance plans almost always come with an **excess** (or deductible). This means you pay for all damages up to that sum, unless they are the fault of another vehicle. The excess you will be quoted applies to collisions with other vehicles; collisions with non-vehicles, such as trees (single-vehicle collisions) will cost you even more. The excess can often be reduced or waived entirely if you pay an additional charge.

National chains often allow one-way rentals, picking up in one city and dropping off in another. There is usually a minimum hire period and sometimes an extra drop-off charge of several hundred dollars.

ON THE ROAD

If you do choose to drive in Manhattan, you must **stay alert** and **know where you are going.** Yellow slow lights last only about four seconds; **both right and left turns on red lights are prohibited.** During rush hours, certain lanes—particularly roads leading to bridges and tunnels—are **closed or reversed.** Most avenues and streets run one-way. Streets usually run east if they're even-numbered and west if they're odd-numbered. Wide transverse streets (125th, 116th, 106th, 96th, 86th, 79th, 72nd, 57th, 42nd, 34th, 23rd, and 14th St.) are two-way. Avenues run north-south, though they get complicated downtown. When traveling outside of Manhattan, make sure to bring a map. **Gasoline** prices vary, but currently average about $3 per gallon.

The **hassle of parking** cancels any convenience of having a car in the city. Don't be surprised if you have to park many blocks from your destination. Read the signs carefully; a space is usually legal only on certain days of the week. The city frequently tows cars, and recovering a towed vehicle can cost $100 or more. Some streets have parking meters that cost 25¢ per 15min., with a time limit of 1-2hr. **Parking lots** are the easiest but the most expensive option. Depending on where you park (midtown being most expensive), garage rates may range from $6 to $15 for the first hour to $40 per day. The cheapest parking lots are **downtown**—try the far west end of Houston St. Many garages have lower weekend rates. Break-ins and car **thefts** happen often, particularly if you have a radio. Never leave anything visible inside your car. You may want to use a steering wheel locking device.

The **AAA Automobile Club of New York,** 1881 Broadway, 2nd fl. (☎212-757-2000, Emergency Service 800-222-4357; www.aaany.com) offers road service and towing.

DRIVING PERMITS AND CAR INSURANCE

You can drive in New York if you are a resident of another state or Canadian province and carry a valid license. New York's minimum driving age is 16. New York State honors all valid foreign licenses; see www.nydmv.state.ny.us/license.htm or call the **New York State Department of Motor Vehicles** (☎212-645-5550; see p. 85 for locations) for details.

Your **International Driving Permit (IDP),** valid for one year, must be issued in your own country before you depart. An application for an IDP usually requires one or two photos, a current local license, an additional form of identification, and a fee. To apply, contact the national or local branch of your home country's automobile association. Be careful when purchasing an IDP online or anywhere other than your home automobile association. Many vendors sell permits of questionable legitimacy for higher prices.

Most credit cards cover standard **car insurance.** If you rent, lease, or borrow a car, you will need an **International Insurance Certificate** (green card) to certify that you have liability insurance and that it applies abroad. Green cards can be obtained at car rental agencies, car dealers (for those leasing cars), some travel agents, and some border crossings. Rental agencies may require you to purchase theft insurance in countries that they consider to have a high risk of auto theft.

KEEPING IN TOUCH

BY EMAIL AND INTERNET

Increasingly, travelers find that taking their laptop computers on the road with them can be a convenient option for staying connected. Laptop users can call an Internet service provider via a modem using long-distance phone cards intended for such calls. Travelers with wireless-enabled computers may be able to take advantage of an increasing number of Internet "hotspots" throughout the city where they can get online for free or for a small fee. Newer computers can detect these hotspots automatically; otherwise, websites like www.jiwire.com, www.wi-fihotspotlist.com, and www.locfinder.net can help you find them. For information on insuring your laptop while traveling, see p. 33.

There are plenty of places to check your email or surf the web in New York. Look for the occasional free Internet terminal at a public library or university, or just visit one of the following wired establishments. For lists of additional cybercafes in New York, check out www.cypercaptive.com and www.netcafeguide.com.

Web2Zone Cyber Center, 52-54 Cooper Sq. (☎212-614-7300; www.web2zone.com), between 3rd and 4th Ave. Ⓢ 6 to Astor Pl.; N, R, W to 8th St. A stand-out choice in the East Village. A huge array of Macs and PCs for Internet use, business applications, and gaming. First 30min. $3, each additional 10min. $1. 9am-noon $3 per hr. Open M-Th 9am-midnight, F-Sa 9am-1am, Su 9am-10pm.

Bryant Park, 6th Ave. (park management ☎212-768-4242; www.bryantpark.org), between 40th and 42nd St., behind the library. Ⓢ B, D, F, V to 42nd St./Ave. of the Americas (6th Ave.); 7 to 5th Ave./42nd St. Free wireless Internet anytime the park is open.

BY TELEPHONE

CALLING HOME FROM NEW YORK

To place an international call from New York, dial: 011 (the international dialing prefix for calls out of the US), then the country code of where you're calling (Australia 61; Ireland 353; New Zealand 64; UK 44), then the area code and local number. The country code for the US is 1. When calling Canada from the US, simply dial the appropriate area code and the local number. To have an operator assist you, dial "0" and ask for the overseas operator.

International calls are cheapest using **prepaid phone cards,** which are available at most convenience stores, drugstores, and pharmacies. These cards range from $5 to $100 and charge a certain per-minute list price (from about 12¢ up) for a set amount of minutes; instructions on the card tell you how to place a call. Make sure any card you buy is issued by a reputable national phone service carrier, or phone service may be spotty. The street vendor-hawked prepaid cards with too good to be true rates usually are: many have unreliable service, and they may have hidden hardware and dial-up charges that make the prices no better than the more "reputable" cards sold at convenience stores and pharmacies. No matter how you place a call, national and international phone rates tend to be highest in the morning, lower in the evening, and lowest on Sunday and at night.

PLACING INTERNATIONAL CALLS: To call the US from home or to call home from the US, dial:

1. The **international dialing prefix.** To call from **Australia,** dial 0011; **Canada** or the **US,** 011; **Ireland, New Zealand,** or the **UK,** 00.

2. The **country code** of the country you want to call. To call **Australia,** dial 61; **Canada** or the **US,** 1; **Ireland,** 353; **New Zealand,** 64; the **UK,** 44.

3. The **city/area code.**

4. The **local number.**

You can usually make **direct international calls** from pay phones, but if you aren't using a calling card, you may need to drop a lot of coins. Prepaid phone cards and occasionally major credit cards can be used for direct international calls. Placing a **collect call** through an international operator is even more expensive, but may be necessary in case of emergency. You can place collect calls through the service providers listed below even if you don't have one of their phone cards. Before settling on a calling card plan, be sure to research your options in order to pick the one that best fits both your needs and your destination.

COMPANY	TO OBTAIN A CARD:	TO PLACE A CALL FROM NEW YORK:
AT&T (US)	800-364-9292 or www.att.com	800-CALL-ATT
Canada Direct	800-561-8868 or www.infocanadadirect.com	800-555-1111
MCI (US)	800-777-5000 or www.minutepass.com	800-888-8000
Telecom New Zealand Direct	www.telecom.co.nz	800-248-0064
Telstra Australia	1800 676 638 or www.telstra.com	800-682-2878

CALLING WITHIN NEW YORK

The three-digit telephone (or city) prefixes in the US are called "area codes." The area codes for Manhattan are ☎212, 347, 646 and 917. For Brooklyn, Queens, the Bronx, and Staten Island, the area codes are 718 and 347. The 917 area code is also used for many cellular phones and pagers in all five boroughs. All New York City calls made within and between the five area codes must be dialed using **1 + area code + the seven-digit telephone number.** Toll-free numbers are used by businesses to encourage requests for information, and are usually accessible only within the US. These numbers are preceded by the area codes ☎800, 888, 866, and 877.

For local or national directory assistance, dial ☎411. If you want to charge a long-distance call to the person you're calling, call collect by dialing "0" instead of "1" before the 10-digit number, and an operator will come on the line to assist you (the person you're calling has the right to refuse the call). For **emergency** services, dial ☎**911.**

The cheapest way to place a call to anywhere in the Greater New York area is to use a coin-operated **pay phone,** available on street corners and in hotel lobbies, bars, restaurants, and subway stations. Cost per local call on most phones is 50¢ for an unlimited amount of time. Don't be surprised, however, if you pick up a receiver and hear no dial tone: New York's pay phones are famously unreliable. A good alternative is to use a prepaid phone card that can be used for local, long-distance, and international calls.

The international standard for cell phones is **Global System for Mobile Communication (GSM).** To make and receive calls in New York you will need a **GSM-compatible phone** and a **SIM (Subscriber Identity Module) card,** a country-specific, thumbnail-sized chip that gives you a local phone number and plugs you into the local network. Many SIM cards are **prepaid,** meaning that they come with calling time included and you don't need to sign up for a monthly service plan. Incoming calls are frequently free. When you use up the prepaid time, you can buy additional cards or vouchers (usually available at convenience stores) to get more. For more information on GSM phones, check out www.telestial.com, www.ustronics.com, www.roadpost.com, or www.planetomni.com. Companies like **Cellular Abroad** (www.cellularabroad.com) rent cell phones that work in a variety of destinations around the world, providing a simpler option than picking up a phone in-country.

TIP **GSM PHONES.** Just having a GSM phone doesn't mean you're necessarily good to go when you travel abroad. The majority of GSM phones sold in the United States operate on a different **frequency** (1900) than international phones (900/1800). Tri-band phones work on all three frequencies (900/1800/1900) and will operate in most of the world. As well, some GSM phones are **SIM-locked** and will only accept SIM cards from a single carrier. You'll need a **SIM-unlocked** phone to use a SIM card from a local carrier when you travel.

TIME DIFFERENCES

New York is 4hr. behind **Greenwich Mean Time (GMT)**, 3hr. ahead of Vancouver and San Francisco, 14hr. behind Sydney, and 16hr. behind Auckland. The US observes **Daylight Saving Time**, and fall and spring switchover times vary.

4AM	7AM	10AM	NOON	2PM	10PM
Vancouver	Toronto	London	Hanoi	China	Australia
Seattle	Ottawa	(GMT)	Bangkok	Hong Kong	
San Francisco	New York		Jakarta	Manila	
Los Angeles	Boston		Phnom Penh	Singapore	

BY MAIL

US mail is controlled by the **US Postal Service** (☎ 800-275-8777; www.usps.com). Hours vary widely according to the branch, although many are open Monday to Friday 9am-5pm; call for details. The city's **General Post Office**, 421 Eighth Ave. (☎ 212-330-3002), at between 31st and 33rd St., is open 24hr.

SENDING MAIL FROM NEW YORK

The **postal rate** for letters under 1 oz. headed anywhere in the **US** is 39¢. Postcards and aerogrammes cost 24¢. Letters and aerogrammes to Canada cost 63¢, postcards 55¢. For Australia, Ireland, New Zealand, and the UK, rates are 84¢ for letters, 75¢ for postcards or aerogrammes. All international mail should be marked "AIRMAIL" or "PAR AVION" on the front, and will arrive by air at their destination in about four to seven days. A post office clerk (or the official online rate calculator at http://postcalc.usps.gov) will give you rates on anything else.

Postage **stamps** for domestic and international letters and postcards can be purchased at all post offices as well as at most convenience stores, drugstores and pharmacies, and even at some ATMs. Note that these stamps will most likely come in 39¢ or 24¢ increments (the amount of domestic postage rates), meaning those sending mail abroad will have to affix more postage than needed to their letters.

Domestic and international mail with proper postage weighing under 15 oz. (that includes letters and postcards) can be dropped in round-topped, dark **blue mailboxes** found on street corners. Postmen usually collect at 1 and 5pm, from Monday to Saturday. The General Post Office is open 24hr.

RECEIVING MAIL IN NEW YORK

If you don't have a mailing address in New York, you can still receive mail via **General Delivery** (known as *Poste Restante* in most other parts of the world). Mail addressed to you at the following address will be held for pick-up for up to 30 days: General Delivery, General Post Office/James A. Farley Station, 421 Eighth Ave., New York, NY 10001. A photo ID is required for pick-up. For US General Delivery, go to 390 Ninth Ave., at W 30th St.

ESSENTIALS

SPECIFIC CONCERNS

TRAVELING ALONE

There are many benefits to traveling alone, including independence and greater interaction with locals. On the other hand, any solo traveler is a more vulnerable target of harassment and street theft. As a lone traveler, try not to stand out as a tourist, look confident, and be especially careful in deserted or very crowded areas. If questioned, never admit that you are traveling alone. Maintain regular contact with someone at home who knows your itinerary. For more tips, pick up *Traveling Solo* by Eleanor Berman (Globe Pequot Press, US$18), visit www.travelaloneandloveit.com, or subscribe to **Connecting: Solo Travel Network,** 689 Park Rd., Unit 6, Gibsons, BC V0N 1V7, Canada. (☎604-886-9099; www.cstn.org. Membership US$30-48.)

WOMEN TRAVELERS

Women exploring on their own inevitably face some additional safety concerns. If you are concerned, consider staying in hostels which offer single rooms that lock from the inside or in organizations with rooms for women only. Stick to centrally located accommodations and avoid solitary late-night treks or subway rides.

Always carry extra money for a phone call, bus, or taxi. **Hitchhiking** is never safe for lone women, or even for two women traveling together. Look as if you know where you're going and approach older women or couples for directions if you're lost or uncomfortable. Generally the less you look like a tourist, the better off you'll be. Wearing a **wedding band** sometimes helps to prevent unwanted overtures.

Your best answer to verbal harassment is no answer at all; staring straight ahead at nothing in particular will do a world of good that reactions usually don't achieve. The extremely persistent can sometimes be dissuaded by a firm, loud, and very public "Go away!" Don't hesitate to seek out a police officer or a passerby if you are being harassed. Memorize the emergency numbers, and consider carrying a whistle on your keychain. A self-defense course will both prepare you for a potential attack and raise your level of awareness of your surroundings (see **Personal Safety,** p. 32).

GLBT TRAVELERS

New York is one of America's most tolerant and welcoming cities, with large, visible GLBT populations, which are hardly confined to Chelsea and Greenwich Village. As everywhere, however, GLBT travelers should trust their instincts and exercise caution, particularly when in more conservative areas of the outer boroughs. The city has a plethora of publications dedicated to the queer community. *Gay City News* is the primary weekly newspaper for the local GLBT population (www.gaycitynews.com). *HomoXtra* (www.hx.com) and *Next* both have listings of nightlife and activities, and are available free at gay hangouts around the city. *Go NYC* promises to be a "cultural roadmap for the city girl." The free *LGNY* (no, that's not *Let's Go NY*, but *Lesbian-Gay NY*) and the *New York Blade News* are community broadsheets and are distributed throughout the boroughs. Free copies of *MetroSource* (www.metrosource.com), a GLBT-oriented magazine with a wider scope including movie reviews, travel, and national news, can be found around Chelsea. The nationally distributed *Advocate* magazine (www.advocate.com) has New York articles in its travel section; also check out the *Village Voice* (www.villagevoice.com) for events, services, and occasional feature articles of interest to gays and lesbians. Some **websites** will give you info that the printed rags don't reveal. Check out www.pridelinks.com for a host of GLBT-related websites.

HEALTH, SUPPORT, AND COMMUNITY SERVICES

Callen-Lorde Community Health Center, 356 W 18th St. (☎212-271-7200; www.callen-lorde.org) between Eighth and Ninth Ave. Ⓢ A, C, E to 14th St.; L to Eighth Ave. Comprehensive general health services for the queer community and those living with HIV/AIDS, plus counseling and a health resource department. Callen-Lorde offers a sliding-scale fee structure for individuals without insurance coverage, and no one is turned away. Open M 8:30am-8pm, Tu 8:30-11:30am and 2:15-8pm, W 12:30-8pm, and Th-F 9am-4:30pm.

Gay Men's Health Crisis (GMHC), 119 W 24th St. (☎212-367-1000; Geffen Center ☎617-367-1100, hotline 800-243-7692 or 807-6655; www.gmhc.org), between 6th and 7th Ave. Ⓢ 1, F to 23rd St. Health care, support groups, physician referrals, and counseling for men and women with HIV and AIDS. Walk-in counseling generally available M-F 11am-8pm, but call to verify hours. GMHC's **Geffen Center** provides free confidential (but not anonymous) HIV testing M-Th. Call to schedule an appointment; walk-in testing also available on certain days. Hotline hours M-F 10am-9pm, Sa noon-3pm.

Gay and Lesbian National Hotline (☎888-843-4564; www.glnh.org). Provides email and phone peer counseling about relationships, coming out, and safe sex. Also maintains large database of gay-friendly businesses, sports leagues, and other resources for the GLBT traveler and those with questions. 24hr. recording. Open M-F 4pm-midnight, Sa noon-5pm.

Lesbian, Gay, Bisexual, and Transgender Community Center, 208 W 13th St. (☎212-620-7310; www.gaycenter.org) between 7th and 8th Ave. Ⓢ A, C, E, to 14th St. The second-largest lesbian, gay, bisexual, and transgender community center in the world, this enormous resource provides information and referral services as well as space for 300 groups, 27 programs, and over 5000 visitors each week. Center hours M-F 9am-9pm. Closed holidays. Lobby open daily 9am-11pm and 5-11pm on holidays.

▼ **ADDITIONAL GLBT RESOURCES**
Spartacus 2005-2006: International Gay Guide. Bruno Gmunder Verlag (US$33).
Damron Men's Travel Guide, Damron Road Atlas, Damron Accommodations Guide, Damron City Guide, and *Damron Women's Traveller.* Damron Travel Guides (US$18-24). For info, call ☎800-462-6654 or visit www.damron.com.
The Gay Vacation Guide: The Best Trips and How to Plan Them, Mark Chesnut. Kensington Books (US$15).
Gayellow Pages USA/Canada, Frances Green. Gayellow Pages (US$20). They also publish smaller regional editions. Visit Gayellow pages online at www.gayellowpages.com.

RELIGIOUS SERVICES

Church of St. Paul and St. Andrew, 263 86th St. (☎212-362-3179; www.spsanyc.org), at West End Ave. Ⓢ 1 to 86th St. Check out the octagonal tower and the angles in the spandrels of this United Methodist church dating from 1897. GLBT-friendly service Su 11am.

Congregation Beth Simchat Torah, 57 Bethune St. (☎212-929-9498; www.cbst.org). Ⓢ A, C, E to 14th St. This synagogue caters to the NY GLBT communities. Main services F at 7pm at the **Church of the Holy Apostle,** at 296 9th Ave. and 28th St. Additional services F at 8:30pm at Bethune St. location. Check website for additional service times and locations as well as holiday information.

Metropolitan Community Church of New York, 446 W 36th St. (☎212-629-7440; www.mccny.org) between 9th and 10th St. [S] A, C, E to 34th St. This Christian church has been serving the queer community for 28 years. Services Su 9am (traditional), 11am (ASL interpreted), and 7pm (praise and worship). W 7pm movie night.

TRAVELERS WITH DISABILITIES

Arrange transportation well in advance to ensure a smooth trip. Hertz, Avis, and National **car rental agencies** have hand-controlled vehicles at some locations. In the US both **Amtrak** and major airlines will accommodate disabled passengers if notified at least 72hr. in advance. Hearing-impaired travelers can contact Amtrak at ☎800-523-6590 (TTD/TTY). Disabled passengers receive a discount when booking in-person or by phone. **Greyhound** buses will provide half-price travel for a companion under certain circumstances; if you are without a fellow traveler, call Greyhound (☎800-752-4841) at least 48hr. before you leave.

New York is much more accommodating to disabled travelers than it used to be, although certain subway journeys are still a challenge. About 75 New York subway stations and all the buses can accommodate wheelchairs. Call **NYC Travel Information** (☎718-596-8585) for details. The **Elevators and Escalator Accessibility Hotline** (☎800-734-6772, TTY 718-596-8273) is available 24hr. for those planning to use public transportation. **Access-A-Ride** door-to-door service is available for some (☎877-337-2017, TTY 718-393-4259, TTY Relay 800-662-1220), and personal care attendants ride free. Those with disabilities should inform airlines and hotels of their disabilities when making reservations, as some time may be needed to prepare special accommodations. Call ahead to restaurants, museums, and other facilities to find out if they are accessible. Guide dog owners must license their dogs; it's free with proper documentation. Contact **Veterinary Public Health Services** for details (☎212-676-2120; www.nyc.gov/html/doh/html/vet/vetdog.shtml).

For those with hearing impairments the **Hands On! Organization** (☎212-740-3087, TTY Relay 711; www.handson.org) arranges sign language interpreting for many cultural events in NYC; **Hospital Audiences** (☎212-575-7676, TTY 212-575-7660; www.hospitalaudiences.org) provides an audio-description service for blind theatergoers. The **Mayor's Office for People with Disabilities** (☎212-788-2830; www.nyc.gov/html/mopd/home.html) will send the book *Access New York* to people who inquire via telephone. The large-type book provides resources and specific accessibility reviews for cultural institutions, theaters, nightlife and sports venues, and tours.

USEFUL ORGANIZATIONS

Accessible Journeys, 35 West Sellers Ave., Ridley Park, PA 19078 (☎800-846-4537; www.disabilitytravel.com). Designs tours for wheelchair users and slow walkers. The site has tips and forums for all travelers.

The Guided Tour, Inc., 7900 Old York Rd., Ste. 114B, Elkins Park, PA 19027 (☎800-783-5841; www.guidedtour.com). Organizes travel programs for persons with developmental and physical challenges in Canada, Hawaii, Ireland, Italy, Mexico, Spain, the UK, and the US.

Mobility International USA (MIUSA), P.O. Box 10767, Eugene, OR 97440 (☎541-343-1284; www.miusa.org). Provides a variety of books and other publications containing information for travelers with disabilities.

Society for Accessible Travel and Hospitality (SATH), 347
York, NY 10016 (☎212-447-7284; www.sath.org). An advocacy
free online travel information and the travel magazine *OPEN WORL*
scription US$13, free for members). Annual membership US$45, stud
seniors US$30.

DIETARY CONCERNS

Vegetarians won't have any problem eating cheap and well in New York. Excellent vegetarian restaurants abound, and almost every non-vegetarian place offers non-meat options (see **Food,** p. 112). The **North American Vegetarian Society,** P.O. Box 72, Dolgeville, NY 13329 (☎518-568-7970; www.navs-online.org), publishes information about vegetarian travel, including the *Vegetarian Journal's Guide to Natural Food Restaurants in the US and Canada.* For more information, visit your local bookstore, health food store, or library. You may want to consult the *Vegan Guide to New York City* by Rynn Berry and Chris A. Suzuki (Pythagorean Books; US$10) and the *Vegetarian Traveler* by Jed and Susan Civic (Larson Publications; US$16).

New York boasts an extensive selection of **halal** food; consult **www.zabi-hah.com** to find your nearest halal restaurant, deli, or grocery. Travelers who keep **kosher** should call a New York synagogue for information (your own synagogue or college Hillel office should have lists of New York Jewish institutions). Chabad houses (centers for Lubavitch Hassidim and outreach) should also be able either to provide kosher food or direct you to it. Columbia's Beit Ayala Chabad Student Center, 510 W 110th St., #5C (☎212-864-5010, ext.44), and the Upper East Side's Chabad *shuckles*, 311 E 83rd St., Ste. B (☎212-717-4613), provide general information, support, and classes for religious visitors.

OTHER RESOURCES

Let's Go tries to cover all aspects of budget travel, but we can't put *everything* in our guides. Listed below are some New York City-related sites to start off your surfing; other web sites are listed throughout the book. Because website turnover is high, use search engines (such as www.google.com) to strike out on your own.

WWW.LETSGO.COM. Let's Go's website features a wealth of information and valuable advice at your fingertips. It offers excerpts from all our guides as well as monthly features on new hot spots in the most popular destinations. In addition to our online bookstore, we have great deals on everything from airfares to cell phones. Our resources section is full of information you'll need before you hit the road, and our forums are buzzing with advice from other travelers. Check back often to see constant updates, exciting new tips, and prize giveaways. See you soon!

www.nycvisit.com. The Convention and Visitors Bureau offers a calendar of events and information for travel professionals.

www.nyc.gov. The official New York City website has a "visitors" section with links to accommodations, food, transportation, and more.

www.nyctourist.com. This website offers a wealth of deals and tips for the New York City tourist.

www.iloveny.state.ny.us. The official New York State tourism website includes listings of attractions, recreation, travel ideas, events, and accommodations.

LIFE AND TIMES

CITY BASICS

New York is the most populous city in the United States, the most densely populated city in North America, and an undisputed world capital. It packs 8.1 million people into its 321 square miles, and some 21 million residents cluster in its greater metropolitan area. The tourist's tendency to think of New York as Manhattan alone is not in fact entirely without historical ground; until 1898, Manhattan was New York, and Brooklyn, across the Hudson River, was the country's second-most populated metropolis. Today, the five boroughs of Manhattan, Brooklyn, Queens, the Bronx, and Staten Island comprise the city, and each is, under a slightly different name, a county of state government. The city's mayor, currently **Michael Bloomberg,** governs along with a 51-member city council, each councilor representing approximately 157,000 residents. Local politics in New York are complex and consequential—and New Yorkers are quick to bemoan the fact that for every dollar the city sends the federal government, it receives only $0.81 in return.

HISTORY

COLONY, CAPITAL, COMMERCE: 1524-1825

The first European eyes to behold the reed- and oyster-filled waterways surrounding the island of Manhattan were those of Italian explorer **Giovanni da Verrazzano,** traveling for the French king François I in 1524, and Englishman **Henry Hudson,** traveling for the Dutch East India Company in 1609. Though both explorers were disappointed in their quest to discover the Northwest Passage, their reports of the island's auspicious location and resources prompted the **Dutch West India Company** to send **Peter Minuit** to establish a trading post on its southern tip. The area had for centuries been populated by Algonquin and Iroquois Indians. Minuit inaugurated the Manhattan tradition of the high-yield real estate investment by purchasing **"Manna-Hata,"** or the "Island of the Hills," for trading goods valued at 60 guilders— the equivalent of about $24 today. Not the last shady New York real estate transaction, Minuit's deal was with a group of Canarsee Delaware Indians, who did not inhabit the island and had no rightful claim to it. Small numbers of Algonquin and Iroquois Indians still live on the Shinnecock reservation on Long Island today.

The Dutch called their small outpost **New Amsterdam,** and it grew to become the Dutch colony of **New Netherland.** The colony's early residents were a rowdy mix of artisans, sailors, trappers, and slaves who drank, gambled, and spoke no fewer than 18 languages. The Dutch appointed the stern Calvinist **Peter Stuyvesant** as colonial governor in hopes of imposing order and religion, yet the colonists despised him so much that

1524
Giovanni da Verrazano is the first European to set foot on Manhattan.

1614
The Dutch establish the first permanent European settlement on Manhattan, with a fort and 30 cabins.

1626
In a real estate deal that would make Donald Trump jealous, Peter Minuit buys Manhattan for trading goods valued at $24.

53

1700
The King's Bridge to the Bronx connects Manhattan's 5000 residents to the mainland for the first time.

1725
The *New-York Gazette*, the city's first newspaper, begins publishing.

1785-90
New York is the first capital of the United States

1776
The Declaration of Independence is read at Bowling Green, prompting an exuberant crowd to topple the statue of George III.

1825
The opening of the Erie Canal makes New York the maritime gateway to the Great Lakes.

1851
The first issue of *The New York Times* is published.

1870
Manhattan's first elevated train line opens.

1873
Central Park—nearly twice the size of the entire country of Monaco—is completed.

when the English attacked in **August of 1664**, they refused to resist. The English took over (despite a brief Dutch re-occupation in 1673-74) and gave the colony its present name in honor of the **Duke of York.**

By the time of the **American Revolution,** New York had become a major commercial port. George Washington tried unsuccessfully to defend the city from the British, who occupied it for most of the war. For a brief period at the Revolution's end, New York became the **first capital of the United States,** hosting the first meeting of Congress and the first sessions of the Supreme Court. The honor soon passed, temporarily of course, to rival Philadelphia.

In the late 1700s, New York's trade and population boomed. With over 33,000 inhabitants in 1790, it became the largest city in the United States. By the mid-1800s, due to the opening of the **Erie Canal** in 1825, New York handled more goods and people than all other American ports combined. Starting in the 1820s, the first waves of German, Irish, and Italian immigrants arrived on New York's shores, doubling its population in the space of a few years and bringing severe outbreaks of yellow fever and cholera. By the time of the outbreak of the Civil War, more than half of New York's residents were first-generation immigrants.

CORRUPTION AND CIVIL WAR: 1826-1899

In the 19th century, New York's exploding population far outpaced the city's ability to manage it. Sewage and animals ran in the streets, and city politics were dominated by cronyism, bribery, and class conflict. The infamous **Tammany Hall,** a fraternal organization formed in 1789, built up a political power base that reached its peak in the 1850s under Democratic **"Boss" William Tweed.** Tweed promised and often provided money and jobs to his immigrant supporters. Tweed expected his kindness to be repaid, of course, and with the complicity of his citywide network, he defrauded government coffers of more than $160 million dollars by exaggerating municipal expenses. Tweed was imprisoned in 1875 in the wake of an exposé in the *New York Times*. Ever wily, however, he escaped from jail and fled to Cuba and then Spain before being tracked down and detained until his death. Tammany Hall remained influential in municipal politics until the 1930s.

The outbreak of the **Civil War** in 1861 brought the class conflicts simmering beneath the surface of New York society to the fore. The city's wealthiest merchants initially hoped to appease the Southern states rather than go to war in order to safeguard trade with the South. Abolitionists and intellectuals succeeded in rallying support for the war effort, but when a new draft law allowing wealthy draftees to buy their way out of service was passed, immigrant resentment spurred the New York City **Draft Riots** of July 1863. Four days of looting and burning, often targeting African Americans, killed more than 2000.

Post-war New York experienced robust economic growth, which molded the city into the recognizable form we know today. **The El,** the first elevated train in lower Manhattan, began running in 1868. **Central Park,** begun in 1857 but stalled by the war and financial worries, was finally completed in 1873. The **Metropolitan Museum of Art** was established in 1872, the **Statue of Liberty** was inaugurated in 1886, and electricity and telephone service arrived in 1882 and 1889. The **1898 Incorporation of New York City** joined Manhattan with the previously independent four outer boroughs, making New York the world's most populous city at the time. The city's first **subway** line began running in 1904.

THE NEW METROPOLIS: 1900-1928

The early 20th century saw the city split between two extremes: big-spending industrialists and flappers on the one hand, and hordes of starving immigrants on the other. Between 1890 and 1930, thousands of Italians, Lithuanians, Russians, Poles, and Greeks fled famine, religious persecution, and political unrest for New York City. Newly liberated Southern blacks also entered the city in droves. Yet New York was hardly the utopia they hoped for. Underpaid workers toiled long hours in unsafe conditions, looked after only by Tammany Hall-influenced "ward bosses." In 1901, a whopping 70% of the city's population lived in tenement housing. Reform movements responding to such miserable conditions inspired national progress. The 1901 **Tenement Law** set basic standards for low-income housing. In 1911, the tragic death of 146 young women in the fire at the **Triangle Shirtwaist Factory** prompted the development of anti-sweatshop laws. The **National Negro Organization,** forerunner to the NAACP, was founded in Harlem in 1909, leading a famous civil rights protest in 1917.

Despite their grim underside (and their lack of legal alcohol), the **Roaring Twenties** fueled a major cultural boom. Radio, Broadway theater, music, journalism, and ballroom dancing all experienced a golden age. Harlem was transformed from a predominantly Jewish neighborhood into a bustling black neighborhood, which, during the **Harlem Renaissance,** gave rise to jazz, poetry, novels, and visual art. Still, the **Cotton Club,** Harlem's most famous nightclub, didn't even allow blacks inside unless they were performing. The 20s were also a golden age of Yankee baseball. When New York bought **Babe Ruth's** contract from the Red Sox in 1920, they inaugurated a tradition of buying World Series success that George Steinbrenner is happy to continue to this day.

RECOVERY AND REFORM: 1929-2001

The epicenter of the Roaring Twenties, New York was also the site of their sudden collapse. On Black Tuesday and Black

1882
Thomas Edison opens New York's first electrical plant, in Lower Manhattan.

1883
The Brooklyn Bridge opens, offering cable car service between Manhattan and Brooklyn.

1886
The Statue of Liberty is inaugurated.

1892
Ellis Island opens its doors.

1898
The Incorporation of New York City—wistfully referred to as "The Great Mistake" in Brooklyn—unites Manhattan and the four outer boroughs.

1900
New York's subway begins running.

1902
The slender and triangular Flatiron Building is completed.

1911
In the Triangle Shirtwaist Fire, 146 immigrant women perish in a sweatshop blaze ignited by a single flicked cigarette.

LIFE AND TIMES

1925
Newly elected mayor Jimmy Walker, a strong proponent of Prohibition, proclaims, "No civilized man goes to bed the same day he wakes up."

1925
The New Yorker, originally conceived as a humorous society magazine, publishes its first issue, proclaiming itself "not edited for the old lady in Dubuque."

1929
The October Wall Street crash turns the Roaring Twenties into the Great Depression overnight.

1931
The Empire State Building is completed.

1957
The Brooklyn Dodgers move to Los Angeles.

1961
Bob Dylan gives legendary early performances at Cafe Wha and other clubs in Greenwich Village.

1973
The 110-story World Trade Center opens in Lower Manhattan.

1989
New York elects its first African-American mayor, David Dinkins.

Thursday in October of 1929, the stock market plummeted, triggering the **Great Depression,** which lasted until American intervention in WWII. In this dark period, the city finally took a stand against Tammany Hall, and it elected as mayor Italian-American **Fiorello LaGuardia**—an enigmatic figure marked by his mother's Judaism, his father's atheism, his own Episcopalianism, and a childhood split among the Bronx, frontier Arizona, Italy, and Hungary. Considered one of New York's greatest mayors, LaGuardia brought reform and non-partisanship to a city in the dire straits of depression.

Post-WWII prosperity brought more immigrants and businesses to the city, but once again, growth provoked conflict and a struggle for increased minority rights. In 1947, **Jackie Robinson** of the Brooklyn Dodgers became the first African American in major-league baseball. In 1969, the gay rights movement fought municipal prejudice with the **Stonewall Riots** in Greenwich Village. During the 1960s, crises in public transportation, education, and housing had heightened both racial tensions and criminal activity. By 1975, the city was pleading unsuccessfully with President Gerald Ford and the federal government to rescue it from impending bankruptcy. The infamous New York **Blackout of 1977** sparked extensive looting and arson, and the Son of Sam serial murders filled the city with fear.

The 80s saw **Wall Street** recovery and growth, but also brought on waves of crime and vandalism that scared off potential tourists. Racial conflict reached an all-time high in the early 90s, with beatings in the outer boroughs. **David Dinkins,** the city's first black mayor, fought hard to dismantle bureaucratic corruption and to encourage racial harmony. The high crime rate persisted, however, and fiscal crises continued to mount. Dinkins's successor **Rudolph Giuliani** is often credited with cleaning and beautifying the city, boosting its morale, and fighting crime, though his critics complain that he excessively infringed civil liberties. Still, Giuliani managed to cut the city's crime rate nearly in half and to transform seedy **Times Square** (p. 179) into a tourist-friendly commercial mecca.

21ST CENTURY CHALLENGES

On **September 11, 2001,** New York was the site of the worst terrorist attack ever to occur on American soil. Al Qaeda terrorists flew two planes into the World Trade Center, one at 8:46am and another at 9:02am. Some 3000 people died, including 343 NYC firefighters, who became symbols of heroism and courage. Though explicit discussion of 9/11 is rarer in the city today than it once was, the event continues to lurk just below the surface of New Yorkers' collective consciousness.

The gaping pit that had once housed New York's tallest buildings became known as **Ground Zero** (p. 158), and it now serves as a pilgrimage site for mourners from around the world. The rebuilding of Ground Zero has been a source of continuing controversy and political wrangling between New York City, New York State, the site's owner, and the Port Authority of New York and New Jersey. The current plan centers around Daniel

Libeskind's 1776-foot **Freedom Tower,** which would become the tallest building in the United States, and would be surrounded by an array of smaller skyscrapers designed by other prominent architects. A portion of the ruins from the Twin Towers will be preserved as a memorial to the victims.

THE CULTURAL CITY

THE MELTING POT

New York has always been a city of immigrants. From 1840-60, Germans and Irish came over in droves, and beginning in 1890, Greeks, Italians, Lithuanians, Poles, and Russians poured in through Ellis Island, often with misspelled names and exotic food. The US Congress restricted immigration in the 1920s, and the Great Depression brought it virtually to a halt. Still, internal American migration continued to bring new residents. When Jim Crow Laws restricted African American life in the South, the city's black population swelled. The 80s and 90s brought new immigrant populations from throughout the globe. Immigrants came from China, the Dominican Republic, Guyana, Jamaica, and the former Soviet Union.

Chinatown, Harlem, the Jewish **Lower East Side,** and **Little Italy** are the most famous ethnic neighborhoods of New York. In addition, lesser-known enclaves are scattered throughout the five boroughs. In Queens, **Astoria** hosts a large Greek community. On **Flushing's** Main St., you could be walking into Korea. Israeli eateries abound on Queens Blvd. in **Forest Hills,** and **Jackson Heights** bustles with Indian and South American populations. In Brooklyn, an Arab community centers around Atlantic Ave. in **Brooklyn Heights.** In **Crown Heights,** West Indians and Hasidim tentatively rub elbows. **Brighton Beach,** dubbed "Little Odessa," boasts a lively Russian enclave, and **Bensonhurst** offers a more authentic taste of Italian-American culture than Manhattan's Little Italy. In the Bronx, **Belmont** also hosts an Italian community. Finally, the **South Bronx,** home to many African Americans and Latinos, is the birthplace of hip-hop.

CITY PLANNING AND ARCHITECTURE

In the early years of European settlement on Manhattan, the city expanded without planning or regulation. The maze of wooden structures that first grew up on lower Manhattan left its mark on the irregular street plan still characteristic of the area. For a taste of old New York, visit **St. Paul's Chapel** (p. 160), and the houses on Charlton St., Vandam St., and in the **South Street Seaport** area (p. 161). Also check out **Old City Hall,** built in 1802 (p. 158).

During the **Revolutionary War,** two large fires burned swaths of the city to the ground. New York hastily rebuilt, but officials realized that greater order would have to be imposed.

1989
New York elects its first African-American mayor, David Dinkins.

2001
The September 11th terrorist attacks destroy the World Trade Center.

2003
New York's iconic subway tokens are phased out entirely, in favor of the MetroCard.

2004
New York's Museum of Modern Art completes a sumptuous renovation and expansion, designed by Yoshio Taniguchi.

2005
Christo and Jean-Claude's two-week Central Park installation "The Gates" delights, puzzles, and provokes New Yorkers.

LIFE AND TIMES

THE BIG OYSTER

Oysters are common enough in New York City today—but most are on the tables of pricey restaurants, flown in daily from far-flung locales. As a recent best-seller explains, however, New York's rivers and harbor once teemed with these mollusks. For centuries, oysters were a staple in the diet of the city's rich and poor alike.

In *The Big Oyster: History on the Half Shell* (Ballantine Books, 2006), Mark Kurlanskey attempts to tell the social history of New York City through its relationship to the oyster. The topic may seem obscure, but, as Kurlanskey notes, New York was famous worldwide in the 19th century as an oyster-eating capital.

After being harvested, New York oysters often traveled only a few blocks before being consumed—sold dirt-cheap on street corners, served on society dinner tables, and offered, along with more lascivious pleasures, in seedy oyster dens. As Kurlanskey explains, longstanding urban legend holds oysters to be an aphrodisiac, perhaps owing to their vaguely vaginal shape. The bivalves were the victual of choice in New York's dens of ill-repute.

But local oysters vanished from New York long before Guilliani determined to clean the city up. The city's last oyster bed closed in 1930, savaged by centuries of pollution and over-harvesting. Any oysters that may still survive in the harbor today are probably best left in the water.

John Randel's 1811 **Randel Plan** required undeveloped portions of Manhattan to be built according to a strict grid pattern—which explains why the cityscape changes so dramatically at 14th St. Between 1820 and 1850, Manhattan's population quadrupled and its ordered density came to seem oppressive. To make room for the 843-acre **Central Park,** conceived as an effort to unite the stately elegance of Europe's gardens with the democratic populism of America, the city had to drain uptown's swamps and demolish the shantytowns of poor immigrants and African Americans that sprawled among them. In the 1930s, urban planner **Robert Moses** became New York's most powerful official, creating 36 parks, a network of roads and highways to make them accessible to the public, 12 bridges and tunnels (including the enormous Triborough Bridge), **Lincoln Center** (p. 192), **Shea Stadium** (p. 211), and numerous housing projects.

Manhattan's most dramatic and memorable feature is its skyline. The modern skyscraper, made possible through the combination of steel-frame construction and the elevator, allowed the city to grow ever skyward, even when available land had long since vanished. In 1889 an 11-story "tower" was called "idiotic"; in 1899 a 30-floor Park Row apartment building became the world's tallest; and by 1913 the 60-floor **Woolworth Building** (p. 160) assumed this honor, dubbing itself the "Cathedral of Commerce." The iconic **Flatiron Building,** with its triangular shape and limestone and terra-cotta facade, rose at Broadway and Fifth Ave. in 1902. The **Chrysler Building's** stainless-steel spire, meant to resemble a radiator cap from a Chrysler car, rose in 1930. One year later, the Art Deco **Empire State Building** (p. 177) began its 42-year reign as the world's tallest building. The **World Trade Center** assumed that honor in 1973. The Twin Towers were an integral part of the Lower Manhattan skyline until their destruction on 9/11.

THE ARTS

LITERATURE

New York's literary history includes such figures as Washington Irving, Herman Melville, Walt Whitman, O. Henry, Theodore Dreiser, John Updike, and Paul Auster, and the city's neighborhoods are entwined with the lives of the authors they have hosted and influenced. Henry James (1843-1916) grew up at **Washington Square** in Greenwich Village, and made it the setting of his novel of the same name. Willa Cather lived at the Square near the turn of the century, and early 20th-century poet Edna St. Vincent Millay also lived nearby. In 1919 the wits of the Round Table—Robert Benchley, Dorothy Parker, Alexander Wolcott, and Edna Ferber—adopted the legendary **Algonquin Hotel** (59 W 44th St.) for their famous weekly meetings. *The New Yorker* magazine, founded by Harold Ross in 1925, was conceived during these boozy luncheons. The African-American artistic flourishing of 1920s **Harlem** gave birth to such classics as Zora Neale Hurston's *Their Eyes Were Watching God*, Nella Larsen's *Passing*, and the poetry of Langston Hughes.

   Columbia University has been an intellectual magnet on the Upper West Side for much of the 20th century. The Beat crowd roved the area in the late 1940s when Allen Ginsberg and Jack Kerouac studied there. **Public School #6,** also on the Upper West Side, boasts J.D. Salinger as an alumnus. The New York School of poets, including Frank O'Hara and John Ashbery, congregated in **Greenwich Village.** Later, the **East Village** became a literary center when Ginsberg and Kerouac moved in next to neighbors Amiri Baraka (Le Roi Jones) and W.H. Auden. Around the same time, poet Dylan Thomas drank himself to death at Greenwich Village's **White Horse Tavern.** Many a writer wiled away his or her dying days in relative obscurity at the **Chelsea Hotel** on 23rd Street between Seventh and Eighth Ave. Among former tenants are Arthur Miller and Vladimir Nabokov.

NEW YORK CITY IN LITERATURE

The Great Gatsby, F. Scott Fitzgerald (1925). Exemplifying, perhaps, the "great American novel," *Gatsby* flits between Long Island's glittering mansions, its industrial-age underside, and an unbearably stuffy suite at the Plaza.

The Catcher in the Rye, J.D. Salinger (1951). Angst-ridden Holden Caulfield wanders the streets of New York—drinking too much, pondering Central Park's ducks, navigating the unsavory characters in his hotel, and not finding whatever it is he's looking for.

The New York Trilogy, Paul Auster (1987). Auster's three short novels weave grim, eccentric narratives from the strange and mysterious pathologies of New York natives.

The Bonfire of the Vanities, Tom Wolfe (1987). Wolfe's scathing portrayal of 80s New York society leaves no stratum untouched—from status-obsessed Wall Street, to corrupt politicians, journalists, and lawyers, to gold-digging mistresses and wives, to the poverty and dishonest racial politics of the South Bronx.

Jazz, Toni Morrison (1992). Set amid the creativity, opportunity, and hardship of 1920s Harlem, the novel interweaves the lyrical story of the birth of jazz with the disappointed dreams of Southern blacks emigrating to Harlem in search of a better life.

'Tis, Frank McCourt (2000). Mirroring the stories of countless Irish immigrants, McCourt's memoir describes his early years in New York—working odd jobs, living in dire conditions, yet ultimately graduating from NYU and teaching English at Stuyvesant High.

VISUAL ART

The **Metropolitan Museum of Art** (p. 229) was founded in 1870 by American businessmen. In 1880, it moved to its current location near Central Park. The present facade was completed in 1926. Many of the city's wealthiest residents donated their private collections to the Met. The museum held its first large show of American art in 1909, but the thriving art communities of the city soon needed exhibition space for more modern art. The **Museum of Modern Art** (p. 225) opened in 1929, the **Whitney** (p. 230) in 1931, and the **Guggenheim** (p. 228), designed by Frank Lloyd Wright, in 1959. These museums contributed to the promotion of such New York movements as the Ashcan School and Abstract Expressionism.

   Much of the art enshrined in New York's museums was produced by artists working nearby. In the 19th century, Manhattan was home to the **Hudson River School,** based at the **Tenth Street Studio** in Greenwich Village. In 1900, famous photographers Alfred Stieglitz and Edward Steichen opened their New York photo gallery. The New York **Armory Show** of 1913 brought in works by artists such as Cézanne, Duchamp, Kandinsky, and Picasso. The show nearly caused riots, and went on to inspire artists for years to come. In the 1950s, the **Abstract Expressionists,** including Jackson Pollock, Willem deKooning, Mark Rothko, and Barnett Newman all congregated downtown, interacting with the **New York School** of poets.

New York today remains a mecca of artistic creativity. SoHo's galleries and studios sprung up after 1971 zoning changes legalized the growing arts community in lofts south of Houston St. The gentrification of recent years, however, has made SoHo's loft prices a little too lofty. Many galleries have shifted their venues to Chelsea. The most recent community of galleries has sprung up in cheaper Williamsburg, Brooklyn.

MUSIC, THEATER, AND DANCE

New York houses the finest classical music in the US. The **New York Philharmonic,** founded in 1842 by a group of local musicians, is the country's oldest symphony orchestra. The **Metropolitan Opera House,** built in 1883, has been stage to the world's finest, including tenor **Enrico Caruso** (1903). New Yorkers take their theater very seriously. The **Astor Place Riot** (May 10, 1849) began when a crowd of some 15,000 people gathered outside the Astor Place Opera House to protest the appearance of the English Shakespearean actor, Charles Macready. The crowd supported Edwin Forrest, an American-born actor. Even then, New Yorkers were sure of their tastes. Broadway—christened "The Great White Way" in 1904 because of its bright moving electric signs—sprang from lowly beginnings as a forum for vaudeville acts to host such American classics as *Oklahoma!* (1943), *West Side Story* (1956), *My Fair Lady* (1958), *The Sound of Music* (1959), and *Hair* (1968).

But chorus lines were not the only forum for dancers. **Martha Graham** opened her dance studio in 1926, and the **New York City Ballet** was founded by George Balanchine and Lincoln Kirstein in 1948. Today, the School of American Ballet continues to train young hopefuls at Lincoln Center Plaza.

The institutionalized arts often took their cue from the street. Long before Benny Goodman played jazz at Carnegie Hall (1938), big band sounds thrived in city clubs. **Minton's Playhouse** in Harlem was home to **Thelonious Monk** and gave rise to bebop, a sophisticated jazz variant. **Miles Davis, Charlie Parker, Dizzy Gillespie,** and many others contributed to the sound of the late 1940s and 50s. New York's most recent contribution to the music scene is the invention of **hip-hop.** In 1973, Bronx **DJ Kool Herc** began prolonging songs' funky drum "break" sections by using two turntables and two copies of the same record, switching and doubling back. Out of the 174th St. area by the Bronx River, Afrika Bambaataa, and Grandmaster Flash joined Kool to birth the art of DJing. In 1981, Grandmaster Flash opened for the Clash, epitomizing the fusion characteristic of the New York music scene

LIFE IN NEW YORK TODAY

NEWSPAPERS AND MAGAZINES

As the undisputed literary capital of the US, New York is the place where many of the nation's most important newspapers, magazines, and books are written, published, and subsequently torn to pieces by reviewers. Though the range of daily papers published in New York has shrunk drastically in recent years, the city nonetheless hosts some 100 daily and weekly newspapers—small and large, English and foreign language. **The New York Times** (www.nytimes.com), nicknamed "the old gray lady" for its sedate restraint, aspires to be the nation's paper of record, and despite a steady stream of scandals in recent years, it continues to provide sophisticated international, national, and municipal coverage. The paper's Wednesday Dining and Sunday Styles sections are trendsetters in the city, and arts coverage throughout the week is extensive. There's a common joke, though, that, while the brainy *New York Times* is written for people who think they should run the world, **The Wall Street Journal** (www.wsj.com), with its financially focused coverage, is written for the people who actually do. The city's two major tabloids, the **New York Post** (www.nypost.com) and **The Daily News** (www.nydailynews.com) are great sources of local color, battling to outdo each other in the size of the headline on their front pages, the gruesomeness of the crimes they describe, and the number of pages they devote to sports. The *Post* tends to be politically conservative, and its gossip column Page Six—inexplicably located at the moment on page 14 of the newspaper—is a salacious record of the latest celebrity foibles. The slim and free **Metro** newspaper (ny.metro.us) is ubiquitous in the subway.

NEW YORK CITY IN THE MOVIES

King Kong, Merian Cooper and Ernest Schoedsack (1933). So low budget it was shot entirely in-studio, the film paints a grim picture of depression-era New York and provides the unforgettable image of a gorilla straddling the Empire State Building.

On the Waterfront, Eliza Kazan (1954). An artful and unflinching portrait of oppressive working conditions, corruption, and mob violence in the dockyards of New York.

Breakfast at Tiffany's, Blake Edwards (1961). Before Paris Hilton came to define the New York socialite, Audrey Hepburn did it with sophistication, class, and far less money. "I don't want to own anything until I find a place where me and things go together. I'm not sure where that is, but I know what it is like. It's like Tiffany's."

West Side Story, Robert Wise and Gerome Robbins (1961). The story of Romeo and Juliet loosely transposed to the gang-dominated Upper West Side of the 1950s.

Annie Hall, Woody Allen (1977). A bittersweet break-up comedy demonstrating the eternal superiority of New York to L.A. "Don't you see the rest of the country looks upon New York like we're left-wing, communist, Jewish, homosexual pornographers? I think of us that way sometimes, and I live here."

Manhattan, Woody Allen (1979). A black-and-white paean to jazz, Manhattan, and the creative, neurotic lifestyle that Allen's persona lives there. "'He was as tough and romantic as the city he loved. Beneath his black-rimmed glasses was the coiled sexual power of a jungle cat.' (I love this.) 'New York was his town, and it always would be....'"

Wall Street, Oliver Stone (1987). Profiling a young Wall Street trader and a savvy older broker, this film depicts the corporate world at its most unseemly—filled with all-consuming greed, lawlessness, and soullessness.

Do the Right Thing, Spike Lee (1989). Set in the Bedford-Stuyvesant neighborhood of Brooklyn, the film tracks the explosive race dynamics on a single neighborhood block on the hottest day of the summer.

When Harry Met Sally, Rob Reiner (1989). A romantic comedy following the rendezvous of Harry and Sally throughout New York, in hopes of answering the question of whether platonic friendship between men and women is possible.

You've Got Mail, Nora Ephron (1998). An exploration of cyber-dating and chain stores on the Upper West Side. "Keep those West Side, liberal, nuts, pseudo-intellectuals.... — 'Readers,' Dad. They're called 'readers.' — Don't do that, son. Don't romanticize them."

THE LOCAL STORY

TAWK LIKE A NEW YAUWKER

Awrange (n.). The color of the leaves in Central Park in the fall; a fruit high in Vitamin C.

Bodega (n.). *From the Spanish.* A small convenience store.

The City (n.). New York City, usually Manhattan. You mean there's another one?

Esscuse me? "I dare you to say that to me again."

Bridge-and-Tunnel (adj.). Describes suburbanites from Jersey or Long Island, who traverse the bridges and tunnels into the City and diminish its coolness.

Fuhgedaboudit. "Based on the premises to which we have agreed, that conclusion does not follow."

Gimme. "May I please have..."

Hero (n.). A submarine sandwich.

Kvetch (v.). *From the Yiddish.* To complain.

Lox and a schmear (n.). A bagel with smoked salmon and cream cheese.

Mad (adv.). An adverb of intensification, as the Boston "wicked."

Mami (n.). *From the Spanish.* A hot, usually Latina, woman.

Nosh (v.). *From the Yiddish.* To snack.

Pie (n.). A pizza.

Tar beach (n.). A rooftop used for sun bathing in Manhattan.

Yous. The second-person plural pronoun; as the Fr. *vous,* but decidedly less elegant.

The Village Voice (www.villagevoice.com), available free at many street corners and newsstands, is the country's largest alternative newspaper. This left-leaning, Greenwich Village-based weekly stages lively political debates, sponsors excellent investigative reporting, and hosts the city's most intriguing set of personal ads. The real estate and nightlife listings are indispensable. The widely respected **New Yorker** (www.newyorker.com) contains invaluable museum, concert, theater, and movie listings for the tourist.

Myriad ethnic papers cater to the African-American, Chinese, Greek, Hispanic, Indian, Irish, and Korean communities, among others. Highlights include **El Diario** (www.eldiariony.com), a comprehensive Spanish-language daily; **Haitian Times** (www.haitiantimes.com); **Irish Echo** (www.irishecho.com); and **Forward** (www.forward.com), a Jewish weekly published in English, Russian, and Yiddish.

EATING

While the food offered in New York is as diverse as its eight million of residents, the city is united by a love of eating—and an interest in virtually every kind of food imaginable. The stereotypes associated with distinctive New York City cuisine tend toward the lowbrow. Be sure to start your day with a **bagel,** perhaps with locks or a "schmear" (that is, of cream cheese). At lunch time, the streets of Manhattan teem with culinary choices from myriad fast-food carts. A New York City **hot dog** usually comes doused in ketchup and mustard and loaded with onion, sauerkraut, or chile. **Pizza** is greasy and thin, making folding the slice into an impromptu sandwich imperative if you care about your shirt. **Falafels, shawarma, burritos, pretzels,** and **knishes** (Eastern European Jewish dumplings with fillings like mashed potatoes, meat, cheese, or spinach) are just some of the ethnically inflected street-cart delicacies that New Yorkers, from construction workers to investment bankers, line up side-by-side for. If you feel like a snack in the afternoon, try a giant salt-encrusted **pretzel** or some roasted **chestnuts.**

In contrast to the democratism of street food, restaurant-going in New York can be elitist. Though the city abounds with restaurants of every stripe, securing a table at a hip new bistro, a sexy sushi bar, or a gastronomic temple can be a blood sport. The heights of decadence reached for at the pinnacle of the New York restaurant world soar ever skyward. Dinner at **Alain Ducasse** purportedly begins with a choice of six types of mineral water and ends with the presentation of a dozen luxury fountain pens for signing the check. **Del Posto,** an Italian restaurant in Chelsea, sits patrons' handbags on specially designed upholstered stools. Power brokers lunching at **The Grill Room** at the Four Seasons Hotel eat alongside an enormous and invaluable Picasso-designed stage curtain.

But between these two extremes lies, thankfully, an enormous and delicious middle ground, always waiting to be explored. The city overflows with cafes specializing in brunch, designer bistros, sedate business-oriented dining rooms, and every type of ethnic restaurant you can imagine. The popular website **Fresh Direct** (www.freshdirect.com) offers next-day delivery of high quality groceries throughout the city, and gourmet grocery stores like **Dean and DeLuca** in SoHo (p. 115) and **Zabar's** on the Upper West Side (p. 141) are a feast for the eyes, even if your wallet can't afford such a feast for your taste buds. The streets of Chinatown abound with fish mongers, butchers, and produce dealers. Farmers' markets set up weekly in 28 locations throughout the five boroughs, with an enormous market four days weekly at Union Square.

GOING OUT

New York nightlife is legendary. Bars are generally in operation by mid-morning, and they aren't required to close until at least 4am. But there's no reason to stop then—the party continues at the many bars and clubs with after-hours licenses, and, since the subway runs all night, it's all too easy to participate in the never-sleeping of this city. Bear in mind that New York nightlife starts late; a hip bar might not fill up before 11pm, and nightclubs don't get going until much later—on the weekends, don't bother showing up before 1 or 2am.

Downtown neighborhoods like SoHo, Chelsea, Greenwich Village, the East Village, and the Lower East Side have the highest density of nightlife spots, but no Manhattan neighborhood lacks its share. A good way to save money—and hang out with a cool, youthful crowd—is to head to up-and-coming neighborhoods outside Manhattan like Williamsburg and Park Slope in Brooklyn. Smoking in virtually all enclosed spaces is banned in the city, so expect to see crowds of chimneys clustered at the entry to most nightspots.

RADIO

New York City's radio spectrum has everything from soulless elevator instrumentals to pirate radio broadcasts of underground sounds and community activism. The lower on the dial, the less commercial the sounds will be.

TYPE	DIAL POSITION
Classical	WNYC 93.9, WQXR 96.3
Jazz	WBGO 88.3, WPSC 88.7, WQCD 101.9
College/Indie/Alternative	WCWP 88.1, WNYU 89.1, WSOU 89.5, WKCR 89.9
Classic Rock	WAXQ 104.3, WNEW 102.7
Top 40	WPLJ 95.5, WRCN 103.9
Hip-Hop/R&B/Soul	WQHT 97.1, WRKS 98.7, WBLS 107.5, WWPR 105.1
Oldies	WCBS 101.1
Foreign Language	WADO 1280AM, WWRV 1330AM, WKDM 1380AM, WZRC 1480AM
News	WABC 770AM, WCBS 880AM, WINS 1010AM, WBBR 1130AM
Public Radio	WNYC 93.9, WNYC 820AM, WBAI 99.5
Sports	WFAN 660AM, WEPN 1050AM
Pirate	88.7 Steal This Radio (Lower East Side)

FESTIVALS AND SPECIAL EVENTS

DATE	NAME, LOCATION, CONTACT INFO	DESCRIPTION
Jan. 6	**Three Kings Parade,** from 5th Ave. and 116th St.	The children of Spanish Harlem celebrate Epiphany by parading through the streets as camels, cattle, and wise men to festive Latin beats.
Late Jan. to early Feb.	**Chinese Lunar New Year,** Chinatown.	Chinatown celebrates the Lunar New Year, whose date varies from year to year, with fireworks, giant floats, and a lavish parade.
Late Jan.	**Restaurant Week** (☎212-484-1222; www.nycvisit.com).	For 1 week in late Jan., and for another in mid-June, gourmet restaurants offer reduced-priced tasting menus that are a great way to sample the city's culinary best.
Early Feb.	**Empire State Building Run-Up,** Empire State Building (☎212-860-4455; www.esbnyc.com).	Runners race to the top of the Empire State Building's 1576 steps. The winner usually scales the skyscraper in under 12min.
Mid-Feb.	**Westminster Dog Show,** Madison Square Garden (☎212-465-6741; www.westminsterkennelclub.org).	If you liked *Best in Show,* or if you just love dogs, then come watch the country's perfectly trained and groomed pets preen.
Early Mar.	**Art Expo New York,** Jacob K. Javits Center (☎888-608-5300; www.artexpos.com).	With more than 500 galleries and dealers under 1 roof, you're sure to see lots of high quality art—and have ample choices if you're in the market to buy.
Mar. 17	**St. Patrick's Day Parade,** 5th Ave. from 44th to 86th St. (☎718-793-1600).	One of the city's biggest parties, the St. Patrick's Day Parade draws the green out of everyone's closet and makes the city's open-container laws seem like a joke.
Late Apr. to early May	**TriBeCa Film Festival,** TriBeCa (☎212-941-2400; www.tribecafilmfestival.com).	Conceived by Robert De Niro as a way to revitalize the physically and emotionally scarred TriBeCa neighborhood in the wake of 9/11, this series of screenings at area cinemas has quickly garnered international fame.
Early May	**Five Boro Bike Tour,** from Battery Park to Staten Island (www.bikenewyork.org).	Billing itself as the largest recreational cycling event in the US, the ride covers 42 miles of traffic-free roads, snaking through all 5 boroughs.
June-July	**Central Park SummerStage,** Rumsey Playfield, Central Park East, north of 69th St. (☎212-360-2756; www.summerstage.org).	An eclectic series of mostly free dramatic, musical, and dance performances in Central Park's Rumsey Playfield.
Mid-June to mid-July	**Shakespeare in the Park,** Delacorte Theater, Central Park West, at 81st St. (☎212-539-8500; www.publictheater.org).	Shakespeare is lovely under the stars. Pick up free tickets at Central Park's Delacorte Theater beginning at 1pm the day of the show, or at The-ater's box office from 1-3pm at 425 Lafayette St.
Mid-June	**Puerto Rican Day Parade,** 5th Ave. from 44th to 86th St. (☎718-401-0404).	This staggeringly patriotic festival draws huge crowds dotted with American and Puerto Rican flags to the Upper East Side.
Mid-June	**Museum Mile Festival,** 5th Ave. from 82nd to 105th St. (www.museummilefestival.org).	One day a year, New York's 9 5th Ave. museums, including the Guggenheim and the Met, open their doors for free and host a mile-long "block party."
Mid-June	**JVC Jazz Festival,** sites throughout the city (www.festivalproductions.net). Tickets sold at venues.	A 2-week festival that hosts big-name international jazz acts in venues ranging from major concert halls, to intimate clubs, to parks and schools.
Mid-June	**Restaurant Week** (see late Jan.).	A repeat of the gourmet deals offered in late Jan.
Late June	**LGBT Pride Week,** parade through Greenwich Village and Chelsea (☎212-80-PRIDE; www.hopinc.org).	One of the nation's largest gay pride celebrations, the week entails a host of festive rallies and dances, and culminates in an enormous march celebrating New York's myriad queer identities.
Late June	**Mermaid Parade,** Coney Island (www.coneyisland.com).	Coney Island's sea-themed parade is wacky, fun, and a favorite activity of the LGBT Pride participants in town the same weekend.

DATE	NAME, LOCATION, CONTACT INFO	DESCRIPTION
July 4	**Macy's 4th of July Fireworks** (☎212-494-4495), exploding on the East River at 34 St., the South Street Seaport, and the Upper NY Harbor.	FDR Drive, Liberty State Park, the top of most Manhattan buildings, and Brooklyn Heights make great viewing areas. Bring a radio and listen to the Philharmonic's musical accompaniment at 1010AM.
Mid-July	**Philharmonic Concerts in the Parks**, parks throughout the five boroughs (☎212-875-5709; www.nyphil.org).	Over the course of a week, the Philharmonic performs outdoor concerts in parks all over the city. The concerts are free and no ticket is required. Check the website for dates and event locations.
Mid-Aug.	**Fringe Festival** (☎212-279-4488; www.fringenyc.org). Check website for venue and ticketing information.	The Fringe Festival showcases offbeat, experimental performance art—more than 200 international companies participate, giving some 1300 performances in 20 venues throughout the city.
Late Aug. to early Sept.	**U.S. Open**, Flushing Meadows, Queens (☎718-760-6200; www.uspen.com).	A 2-week tennis Grand Slam tournament hosting some of the greatest players in the world.
Mid-Sept.	**Howl Festival**, Lower East Side (☎212-505-2225; www.howlfestival.com).	Named in honor of Allen Ginsberg's epoch-making poem, this festival celebrates the Lower East Side's dance, film, music, painting, poetry, sculpture, theater, and food in 8 festive days.
Mid-Sept.	**San Gennaro Festival**, Mulberry St., Little Italy (☎212-768-9322; www.sangennaro.org).	Little Italy at its most carnival-like: expect funnel cake, Italian sausage, cannoli-eating contests, and happy crowds of tourists and locals.
Mid-Sept. to mid-Oct.	**New York Film Festival**, Alice Tully Hall, Lincoln Center (☎212-875-5050; www.filmlinc.com).	The TriBeCa festival's older, more established cousin, this 17-day festival has screened cutting-edge films for nearly 45 years.
Mid-Oct.	**D.U.M.BO. Art Under the Bridge Festival**, Brooklyn (☎718-694-0831; www.dumboartscenter.org).	Brooklyn's D.U.M.B.O. arts district is always a pleasure to visit, but the area is especially alive during this weekend of street exhibitions and open studios and galleries.
Oct. 31	**Halloween Parade**, 6th Ave. from Broome St. to 23rd St. in Greenwich Village (www.halloween-nyc.com).	If you can throw together a creative costume, you can be part of this crazy Greenwich Village parade. Costumes range from artsy, to scary, to sexy.
Early Nov.	**NYC Marathon**, Staten Island to Central Park (☎212-423-2249; www.nycmarathon.org).	Some 35,000 runners run this 26.2-mi. trek through all 5 boroughs, with throngs of cheering spectators lining the entire course.
Late Nov.	**Macy's Thanksgiving Day Parade**, Broadway from 72nd St. to Herald Square (☎212-494-4495).	The New York institution you probably watched on TV when you were a kid, with enormous, artful floats cutting right down Broadway.
Late Nov.	**Rockefeller Center Christmas Tree Lighting** (☎212-632-3975; www.rockefellercenter.com).	Throngs crowd the plaza of Rockefeller Center to ooh and ahh collectively as the 75-ft. Norway Spruce is lit for the first time.
Dec. 31	**New Year's Eve Ball Drop**, Times Square (☎212-768-1560; www.timessquarenyc.org).	New Year's Eve doesn't get any crazier than this. A quarter-million people swarm Times Square to watch the gleaming crystal ball ring in the New Year and to be showered by confetti.
Dec. 31	**Midnight Run**, Central Park (☎212-860-4455; www.nyrrc.org).	DJs, costumes, and fireworks enliven a 4-mi. midnight run through Central Park.

LIFE AND TIMES

BEYOND TOURISM

A PHILOSOPHY FOR TRAVELERS

As a tourist, you're always an outsider. While sightseeing, clubbing, and hotel-living can be great fun, it's worth trying to go *beyond* tourism. Connecting with a place through studying, volunteering, or working can help reduce that tourist-in-a-strange-land feeling and give you deeper insight into a place. Even more importantly, perhaps, you have the potential to make a positive impact on the city. With this Beyond Tourism chapter, *Let's Go* hopes to promote better understanding of New York City and to provide suggestions for those who want to get more than a photo album out of their travels.

New York presents many options to those hoping to go beyond tourism. If you choose to **volunteer** in New York City, you'll almost certainly be responding to serious need. Though its Gotham City facade has in recent years given way to the clean sidewalks of *You've Got Mail*, the city continues to struggle with serious social problems caused by poverty, lack of community infrastructure, and crime. As a volunteer, you can participate in projects from distributing food to the needy, to mentoring at-risk children, to creating affordable housing. Later in this chapter, we recommend organizations that can help you find the opportunities that best suit your interests, whether you're looking to pitch in for a day or a year. **Studying** at one of New York's many institutions of higher learning is another worthwhile option. Even New York's world-famous universities have non-selective summer and continuing education programs that can be fascinating enrichment opportunities. Finally, New York offers numerous short-term **work** opportunities, which range from clerical (mind-numbing) temp work, to opportunities to be seen on the big screen as a movie extra. Those seeking longer commitments can often find jobs as babysitters and nannies, or as waiters and waitresses. Others travel to New York in hopes of climbing the ultimate corporate ladder.

VOLUNTEERING

Though New York is a wealthy city when viewed generally, it has substantial disadvantaged populations that are often hidden by the city's bright lights. Volunteering can be one of life's most fulfilling experiences, especially if you combine it with the thrill of traveling in a new place.

> ## WHY PAY MONEY TO VOLUNTEER?
> Many volunteers are surprised to learn that some organizations require large fees or "donations." While this may seem ridiculous at first glance, such fees often keep the organization afloat, in addition to covering airfare, room, board, and administrative expenses for the volunteers. (Other organizations must rely on private donations and government subsidies.) If you're concerned about how a program spends its fees, request an annual report or finance account. A reputable organization won't refuse to inform you of how volunteer money is spent.
>
> Pay-to-volunteer programs might be a good idea for young travelers who are looking for more support and structure (such as pre-arranged transportation and housing), or anyone who would rather not deal with the uncertainty implicit in creating a volunteer experience from scratch.

Most people who volunteer in New York do so on a short-term basis, at organizations that make use of drop-in or once-a-week volunteers. The best way to find opportunities that match up with your interests and schedule may be to check with New York volunteer agencies and to do Internet searches. There are two main types of volunteer organizations—religious and non-sectarian—though there are rarely restrictions on participating in either. The **Volunteer Referral Center** (☎212-889-4805; www.volunteer-referral.com) places individuals in volunteer positions at organizations throughout the city, based on detailed personal interviews. **New York Cares** (☎212-228-5000; www.nycares.org) also specializes in public service placements. The **Mayor's Volunteer Center** (www.nyc.gov/html/mvc) has an extensive list of community service organizations, and it has teamed up with United Way of New York to organize **VolunteerNYC** (www.volunteernyc.org), a convenient search engine that locates opportunities according to your interests. **Idealist** (www.idealist.org) contains a searchable database of over 27,000 nonprofit and community organizations, including over 1000 in New York City.

HOMELESSNESS

Homelessness is one of New York City's major social challenges. In any given year, some 100,000 New Yorkers experience homelessness for at least one night, and every night of the year, the city's shelters fill with 32,000 people, of whom 12,000 are children. While New York has many organizations seeking to fight homelessness, need for increased support is great.

Common Ground Community, 14 E 28th St., New York, NY 10018 (☎212-389-9365; www.commonground.org). Common Ground runs housing programs seeking to provide permanent homes to the homeless, disabled, elderly, or poor.

Covenant House New York, 460 W 41st St., New York, NY 10036 (☎212-613-0300; www.covenanthouseny.org). Provides food, shelter, health services, counseling, job training, emotional support, and 24hr. crisis assistance to homeless, abused, or at-risk youth. Locations in all 5 boroughs. Wide variety of opportunities for volunteers.

Habitat for Humanity New York City, 334 Furman St., Brooklyn, NY 11201 (☎718-246-5656; www.habitatnyc.org), in Downtown Brooklyn. Through volunteer labor and donations, Habitat builds and rehabilitates simple homes with the help of the future homeowners. Habitat homes, sold to partner families at no profit and financed with no-interest loans, have been built throughout the city.

Neighborhood Coalition for Shelter, 157 E 86th St., New York, NY 10028 (☎212-861-0704, ext. 1; www.ncsinc.org). Offers a variety of services to New York's needy, including housing, 24hr. support, shelter, counseling, and job and education specialists. Volunteers are welcome for short, long, or 1-time commitments.

THE ROCK IS A HARD PLACE
NYC's drug laws and prison population

I know a thing or two about jails. I've spent a night inside Miami-Dade on false arrest for the charge of "unlawful assembly," which was really peaceful protest. Mom and Pop bailed me out, and my charges were dismissed with the help of an ACLU lawyer.

That's not how things go for the 15,000 inmates of "the Rock," as New York's Rikers Island prison is known (San Francisco's Alcatraz goes by the same name). The typical inmate is a black or Latino man held without sentence and unable to post bail. His charge is usually the possession or attempted sale of a narcotic substance, to which he may or may not be addicted.

While I was growing up in New York, I never came close to finding myself in his situation. I wouldn't even have known where he was located—Rikers Island, off the south coast of the Bronx, does not appear on most city maps. I spent my adolescent years at an elite prep school, where the gravest consequence for drug use was a summer in rehab. I belonged to half of the population largely oblivious to the experiences of the other half—in this case, those who have been personally affected by the city's incarceration policies. Most New Yorkers would admit that their overwhelmed criminal justice system probably makes some mistakes. What they are just beginning to realize is that the mistake doesn't lie on the level of individual cases; it rests in the state's drug laws, which have produced the majority of the city and state's jailed population.

I got my first hint of this through my decision to spend the summer working at the Correctional Association of New York, a nonprofit advocacy and research group dedicated to serving inmates. I discovered the existence of the Rockefeller Drug Laws, established by Governor Nelson Rockefeller in 1973. The Rockefeller laws impose harsh minimum sentences for the possession or attempted sale of relatively small quantities of drugs. Ninety-three percent of those jailed under the law are black or Latino, and most enter prison with no prior criminal history. They cost the state around $590 million a year.

I also got to visit the Bronx Criminal Court Complex on 161st St., which is the gateway to Rikers Island. It was a rare chance for somebody who wasn't arrested. The city grudgingly grants this tour to the Correctional Association; other visitors are not allowed. We were taken in the back way past a series of squalid holding cells crammed with people. Some looked panicked, while others looked bored—"the regulars," as a tour guide put it. They were waiting to be processed in the drab, low-ceilinged courtrooms downstairs, where the average hearing lasts a matter of minutes, thanks to the bleak efficiency of public defenders.

If the offense falls under the Rockefeller statutes, plea-bargaining is not an option: mandatory sentencing takes over, and the trial runs like clockwork. The complete lack of sentencing flexibility written into the Rockefeller laws has turned plenty of judges and prosecutors into its most outspoken opponents. The stipulated sentences are among the harshest in the country, and a failure from the perspective of drug prevention policy. Yet they persist despite efforts to repeal them, largely because of the power imbalance between urban Democrats and suburban and rural Republicans in the state Senate. New York City may be the capital of the world, but the state capital remains in Albany, 150 mi. and a world away.

Geographic differences translate into economic and political conflicts. The state's prison population is located mostly upstate, where poor communities want new prisons to be built. They ally with private prison contractors, who provide the backbone of an otherwise dying economy. And although prisoners can't vote, their presence increases upstate population, skewing legislative representation.

The Rockefeller drug laws pit poor urban blacks and Latinos against poor rural whites. Both communities end up suffering from the violence generated by prisons, through guards and former inmates. Until New York can figure out a way to repeal these laws, the Rock around its neck will only drag it further into the muck. And Rikers Island will continue to be the city's most important landmark you'll never visit.

Correctional Association of New York, 135 E 15th St. (☎212-254-5700). Drop the Rock Campaign (www.droptherock.org).

Madeleine Elfenbein graduated from Harvard in 2004 with a degree in Social Studies.

Partnership for the Homeless, 305 7th Ave., New York, NY 10001 (☎212-645-3444; www.partnershipforthehomeless.org). Dedicated to breaking the cycle of homelessness through a variety of programs geared toward families, the elderly, veterans, those affected by HIV/AIDS, and several other at-risk groups. Volunteers staff shelters throughout the city and assist with the Partnership's many programs.

FOOD ASSISTANCE

Hunger is a daily concern for an astonishing number of people in a city as wealthy as New York. More than one million New Yorkers require food assistance annually, and one in four New York City children live below the poverty line. New York has more than 1000 food banks, yet they continually struggle with cutbacks in governmental and charitable support.

City Harvest, 575 8th Ave., 4th fl., New York, NY 10018 (☎917-351-8700; www.cityharvest.org). Founded in 1981, the largest and oldest nonprofit food-rescue program in the world. Committed to feeding hungry people in NYC using innovative, practical, and cost-effective methods. They rescue food that otherwise would be wasted and deliver it to those who serve the hungry. Volunteer opportunities vary widely in nature and level of commitment—you can pick up food donations from the city's vendors and markets, drive the truck that collects the food, or provide administrative support.

Food Bank for New York City, 90 John St., Ste. 702, New York, NY 10038 (☎212-566-7855; www.foodbanknyc.org), in the Bronx, Brooklyn, Manhattan, and Queens. Supplies over 200,000 meals daily to those in need. Volunteer opportunities are available sorting food, working events, or assisting at one of its 1000 community food programs.

God's Love We Deliver, 166 Ave. of the Americas, New York, NY 10013 (☎212-294-8104; www.godslovewedeliver.org). Prepares and delivers fresh, nutritious meals to those living with AIDS, cancer, and other serious illnesses, who cannot shop and cook for themselves. Internships and volunteer opportunities for students.

Yorkville Common Pantry, 8 E 109th St., New York, NY 10029 (☎212-410-2264; www.ycp.org). Serves 1200 hot meals each week. Also offers a girls' youth program, showers, laundry service, psychiatric help, and after-school programs. Volunteers help prepare and serve meals, and assist with the pantry's other services.

YOUTH AND COMMUNITY PROGRAMS

Though all five of New York City's boroughs boast exciting highlights, there is a great disparity in resources and opportunities from neighborhood to neighborhood. Many poorer communities lack strong educational and recreational programs, support services, and career counseling. Contributing to a community support organization can make a tremendous difference, if only in one child's life.

Big Brothers, Big Sisters, 223 E 30th St., New York, NY 10016 (☎212-686-2042; www.bigsnyc.org). By spending only 4hr. every other week hanging out with a local child, volunteers become mentors and friends to at-risk kids in an effort to support children growing up in single-parent households. At least a 1-year commitment required.

City Year, 20 W 22nd St., New York, NY 10010 (☎212-675-8881; www.cityyear.org). Volunteers participate in a broad range of public service programs primarily in the South Bronx, East Harlem, and Lower East Side. Service work focuses primarily on youth development and enrichment, and mentoring. Participants must be US citizens.

East Harlem Tutor Program (EHTP), 2050 2nd Ave., New York, NY 10029 (☎212-831-0650; www.ehtp.org). This nonprofit program offers local Harlem children lessons in math, reading, writing, and computers. Need for volunteers is great; there is a waiting list for kids seeking tutors.

Forest Hills Community House, 108-25 62nd Dr., Forest Hills, NY 11375 (☎718-592-5757; www.fhch.org). Supports the community through youth and elderly programs, and local support and education services. Volunteers are encouraged to participate in its wide range of programs that include tutoring, employment support, homelessness prevention, early childhood development, and youth outreach.

The Point Community Development Center, 940 Garrison Ave., Bronx, NY 10474 (☎718-542-4139; www.thepoint.org). A nonprofit organization operating in Hunts Point that is committed to promoting youth development, as well as cultural and economic revitalization. It offers South Bronx residents after-school programs, music instruction, visual arts workshops, entrepreneurial opportunities, community leadership projects, and much more.

Union Settlement Association, 237 E 104th St., New York, NY 10029 (☎212-828-6018; www.unionsettlement.org). With 16 locations in Harlem, Union Settlement's after-school, childcare, summer job placement, nutrition, and economic development programs have a positive impact on nearly 12,000 people per year.

OTHER CONCERNS

City of New York Parks and Recreation, The Arsenal, Central Park, 830 5th Ave., New York, NY 10021 (☎212-NEW-YORK; www.nycgovparks.org). If you're 18 or older, you can be an Urban Park Ranger Volunteer in parks throughout the city. Participants research local history, greet visitors, seek donations, write grants, and more.

Guggenheim Museum, 1071 5th Ave., New York, NY 10128 (☎212-423-3648; www.guggenheim.org). Volunteer opportunities are available in the curatorial, public affairs, visitor information, education, finance, and special events departments. Volunteers may also assist with the museum's outreach program, *Learning Through Art.*

New York Civil Rights Coalition, 3 W 35th St., New York, NY 10001 (☎212-563-5636; www.nycivilrights.org). College, law, and graduate students participate in the Coalition's efforts to defend civil rights and improve race relations through its Unlearning Stereotypes program. Volunteers in groups of 2 teach semester-long courses in local schools.

Sanctuary for Families, P.O. Box 1406, Wall St. Station, New York, NY 10268 (☎212-349-6009; www.sanctuaryforfamilies.org). Sanctuary for Families provides shelter, support, and clinical and legal services to victims of domestic violence and their children. Volunteers participate in many of the organization's programs including childcare, tutoring, special events coordination, and *pro bono* services (for professionals).

STUDYING

New York has more institutions of higher education than any other city in the world. Some 500,000 students worldwide flock to its 95 major universities, small colleges, and professional and specialty schools. Many schools, such as **NYU** and **Columbia,** have summer programs for visiting students, while the **Cooper Union for the Advancement of Science and Art** and the **Juilliard School** offer respected adult-education programs (p. 73). For a complete list of academic institutions in the city, visit the official New York City website (www.nyc.gov). Schools listed below all offer summer or extension programs. Some of these schools may be helpful in finding long-term accommodations. Call for details.

UNIVERSITIES, DESIGN SCHOOLS, AND EXCHANGE PROGRAMS

Association for International Practical Training, 10400 Little Patuxent Pkwy., Ste. 250, Columbia, MD 21044 (☎410-997-2200; www.aipt.org). 8- to 12-week programs in New York and across the US for international college students with 2 years of experience in technical study. US$25 application fee.

> **VISA INFORMATION.** Two types of study visas are available: the **F-1,** for academic studies (including language school), and the **M-1,** for non-academic and vocational studies. To secure a study visa, you must already be accepted into a full course of study at an educational institution approved by the Immigration and Naturalization Services (INS). F-1 applicants must also prove they have enough readily available funds to meet all expenses for the first year of study, and that adequate funds will be available for each subsequent year of study; M-1 applicants must have evidence that sufficient funds are immediately available to pay all tuition and living costs for the entire period of intended stay. Be prepared to show transcripts and standardized test results, and make sure your passport is valid for at least six months after entry. See www.united-statesvisas.gov for more information. Applications should be processed through the American embassy or consulate in your country of residence (see **Visas, Invitations, and Work Permits,** p. 27).

Columbia University Continuing Education, 303 Lewisohn Hall, 2970 Broadway, Mail Code 4110, New York, NY 10027 (☎212-854-9699; www.ce.columbia.edu). Columbia's 35-acre campus boasts one of the largest library collections in the nation and modern gym and recreational facilities (p. 194). The university also has continuing-education options for those not enrolled in degree programs—students can enroll in individual classes or participate in other programs (Second Majors, Summer Session, Creative Writing Studies, or Auditing). Info center open M-F 9am-6pm.

The Cooper Union for the Advancement of Science and Art, Cooper Sq., New York, NY 10003 (☎212-353-4100; www.cooper.edu). The Adult Education department at Cooper Union (p. 170) offers non-credit classes in art, design, photography, language, and urban studies; the school also offers an extensive range of free and inexpensive public lectures, debates, cultural events, symposia, concerts, tours, and other community-oriented activities. Fall, spring, and summer sessions.

The New School, 66 W 12th St., New York, NY 10011 (☎212-229-5600; www.newschool.edu). The Adult Education department (p. 168) offers more than 1500 credit and non-credit courses each semester. Courses for adults are offered in: business and career education, writing, social sciences, humanities, culinary arts, and foreign languages, among others. Most summer adult education courses begin in early June.

New York University (NYU), 22 Washington Sq. N, New York, NY 10003 (☎212-854-9699, registration 212-998-2292; www.nyu.edu). In addition to degree-program students, students from other colleges and universities and adults who want to earn college credit can register for summer classes at this Greenwich Village institution. Courses are usually 6 weeks (late May to mid-June), and housing in residence halls is available for an additional fee. The university also hosts a School of Continuing and Professional Studies (☎212-998-7200).

Parsons School of Design, 66 5th Ave., New York, NY 10011 (☎212-229-8910 or 800-252-0852; www.parsons.edu). Offers a number of non-degree program options. Individual classes and summer intensives for credit and non-credit. Courses cover such topics as digital design, fashion studies, fine arts, floral design, graphic design, and architecture. Students can enroll in continuing education classes or take 6-week studio classes ("short courses"). 1-month summer intensive programs geared for high-school and college students also available (June and July sessions).

School of Visual Arts, 209 E 23rd St., New York, NY, 10010 (☎212-592-2000; www.schoolofvisualarts.edu). Offers continuing education courses, programs, and workshops. Subjects range from studio arts classes in advertising, computer art, film, interior design and photography, to liberal-arts classes in art history, humanities, English as a Second Language, and cinema studies. The School of Visual Arts also offers Arts

Abroad, Arts for Kids, and pre-college art programs. Student housing may be available for an additional fee.

FILM, THEATER, AND MUSIC SCHOOLS

New York hosts a large number of prestigious performing-arts schools, though most of them are for full-time students only. Such schools include the **Columbia University School of the Arts** (☎ 212-854-2815; www.columbia.edu/cu/arts/film), **The American Musical and Dramatic Academy** (☎ 212-787-5300 or 800-367-7908; www.amda.edu), and **New York University, Department of Film and Television** (☎ 212-998-1600; filmtv.tisch.nyu.edu/page/home). Still, these schools often cast non-students for short films and can provide valuable networking opportunities. The following schools, on the other hand, offer short-term programs:

American Academy of Dramatic Arts (AADA), in New York, 120 Madison Ave., New York, NY 10016 (☎ 212-686-9244 or 800-463-8990; www.aada.org). The Academy has provided stage, film, and television training for over a century. Evening, summer, and Sa classes offered.

Circle in the Square Theatre School, 1633 Broadway, New York City, NY 10019 (☎ 212-307-0388; www.circlesquare.org). Besides its regular and evening curriculum, offers a 7-week (July-Aug.) program with an intensive, professionally oriented curriculum of acting classes. Musical track also available.

The Juilliard School Evening Division, 60 Lincoln Center Plaza, New York, NY 10023-6588 (☎ 212-799-5040; www.juilliard.edu/evening/evening.html). World-famous performing-arts institution also offers evening classes to the public (p. 250). Classes are taught by renowned experts in the music and performing-arts worlds, including faculty members from the College Division. Class levels range from beginning to advanced. Most classes start after 5:30pm and finish by 8pm. Fall and spring semesters offered.

Mannes College of Music, 150 W 85th St., New York, NY 10024 (☎ 212-580-0210; www.mannes.edu). Newly offered extension school classes include basic theory and jazz piano for pianists.

New York Film Academy, 100 E 17th St., New York, NY 10003 (☎ 212-674-4300; www.nyfa.com). Offers classes in filmmaking, digital editing, film acting, screenwriting, and 3D animation. Courses last 4 weeks to 1 year. Evening and summer classes offered.

The School for Film and Television, 39 W 19th St., 12th fl., New York, NY 10011 (☎ 212-645-0030 or 888-645-0030; www.filmandtelevision.com). Accredited film acting school. The full-time program lasts 2 years, but the Summer Acting Intensives program allows high-school and college students to earn college credits while learning cutting-edge, on-camera performance techniques. 9-month part-time certificate programs also offered.

TVI Actors Studio, 165 W 46th St., Ste. 509, New York, NY 10036 (☎ 212-302-1900 or 800-884-2772, ext. 2; www.tvistudios.com). Offers summer programs and year-round classes. Courses run for 2-10 weeks.

WORKING

Some travelers want long-term jobs that allow them to get to know New York as a member of the community, while others seek short-term work to finance their travels. In New York City, those looking for long-term jobs should check out childcare, waitstaff, bartending, and internship opportunities. For shorter commitments, the best bet is probably temp work. Check the **classifieds** of New York's newspapers, particularly in the *Village Voice, New York Press*, and the Sunday edition of *The New York Times*. Also check **bulletin boards** in local coffee shops, markets, librar-

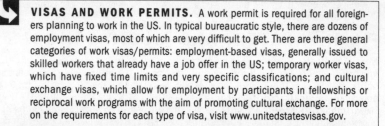

VISAS AND WORK PERMITS. A work permit is required for all foreigners planning to work in the US. In typical bureaucratic style, there are dozens of employment visas, most of which are very difficult to get. There are three general categories of work visas/permits: employment-based visas, generally issued to skilled workers that already have a job offer in the US; temporary worker visas, which have fixed time limits and very specific classifications; and cultural exchange visas, which allow for employment by participants in fellowships or reciprocal work programs with the aim of promoting cultural exchange. For more on the requirements for each type of visa, visit www.unitedstatesvisas.gov.

ies, and community centers for help wanted posters (for a list of community centers, see **Community Centers,** p. 83). In addition, all of New York's colleges and universities have **career and employment offices;** even if you can't get into the office itself (some may require a school ID to enter), most have bulletin boards outside (for a list of colleges and universities in New York, see **Studying,** p. 71). Sometimes a restaurant or store will post a sign in the window—keep your eyes peeled. As a last resort, it can be fruitful to **go door-to-door with your résumé** and a cover letter, particularly if you're targeting a type of establishment that is concentrated in a given area (this works well in an area like SoHo, for example, for someone interested in finding work at a gallery). When finding a job in New York, the **Internet** is your best friend.

LONG-TERM WORK

If you're planning on spending more than three months working in New York City, search for a job well in advance. Be wary of advertisements or companies that claim the ability to get you a job for a fee—often the same listings are available online or in newspapers, or are out-of-date. For foreigners looking to find work in New York, **The Council on International Educational Exchange (CIEE)** is a reputable organization with offices at 3 Copley Pl., 2nd Fl., Boston, MA 02116 (☎617-247-0350; www.ciee.org) and 7 Custom House St., 3rd fl., Portland, ME 04101 (☎207-553-7600; www.ciee.org).

INTERNET RESOURCES

Careerbuilder (www.careerbuilder.com). Over 400,000 jobs in database.

Craigslist (newyork.craigslist.org). Post your résumé and search available jobs. Also provides community and apartment listings.

Foreignborn (www.foreignborn.com/career_ctr.htm). Foreignborn's career center lets you submit your résumé for viewing by US-based companies looking specifically for foreign-born employees. Also has visa information.

Monster (www.monster.com). Search database, post résumé on site.

Yahoo HotJobs (hotjobs.yahoo.com). Allows potential employees to post résumés and search a huge job database.

INTERNSHIPS

New York City hosts the headquarters of just about every industry and nonprofit sector imaginable, with the exception of government (and even then, there's the high-profile Mayor's Office and City Hall). In particular, New York City is the primary American home for publishing, advertising, theater, television, finance, fashion, and museum curating. It also houses offices for most international and nationwide nonprofit organizations. While it's difficult to get paid, short-term positions at these offices, most are eager for unpaid interns; still, even interning and volunteering in the Big Apple can be fiercely competitive. Be sure to contact your organization of choice early (3-6 months before you plan to arrive), and be prepared for an extensive application process.

Many websites provide nationwide databases of internship opportunities: **Internjobs.com** (www.internjobs.com); **Internsearch.com** (www.internsearch.com); **Internweb.com** (www.internweb.com); **Rising Star Internships** (www.rsinternships.com); **Studentintern.com** (www.studentintern.com); and **Wetfeet.com** (www.wetfeet.internshipprograms.com) all let you search their postings and post your résumé for free. Don't overlook websites more dedicated to your field of interest, however. **Journalismjobs.com** (www.journalismjobs.com), for instance, focuses entirely on media jobs, while **Studentjobs.gov** (www.studentjobs.gov)—a joint project between the US Office of Personnel Management (OPM) and the US Department of Education's Student Financial Assistance office—lists jobs and internships with the federal government. The **Council on International Educational Exchange (CIEE)** may also be useful in finding an internship (p. 74). The list below includes some (but definitely not all) internships that are unique to New York City.

City of New York Parks and Recreation, the Arsenal, Central Park, 830 5th Ave., New York, NY 10021 (☎212-NEW-YORK; www.nycgovparks.org). The Parks Department works to keep the city's parks and playgrounds clean and safe, while organizing cultural, social, and athletic activities such as nature walks, historic tours, and concerts. A wide range of internship opportunities are available.

Government Scholars Program, NYC Department of Citywide Administrative Services, 1 Center St., Rm. 1340, New York, NY 10007 (☎212-669-4163; www.nyc.gov/html/dcas/html/resources/mgsp.shtml). College sophomores and juniors are eligible to participate in the Government Scholars Program, which combines an internship in city government with seminars on its workings. Interns receive a $3500 stipend for the 10-week summer program.

Guggenheim Museum, 1071 5th Ave., New York, NY 10128 (☎212-423-3500; www.guggenheim.org). Offers a variety of academic year and summer internships to undergraduates and graduates studying art history, conservation, and similar fields. Sometimes stipends are awarded. International students are encouraged to apply.

New York City Government Summer Internship Program, NYC Department of Citywide Administrative Services, 1 Center St., 24th fl., New York, NY 10007 (☎212-NEW-YORK; www.nyc.gov/html/dcas/html/employment/summerintern.shtml). Summer internships are available to college and graduate students in a long list of government departments, including Homeless Services, Human Rights, and Fire departments. The availability of stipends, and length of the internship (up to 13 weeks) varies with placement.

CHILDCARE

Childcare can be a lucrative field; babysitters and nannies are always in demand. Make sure you know what you're getting into, though, as some parents also expect you to do housework. Websites such as **Craigslist** (newyork.craigslist.org) let both parents and potential babysitters advertise for free. If you go through an agency, make sure you research the company thoroughly, as many of them make a killing on fees while providing little service or support to you. Major childcare agencies, not necessarily endorsed by *Let's Go,* include:

Adele Poston Domestic Agency, 16 E 79th St., New York, NY 10021 (☎212-879-7474; www.adelepostonagency.com). In addition to childcare, provides butler, chauffeur, laundress, bartender, waiter/waitress, and housekeeper services. Call for details. Fees are 8 week's salary for permanent placement, and—when placement is short-term—30% of salary (up to 8 weeks) for the length of employment.

The Baby Sitters' Guild, 60 E 42nd St., Ste. 912, New York, NY 10165 (☎212-682-0227; babysittersguild.com). References required. Open daily 9am-9pm.

Childcare International, Ltd., Trafalgar House, Grenville Pl., London NW7 3SA (☎+44 020 8906 3116; www.childint.co.uk). Specializes in au pair work for those aged 18-27, who work as live-in nannies caring for children and doing light housework in exchange for room, board, and a small stipend.

InterExchange, 161 6th Ave., New York, NY 10013 (☎212-924-0446; www.interexchange.org). Specializes in au pair work.

FOOD SERVICE

The highest-paid food-service employees are generally **waiters** and **waitresses**. Waitstaff in New York City make $80-200 per shift, on average about $150 per shift or about $600-700 per week. Experienced professionals usually make more, depending on the restaurant. **Bartenders** can make up to $300 per shift.

Food service employees often make less than minimum wage, but their salary is supplemented with tips, which can average upwards of $15 per hour. Since tipping is 15-20% of the bill, the more expensive the restaurant, the more tips for the waitstaff (although higher-class restaurants want experienced staff). If you are working as a **cashier** or **host**, you won't make much in tips and your salary will be close to minimum wage. **Bartenders** make great tips, but they work late and usually need certification and previous experience. The **American Bartending School,** 68 W 39th St., New York, NY 10018 (☎800-532-9222; www.newyorkbartendingschool.com) provides a one- to two-week 40-hour bartending course, as well as job placement. For food-service job listings, check out the search engines listed under **Internet Resources** (p. 74). You may also want to check **www.bartender.com** and read the classified ads in the papers listed on p. 60.

SHORT-TERM WORK

Traveling for long periods of time can get expensive. Some travelers try their hand at odd jobs for a few weeks at a time to make some extra cash to carry them through another month or so. For extra cash, take on a temp position, or, if you're feeling lucky, register to act as a movie extra.

TEMPORARY WORK

One of the easiest ways to earn money is as a temp worker. Offices often hire employees for short periods (anywhere from a few days to several months) through New York's many temp agencies. Most jobs are secretarial in nature: data entry, filing, answering phones, etc. Those with computer skills make the most money in the temping industry. After a few weeks, agencies may be able to place you in full-time work; health insurance is then often included. Other companies may offer direct deposit, referral bonuses, and/or vacation pay. It is rare to find an agency which offers all these benefits, and if it does, the pay is usually rather low. The **Red Guide to Temp Agencies** (www.panix.com/~grvsmth/redguide) provides great reviews of the city's temp agencies. The following temp agencies are not necessarily endorsed by *Let's Go:*

Atrium Staffing, 420 Lexington Ave., Ste. 1410, New York, NY 10170 (☎212-292-0550; www.atriumstaff.com). Assignments in support and finance.

Canine Creative Staffing (☎212-699-6450; www.caninecreative.com). Specializes in tech and creative temp jobs in the NYC area.

Snelling Downtown, 150 Broadway, Ste. 902, New York, NY 10038-4381 (temping ☎212-331-9200, permanent jobs 212-227-6705; www.snelling.com). Business, IT, and office temps.

The Supporting Cast, 10 E 40th St., #1300, New York, NY 10016 (☎212-532-8888; www.supportingcast.com). Also offers permanent jobs.

Tiger Information Systems, 130 William St., New York, NY 10038 (☎212-412-0600; www.tigerinfo.com). Offers temporary and permanent desktop, IT, project management, and creative staffing.

ACTING AND MOVIE EXTRA OPPORTUNITIES

New York boasts hosts of small theaters and low-budget independent film companies that offer opportunities for unknown actors. **Backstage** (www.backstage.com) features **casting notices** for features, stage, indie-film, and TV productions. Keep in mind, though, that the entertainment industry is fickle: look for a day job as well.

Many film producers select **extras** from a casting agency's album of headshots; registration fees at casting agencies are usually around $15-30. You don't have to belong to a union to land a gig, but union members do earn more than non-union extras—up to $200 for 8hr. of work if they make it into the movie, television show, or commercial. The **Screen Actors Guild** office is located at 360 Madison Ave. 12th floor, New York, NY 10017 (☎212-944-1030; www.sag.org). Still, non-union members can pick up about $50 a day. Below is a list of agencies that cast background actors in New York; see **www.nycasting.com** or **www.assistantdirectors.com** for more.

Actors Reps of New York, 1501 Broadway, Ste. 308, New York, NY 10036 (☎212-391-4668; www.actorsreps.com). Casts extras for all areas. Auditions M-F 11:30am-1pm and 4-5:30pm, Sa 11am-1pm.

Impossible Casting, 111 W 17th St., New York, NY 10011 (☎212-255-3029).

Kee Casting, 424 Park Ave. S, #128, New York, NY 10016 (☎212-725-3775). Casts films and commercials.

Liz Lewis Casting Partners, 129 W 20th St., New York, NY 10011 (☎212-645-1500).

Stark Naked Productions (Elsie Stark Casting), 39 W 19th St., 12th fl., New York, NY 10011 (☎212-366-1903). Casts commercials and films.

FOR FURTHER READING ON BEYOND TOURISM.

Alternatives to the Peace Corps: A Directory of Third World and U.S. Volunteer Opportunities, by Jennifer S. Willsea. Food First Books, 2003 (US$10).

Back Door Guide to Short-Term Job Adventures: Internships, Extraordinary Experiences, Seasonal Jobs, Volunteering, Working Abroad, by Michael Landes. Ten Speed Press, 2002 (US$22).

Green Volunteers: The World Guide to Voluntary Work in Nature, by Ausenda and McCloskey. Universe, 2003 (US$15).

How to Get a Job in Europe, by Sanborn and Matherly. Planning Communications, 2003 (US$22).

How to Live Your Dream of Volunteering Overseas, by Collins, DeZerega, and Heckscher. Penguin Books, 2002 (US$17).

International Directory of Voluntary Work, by Whetter and Pybus. Peterson's Guides and Vacation Work, 2000 (US$16).

International Job Finder: Where the Jobs Are Worldwide, by Daniel Lauber. Planning Communications, 2002 (US$20).

Invest Yourself: The Catalogue of Volunteer Opportunities, published by the Commission on Voluntary Service and Action (☎646-486-2446).

Live and Work Abroad: A Guide for Modern Nomads, by Francis and Callan. Vacation-Work Publications, 2001 (US$16).

Make a Difference: America's Guide to Volunteering and Community Service, Arthur I. Blaustein. John Wiley and Sons, 2003 ($13).

Overseas Summer Jobs 2002, by Collier and Woodworth. Peterson's Guides and Vacation-Work, 2002 (US$18).

Volunteer Vacations: Short-term Adventures That Will Benefit You and Others, by Cutchins and Geissinger. Chicago Review Press, 2003 (US$18).

Work Abroad: The Complete Guide to Finding a Job Overseas, by Hubbs, Griffith, and Nolting. Transitions Abroad Publishing, 2002 (US$16).

Work Your Way Around the World, by Susan Griffith. Vacation-Work Publications, 2003 (US$18).

PRACTICAL INFORMATION

TOURIST AND FINANCIAL SERVICES

CONSULATES

Australia, 150 E 42nd St. (☎212-351-6500), 34th floor, at Broadway. No visa services.

British Commonwealth, 800 2nd Ave. (☎212-599-8478), at Broadway.

Canada, Main Concourse Level, 1251 Ave. of the Americas/6th Ave. (☎212-596-1700), between 49th and 50th St.

Germany, 871 UN Plaza (☎212-610-9700), 49th St., at 1st Ave.

France, 934 5th Ave. (☎212-606-3600/3680), between 74th and 75th St. Visa services, 10 E 74th St. (☎212-606-3681/3644), between 5th and Madison Ave.

Ireland, 345 Park Ave. (☎212-319-2555).

Israel, 800 2nd Ave. (☎212-499-5000), at Broadway.

New Zealand, 222 E 43rd St., Ste. 2510 (☎212-832-4038). Also at 780 3rd Ave., Ste. 1904, at E 48th St.

South Africa, 333 E 38th St., 9th floor (☎212-213-4880), between 1st and 2nd Ave.

UK, 845 3rd Ave. (☎212-745-0200), between 51st and 52nd St.

CURRENCY EXCHANGE

American Express (☎800-AXP-TRIP; www.americanexpress.com):

Macy's Herald Square, 151 W 34th St. (☎212-695-8075), at 7th Ave., on Macy's balcony level. Open M-F 9am-5pm.

822 Lexington Ave. (☎212-758-6510), at 63rd St. Open M-F 9am-6pm, Sa 10am-4pm.

374 Park Ave. (☎212-421-8240), at 53rd St. Open M-F 9am-5:30pm.

1185 6th Ave. (☎212-398-8585), at 47th St. Open M-F 9am-6pm.

111 Broadway (☎212-693-1100), near Pine St. Open M-F 8:30am-5:30pm.

200 5th Ave. (☎212-691-9797), at 23rd St. Open M-F 8:30am-5:30pm, Sa 10am-4pm.

New York Marriot Marquis, 1535 Broadway (☎212-575-6580), between 45th and 46th St., in 8th floor lobby. Open M-F 9am-5pm.

Bank Leumi, 579 5th Ave. (☎917-542-2343; www.bankleumiusa.com), at 47th St. Open M-F 9am-3:30pm.

Chequepoint USA, 1568 Broadway (☎212-750-2400; www.chequepointusa.visual-net.com), at 47th St. Call for locations of other branches. Open daily 8am-7pm.

Travelex and Thomas Cook, 29 Broadway (☎800-287-7362; www.thomascook.com), at Morris St. Open M-F 9am-5pm.

TRANSPORT INFORMATION

AIRLINES

All major airlines have Manhattan offices; call for the closest location.

American, ☎800-433-7300; www.aa.com.

Continental, ☎800-525-0280; www.continental.com.

Delta, ☎800-221-1212; www.delta.com.

Northwest, ☎800-225-2525; www.nwa.com.

United, ☎800-241-6522; www.united.com.

US Airways, ☎800-428-4322; www.usairways.com.

AIRPORTS
See p. 38 for directions.

John F. Kennedy Airport (JFK), ☎718-244-4444; www.panynj.gov. In Jamaica, Queens.

LaGuardia Airport (LGA), ☎718-533-3400; www.panynj.gov. In East Elmhurst, Queens.

Newark Liberty Int'l Airport (EWR), ☎973-961-6000; www.newarkairport.com. In NJ.

Islip Long Island MacArthur Airport (ISP), ☎631-467-3210; www.macarthurairport.com. In Ronkonkoma, NY.

AIRPORT TRANSPORT
See p. 38 for airport transport information.

New York Airport Service, ☎212-875-8200; www.nyairportservice.com. Serves JFK and LaGuardia.

Olympia Airport Express, ☎212-964-6233; www.olympiabus.com. Serves Newark.

SuperShuttle, ☎800-258-3826; www.supershuttle.com. Serves JFK, LaGuardia, and Newark.

AUTO ASSOCIATIONS

American Automobile Association (AAA) Travel Related Services, ☎800-222-4357; www.aaa.com. Provides travel services, maps, and guides to members, and emergency road service to all.

AUTO RENTAL

AAmcar Discount Car Rentals, 330 W 96th St. (☎212-222-8500; www.aamcar.com), by Riverside Dr. Open M-F 7:30am-7:30pm, Sa 9am-5pm, Su 9am-7pm. Also at 506 W 181st St. (☎212-927-7000), at Amsterdam Ave.

Avis, ☎800-230-4898; www.avis.com. 18+. Under 25 extra fee.

Dollar, ☎800-800-4000; www.dollar.com. 21+.

Enterprise, ☎800-736-8222; www.enterprise.com. 18+. Under 21 extra fee.

Hertz, ☎800-654-3131, 800-831-2847; www.hertz.com. 18+. Under 25 $51 extra fee per day.

National, ☎800-227-7368; www.nationalcar.com.

Zipcar, www.zipcar.com.

BICYCLE RENTAL
See **Entertainment,** p. 270.

BUSES
Also see **By Bus,** p. 87.

Chinatown Buses, www.chinatown-bus.com. Assorted cheap rides to Boston, Philadelphia, DC.

Fung Wah, ☎212-925-8889; www.fungwahbus.com. Chinatown bus to Boston. $15.

Green Bus Lines, ☎718-995-4700; www.greenbus.com. Serves Jamaica and central Queens.

Greyhound, ☎800-229-9424; www.greyhound.com. In- and out-of-state travel.

Jamaica Buses, Inc., ☎ 718-526-0800; www.jamaicabus.com. Serves Jamaica and Far Rockaway.

Liberty Lines Express, ☎ 718-652-8400; www.libertylines.com. Serves the Bronx.

MTA/Long Island Bus, ☎ 516-228-4000; www.mta.nyc.ny.us/nyct/bus.

New York Bus Service, ☎ 718-994-5500; www.nybus.com. Serves the Bronx.

Port Authority Terminal, ☎ 212-435-7000; www.pannynj.gov. Departure center for most buses to the city.

Queens Surface Corp., ☎ 718-445-3100; www.qsbus.com. Serves Queens.

TriBoro Coach Corp., ☎ 718-335-1000; www.triborocoach.com. Serves Forest Hills, Ridgewood, Jackson Heights, and Midtown.

SUBWAY

See also **Airport Transport,** p. 80; **Buses,** p. 80; and **Trains,** p. 81.

Bus Info, ☎ 718-330-3322.

General Info, English ☎ 718-330-1234, other languages 718-330-4847.

MetroCard Info, ☎ 800-638-7622 or 212-638-7622; www.mta.nyc.ny.us.

Reduced Fare Info, ☎ 718-243-4999, TDD 718-596-8273.

TAXIS

All City Taxis, ☎ 718-402-2323.

Allstate Car Service, ☎ 800-453-4099.

B Taxi Management, ☎ 212-957-0033.

Brothers & Sisters Car Services, ☎ 718-815-4400. Serves Staten Island.

Gateway Transportation Services, ☎ 718-273-6363. Serves Staten Island.

Taxi Commission, 40 Rector St. (☎ 212-676-1000, 24hr. 212-692-8294). Open M-F 9am-4:30pm.

Dial 7 Car and Limousine Service, ☎ 212-777-7777.

Tri-State Limousine, ☎ 212-777-7171.

TRAINS

Amtrak, ☎ 800-872-7245; www.amtrak.com.

Long Island Railroad (LIRR), ☎ 718-217-5477 or 516-822-5477; www.lirr.org.

Metro-North Commuter Lines, ☎ 800-638-7646; www.mta.nyc.ny.us/mnr.

NJ Transit, ☎ 973-762-5100 or 800-772-2222; www.njtransit.com.

PATH, ☎ 800-234-7284; www.panynj.gov/path.

TOURIST INFO AND AID

Big Apple Greeter, 1 Centre St. (☎ 212-669-8159; www.bigapplegreeter.org). This free service pairs enthusiastic and friendly New Yorkers with tourists. The volunteer greeters do not accept tips and seek to help tourists get more from their visit to the city.

34th Street Partnership, 250 W 34th St. (☎ 212-967-3433), Penn Station, on south side of Amtrak Rotunda. Open daily 9:30am-6:30pm.

Downtown Alliance, 120 Broadway (☎ 212-566-6700, 24hr. security hotline 212-306-5656; www.downtownny.com), Ste. 3340.

Lower East Side Visitor's Center, 261 Broome St. (☎ 212-226-9010; www.lowereastsideny.com). Open daily 10am-4pm.

PRACTICAL INFO

Manhattan Mall Info Booth, (☎212-465-0500), 1st floor, Herald Sq., at 6th Ave. and 33rd St. Open M and Th-F 10am-8pm, Tu-W and Sa 10am-7pm, Su 11am-6pm.

NYC & Company, 810 7th Ave. (☎212-484-1222; www.nycvisit.com), at 53rd St. Open M-F 8:30am-6pm, Sa-Su 9am-5pm.

Times Square Visitor Center, 1560 Broadway (☎212-869-1890; www.timsesquare-bid.org), at W 46th St. Open daily 8am-8pm.

Travelers' Aid of NY & NJ (☎718-656-4870), at JFK Airport, in Terminal 6. Open daily 9am-8pm.

SIGHTSEEING TOURS

WALKING TOURS

▓ **Joyce Gold's Tours** (☎212-242-5762; www.nyctours.com). Ms. Gold has read over 900 books on the history of Manhattan, the subject she teaches at NYU and The New School. On 45 days out of the year, she and a company of adventurers give tours focused on architecture, history, and ethnic groups within the city. About 2-2½hr., depending on the subject. $12. Reservations not required.

Radical Walking Tours (☎718-492-0069; www.he.net/~radtours). Historian and activist Bruce Kayton leads tours that cover the alternative history of NYC. For example, tours of Greenwich Village highlight radicals and revolutionaries John Reed and Emma Goldman, and the artistic and theatrical movements they inspired. Trips to Harlem, the Lower East Side, and Central Park are also available. Even locals will learn fascinating details about the city's history. Call for schedule and departure sites. 2-3hr. $10.

Big Onion Walking Tours (☎212-439-1090; www.bigonion.com). Grad students in American history from Columbia and NYU lead tours of historic districts and ethnic neighborhoods. Themed excursions include "Brooklyn Bridge to Brooklyn Heights," "Before Stonewall: A Gay and Lesbian History Tour," "Immigrant New York," "Historic Harlem," and the "Multi-Ethnic Eating Tour," which explores the gastronomical delights of neighborhoods like Chinatown and Little Italy. Tours average 2hr. Group tours and bus tours available. $15, seniors $12, students $10. "Show-up" tours June-Aug. Th-Su; Sept.-May Sa-Su.

Lower East Side Tenement Museum Walking Tours (☎212-431-0233; www.tene-ment.org). See p. 223 for museum info and directions. Neighborhood heritage tour guides you through the Lower East Side and examines how different immigrant groups have shaped the area. Call for tour dates and times. Apr.-Dec. $9, students and seniors $7. Combination tickets available for walking tours and tenement tours.

Municipal Art Society (☎212-439-1049; www.mas.org). Guided walking tours. Destinations vary but include most major Manhattan districts, such as SoHo and Times Square. Free tour of Grand Central Station W 12:30pm, at info booth on the main concourse. Other tours $12-15. Call in advance.

92nd St. Y, 1395 Lexington Ave. (☎212-415-5628; www.92ndsty.org), at 92nd St. The Y leads an astounding variety of walking tours covering all boroughs. Learn about the Garment District, SoHo artists, and the brownstones of Brooklyn through literary tours, museum visits, and even excursions by candlelight. Tours vary in length. $20-60.

BOAT TOURS

Circle Line Tours, W 42nd St. (☎212-563-3200; www.circleline.com), on the Hudson River, at Pier 83. 3hr. full-circle boat tour around Manhattan island $29, seniors $20, children $16; 2hr. semi-circle tour $24, seniors $20, children $13. No reservations necessary; arrive 30-45min. before tour starts. Call or check online for schedule.

BUS TOURS

Gray Line Sight-Seeing, 42nd St. and 8th Ave. (☎212-445-0848 or 800-669-0051; www.graylinenewyork.com), at the Port Authority Terminal. This huge bus tour company offers many trips, including jaunts throughout Manhattan and gambling trips to Atlantic City. The Downtown Tour (frequent departures daily beginning at 8:20am; $34, children ages 5-11 $24) and Uptown Tour (frequent departures daily 8:30am-5pm; $34, children ages 5-11 $24) allow you to get on and off the bus at various points of interest to explore on your own. The night tour (daily every 15min. 6-9pm; $34, children $24) emphasizes sights that look their best lit-up. Reservations aren't required for in-city tours, but arrive at the terminal 30min. early.

On Location Tours, 347 5th Ave. (☎212-683-2027, tickets 212-209-3370; www.sceneontv.com). Tours that showcase New York as it has appeared in films and on TV. The "New York TV and Movie Tour" takes you to a host of locations seen in shows like *Friends, Seinfeld,* and *The Cosby Show* and films such as *Spiderman* and Woody Allen's *Manhattan.* Departs daily 11am from near Broadway and 51st St.; $34. "*Sex and the City* Hotspots" tour leaves M-F 11am and 3pm, Sa-Su 10, 11am, and 3pm from near 5th Ave. and 58th St.; $38. "*Sopranos* Sights" leaves Sa-Su 2pm from near 7th Ave. and 39th St.; $42. "Central Park Movie Sights," the company's only walking tour, leaves F 3pm and Sa noon from 59th St., between 5th and 6th Ave.; $17. All tours require advance reservations.

Harlem Spirituals, 690 8th Ave. (☎212-391-0900; www.harlemspirituals.com), between 43rd and 44th St. Offers tours of Manhattan, Brooklyn, and the Bronx. Tours of upper Manhattan, like "Harlem on Sunday" (4hr.; Su 9:15am; $45) and "Gospel on a Weekday" (4hr.; W 8:45am; $45), include trips to historic homes and Baptist services. "Soul Food and Jazz" (M, Th, Sa 7pm-midnight; $99) features a tour of Harlem, a filling meal at a Harlem restaurant (usually Sylvia's, p. 144), and an evening at a jazz club. Reserve in advance.

Heart of Brooklyn Trolley (☎718-282-7789; www.heartofbrooklyn.org). This trolley system connects major sights around Prospect Park, including the Brooklyn Museum of Art (p. 235) and the Botanic Garden (p. 204). Wheelchair accessible. Sa-Su noon-6pm. Free.

LOCAL SERVICES

COMMUNITY CENTERS

Alliance for Downtown New York, ☎212-566-6700; www.downtownny.com. The Alliance's **NYPD Downtown Center** (☎212-306-5656) is available 24hr. for security concerns.

United Community Centers, 613 New Lots Ave. (☎718-649-7979) between Hendrix St. and Schenck Ave., Brooklyn.

United Neighborhood Houses of New York (UNH), 70 W 36th St., 5th floor (☎212-967-0322; www.unhny.org). Partnerships with community centers throughout the 5 boroughs.

DENTISTS

Emergency Dental Associates, ☎800-439-9299. Open 24hr.

NYU College of Dentistry, ☎212-998-9800; www.nyu.edu/dental. Open M-Th 9am-7pm, F 9am-3pm.

DISABLED RESOURCES

Access-A-Ride, ☎718-330-3322 or 718-337-2017. For public transport.

PRACTICAL INFO

MTA Elevators and Escalators Service, ☎800-734-6772. Open 24hr.

Moss Rehab Hospital Travel Information Service, ☎800-225-5667; www.mossresourcenet.org. Resources for accessible travel.

Society for Accessible Traveler Hospitality (SATH), 347 5th Ave., Ste. 610 (☎212-447-7284; www.sath.org), New York, NY 10016.

Transit Authority Access, ☎718-596-8585. Provides information about disabled access to New York City public transportation.

DRY CLEANERS

Midnight Express Cleaners, ☎212-921-0111. Pick-up service available. Open M-F 8am-8pm, Sa 9am-noon; closed Sa July-Aug.

ENTERTAINMENT INFO

See also **Ticket Services,** p. 85.

MovieFone, ☎212-777-3456; www.moviefone.com.

Parks & Recreation Special Events Hotline, ☎212-360-3456 or 888-NY-PARKS (697-2757). Open 24hr.

GLBT RESOURCES

Act Up! New York, 332 Bleecker St. (www.actupny.org).

GLBT National Help Center, ☎888-THE-GLNH; www.glnh.org.

Gay Men's Health Crisis-Geffen Clinic, 119 W 24th St. (☎212-807-6655; www.gmhc.org), between 6th and 7th Ave. Open M-F 11am-8pm.

The Lesbian, Gay, Bisexual, and Transgender Community Center, 208 W 13th St. (☎212-620-7310), at 7th Ave.

New York City Gay and Lesbian Anti-Violence Project, 240 W 35th St. (☎212-714-1141; www.avp.org).

INTERNET ACCESS

See also **By Email and Internet,** p. 47.

Alt.Coffee, 139 Ave. A (☎212-529-2233), between 8th and 9th St. $10 per hr. Open M-F 7:30-1:30am, Sa-Su 10-2am.

Kinko's, ☎800-254-6567; www.fedex.kinkos.com. About $0.20 per min., but varies according to branch. Over 30 locations. Open 24hr.

LIBRARIES

Bronx Reference Center, 2556 Bainbridge Ave. (☎718-579-4257), at Dr. Sandy F. Ray Blvd. Open M and W 10am-8pm, Tu and Th 10am-6pm, F noon-6pm, Sa 10am-5pm.

Brooklyn Public Library, Grand Army Plaza (☎718-230-2100; www.brooklynpubliclibrary.org), Brooklyn. Open M-Th 9am-8pm, F-Sa 9am-6pm.

Donnell Library Center, 20 W 53rd St. (☎212-621-0618; www.nypl.org), between 5th and 6th Ave. Open M and W, F 10am-6pm, Tu and Th 10am-8pm, Sa 10am-5pm.

Mid-Manhattan Library, 455 5th Ave. (☎212-340-0833; www.nypl.org), at 40th St. Open M, and W-Th 9am-9pm, Tu 11am-7pm, F-Sa 10am-6pm.

New York Humanities and Social Sciences Library, 11 W 40th St. (☎212-930-0830 or 869-8089; www.nypl.org). Entrance on 5th Ave. at 42nd St. Open M and Th-Sa 10am-6pm, Tu-W 11am-7:30pm.

New York Public Library for the Performing Arts, 40 Lincoln Center Plaza (☎212-870-1630; www.nypl.org). Open M and Th noon-8pm, Tu-W and F-Sa noon-6pm.

Queens Borough Public Library, 89-11 Merrick Blvd. (☎718-990-0700; www.queenslibrary.org), at 89th St., in Jamaica, Queens. Open M-F 10am-9pm, Sa 10am-5:30pm; mid-Sept. to mid-May Su noon-5pm.

Schomburg Center for Research in Black Culture, 515 Malcolm X Blvd. (6th Ave.) (☎212-491-2200; www.nypl.org), on the corner of 135th St. Library open M and W noon-7pm, Tu and Th-F noon-6pm, Sa 10am-6pm; archives M-Tu and F-Sa noon-5pm.

St. George Library Center, 5 Central Ave. (☎718-442-8560; www.nypl.org), at Hyatt St., on Staten Island. Open M and Th noon-8pm, Tu-W 10am-6pm, F noon-6pm, and Sa 10am-5pm.

REGISTRY OF MOTOR VEHICLES

All **DMV** branches below can be reached at ☎212-645-5550 or 718-966-6155.

11 Greenwich St. (☎212-645-5550 or 718-966-6155) Battery Park Pl. and Morris St. Open M-F 8:30am-4am. Many other locations in city; most use the same phone numbers, so call for the one nearest you.

TICKET SERVICES

See also **Entertainment Info,** p. 86.

Tele-Charge, ☎212-239-6200 or 800-545-2559; www.telecharge.com. 24 hr.

Ticket Central, ☎212-279-4200. Open daily 1-8pm.

Ticketmaster, ☎212-307-4100; www.ticketmaster.com.

TKTS, ☎212-221-0031.

WOMEN'S HEALTH

See also **Crisis and Help Lines,** p. 85; **Hospitals,** p. 86; and **Medical Clinics,** p. 87.

Eastern Women's Center, 38 E 30th St. (☎212-686-6066 or 800-346-5111), between Park and Madison Ave. Exams by appointment only; walk-in pregnancy testing. Facility open Tu-Sa 7:30am-4:30pm; free pregnancy testing Tu-Sa 11am-4pm; switchboard open M-Sa 8am-5pm, Su 9am-4pm.

Planned Parenthood, Margaret Sanger Center, 26 Bleecker St. (☎212-965-7000; www.plannedparenthood.org), at Mott St. Also at: 44 Court St., Brooklyn and 349 E 149th St., at Cortland Ave., the Bronx.

Women's Health Line, New York City Department of Health (☎212-230-1111). Open M-F 9am-9pm, Sa 8am-6pm.

EMERGENCY AND COMMUNICATIONS

CRISIS AND HELP LINES

See also **Emergency,** p. 86; **Hospitals,** p. 86; **Medical Clinics,** p. 87; and **Women's Health,** p. 85.

Alcohol and Substance Abuse Info Line, ☎800-274-2042. Info and referrals 24hr.

CDC AIDS Hotline, ☎800-342-AIDS/2437 or 800-825-5448. Open daily 9am-9pm. 24hr. recording.

Crime Victims' Hotline, ☎212-577-7777. 24hr. counseling and referrals.

GLBT National Help Center, ☎888-THE-GLNH; www.glnh.org.

Help Line New York, ☎212-532-2400; www.helpline.org. Crisis counseling and referrals. Open 24hr.

National Abortion Federation, ☎800-772-9100; www.prochoice.org. Family planning counselling and abortion information available M-F 8am-10pm, Sa-Su 9am-5pm.

Poison Control Center, ☎212-764-7667. Open 24hr.

Roosevelt Hospital Rape Crisis Center, ☎877-665-7273. Open 24hr.

Samaritans, ☎212-673-3000 or 800-SUICIDE; www.samaritansnyc.org. Suicide prevention hotline. Open 24hr.

Sex Crimes Report Line, ☎212-267-7273. NYPD-related. 24hr. information and referrals.

Terrorism Hotline, in New York City ☎888-NYC-SAFE, in New York State 866-SAFE-NYS; security.state.ny.us. Accepts reports of suspicious activity 24hr.

EMERGENCY

In an emergency, dial ☎911. See also **Crisis and Help Lines,** p. 86; **Hospitals,** p. 86; **Medical Clinics,** p. 87; **Women's Health,** p. 85.

Police (non-emergency): ☎646-610-5000 or 311.

HOSPITALS

See also **Crisis and Help Lines,** p. 85; **Emergency,** p. 86; **Medical Clinics,** p. 87; **Women's Health,** p. 85.

Bellevue Hospital Center, 462 1st Ave. (☎212-562-4141, adult ER 212-562-3015, pediatric ER 212-562-3025; www.med.nyu.edu), at 27th St.

Beth Israel Medical Center, 1st Ave. (☎212-420-2000, adult ER 212-420-2840, pediatric ER 212-420-2860), at E 16th St.

Bronx-Lebanon Hospital Center, 1650 Grand Concourse (☎718-590-1800; www.bronxleb.org), at Cross-Bronx Expwy., the Bronx. 2 ERs: 1650 Grand Concourse (☎718-518-5120), and 1276 Fulton Ave. (☎718-960-8700), between E 168th and 169th St.

Brooklyn Hospital Center, 121 DeKalb Ave. (☎718-250-8000, ER 718-250-8075; www.tbh.org), near Ashland Pl., in Brooklyn.

Interfaith Medical Center, 1545 Atlantic Ave. (☎718-613-4000; www.interfaithmedical.com), in Brooklyn. 555 Prospect Pl. (☎718-935-7000), near Franklin St., Brooklyn. 2 ERs: St. Marks (☎718-935-7110) and Atlantic Ave. (☎718-613-4444).

Jacobi Medical Center, 1400 Pelham Pkwy. S. (☎718-918-5000, adult ER 718-918-5800, pediatric ER 718-918-5875, psychiatric ER 718-918-4850), at Seymour Ave. in the Bronx.

Jamaica Hospital Medical Center, 8900 Van Wyck Expwy. (☎718-206-6000, ER 718-206-6066; www.jamaicahospital.org), at 89th Ave., in Jamaica, Queens.

Mount Sinai Medical Center, 5th Ave. (☎212-241-6500, ER 212-241-7171; www.mountsinai.org), at 100th St.

New York Columbia-Presbyterian Medical Center, 622 W 168th St. (☎212-305-2500, ER 212-305-6204; www.nyp.org), between Fort Washington Ave. and Broadway.

New York University Downtown Hospital, 170 William St. (☎212-312-5000; www.nyudh.org), between Spruce and Beekman St.

New York University Medical Center, 560 1st Ave. (☎212-263-7300; ER 212-263-5550; www.med.nyu.edu), between 32nd and 33rd St.

MEDICAL CLINICS

See also **Crisis and Help Lines,** p. 85; **Dentists,** p. 86; **Emergency,** p. 86; **Hospitals,** p. 86; **Pharmacies,** p. 87.

Callen-Lorde Community Health Center, 356 W 18th St. (☎212-271-7200; www.callen-lorde.org), between 8th and 9th Ave. Provides health services to New York's GLBT community. Open M 12:30-8pm, Tu and Th-F 9am-4:30pm, W 8:30am-1pm and 3-8pm.

D*O*C*S, 55 E 34th St. (☎212-252-6000), at Park and Madison Ave. Also at: 1555 3rd Ave. (☎212-828-2300), at 88th St.; 202 W 23rd St. (☎212-352-2600), at 7th Ave. Open M-Th 8am-8pm, F 8am-7pm, Sa 9am-3pm, Su 9am-2pm.

Doctors Walk-in Clinic, 55 E 34th St. (☎212-252-6001, ext. 2), between Park and Madison Ave. Open M-Th 8am-8pm, F 8am-7pm, Sa 9am-3pm, Su 9am-2pm. Last walk-in 1hr. before closing.

Gay Men's Health Crisis-Geffen Clinic, 119 W 24th St. (☎212-807-6655; www.gmhc.org), between 6th and 7th Ave. Open M-F 11am-8pm.

PHARMACIES

See also **Medical Clinics,** p. 87.

CVS, ☎800-746-7287; www.cvs.com.

Duane Reade, 224 57th St. (☎212-541-9708; www.duanereade.com), at Broadway. Open 24hr. Also at: 2465 Broadway (☎212-799-3172), at 91st St.; 1279 3rd Ave. (☎212-744-2668), at 74th St.; 378 6th Ave. (☎212-674-5357), at Waverly Pl.

Rite-Aid, 81 1st Ave. (☎800-748-3243; www.riteaid.com.), at E 5th St. Many other locations.

POSTAL SERVICES

US Postal Service Customer Service Assistance Center, ☎212-967-8585 (M-F 8:30am-6pm), ☎800-725-2161 (24hr.).

General Post Office, 421 8th Ave. (☎212-330-3002; www.usps.com), at W 32nd St., occupying the block. Use website to locate other post offices. Open 24hr.

PRACTICAL INFO

ACCOMMODATIONS

HOTELS

In a typical trip to New York City, accommodations almost always make up the biggest expense. Space is notoriously at a premium in Manhattan—rooms are small, rents are high, and plumbing, cleanliness, and amenities might not match your expectations given what you're paying. Bare-bones hotel singles in New York City start around $60-100 per night, doubles around $70-120. In the cheapest hotels, you'll typically share a hall bathroom. Of course, the sky's the limit in this city when it comes to luxuries and prices. Often, though, it's best to settle on a relatively low-end room, and spend your money elsewhere.

The Internet can be a worthwhile tool for finding hotel deals in New York. Most hotels listed in this chapter have websites, and some offer discounts for booking online—always ask when calling. Sites like **Hotwire** and **Priceline** often harbor deeply discounted rates, but they present a certain amount of risk because they provide only a general description of a hotel (not its name) until after you make your purchase. By keeping the hotel's name secret until after you buy, such websites allow hotels to fill their rooms at deeply discounted rates, without diminishing their prestige and market value by posting cut-rate prices publicly.

BED AND BREAKFASTS

Bed and Breakfasts (private homes that rent out one or more spare rooms to travelers) can be a great alternative to impersonal hotel and motel rooms. Many don't have phones, TVs, or showers with their rooms, though others can be quite luxurious. Reservations should be made a few weeks ahead, and they usually require a deposit. Some B&Bs are "hosted," while others are "unhosted"; the people renting you the room may or may not live on-site. **All Around the Town** (☎212-675-5600 or toll-free from within the US 800-443-3800) specializes in short-term furnished apartments, and **Bed and Breakfast of New York** (☎212-645-8134) offers weekly and monthly rates.

HOSTELS

> **BOOKING HOSTELS ONLINE.** One of the easiest ways to ensure you've got a bed for the night is by reserving online. Click to the **Hostelworld** booking engine through **www.letsgo.com,** and you'll have access to bargain accommodations from Argentina to Zimbabwe with no added commission.

Many hostels are laid out dorm-style, often with large single-sex rooms and bunk beds, although private rooms that sleep anywhere from one to four people are becoming more common. Hostels often offer kitchens and utensils for your use, bike or moped rentals, storage areas, affordable airport transportation, breakfast and other meals, laundry facilities, and Internet access. Guests must sometimes rent or bring their own sheets or "sleepsacks" (two sheets sewn together); sleeping bags are usually not adequate.

There can be drawbacks to hostel living. Some hostels close during certain daytime "lockout" hours, have a curfew, don't accept reservations, impose a maximum stay, or, less frequently, require that you do chores. In New York City, a dorm bed in a hostel will average around $35 and a private room around $45. Most hostels place caps on maximum stays. The **De Hirsch Residence,** however, on the Upper East Side, rents rooms by the month (p. 102). The **Flushing YMCA** also allows long-term stays with advance notice (p. 107).

> ■ **A HOSTELER'S BILL OF RIGHTS.** There are certain standard features that we do not include in our hostel listings. Unless we state otherwise, you can expect that every hostel has no lockout, no curfew, a kitchen, free hot showers, some system of secure luggage storage, and no key deposit.

YMCAS AND YWCAS

Young Men's Christian Association (YMCA) lodgings are usually cheaper than a hotel but more expensive than a hostel. Not all YMCA locations offer lodging. Many YMCAs accept women and families; some will not lodge those under 18 without parental permission.

YMCA of the USA, 101 North Wacker Dr. (☎888-333-9622 or 800-872-9622; www.ymca.net), Chicago, IL 60606 USA. Provides a listing of the nearly 1000 Ys across the US and Canada. Offers info on prices, services, telephone numbers, and addresses.

The Y's Way, 224 E 47th St. (☎212-308-2899; ymcanyc.org), New York, NY 10017. New York City contact for information and reservations.

YWCA of the USA, 1015 18th St. NW (☎202-467-0801 or 800-YWCA-US1; www.ywca.org), Ste. 1100, Washington, DC 20036 USA. Provides a directory of YWCAs across the USA.

LONG-TERM ACCOMMODATIONS

Travelers planning to stay in New York for extended periods of time may find it most cost-effective to rent an **apartment.** A basic one-bedroom (or studio) apartment in Manhattan will cost $900-2600 per month. In addition to the rent, tenants usually are required to front a security deposit (often one month's rent) and the last month's rent. ■**Craig's List** (www.craigslist.org) is far-and-away the best source for apartment listings in all neighborhoods and price ranges.

If house-hunting on your own gets too exhausting, some sites will help you find a place—for a fee. **Manhattan Lodgings** (☎212-677-7616; www.manhattanlodgings.com) puts visitors in contact with New York apartment tenants who want to rent out their respective pads for a few days or weeks. **New York Habitat,** 307 Seventh Ave., Ste. 306 (☎212-255-8018; www.nyhabitat.com) finds sublets, roommates and apartment rentals. For help with everything from finding an apartment to renting a moving van, check out **www.relocationcentral.com.** If you need to find a roommate in the city, **www.roomiematch.com** aims to match individuals together based on their likely compatibility.

If you're moving to New York and want help finding a **gay, lesbian, bisexual, or transgendered roommate, Rainbow Roommates,** 268 W 22nd St., between Seventh and Eighth Ave., can be an excellent resource. (☎212-627-8612; www.rainbowroommates.com. Open hours Tu-Sa 11am-7pm.) This subscription-based service provides you with personalized listings according to criteria that you specify.

UNIVERSITY DORMS

Many universities in New York rent out their vacant dorms to summer visitors. The length of stay varies depending on the school, but often you can stay for the entire summer. **NYU** (p. 94) and **Columbia** (p. 105) provide good summer housing for non-affiliates. The following schools also offer summer housing opportunities, though they are not necessarily endorsed by *Let's Go*:

Fordham University, 315 Keating Hall, 441 East Fordham Rd., Bronx, New York 10458 (☎718-817-4665; www.fordham.edu/summer).

Long Island University, 1 University Plaza (☎718-488-1011; Resident Hall Director 780-1552), Brooklyn, NY 11201. Rates average $50 per night, depending on length of stay.

New School University, Office of the Vice President for Student Affairs (☎212-229-5350; downtown@newschool.edu), 66 W 12th St., 8th fl., New York, NY 10011.

HOME EXCHANGE AND RENTAL

For short stays, home exchange and rental can be cost-effective options, particularly for families with children. Home rentals are much more expensive than exchanges, although they are cheaper than an extended stay at a comparably serviced hotel. In New York, most home exchanges and rentals come with kitchen, cleaning service, telephones, and TV. Unfortunately, it can be difficult to arrange an exchange or rental for longer than one month. Rentals and exchanges are organized by the following services:

HomeExchange.com, P.O. Box 30085 (☎800-877-8723; www.homeexchange.com), Santa Barbara, CA 93130.

The Invented City: International Home Exchange, 41 Sutter St. (☎800-788-2489 in the US, 415-252-1141 elsewhere; www.invented-city.com), Ste. 1090, San Francisco, CA 94104. For $50, your offer is listed in a catalog and you have access to a database of thousands of homes for exchange.

ACCOMMODATIONS BY NEIGHBORHOOD

$40 AND UNDER (❶)	
Big Apple Hostel	(101)
🖾 Central Park Hostel	(104)
Chelsea Center Hostel	(96)
Chelsea International Hostel	(99)
🖾 Chelsea Star Hotel	(96)
De Hirsch Residence	(102)
Harlem YMCA Claude McKay Residence	(105)
International Student Center	(105)
🖾 Jazz on Harlem	(105)
🖾 Jazz on the Park	(104)
Jazz on the Town	(94)
🖾 New York Int'l HI-AYH Hostel	(104)
New York University	(94)

$41-80 (❷)	
American Dream Hostel	(100)
Amsterdam Inn	(105)
🖾 Carlton Arms Hotel	(99)
Columbia University	(105)
Flushing YMCA	(107)
Hotel 17	(100)
Hotel Pickwick Arms	(102)
🖾 Larchmont Hotel	(94)
Murry Hill Inn	(100)
SoHotel	(92)
St. Mark's Hotel	(94)
West Side YMCA	(104)

$81-100 (❸)	
🖾 Broadway Inn	(101)
🖾 Chelsea Pines Inn	(96)
Chelsea Savoy Hotel	(99)
🖾 Colonial House Inn	(96)
🖾 Gershwin Hotel	(99)
Larchmont Hotel	(94)
Herald Square Hotel	(101)
Hotel Belleclaire	(104)
Hotel Grand Union	(100)
🖾 Hotel Newton	(104)
🖾 Hotel Pickwick Arms	(102)
🖾 Hotel Wolcott	(101)
Vanderbilt YMCA	(102)

$101-120 (❹)	
🖾 Hotel Belleclaire	(104)
Hotel Grand Union	(100)
🖾 Hotel Stanford	(100)
The Marcel	(100)
🖾 Novotel	(101)

$121 AND UP (❺)	
🖾 Bed & Breakfast on the Park	(106)
🖾 Hotel Chelsea	(96)
Sheraton LaGuardia East Hotel	(107)
🖾 ThirtyThirty	(99)

Let's Go lists prices excluding tax, unless otherwise noted. Quality, value, and safety have been taken into account in ranking. Unless otherwise noted, all establishments accept major credit cards.

NOLITA

Though accommodations options here are relatively scarce, the emerging Nolita district provides a great location and a cool vibe.

SoHotel, 341 Broome St. (☎212-226-1482; www.sohotel-ny.com), between Elizabeth St. and the Bowery. Ⓢ J, M, Z to Bowery; B, D to Grand St. This 100-year-old building is a

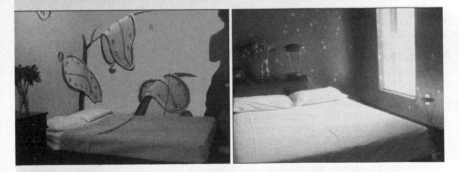

good value for those looking to take advantage of the nearby nightlife without paying exorbitant rates. All rooms have high ceilings, hardwood floors, sinks, private bathrooms, A/C and flat-screen TVs. $10 key deposit. Check-in 3pm. Check-out 11am. Reservations recommended 6 weeks in advance in high season. Singles and doubles from $119. ❷

GREENWICH VILLAGE

NYU's dorms make an excellent value in the summer, putting you right in the heart of the Washington Square scene.

Larchmont Hotel, 27 W 11th St. (☎212-989-9333; www.larchmonthotel.com), between 5th and 6th Ave. Ⓢ 4, 5, 6, L, N, Q, R, W to 14th St./Union Sq. Clean, European-style rooms in a whitewashed brownstone on a quiet block. A/C, closets, desks, phones, TVs, and wash basins in all rooms. Wear your cotton robe and slippers to the shared bath. Continental breakfast included. Check-in 3pm. Check-out noon. Reserve 4-6 weeks ahead. Singles $80-115; doubles $109-135; queens $129-145. ❸

DORMITORY

New York University, 14a Washington Pl., between Mercer and Green (☎212-998-4621; www.nyu.edu/housing/summer). Ⓢ N, R, W to 8th St./NYU. You don't have to be enrolled in NYU summer school to get housing, but summer school students get priority and lower rates. Rolling applications accepted beginning in July; housing applications for non-NYU students generally not accepted after Apr. Housing only available for individuals. Options in the East, Greenwich, and West Villages as well as near South Street Seaport. "Traditional" rooms are dorm style and don't have air-conditioning, but can be cheaper. 17+, unless an approved summer-school student. Meal plan ($90-100 per week) available but not required. Reception mid-May to mid-July M and Th 9am-5pm, Tu and W 9am-7pm, F 9am-4pm, Su 10am-3pm. Rest of year M-F 9am-5pm. 3-week (consecutive) min. stay. 11- to 12-week max. stay. Call for prices. Doubles and triples $130-280 per week depending on residence hall and enrollment status. Singles $165-285 per week. ❶

EAST VILLAGE

Though people don't usually think of the East Village as a place to sleep, its proximity to awesome nightlife makes it a worthwhile choice if you can snag a room.

Jazz on the Town, 307 E 14th St. (☎212-228-2780), at 2nd Ave. This new hostel from the owners of Jazz on the Park and Jazz on Harlem provides a cool downtown location at unbeatable prices. All rooms have A/C and private baths, and there's a friendly social terrace. Linens and towels provided. Reception 24hr. Dorms $32-36 per person. ❶

St. Mark's Hotel, 2 St. Mark's Pl. (☎212-674-0100; www.stmarkshotel.qpg.com), at 3rd Ave. Ⓢ 6 to Astor Pl. Clean, no-frills rooms with tiny sinks and emerald green carpet. The building is a bit run-down on the whole, but the location is exciting enough that you won't be spending much time in your hotel anyway. All 64 rooms have cable TV and private baths. Room with full bed $110; queen-size $120; 2 twins $130; 2 full-size $140. Cash and traveler's checks only. ❷

CHELSEA

Chelsea is home to a wide range of high-quality and often affordable accommodations. GLBT-friendly inns and B&Bs dot the area and are great places to meet oth-

ers looking to enjoy the area's nightlife. In addition to some historic, one-of-a-kind hotels, the neighborhood also hosts several no-frills hostels.

Colonial House Inn, 318 W 22nd St. (☎212-243-9669 or 800-689-3779; www.colonialhouseinn.com), between 8th and 9th Ave. [S] C, E to 23rd St. This Chelsea brownstone was the original headquarters of New York's pioneering Gay Men's Health Crisis. Today, it's a classy and comfortable gay-oriented B&B. All rooms have A/C, cable TV, and phones; some have baths and fireplaces. There's a "clothing optional" sun deck with lounge chairs and a privacy fence. Continental breakfast, served in the lounge, is included. Internet access $0.20 per min. in the lobby. Reception 24hr. Check-in 2pm. Check-out noon. Reservations are encouraged and require 2 nights' deposit within 10 days of reservation. Rates reduced Jan. to mid-Mar. Double-bed economy room $85-104; queen-size bedroom $104-130, with private bath and fridge $135-150. [3]

Chelsea Pines Inn, 317 W 14th St. (☎212-929-1023; www.chelseapinesinn.org), between 8th and 9th Ave. [S] A, C, E to 14th St.; L to 8th Ave. Every room in this friendly gay-owned and operated inn has a movie-star theme, and vintage movie posters are everywhere. There's a small courtyard and "greenhouse" with free Internet access out back. The cozy rooms have A/C, cable TV (with HBO, Showtime, and LOGO), phones, refrigerators, and showers. Continental breakfast (with fresh-baked bread) included. 3-day min. stay on weekends. Reception 24hr. Reservations are essential. Rooms with private showers and shared toilet from $89; with queen-size bed, private bath, day bed, stereos, and breakfast area $129. Extra person $20. [3]

Chelsea Star Hotel, 300 W 30th St. (☎212-244-7827 or 212-877-6969; www.starhotelny.com), at 8th Ave. [S] A, C, E to 34th St./Penn Station/8th Ave. The hallways at this coveted budget find are a cool industrial-grade metal, and many of the rooms have themes, like Salvador Dali-style decor. There's also a Madonna-themed room; the star supposedly stayed here once when she was a struggling artist. All rooms have shared bathrooms (4 rooms per bath) and A/C. A relaxing roof terrace is a great lounge area for guests. Linens provided. Safe deposit box $5. 14-night max. stay. Reception 24hr. Check-in 1pm. Check-out 11am. Reserve at least 1 month ahead. Dorms $35; singles $79-89; doubles $95-105; quads $119-129; queens with bath $169-189. [1]

Hotel Chelsea, 222 W 23rd St. (☎212-243-3700; www.hotelchelsea.com), between 7th and 8th Ave. [S] 1 to 23rd St./7th Ave. This classy art-filled gem is the grande dame of bohemian New York hotels. Staff is accommodating, and decor is one-of-a-kind. See p. 172 for more about the hotel's history and famous literary guests, such as Mark Twain and Dylan Thomas. All rooms have A/C, cable, bathrooms, showers, and phones; many have kitchens. Free wireless Internet in the cushy lobby. Fashion catalogues routinely shoot here. Reservations recommended, but cancel 72hr. ahead to avoid penalty. Singles from $195; doubles from $235; suites from $350. [5]

Chelsea Center Hostel, 313 W 29th St. (☎212-643-0214; www.chelseacenterhostel.com), between 8th and 9th Ave. [S] A, C, E to 34th St./Penn Station/8th Ave.; 1, 2, 3, 9 to 34th St./Penn Station/7th Ave. A small, friendly hostel in a great but inconspicuous location. Know the address—there's no sign out front, just a buzzer like at an ordinary apartment. 15 stay in a spacious basement dorm with a summer-camp feel, others in a slightly cramped bedroom on the main floor. There's a lovely garden in back where guests can hang out. Light breakfast included. 2 showers. Passport required. Luggage storage. Safe available. Linens provided. Check-in 8:30am-10:45pm. Check-out 11am. Flexible lockout 11am-5pm. Dorms $33. Cash and traveler's checks only. [1]

Chelsea International Hostel, 251 W 20th St. (☎212-647-0010; www.chelseahostel.com), between 7th and 8th Ave. [S] 1 to 23rd St./7th Ave.; C, E to 23rd St./8th Ave. Full of funky young (mostly European) travelers, this bare-bones hostel offers small, sparsely furnished dorms at unbeatable prices. The neighborhood is considered safe, and there's a police station right across the street. Free pizza W night. Enclosed courtyard. Kitchens, laundry room, and TV rooms. Internet access $1 per 8min. Key deposit $10. Passport required. Reception 24hr. Check-out noon. Reservations recommended 1-3 months in advance. $28 for rooms without bathrooms, $32 for rooms with bathrooms. ❶

Chelsea Savoy Hotel, 204 W 23rd St. (☎212-929-9353; www.chelseasavoynyc.com), at 7th Ave. [S] 1 to 23rd St./7th Ave.; C, E to 23rd St./8th Ave. Clean, functional rooms, all with A/C, cable TV, hair dryers, irons, and private baths, in an excellent Chelsea location. Reception 24hr. Check-in 3pm. Check-out 11am. Group rates available. Weekly specials available by phone. Reservations recommended 2-3 months in advance for weekends. Wheelchair accessible. Singles $99-125; doubles $135-250; quads $145-250. ❸

UNION SQUARE, THE FLATIRON DISTRICT, AND MURRAY HILL

To the east of lower Midtown, you'll find a high concentration of affordable hotels. The area doesn't necessarily have the residential charm others do, but it's got plenty of restaurants and is close to major attractions like the Empire State Building, Rockefeller Center, and the Museum of Modern Art. It's a good neighborhood if you're looking to save on accommodations—but be forewarned that you'll be a short cab ride or subway trip away from the best nightlife and entertainment.

👍 **Gershwin Hotel,** 7 E 27th St. (☎212-545-8000; www.gershwinhotel.com), between Madison and 5th Ave. [S] N, R, W to 28th St./Broadway; 6 to 28th St./Park Ave. S. This budget boutique hotel's red facade is ornamented with stunning glass, and its modern lobby has a Warhol vibe. The modestly sized rooms have bathrooms, cable TV, A/C, and phones. Wireless Internet $10 per day, $35 per week. Reception 24hr. Check-in 3pm. Check-out 11am. 6- to 10-bed dorms $33-45; singles and doubles $109-249. ❸

👍 **Thirty Thirty,** 30 E 30th St. (☎212-689-1900 or 800-497-6028; www.thirtythirty-nyc.com), between Park Ave. S and Madison Ave. [S] N, R, W to 28th St./Broadway; 6 to 28th St./Park Ave. S. This upscale hotel has modern style, a prime location, and rooms with A/C, cable TV, hair dryers, irons, and phones. There's also an attached restaurant and evening cocktail bar. Pet friendly. Reception 24hr. Check-in 3pm. Check-out 11am. Singles and doubles $169-229. ❺

👍 **Carlton Arms Hotel,** 160 E 25th St. (☎212-679-0680; www.carltonarms.com), between 3rd and Lexington Ave. [S] 6 to 23rd St. An unconventional and hip hostel with a dose of spunky attitude. The hostel's insignia shield sports the Latin for "there's no mint on your pillow." What it lacks in mints, TV, and phones, however, it makes up for in cool decor. Each room is decorated by a different artist. Room 11C is "good daughter/bad daughter"-themed; half is festooned in teeny-bopper posters, the other in horror-movie pics. All rooms have A/C and a sink; some have private baths. The hostel is popular with budget-conscious Europeans. Check-in 10am. Check-out 11:30am. Reserve for summer 1 month ahead; confirm on date specified during initial reservation or risk losing room. Single rooms $70, with bath $87; doubles $87/101; triples $112/122; quads $132/142. Pay for 7+ nights up front and get a 10% discount. ❷

Hotel 17, 225 E 17th St. (☎212-475-2845; www.hotel17ny.com), between 2nd and 3rd Ave. Ⓢ L to 3rd Ave. This historic, 120-room hotel served as the setting for Woody Allen's *Manhattan Murder Mystery.* Today, the friendly staff and recently renovated lobby make it a good no-frills choice. Rooms have high ceilings, A/C, and cable TV. Most have shared baths; some have fireplaces. The hotel is popular with foreigners. Check-in 3pm. Check-out noon. No visitors are allowed in guest rooms after 10pm. Reception 24hr. Singles $75-99; doubles $89-120; triples $120-150. Rooms with private bath $120. ❷

The Marcel, 201 E 24th St. (☎212-696-3800 or 888-66-HOTEL; www.nychotels.com), at 3rd Ave. Though not exactly at the bottom of the budget price range, this cute, modern hotel provides excellent value. The clean, modern interior looks like it could be an Ikea showroom. Rooms have TVs and squeaky-clean bathrooms. Singles and doubles from $117-250. Free upgrade if you book online. ❹

American Dream Hostel, 16 E 24th St. (☎212-260-9779), between Lexington and 3rd Ave. A basic, no-frills hostel catering to an international crowd. Though the lobby doesn't have A/C, all rooms do; most have TVs, some have private bath. Continental breakfast included. Internet $2.50 for 30min. Reception 8am-midnight. 4-person dorms $45; singles $66; doubles $88. ❷

Hotel Grand Union, 34 E 32nd St. (☎212-683-5890; www.hotelgrandunion.com), between Park Ave. S and Madison Ave. Ⓢ 6 to 33rd St. This functional, centrally located hotel offers relatively spacious rooms with A/C, cable TV, mini-fridge, bathrooms, and phones. Internet access $2 per 10min. Wi-Fi available in lobby; $5 for 3hr. Multilingual staff make this a popular option with international travelers. 24hr. security. Wheelchair accessible. Ask for a recently renovated room for the best value. Check-in 2pm. Check-out noon. Singles and doubles $140-160; twins and triples $165-185; quads $190-220. Lower summer rates available online. ❸

Murray Hill Inn, 143 E 30th St. (☎212-683-6900 or 888-996-6376; www.nyinns.com), between 3rd and Lexington Ave. Ⓢ N, R, W to 28th St./Broadway; 6 to 28th St./Park Ave. S. Five floors of clean, well-maintained rooms, but no elevator. Rooms have A/C, cable TV, and phones; some have private baths. 21-night max. stay. Check-in 3pm. Check-out noon. Small doubles $119-159; standard doubles $129-169. ❷

MIDTOWN WEST

Smack dab in the center of Midtown's bustle, hotels around Times Square, the Theater District, and Herald Square can make a surprisingly good value. For centrality, accommodations here can't be beat.

▨ **Hotel Stanford,** 43 W 32nd St. (☎212-563-1500 or 800-365-1114; www.hotelstanford.com), between 5th Ave. and Broadway. Ⓢ B, D, F, N, Q, R, V, W to 34th St./Herald Sq. This surprisingly affordable Herald Sq. hotel's lobby has sparkling ceiling lights, a polished marble floor, and a front desk with great service. Rooms have comfortable beds and A/C, private bathrooms, cable TV, phones, hair dryers, safes, and fridges. Continental breakfast included. The hotel also houses a Korean bakery and a bustling 24hr. Korean eatery. Multilingual concierges. Wireless Internet $10 for 24hr. Check-in 3pm. Check-out noon. Reservations recommended 2 weeks in advance. Singles $109-129; doubles $119-149; suites from around $169. ❹

▨ **Hotel Wolcott,** 4 W 31st St. (☎212-268-2900; www.wolcott.com), between 5th Ave. and Broadway. Ⓢ B, D, F, N, Q, R, V, W to 34th St./Herald Sq. The Wolcott's grand, lobby is a pleasant surprise in a hotel this affordable. The building has a long history— 50s rock-and-roll legend Buddy Holly recorded 2 hit albums here in now-defunct studios. 170 clean, functional rooms have A/C, bath, cable TV, irons, hair dryers, and phones. Fitness center. Free coffee and muffins for breakfast. Safe deposit boxes. Self-service laundry. In-room wireless Internet $8 per 24hr. Reception 24hr. Check-in 2pm. Check-out 12:30pm. Reserve at least 1 month in advance. Singles and doubles from $120; triples from $140; suites for 3 from $150. ❸

▨ **Broadway Inn,** 264 W 46th St. (☎212-997-9200, 800-826-6300; fax 212-768-2807), between 8th Ave. and Broadway. Ⓢ 1, 2, 3, 7, N, Q, R, S, W to 42nd St./Times Sq. Spotless suites, a cozy lobby, and a friendly atmosphere. A/C, data jacks, private baths, and TVs in all rooms. Free wireless Internet in lobby. Continental breakfast included. Parking $25 per day. Discounts on Broadway shows and some local restaurants. No elevator. Check-in 3pm. Check-out noon. Singles $129-299; doubles $140-160; suites $199-275. Book 2-3 weeks in advance, if possible. ❸

▨ **Novotel,** 226 W 52nd St. (☎212-315-0100), at Broadway. A large, well-located hotel run by a French chain. It's hardly cheap, but the hotel is a good value for those looking for a relatively upscale experience without breaking the bank. The lobby is stylish, and rooms are comfortable. Double rooms from $167 per night; most nights $200-250. ❺

Big Apple Hostel, 119 W 45th St. (☎212-302-2603; www.bigapplehostel.com), between 6th and 7th Ave. Ⓢ 1, 2, 3, 7, N, Q, R, S, W to 42nd St./Times Sq. This centrally located hostel provides a clean place to sleep in an unbeatably central location. Kitchen with refrigerator, luggage room, big deck with grill, common rooms, and laundry facilities. When reserving, make sure to mention any health problems or age concerns to avoid being put on one of the higher floors—there's no elevator. Bring your own towels. Internet access $1 per 8min. Safe deposit at reception. 21-day max. stay. Reception 24hr. Check-in and check-out 11am. Aug.-Sept. reservations only accepted on website. 4-person dorms $28 (same-sex available); private rooms with double bed and cable TV $77. ❶

Americana Inn, 69 W 38th St. (☎212-840-6700; www.theamericanainn.com), between 5th and 6th Ave. Ⓢ B, D, F, N, Q, R, V, W to 34th St./Herald Sq.; B, D, F, V to 42nd St./Ave. of the Americas. A no-frills budget hotel, 1 floor up from the street. Each of the 50 simple rooms has A/C, sink, and TV. 5 shared baths and a kitchenette on each floor. Internet access available. Check-in 1pm. Check-out noon. Singles $115; doubles $125; triples $145. ❸

Herald Square Hotel, 19 W 31st St. (☎212-279-4017 or 800-727-1888; www.heraldsquarehotel.com), between 5th Ave. and Broadway. Ⓢ B, D, F, N, Q, R, V, W to 34th St./Herald Sq. In a building that served as the original home for Life magazine, this hotel offers 120 clean, small rooms, all with A/C, satellite TV, phones, high-speed wireless Internet, and safes. Staff is friendly and accommodating. Internet available in lobby; $1 per 5min. Reception 24hr. Check-in 2pm. Check-out noon. Reserve 2-3 weeks ahead. Singles $89, with bath $109; doubles $169-199; triples $209; quads $219. 10% discount with ISIC. ❸

MIDTOWN EAST

Accommodations in Midtown East tend to be stately and super-expensive four-star hotels, catering primarily to business travelers. Still, you do have a couple of more affordable options.

👍 **Hotel Pickwick Arms,** 230 E 51st St. (☎212-355-0300 or 800-742-5945; www.pickwickarms.com), between 2nd and 3rd Ave. [S] 6 to 51st St.; E, V to 53rd St./Lexington Ave. The chandelier-lit marble lobby of this recently renovated hotel contrasts with the new-age decor of the small but efficient bedrooms, some of which come with iPod docks. A/C, flat-screen TVs, phones, wireless Internet, and voicemail in all rooms. Roof garden. Check-in 2pm. Check-out 1pm. Singles from $109, with bath from $129; doubles with bath from $159; studios with queen-sized bed and sofa from $249. ❸

Vanderbilt YMCA, 224 E 47th St. (☎212-756-9600; www.ymcanyc.org), between 2nd and 3rd Ave. [S] 6 to 51st St.; E, V to Lexington Ave./53rd St. A convenient location on a busy city block. The clean, brightly lit lobby bustles with international visitors, and the small rooms have A/C and cable TV. There's a 24hr. guard on duty, and the women's bathrooms require a code for entry. Bathrooms and showers on each floor. Free well-equipped gym and safe-deposit boxes. Several shuttles per day to airports. Luggage storage until departure $1 per bag. 25-night max. stay. Check-in 3pm. Check-out 11am. Reserve 2-3 weeks ahead with credit card. Singles and doubles $72-89 with shared bath, $105-140 with private bath. ❸

UPPER EAST SIDE

With one exception, the Upper East Side is not the place to look for budget-friendly accommodations. If you're looking for dorm-like quarters for a long-term stay, the De Hirsch Residence makes a good choice. Apply well in advance if you're serious about staying here.

De Hirsch Residence, 1395 Lexington Ave. (☎212-415-5650 or 800-858-4692; www.dehirsch.com), at 92nd St. [S] 6 to 96th St. This large, clean, and convenient hostel (affiliated with the 92nd St. YMHA/YWHA) has the feel of a college dorm. Catering only to those staying a month or longer, the residence requires that guests be going to school or working full-time. Over 300 dormitory-style rooms, all with A/C; choose from singles and small or large doubles. Huge bathrooms, fully equipped kitchens, and laundry machines on every other floor. Organized activities such as walking tours of New York. Discounted access to the 92nd St. Y's many facilities ($99 per month) and reduced rates for concerts. All residents have their own lockable closet. Linens provided; bring your own towels. Free internet access in the library. 1-month min. stay. 1-year max. stay. 24hr. access and high security. Single-sex floors, strictly enforced, but visitors of the opposite sex allowed as long as they sign in at the front desk. Wheelchair accessible. Apply several months ahead, as getting in is highly competitive. Singles $1280-$1380 per month; shared rooms $950-1080 per person per month. ❶

UPPER WEST SIDE

The Upper West Side is budget-accommodations central for Manhattan. You'll find an abundance of quality hostels and some excellent hotel values. Be careful, though, when selecting your digs here. The area is rife with apartment buildings operating as cheap hotels, often with only marginal legality, and often catering to significant numbers of long-term residents. Many a veteran visitor to New York can tell horror stories of malfunctioning climate-control systems, bug-infested rooms, and sketchy permanent residents in these dives.

👍 **Hotel Newton,** 2528 Broadway (☎212-678-6500 or 888-468-3558; www.newyorkhotel.com), between 94th and 95th St. [S] 1, 2, 3 to 96th St./Broadway. Likely one of the best values in Manhattan, this classy, recently renovated hotel boasts clean and spa-

cious rooms with A/C, TVs, and private baths. Internet access $1 per 9min. Check-in 2pm. Check-out noon. Children 17 and under stay free. Singles and doubles from $99. Additional person $15. Prices lowest on weekdays. ❸

👍 **New York International HI-AYH Hostel,** 891 Amsterdam Ave. (☎212-932-2300; www.hinewyork.org), at 103rd St. [S] 1 to 103 St./Broadway; B, C to 103rd St./Central Park W. The largest youth hostel in the US, housed in a block-long landmark building with 96 dorm-style rooms and 624 beds. Soft carpets, tight security, spotless bathrooms, and A/C. Kitchens, dining rooms, communal TV lounges, and large outdoor garden. Internet access $2 per 20min. Linen and towels included. 27-night max. stay. Check-in 4pm. Check-out 11am. Credit card reservations required. 10- to 12-bed dorms $30; 6- to 8-bed dorms $32-35; 4-bed dorms $35. Non-members $3 more. Family room with 1 queen and 2 bunk beds and shared bath $120. ❶

👍 **Hotel Belleclaire,** 250 W 77th St. (☎212-362-7700 or 877-468-3522; www.hotelbelleclaire.com), at Broadway. [S] 1 to 79th St. In a landmark building with marble staircases and an attractive modern lobby, this Scandinavian-chic boutique hotel offers fluffy comforters on sleek white beds. Service is friendly and professional, and room service is available from a nearby diner. All 237 rooms have A/C, cable TV, and fridges. Full gym. Check-in 3pm. Check-out noon. Single and double economy rooms with sink, fridge, TV, and shared bath $109-119; doubles with private bath $199-219; family suites with 3 full beds $229-289. Prices lowest on weekdays. ❹

👍 **Central Park Hostel,** 19 W 103rd St. (☎212-678-0491; www.centralparkhostel.com), between Manhattan Ave. and Central Park W. [S] B, C to 103rd St./Central Park W. This classic 5-story brownstone walk-up boasts hand-painted murals in the lobby, a funky tiled floor, spotless rooms with A/C, and a nice downstairs TV lounge. Lockers available. Linens provided; bring your own towels. Internet access $2 per 20min. Shared bathrooms. Key deposit $2. 13-night max. stay. Booking at least 2 weeks in advance recommended. Dorms $26-35; private doubles $85-95; studio apartments with private bath and kitchenette $109-149. ❶

👍 **Jazz on the Park,** 36 W 106th St./Duke Ellington Blvd. (☎212-932-1600; www.jazzonthepark.com), between Manhattan Ave. and Central Park W. [S] B, C to 103rd St./Central Park W. A brightly colored hostel with funky, fun decor and live jazz in the lounge on weekends. Rooms are small but quiet. A/C and lockers. Internet access $1 per 9min. Linen, towels, and breakfast included. Laundry on premise. Check-in 11am. Check-out 1pm. Reservations essential June-Oct. 10- to 12-bed dorms $27; 6- to 8-bed dorms $29; 4-bed dorms $32; doubles or twins $75, with bath $130. ❶

> **!** There are tons of cheap sleeps on the Upper West Side, but if you're returning to a hotel or hostel north of 90th St. late at night, be careful. Travel in groups, stick to major streets, or take a cab.

West Side YMCA, 5 W 63rd St. (☎212-875-4281 or 917-441-8800; www.ymcanyc.org), at Central Park W. [S] 1, A, B, C, D to 59th St./Columbus Circle. Behind the Y's impressive Moorish facade stand 450 basic, small rooms off dorm-style halls. The atmosphere is young and convivial, the location is ideal, and there is free access to a 65,000 sq. ft. gym with 2 pools, aerobics classes, steam room/sauna, and well-equipped fitness center. All rooms have A/C and cable TV. Wheelchair accessible. 25-night max. stay. Check-in 2:30pm. Check-out 11am. 24hr. security desk. Singles with shared bath $67-90, with private bath $99-130. ❷

International Student Center, 38 W 88th St. (☎212-787-7706), between Central Park W and Columbus Ave. [S] B, C to 86th St./Central Park W. An aging brownstone in a central Upper West Side location, this hostel has lots of stairs and no frills. Tolerable dorms with showers and sheets. Bring your own towel. Open only to those aged 18-35 (American non-NYC residents allowed); you must show a passport or a driver's license. Large basement TV lounge with kitchen, fridge, and an affable atmosphere. Key deposit $10. Reception daily 8am-11pm. Reserve on website to guarantee room for $3 fee. June-Aug. 7-night max. stay; Sept.-May 14-night max. stay. 8- to 10-bed dorm $30. ❶

The Amsterdam Inn, 340 Amsterdam Ave. (☎212-579-7500; www.nyinns.com), at 76th St. [S] 1 to 79th St. Though it calls itself a "boutique hotel for the budget minded," The Amsterdam Inn ain't the W, yet its location in the heart of the Upper West Side makes it worth considering. The 28 rooms are small, basic, and clean. All rooms have A/C, color TV, and WiFi Internet access; some have sink and microwave. The lobby is on the second floor. Check-in 2pm. Check-out noon. Single with shared bath $69-89; double with bath $129-169. ❷

MORNINGSIDE HEIGHTS

Particularly if their Uptown address suits your needs better than NYU's Greenwich Village location, Columbia dorms make an excellent summer choice.

Columbia University, 1230 Amsterdam Ave. (☎212-678-3235; fax 678-3222), at 120th St. [S] 1 to 116th St. Whittier Hall sets aside clean rooms, equipped with full beds, year-round. 24hr. security. The outlying neighborhood is not the safest, but it's well-populated until fairly late at night. Private bathroom, cable TV, heat and A/C. One-week max. stay. Four-person max. in room. Reserve in Mar. for May-Aug., in July for Sept.-Dec. $85-125 per night. Credit card deposit required. ❷

HARLEM

Harlem is a convenient home base if you're planning on visiting sights on the Upper West Side and in the Bronx, and the setting makes for an interesting and atypical New York experience. Downtown is far away, though. Also, when booking your room, think about how close you'll be to a subway stop. Although the area has become markedly safer in recent years, it's still best to avoid walking on deserted side streets at night.

👍 **Jazz on Harlem,** 104 W 128th St. (☎212-222-5773; www.jazzonthepark.com), near Lenox (6th) Ave. [S] 2, 3 to 125th St./Lenox (6th) Ave. This new hostel from the owners of the Jazz on the Park hostel on the Upper West Side (p. 104) was recently converted from a brownstone apartment complex. It offers clean, secure lodging in the heart of Harlem, a short walk from neighborhood sights and the subway. Sparkling hardwood floors, new furniture, and A/C. make for a comfortable stay. Rooms vary dramatically in size. Free morning coffee. TV lounge, lockers, and luggage storage. Internet available. 14-night max. stay. Reception 24hr. 10- to 14-person dorms $24; 4- to 6-person dorms $28; singles $85; doubles with bunk bed $102. ❶

The Harlem YMCA Claude McKay Residence, 180 W 135th St. (☎212-281-4100 x218; www.ymcanyc.org/reservations), between Adam Clayton Powell Jr. Blvd. (7th Ave.) and Lenox (6th) Ave. [S] 2, 3 to 135th St./Lenox (6th) Ave. In the era of segregation, this was New York's "colored" YMCA, and it housed legends like Langston Hughes and Claude McKay. Today, boasting tight security and good facilities, it makes a wise budget choice for tour groups and individual travelers alike. Guests have access to an excellent swimming pool and fitness center. Rooms include TV, A/C, and refrigerator.

Reserve well in advance in summer. Linens and towels provided. 28-day max. stay. Singles $60, with private bath $100; doubles $90, with private bath $115. Students with ID and letter of enrollment $213 per week for singles with shared bath. Seniors 65+ $171 per week for singles. ❶

BROOKLYN

If you're looking to splurge in New York, your accommodations dollar might just stretch farthest at this lovely B&B on Prospect Park.

🏛 **Bed & Breakfast on the Park,** 113 Prospect Park W (☎718-499-6115; www.bbnyc.com), between 6th and 7th St., in Prospect Park. Ⓢ F to 7th Ave./9th St., then 2 blocks east and 2 blocks north. Behind the unmarked doors of this magnificently restored brownstone lies a stunningly elegant B&B lacking only horse stables and gas lighting. Museum-quality Rococo armoires, oriental carpets, and damask fill the public areas and bedrooms. The complimentary gourmet breakfast in the common room includes treats like stuffed french toast, artichoke frittatas, smoothies, and pastries. Pricier than a typical *Let's Go* pick, but worth every penny. Most, but not all, rooms have private baths. A/C and cable TV. Singles and doubles $155-300. ❺

QUEENS

Choosing to stay in Queens means you'll be far from Manhattan's attractions (though close to LaGuardia and JFK airports). As in the other outer-borough neighborhoods, you'll get more amenities for your money by staying here.

Sheraton LaGuardia East Hotel, 135-20 39th Ave. (☎718-460-6666 or 888-268-0717; www.sheraton.com/laguardia), off Main St., Flushing. [S] 7 to Flushing/Main St. A surprisingly affordable, surprisingly luxurious alternative to Manhattan hotels. Whether you're flying in and out of nearby LaGuardia, or you just want to get more bang for your buck than you ever will in Manhattan, this hotel makes a good choice. The swank lobby has several stores and an attentive staff. Cable TV, A/C, phone. Continental breakfast included. Check-in 3pm. Check-out noon. Doubles (sleep 4 with no extra charge) $189-289. Call for cheaper rates based on availability and season. ❺

Flushing YMCA, 138-46 Northern Blvd. (☎718-961-6880; fax 718-461-4691), between Union and Bowne St., Flushing. [S] 7 to Flushing/Main St.; from there walk 10min. north on Main St. and turn right onto Northern Blvd. In an out-of-the-way location not likely to be convenient for most tourists, the Flushing Y offers budget rooms and a youthful atmosphere. Rooms are small, with cable TV and A/C. Shared bathrooms. Access to all Y facilities (gym, squash courts, and swimming pools) included. Key deposit $10. Check-in 3pm. Check-out noon. Reserve at least 1 month ahead for summer, 1 week otherwise. 25-night max. stay. Singles $50; doubles $70; triples $80. ❷

FOOD

New York is a diner's paradise, with virtually every kind of food imaginable on offer and new flavor combinations being created in the city's kitchens and on its street corners all the time. Standards like pizza and bagels pervade every neighborhood, of course, but the city's myriad ethnic communities all offer their own culinary expertise. Street food specialties like roasted peanuts in the winter, mustard- and sauerkraut-slathered hotdogs year-round, and rainbow-colored ice cones are distinctively New York treats. Of course, on the other end of the spectrum, New York is home to many of the world's best chefs and swankiest dining rooms. Don't automatically assume that a gourmet meal here is out of your reach. In both February and July, many of New York's best restaurants participate in **Restaurant Week,** during which they offer amazingly affordable fixed-price meals. In 2006, participating restaurants charged just $24.07 for a three-course lunch and $35 for a three-course dinner. For details on Restaurant Week, call ☎ 212-484-1200, or visit www.nycvisit.com.

ORGANIZATION
We have prefaced the food listings with a chart of restaurants categorized by **type of cuisine.** Appraisals are based on price, quality, and atmosphere. The *Let's Go* Picks feature an extraordinary marriage of low prices with high quality. For more complete listings of good eats, turn to the **By Neighborhood** section.

❶	❷	❸	❹	❺
under $7	$7-12	$13-20	$21-34	$35+

FOOD BY TYPE

AFRICAN

Keur N'Deye (p.147)	BR ❷
🗺 Madiba Restaurant (p.146)	BR ❸
Massawa (p.142)	MH ❷

AMERICAN, STANDARD

🗺 Big Nick's Burger and Pizza (p.139)	UWS ❷
Blue 9 Burger (p.128)	EV ❶
Brooklyn Moon (p.147)	BR ❶
🗺 Bubby's (p.113)	SoT ❷
🗺 Cafeteria (p.130)	CHE ❷
Chat 'n' Chew (p.133)	USQ ❷
Christie's Bakery (p.149)	BR ❶
🗺 Clinton St. Baking Company (p.121)	LES ❷
Crif Dogs (p.129)	EV ❶
🗺 Diner (p.145)	BR ❷
🗺 Diner 24 (p.130)	CHE ❷
🗺 Dizzy's (p.149)	BR ❷
EJ's Luncheonette (p.137)	UES ❷
🗺 elmo (p.130)	CHE ❸

AMERICAN, STANDARD, CON'T.

Empire Diner (p.131)	CHE ❷
Good Enough to Eat (p.138)	UWS ❷
Gray's Papaya (p.140)	UWS ❶
Hourglass Tavern (p.135)	MW ❸
Island Burgers and Shakes (p.135)	MW ❷
Jackson Hole (p.137)	UES ❷
Jerry's (p.114)	SoT ❷
Johnny's Reef (p.153)	BX ❷
🗺 Junior's (p.146)	BR ❷
🗺 Kitchen 22 (p.132)	USQ ❹
Mama's Food Shop (p.129)	EV ❷
🗺 Nathan's (p.150)	CIB ❶
Peanut Butter & Co. (p.125)	GV ❶
Rush Hour (p.122)	LES ❶
Schnack (p.148)	BR ❶
🗺 Shake Shack (p.132)	USQ ❶
🗺 Tom's Restaurant (p.149)	BR ❶
Tom's Restaurant (p.142)	MH ❶

AMERICAN, NEW
🏶 Barking Dog Luncheonette (p.136) UES ❷
The Bridge Cafe (p.113) LM ❹
🏶 Cafe Colonial Restaurant (p.120) LIT ❸
🏶 Chef & Co. (p.131) CHE ❷
Chestnut (p.148) BR ❸
🏶 DuMont Restaurant (p.145) BR ❷
🏶 Esperanto Cafe (p.126) GV
Essex (p.121) LES ❸
🏶 Freeman's (p.121) LES ❸
🏶 HQ (p.114) SoT ❹
New Leaf Cafe (p.143) H ❷
Pink Pony (p.124) LES ❷
Pink Tea Cup (p.125) GV ❷
Pop Burger (p.131) CHE ❶
🏶 Schiller's Liquor Bar (p.121) LES ❷
Toast (p.142) MH ❷

ASIAN, MISCELLANEOUS
Ivy's Chinese and Japanese (p.140) UWS ❷
Kelley and Ping Asian Grocery (p.114)SoT ❸
Pakistan Tea House (p.114) SoT ❶
🏶 Rice (p.120) LIT ❷
Republic (p.133) USQ ❶
🏶 Sea (p.145) BR ❷
Spice Market (p.126) MPD ❹

BAGELS AND BIALYS
Ess-a-Bagel (p.135) ME ❶
🏶 Kossar's Bialys (p.122) LES

BAKERIES
🏶 Beard Papa Sweets Cafe (p.141) UWS
🏶 Buttercup Bake Shop (p.141) UWS
Christie's Bakery (p.149) BR ❶
The City Bakery (p.134) USQ
🏶 Doughnut Plant (p.122) LES
🏶 Egidio's Pastry Shop (p.153) BX
Galaxy Cafe (p.151) QU
🏶 The Hungarian Pastry Shop (p.142) MH
🏶 Le Pain Quotidien (p.136) UES ❷
🏶 Little Pie Co. (p.132) CHE
🏶 Madonia Bakery (p.153) BX
🏶 The Magnolia Bakery (p.126) GV
🏶 Nussbaum & Wu (p.142) MH
Silver Moon Bakery (p.141) UWS
🏶 Sugar Sweet Sunshine (p.122) LES
🏶 Taipan Bakery (p.118) CHI
🏶 Veniero's (p.130) EV
Wimp's Southern Style Bakery (p.144) H
Yi Mei Fung Bakery (p.152) QU

CAFES
🏶 Alice's Tea Cup (p.141) UWS
Alt.Coffee (p.130) EV
Arthur Avenue Cafe (p.153) BX ❷
Cafe La Fortuna (p.141) UWS

CAFES, CON'T.
Cafe Lalo (p.141) UWS
Caffe Dante (p.126) GV
Caffe Pane e Cioccolato (p.126) GV
🏶 Downtown Atlantic (p.146) BR ❸
🏶 DT.UT (p.138) UES
🏶 The Grey Dog (p.126) GV
La Bella Ferrara (p.119) LIT
🏶 Mudspot (p.130) EV
Payard (p.138) UES
🏶 Serendipity 3 (p.137) UES
Settepani (p.144) H
Sunburst Espresso Bar (p.134) USQ
Yaffa Cafe (p.129) EV ❶

CARIBBEAN
Cafecito (p.128) EV ❶
Cafe Habana (p.120) LIT ❶
🏶 Cubana Cafe (p.114) SoT ❷
El Rey De Los Caridad (p.144) H ❷
La Fonda Boricua (p.144) H ❷
Negril (p.131) CHE ❸

CENTRAL/EASTERN EUROPEAN
Djerdan (p.151) QU ❶
🏶 Primorski Restaurant (p.150) CIB ❷
Varenichnaya (p.150) CIB ❶
Veselka (p.128) EV ❶
Yonah Schimmel Knishery (p.122) LES
🏶 Zum Schneider (p.127) EV ❷

CHINESE
Big Wong King Restaurant (p.117) CHI ❷
Chanoodle (p.117) CHI ❷
Chao Zhau Restaurant (p.151) QU ❶
Excellent Dumpling House (p.116) CHI ❶
🏶 Flushing Noodle (p.151) QU ❶
🏶 Fried Dumpling (p.115) CHI ❶
Hop Kee (p.117) CHI ❸
Joe's Ginger (p.116) CHI ❷
🏶 Joe's Shanghai (p.115) CHI ❸
🏶 Joe's Shanghai (p.151) QU ❷
New Green Bo (p.117) CHI ❷
Shanghai Cuisine (p.117) CHI ❷
Shanghai Pavilion (p.137) UES ❷
Sweet-n-Tart Cafe (p.117) CHI ❷/❶
Szechuan Gourmet (p.152) QU ❷
X.O. Cafe & Grill (p.117) CHI ❶

DELICATESSENS
🏶 Barney Greengrass (p.139) UWS ❷
Di Palo's (p.119) LIT
Katz's Delicatessen (p.122) LES ❷
Mangia (p.136) ME ❶
Milano Market (p.143) MH
🏶 The Pickle Guys (p.122) LES

DESSERT
ChikaLicious Dessert Bar (p.128) EV ❷

EUROPEAN, MISCELLANEOUS

F&B (p.131) — CHE ❶
Markt (p.127) — MPD ❹
🍴 Pommes Frites (p.127) — EV ❶
🍴 Smorgas Chef (p.113) — LM ❸

FRENCH

🍴 Alouette (p.139) — UWS ❹
🍴 Artisanal Fromagerie (p.133) — USQ ❸
🍴 Chez Brigitte (p.125) — GV ❷
Jules (p.129) — EV ❸
🍴 Mon Petit Café (p.136) — UES ❸
Pastis (p.127) — MPD ❹
Provence en Boite (p.148) — BR ❽
🍴 Restaurant Florent (p.126) — MPD ❸
Robin des Bois (p.148) — BR ❷
Tartine (p.125) — GV ❷

FUSION

🍴 Bistro Itzocan (p.143) — H ❷
🍴 Chip and Curry Shop (p.149) — BR ❷
La Caridad 78 Restaurant (p.140) — UWS ❷
La Marmite (p.144) — H ❷
🍴 Zen Palate (p.132) — USQ ❷

GOURMET SHOPS

Dean and Deluca (p.115) — SoT
Grace's Marketplace (p.138) — UES
Rice to Riches (p.120) — LIT
🍴 Zabar's (p.141) — UWS

GREEK AND MEDITERRANEAN

🍴 Antique Garage (p.114) — SoT ❹
🍴 Elias Corner (p.150) — QU ❷
Symposium (p.142) — UWS ❷
🍴 Telly's Taverna (p.150) — QU ❷
🍴 Uncle George's (p.150) — QU ❷
Zygos Taverna (p.151) — QU ❷

ICE CREAM AND CANDY

Aji Ichiban (Munchies Paradise) (p.118) — CHI
🍴 Brooklyn Ice Cream Factory (p.147) — BR
🍴 Chinatown Ice Cream Factory (p.118) — CHI
🍴 Ciao Bella (p.119) — LIT
🍴 Dylan's Candy Bar (p.138) — UES
Economy Candy (p.124) — LES
Il Laboratorio del Gelato (p.124) — LES
🍴 Jacques Torres Chocolate (p.147) — BR
🍴 La Maison du Chocolat (p.138) — UES
🍴 The Lemon Ice King of Corona (p.152) — QU
🍴 Teuscher Chocolatier (p.136) — ME

INDIAN

🍴 Bread Bar at Tabla (p.133) — USQ ❹
🍴 Chola (p.135) — ME ❸
Jackson Diner (p.151) — QU ❷
Minar (p.131) — CHE ❶
Mughai (p.140) — UWS ❸

INDIAN, CON'T.

Salaam Bombay (p.113) — SoT ❸
Spice Cove (p.128) — EV ❸

ITALIAN

🍴 Becco (p.135) — MW ❹
Cucina di Pesce (p.128) — EV ❷
🍴 Dominick's (p.152) — BX ❸
🍴 Falai (p.121) — LES ❹
🍴 Frank (p.127) — EV ❷
Il Vagabondo (p.137) — UES ❹
La Mela (p.119) — LIT ❷
🍴 Le Zie (p.130) — CHE ❸
Mario's (p.153) — BX ❹
Palmira's Ristorante (p.146) — BR ❷
Pasquale's Rigoletto (p.153) — BX ❹
Portofino Ristorante (p.153) — BX ❹
Rocky's Italian Restaurant (p.119) — CHI ❸

JAPANESE AND SUSHI

Mottsu (p.120) — LIT ❷
Sapporo (p.135) — MW ❷
Sushi Samba (p.134) — USQ ❹
Tomoe Sushi (p.125) — GV ❸

KOREAN

Dong Hae Ru (p.151) — QU ❷
🍴 Kum Gang San (p.151) — QU ❷

KOSHER

🍴 Moishe's Bake Shop (p.129) — EV
🍴 Second Avenue Delicatessen (p.128) — EV ❷
Wolf and Lamb (p.135) — ME ❸

LATIN AMERICAN

🍴 Alma (p.148) — BR ❸
Beso (p.149) — BR ❷
Bonita (p.145) — BR ❶
🍴 Empanada Mama (p.134) — MW ❶
🍴 Kitchen/Market (p.131) — CHE ❷
Lupe's East L.A. Kitchen (p.113) — SoT ❷
Mama Mexico (p.140) — UWS ❸
Rincon Salvadoreño (p.152) — QU ❷
🍴 Rosa Mexicano (p.130) — CHE ❸
Ruben's Empanadas (p. 113/114) — LM/SoT ❶
Santa Fe Grill (p.149) — BR ❷

MARKETS

Arthur Avenue Retail Market (p.153) — BX
🍴 Fairway (p.144) — H
🍴 Garden of Eden Gourmet (p.132) — CHE
🍴 Hing Long Supermarket (p.152) — QU
Tino's Salumeria (p.153) — BX
Yong Da Fung Health Food (p.152) — QU

MIDDLE EASTERN

🍴 Amir's Falafel (p.142) — MH ❶
Chickpea (p.129) — EV ❶
Moustache (p.125) — GV ❶

FOOD

MIDDLE EASTERN, CON'T.

Rainbow Falafel (p.133)	USQ ❶
🍴 Sahadi Importing Company (p.147)	BR

PIZZA

🍴 Adrienne's Pizza Bar (p.113)	LM ❷
🍴 Arturo's Pizza (p.125)	GV ❸
🍴 Giovanni's (p.152)	BX ❷
🍴 Grimaldi's (p.146)	BR ❷
🍴 Lombardi's Coal Oven Pizza (p.118)	LIT ❷
Totonno Pizzeria Napolitano (p.150)	CIB ❶

SANDWICHES AND SALADS

Bread (p.120)	LIT ❷
🍴 Cafe Gitane (p.119)	LIT ❷
Fresco by Scotto (p.136)	ME ❷
Miro Cafe (p.115)	SoT ❷
Roll n' Roaster (p.150)	CIB ❶
🍴 Say Cheese! (p.134)	MW ❶

SOUTHEAST ASIAN

Chai (p.145)	BR ❷
🍴 Doyers Vietnamese (p.115)	CHI ❷
Faan (p.148)	BR ❷
Land Thai Kitchen (p.140)	UWS ❷
Nyonya (p.116)	CHI ❷
Pad Thai Noodle Lounge (p.131)	CHE ❷
Ping's (p.117)	CHI ❸
Thai Pavilion (p.151)	QU ❷
Vermicelli (p.137)	UES ❷
Watana Siam (p.149)	BR ❷

SOUTHERN

Blue Smoke Barbecue (p.133)	USQ ❸
Brother Jimmy's BBQ (p.137)	UES ❷
Charles' Southern-Style Kitchen (p.142)	MH ❷
🍴 Dinosaur BBQ (p.143)	H ❷
JRG Fashion Cafe (p.147)	BR ❸
🍴 Manna's Soul Food Restaurant (p.143)	H ❶
🍴 Miss Maude's Spoonbread Too (p.143)	H ❷
Shark Bar and Restaurant (p.140)	UWS ❸
Sylvia's (p.144)	H ❷

SPANISH

Pipa (p.133)	USQ ❹
Suba (p.121)	LES ❹

TEA

Ten Ren's Tea and Ginseng (p.118)	CHI

VEGETARIAN/VEGAN/HEALTH

Better Burger (p.131)	CHE ❶
Bliss (p.145)	BR ❶
Cafe Kai (p.148)	BR ❶
🍴 Candle Cafe (p.136)	UES ❸
Josie's Restaurant and Juice (p.140)	UWS ❸
Kate's Joint (p.129)	EV ❷
🍴 Sacred Chow (p.124)	GV ❷
Soy Luck Club (p.125)	GV ❶
🍴 Teany (p.124)	LES ❷
The V-Spot (p.149)	BR ❷
🍴 Vegetarian Dim Sum House (p.116)	CHI
	❶

BR Brooklyn; **BX** Bronx; **CHE** Chelsea; **CHI** Chinatown; **CIB** Coney Island, Brighton Beach; **EV** East Village; **GV** Greenwich Village; **H** Harlem; **LES** Lower East Side; **LIT** Little Italy, Nolita; **LM** Lower Manhattan; **MW** Midtown West; **ME** Midtown East; **MH** Morningside Heights; **MPD** Meatpacking District; **QU** Queens; **SoT** SoHo, Tribeca; **UES** Upper East Side; **USQ** Union Square, Flatiron District, Murray Hill; **UWS** Upper West Side.

FOOD BY NEIGHBORHOOD

Neighborhoods are listed in geographical order (from south to north in Manhattan and from north to south in Brooklyn). Within each area, restaurants are listed in the order in which *Let's Go* likes them.

LOWER MANHATTAN

Lower Manhattan eateries tailor their service to the tightly scheduled lives of Wall St. brokers and bankers. Street carts and fast food joints selling falafels, burritos, and gyros line Broadway near Dey and John St. Upscale, power-dining spots are tucked amid the fray, often in luxury hotels. Stone St., between William St. and Coenties Alley, and historic Water St. offer a welcome selection of cute cafes and restaurants.

FOOD

■ **Smorgas Chef,** 53 Stone St. (☎212-422-3500; www.smorgaschef.com). Ⓢ 4, 5 to Bowling Green; 1 to South Ferry. Scandinavian cooking may be one of the few under-represented cuisines in New York City, but Smorgas Chef is an outstanding exception. Menu selections cater both to die-hard nordic palettes (herring sampler with lefsa $15; Swedish meatballs with lingonberries $16) and to less adventurous ones (burger $13; Alaskan salmon $18). The weekend brunch (Sa-Su 10am-5pm) is one of the best in the city. Additional locations at 283 W 12th St. in the West Village and at 924 2nd Ave. in Midtown. Open M-Th 11am-10:30pm, F-Sa 11am-11pm. ❸

■ **Adrienne's Pizza Bar,** 54 Stone St. (☎212-248-3838). Ⓢ 4, 5 to Bowling Green; 1 to South Ferry. A popular spot for refueling before or after a visit to the Statue of Liberty, Adrienne's serves mouth-watering thin-crust pizza topped with fresh Italian cheese. Sit outside in the cobblestone alley in nice weather. Salads $5-9. Pizzas $9-15. Open M-Sa 11:30am-midnight, Su 11:30am-10pm. ❷

The Bridge Cafe, 279 Water St. (☎212-227-3344). Ⓢ 4, 5, 6 to Brooklyn Bridge/City Hall; J, M, Z to Chambers St./Centre St. This well-known eatery in the shadow of the Brooklyn Bridge is as historic as Water St. itself. Dating from 1794, it claims to be the oldest continuously operating tavern in the city. Its history goes back even farther—in New York's rowdier past, it housed a brothel. Today, it's gone decidedly upscale. The gourmet New-American cuisine is expensive, but it's a good splurge. Provolone- and panko-crusted chicken $22. Almond-coated Atlantic halibut $25. Open M and Su 11:45am-10pm, Tu-Th 11:45am-11pm, F 11:45am-midnight, Sa 5pm-midnight. ❹

Ruben's Empanadas, 64 Fulton St. (☎212-962-5330). Ⓢ 2, 3, 4, 5, A, C, J, M, Z to Fulton St./Broadway/Nassau St. This outpost of the justifiably popular chain serves empanadas with a wide selection of fillings, including corn, veggie chili, spicy tofu, argentine sausage, and shrimp ($3.50-4). Open M-F 8am-7:40pm, Sa-Su 11am-6pm. Additional location at 505 Broome St. (☎212-334-3351; p. 114), between Thompson St. and W Broadway. ❶

SOHO AND TRIBECA

TRIBECA

TriBeCa's tangled streets are chockablock with restaurants and cafes. Close to Wall Street, the area does a busy lunch trade and hosts many a loosened-tie dinner. A meal here is pricey, though, and, while celebrity sightings are frequent, better neighborhoods exist for a splurge. Still, there are several affordable options.

■ **Bubby's,** 120 Hudson St. (☎212-219-0666; www.bubbys.com), at N Moore St. Ⓢ 1 to Franklin St. An airy, brick-walled, and stylishly simple cafe, known for its fresh, home-style comfort food. The weekend brunch is great, and the homemade pies ($6) are out of this world. Entrees $11-13. Su kids under 8 eat free at dinner. Open M-Th 8am-11pm, F 8am-midnight, Sa 9am-midnight, Su 9am-10pm. ❷

Salaam Bombay, 317 Greenwich St. (☎212-226-9400; www.salaambombay.com), at Reade St. Ⓢ 1, 2, 3 to Chambers St. A highly regarded Indian restaurant, serving off-beat and flavorful fare in an intimate atmosphere. Vegetarian options are plentiful. Tandoori vegetables $14. *Methi gosht* (lamb with tomatoes, onions, and spices) $17. Unbeatable lunch buffet $13. Box lunches $8. Full bar. Open M-F 11:30am-3pm and 5:30-11pm, Sa-Su noon-3pm and 5:30-11pm. ❸

Lupe's East L.A. Kitchen, 110 6th Ave. (☎212-966-1326; www.lupeskitchen.com), at Watts St. Ⓢ 1 to Canal St./Varick St.; A, C, E to Canal St./Ave. of the Americas (6th Ave.); C, E to Spring St./Ave. of the Americas (6th Ave.). This small, sparsely furnished Mexican cantina serves excellent and filling burritos and enchiladas ($8-10). Chicken mole $9. Stuffed *camarones chipotle* (sauteed spicy shrimp) $12. Four types of hot-

FOOD

pepper sauce are available. Free delivery. Open M-Tu and Su 11:30am-11pm, W-Sa 11:30am-midnight. Cash only. ❷

SOHO

SoHo's once impossibly hip scene has cooled slightly in recent years, and by and large that's good news for diners, who can expect high quality—and still a healthy dose of attitude—from a meal here. SoHo's cooking often serves as a precursor to a night out in one of its many bars and lounges.

👍 **HQ,** 90 Thompson St. (☎212-966-2755; www.hqrestaurant.com), between Spring and Prince St. [S] C, E to Spring St. Quiet and intimate, with an attentive staff, this new-American bistro is an ideal spot for a splurge. Admire the copper-plated wall from the circular booth in the back, or sit near the open-air windows in front during the summer. Irish organic salmon $21. Crisped Long Island duck breast $23. Open M-Th noon-3pm, 5pm-1am, F noon-3pm and 5pm-midnight, Sa noon-4pm and 5pm-midnight, Su noon-4pm and 6-9pm. ❹

👍 **Cubana Cafe,** 110 Thompson St. (☎212-966-5366), between Prince and Spring St. [S] 1 to Canal St. This Havana-style diner serves great Cuban specialities like pulled pork with whipped plantains ($9) and *Picadillo cubano* (ground beef sofrito with olives, raisins, yuca, and cumin) $8. Pineapple Jarritos soda $2.50. Excellent mojitos $6. Delivery. Open daily noon-11pm. Cash only. ❷

👍 **Antique Garage,** 41 Mercer St. (☎212-219-1019, www.antiquegaragesoho.com), between Broome and Grand St. [S] J, M, N, Q, R, W, Z, 6 to Canal St. Formerly an auto garage, this antique-filled restaurant still has its garage door, which opens in the summer to let in the fresh air. The Mediterranean menu features an excellent array of appetizers–from a simple bowl of olives ($6) to Aegean Sea sardines wrapped in grape leaves ($16). Entrees are just as good; try the grilled Turkish meatballs or the shrimp casserole ($20). Su live-jazz brunch. Open daily noon-midnight. ❹

Jerry's, 101 Prince St. (☎212-966-9464; www.jerrysnyc.com), between Mercer and Greene St. [S] N, R, W to Prince St. A slick and stylish lounge serving a variety of tasty sandwiches and salads. Jerry's Hamburger ($13.50) comes on onion brioche, and the chicken salad ($13) is anointed with truffle oil. Open M-W 9am-11pm, Th-F 9am-11:30pm, Sa 10:30am-11:30pm, Su 10:30am-5pm. ❷

Ruben's Empanadas, 505 Broome St. (☎212-334-3351), between Thompson St. and W Broadway. [S] C, E to Spring St. This counter-service snack shop has been a local favorite since 1975 for its empanadas of every variety, including spinach, spicy tofu, and Argentine sausage ($3.50-4). Save room for the dessert empanadas, like cherry and apple. Miniature empanadas are also available (12 for $9). Delivery available. Open M-F 8am-8pm, Sa-Su 9am-7pm. Additional location at 64 Fulton St. (☎212-962-5330; p. 113). ❶

Kelley and Ping Asian Grocery and Noodle Shop, 127 Greene St. (☎212-228-1212), between W Houston and Prince St. [S] N, R, W to Prince St. This cafeteria-style lunch destination goes slightly upscale at night. Lemongrass chicken $13.50. Crispy boneless duck glazed with soy, ginger, and tamarind sauce $17.50. The upstairs bar serves a variety of specialty cocktails. Blueberry Mojotini $9. Open daily 11:30am-11pm. ❸

Pakistan Tea House, 176 Church St. (☎212-240-9800), between Duane and Reade St. [S] C, E to Spring St. This small eatery serves outstanding tandoori dishes and other Pakistani favorites. Combo plates ($6-9) make an amazing deal. Try the spicy lamb curry ($10), and the homemade *kulfi* (Indian ice cream; $2) for dessert. All meat is halal. Takeout and sit-down service available. Open daily 9am-4am. ❶

Cafe Bari, 529 Broadway (☎212-431-4350), at Spring St. [S] N, R, W to Prince St. A first-floor coffee bar sits beneath this second-floor restaurant, which serves a healthy menu of sandwiches (spicy chunk tuna with homemade mozzarella and basil $12), pizzas (from $12), and pastas (penne with yellowfin tuna $15). Great at lunchtime when you need a break from shopping. Open M-Th noon-11pm, F-Sa noon-midnight, Su 11am-5pm. ❷

Miro Cafe, 474 Broadway (☎212-431-9391), between Broome and Grand St. [S] N, R, W to Prince St. This airy and unpretentious cafe serves heaping sandwiches on fresh-baked bread ($8-11), along with a good selection of coffee ($1.50-5), beer ($5), and wine ($6). Open daily 7am-9pm. ❷

SHOPS

Dean and Deluca, 560 Broadway (☎212-226-6800; www.deandandeluca.com), at Prince St. [S] N, R, W to Prince St. A New York institution for gourmet groceries that has grown into a chain. The high-ceilinged, marble-floored space has all the culinary ingredients (quail eggs $0.50), tools (waffle irons $45), and recipes (cookbooks from $15) your gourmet heart could desire. Abundant free samples make a trip here worthwhile whether you're actually shopping or not. Store open daily 10am-8pm. Espresso bar open M-F 7am-8pm, Sa 8am-8pm, Su 8:30am-8pm.

CHINATOWN

Have you been unsuccessfully scouring New York for fresh eel or live squid? Look no further than Chinatown's open-air markets, which spill onto the sidewalks above Canal and Mott Streets and offer every conceivable kind of Asian produce, seafood, meat, and prepared food. The neighborhood's 300-plus restaurants serve wonderfully diverse East- and Southeast-Asian cuisines at prices agreeable to the most frugal diner. Be patient with waiters and salespeople; English is a second language for most. Most restaurants are cash only, and many don't serve alcohol.

👍 **Joe's Shanghai,** 9 Pell St. (☎212-233-8888; www.joeshanghairestaurant.com), between the Bowery and Mott St. [S] 6, J, M, N, Q, R, W to Canal St. From fried turnip cakes ($3.25) to crispy whole yellowfish ($14), the Shanghai specialties served here draw huge crowds. Joe's is so well known for it's *xiao long bao* (soup dumplings) that the waiter will probably ask you if you want to order them immediately after you sit down. They're made-to-order and absolutely delicious. Communal tables give the restaurant a friendly feel. Though prices are slightly higher than at a typical Chinatown restaurant, Joe's is worth every penny. Expect long lines on weekends. If this Joe's is crowded, head to Joe's Ginger (see below), under the same ownership. Be sure to check out Joe's original Queens location, 13621 37th Ave., Flushing. Open daily 11am-11pm. Cash only. ❸

> [TIP] **TAKE IT SLOW.** Order gradually throughout the evening at restaurants in Chinatown. Ordering everything at the same time will result in a barrage of food, and most of it will get cold while you sift through. Gradual ordering keeps the food coming and lets your appetite keep up.

👍 **Fried Dumpling,** 106 Mosco St. (☎212-693-1060), between Mulberry and Mott St. [S] 6, J, M, N, Q, R, W to Canal St. For half the price of a subway ride, you can get either 5 dumplings or 4 pork buns ($1). Delicious, dirt-cheap food from a tiny hole in the wall with no A/C and a tiny counter with about 4 stools; most dumplings are sold for take-out. Other available items include soy milk ($1) and a very good hot-and-sour soup ($1). When you buy $5 worth of dumplings, there's a slight discount (as if you needed one). Cash only. ❶

👍 **Doyers Vietnamese Restaurant,** 11 Doyers St. (☎212-693-0725), between the Bowery and Pell St. [S] 6, J, M, N, Q, R, W to Canal St. One of those staircases-beneath-the-

CRAZY ABOUT *XIAO LONG BAO*

Xiao long bao—Chinese soup dumplings or soup buns, a common component of traditional *dim sum* spreads—have become a Chinatown craze in recent years. Soup dumplings are what draw many New Yorkers to Chinatown, and they're so popular they've fueled the expansion of numerous local restaurants, including Joe's Shanghai (p. 115), which had to open nearby Joe's Ginger (p. 116) to keep up with the craze. *Xiao long bao* are a delicious addiction—but one that many New Yorkers only feel comfortable feeding in secret. After all, these juicy dumplings—usually filled with soup broth and pork or crab meat—pose a definite projectile risk. How exactly can they be safely consumed?

Relax—there's a quick and easy way to savor these explosive treats, while keeping your clothes and your dining companions dry. It's just a matter of putting the right utensils to their proper use. Use the tongs that you received to place a dumpling in the large plastic spoon which your server has given you. Now use a chopstick to puncture the dumpling so that the broth drains into the spoon, and slurp it all down. With the liquid risk minimized, you can safely move on to what's left of the dumpling.

sidewalk, so characteristic of Chinatown, leads to this delicious Vietnamese restaurant. The staff is friendly, and the service is quick. You don't come here for the decor, which includes palm trees, year-round Christmas decorations, and (as at many restaurants in Chinatown) prominently displayed posters illustrating the Heimlich Maneuver. Appetizers here are delicious and often unusual—try the shrimp paste grilled on sugar cane ($6.25). Also excellent are the hot-pot soups, full of simmering meat, vegetables, and seafood. Serves beer, wine, and sake. Open M-Th and Su 11am-9:30pm, F-Sa 11am-10:30pm. Cash and AmEx only. ❷

Vegetarian Dim Sum House, 24 Pell St. (☎212-577-7176; www.vegetariandshouse.com), at Doyers St. Ⓢ 6, J, M, N, Q, R, W to Canal St. No animals are on the menu in this small eatery, but don't assume you'll find only straightforward veggie stir-fries. Much of the menu consists of mock meat dishes produced through creative combinations of soy, wheat, and mushroom by-products, providing a great opportunity for vegetarians and meat-lovers alike to enjoy dim sum. Vegetarian spring rolls $2.75. Fantastic dumplings $3. Most entrees from $11. Noodle and rice dishes can be ordered with whole-wheat noodles or brown rice for the carb-conscious. Open daily 10:30am-10:30pm. Cash only. ❶

Nyonya, 194 Grand St. (☎212-334-3669), between Mulberry and Mott St. Ⓢ 6, J, M, N, Q, R, W to Canal St. Dishes at this popular Malaysian restaurant are more unusual than your typical Chinatown choices, and most of the entrees are quite spicy. Try the *nasi lemak* ($5), chili anchovies and curry chicken in a bed of coconut rice. Seafood is also a speciality; that large fish tank in the dining room is not there for aesthetic purposes. If you're really adventurous, try the "deep fried squids ball" ($5.50). Nyonya's most popular drink is a whole coconut with a straw in it ($3.50); when you finish drinking the milk, the server will cut it in half so you can eat the inside. Beer and wine available, along with a variety of interesting fruit juice blends. Open M-Th and Su 11am-11:30pm, F-Sa 11am-midnight. Delivery and takeout available. Cash only. ❷

Joe's Ginger, 113 Mott St. (☎212-966-6613), at Hester St. Ⓢ 6, J, M, N, Q, R, W to Canal St. The same famous soup dumplings as at Joe's Shanghai (8 for $6.25). Cheap, excellent Shanghai cuisine in a comfortable environment with good service. Try the crispy yellowfish fingers with dry seaweed ($13). Open M-Th 11am-10:30pm, F-Sa 11am-11:30pm, Su 11am-10pm. Cash only. ❷

Excellent Dumpling House, 111 Lafayette St. (☎212-219-0212), just south of Canal St. Ⓢ 6, J, M, N, Q, R,

W to Canal St. Small, unassuming, and crowded during peak hours. The dumplings (8 for $4.25) are, in fact, excellent. Also features noodle soups ($4.25-6.50). Open daily 11am-9pm. Cash only. ❶

New Green Bo, 66 Bayard St. (☎212-625-2359), between Mott and Elizabeth St. Ⓢ 6, J, M, N, Q, R, W to Canal St. Another opportunity to try those delicious soup dumplings (8 for $6.25). Entrees $8-15. Open daily 11am-midnight. Cash only. ❷

> ❗ Dining late in Chinatown? Though your restaurant will probably stay open into the wee hours, virtually all of the shops and market stalls close between 7-8pm, leaving side streets empty and dark. When walking at night, exercise caution, travel in groups when possible, and stay on the main streets.

Ping's, 22 Mott St. (☎212-602-9988), at Mosco St. Ⓢ 6, J, M, N, Q, R, W to Canal St. One of Chinatown's more upscale restaurants, Ping's specializes in seafood and hot pots (stewed clams with spicy sauce, $14), but they also have the more traditional dim sum (from $4). The clientele here tends to come well dressed. Open M-F 10am-midnight, Sa-Su 9am-midnight. ❸

Sweet-n-Tart Cafe, 20 Mott St. (☎212-334-8088; www.sweetntart.com), near Mosco St. Ⓢ 6, J, M, N, Q, R, W to Canal St. With separate upstairs and downstairs settings, Sweet-n-Tart lets you choose the environment in which you want to enjoy fresh and delicious Chinese food. Upstairs is a formal restaurant, with linen tablecloths and so forth, while downstairs you'll find a laid-back cafe setting. The menu features traditional Chinese fare and a variety of fresh juice combinations (try the "Titanic"—watermelon, kiwi, banana, and apple in cream soda; $3.75) and some unusual desserts (coconut milk with Chinese jello $4.25). ❷ and ❶

Big Wong King Restaurant, 67 Mott St. (☎212-964-0540), between Canal and Bayard St. Ⓢ 6, J, M, N, Q, R, W to Canal St. Though spartan in the way of decoration, this restaurant has delicious food and, crucially in the summer, A/C. Try the Seafood Delight (shrimp, squid, fish cake, crab, and scallop in garlic sauce; $12.50) or the barbecued spare ribs ($5.25). Open daily 8:30am-9pm. Cash only. ❷

Hop Kee, 21 Mott St. (☎212-964-8365), downstairs, at the corner of Mosco and Mott St. Ⓢ 6, J, M, N, Q, R, W to Canal St. A quality Chinese restaurant with more space than most in Chinatown. Spicy beef chow fun $6. Chop suey from $9. Delicious roast pork with oyster sauce $11.25. Open daily 11am-1am. Cash only. ❸

Shanghai Cuisine, 89 Bayard St. (☎212-732-8988), at Mulberry St. Ⓢ 6, J, M, N, Q, R, W to Canal St. The house specialty is braised soy duck with 8 treasures ($36), which must be ordered 1 day in advance. It might be the richest dish you'll ever taste, so attack it only in large groups. Less intense dishes include spicy pepper salt prawns ($13), juicy meat dumplings ($6.25), and mixed vegetables ($7). Serves beer and wine. Open daily 11:30am-10:30pm. Kitchen closes at 10:15pm. Cash only. ❷

X.O. Cafe & Grill, 96 Walker St. (☎212-343-8339), between Centre and Lafayette St. Ⓢ 6, J, M, N, Q, R, W to Canal St. A Chinatown restaurant that actually puts some effort into its decor. The menu features many kinds of *congee* (rice porridge), from beef ($4), to fresh clam with chicken ($7). The drinks (fresh juices $2) and desserts (fried ice cream $3) here are especially delicious. The chef will perform cooking demonstrations for small groups on request. Open M-Th and Su 11am-10:30pm, F -Sa 11am-11pm. Cash only. ❶

Chanoodle, 79 Mulberry St. (☎212-349-1495), between Canal and Bayard St. Ⓢ 6, J, M, N, Q, R, W to Canal St. Delicious food in a crowded, fast-paced setting. Try the crispy fried soft-shell crab ($4.75), with some cool tapioca bubble tea ($2.50). Open M-Th and Su 8:30am-9pm, F-Sa 8:30am-10pm. Cash only. ❷

FOOD

SHOPS

■ **Chinatown Ice Cream Factory,** 65 Bayard St. (☎212-608-4170; www.chinatown-icecreamfactory.com), at Elizabeth St. Ⓢ 6, J, M, N, Q, R, W to Canal St. Unbeatable creative and delicious homemade ice cream in exotic flavors. The menu currently includes passion fruit, green tea, red bean, and wasabi ice creams, as well as assorted sorbets. 1 scoop $3, 2 scoops $4.65, 3 scoops $5.75. Crowded, but the line moves quickly. Open daily 11am-11pm.

■ **Taipan Bakery,** 194 Canal St. (☎212-732-2222; www.taipan-bakery.com), between Mott and Mulberry St. Ⓢ 6, J, M, N, Q, R, W to Canal St. Don't let the ridiculously low prices at this Chinese bakery fool you—the pastries here are spectacular. Try the popular egg custard tarts ($0.80) or the Green Tea Sweetheart ($1.50), a green-tea flavored, custard-filled cake. Open daily 7:30am-8:30pm. Cash only.

Aji Ichiban (Munchies Paradise), 37 Mott St. (☎212-233-7650), at Pell St. Ⓢ 6, J, M, N, Q, R, W to Canal St. This Japanese chain sells dried and spiced fruit (preserved plums $3.50-5 per ½ lb.) and a mouth-watering selection of Japanese and American candies (flavored rice cakes $3 per lb.). If you're feeling brave, try the dried fish, which are quite literally what they sound like; they're textured vaguely like potato chips (dried puffer fish $12 per ½ lb.). Open daily 10am-8pm.

Ten Ren's Tea and Ginseng Company, 75 Mott St. (☎212-349-2286; www.tenren.com), between Canal and Bayard St. Ⓢ 6, J, M, N, Q, R, W to Canal St. This comfortable and classy tea emporium boasts a huge selection of rare teas, teapots, teabags, and ginseng root. Prices range from the inexpensive (teabag $0.50) to hefty (ginseng $10-200 per ½ lb.). Open M-Th and Su 11am-10pm, F-Sa 11am-11pm. Up the street at 70 Mott St., a cafe called **Ten Ren's Tea Time** serves a huge variety of bubble teas at great prices ($3-5).

LITTLE ITALY AND NOLITA

In recent decades, as the allure of the classic spaghetti-with-garlic-bread type of Italian cuisine has faded, the size of New York's Little Italy neighborhood has shrunk considerably. To the south, Chinatown has expanded onto blocks that once were Italian territory, and, to the north, the newly minted Nolita ("North of Little Italy") district—an appellation invented by Manhattan real estate investors to boost the neighborhood's cachet—has recently come in vogue, replacing checkered tablecloths and Chianti with designer boutiques and specialty martinis. While it's still fun to soak up Little Italy's carnival-like atmosphere in the evening, head to Nolita to escape the tourists, find creative gourmet cuisine, and, believe it or not, pay less.

LITTLE ITALY

Little Italy endures today on the three blocks of **Mulberry Street** between Grand and Canal St. The best Italian cuisine in New York is definitely not to be found here, and a full meal in one of the many restaurants can easily run $60-70 per person if wine is involved. But the area does retain a certain historical charm, and you can still find a few small, authentic Italian food stores. The restaurants listed below are low-brow and unpretentious, sure to deliver a boisterous and fun evening.

■ **Lombardi's Coal Oven Pizza,** 32 Spring St. (☎212-941-7994), between Mott and Mulberry St. Ⓢ 6 to Spring St./Lafayette St. Recognized as the nation's oldest pizzeria (1905), Lombardi's claims to have created the NY-style coal-oven pizza, and it has the checkered-tablecloth-and-exposed-brick atmosphere to match. If you're willing to brave Lombardi's inevitable crowds, its pizzas—from standard mozzarella and tomato to more exotic specialties like clam pie—won't disappoint. A large pizza ($15.50) feeds 2. Try to visit during off-peak hours; the line is invariably out the door. Open M-Th 11:30am-11pm, F-Sa 11:30am-midnight, Su 11:30am-10pm. Delivery and takeout available. Cash only. ❷

La Mela, 167 Mulberry St. (☎212-431-9493; www.lamelarestaurant.com), between Broome and Grand St. Ⓢ 6 to Spring St./Lafayette St.; 6, J, M, N, Q, R, W, Z to Canal St. Enormous La Mela is old-school Little Italy at its best, with family-style portions, long communal tables, chummy staff, and heaps of pasta drenched in red sauce. It's a great choice for a rowdy evening with a large group. 4-course dinner $28 per person, 3-course $19; 2-person min. 1.5L house wine $26. Pasta $11-16. House's huge dessert concoction (ice cream, cake, coconut, glazed bananas) $6 per person. Family-style only after 6pm. Open M-Th and Su noon-2am, F-Sa noon-3am. ❷

Rocky's Italian Restaurant, 45 Spring St. (☎212-274-9756), at Mulberry St. Ⓢ 6 to Spring St./Lafayette St. The food at this Little Italy classic is hardly cutting-edge, but it's served in a friendly neighborhood ambience that draws everyone from families, to elderly friends, to first dates. The lunch menu (until 5pm) offers huge hero sandwiches ($5.50-9). Pasta $8-17. Entrees $11-25. Carafe of wine $16. Open Tu-Su 11am-11pm. Kitchen closes at 10:30pm. ❸

SHOPS

🏷 **Ciao Bella,** 285 Mott St. (☎212-431-3591), between Prince and Spring St. Ⓢ 6 to Spring St./Lafayette St.; B, D, F, V to Broadway/Lafayette St. The *gelato* here, made according to a family recipe from Turin, Italy, is some of the best in New York: dense, smooth, rich, and flavorful. Flavors range from the classic (cookies 'n cream, coffee, pistachio, amaretto) to the exotic (chocolate jalapeno, lemon curd, red bean, ginger). The shop is little more than a storefront, but it's easy to find a bench nearby to enjoy your treat. Small $4.50; large $6. Gourmet smoothies $7. Open M-Sa 11am-11pm, Su 11am-10pm. Cash only.

Di Palo's, 206 Grand St. (☎212-226-1033), at Mott St. Ⓢ 6 to Spring St./Lafayette St.; 6, J, M, N, Q, R, W, Z to Canal St. This gourmet Italian food shop is a great place to come if you're craving cheese—homemade mozzarella, goat cheese, and ricotta fresca are mainstays. If you're lucky, you'll get a free cheese sample while you wait in line. Open M-Sa 9am-6:30pm, Su 9am-3:30pm.

CAFES

La Bella Ferrara, 110 Mulberry St. (☎212-966-1488), between Canal and Hester St. Ⓢ 6 to Spring St./Lafayette St.; 6, J, M, N, Q, R, W, Z to Canal St. Come to this neighborhood cafe for a leisurely cappuccino or a delicious Italian dessert. The shaded outdoor seating is delightful in the summer. Pastries $2-2.50. Cappuccino $3.75. Gelato and ices $2.50-4. Open daily 10am-midnight.

NOLITA

Nolita, which has become a Manhattan restaurant destination in its own right in recent years, is packed with beautiful people dressed more fashionably than you'll ever be—and restaurants serving hip, delicious cuisine at prices you can afford.

🏷 **Cafe Gitane,** 242 Mott St. (☎212-334-9552), at Prince St. Ⓢ 6 to Spring St./Lafayette St. B, D, F, V to Broadway/Lafayette St. A chill cafe with a Euro vibe, filled with fashionable shoppers. Especially good for brunch, Cafe Gitane offers a wonderful selection of fresh-baked breads, delicious breakfasts such as baked eggs with salmon ($7), lovely snacks like brie with apples ($5.50), and designer salads such as cucumber, yogurt, and mint with hummus ($7.50), at highly affordable prices. Open daily 9am-midnight. Delivery available. Cash only. ❷

■ **Rice,** 227 Mott St. (☎212-226-5775; www.riceny.com), between Prince and Spring St. Ⓢ 6 to Spring St./Lafayette St.; B, D, F, V to Broadway/Lafayette St. Rice offers every permutation of its namesake you can imagine, and others that you probably haven't but will love, served in a subdued, chic atmosphere. The basics—basmati, brown, sticky, and Japanese—are all here, along with more exotic specimens like Bhutanese red and green rice, grown at a high altitude and supposedly rich in healthy minerals. Sauces range from mango chutney to aleppo yogurt. The menu offers a variety of original items you won't find elsewhere, such as butternut squash chowder ($4.50) and warm pear cider ($3). Salads are also a treat; try the tea-smoked salmon salad on mixed greens with ginger hoisin vinaigrette and grilled scallion mayonnaise ($9). Rice entrees $4-9.50. Open daily noon-midnight. Delivery available. Cash only. ❷

■ **Cafe Colonial Restaurant,** 276 Elizabeth St. (☎212-274-0044; www.cafecolonialny.com), at Houston St. Ⓢ 6 to Spring St./Lafayette St.; B, D, F, V to Broadway/Lafayette St. This colorful and laid-back Brazilian cafe serves great sandwiches and salads ($8.50-11) and fuller entrees at dinner (grilled salmon $17; Brazilian-style pork ribs $18). For dessert, the Brazilian flan pudding ($6.75) is scrumptious. Breakfast here, served 8am-4pm, is a treat (french toast, made with a baguette, $6.75). Indoor and outdoor seating. Open daily 8am-11pm. ❸

Cafe Habana, 17 Prince St. (☎212-625-2002; www.ecoeatery.com), on the corner of Elizabeth and Prince St. Ⓢ 6 to Spring St./Lafayette St.; B, D, F, V to Broadway/Lafayette St. Local artsy types call this inexpensive and retro-styled place home on summer evenings. The line spills onto the street, but the newly added takeout section next door takes the edge off. The Mexican-grilled corn-on-the-cob ($1.80) is a favorite. Preparation of the food takes time, but it's worth it. Cuban sandwiches $6.75. Tostadas de pollo $7.75. Vegetarian plate $8. Handmade corn cake stuffed with goat cheese, sun-dried tomatoes, and black beans $9.25. Open daily 9am-midnight. Takeout open noon-10pm. ❶

Bread, 20 Spring St. (☎212-334-1015), between Elizabeth and Mott St. Ⓢ 6 to Spring St./Lafayette St.; B, D, F, V to Broadway/Lafayette St. So you think you're cool? See if your hipness matches up against Bread's, with its minimalist interior (lit only by votive candles at night), world-weary waitstaff, and trendy clientele. Even if the design team has been trying a little too hard here, the cuisine is delicious, focused on fresh, gourmet sandwiches ($7-9), which come with salad and are served, of course, on freshly baked bread (from nearby Balthazar). Try the shrimp with arugula, avocado, and salsa rosa on ciabatta ($9.50) or the gorgonzola dolce with Golden Delicious apples and honey on cranberry raisin bread ($9). Open M-Th and Su 10:30am-noon, F-Sa 10:30am-1am. ❷

Mottsu, 285 Mott St. (☎212-343-8017), between E Houston and Spring St. Ⓢ 6 to Spring St./Lafayette St.; 6, J, M, N, Q, R, W, Z to Canal St.; F to E Broadway; B, D, F, V to Broadway/Lafayette St. One of the neighborhood's few Japanese restaurants, serving fresh and reasonably priced sushi and sashimi in a quiet, intimate atmosphere. Tuna rolls $5.75. Eel and avocado rolls $6.25. Chicken teriyaki with mushrooms $14.50. M-Th noon-3pm and 5-11pm, F noon-3pm and 5-11:30pm, Sa 5-11:30pm, Su 5-10pm. ❷

SHOPS

Rice to Riches, 37 Spring St. (☎212-274-0008; www.ricetoriches.com), between Mott and Mulberry St. Ⓢ 6 to Spring St./Lafayette St. Where else but New York can you find a shop selling 20-some varieties of rice pudding—and with decor so space-age the tables hang from the ceiling and the menu is displayed on flat-screen TVs? The flavors have fun names like Rest in Peach, Almond Schmalmond, and Sex, Drugs, & Rocky Road; be sure to sample a few before making your final decision. Toppings like Nudge (chilled espresso with cocoa; $0.50) make the pudding taste even better. Open M-W and Su 11am-11pm, Th-Sa 11am-midnight. Under $20 cash only.

FOOD

LOWER EAST SIDE

Most members of the Lower East Side's Jewish community have moved elsewhere, but the pickles, reubens, and knishes remain. Alongside family-run shops are trendy restaurants and cafes catering to the artists and night-owls who now call the area home. Many of these cluster along Ludlow, Clinton, and Rivington St.

👍 **Freeman's,** at the end of Freeman Alley (☎212-420-0012; www.freemansrestaurant.com), off Rivington St., between the Bowery and Chrystie St. [S] F, V to 2nd Ave. Finding this restaurant, tucked away at the end of a narrow alley, is nearly as fun as eating here. Nosh on traditional American cuisine in what looks like a hunting lodge, complete with antlers and stuffed geese. Three-cheese macaroni $12. Whole grilled trout with thyme, garlic, and lemon $16. Brunch specialties like poached eggs, lamb sausage, and watercress ($9) and waffles with *crème fraiche* and banana-maple syrup ($8) are crowd-pleasers. Open M-F 6:30-11:30pm and Sa-Su 11am-4pm and 6:30-11:30pm. ❸

👍 **Schiller's Liquor Bar,** 131 Rivington St. (☎212-260-4555), at Norfolk St. [S] F, J, M, Z to Delancey St./Essex St. Schiller's owner, also responsible for popular Balthazar and Pastis, sought to create his own "low-life restaurant and bar" on the Lower East Side. The result is somewhere between a dive bar and a French bistro. Welsh rarebit $11. Mac and cheese $12. Brunch, available Sa-Su 10am-5pm, features fresh-fruit waffles ($9), *huevos rancheros* ($10), and croissants ($2). The wine list is divided by budget: cheap ($5), decent ($6), and good ($7). Free wireless Internet. Open M-Tu 11am-1am, W-Th 11am-2am, F 11am-3am, Sa 10am-3am, Su 10am-1am. ❷

👍 **Clinton St. Baking Company,** 4 Clinton St. (☎646-602-6263; www.clintonstreetbaking.com), between E Houston and Stanton St. [S] F, J, M, Z to Delancey St./Essex St. Six years ago, Clinton St. Baking Co. was just a small muffin shop with a loyal following. Today, it's a full-service American restaurant with some of the best baked goods in the city. Lines form early on weekends for famous wild-blueberry or banana-walnut pancakes ($10) and buttermilk-biscuit sandwiches ($8). M-Th 6-8pm Brooklyn lager and a burger on a brioche bun $10. Classic hot fudge sundaes with Brooklyn-made ice cream $8. Free delivery with $10 minimum. Open M-F 8am-4pm and 6-11pm, Sa 10am-4pm and 6-11pm, Su 10am-4pm. ❷

👍 **Falai,** 68 Clinton St. (☎212-253-1960; www.falainyc.com), between Stanton and Rivington St. [S] F, J, M, Z to Delancey St. This modern Italian restaurant is a trendy splurge, sure to please even the pickiest of foodies. Somehow the hyper-white decor still manages to be warm. Sea-salt foccacia and black-cabbage rolls are complimentary. Pastas are hand-cut; try the flat noodles with beef au jus and spinach ($16). Most entrees $16-26. Open Tu-Th and Su 6-11:30pm, F-Sa 6-11pm. ❹

Suba, 109 Ludlow St. (☎212-982-5714; www.subanyc.com) between Rivington and Delancey St. [S] F, J, M, Z to Delancey St./Essex St. One of the most dramatic dining spaces in the city, worth a trip even though the food doesn't always match up with the decor. From the ground-floor tapas lounge, you can descend to a "grotto" with exposed brick walls and a water-filled moat, followed by a sky-lit dining room with 14 ft. ceilings. The Spanish menu features tapas ($6-10) and 7 kinds of sangria (glass $11, pitcher $35-45). M classic film screenings (3-course dinner and film $35). Suba transitions into a lounge F and Sa nights, with DJs spinning Latin and world pop and house 11pm-4am (cover $20; includes 2 drinks). Su live flamenco performances (food-and-drink min. $30; reservations required). Open M-Th and Su 6pm-midnight, F-Sa 6pm-4am. ❹

Essex, 120 Essex St. (☎212-533-9616; www.essexnyc.com), between Delancey and Rivington St. [S] F to Delancey St.; J, M, Z to Delancey St./Essex St. Essex's mix of Jewish and Latin cooking pays homage to the ethnically diverse roots of the Lower East Side. The lofty, whitewashed space is a perfect place to devour potato pancakes ($6), goat-cheese-stuffed chicken breast ($15), and chipotle pork loin ($14) amid an artsy local crowd. The fantastic Su brunch ($15) gets you 3 bloody marys, mimosas, or screwdrivers with your challah french toast, lobster benedict, grilled sirloin burger, or cubano sandwich. Get there early or make reservations; the wait can be quite long. W whole lobsters with 2 sides $14. Open Tu-Th 6pm-midnight, F 6pm-1am, Sa 11:30am-4:30pm and 6pm-1am, Su 11:30am-4:30pm. ❸

Katz's Delicatessen, 205 E Houston St. (☎212-254-2246), between Orchard and Ludlow St. [S] F, V to Lower East Side/2nd Ave. A Lower East Side institution since 1888, Katz has served salami to every president in the last 3 decades. The pastrami and reuben sandwiches are orgasmic (as Meg Ryan confirmed in *When Harry Met Sally*). Though Katz's caters to a touristy crowd and its reputation comes at a premium price, it remains the prototype of the New York delicatessen. Knishes and franks $2.50. Potato latkes $6.75. Tongue sandwich $12.50. Open M-Tu and Su 8am-10pm, W-Th 8am-11pm, F-Sa 8am-3am. ❷

Rush Hour, 134 Ludlow St. (☎212-979-9211), between Rivington and Stanton St. [S] F, J, M, Z to Delancey St./Essex St.; F, V to Lower East Side/2nd Ave. A late-night crowd cures its munchies in Rush Hour's graffiti-covered back room or takes the greasy food out to the street. Burgers ($5.25-8) are the specialty, and are served 18 different ways from "classic" to "Israeli" (sauteed veggies and herb tahini) to "Caribbean" (fresh pineapple and leafy greens). Open M-Th and Su 11am-2am, F-Sa 11am-4am. ❶

SHOPS

🛍 **The Pickle Guys,** 49 Essex St. (☎212-656-9739; www.nycpickleguys.com), between Grand and Hester St. [S] F, J, M, Z to Delancey St./Essex St. Glorious pickled onions, mushrooms, and peppers, along with standard pickled cucumbers, ranging in flavor from super-sour to super-sweet—all sold straight out of the barrel. Made under the supervision of Rabbi Shmuel Fishelis. The straight-up sour dill is a bestseller. Individual pickle $0.50, quart $5.75. Open M-Th and Su 9am-6pm, F 9am-4pm.

🛍 **Doughnut Plant,** 379 Grand St. (☎212-505-3700; www.doughnutplant.com), at Norfolk St. [S] F, J, M, Z to Delancey St./Essex St. In 1994, Mark Israel made his first batch of doughnuts from his grandfather's recipe. Israel sold the doughnuts wholesale, using the basement of a tenement building as his kitchen and his bicycle as the delivery truck. Today, the Doughnut Plant churns out flaky, handmade, and organic doughnuts ($1.50-2.50) by the hundreds to a zealously loyal clientele. New Yorkers line up early each morning for these treats and call all day to hear what's left on the shelves. Try a cake doughnut dipped in bittersweet orange glaze or a ginger doughnut made especially for Chinese New Year. Open 6:30am until supplies run out (3-7pm).

🛍 **Kossar's Bialys,** 367 Grand St. (☎212-473-4810), between Essex and Norfolk St. [S] F, J, M, Z to Delancey St. New York's best bialy emporium. What are bialys, you ask? Polish-Jewish baked rolls somewhere between an English muffin and a bagel, coming in delicious flavors like onion and garlic. $0.60 each, 13 for $7.20. Open M-Th and Su 6am-8pm, F 6am-sunset.

🛍 **Sugar Sweet Sunshine,** 126 Rivington St. (☎212-995-2960), between Essex and Norfolk St. [S] F, V to Lower East Side/2nd Ave.; F, J, M, Z to Delancey St./Essex St. Owned by a pair of former employees of the West Village's Magnolia Bakery (p. 126), Sugar Sweet serves buttercream-iced cupcakes ($1.50), layer-cakes ($4.25 per slice), and cookies ($0.50). Unlike Magnolias, Sugar Sweet Sunshine has a seating area, with throwback 50s decor. Open M-Th 8am-10pm, F 8am-11pm, Sa 10am-11pm, Su 10am-7pm.

Yonah Schimmel Knishery, 137 E Houston St. (☎212-477-2858; www.yonahschimmel.com), between Forsyth and Eldridge St. [S] F, V to Lower East Side/2nd Ave. Rabbi Schimmel opened this storefront in 1910, and 95 years later it serves unbeatable knishes in a store that has barely changed since then. The Eastern European potato-filled pastries come with a variety of additional fillings, including vegetables, fruit, and

Chef Rick Moonen Explores Manhattan's Unexpected Bounty

Televised cooking shows make professional food preparation look so simple and organized. The real professional kitchen is more hectic—but also more inspiring. As the executive chef and owner of RM restaurant in Manhattan, I have been working in the restaurant business for over 27 years. Manhattan is a treasure for the professional chef. With its tall buildings and gridlocked streets, it may not seem like the place for fresh produce and seafood. But the city has a way of providing inspiration when you least expect it.

For the past 17 years, I have run restaurants focused on seafood. I've developed a reputation in the industry for handling fish. In January of 1998, I was called on to write an article on Chilean seafood for *Wine and Spirits* magazine.

Four months after the article appeared, I received a phone call from a gentleman named Patricio Osses. He said he had read my article, and wanted to set up an appointment to show me his selections of fresh seafood from Chile. We agreed on a day and time that following week.

At the time, I was the chef and partner of a very busy, high-end seafood restaurant in midtown Manhattan. Every lunch service was bustling, and if I wasn't ready for the onslaught of business, I would have a disaster on my hands. Our lunch customers were mainly businessmen with very tight schedules. They wanted great food, and they wanted it right away. I was responsible for feeding 100 guests three courses within a 90min. window of time. Between noon and 1:30pm, I was not a person whose path you'd want to cross.

Patricio showed up in my kitchen at 11:45am with a huge smile on his face. This was not what we had planned. Lunch started in 15min. Mildly irritated, I asked him to bring some samples into my kitchen. Patricio just laughed. He said he had a full truck parked outside. On a normal day, I would have thrown him out of my kitchen. For some reason, instead, I chose to follow him up the back stairs to his white van, complaining the entire way that he was crazy to show up so close to lunch. He opened the back doors of his van, revealing a wall of Styrofoam boxes covered in airline stickers.

Patricio began carefully removing one box after another, and opened them right on the sidewalk. My patience was waning. But as he opened the boxes, my irritation turned into amazement. Each box revealed the most unusual and beautiful array of seafood I had ever seen.

Within a short period of time, the sidewalk was covered with open boxes. There were picorocos,

giant live barnacles weighing over 1 lb.each. They resembled 8 in. tall volcanoes with sharp, thorn-shaped claws moving around inside. There were small sea urchins with perfectly formed divots, and grenadier fish with huge eyes, long beards, and whip-like tails. Patricio pulled out a clear plastic bag filled with piures, or sea squirts, deep red mollusks that had been shucked from their shell.

My mind wandered all over the place. What could I possibly do with these things, and what was their traditional preparation? I ran back into the kitchen to snatch a large plastic bin. I grabbed an elephant fish, with a long snout and fins. I seized some *choros zapatos*, shoe mussels the size of my hand. I nabbed a *merluza*, or Antarctic queen, the one fish I had heard of. (The *merzula* is related to the codfish, and is a main staple in Spain.) Finally, I couldn't resist a *congrio*, or cusk eel, long and slippery with mottled pink skin. I took out my small pocket notebook, and began scribbling down names and notes on preparation. My bin was filling up quickly.

It was now 12:15. I realized that, in all of this frenzy, I was risking a disastrous lunch service. I shook Patricio's hand with my now slime-coated palm, and told him I would call him later. I lifted my overloaded bin of new fish, and headed back to the kitchen to stash my grab bag in the refrigerator for playtime later that day. My crew's curiosity was piqued. Everyone in the kitchen had their eyes fixed on that bin. I don't think Steven Spielberg could have dreamed up a more bizarre-looking array of what appeared to be mutants.

Toward the end of lunch service, someone rushed in to announce that a letter had been hand delivered to the general manager. It was a typed and signed complaint from the owner of a real-estate office a few doors from my restaurant. She was outraged at the awful display she had observed before her store front earlier that afternoon. "Your chef is trying to turn our block into his own personal fish market, and it is detrimental to the image of this fine neighborhood." I had to laugh. I knew she was probably right. To me, these white Styrofoam boxes were excitement beyond my dreams. To the Midtown pedestrian, they were obstructions filled with slimy objects with fishy odors.

In my excitement over cooking, I had forgotten the world around me. New York City is wonderful this way. In the middle of the busiest day on the busiest sidewalk, a chef can be transported, like a lover caught in a passionate embrace in the middle of a crowd.

Rick Moonen has worked as head chef at New York restaurants Oceana and RM. He is currently at work on a cookbook.

chocolate. Overnight delivery to anywhere in the continental US available. Open M-Th and Su 9am-8pm, F-Sa 9am-midnight.

Il Laboratorio del Gelato, 95 Orchard St. (☎212-343-9922; www.laboratoriodelgelato.com), between Broome and Delancey St. Ⓢ F, V to Lower East Side/2nd Ave.; F, J, M, Z to Delancey St./Essex St. A perfect stop after a visit to the Lower East Side Tenement Museum, this immaculate white gelato "lab" mainly sells wholesale, supplying some of Manhattan's best restaurants. The gelato is made in small batches from fresh ingredients, such as blueberry, mint, hazelnut, and papaya. At the tiny counter in front, you can choose from 20 rotating flavors. 2 flavors $3.25, 4 flavors $5.25. Open M and Su 10am-6pm, Tu-Sa 10am-7pm.

Economy Candy, 108 Rivington St. (☎212-254-1531), between Ludlow and Essex St. Ⓢ F, J, M, Z to Delancey St./Essex St. A 1-room candy warehouse, stocked floor-to-ceiling with imported chocolates, jams, teas, nuts, and confections at rock-bottom prices. 10 lb. bag of assorted candy $12. M&Ms $6 per lb. Giant Bart Simpson Pez dispenser $18. Open M-F and Su 9am-6pm, Sa 10am-5pm.

CAFES

▨ **Teany,** 90 Rivington St. (☎212-475-9190), between Orchard and Ludlow St. Ⓢ F, V to Lower East Side/2nd Ave.; J, M, Z or F to Delancey St./Essex St. Musician Moby and his (now former) girlfriend Kelly started Teany as a vegetarian and vegan cafe that even meat-lovers could enjoy. Since then, this cafe and tea shop has changed hands, but the formula is still a success. Breakfast breads ($3.50), oatmeal ($6), non-turkey clubs ($8), and strawberry shortcake ($5) are served in a sunny, contemporary space. The selection of teas is fantastic. Espresso drinks $2-4. Beer $5. Wine $8. Open M-Th and Su 9am-midnight and F-Sa 9am-1am. ❷

Pink Pony, 176 Ludlow St. (☎212-253-1922), between E Houston and Stanton St. Ⓢ F, J, M, Z to Delancey St./Essex St.; F, V to Lower East Side/2nd Ave. The walls may be book-lined and the waitstaff may be foreign, but this spacious cafe is as unpretentious as it gets. A lovely spot for reading the paper or chatting with friends. The menu features gourmet specialties such as escargot ($9) and goose-liver pâté ($8). Less intimidating lunch fare includes turkey and brie sandwiches ($9) and vegetable lasagna ($10). Lots of beer and wine. Open daily 10am-2am. Cash or traveler's checks only. ❷

GREENWICH VILLAGE

Restaurants in the Village are as diverse as its inhabitants, and the local artistic flair definitely shows up in the food. Most restaurants are delightfully budget-friendly, and many are one-of-a-kind. Italian restaurants cluster around the intersection of Bleecker and Carmine St. On Hudson St., you'll find a number of gourmet shops with great sandwiches. The neighborhood's many cafes are the perfect place to get started writing that screenplay you've had kicking around.

▨ **Sacred Chow,** 227 Sullivan St. (☎212-337-0863; www.sacredchow.com), between W 3rd St. and Bleecker. Ⓢ A, B, C, D, E, F, V to W 4th St./Washington Sq. This delightful vegan restaurant, with a logo depicting a meditating cow, serves creative and delicious cuisine—without any animal products, refined sugar, or white flour. Mix and match from the tapas selection (tofu in sunflower pesto, Mama's Soy Meatballs, dijon-marinated raw kale, root vegetable pancakes with Indonesian date butter; 3 for $12), or go for one of the heaping hero sandwiches ($8.50). There's a big selection of smoothies, energy drinks, and organic beer and wine. Desserts like triple chocolate brownies, nougatines, and the Sacred Sundae make guilt-free treats ($2-6). Open M-Th 11am-10pm, F-Sa 11am-11pm. ❷

👍 **Arturo's Pizza,** 106 W Houston St. (☎212-677-3820), at Thompson St. [S] 1 to Houston St. Arturo's has provided the Village with outstanding pizza and divey class for decades, and many aficionados consider it the best pizza in the city. Big cheesy pies $14-21. Entrees $12-28. Live jazz starting M-F at 5pm, Sa-Su at 6pm. Open M-Th 4pm-1am, F-Sa 4pm-2am, Su 3pm-midnight. ❸

👍 **Chez Brigitte,** 77 Greenwich Ave. (☎212-929-6736), between 7th Ave. and Bank St. [S] 1, 2, 3 to 14th St./7th Ave. This hole-in-the-wall French bistro has no pretensions and a selection friendly to even the most strapped budget. As its menu boasts, it "serves 250 people, 11 people at a time" from its counter daily. The hearty weekday lunch special ($6.45) of beef, chicken, or veal stew with rice and potatoes, sweet peas, soup or salad, and a drink is a great deal. Meat and fish sandwiches on French bread $5-7. Entrees $8-9.50. Fixed-price brunch Sa-Su 11:30am-5pm $6.45. Delivery free with $10 min. Open daily 11am-10pm. Cash only. ❷

Peanut Butter & Co., 240 Sullivan St. (☎212-677-3995; www.ilovepeanutbutter.com), at 3rd St. [S] A, B, C, D, E, F, V to W 4th St. If you find yourself craving the PB&J sandwiches you carried to middle school in a Ninja Turtles lunchbox, Peanut Butter & Co. will deliver a delightful flashback. You'll find a huge array of peanut-butter-based sandwiches, all served with potato chips and carrot sticks. Classics include the Elvis (peanut butter, bananas, and honey; $6.50, with bacon $7.50) and the Ants on a Log (celery, peanut butter, and raisins; $5). Still, you'll know you're not in middle school anymore—peanut butters are made daily from fresh-ground peanuts, and they come in gourmet flavors like cinnamon raisin and white chocolate. More adventurous sandwiches like The Heat is On (spicy peanut butter, grilled chicken, and pineapple jam; $8) are surprisingly good. Free delivery. Open M-Th and Su 11am-9pm, F-Sa 11am-10pm. ❶

Pink Tea Cup, 42 Grove St. (☎212-807-6755), between Bleecker and Bedford St. [S] A, C, E, L to 14th St./8th Ave.; 1, 2, 3 to 14th St./7th Ave. Delightful smells waft from this soul food restaurant, and they always draws crowds. Amazing pecan pancakes $6.25. Fried chicken and apple fritters $10. Salmon croquettes $12. All entrees come with soup, salad, veggies, and bread pudding or Jello. M-F lunch entrees $7. Dinner entrees $10-15. Open M-Th and Su 8am-midnight, F-Sa 8am-1am. Cash only. ❷

Soy Luck Club, 115 Greenwich Ave. (☎212-229-9191; www.soyluckclub.com), at Jane St. [S] 1, 2, 3 to 14th St./7th Ave. This comfy orange-and-white space is a cool place to hang out, and it's heaven if you like soy. There's a wide selection of grilled panini, topped with tuna, turkey, apple, or avocado, and delicious soy condiments ($8-9). The iced vanilla mint soy latte or chai soyafrost ($4-5) go well with a wheat-free entree crepe ($9). Top things off with a honey-and-apple dessert crepe ($6). Free wireless Internet. Open M-F 8:30am-9:30pm, Sa-Su 9:30am-9:30pm. ❶

Tartine, 253 W 11th St. (☎212-229-2611), at W 4th St. [S] 1, 2, 3 to 14th St./7th Ave.; 1 to Christopher St. Bring your own wine to complement a fine continental brunch, lunch, or dinner at this secluded but always-crowded bistro. Sidewalk seating when the weather's warm. Endive salad with Roquefort $8.50. Chicken pot pie $16. Open M-F 9am-4pm and 5:30-10:30pm, Sa 9am-4pm and 5:30-10:30pm, Su 9am-10pm. Strictly coffee and pastries 9-10:30am and 4-5:30pm. Cash only. ❷

Tomoe Sushi, 172 Thompson St. (☎212-777-9346), between Bleeker and Houston St. [S] A, B, C, D, E, F, V to W 4th St./Washington Sq. Young crowds happily endure long waits to enjoy some of the freshest sushi in New York. The fish is affordable and the atmosphere is plain but unpretentious. 8-piece sushi assortment $21. Open M-Tu 5-11pm, W-Sa 1-3pm and 5-11pm. ❸

Moustache, 90 Bedford St. (☎212-229-2220), between Barrow and Grove St. [S] 1 to Christopher St. Delicious Middle Eastern fare served on copper tabletops in a cute setting. Try the succulent Leg of Lambwich ($9). Lentil soup $4. Open M-Sa noon-11pm, Su noon-10:30pm. Additional location at 265 E 10th St. in the East Village. ❶

CAFES

👍 **The Grey Dog,** 33 Carmine St. (☎212-462-0041; www.thegreydog.com), between Bleecker and Bedford St. [S] A, B, C, D, E, F, V to W 4th St. Exposed brick and dark wood provide a studious ambience during the day; at night, the addition of candlelight makes it perfect for a romantic date. Dogs are everywhere, covering the walls and leaving their (painted) tracks on the tables. Salads and sandwiches with smoked turkey, brie, black forest ham, sliced apple, or roasted peppers $6-9.50. Some of the best regular coffee (large $1.75) in the city. Open M-Th 6:30am-11:30pm, F 6:30am-12:30am, Sa 7:30am-12:30am, Su 7:30am-11:30pm.

👍 **Esperanto Cafe,** 114 MacDougal St. (☎212-475-2525), between Bleecker St. and W 3rd St. [S] A, B, C, D, E, F, V to W 4th St. Village hippies, young poets, and would-be intellectuals wax philosophical here, enjoying espresso ($2.25) on the same hallowed ground as Bob Dylan once did. Mozzarella, turkey, and tuna sandwiches $5.50. Pumpkin-ginger cheesecake $4.50. Free wireless Internet. One computer with free Internet available for patrons' use. Open 24hr.

Caffe Pane e Cioccolato, 10 Waverly Pl. (☎212-473-3944), at Mercer St. [S] N, R, W to 8th St. A romantic European cafe with high ceilings and marble tables serving well-made espresso drinks. A congenial waitstaff serves a mix of breakfast items (omelets and eggs, $6.50), salads ($9-11), and pastas (fettucine al salmon $11). Opera singers grace the small stage F-Sa 9pm-1am. Open M-Th and Su noon-10pm, F-Sa noon-1am. Brunch Sa-Su noon-4pm. Cash only.

Caffe Dante, 79-81 MacDougal St. (☎212-982-5275), between W Houston and Bleecker St. [S] A, B, C, D, E, F, V to W 4th St. A Village staple, with black-and-white photos of Italy and atmospheric lighting. Heavenly homemade tiramisu ($5.75), espresso drinks ($2-6), and prosciutto sandwiches ($8). Outdoor tables are a prime people-watching locale. No laptops allowed. Open M-Th and Su 10am-2am, F-Sa 10am-3am.

SHOPS

👍 **The Magnolia Bakery,** 401 Bleecker St. (☎212-462-2572), at W 11th St. [S] 1 to Christopher St. The cupcakes at this West Village corner bakery are so famous that they're sold with a quota (1 dozen per person, $1.75 each). On the weekends, the line can be 20min. long—a small price to pay for sweet frosting and spongy cake. Brownies and cheesecakes $2-4. Open M noon-11:30pm, Tu-Th 9am-11:30pm, F 9am-12:30am, Sa 10am-12:30am, Su 10am-11:30pm.

MEATPACKING DISTRICT

The Meatpacking District is hot restaurant territory. Seemingly every big-name New York restauranteur has set up shop amid the fashionably grimy warehouses of this once-seedy neighborhood. Though you can certainly have an excellent meal here, this isn't an optimal destination for the budget-minded gourmand. Prices are high, and they're as much about the scene as they are about the food. Most spots cater to a well-dressed crowd gaming up for a big night out.

👍 **Restaurant Florent,** 69 Gansevoort St. (☎212-989-5779; www.restaurantflorent.com), between Greenwich and Washington Ave. [S] 1, 2, 3 to 14th St./7th Ave; A, C, E, L to 14th St. The board above the counter at this funky diner reads, "Go Out Your Nightlife Needs U," and the French bistro fare is sure to keep the hipsters energized. The food is good, and the prices are affordable. Goat cheese and apple plate $8. *Salade niçoise* $15. *Steak frites* $21. Wine from $6. Delivery M-F 11am-3:15pm and daily 6pm-midnight. Open 24hr. Cash only. ❸

Spice Market, 403 W 13th St. (☎212-675-2322), at 9th Ave. A, C, E, L to W 14th St./8th Ave.; 1, 2, 3 to W 14th St. A worthwhile splurge, Spice Market is the latest effort of celebrity chef Jean-Georges Vongerichten, who, despite his French roots, here pays homage to Asian street food. The enormous space is beautifully appointed with a club-like decor, and service is skilled. However low-brow the origin of the cuisine, you're in the hands of a master chef. Vongerichten's updates on Asian appetizers, like mushroom-stuffed egg rolls and chicken samosas in a cilantro yogurt sauce, may be the best part of the meal ($8-12). Entrees $15-29. Open M-F noon-3pm and 5:30pm-midnight, Sa-Su noon-4pm and 5:30pm-midnight. ❹

Pastis, 9 9th Ave. (☎212-929-4844), at 12th St. One of the original cornerstones of the Meatpacking District's rebirth, always-mobbed Pastis recreates the atmosphere of a classic Parisian *brasserie*. The owner scoured French flea markets for months looking for perfectly distressed lamps, newspaper racks, and mirrors to complete the decor, and the menu is filled with faithful renditions of French stalwarts. It's one of the best brunch spots in New York, and it's a hip scene late. Mussels and fries in a Pernod sauce $18. Pan-seared organic salmon $25. Open M-Th 9am-2am, Sa-Su 9am-2:30am. ❹

Markt, 401 W 14th St. (☎212-727-3314; www.marktrestaurant.com), at 9th Ave. S A, C, E, L to 14th St./8th Ave. An enormous space with a classy retro feel, this Belgian *brasserie* serves delicious if pricey Belgian classics. Mussels $15-16. Belgian beef stew $15. Poached salmon with lobster stoemp $19. Grilled lobster in a Hoegaarden cream sauce $32. The enormous bar is a chill place to begin a night out. Open M-Th and Su 11:30am-midnight, F-Sa 11:30am-1am. ❹

EAST VILLAGE

Dining opportunities in the East Village are as diverse as its residents—and that makes it a top culinary destination for budget travelers and gourmets alike. St. Mark's Pl. hosts a slew of inexpensive and popular Village institutions. Ave. A throbs with bars and sidewalk cafes at night. For great ethnic choices, visit the row of Indian restaurants that line E Sixth St. between First and Second Ave., the Japanese eateries on E Ninth and Stuyvesant St., between Second and Third Ave., and the Eastern European restaurants along Second Ave.

▨ **Frank,** 88 2nd Ave. (☎212-420-4900; www.frankrestaurant.com), between E 5th and 6th St. S 6 to Astor Pl. An Italian neighborhood favorite, with outdoor seating surrounded by a white picket fence and flower boxes. Inside, homey and close quarters guarantee an intimate dining experience—and often a wait. Try the roasted rosemary chicken with mashed potatoes, gravy, olives and slow-cooked tomatoes ($13), the *prosciutto di parma* sandwich ($9), or Uncle Tony's gnocchi ($11). Delivery available. Open M-Th 10:30am-4pm and 5pm-1am, F-Sa 10:30am-2am, Su 10:30am-midnight. Cash only. ❷

▨ **Zum Schneider,** 107 Ave. C at 7th St. (☎212-598-1098). S 6 to Astor Pl.; N, R, W to 8th St. Alphabet City's Bavarian beer garden—complete with wall-hugging fake trees and exposed rafters. Most importantly, there's tons of German beer to choose from. This is the place for yearly Oktoberfest celebrations and Lederhosen spottings. Try the *Wiener Schnitzel* with potato and cucumber-dill salads ($16), organic *Schweinebraten* (roast pork in beer gravy with potato dumplings and Bavarian salad; $17), *Blut-* and *Leberwurst* (blood and liver sausages; $13), or the vegetarian *Käsespätzle* (spaetzle with cheese and onions; $13). Wash it all down with some Pilsner (small $4, regular $6, large $12). A full German breakfast of cold cuts and cheeses with strawberry jam, soft boiled egg and bread basket ($9) is served Sa-Su 1-5pm. German pancakes $6. Outdoor seating when the weather's warm. Kitchen open M-Th 5-11pm, F 4-11pm, Sa-Su 1-11pm. Bar open M-Th 5pm-2am, F 4pm-4am, Sa 1pm-4am, Su 1pm-2am. Cash only. ❷

▨ **Pommes Frites,** 123 2nd Ave. (☎212-674-1234), between E 7th St. and St. Mark's Pl. S 6 to Astor Pl. This hole-in-the-wall takeout eatery does one thing—delicious Belgian fries, served in paper cones—and does it very well. Choose from over 30 gourmet sauces, including tandoori mayo and mango chutney ($0.75 each, 3 for $1.25). Great for a late-night snack. Regular fries $4, large $6.25. Open M-Th and Su 11:30am-1am, F-Sa 11:30am-3:30am. ❶

■ **Second Avenue Delicatessen,** 156 2nd Ave. (☎212-677-0606), at 10th St. Ⓢ 6 to Astor Pl. The definitive New York deli. See p. 171 for historical info. The Lebewohl family maintained this strictly kosher joint from 1954 until its closing in early 2006. While some sources maintain that it will re-open at some point in the future, there are no immediate plans for re-opening; rumor has it that a bank will soon be moving in. See p. 171 for historical info. If you can't shake your craving for a mean pastrami sandwich, we suggest heading over to Katz's Deli in the Lower East Side (p. 122).

Spice Cove, 326 E 6th St. (☎212-674-8884), between 1st and 2nd Ave. A stand-out Indian restaurant in a neighborhood that's full of them. The lunch special ($7) is a spectacular deal, and the multi-course $17 Spice Cove Dinner is a good value as well. Delicious mango lassis $3. Open M 4:30-11:30pm, Tu-Th noon-11:30pm, F-Sa noon-midnight, Su noon-11:30pm. ❸

ChikaLicious Dessert Bar, 203 E 10th St. (☎212-995-9511), at 2nd Ave. A sleek, date-worthy restaurant devoted entirely to everyone's favorite part of the meal. The multi-course $12 fixed-price menu includes an "amuse," such as yogurt sorbet in lavendar soup; a dessert "main course," like rhubarb brulée with vanilla sorbet or warm chocolate tart; and a selection of petit-fours. Well-selected wine-pairings compliment each course for an additional $7. Individual desserts Open W-Su 3-10:45pm. ❷

Veselka, 144 2nd Ave. (☎212-228-9682), at E 9th St. Ⓢ 6 to Astor Pl. When a late-night *borscht* craving gets the better of you, head straight for this Ukrainian diner, adorned inside and out with big, beautiful murals. The thick menu features soups ($3.25), salads ($8-11), *blintzes* ($7.25), and Ukrainian meatballs ($8.25). Combo specials ($9.75-11) get you soup, salad, stuffed cabbage, and 4 *pierogis* (vegetarian or meat). Breakfast is a big draw, with waffles ($5-6) and omelets ($4-5) served at all hours. Sidewalk tables are available in warm weather. Open 24hr. ❶

Cucina di Pesce, 87 E 4th St. (☎212-260-6800; www.cucinadepesce.com), between 2nd and 3rd Ave. Ⓢ 6 to Astor Pl. A pretty, classy Italian place with oil paintings, rosily lit nooks, a beautiful garden, fireplace, skylight, and sidewalk seating. The high-quality cooking comes in huge portions. Spinach penne (with asparagus, sundried tomatoes, and fontina cheese) $9. Salmon with sauteed mushrooms and pasta $13. Free mussels at the bar. Early-bird dinner special of soup, entree, and glass of wine $11 daily 2:30-6:30pm. Free delivery. Open M-Th and Su 2:30-11pm, F-Sa 2:30pm-midnight. AmEx or cash only. ❷

Blue 9 Burger, 92 3rd Ave. (☎212-979-0053), between E 12th and E 13th St. Ⓢ 6 to Astor Pl. Modeled after the California success of the famous In-N-Out Burger, Blue 9 sticks to what it does well—hamburgers, fries, and milkshakes. French fries are made from scratch from only the freshest ingredients. The "Blue 9" double cheeseburger costs just $4.50. The mango-chili sauce for the fries is holy to those who love it. Open M and Su 11am-12:30am, Tu-W 11am-1:30am, Th 11am-2am, F-Sa 11am-4pm. ❶

Cafecito, 185 Ave. C (☎212-253-9966), between 11th and 12th St. Ⓢ 6 to Astor Pl.; N, Q, R, W to 8th St. Authentic Cuban cuisine in an Old Havana setting. At dinner, dim candles and Latin music make for a romantic scene. Delightful *bocadillos* ($5-7.25) include the Cubano (smoked ham, roast pork, swiss cheese, pickles), and the Vegetariano (red beans, avocado, swiss). Entrees like breaded sirloin steak ($10.25) or mojo marinated pork ($9) come with rice and beans and a choice of plantains or *tostones*. Flan ($3.50) and *tres leches* with roasted pineapple salsa ($4.75) make great desserts. Exotic fruit juices $3.25-3.75. Beer $4. Mojitos $5. Open M-Th 11am-11pm, F 11am-midnight, Sa noon-midnight, Su noon-10pm. Cash only. ❶

Yaffa Cafe, 97 St. Mark's Pl. (☎212-677-9001), between 1st Ave. and Ave. A. Ⓢ 6 to Astor Pl. This late-night hangout is somewhere between a garden cocktail party and a Middle Eastern leisure lounge. Cowprint adorns the outside tables; framed pictures of Elvis and Mick Jagger grace the inside walls. Though menu items can't always keep pace with the flamboyant surroundings, they're good, and they seem to get better as the evening wears on. Sandwiches $7-9. Salads around $7.50. Veggie entrees $8. Super weekend brunch $9. Wine $5-7. In the summer months, the basement cafe opens onto a lovely backyard garden. Delivery available with $10 min. Open 24hr. Cash only under $20. ❶

Crif Dogs, 113 St. Marks Pl. (☎212-614-2728), between 1st Ave. and Ave. A. Ⓢ 6 to Astor Pl.; L to 1st Ave. An impressive array of hot dog variations, served under disco ball lighting. Try a Spicy Redneck dog with bacon, jalapeños, and cheese ($4). Simple Crif Dog $2. Two dogs and a soda $3.75. Hamburgers ($3.50) are also available for the dog-averse. PBR $2. Bud $3.50. According to a sign posted at the counter, prices are subject to change according to customer attitude. Free delivery with $10 min. Open M and Su noon-midnight, Tu-Th noon-2am, F-Sa noon-4am. ❶

Jules, 65 St. Mark's Pl. (☎212-477-5560), between 1st and 2nd Ave. Ⓢ 6 to Astor Pl.; L to 1st Ave. The bar of this dimly lit French bistro was shipped over from the old country. The grilled sea scallops with marinated *bacalao* and cranberry beans ragout ($21) go well with the white-wine sangria and house wine ($6). But the real attraction here is the nightly jazz: Afro-Latin, Brazilian, and ragtime grooves. Post-theater crowds make reservations a good idea on weekend nights. Brunch served Sa-Su noon-4pm. Open M-Th 11am-4pm and 5:30pm-1am, F 11am-2am, Sa 10am-2am, Su 10am-1am. Music begins 8-9pm. AmEx or cash only. ❸

Kate's Joint, 56 Ave. B (☎212-777-7059), at E 4th St. Ⓢ F, V to Lower East Side/2nd Ave. Spacious, couch-lined, and chill, Kate's Joint serves vegetarian fare like tofu teriyaki ($11), Southern-fried unchicken cutlets ($11), and the McKate ("two unbeef patties with special sauce and toppings on a whole wheat sesame seed bun"; $10). Beer $4. Wine $5-6. Vegan white russians $7. Breakfast served M-F 9am-4pm. Open M-Th 11am-11pm, F 11am-1am, Sa 10am-1am, Su 10am-11pm. Cash only under $10. ❷

Mama's Food Shop, 200 E 3rd St. (☎212-777-4425), between Ave. A and B. Ⓢ F, V to Lower East Side/2nd Ave. Home-style comfort food in a living room-like setting, with portrait-lined walls and upholstered armchairs. Enjoy fried chicken or salmon ($9) with sides like honey-glazed sweet potatoes and broccoli ($1 each). Macaroni and cheese and mashed potatoes are local favorites (each $1 for ½ pint). Vegetarian dinner $7. Bread pudding or cobbler $3. Outdoor seating in nice weather. BYOB. Open M-Sa 11am-10pm. ❷

Chickpea, 23 3rd Ave. (☎212-228-3445), between E 9th St. and St. Mark's Pl. Chickpea serves Middle Eastern fare that's a cut above what you'll find at your ordinary falafel stand. They do have falafel, and they do have *shawarma;* but where else can you find "shawafel" (falafel and *shawarma;* $5.50)? You'll also find a healthy assortment of veggie salads ($6.50-8.25). Open M-W 10am-3am, Th-F 10am-5am, Su 10am-1am. ❶

SHOPS

🔳 **Moishe's Bake Shop,** 115 2nd Ave. (☎212-505-8555), between E 6th and 7th St. Ⓢ 6 to Astor Pl. For 30 years this unassuming bake shop has served up outstanding homemade breads ($1-2 per lb.), pastries ($1-3) and cookies ($0.50-1.50). The challah ($2.75) is superb. This bakery is one of the surviving strictly kosher establishments in the city. No seating. Open M-Th and Su 7am-9pm, F 7am until 1hr. before sunset.

FOOD

■ **Veniero's,** 342 E 11th St. (☎212-674-7070; www.venierospastry.com), between 1st and 2nd Ave. Ⓢ L to 1st Ave. This Italian pastry shop, established in 1894, is a city classic. If you want a cake too pretty to eat (but too tasty to just look at) you'll find your culinary quandary here. Goodies can be bought at the counter or enjoyed in the wait-service seating area. The giant bakery cases are filled with indecision-inducing options. Cannolis $2.75. Tiramisu $4.25. Slice of black forest cake $3.75. Gelato $3-4.75. Good selection of coffee drinks. Open M-Th and Su 8am-midnight, F-Sa 8am-1am.

CAFES

■ **Mudspot,** 307 E 9th St. (☎212-228-9074), between 1st and 2nd Ave. A cool, cheery, orange-walled indie coffee shop, serving strong coffee and excellent pastries and sand-wiches. The flower-filled patio is a lovely place to hang out on a sunny day. Beer and wine available, in addition to the usual caffeinated choices. Open M-F 8am-midnight, Sa-Su 9am-midnight.

■ **Alt.Coffee,** 139 Ave. A (☎212-529-2233), at E 9th St. Ⓢ 6 to Astor Pl. In its own words, Alt.Coffee has been "serving derelicts for a decade." It's a haven for artists, anarchists, and alterna-types galore. All sorts of (non-alcoholic) drinks ($1.50-3.75), vegan cook-ies ($2.50), and dessert bars ($3). Use the Internet terminals for $10 per hr. or bring your own computer to take advantage of free wireless. Local art on walls. Lounge on comfy 70s-motif couches or upright tables and chairs. A Simpsons pinball machine awaits if you're wired on caffeine. Open M-Th 7:30am-1am, Sa-Su 9:30am-1am.

CHELSEA

Dining in Chelsea is closely tied to its nightlife. Many restaurants here morph into lounges as the night wears on. The area is also home to what is likely the city's highest concentration of 24hr. eateries—which can be life-savers (and an enter-taining scene) at 5am. You'll also find tons of excellent and fun ethnic restaurants.

■ **elmo,** 156 7th Ave. (☎212-337-8000; www.elmorestaurant.com). Ⓢ 1 to 23rd St.; 1, 2, 3 to 14th St. A fashionable crowd fills this minimalist setting for fresh takes on Amer-ican classics. Sample the gourmet macaroni and cheese ($7), fried chicken ($15), or country beef stew ($16). Cucumber and watermelon salad with fresh ricotta and a gin-ger-citron vinaigrette $8. Wine $6-9. Mixed drinks $10. Open M-Th 11am-1am, F 11am-2am, Sa 10am-2am, Su 10am-1am. ❸

■ **Cafeteria,** 119 7th Ave. (☎212-414-1717; www.cafeteriagroup.com), at 17th St. Ⓢ 1 to 18th St. A stylish, starkly white 24hr. restaurant and bar that serves delicious food to a mixed clientele. Meticulously prepared BLTs $10. Hugely popular crab burger $12. Silver dollar pancakes $7. The hefty drink menu includes lychee mojitos (from $11) and passion-fruit cosmopolitans ($10). Open 24hr. ❷

■ **Le Zie,** 172 7th Ave. (☎212-206-8686; www.lezie.com) between 20th and 21st St. Ⓢ 1 to 18th St. or 23rd St. This candlelit trattoria is a Chelsea standby. Start with the baked goat cheese with tomato sauce and garlic croutons ($6). The tuna ravioli with light tomato, tarragon broth, and crispy ginger ($14) is excellent. Don't be alarmed by the rumble you might feel beneath your table; the 1, 2, and 3 trains run directly under-neath the restaurant. Most entrees $11-15. Open daily noon-11:30pm. ❸

■ **Rosa Mexicano,** 9 E 18th St. (☎212-533-3350; www.rosamexicano.com) between 5th Ave. and Broadway. Extraordinary Mexican cuisine in a romantic setting. *Flautas de pollo* (crispy rolled chicken tacos) $7.50. *Alambre de camarones* (grilled shrimp in a garlic vinaigrette with onions, tomatoes, peppers, and Yucatan *pico de gallo*) $24. Open M-Tu 11:30am-10:30pm, W-Sa 11:30am-11:30pm, Su 11am-10pm. ❸

■ **Diner 24,** 102 8th Ave. (☎212-242-7773; www.diner24.com), at 15th St. Ⓢ 1, 2, 3, A, C, E, L to 14th/8th Ave. Diner 24 is fun—whether you're looking for a calm lunch or a second dinner at 4am to soften your hangover. Grilled cheese with tomato and bacon $8. Grilled portobello sandwich with cheddar $9. Open 24hr. ❷

■ **Chef & Co.,** 8 W 18th St. (☎646-336-1980; www.chefandco.com), between 5th Ave. and 6th St. Ⓢ N, R, W to 23rd St. Chef & Co. is a world-famous catering business, serving 30-40 events around New York daily. Leftovers go to this Chelsea store—an extraordinary budget deal with a huge selection every afternoon. You'll find a wide array of gourmet treats like couscous paella, sushi, and chopped salads—all for $10.50 per lb. Delicious cookies from $1.75. Candy-adorned cupcakes $3. The store is an ideal place to supply a picnic basket, but there are a few tables in front. Everything is half-price 3-4pm. Open M-F 11am-4pm. ❷

Kitchen/Market, 218 8th Ave. (☎212-243-4433; www.kitchenmarket.com), at 21st St. Ⓢ C, E to 23rd St./8th Ave. Primarily a gourmet Mexican food and spice shop, Kitchen/Market also offers delicious prepared food for takeout. Burrito stuffed with roasted eggplant, BLT, or barley corn salad, served with pinto beans, rice, and green salsa $8. Black bean soup $3.25. Chocolate bread pudding $3.50. Open M-F 9am-10:30pm, Sa-Su 11am-10:30pm. ❷

Pop Burger, 58-60 9th Ave. (☎212-414-8686; www.popburger.com), between 14th and 15th St. Ⓢ 1, 2, 3 to 14th St./7th Ave; A, C, E, L to 14th St. In front, a hip faux-formica counter-service setting for artery-clogging burgers (2 for $5) and milkshakes ($4.75). In back, a lounge and pool room that are cool nightspots in their own right. Counter open daily 11am-1am. Lounge open M-Tu and Su 5pm-2am, W-Sa 5pm-4am. ❶

F&B, 269 W 23rd St. (☎212-486-4441; www.gudtfood.com), between 7th and 8th Ave. Ⓢ 1 to 23rd St./7th Ave.; C, E to 23rd St./8th Ave. A concept-driven, Euro take on American street food, F&B sells an array of designer hot dogs. Options include a "Bavarian" veal-and-pork dog with sauerkraut and mustard and a "Norwegian" salmon dog with tomato and horseradish ($3.75). Plenty of vegetarian options are also available. Open M 11:30am-10pm, Tu-F 11:30am-11pm, Sa-Su noon-11pm. ❶

Better Burger, 178 8th Ave. (☎212-989-6688; www.betterburgernyc.com). Ⓢ C, E to 23rd St./8th Ave. Organic beef burgers ($6) and antibiotic- and hormone-free chicken and turkey burgers ($6). Toppings include organic or soy cheese, natural pork or veggie Canadian bacon, spicy BBQ onions, marsala mushroom, or guacamole. The guilt-free Better Fries ($2.50) are baked, not fried. Even the condiment bar features organic variations on the classics, including stone-ground mustard, Cajun ketchup, and vegan mayo. Free delivery. Open M-Th and Su 11am-midnight, F-Sa 11am-1am. ❶

Empire Diner, 210 10th Ave. (☎212-243-2736), at W 22nd St. Ⓢ C, E to 23rd St./8th Ave. Chelsea's take on the 50s classic, black-and-chrome Empire Diner attracts an eclectic crowd that keeps the people-watching interesting. $6 breakfast special of eggs, bacon, English muffin, and OJ 6-10am. Lentil burgers, BLTs, and turkey club sandwiches $7-11.50. Root beer floats $5. Microbrews $5.50-6.50. Open 24hr. ❷

Minar, 5 W 31st St. (☎212-684-2199), between 5th Ave. and Broadway. Ⓢ B, D, F, N, Q, R, V, W to Herald Sq. A long and narrow Indian restaurant serving tasty and budget-friendly Indian food. Spicy vegetable and chicken curries $5-6. Free delivery. Open daily 10:30am-7:30pm. ❶

Negril, 362 W 23rd St. (☎212-807-6411), between 8th and 9th Ave. Ⓢ C, E to 23rd St./8th Ave. Colorful decor, great Jamaican food, and a lively bar serving great coladas and martinis ($7-9). Tender and spicy jerk chicken $10. Most entrees $15-24. Open M-Th and Su noon-midnight, F-Sa noon-1am. ❸

Pad Thai Noodle Lounge, 114 8th Ave. (☎212-691-6226), between 15th and 16th St. Ⓢ A, C, E, L to 14th St./8th Ave. A plush restaurant with fuchsia chairs, a neon-pink-lit bar, and great pad Thai (lunch $7, dinner $9). Open daily noon-11pm. ❷

F
O
O
D

SHOPS

■ **Little Pie Co.**, 407 W 14th St. (☎212-414-2324; www.littlepiecompany.com), between 9th and 10th Ave. Ⓢ A, C, E, L to 14th St./8th Ave. A New York favorite for fresh-baked pie. Sour cream apple walnut with crumble topping and a buttery crust is the house specialty. Pies come in 5, 8, and 10 in. sizes; grab a 5 in. ($6) at the red diner-style counter. Open M-F 9am-7pm, Sa 10am-7pm, Su 11am-6pm.

■ **Garden of Eden Gourmet Marketplace**, 162 W 23rd St. (☎212-675-6300; www.edengourmet.com), between Ave. of the Americas (6th Ave.) and 7th Ave. Ⓢ 1, F, V, N, R, 6 to 23rd St. A grocery store, Chelsea-style, Garden of Eden has bountiful baskets hanging from the ceilings, dozens of gourmet meats, cheeses, and other ingredients (23 kinds of olives, anyone?), and zero fluorescent lighting. There are pre-packaged salads to go, or you can make your own ($5-8). Open M-Sa 7am-10pm, Su 7am-9:30pm.

UNION SQUARE, THE FLATIRON DISTRICT, AND MURRAY HILL

Pakistani and Indian restaurants cluster on Lexington and Third Ave. in the upper 20s and lower 30s; the area is jocularly known as **Curry Hill**. Trendy upscale restaurants cluster around Union Sq. and Park Ave. S. The open space at Union Square's north end hosts the ■**Union Square Greenmarket** (open M, W, F-Sa 6am-8pm), where dozens of small businesses and farms bring fresh-baked goods and produce to the area. Products vary with the season, but you can almost always expect to find slabs of focaccia, homemade jams, and a wide selection of organic fruit.

■ **Zen Palate**, 34 Union Sq. E (☎212-614-9291; www.zenpalate.com), at E 16th St. Ⓢ 4, 5, 6, L, N, Q, R, W to 14th St./Union Sq. This casual but tranquil restaurant serves some of the best vegetarian cooking in the city. The 1st floor cafe and noodle bar offers a bustling and informal setting for an affordable lunch or dinner. Delicious entrees come with 2 sides; try the taro spring rolls and the red and brown rice. Battered soy protein in sweet-and-sour sauce on a bed of steamed broccoli $8.75. *Moo shu*, Mexican style $9.25. Mini veggie-loaf (tofu, chestnut, and cilantro croquettes over spaghetti in a tomato sauce) $9. The upstairs dining room serves similar food in a more elegant setting; entrees $14-18. Free delivery with a $10 min. Downstairs open M-Sa 11am-10:45pm, Su noon-10:30pm. Upstairs open M-Sa 11:30am-3:30pm and 5:30-10:30pm, Su 5:30-10:30pm. Reservations recommended upstairs. Additional locations: 2170 Broadway between 76th and 77th St., near Lincoln Center; and 663 9th Ave., at 46th St. in the Theater District. ❷

■ **Shake Shack**, at the southeast corner of Madison Sq. Park (☎212-889-6600; www.shakeshacknyc.com). Ⓢ N, R, 6 to 23rd St. A good, old-fashioned burger-and-shake stand beneath the leafy trees of Madison Sq. Park. Burgers are spiced and cooked to perfection; the frozen custards, which come in always-changing flavors like fig, chocolate spice, and peanut butter chocolate chip, are to-die-for. The Shake Shack draws huge crowds, and they come for a reason. Shack burger with lettuce, tomato, and Shack Sauce $4.50. French fries $2. Open in summer daily 11am-11pm. ❶

■ **Kitchen 22**, 36 E 22nd St. (☎212-228-4399; www.charliepalmer.com), between Broadway and Park Ave. S. Ⓢ 6, N, R, W to 23rd St. This classy American bistro serves delicious gourmet cuisine at surprisingly affordable prices. The fixed-price 3-course dinner is an excellent value at $29. Starters include lox and cream cheese, heirloom tomato carpaccio, and watermelon salad. Entrees include chicken and grits and grilled bluefish. M $5 margaritas. Tu 2-for-1 drinks. W bottles of wine $10. Open M-Th 5-10:30pm, F-Sa 5-11pm. ❹

👍 **Bread Bar at Tabla,** 11 Madison Ave. (☎212-889-0667; www.tablany.com), at 25th St. [S] 6 to 23rd St. The affordable downstairs patio of its expensive brother, Tabla, this Indian-fusion restaurant offers creative and delicious cuisine. Feast on a few small plates for the best variety. Rosemary *naan* ($4), *saag paneer* pizza ($13), and *bhoondi raita* (crispy chickpeas in cumin-yogurt sauce; $6) are all excellent. The most popular entree is the chicken tikka ($18), which combines organic chicken marinated in curry leaf, ginger, and chilies with a fantastic mango chutney. If there's a wait for a table, check out the unique mixed drinks–the Tamarind Margarita ($12) is made with Sauza, Cointreau, tamarind, fresh lime, and orange. Or, head upstairs for Tabla's fixed-price 3-course lunch, a great value at $25-32. Bread Bar open M-Sa noon-11pm, Su 5:30-10:30pm. Tabla open M-F noon-2pm and 5:30-10:30pm, Sa 5:30-10:30pm, Su 5:30-10pm. ❹

Republic, 37 Union Sq. W (☎212-627-7172), between 16th and 17th St. Huge, youthful crowds come to this crisp modern space for dirt-cheap noodle dishes, cooked in a wide variety of Asian styles. Nothing on the menu costs more than $9. Grilled Japanese eggplant $5. Curried duck noodles $7. Open M-W and Su 10:30am-10:30pm, Th-Sa 11:30am-11:30pm. ❶

Artisanal Fromagerie and Bistro, 2 Park Ave. (☎212-725-8585), at 32nd St. Push open the door of this cavernous French bistro, and the smell of cheese might just knock you over. The standard bistro fare (fish soup $9.50; tuna niçoise $19.50; organic trout $25.50) is good, but the standout here is handcrafted cheese, in all its stinky variety. Fondue pot $23; serves 1-3. Assorted meat and cheese plate $35; serves 1-3. Cheeses can be paired with over 160 wines by the glass, and there's also a retail counter selling cheese to take home. Open M-Th 11:45am-11pm, F 11:45am-midnight, Sa 11am-midnight, Su 11am-10pm. ❸

Blue Smoke Barbecue, 116 E 27th St. (☎212-447-7733; www.bluesmoke.com), between Park Ave. S and Lexington Ave. A stand-out barbecue joint with a jazz club beneath it. Come for the mouth-watering hush puppies with jalapeno marmalade ($3.50), pulled-pork sandwiches ($10.50), and barbecued ribs (half-slab $16); stay for the great music in Jazz Standards downstairs (sets daily 7:30, 9:30pm; F-Sa additional set 11:30pm). Restaurant open M 11:30am-10pm, Tu-Th 11:30am-11pm, F 11:30am-1am, Sa noon-1am, Su noon-10pm. ❸

Chat 'n' Chew, 10 E 16th St. (☎212-243-1616; www.chatnchewnyc.com), between 5th Ave. and Union Sq. W. [S] 4, 5, 6, L, N, Q, R, W to 14th St./Union Sq. Real American homestyle cooking in a funky 50s-style diner. The friendly staff serves crowds of families and young people. Heaping portions of macaroni and cheese $8. Classic grilled cheese with tomato $7. Too full to chew? Specialty drinks like Mama May's Sangria Margarita and the Sassy Sour (both $7) make great Booze 'n' Chew options. Delicious milkshakes $5. Free delivery with $12 min. Open M-F 11am-midnight, Sa 10am-midnight, Su 10am-11pm. ❷

Pipa, 38 E 19th St. (☎212-677-2233), between Park and 5th Ave. [S] 6 to 23rd St.; 4, 5, 6, L, N, Q, R, W to 14th St./Union Sq. Excellent Spanish tapas served on rustic wooden tables beneath lavish chandeliers–most of which are for sale at the adjacent ABC Carpet and Home. Latin music complements the bustling and romantic atmosphere. Great *piquillos* (peppers stuffed with crab and shrimp; $12), mini *chorizo* ($9), and calamari ($12). Pitcher of red or white sangria $32. Brunch specials Sa-Su include banana French toast ($8) and *churros con chocolate* ($8). Open M-Th noon-3pm and 5:30-11pm, F noon-3pm and 5:30pm-midnight, Sa 10am-3pm and 5:30pm-midnight, Su 10am-3pm and 5:30-11pm. ❹

Rainbow Falafel and Shawarma, 26 E 17th St. (☎212-691-8641), at Union Sq. W. [S] 4, 5, 6, L, N, Q, R, W to 14th St./Union Sq. This no-nonsense falafel stand does a franticly busy business at lunch hour. There's room for only 4 customers and 3 employees inside at a time; plan on taking your food to go. Falafel sandwiches $3.50. Platters $7.50. Hummus and *baba ghanoush* sandwiches $3.75. Spinach and meat pies $2-3. Open M-Sa 11am-6pm. ❶

Sushi Samba, 245 Park Ave. S (☎212-475-9377; www.sushisamba.com), between 19th and 20th St. Ⓢ 6, N, R, W to 23rd St. This stylish sushi restaurant is worth a splurge. Innovative takes on traditional rolls include the Inca (Japanese squash, shiitake mushroom, burdock, red *shiso* rice, and crispy tofu skin; $9.50) and the Yamato (tuna sushi with *foie gras*, osetra caviar, and gold leaf; $19). Sashimi ceviche ($11-16) includes salmon, lobster, heart of palm, and pineapple. Bottles of sake from $23. Sushi lunch combos $20, lunch bento boxes $13-15. Open M-W 11:45am-1am, Th-Sa 11:45am-2am, Su 1pm-midnight. Additional location at 87 7th Ave. (☎212-691-7885). Open M-W 11:45am-1am, Th-Sa 11:45am-2am, Su 12:15pm-midnight. ❹

CAFES AND SHOPS

Sunburst Espresso Bar, 206 3rd Ave. (☎212-674-1702), at 18th St. Ⓢ 6 to 23rd St. This corner coffee shop has free wireless and an ambitious menu. It's a good place to work or study while munching on paninis ($6-6.50), wraps ($6.50), and pasta dishes (most $8 with soup or salad). H&H bagels with cream cheese $1.25. Low-fat muffins $1.75. Also serves beer and smoothies. Open M-Th 7am-11pm, F-Sa 7am-midnight, Su 8am-11pm.

The City Bakery, 3 W 18th St. (☎212-366-1414), between 5th and 6th Ave. Ⓢ N, R, W to 23rd St. This American deli serves gourmet prepared food to a well-heeled crowd. The baked goods are nearly perfect; pretzel croissants, cheese Danishes, and chocolate tarts sell like hotcakes. But buffet-style salads and entrees make this more than a dessert shop. On the weekends, it's worth battling the crowds for brunch dishes like cornbread pudding ($10 per lb.), baked salmon, organic chicken, caesar salad, and gazpacho (all $12 per lb.) Signature homemade marshmallows come floating in steaming hot chocolate that's nearly as thick as soup ($4). Two floors of seating. Open M-F 7:30am-7pm, Sa 7:30am-6:30pm, Su 9am-6pm.

MIDTOWN WEST

The super-sized chain restaurants in Times Square cater mostly to tourists. Neighboring Hell's Kitchen is a different destination entirely, and its many quirky and affordable restaurants, lining Ninth Ave., between 42nd and 52nd St., are great pre-Broadway destinations. If you're willing to spend more, try a meal on posh Restaurant Row, along 46th St., between Eighth and Ninth Ave. The block caters to a pre-theater crowd; arriving after 8pm will make it easier to get a table. (Ⓢ 1, 2, 3, 7, N, Q, R, S, W to 42nd St./Times Sq.; A, C, E to 42nd St./Port Authority.)

▧ **Empanada Mama,** 763 9th Ave. (☎212-698-9008), between 51st and 52nd St. *Empanadas* are an artery-clogging Latin American speciality—some combination of meat, cheese, and vegetables wrapped in dough and fried. Empanada Mama, a narrow, always-jammed Hell's Kitchen find, offers over 40 variations, from the Pizza (mozzarella and cheese; $2), to the Viagra (crab meat, scallops, and shrimp; $3). Don't miss the dessert *empanadas*, like the Elvis (peanut butter and bananas; $2). Beer, wine, and sangria $4.25. Open daily 10am-midnight. ❶

▧ **Say Cheese!,** 649 9th Ave. (☎212-265-8840), between 45th and 46th St. This cute Hell's Kitchen soup-and-sandwich joint looks like a funky Kindergarten cafeteria and smells like home. It specializes in all permutations of grilled-cheese sandwiches ($4.25-7.50). If you're feeling low, try Mama's Special, a bowl of rich tomato soup with grilled cheese on sourdough ($6.50). Open M-F noon-9pm, Sa-Su 10am-9pm. ❶

■ **Becco,** 355 W 46th St. (☎212-397-7597; www.becconyc.com), between 8th and 9th Ave. This Restaurant Row standby serves huge portions of Italian food and offers 70 wines priced at $25 per bottle. The $17 fixed-price lunch (dinner $22) gets you a gourmet antipasto platter or caesar salad and unlimited servings of the 3 pastas of the day. Food minimum lunch $14, dinner $18. Try the mesclun salad with Tuscan beans and ripe tomatoes, tossed with an aged Chianti vinaigrette ($8). Reservations strongly recommended. Open daily noon-3pm and 5pm-midnight. ❹

Sapporo, 152 W 49th St. (☎212-869-8972), between 6th and 7th Ave. Ⓢ B, D, F, V to 47th-50th St./Rockefeller Ctr. Serving big portions of Japanese food in an unassuming setting, Sapporo is popular with Broadway cast members. Most dishes ($7-9) come with miso soup. Try the pan-fried noodles with diced pork ($7), and don't miss the Japanese dumplings ($4.25). Open M-Sa 11am-11pm, Su 11am-10pm. Cash only. ❷

Island Burgers and Shakes, 766 9th Ave. (☎212-307-7934), between 51st and 52nd St. Island offers more than 50 kinds of burgers ($5-8) on the menu, and they serve more than 150 lb. of hamburger meat a day. Try the Hippo Burger ($8), served with curried sour cream, bacon, cheddar, onion, scallions, and guacamole in a pita. They don't serve fries, but the black-and-white milkshakes are to-die-for. Open M-Th and Su noon-10:30pm, F noon-11pm. Cash only. ❷

Hourglass Tavern, 373 W 46th St. (☎212-265-2060), between 8th and 9th Ave. A dark, crowded, 3-floor restaurant serving good if unadventurous cuisine. Servers flip an hourglass at your table when you sit down, and the 59min. time limit is strictly enforced when crowds are waiting. You'll get to the theater on time. Changing entrees ($14-22) usually include fresh fish and filet mignon, plus seasonal veggies and a great selection of homemade soups. Fixed-price dinner $18, with appetizer, soup or salad, bread, entree, dessert, and coffee. Open daily 3:30pm-midnight. ❸

MIDTOWN EAST

In Midtown, cash is king. Here, corporate executives wine and dine their clients, and socialite shoppers drop as much money on lunches as on their Fendi totes. Budget travelers, however, needn't despair; there are plenty of delis and cafes catering to those impoverished junior execs.

■ **Chola,** 232 E 58th St. (☎212-688-4619), between 2nd and 3rd Ave. Ⓢ 4, 5, 6, N, R, W to Lexington/59th St. In a neighborhood of good Indian restaurants, elegant Chola is a standout. Its menu emphasizes recipes from Calcutta's Jewish community. Signature dishes include chicken *korma* ($18) and *chingri malai* (spiced shrimp with raisins, ginger, and fennel-infused tomato-coconut sauce; $22). Wonderful appetizers include vegetable fritters ($6) and some of the best *dosas* ($9) around. The $14 buffet lunch, served daily, is an incredible value. Open M-Th and Su noon-3pm and 5-10:30pm, F-Sa noon-3pm and 5-11pm. ❸

Wolf and Lamb, 10 E 48th St. (☎212-317-1950) between 5th and Madison Ave. Ⓢ E, V, 6 to 51st St. Whether you keep Kosher or you just like traditional Jewish cuisine, Wolf and Lamb is sure to satisfy your hunger. They have a large selection of affordable sandwiches (hot corn beef $11; Serious Schnitzel $14), but the house specialty is steak (8 oz. ribeye $22, Jack Daniel's whiskey steak $24). Appetizers here are especially good. Meat knisches $5.50. Chicken soup with matzah ball $6. Open M-Th 11:30am-10pm, F 11:30am-2:30pm. ❸

Ess-a-Bagel, 831 3rd Ave. (☎212-980-1010; www.ess-a-bagel.com), between 50th and 51st St. Ⓢ 6 to 51st St.; E, V to 5th Ave./53rd St. Bagels here are hand rolled and baked on the premises each morning. Sandwiches are fat, stuffed with flavored cream cheeses, cold cuts, or smoked fish ($4-10.45). A number of low-carb options are avaialble. Open M-F 6am-9pm, Sa-Su 8am-5pm. ❶

Fresco by Scotto, 34 E 52nd St. (☎212-935-3434; www.frescobyscotto.com), between Park and Madison Ave. [S] 6 to 51st St.; E, V to 5th Ave./53rd St. A beautiful restaurant serving Italian staples in an intimate atmosphere. Pizza margarita $20. Homemade ravioli $24. Grilled lamb chops $40. Next door, **Fresco by Scotto on the Go** serves good sandwiches ($6.50-12) to go. Restaurant open M-F 11am-3pm and 5:30-11pm, Sa 5-11pm. Sandwich shop open M-F 6:30am-6pm. ❷

Mangia, 16 E 48th St. (☎212-754-7600; www.mangiatogo.com), between Madison and 5th Ave. [S] E, V, 6 to 51st St. An upscale prepared-food chain with hearty sandwiches ($3.50-12). Try the gruyère and wood-smoked ham panini ($4) or the fresh mozzarella and oven-dried tomato sandwich on rosemary ciabatta ($6.75). Pretty cakes, pies, and candy tidbits. Fresh-pressed cantaloupe, red grape, and lime juice $2.85 for 10 oz., $3.85 for 12 oz. Shop open M-F 7am-7pm. Restaurant open M-F 11:30am-4pm. ❶

SHOPS

👍 **Teuscher Chocolatier,** 620 5th Ave. (☎212-246-4416; www.teuscherchocolate.com), on the promenade at Rockefeller Center. [S] B, D, F, V to 47th-50th St./Rockefeller Center. This chocoholic's paradise features chocolates flown in from Zurich weekly. Marvelous champagne truffles $66 per lb. Open M-Sa 10am-6pm.

UPPER EAST SIDE

On Madison Ave., designer boutiques neighbor equally expensive cafes, which can hurt your wallet almost as much as a pair of Manolos. If you want a cheap(er) bite to eat, move east of Madison, and you'll find plenty of great places along Lexington, Third, and Second Avenues.

👍 **Barking Dog Luncheonette,** 1678 3rd Ave. (☎212-831-1800), at 94th St. [S] 6 to 96th St. A haven for Upper East Siders and their 4-legged friends (who are permitted to eat on the patio), the Barking Dog is known for its tasty American comfort food, served in a homey, dog-festooned setting. Try the buttermilk-battered half chicken ($13), which comes with mashed potatoes, gravy, and homemade biscuits. Daily sunset specials (M-F 5-7pm; $13-17) include soup or salad and dessert. There's also an appealing selection of lighter dinner options; try the pan-seared crabcake with corn relish ($10). Sandwiches $6-8. Takeout and delivery available. Open daily 8am-11pm. Also at York Ave. and 77th St. (☎212-861-3600). Cash only. ❷

👍 **Mon Petit Café,** 801 Lexington Ave. (☎212-355-2233) at 62nd St. [S] N, R, W, 4, 5, 6 to 59th St., F to Lexington Ave./63rd St. This welcoming and unpretentious Parisian-style bistro is the perfect place to relax after a day of shopping. While dinner entrees ($16.50-20) aren't cheap, breakfast and lunch here make a delicious value. Omelettes $7.25-11. Escargot $8. *Croque monsieur* $10.75. Salmon and spinach crêpe $12.50. *Steak frites* $18.75. *Fondant au chocolat* $9. Some nights feature live music. Open M-Sa 8am-11pm, Su 11am-6pm. ❸

👍 **Candle Cafe,** 1307 3rd Ave. (☎212-472-0970; www.candlecafe.com), at 75th St. [S] 6 to 77th St. This vegetarian and vegan heaven serves fresh, creative, and delicious cuisine. Try the caesar salad with tempeh bacon and herbed croutons ($13), or the seasonal vegetable lasagna with artichoke pasta, tempeh ragout, and spinach-herb tofu ricotta ($16). Specialty drinks like the Carrot Apple Snap with fresh ginger ($4) or the Green Goddess with mixed greens, apple, lemon, and ginger ($4) are a refreshing change of pace. Open M-Sa 11:30am-10:30pm, Su 11:30am-9:30pm. ❸

👍 **Le Pain Quotidien,** 1131 Madison Ave. (☎212-327-4900), between 84th and 85th St. [S] 4, 5, 6 to 86th St. This boutique bakery chain from Belgium makes some of New York's best bread. Sit at the famous communal tables and enjoy soup, salad, sandwiches, and pastries. The environment is hip, but the prices are affordable. Open M-F 7:30am-7pm, Sa-Su 8am-7pm. ❷

EJ's Luncheonette, 1271 3rd Ave. (☎212-472-0600), at 73rd St. Ⓢ 6 to 68th, 77th St. Be prepared to wait for a seat during peak hours at this classic 50s diner, which serves scrumptious all-day breakfast, ice cream, and lunch. The black-and-white malt ($4.75) is a crowd-pleaser. Fluffy buttermilk or multigrain pancakes $6.60. Burgers from $8. Open M-Sa 8am-11pm, Su 8am-10:30pm. Other locations: 447 Amsterdam Ave. (☎212-873-3444), between 81st and 82nd St.; 432 6th Ave. (☎212-473-5555), between 9th and 10th St. Cash only. ❷

Il Vagabondo, 351 E 62nd St. (☎212-832-9221; www.ilvagabondo.com), between 1st and 2nd Ave. Ⓢ N, R, W, 4, 5, 6 to 59th St. This classy old-school Italian restaurant, complete with an indoor bocce court and mafia photographs on the walls, has been an East Side staple since 1971. You won't find many tourists here, but the regulars have been coming for decades. Come dressed in something nicer than jeans. Baked stuffed mushrooms $7.50. Veal scallopine $18.75. Entrees $17-29. Open M-F noon-3pm and 5:30-11:30pm, Sa 5:30-11:30pm, Su 5:30-11pm. ❹

Brother Jimmy's BBQ, 1485 2nd Ave. (☎212-545-7427; www.brotherjimmys.com), between 77th and 78th St. Ⓢ 6 to 77th St. This greasy-chops South Carolina kitchen serves barbecue and boozy drinks to rowdy crowds. It may seem strange that a Southern-themed bar with a rustic interior and idiosyncratic menu items ("frickles," for example, are fried pickles) is popular in New York City, but it's hard to resist Brother Jimmy's friendly communal atmosphere. The house concoctions, like Charlotte Tea (made with 5 kinds of alcohol; $8) are for serious drinkers only. On "white trash Wednesdays," southerners with ID get 25% off. Fried green tomatoes $6.75. All-you-can-eat-ribs $23. Delivery available. Open M-Th and Su noon-midnight, F-Sa noon-1am. Bar open M-Sa until 4am, Su until 1am. Also at 1644 3rd Ave. (☎212-426-2020) and at 92nd St. and 428 Amsterdam Ave. (☎212-501-7515), between 80th and 81st St. ❷

Jackson Hole, 232 E 64th St. (☎212-371-7187; www.jacksonholeburgers.com), between 2nd and 3rd Ave. Ⓢ 6 to 68th St. Stop by at either of the East Side locations after 3pm, and prepare to face hordes of kids munching on the famous 7 oz. burgers and fries. Open since 1972, Jackson Hole is a local favorite. Burger platters $8-15. Chicken sandwiches from $5.55. Salads from $5. Burritos and quesadillas from $8. Open M-Th 10:30am-1am, F-Sa 10:30am-1:30am, Su 10:30am-midnight. Other locations: 91st St. and Madison Ave. (☎212-427-2820); 85th St. and Columbus Ave. (☎212-362-5177); 70th St. and Astoria Blvd. (☎718-204-7070). ❷

Shanghai Pavilion, 1378 3rd Ave. (☎212-585-3388), between 78th and 79th St. Ⓢ 6 to 77th St. Chinese cooking meets Upper East Side sensibilities at this beautifully decorated restaurant, noted for its fresh ingredients, great seafood, and phenomenal appetizers. Tender crab and juicy pork dumplings $7. Crispy baby chicken glazed with brown spicy sauce $18. Lunch special $7 M-F until 4pm. Open M-F 11:30am-11pm, Sa-Su noon-11pm. ❷

Vermicelli, 1492 2nd Ave. (☎212-288-8868; www.vermicellirestaurant.com), between 77th and 78th St. Ⓢ 6 to 77th St. A pleasant Vietnamese restaurant with open-air seating. The $6 box lunches, served with vegetables, soup, salad, and steamed rice, are a popular eat-on-the-go option. Spring rolls with warm vermicelli, coriander, and roasted peanuts from $6. Spicy lemongrass chicken with peppers $12. Open daily 11:30am-10:30pm. ❷

CAFES

▨ **Serendipity 3,** 225 E 60th St. (☎212-838-3531; www.serendipity3.com), between 2nd and 3rd Ave. Ⓢ 4, 5, 6 to 59th St. This "restaurant and general store" has been satisfying New York's sweet tooth for more than 50 years. As the invariable lines out the door

FOOD

attest, this isn't some off-the-beaten-path find—everybody from Oprah to John Travolta to Rudy Guiliani has been spotted here. The "Frrrozen Hot Chocolate" ($7.50) is the stupendously rich cornerstone on which Serendipity's reputation has been built. Pies $6.50. Outrageous banana split $18.50. Open M-Th and Su 11:30am-midnight, F 11:30am-1am, Sa 11:30am-2am.

🄳 **DT.UT,** 1626 2nd Ave. (☎212-327-1327; www.dtut.com), between 84th and 85th St. Ⓢ 4, 5, 6 to 86th St. By day, this laid-back coffee shop looks just like Central Perk—though, in contrast, it serves great food to crowds of 20-somethings, and it offers free wireless. After 5pm, the lights go down, the music goes up, and the place morphs into a chill singles lounge with low couches, heavy curtains, mismatched coffee tables, and amazing desserts ($1.75-5). Try the make-your-own s'mores (serves 2; $11) or the brick-sized rice crispie bars ($3.75). Tu night live music. W open-mic night. Open M-Th and Su 8am-midnight, F-Sa 8am-2am.

Payard, 1032 Lexington Ave. (☎212-717-5252; www.payard.com), between 73rd and 74th St. Ⓢ 6 to 77th St. Catering to a crowd of socialite regulars, this French bakery-cafe serves up deliciously decadent desserts in an elegant setting. To-die-for fruit tarts from $5. Gourmet sandwiches and savory tarts from $13. Larger entrees are also available; try the sauteed soft-shell crab with oakwood Shiitake, baby bok choy, pickled ginger, and ginger scallion dressing $15. Open M-Th noon-3pm and 5:45-10:30pm, F-Sa noon-3pm and 5:45-11pm.

SHOPS

🄳 **Dylan's Candy Bar,** 1011 3rd Ave. (☎646-735-0078; www.dylanscandybar.com), at 60th St. Ⓢ 4, 5, 6 to 59th St. This giant, 2-story, out-of-control candy extravaganza—the brainchild of Ralph's daughter Dylan Lauren—is a must-see sight, if only as a monument to excess. Candy is everywhere—inlaid in the tables and stairs, infused into shampoos and lip gels, hidden in a secret compartment in special Dylan's flip-flops. You can buy every imaginable kind of candy for around $10 per pound. Dylan's also serves ice cream and some 20 varieties of hot chocolate. This being the Upper East Side, children can even hire their own personal candy shopper if they so desire. Open M-Th 10am-9pm, F-Sa 10am-11pm, Su 11am-8pm.

🄳 **La Maison du Chocolat,** 1018 Madison Ave. (☎212-744-7117; www.lamaisonduchocolat.com), between 78th and 79th St. Ⓢ 6 to 77th St. A library-like hush enshrouds this sanctuary of rich and elegant chocolate creations, where clerks in designer chocolate-brown dresses patiently wait for customers to stop salivating long enough to order. The chocolate ice cream ($3.50 per scoop) elicits moans from everyone who tastes it. Open M-F 9:30am-7pm, Sa 10am-7pm, Su noon-6pm.

Grace's Marketplace, 1237 3rd Ave. (☎212-737-0600; www.gracesmarketplace.com), at 71st St. Ⓢ 6 to 68th St. This high-end grocery store stocks fresh, imported, gourmet goodies with hefty price tags. The deli makes delicious prepared food to go. Open M-Sa 7am-8:30pm, Su 8am-7pm.

UPPER WEST SIDE

Though not known for culinary innovation, the Upper West Side is home to a diverse range of restaurants: trendy brunch spots, ethnic outposts of every stripe, 24hr. greasy spoons, and quaint cafes. The Upper West Side is also an especially great place to furnish a picnic lunch. Browse its gourmet grocery stores, old-fashioned delis, and mouth-watering bakeries, and then head straight for Riverside or Central Park, where you're sure to find a beautiful spot to eat and relax.

🄳 **Good Enough to Eat,** 483 Amsterdam Ave. (☎212-496-0163; www.goodenoughtoeat.com), between 83rd and 84th St. Ⓢ 1 to 86th St. Vermont cabin-style decor, complete with miniature white picket fences, quilts, and mismatched cow-motif dishware, is the perfect match for the homey American cuisine at this Upper West Side gem. Try the traditional turkey dinner ($17.50) or the macaroni and cheese ($11). Brunch is a mob scene, but it's worth the wait. All desserts, ice creams, and breads are made on-site. Full bar. Open M-Th 8am-4pm and 5:30-10:30pm, F 8am-4pm and 5:30-11pm, Sa 9am-4pm and 5:30-11pm, Su 9am-4pm and 5:30-10:30pm. Breakfast available M-F 8am-4pm, Sa-Su 9am-4pm. Free delivery. ❷

■ **Barney Greengrass,** 541 Amsterdam Ave. (☎212-724-4707; www.barneygreengrass.com), between 86th and 87th St. Ⓢ 1 to 86th St. This classic family-run deli, in business since 1908, proclaims itself the "Sturgeon King" of New York. Weekend crowds flock for home-made matzo ball soup ($4), lox scrambled with eggs and onions ($12), and pastrami sandwiches ($8). Open Tu-Su 8am-6pm. Cash only. ❷

■ **Big Nick's Burger and Pizza Joint,** 2175 Broadway (☎212-362-9238; www.bignicksnyc.com), at 77th St. Ⓢ 1 to 79th St. This vintage dive has satisfied West Siders' comfort-food cravings for more than 40 years. Its reputation rivals its 27-page menu in size. Burgers and pizza rule the day, but you can also get all-day breakfast, or vegan and vegetarian options. If you're craving something, it's probably on the menu, and it probably comes with waffle fries. Wrestle with a plate-sized burger ($5-7.50), a homestyle Italian dinner ($9-15), or crispy sweet-potato fries ($2.75). Open 24hr. Cash only. Second location 70 W 71st St. (☎212-799-4444), at Columbus Ave. ❷

■ **Alouette,** 2588 Broadway (☎212-222-6808; www.alouettenyc.com), between 97th and 98th St. Ⓢ 1, 2, 3 to 96th St. This cozy French bistro is a favorite of neighborhood couples and Columbia students. The atmosphere is romantic without being pretentious, many of the waitstaff are French, and the food is delicious and reasonably priced. The 3-course fixed-price dinner, available M-Th and Su 5:30-7pm and F-Sa 5:30-6:30pm, is an amazing deal ($24). Succulent sirloin steak with *pommes frites* and pepper sauce $22. Open M-Sa 5:30-11pm, Su 11am-3pm and 5:30-10pm. ❹

Josie's Restaurant and Juice Bar, 300 Amsterdam Ave. (☎212-769-1212; www.josiesnyc.com), at 74th St. Ⓢ 1, 2, 3 to 72nd St. Josie's serves healthy, mostly organic food emphasizing whole grains, free-range chicken, and hand-raised fish in a feng shui sort of setting. Try the ginger-grilled calamari ($8 lunch; $10 dinner) as an appetizer, or go for the yellowfin tuna wasabi burger ($17 lunch; $19 dinner). Calorie counters will love the air-baked Belgian fries and "un-fried" rice. Full

LUNCH AT NOUGATINE

Four-star dining in New York has never been an inexpensive venture. It's easy to drop $60 on a mediocre meal, and tabs in the upper echelons of the gourmet world can easily exceed $200 per person. Budget-minded gourmets have long known that to stretch their dollars farthest, it pays to visit fine restaurants for lunch, rather than dinner.

Nougatine—the casual fine dining cafe operated by celebrity chef Jean-Georges Vongerichten next to his four-star Jean-Georges flagship in the Trump International Tower—offers a gourmet lunchtime deal that's a cut above the rest. Nougatine shares Jean-Georges's kitchen, and especially at lunchtime, their menus are much alike. The restaurant showcases Vongerichten's genius for unexpected flavor combinations and provides attentive service and a beautiful setting. Best of all, the price is a steal—a mere $24 for three courses.

A recent lunch at Nougatine began with a cold asparagus soup assembled tableside from potatoes and vegetables, creatively chosen spices, and asparagus broth. The main course featured a succulently moist chicken breast, Asian noodles, and red cabbage. Dessert, however, was the standout—fresh mango sorbet interlaced with rich dark chocolate.

(☎ 212-299-3900; www.jeangeorges.com. $24 fixed-price lunch served M-Sa noon-3pm.)

bar. Takeout and delivery available. Open M-Th noon-11pm, F noon-midnight, Sa 11am-midnight, Su 10:30am-10:30pm. Second location at 565 3rd Ave. ❸

Mama Mexico, 2672 Broadway (☎212-864-2323; www.mamamexico.com), at 102nd St. Ⓢ 1 to 103rd St. This lively Mexican diner with colored lanterns, hand-painted tiles, murals, and a loud mariachi band every night, serves amazing margaritas in 16 tropical flavors, including pomegranate and papaya ($9). Entrees ($8-29) include a large selection of creative fajitas ($17-26). Reservations recommended on weekends. Open M-Th and Su noon-11:30pm, F-Sa noon-2am. ❸

Gray's Papaya, 2090 Broadway (☎212-799-0243), at 72nd St. Ⓢ 1, 2 to 72nd St. This 24hr. "hot doggery" serves up all-beef franks in a loud, tacky, and fun space. Tom Hanks and Meg Ryan come here in *You've Got Mail*. Locals line up for the "recession special" at lunchtime: 2 hot dogs and a fruit drink (banana daquiri, pineapple, piña colada, or papaya) for a mere $2.75. Coffee ($0.25 per cup) is a steal from 6-11am. Eat standing up at counters beneath oversized hanging fruit or take the food to go. Additional locations at 539 8th Ave. and 402 6th Ave. ❶

Ivy's Chinese and Japanese Cafe, 154 W 72nd St. (☎212-787-0165; www.ivyscafenyc.com), between Broadway and Columbus Ave. Ⓢ 1, 2, 3 to 72nd St./Broadway; B, C to 72nd St./Central Park W. This Chinese-Japanese restaurant once provided People's Republic President Jiang Zemin with takeout for 10 straight days. Locals rave about the steamed buns (6 for $4.25) and the Lotus Delight ($11), a mixture of sliced lotus, black mushrooms, and tofu. The Japanese menu includes excellent tempura and a wide selection of sushi rolls ($4-11). Lunch specials $5-10. Free delivery. Open M-Th 11:30am-11:30pm, F-Sa 11:30am-midnight, Su noon-11:30pm. ❷

Mughai, 320 Columbus Ave. (☎212-724-6363), at 75th St. Ⓢ 1, 2, 3 to 72nd St. A local Indian favorite with quick service, reasonable prices, and a pleasant ambience. The tender, creamy lamb *pasanda* ($16) is the management's pride. If you're looking for a little more zip, try the chicken vindaloo ($14). Open M-Th 5-11:30pm, F-Sa noon-midnight, Su noon-11pm. ❸

Land Thai Kitchen, 450 Amsterdam Ave. (☎212-501-8121; www.landthaikitchen.com), between 81st and 82nd St. Ⓢ 1 to 79th St. This sleek, modern Thai restaurant is a local favorite. It doesn't accept reservations, and a line is almost guaranteed; sip a beer at the Dead Poet next door while you wait. Fixed-price lunch (noon-3:30pm) including appetizer and entree $8. Green curry with chicken $10. Wok basil with beef $11. Pad Thai with shrimp $10. Delivery available M-Sa until 10:45pm, Su until 10:30pm. $10 delivery min. Open M-Th and Su noon-10:45pm, F-Sa noon-11:45pm. ❷

Shark Bar and Restaurant, 307 Amsterdam Ave. (☎212-874-8500), between 74th and 75th St. Ⓢ 1, 2, 3 to 72nd St. Mellow jazz accompanies quiet conversations at this popular soul-food restaurant. Louisiana deep-fried crab cakes $8.25. Seafood okra gumbo $18.75. Honey-dipped Southern fried chicken $15.25. Open M-Tu 5-11:30pm, W 11:30am-3pm and 5-11:30pm, Th 11:30am-3pm and 5pm-12:30am, F-Sa 11:30am-3pm and 5pm-1:30am, Su 11:30am-11:30pm. ❸

La Caridad 78 Restaurant, 2197-2199 Broadway (☎212-874-2780), at 78th St. Ⓢ 1 to 79th St. You don't find many city diners where *egg foo young* and *huevos revoltillos* turn up on the same menu, but this Cuban and Chinese canteen has tasty offerings for a wide variety of tastes. The no-frills food isn't some fancy-pants effort at culinary fusion, but the authentic cuisine of the Chinese population that emigrated to Cuba in the 19th century. The Cuban dishes here are standouts, while the Chinese dishes are more ordinary. Good selection of lunch specials ($6-7) served M-F 11:30am-4pm. The red beans, rice, and chopped beef ($6) won't disappoint. Open M-Sa 11:30am-midnight, Su 11:30am-10:30pm. Cash only. ❷

CAFES

👍 **Alice's Tea Cup,** 102 W 73rd St. (☎212-799-3006, www.alicesteacup.com), at Columbus Ave. [S] 1, 2, 3 to 72nd St. This frilly "Alice in Wonderland"-themed tea room, a favorite for mother-daughter outings, has doors with oversized keyholes and a "Take Me" menu. Delicious scones come with homemade preserves. Try a pot of any of Alice's 120 varieties of tea ($5-7), à la carte or as part of afternoon tea. For lunch, try the *lapsang souchong* chicken breast sandwich with apples and herbed goat cheese ($11). If you love the decor, you might want to pick up a tiara or fairy costume at the gift shop on your way out. Open M-Th and Su 8am-8pm, F and Sa 8am-10pm. Second location at 156 E 64th St.

Cafe Lalo, 201 W 83rd St. (☎212-496-6031; www.cafelalo.com), between Broadway and Amsterdam Ave. [S] 1 to 79th St., 86th St. Ever since Meg Ryan got stood up here in *You've Got Mail,* this European-style cafe has been packed with tourists. Still, it's worth a visit for its excellent desserts and coffees. Snag seating by the French windows if you can, sip an iced cappuccino ($3.75), and choose from the immense selection of cakes, pies, and tarts ($6.50 per slice). Try the decadent Belgian chocolate cake. Full bar. Open M-Th 8am-2am, F 8am-4am, Sa 9am-4am, Su 9am-2am. Credit cards accepted only for whole cakes and T-shirts.

Cafe La Fortuna, 69 W 71st St. (☎212-724-5846), at Columbus Ave. [S] 1, 2, 3 to 72nd St./Broadway; B, C to 72nd St./Central Park W. John Lennon used to frequent this cafe, which calls itself the oldest on the Upper West Side. The sandwiches are nothing special, but the strong coffees (espresso $2.75), flaky pastries ($2.50), and homemade Italian ices (cherry, coffee, mango, etc. $4.50) are as Italian as the waitresses' accents. Homemade pie, beer, and wine make this a good after-dinner stop. On warm evenings the high-walled garden out back is a great place to relax. Open M-Th and Su noon-midnight, F noon-1am, Sa noon-1:30am. Cash only.

SHOPS

👍 **Zabar's,** 2245 Broadway (☎212-787-2000 or 800-697-6301; www.zabars.com), between 80th and 81st St. [S] 1 to 79th St. This Upper West Side institution is packed floor-to-ceiling with gourmet delicacies. At the very least, come here to feast on the legendary free samples, or pick up a salad or sandwich ($8-9) from the deli. On weekday mornings, masses of hungry New Yorkers stand in line for bagels, pastries, and coffee. The attached cafe is delicious and cheep. Open M-F 8am-7:30pm, Sa 8am-8pm, Su 9am-6pm. Cafe open M-F 7am-7pm, Sa 7:30am-7pm, Su 8am-6pm. Housewares open M-Sa 9am-7:30pm, Su 9am-6pm.

👍 **Beard Papa Sweets Cafe,** 2167 Broadway (☎212-799-3770; www.muginohousa.com), between 76th and 77th St. [S] 1, 2, 3 to 72nd St. This Japanese bakery has created a near-perfect puff pastry—and the whole Upper West Side knows it. Lines often snake out the door for these flaky gems, sprinkled with powdered sugar and filled with vanilla custard just before serving. It's messy, delicious, and just 220 calories. Cream puff pastry $1.45. Special flavors change weekly. Open daily 10am-8pm. Second location at 740 Broadway.

👍 **Buttercup Bake Shop,** 141 W 72nd St. (☎212-787-3800; www.buttercupbakeshop.com), between Columbus and Amsterdam Ave. [S] 1, 2, 3 to 72nd St. Featuring colorful chocolate and vanilla cupcakes topped with buttercream frosting, this newly opened bakery is the perfect place to relive the elementary-school birthday parties of your youth. Just remember to adhere to the rules: no more than 24 cupcakes can be purchased at one time. Large orders must be placed by 2pm the day before pick-up. Delivery available in cupcake emergencies. Open M-W 8am-8pm, Th-F 8am-10pm, Sa 9am-10pm, Su 10am-7pm. Under $10 cash only.

Silver Moon Bakery, 2740 Broadway (☎212-866-4717; www.silvermoonbakery.com), at 105th St. [S] 1 to 103rd St. Serving delicious fresh breads and pastries, this bakery doubles as a pleasant sidewalk cafe in the summer. Popular items include crusty Parisian baguettes ($2.25) and warm croissants ($1.85). The well-stuffed gourmet sandwiches on freshly made bread ($6.50) sell like hotcakes. Cookies, cakes, and pastries $2-5. Open M-F 7:30am-8pm, Sa-Su 8:30am-7pm.

MORNINGSIDE HEIGHTS

Largely catering to the Columbia University community, Morningside Heights has a great, budget-friendly range of restaurants, from romantic Italian to Chinese fast food, and plenty of old-fashioned coffee shops that stay open late.

👍 **Amir's Falafel,** 2911A Broadway (☎212-749-7500), between 113th and 114th St. [S] 1 to 110th St., 116th St. This top-notch falafel stand also serves Middle Eastern staples like *schawarma* and *baba ghanoush.* Substantial vegetarian selections (platters from $5.50). Falafel $3.50. Open daily 11am-11pm. Free local delivery. Cash only. ❶

Symposium, 544 W 113th St. (☎212-865-1011), between Broadway and Amsterdam. [S] 1 to 110th St. The Classics students at nearby Columbia know that, despite its academic connotation today, the word "symposium" originally meant a drinking party. Plenty of that goes on at this superb little Greek restaurant, with hand-painted murals on its walls and a roofed garden with lanterns and trees in back. Delicious dips $5. For a little bit of everything, get the Greek sampler ($15). ❷

Charles' Southern-Style Kitchen, 2841 8th Ave. (Frederick Douglass Blvd.) (☎212-926-4313), at W 152nd St. [S] A, B, C, D to 145th St. Fantastic Southern soul food in a counter-service setting. Dishes come with fried chicken, okra, catfish, black-eyed peas, oxtail stew, and cornbread. Corn on the cob $1.50. Barbecue ribs $9.21. Macaroni and cheese $3. Open Tu-F noon-10pm, Sa noon-11pm, Su noon-7pm. Hours can be erratic; call ahead. ❷

Massawa, 1239 Amsterdam Ave. (☎212-663-0505), at 121st St. [S] 1 to 116th St., 125th St. Though it's in a slightly out-of-the-way location, Massawa serves delicious Ethiopian and Eritrean cuisine. Meat and veggie dishes ($10.50-14) are served with spongy *injera* bread or rice. Beef sauteed with tomatoes, jalapenos, and peppers $12. Lunch specials ($8-9) include entree, vegetable, salad, and *injera.* 10% off with a Columbia ID. Open daily 11:30am-midnight. ❷

Toast, 3157 Broadway (☎212-662-1144; www.toastnyc.com), between Tiemann Pl. and La Salle St., near 125th St. [S] 1 to 125th St. This new-American restaurant caters to artsy collegiate regulars, who enjoy its fresh sandwiches and monkey-themed artwork. Mozzarella, roasted peppers, sun-dried tomatoes, and basil sandwich $7.50. Fries with melted cheese and gravy $3.50. Brunch specials Sa-Su 10am-4pm. Beer on tap $5. Open M-W and Su 11am-11pm, Th-Sa 11am-midnight. ❷

Tom's Restaurant, 2880 Broadway (☎212-864-6137; www.toms-diner.com), at 112th St. [S] 1 to 110th St. Mostly famous for its facade (prominently featured in *Seinfeld*), Tom's serves decent food in a surprisingly untouristy environment. Breakfast items served all day include huge pancakes ($5.35) and 3-egg omelets (from $6). Open M-Th 6am-1:30am, F-Sa 24hr., Su closes at 1:30am. Cash only. ❶

SHOPS

👍 **The Hungarian Pastry Shop,** 1030 Amsterdam Ave. (☎212-866-4230), at 111th St. [S] 1 to 110th St. Everyone from neighborhood teenagers to little old Hungarian ladies comes here for eclairs, croissants, and cake slices ($2-3.50). The pleasant outdoor seating is popular during the summer. Open M-F 8am-11:30pm, Sa 8:30am-11:30pm, Su 8:30am-10:30pm. Cash only.

👍 **Nussbaum & Wu,** 2897 Broadway (☎212-280-5344). This small bakery cafe lies on the western side of the Columbia campus and provides the sugar-rush sustenance to college kids pulling all-nighters. Sandwiches are everything from simple (cheese $1.50) to complex (turkey, ham, swiss cheese, cole slaw, and Russian dressing $7.50). Pastries are the bakery's true niche. Crepes, tiramisu, crumb cake, and out-of-this-world profiteroles. Open daily 6am-midnight.

Milano Market, 2892 Broadway (☎212-665-9500), between 112th and 113th St. Ⓢ 1 to 110th St. Italian imports, including chocolate bars and other rich treats. Gourmet sandwiches (around $6), are made with fresh cheeses at the deli counter. Great baked goods. Gloppy squares ($3) are topped with gooey chocolate, nuts, caramel and fudge. Open daily 7am-1am.

HARLEM

Harlem's cuisine ranges from East and West African to Caribbean and Creole, but the neighborhood is famous for its soul food, some of the best north of the Mason-Dixon line. As Harlem gentrifies, upscale restaurants have begun to pop up along Lenox Ave., between 125th and 135th St. In Spanish Harlem, you'll find delicious Puerto Rican food. Washington Heights has authentic and inexpensive Latin fare.

▨ **Miss Maude's Spoonbread Too,** 547 Lenox (6th) Ave. (☎212-690-3100; www.spoonbreadinc.com), between 137th and 138th St. Ⓢ 2, 3 to 135th St. Heaping portions of delicious, down-home soul food. The restaurant is famous for spoonbread and sweet potato pie ($3.50), and the macaroni and cheese ($3.50) is to-die-for. Entrees include Louisiana catfish ($13), southern fried chicken ($11), and Jamaican jerk chicken ($12) and come with 2 sides. Delivery available; $15 min. Open M-Th noon-9:30pm, F-Sa noon-10:30pm, Su 11am-9:30pm. ❷

▨ **Dinosaur BBQ,** 646 W 131st St. (☎212-694-1777; www.dinosaurbarbque.com), at 12th Ave., 1 block south of Fairway Supermarket, 1 block north of 125th St. Ⓢ 1 to 125th St. This jumbo-sized rib joint serves some of the best barbecue in the city. The decor screams biker bar, with flames on the walls and a motorcycle hanging from the ceiling. "Big-ass pork plate" with 2 sides and cornbread $14. Excellent brisket sandwiches $11. Jazz in Deep Blues Lounge Th-Sa 10pm-1am; no cover. Free neighborhood delivery; $15 min. Kitchen open Tu-Th 11:30am-11pm, F-Sa 11:30am-midnight, Su noon-10pm. ❷

▨ **Bistro Itzocan,** 1575 Lexington Ave. (☎212-423-0255), at 101st St. Ⓢ 6 to 103rd St./Lexington Ave. This tiled bistro combines Mexican flavors with French culinary techniques to produce some of the most innovative (and delicious) food around. Wild mushroom *huitlacoche* crepes $14. Steak with tequila and green peppercorn sauce $17. For dessert, try the brown sugar kahlua *pot de creme* or the chocolate pear goat's milk tart with caramel sauce (both $5). Fixed-price weekend brunch with coffee and entree $8.50. Free delivery. Open M-F 5-11pm, Sa-Su noon-3pm and 5-11pm. Cash only. ❷

New Leaf Cafe, 1 Margaret Corbin Dr. in Fort Tryon Park (☎212-568-5323; www.nyrp.org/newleaf). Ⓢ 1 to 191st St./St. Nicholas Ave.; A to 190th St./Fort Washington Ave. This Fort Tryon Park oasis serving gourmet new-American cuisine makes a romantic post-Cloisters stop. The restaurant is part of Bette Midler's New York Restoration Project; proceeds help reclaim and develop parks and gardens throughout the city. Lunch sandwiches include grilled chicken breast ($11) and goat cheese and wild vegetable ($11). For dinner, try the wild mushroom risotto ($19) or the orange-glazed duck breast ($24). Live jazz Th-F 8-11pm. Open Tu-Sa 9am-3pm and 6-10pm, Su 5:30-9:30pm. Brunch Su 11am-4pm. Bar open Tu-Su noon-11pm. ❷

Manna's Soul Food Restaurant, 486 Lenox (6th) Ave. (☎212-234-4488), between 134th and 135th St. Ⓢ 2, 3 to 135th St./Lenox (6th) Ave. This highly affordable soul-food buffet and salad bar offers classic standards and an unusually good selection of fresh fruit. Mix and match from mac and cheese, barbecued ribs, fried chicken, mashed potatoes, corn, fruit, and prepared salads. $5 per pound. Open M-Sa 8am-9:30pm, Su 10am-8pm. Cash only. ❶

La Marmite, 2264 Frederick Douglass Blvd. (8th Ave.) (☎212-666-0653), between 121st and 122nd St. Ⓢ A, B, C, D to 125th St./St. Nicholas Ave. A tiny restaurant serving authentic and very spicy French-African cuisine. Popular $8 lunch dishes (available until 4pm) include *thiebou djeun* (a Senegalese dish of fried rice, fish, and vegetables), *mafe* (lamb cubes in peanut sauce), and *thiou* (fish balls in a tomato onion sauce). Dinner options include *crevette* (sauteed black tiger shrimp; $11), *gigot* (roasted lamb shank; $11), and *poisson braisé* (whole fish served with *attieke* and onion sauce; $11). Open daily noon-5am. ❷

El Rey De Los Caridad, W 184th St. (☎212-781-0431), at Broadway. Ⓢ 1, 9 to 181st St./Broadway. One of the best of New York's ubiquitous "Caridad" Dominican restaurants, with both a cafeteria-style counter and a colorful and comfortable wait-service area. Steak, pork, and BLT sandwiches $3-4.50. Entrees include pepper steak ($9.45), lobster creole ($20.50), and seafood paella ($28). Lunch specials (11am-4pm; $4.50-6.50) feature oxtail stew or spaghetti with chicken, plus sides. Salsa and merengue jukebox. Free delivery. Open daily 7am-midnight. Under $10 cash only. ❷

La Fonda Boricua, 169 E 106th St. (☎212-410-7292; www.fondaboricua.com), between Lexington and 3rd Ave. Ⓢ 6 to 103rd St./Lexington Ave. A good place to practice your Spanish, this is a friendly Puerto Rican restaurant and community hangout with lively music. There's no menu here, but there are always plenty of choices. Chicken with rice and beans $5. Catfish $7. Octopus and shrimp salad $10. Beer $4. Mixed drinks $7-8. Open M-Su 11am-10pm. ❷

Sylvia's, 328 Lenox (6th) Ave. (☎212-996-0660), between 125th and 126th St. Ⓢ 3 to 125th St./Lenox (6th) Ave. Sylvia's has grown from a beloved local soul-food restaurant to a citywide tourist destination jammed with busloads of tourists. Southern fried chicken with eggs $8.75. "World-Famous Talked-About BBQ Ribs Special" with "Sassy Sauce" $13. Wash it all down with Harlem's own Sugar Hill brew $5. Sa free live jazz. Su Gospel brunch 12:30-4pm. Open M-Sa 8am-10:30pm, Su 11am-8pm. ❷

SHOPS

▩ **Fairway,** 2328 12th Ave. (☎212-234-3883; www.fairwaymarket.com), at W 132nd St., on the Hudson River. Ⓢ 1 to 125th St./Broadway. A spectacular supermarket with a fabulous selection at wholesale prices. Bakery, gourmet cheeses, fruit, and deli. The store reportedly has the highest turnover of fresh fruit and produce in all of New York. Open daily 8am-11pm. Delivery available ($4-5 charge); see website for details. Additional locations at 2127 Broadway (☎212-595-1888), between W 74th and W 75th St. (open daily 9am-9pm) and 480-500 Van Brunt St. in Redhook (open daily 8am-10pm).

Wimp's Southern Style Bakery, 29 W 125th St. (☎212-410-2296; www.wimpsbakery.com), between Lenox (6th) and 5th Ave. Ⓢ 2, 3 to 125th St./Lenox (6th) Ave. This bakery sells pies, cobblers, puddings, and cakes the size of small tires. Sweet potato, coconut custard, apple crumb, and pecan pies come in 4 sizes, from small (5 in.; $2.50-3.50) to large (10 in.; $16-20). Banana pudding and fruit cobblers $5 per lb. Slice of cheesecake $3.50. Pre-ordered full cakes $30-170. Open M-Th 11am-8pm, F-Sa 10am-9pm, Su noon-7pm.

CAFES

Settepani, 196 Lenox (6th) Ave. (☎917-492-4806; www.settepani.com), at 120th St. Ⓢ 2, 3 to 116 St./Lenox (6th) Ave. This comfortable bakery and cafe specializes in fine Italian breads and pastries. It's the perfect place to relax with the morning paper. Outdoor seating in good weather. Oatmeal with fresh fruit $7.50. Omelettes $8-10. Open M-Th 7am-10pm, F-Su 7am-11pm. Additional location at 602 Lorrimer St. in Brooklyn.

BROOKLYN

WILLIAMSBURG AND GREENPOINT

Williamsburg's artists are definitely not of the starving variety—the area has a huge array of offbeat and affordable restaurants, many housed in converted industrial locales. Greenpoint is home to authentic Polish fare, plus an increasing concentration of Thai and Japanese restaurants.

👍 **DuMont Restaurant,** 432 Union Ave. (☎718-486-7717), at Devoe St. [S] L to Lorimer St. One of the best of Williamsburg's many brunch spots, DuMont is a magnet for locals looking to drink mimosas ($8) and munch on favorites like *huevos rancheros* and smoked trout salad in the early afternoon. At dinner, the signature DuMac and Cheese ($12) and specials like pancetta-wrapped monkfish ($16) are fresh and delicious. The service is excellent, the wine list is solid, and the garden areas in back couldn't be more pleasant when the weather's warm. Open daily 11am-3pm and 6-11pm. ❷

👍 **Diner,** 85 Broadway (☎718-486-3077), at Berry St. [S] J, M, Z to Marcy Ave. In a gritty neighborhood of warehouses and auto mechanics, Diner, housed in an old railroad car, caters to an artfully disheveled crowd. Rotating specials include grouper with oyster sauce and goat-cheese tarts. The chocolate cake ($6) is locally famous. Delicious burgers $9.50. Mussels with fries $12.50. Marlow & Sons, a cafe and gourmet grocery next door under the same ownership, has a friendly and informal terrace. Open M-Th and Su 11am-midnight, F-Sa 11am-1am. ❷

👍 **Sea,** 114 N 6th St. (☎718-384-8825; www.searestaurant.com), between Berry St. and Wythe St. [S] L to Bedford Ave. Sleek and chic, with fluorescent lighting and thumping music, this Thai restaurant centered around a reflecting pool and floating flower boat feels as much like a dance club as it does a place to eat. But the food won't disappoint. The lunch special ($6.50-7.50) is an unbeatable value; entrees come with an appetizer and a mountain of rice. Pad thai $7. Duck with curry sauce $13. 2 bars. DJ Th-Su. Open M-Th and Su 11:30am-11:30pm, F-Sa 11:30am-2am. ❷

Bonita, 338 Bedford Ave. (☎718-384-9500), between S 2nd and 3rd St. [S] L to Bedford Ave. This mosaic-covered Mexican cafe serves great tacos ($7-8.50), *huevos rancheros* ($7), and chopped salad ($6-8.50). Counters at the window and bar make lovely spots for a meal or drink. Mexican beers $4-5. Sangria $5. Open M-Th 9am-11pm, F-Su 11am-midnight. ❶

Bliss, 191 Bedford Ave. (☎718-599-2547), between N 6th and 7th St. [S] L to Bedford Ave. A vegan-friendly wait-service cafe with a homey ambience. Dishes include tofu clubs ($8), grilled portobello sandwiches ($8), and meat-free chili ($6). The specialty Bliss Bowl ($8) comes with vegetables, rice, potatoes, tofu, and more. BYOB. Organic iced coffee $2. Organic iced tea $1. Delivery available 6-11pm. Open M-F 8:30am-11pm, Sa-Su 9:30am-11pm. Su brunch 9:30am-4pm. Cash only. ❶

Chai, 124 N 6th St. (☎718-599-5889), between Bedford Ave. and Berry St. [S] L to Bedford Ave. This mellow, meditative Thai restaurant centers on a reflecting pond with floating blossoms. The inventive menu features crab cakes ($6) and *pla ginger* (crispy whole red snapper with ginger; $14). Lunch specials (noon-4pm, $6) include entree (chicken, beef, or tofu pad thai), soup, and salad or spring roll. Sake $7. Free delivery. Open M 4pm-midnight, Tu-Su noon-midnight. Cash only. ❷

BROOKLYN HEIGHTS AND DOWNTOWN

Brooklyn is famous for its pizza, and in Brooklyn Heights you'll find scores of no-frills pizzerias, serving some of the best thin-crust this side of the Atlantic. But the area's changing population has brought dozens of ethnic eateries, which are sure to get you out of a culinary rut.

NEW YORK'S SWEET TOOTH

Though you might not realize it if you don't live in the city, nothing says New York like its classic desserts: black-and-white cookies, Brooklyn egg creams, and New York-style cheesecake. These three sweet treats—all developed, incidentally, in Jewish immigrant communities around the turn of the last century—can be ordered over the Internet today and delivered anywhere in the country. But it's a lot more fun to save yourself the shipping and sample them while you're here.

Black-and-white cookies are more like a chewy, flat cake than what you usually think of as a cookie. An indelible childhood memory in the minds of countless New Yorkers, the circular treats are dipped in vanilla frosting on one side and chocolate frosting on the other; according to Jerry Seinfeld, a proper bite must include a taste of each. **William Greenberg Jr. Desserts,** 1100 Madison Ave., between 82nd and 83rd St., has been making these cookies by hand since 1946. (☎ *212-873-7100;* *www.wmgreenbergdesserts.com.* *Open M-F 8am-6:30pm, Sa* *8:30am-6pm, Su 10am-4pm.)*

The Brooklyn egg cream is a soda-fountain concoction credited to Louis Auster, an enterprising Brooklyn candy-shop owner who took his original recipe for the drink to his grave. Only one surviving relative knows the exact

Grimaldi's, 19 Old Fulton St. (☎ 718-858-4300; www.grimaldis.com), between Front and Water St. Ⓢ A, C to High St. Once a favorite of Frank Sinatra, Grimaldi's serves classic brick-oven New York-style pizza, with wonderfully fresh mozzarella. Small pies $12, large $14. Toppings from $2 each. Wine by the glass $4. Open M-Sa 11:30am-10:45pm, Su noon-11:45pm. Cash only. ❷

Madiba Restaurant & Shebeen, 195 DeKalb Ave. (☎ 718-855-9190; www.madibarestaurant.com), between Carlton and Adelphi St. Ⓢ C to Lafayette Ave. New York's only South-African restaurant recreates the atmosphere of Africa's corner *shebeens,* or social halls, offering fun times to a diverse crowd. The cuisine is delicious and often unusual. Fish and chips $16. Baby-back ribs basted with monkey-gland sauce $20. Traditional African stew $22. F South-African live music. Occasional lectures and screenings of South-African films. Nightly DJ spins African, reggae, house, and jazz. Open M-Th 10am-midnight, F 10am-1am, Sa 10:30am-1am, Su 10:30am-midnight. ❸

Downtown Atlantic, 364 Atlantic Ave. (☎ 718-852-9945; www.downtownatlantic.com), between Hoyt and Bond St. Ⓢ A, C, G to Hoyt-Schermerhorn St.; F, G to Bergen St. Both relaxed and gourmet, this neighborhood cafe offers a wide spectrum of choices, from delicious sandwiches (lemon pepper salmon $9), to full-scale entrees (crispy roasted pork shank $20), to decadent cupcakes ($3.50) and other desserts (chocolate mousse cake $5.50). Open Tu-Th noon-4pm and 5-10pm, F noon-4pm and 5-11pm, Sa 11am-3pm and 5-11pm, Su 11am-3pm and 4-10pm. ❸

Junior's, 386 Flatbush Ave. Extension (☎ 718-852-5257; www.juniorscheesecake.com), at DeKalb Ave. Ⓢ B, M, Q, R to DeKalb Ave. A 1970 *New York* magazine article touted this Brooklyn institution as the home of "the world's finest cheesecake," and the crowds that devour thousands of slices here every week seem to agree. The famous cake comes in plain, blueberry, pineapple, chocolate mousse, and strawberry flavors (slices $5; whole cakes $10.50-17). Past the takeout counters lies a classic diner-style restaurant serving a full dinner menu. Entrees $12-30. Open daily 8am-7pm. ❷

Palmira's Ristorante, 41 Clark St. (☎ 718-237-4100), at Hicks St. Ⓢ 2, 3 to Clark St. Nestled in a residential brownstone neighborhood, this is a classic Brooklyn Italian restaurant, where guests sit in comfortable booths and enjoy stuffed mushrooms ($5), baked clams ($10), or fettucine alfredo ($13). Hero sandwiches $7-14. Pizza from $8. Open M-Th and Su 11am-10:30pm, F-Sa 11am-12:30am. ❷

JRG Restaurant, Bar, and Fashion Café, 17 / Flatbush Ave. (☎718-399-7079) at Pacific St. Ⓢ 2, 3, 4, 5, B, D, M, N, R Q to Atlantic Ave./Pacific St. A gem hidden on Flatbush Ave., JRG was opened by a fashion-show promoter who furnished it with runway photos and mannequins sporting exotic dresses. The menu features codfish cakes ($7), jerk chicken ($15), and sides of okra ($3). The upscale bar serves drinks to a well-dressed local clientele. Open M-Th and Su 1:30pm-midnight, F-Sa 4pm-3am. ❸

Keur N'Deye, 737 Fulton St. (☎718-875-4937), at S Elliott Pl., in Fort Greene. Ⓢ G to Fulton St.; C to Lafayette Ave. A Senegalese restaurant with a comfortable back garden and excellent food, including unbelievably good french fries. *Tiebou dieun* (bluefish with vegetables stewed in a tomato sauce) $12. Sweet-potato pie $5. Open Tu-Th 4-10:30pm, F 4-11:30pm, Sa 11am-11:30pm, Su 11am-10:30pm. ❷

Brooklyn Moon, 745 Fulton St. (☎718-243-0424), at S Elliott Pl., in Fort Greene. Ⓢ G to Fulton St.; C to Lafayette Ave. A comfy cafe and restaurant with mismatched furniture, green walls, and good food. Many of the menu items, like the salmon burger with spicy fries, cost only $5 before 6pm. Fried whiting $9.75. F 10:30pm open mic night featuring poetry and occasional performances. Open M-Th noon-11:30pm, F-Sa 11:30am-2am, Su 11:30am-11:30pm. Cash only. ❶

SHOPS

▨ **Brooklyn Ice Cream Factory** (☎718-246-3963), at Fulton Ferry Pier, at Old Fulton and Water St. Ⓢ 2, 3 to Court St.; A, C to High St. This small, busy shop sits on the Fulton Ferry Landing and serves homemade ice cream (1 scoop $3) in basic but delicious flavors. There are only a few seats inside, but the outside benches offer a spectacular view of the Manhattan and Brooklyn Bridges and the Downtown skyline. Open M-W noon-10pm, Th-Su noon-11pm. Cash only.

▨ **Jacques Torres Chocolate,** 66 Water St. (☎718-875-9772), between Dock and Main St. Ⓢ A, C to High St.; F to York St. A beautiful store serving both traditional and exotic chocolate treats. Patrons can watch chefs preparing the creations; the larger masterpieces are signed by Jacques Torres himself. Small bag of chocolate-covered almonds $6. Chocolate-covered fortune cookies $10. High-heeled shoes sculpted from white chocolate $25. Hot chocolate from $2.50. Open M-Sa 9am-7pm, Su 10am-6pm.

Sahadi Importing Company, 187-189 Atlantic Ave. (☎718-624-4550; www.sahadis.com), between Court and Clinton St. Ⓢ 2, 3, 4, 5, M, R to Court St./Borough Hall. This popular Middle-Eastern emporium stocks a

ingredients Auster used; he claims the authentic mix contains neither eggs nor cream. Most restaurants today make Brooklyn egg creams with seltzer, chocolate syrup, and whole milk. Success in preparation depends as much on proper mixing technique as it does on the right ingredients. An authentic egg cream should taste like an ice-cream soda and have a foamy, egg-white-like head. To sample a great one, head to **Gem Spa,** 131 2nd Ave., at St. Mark's Pl. in the East Village. (☎212-995-1866. Open 24hr.)

Cheesecake has been around since Roman Times, but the New York-style version we know today (likely the most nationally popular of the three desserts discussed here) was developed around the beginning of the 20th century. The characteristic graham-cracker crust is a New York innovation. The authentic filling has no fancy ingredients inside or on top—it's just pure cream cheese, eggs, cream, and sugar. The cake should be moist and have a uniform texture, free of cracks or crevices. **Junior's Cheesecake,** 386 Flatbush Ave. Extension, at DeKalb Ave. in Brooklyn has been a beloved cheesecake institution since 1950. Until recently, Junior's recipe was known to only three people on earth. (☎718-852-5257; www.juniorscheesecake.com. Open daily 8am-7pm.)

variety of spices and seasonings ($3-12 per lb.), dried fruits, hummus, and *baba ghanoush.* Olive bar $3-5.25 per lb. Seafood salad with octopus tentacles $9.50 per lb. Open M-Sa 9am-7pm.

CARROLL GARDENS AND RED HOOK

Sometimes referred to as Brooklyn's new "Restaurant Row," Carroll Gardens' **Smith Street** seems to witness the opening of a new restaurant every week.

👍 **Alma,** 187 Columbia St. (☎ 718-643-5400; www.almarestaurant.com), at Degraw St. [S] F, G to Carroll St. Haute Mexican cuisine, a lengthy tequila list, and a spectacular rooftop view of the Red Hook shipyard and Lower Manhattan make this a local favorite. Variations on Mexican basics include *camarones asados* (grilled shrimp; $15), *mole poblano al pollo* ($15), and fajitas ($16). The notoriously strong margaritas might make negotiating the stairs difficult. Enter the restaurant through Bar B61. Reserve in advance to secure rooftop seating. Open M-Th and Su 11:30am-2:30pm and 5:30-10:30pm, F-Sa 11:30am-2:30pm and 5:30-11:30pm. ❸

Robin des Bois, 195 Smith St. (☎ 718-596-1609; www.sherwoodcafe.com), between Baltic and Warren St. [S] F, G to Bergen St. This French-themed cafe is full of eclectic antiques—gilded mirrors, stuffed marlins, religious icons, a Playboy pinball machine, to name just a few—and they're all for sale, along with a classic selection of French fare. *Croque Monsieur* $8.50. *Salade Niçoise* $13.50. Good French wine list ($5-7 per glass). Open M-Th 4pm-midnight, F noon-1am, Sa 11am-1am, Su 11am-midnight. ❷

Cafe Kai, 151 Smith St. (☎ 718-596-3466), between Bergen and Wyckoff St. [S] F, G to Bergen St. A counter-service vegan cafe with lots of fresh juice—grapefruit ($2.75), mixed vegetable ($3.75), wheat grass shot ($1.75). Sandwich favorites include hummus with veggies and miso dressing ($3.50). Green salad with dried ginger, mango, beets, and tofu $7.50. Vegetarian burgers $6-8. Delivery available. Open M-F 8am-9pm, Sa 10:30am-9pm, Su 11am-6pm. ❶

Chestnut, 271 Smith St. (☎ 718-243-0049; www.chestnutonsmith.com), at Degraw St. [S] F, G to Bergen St. A wood-floored, brick-walled escape from the bustle of Smith St., Chestnut offers a seasonal menu featuring local and organic fruits and vegetables. Past creations have included appetizers like haystack shrimp with cilantro puree ($11) and charred octopus salad ($12), along with entrees like chicken breast with caramelized onions ($19) and braised-greens ravioli ($17). Seating is available in a beautiful outdoor garden when weather permits. Open Tu-Sa 5:30-11pm, Su 5:30-10pm. ❸

Schnack, 122 Union St. (☎ 718-855-2879; www.schnackdog.com), at Columbia St. [S] F, G to Carroll St. Schnack's motto is "Hot Dogs, Cold Beer, It's Not Complicated," and it's a formula for success. Famous mini burgers $1.65. Hot dogs $3-5. PBR $3, $1.50 in summer. 8-25 people can eat and drink all they can for 2hr. for $30 per person M-F, $35 per person Sa-Su. Open daily 11am-1am. ❶

Provence en Boite, 263 Smith St. (☎ 718-797-0707) at Degraw St. [S] F, G to Carroll St. The French owners of this family-run pastry shop and bistro will likely know your name before you leave. Delectable crepes, fruit tarts ($6.50), and strong coffee make this an excellent stop for dessert, but the main courses are excellent too. *Steak frites* $17. Cheese plate with bread and mixed greens $9.50. Fixed-price brunch Sa-Su $12. Open M-F 8am-4pm and 5-10pm, Sa-Su 8am-3:30pm and 5-10pm. ❷

Faan, 209 Smith St. (☎ 718-694-2277), at Baltic St. [S] F, G to Bergen St. Excellent Thai standards and superb sushi join fusion dishes like Asian seafood paella ($13) in a funky pagoda-like space. Lunch special (M-F 11am-3pm; $5) offers entrees like *bo xao xa* (beef and lemongrass in chili sauce with rice) and *pad see yu* (Thai country noodles with chicken, egg, and vegetables) with salad. The glass-enclosed front patio, with branches and mini-birdhouses hanging from the ceiling, has open windows in the summer. Free delivery. Open M-Th and Su 11am-midnight, F-Sa 11am-1am. ❷

PARK SLOPE AND PROSPECT PARK

Park Slope has grown into one of the best dining destinations in Brooklyn, and though many restaurants are more upscale than elsewhere in the borough, a host of excellent budget options remain.

▨ **Dizzy's,** 511 9th St. (☎ 718-499-1966), at 8th Ave. Ⓢ F to 7th Ave. This "finer diner" has colorful artwork on the walls, newspapers on the tables, and crayons out for the kids. This is one of the best brunch deals in the Slope, and everyone within a 10 mi. radius knows it. Fixed-price meals ($10-13) include muffins, biscuits, juice, coffee, and a choice of entrees like lox and waffles. For dinner, try the margarita barbecue ribs ($15). Free delivery. Open M-F 7am-10pm, Sa-Su 9am-4pm and 6-10pm. ❷

▨ **Chip and Curry Shop,** 381 5th Ave. (☎ 718-832-7701), at 6th St. Ⓢ F, M, R to 4th Ave./ 9th St. Downstairs, this restaurant is properly British as can be, with yellow walls, royal paraphernalia, and excellent fish and chips ($10.50-11.50). Upstairs is Bali-inspired, with red walls and succulent chicken *korma* ($9). Open M-Th noon-10pm, F noon-11pm, Sa 11am-10pm, Su 11am-11pm. Cash only. ❷

▨ **Tom's Restaurant,** 782 Washington Ave. (☎ 718-636-9738), at Sterling Pl. Ⓢ 2, 3 to Eastern Pkwy. The perfect place to have breakfast or lunch before a visit to the Brooklyn Museum of Art or the Botanic Garden. Open since 1936 and family-owned, Tom's might very well be the friendliest diner in all of New York. Staff brings free lollipops, oranges, and cookies while you await your eggs and pancakes ($3-7). The most authentic Brooklyn egg cream ($2.25) money can buy. Free delivery. Open M-Sa 6am-4pm. ❶

Christie's Bakery, 387 Flatbush Ave. (☎ 718-636-9746), at Sterling Pl. Ⓢ Q to 7th Ave.; 2, 3 to Grand Army Plaza. A tiny counter-service shop serving a soul-satisfying spicy beef patty in a coco-bread pastry shell ($2). Curried goat and oxtail $7.50. Open M-Sa 10:30am-10:00pm, Su 10:30am-8pm. ❶

Beso, 210 5th Ave. (☎ 718-783-4902), at Union St. Ⓢ M, R to Union St. Dinner is good, but brunch is something special at this Latin restaurant serving breakfast burritos ($7.50), *tortilla de huevos* ($11), and salmon omelets ($11). Try the daily specials ($10-12), and wash them down with one of the many inventive mimosas (glass $5, pitcher $15). End the meal with some *dulce de leche* flan with cinnamon bonbons ($6). Happy hour daily 5-7pm; margarita pitchers $10. Open daily 10am-3pm and 5-10pm. Bar open until 2am. ❷

Santa Fe Grill, 62 7th Ave. (☎ 718-636-0279), at Lincoln Pl. Ⓢ Q to 7th Ave.; 2, 3 to Grand Army Plaza. A beloved neighborhood Mexican joint, serving bottomless chips and salsa, strong margaritas ($6-7), and nightly specials like chicken and sausage enchiladas ($10) and red snapper filet ($14). Beer $4-5. Tequilas $6.50-8. Sangria $5.50. Open M-Th 5-11pm (bar until 12:30am), F 5pm-midnight (bar until 2am), Sa 3pm-midnight (bar until 2am), Su 3-11pm (bar until 1am). ❷

The V-Spot, 156 5th Ave. (☎ 718-622-2275), between Douglass and Degraw St. Ⓢ M,R to Union St. A delicious and affordable vegetarian cafe, with a modern decor and a comfortable outdoor patio. Soups and salads $6-9. Imitation meatloaf with mashed potatoes and corn $10. Open Tu-F 11am-10pm, Sa 11am-11pm, Su 11am-9pm. ❷

Watana Siam, 420 7th Ave. (☎ 718-832-1611), at 3rd St. Ⓢ F to 7th Ave. A stylish and affordable Thai restaurant that makes a great spot for a casual date. Appetizers $4-6. Pad Thai $8. Open M-Th and Su noon-11pm, F-Sa noon-midnight. ❷

CONEY ISLAND AND BRIGHTON BEACH

Unless you consider funnel cake a food group, Coney Island is not the place to go for a nutritious meal. On the other hand, Brighton Beach is full of delicious Russian and Ukrainian restaurants, which are so authentic you may not be able to read the menus.

F O O D

Nathan's, 1310 Surf Ave. (☎718-946-2202; www.nathansfamous.com), between Stillwell and 15th St., in Coney Island. S D, F, Q to Coney Island. 74 years ago, Nathan Handwerker became famous for outdoing his competitors on the Coney Island boardwalk. Handwerker's hot dogs cost a nickel, theirs a dime. His dogs have since become famous world-over. Nathan's is now franchised, but the original is still worth a visit. Every year, on July 4th, Nathan's hosts an international hot-dog eating contest. Hot dogs from $2.50. Cheeseburger meal with fries $5.50. Sauerkraut and fried onions available upon request. Open M-Th 6am-2am, F-Su 6am-4am. ●

Primorski Restaurant, 282 Brighton Beach Ave. (☎718-891-3111; www.primorski.net), between 2nd and 3rd St. S Q to Brighton Beach. By day, it's a mild-mannered Russian restaurant with a great $5.50 lunch special (M-F 11am-5pm, Sa-Su 11am-4pm). By night, you're in the loudest karaoke-disco-variety show west of the Volga. For the adventurous, the menu also features roasted eel ($15) and black caviar ($30). Russian music and disco M-Th 8pm-midnight, F-Sa 9pm-2am, Su 8pm-1am. Open daily 11am-2am. Cash only. ❷

Varenichnaya, 3086 Brighton 2nd. St. (☎718-332-9797), off Brighton Beach Ave. S Q to Brighton Beach. Fluency in Russian is not completely necessary, but it would probably help to know what you're ordering. You may not understand anything on the menu, but you'll love the dirt-cheap *pelmeni* (Siberian meat dumplings; $4.75) and *vareniki* (stuffed Ukranian potato dumplings; $4.75). Open daily 10am-9pm. ●

Totonno Pizzeria Napolitano, 1524 Neptune Ave. (☎718-372-8606), between 15th and 16th St. S D, F, Q to Coney Island. A Coney Island legend, serving pizza by the pie ($16-17.50). No slices. Open W-Su noon-8pm. Cash only. ●

Roll n' Roaster, 2901 Emmons Ave. (☎718-769-6000; www.rollnroaster.com), at Nostrand Ave. S Q to Sheepshead Bay. Serves the classic Brooklyn sandwich—roast beef on a kaiser. Regular patrons play "Spin 'n' Win," the in-house lottery. Serves beer. Open M-Th and Su 11am-1am, F-Sa 11am-3am. ●

QUEENS

Multicultural Queens offers visitors some of the best low-priced ethnic cuisine in town. Keep an eye out for delicacies like Greek *souvlaki*, Indian *dal*, Italian ices, and Jamaican beef. Outdoor market stalls frequently spring up along major thoroughfares, and grocery stores selling ethnic goods are on almost every corner.

ASTORIA AND LONG ISLAND CITY

Greek restaurants in Astoria proliferate around the elevated station at Broadway and 31st St. You can catch the N and W trains north to Ditmars Blvd., commonly known as "Little Athens" for even more Greek options.

Elias Corner, 24-02 31st St. (☎718-932-1510). S N, W to Astoria Blvd. A fantastic seafood restaurant with a distinctly Greek character, Elias Corner has no fixed menu, just an ever-changing selection of fish caught the morning of your dinner. Try the *tsatziki*, calamari, or grilled octopus as *mezedes*. Reservations aren't accepted; arrive early to guarantee that you get a table. Prices depend on the catch of the day, but the average meal starts around $10. Open daily 4-11pm or midnight. Cash only. ❷

Uncle George's, 33-19 Broadway (☎718-626-0593; www.unclegeorges.us), at 34th St. S N, W to Broadway; G, R, V to Steinway St. A diner gone Greek, this Astoria institution serves hearty fare at all times of the day and night. Whole animals turn slowly on spits behind the counter. Stuffed grape leaves $8.75. Roast leg of lamb $11. Open 24hr. ❷

Telly's Taverna, 28-13 23rd Ave. (☎718-728-9056). S N, W to 30th Ave. A really big, really popular, and really Greek fish and steak house. Try the octopus ($10) and *saganaki* ($9). Open M-Th 3pm-midnight, F-Sa 3pm-1am, Su noon-midnight. ❷

Zygos Taverna, 22-55 31st St. (☎718-728-7070). $\boxed{S}$ N, W to Broadway. This cheerily decorated restaurant serves delicious Greek fare like thinly sliced leg of lamb with lemon potatoes ($12.75), grilled baby octopus ($12.50), and *moussaka* (eggplant, ground beef, and bechamel sauce; $13). Open daily 11am-midnight. ❷

Jackson Diner, 37-47 74th St. (☎718-672-1232), between 37th and 38th Ave. $\boxed{S}$ E, F, G, R, V to Jackson Heights/Roosevelt Ave.; 7 to 74th St./Broadway. Modern art and a giant TV playing Bollywood music videos make for a quirky, always-busy setting for delicious Indian food. Great *saag gosht* (lamb with spinach, tomato, ginger, and cumin; $14) and samosas ($4). Specials from $10. The lunch buffet (11:30am-4pm) is a steal at $9. Open M-F 11:30am-10pm, Sa-Su 11:30am-10:30pm. Cash only. ❷

Thai Pavilion, 37-10 30th Ave. (☎718-777-5546). $\boxed{S}$ N, W to 30th Ave. A simple but elegantly furnished setting for good Thai food. Masaman shrimp (with coconut milk, peanuts, and avocado; $11). Amazing pad Thai $8. Stick around for dessert; the pumpkin custard is out of this world. Open daily noon-11pm. ❷

Djerdan, 34-04 31st Ave. (☎718-721-2694) $\boxed{S}$ N, W to 30th Ave. This hole-in-the-wall Bosnian restaurant serves wonderful Balkan mainstays, like meal-sized *burek* (phyllo stuffed with cheese, meat, and vegetables, then coiled and baked; from $4.25). Baklava $1.50. Open daily 11am-10pm. ❶

CAFES

Galaxy Cafe, 37-11 30th Ave. (☎718-545-3181). $\boxed{S}$ N, W to 30th Ave. A popular hangout for young locals, this cafe serves delicious pastries (baklava $3.50, canoli $4.25, tiramisu $4.50), really cheap entrees (chicken souvlaki $3), and great cappucino ($3.50). Open daily 7am-1am. Cash only.

ELMHURST, CORONA, AND FLUSHING

Flushing has excellent, authentic, and cheap Chinese and Korean eateries. Thai, and Vietnamese options abound in Elmhurst, around Broadway and Elmhurst Ave. Seafood sold in the area markets isn't just fresh—it's live.

🦐 **Kum Gang San,** 138-28 Northern Blvd. (☎718-461-0909; www.kumgangsan.net). $\boxed{S}$ 7 to Flushing/Main St.; walk north on Main St. and take a right on Northern Blvd. An elegant, marble-floored restaurant off the bustle of Main St., with individual grills at each table for great Korean barbecue ($15-22). Though it's not cheap, dinner here is a good value. If you want to splurge, order the *chulpan gui* ($43, serves 2), an assortment of seafood marinated in the restaurant's special sauce and barbecued at your table. Lunch special includes chicken teriyaki with salad, noodles, California roll, and dumplings ($7-9). Warm weather outdoor seating by a lovely little waterfall. Open 24hr. ❷

🦐 **Joe's Shanghai,** 136-21 37th Ave. (☎718-539-3838; www.joesshanghai.com). $\boxed{S}$ 7 to Flushing/Main St. The original Queens location of the famous Shanghai eatery. The *xiao long bao* dumplings are known throughout New York; try the crab and pork ($7). The grilled yellowfish fingers in seaweed ($14) are also excellent. Open M-Th and Su 11am-11pm, F-Sa 11am-midnight. Cash only. ❷

🦐 **Flushing Noodle,** 135-42 Roosevelt Ave. (☎718-353-1166). $\boxed{S}$ 7 to Flushing/Main St. One of Flushing's best Chinese noodle shops. Try the spare ribs ($8) and noodles (from $3.25). Lunch special $5.50 11am-3:30pm, with 37 entree choices. Limited seating, and it's always packed. Takeout available. Open daily 9am-10pm. Cash only. ❶

Dong Hae Ru, 36-26 Union St. (☎718-358-3869). $\boxed{S}$ 7 to Main St. Friendly Korean ladies prepare pork- and leek-stuffed dumplings (from $6) and Korean-Chinese *jjajjang-myun* (noodles in black bean sauce; $5). Open daily 10:30am-10:30pm. ❷

Chao Zhau Restaurant, 40-52 Main St. $\boxed{S}$ 7 to Main St. A plain Chinese restaurant with communal tables, delicious noodle soups, and creamy milk teas. Quick, attentive service and good lunch specials (M-F $7, Sa-Su $9). Open daily 7:30am-4am. ❶

F O O D

Szechuan Gourmet, 135-15 37th Ave. (☎718-888-9388). Ⓢ 7 to Main St. Gourmet Szechuan food with a nod to the intricacies of regional cuisine. Crispy fried duck (½ duck $10) is tender and juicy, and jellyfish with hot-and-sour sauce ($5) is a succulent delicacy. Lunch specials (11:30am-4pm) $5.25. Open M-W 11:30am-11pm, Th-F and Su 11:30am-11:30pm, Sa 11:30am-midnight. ❷

SHOPS

🍲 **Hing Long Supermarket,** 41-22 Main St. (☎718-358-8889). Ⓢ 7 to Main St. A huge selection of mangoes, cherries, papayas, and other exotic fruits. The seafood is so fresh it's often killed inside, right before your eyes. It's a little hard to maneuver around the determined locals, but the experience is worth it for the people-watching alone. Don't miss the worker outside at the fruit stand incessantly shouting, "Cherry! Cheeeeerry!" When one tires, another one takes over. Open daily 8am-9pm.

🍲 **The Lemon Ice King of Corona,** 52-02 108th St. (☎718-699-5133), Corona Ave., near Flushing Meadow-Corona Park. Ⓢ 7 to 111th St.; walk 1 block to 108th and south 10 blocks. One of Queens's most famous sites, with juicy frozen treats served outdoors at a storefront counter since 1944. Their vast flavor selection includes bubble gum, blueberry, cantaloupe, cherry, and, of course, lemon. A decent-sized medium is $1.75. Open daily 10am-12:30am; sometimes closes earlier in winter.

Yi Mei Fung Bakery, 135-38 Roosevelt Ave. (☎718-886-6820) Ⓢ 7 to Main St. A small Chinese bakery serving gorgeous, delicious treats. Lemon cake rolls $1.50. Honey puffs $2. Loaves of delicious raisin bread ($2) line the wall. Cash only.

Yong Da Fung Health Food Herbal Products Inc., 41-53A Main St. (☎718-539-6143). Ⓢ 7 to Main St. Herbal roots, teas, and rubs provide the natural cure for any ailment. Seek the advice of the wise staff. Between dragon's ears and deer's tail extract, you'll find everything you need in this maze of pungent bins. Open 9am-8pm.

JAMAICA AND THE ROCKAWAYS
Jamaica boasts West Indian, Central American, and Caribbean cuisine. Linden Blvd. and Jamaica Ave. are the best bets for tropical tastes.

Rincon Salvadoreño, 92-15 149th St. (☎718-526-3220), at Jamaica Ave. Ⓢ E, J, Z to Jamaica Center/Parsons/Archer Ave. This popular neighborhood restaurant serves heaping portions of El Salvadorean specialties like *pupusas* (cornmeal patties with pork, cheese, or beans; from $1.50). Meat entrees from $10. Try to get anything with the *frijoles fritos* (refried beans)—they are to die for. Live music F-Sa 8pm-1am. ❷

THE BRONX
Belmont's Arthur Ave. offers a one-of-a-kind cluster of Italian restaurants. Far superior to Manhattan's disappointing and over-priced Little Italy, the area brims with pastry shops, pizzerias, restaurants, and mom-and-pop Italian shops. Sea-side City Island makes a good destination for *al fresco* dining in the summer.

BELMONT

🍲 **Dominick's,** 2335 Arthur Ave. (☎718-733-2807), near E 186th St. This wood-paneled Italian gem has family-style seating and no fixed menu. The ever-changing house specials ($12-20) include linguine with mussels and roast veal. On weekends, arrive before 6pm or after 9pm unless you're willing to wait. Open M, W-Th, and Sa noon-10pm; F noon-11pm, Su 1-9pm. Cash only. ❸

🍲 **Giovanni's,** 2343 Arthur Ave. (☎718-933-4141), between E 186th St. and Crescent Ave. Great brick-oven pizza served by a gregarious staff. Check out the celebrity-filled photo wall; everybody from George Bush to Bill Clinton has been here. Individual pizzas $9-11. Full-sized pies $15-20. Free delivery. Open M-Sa 11am-11pm, Su noon-11pm. ❷

> **!** In the Bronx, unlicensed "gypsy" cabs make up for the lack of official taxis on the streets, but it's best to avoid these altogether, especially if you're alone; drivers have been linked to sexual assaults and other violent crimes. If you're dining in the Bronx, ask your waiter to call you a cab before you leave your table.

Pasquale's Rigoletto, 2311 Arthur Ave. (☎718-365-6644), near E 186th St. Sumptuous arias, classy decor, and free bruschetta. Ask to have your favorite song played, or sing it yourself on Sa amateur night (reserve 1 week ahead; begins at 8:30pm). Star customer Joe Pesci's photos adorn the front door. Pasta $14. Meat dishes $17-19. Open M-Th noon-9:30pm, F-Sa noon-10:30pm, Su noon-8:30pm. ❹

Mario's, 2342 Arthur Ave. (☎718-584-1188), near E 186th St. This popular restaurant serves massive portions of spicy southern-Italian cuisine. The starched-linen decor is dated and a little tired, but the excellent food makes up for it. Try the broiled half spring chicken ($16.25) or the Alaskan king crab with oregano ($22.50). Pasta $11-13. Seafood $15-29. Open Tu-Su noon-11pm. ❹

CAFES

Arthur Avenue Cafe, 2329 Arthur Ave. (☎718-562-0129), near E 186th St. A neighborhood coffee shop, with great tiramisu, gelato, and tarts ($1.25-4.50). Linger here with a cappuccino and enjoy the opera music in the background. Italian sandwiches $6.75-10. House special veggie lasagna $10. Sidewalk seating in nice weather. Open daily 8:30am-9pm. ❷

SHOPS

Egidio's Pastry Shop, 622 E 187th St. (☎718-295-6077). This dangerously tempting pastry shop is where Fordham students gain their "freshman 15." Famous fried cartoccios (hollow, doughnut-like pastries filled with sweet cream) $1.75. Open daily 7am-8pm.

Madonia Bakery, 2348 Arthur Ave. (☎718-295-5573), between E 186th St. and Crescent Ave. The Madonia family has been baking acclaimed Italian breads and pastries since 1918. Stop in for fresh biscotti, cookies, and a range of freshly baked breads. Jalapeno-cheddar, proscuitto, fougasse, and olive bread are all favorites. Reputed to have the best cannolis in town. Open M-Sa 6am-7pm, Su 6:30am-6pm.

Arthur Avenue Retail Market, 2334 Arthur Ave., between 186th St. and Crescent Ave. Open since the 1940s, this Little Italy Bronx market is fun for browsing and features a massive selection of fresh fruits and vegetables, meats, cheeses, gelato, and kitchenwares. Open M-Sa 7am-6pm.

Tino's Salumeria, 2410 Arthur Ave. (☎718-733-9879), near 187th St. One-stop Italian grocery store with a good selection of cheeses and meats, many hanging from the ceiling. Try a sandwich (most under $6) or one of many hot Italian entrees like baked ziti ($5) and stuffed shells ($5). A friendly atmosphere for a casual meal. Open M-Sa 6:30am-7:30pm, Su 8:30am-7:30pm.

CITY ISLAND

Johnny's Reef, 2 City Island Ave. (☎718-885-2086). Ⓢ 6 to Pelham Bay Park, then Bx29 to City Island. Delicious fresh steamed or fried seafood served to crowds that swarm like seagulls in the summer. Fish and chips $9-11. Beer $2. Open M-Th and Su 11am-midnight, F-Sa 11am-1am. Cash only. ❷

Portofino Ristorante, 555 City Island Ave. (☎718-885-1220; www.portofinocityisland.com). A local favorite for upscale Italian food, with a prime outdoor patio. Lunch specials M-F noon-3pm include linguine with clams ($16) and veal scalloppine ($15). Live music F-Sa 8:30pm-midnight. Open M-F noon-10pm, Sa-Su noon-midnight. ❹

FOOD

SIGHTS

MANHATTAN

LIBERTY AND ELLIS ISLANDS

A pair of specks in New York Harbor just off the tip of Lower Manhattan, the Statue of Liberty and Ellis Island have for over a century made up the symbolic and sometimes idealized face that the United States first shows to the outside world. Regular ferry service, running in a loop between Battery Park and the two islands, provides jaw-dropping views of the Lower Manhattan skyline, the Brooklyn Bridge, and, of course, the Statue itself.

THE STATUE OF LIBERTY. The Statue of Liberty stands as a symbol of the freedom, opportunity, and democracy that the United States aspires to and that the immigrants who arrived at nearby Ellis Island longed for. Lady Liberty today draws tourists from all over the globe, to the tune of five million people per year.

The roots of this American icon stretch back into the Old World. In the mid-19th century, many French intellectuals saw America as the model of a successful republic, and in 1865 French leftist Edouard-René de Laboulaye conceived a monument that would celebrate America's success, embody his hopes for a French republic, and strengthen the Franco-American friendship established during the US Revolutionary War. **Frederic-Auguste Bartholdi** was commissioned to construct the statue in Paris with the aid of **Gustave Eiffel** (yes, *that* Eiffel). The statue was presented to the American ambassador to France on July 4, 1884. It was then disassembled and sent across the Atlantic in 220 crates.

Had it not been for **Joseph Pulitzer,** the tycoon publisher of the *New York World*, Lady Liberty might have remained in pieces forever. Funding for assembly was slow to come, and the Statue did not (literally) get off the ground until Pulitzer took control of fundraising for construction. Pulitzer used his paper to berate New Yorkers for failing to contribute funds for the construction of a pedestal, and he pledged to publish in his paper the name of all donors, no matter how small their contribution. His efforts were successful, and in 1886, the pedestal received its final touch: the now-famous words of welcome by poet **Emma Lazarus.**

Since that time this beacon of freedom has served as a magnet for a variety of lunatic stunts. In 1986, an Australian stuntman parachuted off the torch and landed safely. (Charged with parachuting without a license, he said, "I just couldn't help myself.") In 1990, a New Yorker used a mountain climbing rope to descend from the observation deck as protest against the conviction of Native American activist Leonard Peltier. In summer 2001, a daredevil Frenchman named Thierry Devaux tried to use a motorized parachute to land on the Statue of Liberty's torch. He got snagged on the gilded flame and clung to Lady Liberty's arm for 30min. before police pulled him to safety and slapped on the handcuffs.

Until 2001, visitors could ascend to the observation deck atop the pedestal, its second-floor museum, and the statue's crown. Heightened security precautions following the 9/11 terrorist attacks have closed access to the crown and limited access to the pedestal to those with advance reservations. Call for information and to reserve tours. If you plan to make a day of it on Liberty Island, **Crown Cafe** serves surprisingly decent food at a fair price (pizza from $5.50, salads from $6, cheeseburgers $7). *(Liberty Island in New York Harbor, about 1 mi. southwest of Manhattan.* $\mathbb{S}$ *4, 5 to*

Bowling Green; R, W to Whitehall St.; 1, 9 to South Ferry. ☎ 212-363-3200; www.statueofliberty.org; www.nps.gov/stli. Liberty Island open daily 9am-5pm; longer hours in summer. Free 20min. and 45min. ranger-guided tours throughout the day; check at the information booth for details. Audio tour of Liberty and Ellis Islands $6. Ferries leave for Liberty Island from the piers at Battery Park every 30min. M-F 9:15am-3:30pm, Sa-Su 9am-4pm. Ferry reservations ☎ 212-269-5755 or 866-782-8834; www.statuereservations.com. If you don't have reservations, buy tickets in Castle Clinton's central courtyard, just to the right of the ferry dock as you face the harbor. Ferry tickets $11.50, seniors $9.50, ages 4-12 $4.50, under 4 free.)

 PLANNING YOUR VISIT. Trying to avoid the line for the Liberty-Ellis Island ferry? While you may think that getting to the boat early is the way to avoid the crowds, sometimes waiting until the afternoon results in much shorter lines. Though it's not a sure bet, coming then could cut your wait time substantially.

■ **ELLIS ISLAND.** Between 1892 and 1954, over 22 million people entered the US through Ellis Island. Each day, as many as 5000 immigrants would wait in the Main Building's vaulted Registry Room until they were called forward to be questioned by inspectors. Despite the long wait and the often harrowing medical exams that they were forced to undergo, only 1-2% of immigrants failed to pass inspection. Of those that were granted entry to the US, one-third would settle in New York City. Over 30% of all living Americans can trace their roots to an ancestor who came through the island.

Ellis Island opened as a museum in 1990 after multimillion-dollar renovations, seeking to commemorate the site's history and the immigrant experience in America more generally. The museum is housed in the island's grand brick and stone building, constructed in 1900 and now restored to its original grandeur. The building's four copper-domed towers evoke a military fortress, and two bald eagles, symbols of the US, perch over the central entrance.

Visitors pass through the surprisingly small Registry Room on their way to a restored dormitory room and the "Treasures from Home" exhibit, which features a collection of clothing, letters, religious icons, and other possessions donated by families who passed through Ellis Island. Tucked away on the third floor is the Oral History Project Library, which houses over 1700 audio-recorded and transcribed interviews with Ellis Island immigrants.

Since 2001, visitors have had access to the first-floor **American Family Immigration History Center's** user-friendly, computerized database of immigrants who passed through Ellis Island. Would-be genealogists pay for 35min. of computer time ($5) to search through ship records and arrival papers. Visitors can search by name, gender, country of origin, and age upon arrival. The friendly staff are eager to help you with your search. Those who find an ancestor can print a picture of the ship on which he or she arrived ($12.50) or a copy of the ship's manifest ($25).

The Main Building's first-floor right wing houses a stand selling a variety of fresh fudge and a cafeteria with similar offerings and prices to that on Liberty Island. *(For instructions on getting to Ellis Island, see the Statue of Liberty. ☎ 212-363-3200; www.ellisisland.org. 30min. video shown in 2 theaters, 1 with a preceding 15min. talk by a ranger. Free tickets from the info desk required. Library ☎ 212-363-3200, ext. 158. American Family Immigration History Center ☎ 212-561-4500; www.ellisislandrecords.org. 30min. theatrical play with rotating features performed daily Mar. to early Nov. $5. Audio tour $5; seniors, students, and children under 17 $4. 45min. ranger-guided tours of main building throughout the day. Free.)*

LOWER MANHATTAN

FINANCIAL DISTRICT

Once a dock where oystermen shucked their daily catch, Pearl St. is now one of the richest streets in the world. Wall St., the cornerstone of the district and the financial universe, once served as the northern border of the New Amsterdam settlement, taking its name from the wall built in 1653 to shield the Dutch from British attacks. Thanks to an influx of funding following the September 11th attacks, the area is one of the fastest-growing parts of New York City. Even so, the bustle is mainly reserved for weekdays; its power-lunch and after-work crowds clear out on the weekends.

BATTERY PARK. Battery Park is located at the southernmost tip of Manhattan. The earth under your feet is actually the accumulation of landfills that filled New York Harbor between State St. and the formerly offshore **Castle Clinton.** Castle Clinton served as an immigrant processing depot from 1835 to 1890 and now acts as a visitors center and ticket booth for the ferry to the Statue of Liberty and Ellis Island. The park features beautiful views of Brooklyn and the Statue of Liberty, and some elaborately landscaped gardens. **New York Unearthed,** an urban archaeology museum and part of the South Street Seaport, is across from the park's northern border between Pearl and Whitehall St. Recent exhibits have included a look at surviving artifacts of the 19th-century neighborhood of Five Points, which inspired the film *Gangs of New York.* Call ahead for info on the museum's free exhibits. *(Located on the southern tip of Manhattan.* Ⓢ *4, 5 to Bowling Green; R, W to Whitehall St. CASTLE CLINTON: Open daily M-F 8am-5pm. Tours of the Castle by request. Free. NEW YORK UNEARTHED: 19 State St.* ☎ *212-748-8753; www.southstreetseaportmuseum.org. Open M-F noon-5pm. Free.)*

BOWLING GREEN. This tiny, triangular piece of land is Manhattan's oldest park. It's a perfect perch for the Peregrine falcons who have a nest on Wall St. and occasionally light here in the summer months. The commanding statue in the park is *Charging Bull,* a shrine to the god of strong stock markets. *(Intersection of Battery Pl., Broadway, and Whitehall St.* Ⓢ *4, 5 to Bowling Green.)*

US CUSTOM HOUSE. The Custom House was completed in 1907, when the city still derived most of its revenue from customs. In 1979, it was narrowly saved from demolition, and it has since been transformed into the Smithsonian's **National Museum of the American Indian** (see **Museums,** p. 222). The magnificent Beaux Arts building, designed by Cass Gilbert, is fronted by sculptures of four women representing Africa, America, Asia, and Europe. The face of the god Mercury crowns each of the building's 44 columns, which pay homage to the most successful city-states in history. The rotunda holds a series of 1936 murals by Reginald Marsh depicting famous explorers and New York's port. *(1 Bowling Green.* Ⓢ *4, 5 to Bowling Green.)*

NEW YORK STOCK EXCHANGE. In 1792, 24 stockbrokers met beneath a buttonwood tree outside **68 Wall Street** and signed a trade agreement, which formed the precursor to the world's largest stock exchange. The NYSE in its present form was incorporated in 1817, moving to its current site in 1865 and moving to its current building in 1903. Designed by George B. Post in Classical Revival style, the building is closely modeled on a Roman temple, ringed by imposing Corinthian columns and clothed in reliefs representing commerce. Over two billion shares change hands here every day. The trading floor has been enclosed in glass since 1967, when the radical activist Abbie Hoffman and his merry band of "Yippies" dumped hundreds of dollar bills on the floor, causing the traders to stop their work to snatch up the money. The anti-capitalist Hoffman saw the event as a vivid drama-tization of what happens on the trading floor every day. Prior to 2001, the NYSE was one of New York's most popular tourist attractions, but it has been closed to the public since the 9/11 attacks, with some exceptions made for large groups. Security here is among the tightest in the Financial Center. *(18 Broad St., between Wall St. and Exchange Pl.* Ⓢ *2, 3 to Wall St./William St.; 4, 5 to Wall St./Broadway; 1, R, W to Rector St.; J, M, Z to Broad St.* ☎ *212-656-5165 or 212-656-5168; www.nyse.com. Closed indef-initely to the public.)*

▨**TRINITY CHURCH.** Around the corner from the NYSE sits this Gothic Revival Epis-copal church, which actually owns much of the land on which its towering, hyper-wealthy neighbors sit. At the time of its construction in 1846, the Gothic spire of Trinity Church was the tallest structure in all of New York. The church's sanctuary and ceme-tery (site of Alexander Hamilton's grave) are peaceful oases in the midst of the biggest rat race in the world. *(Broadway, at Wall St.* Ⓢ *1, 2, 4, 5 to Wall St./Broadway; 1, R, W to Rec-tor St.* ☎ *212-602-0800; www.trinitywallstreet.org. Open M-F 7am-6pm. Museum open M-F 9-11:45am and 1-3:45pm, Sa 10am-3:45pm, Su 1-3:45pm. Concerts most Th at 1pm. Su Eucha-rist 9, 11:15am. Free tours daily at 2pm, and following Su 11:15am Eucharist.)*

❗ From 2006 to 2009, weekend service on some lower Manhattan subway lines may be suspended for the construction of the Fulton Transit Center and the new South Ferry Terminal. For up-to-date subway information, check www.mta.info.

FEDERAL HALL NATIONAL MEMORIAL. George Washington stands guard in front of this 1703 Parthenon look-alike, which housed the original City Hall. It was renamed Federal Hall in 1789, when Washington took his Oath of Office here. The hall served as the first seat of government of the United States. James Madison presented the Bill of Rights to Congress here. The original structure was demol-ished in 1812, but was later rebuilt to house numerous federal agencies. A recently renovated and expanded museum features the Bible that Washington swore upon at his inauguration and a piece of flooring he stood on during the ceremony. The first floor houses a new Lower Manhattan visitors center with information about nearby parks and museums. *(26 Wall St., between Nassau and William St. Wheelchair-accessible entrance at 15 Pine St.* Ⓢ *1, R, W to Rector St.; 2, 3 to Wall St./William St.; 4, 5 to Wall St./Broadway; J, M, Z to Broad St.* ☎ *212-825-6888; www.nps.gov/feha. Open M-F 9am-5pm. Call for tour times.)*

THE FEDERAL RESERVE BANK OF NEW YORK. This mammoth neo-Renaissance building, completed in 1924, occupies an entire city block. Modeled after the Palazzo Strozzi, the home of a 15th-century Florentine banking family, its stern facade protects one-fourth of the world's gold bullion; the building is the most heavily fortified in the city. The gold, much of which is foreign, is secured by 121 triple-locked compartments and a 90-ton steel door in a vault five stories under-ground. On the second floor of the building, there is a shooting range where the building's security personnel maintain their aim. Despite the heavy security, a tour of the building is surprisingly fun. Current exhibits include *FedWorks: Money, Banking, and the Federal Reserve System* and *Drachmas, Doubloons, and Dollars: The History of Money.* Call at least five days in advance to reserve a place on the tour of the vault. *(33 Liberty St., between Nassau and William St.* Ⓢ *2, 3, 4, 5, A, C, J, M, Z to Fulton St./Broadway/Nassau St.* ☎ *212-720-6130; www.newyorkfed.org. Free tours M-F 9:30, 10:30, 11:30am, 1:30, and 2:30pm. Arrive 15min. early for security screening and bring ID. Reservations required at least 5 days in advance.)*

WORLD TRADE CENTER SITE (GROUND ZERO). The site where the World Trade Center once stood is a sobering one. The poignancy of the conspicuously empty landscape can only be understood in person. But it won't remain empty for long. Construction of a memorial, *Reflecting Absence*, began in the summer of 2006, and it is scheduled to be completed by the eighth anniversary of the attacks on September 11, 2009. Until then, the Tribute Center across the street from Ground Zero tells the story of the victims and their families through two floors of images, audio, and video. The planned Freedom Tower (see **Ground Breaking at Ground Zero,** at right) is currently scheduled to be completed by 2011. *(On the corner of Liberty and West St.* [S] *E to World Trade Center; R, W to Cortlandt St.; 2, 3, 4, 5, A, C, J, M, Z to Fulton St./Broadway/Nassau St. TRIBUTE CENTER: 120 Liberty St., between Church and Greenwich St. ☎ 212-422-3520; www.tributenyc.org. Open M and W-Sa 10am-6pm, Tu and Su noon-6pm. 1hr. walking tours of the site, led by those affected by the attacks, are held M-F 1 and 3pm; Sa-Su at noon, 1, 2, and 3pm. $10, children under 12 free. Reserve walking tours at www.telecharge.com.)*

■ **BATTERY PARK CITY.** When the World Trade Center was being constructed in the 1970s, millions of tons of soil were deposited west of West St. The **World Financial Center,** on West St. between the World Trade Center and the Hudson River, was built on this landfill. The 45,000 sq. ft. **Winter Garden,** a grand public space and a popular lunchtime relaxation zone for downtown office workers and tourists, is its centerpiece. The garden suffered severe damage on its east side on September 11. Some 2000 panes of the arched glass ceiling, half of the grand staircase, the marble flooring, and all 16 of the 40 ft. palm trees had to be replaced. Today, the second-floor observation area is the best all-weather perch from which to view Ground Zero. The garden, which faces the river, hosts free year-round festivals and performances (schedules and information www.worldfinancial-center.com). The most well-known of these is the spectacular **New York International Orchid Show,** held in mid-spring each year. The re-opened **Liberty Street Bridge,** formerly known as South Bridge, connects Battery Park City to the rest of Lower Manhattan. Two spectacularly beautiful parks are also within Battery Park City limits. Recently opened **Wagner Park** is an ideal place for sunbathing near the water, with unobstructed views of the Statue of Liberty, sailboats, and speeding jet skis. Nearby **Rockefeller Park** is a popular spot for children. The Battery Park City Authority (www.batteryparkcity.org) sponsors chess lessons, volleyball tournaments, tai chi lessons, and a range of other activities. *(*[S]* E to World Trade Center; 2, 3 to Wall St./William St.; 4, 5 to Wall St./Broadway; 1, R, W to Rector St.; 1, 2, 3 to Chambers St./W Broadway; A, C to Chambers St./Church St.; 2, 3 to Park Pl. ☎ 212-945-0505.)*

GROUND BREAKING AT GROUND ZERO

Few questions in the history of city planning have been as fraught with controversy as what to do with the site once occupied by the World Trade Center. The competing interests of architects, city planners, real estate developers, city and state politicians, and the victims' families have made the planning process unwieldy and miasmic. Can the memory of the victims be honored in a way that still makes productive use of prime Lower Manhattan real estate? Can site design be bold yet still conscious of the security risks of the post-9/11 era?

After years of back-and-forth negotiation, construction finally began on a tower and memorial complex at the site in April of 2006. *Freedom Tower,* designed by Polish-born architect Daniel Libeskind, will be the largest edifice on the site—76 floors topped with a 1776 ft. spire.

The site will also include a memorial to the victims called *Reflecting Absence,* designed by Michael Arad. Sitting in the footprint of the original World Trade Center, it will include a garden at street-level; twin, waterfall-fed reflecting pools where the towers once stood, with the names of all 2979 victims inscribed along their edges; the foundation and slurry wall of the original Twin Towers at the bedrock level; and a small museum and visitors center.

CIVIC CENTER

New York City's center of government is located immediately north of its financial district. Courthouses, municipal buildings, and federal buildings revolve around City Hall. Sights are listed roughly from south to north. *([S] 2, 3 to Park Pl.; R, W to City Hall; 4, 5, 6 to Brooklyn Bridge/City Hall; J, M, Z to Chambers St./Centre St.)*

ST. PAUL'S CHAPEL. Inspired by the design of London's St. Martin-in-the-Fields, this modest chapel was completed in 1766; its clock tower and spire were added in 1794. It is Manhattan's oldest church—George Washington prayed here regularly—and its structure has been altered little since Revolutionary times. In 2001-2002, the gates surrounding the "Little Church that Stood" served as a de facto memorial to the victims of the 9/11 attacks. Mourners left mementos and messages of grief and hope. The many cards, photographs, and other items left at the chapel have been stored for display in a museum that is to be built near the former site of the World Trade Center. Today, the *Unwavering Spirit* exhibit chronicles the Chapel's year-long ministry to WTC recovery workers. Pictures of Ground Zero, messages to those who died in the collapse, and tributes to the hundreds of men and women who risked their lives to rescue others can be seen in the sanctuary. *(Broadway, between Fulton and Vesey St. ☎212-233-4164; www.saintpaulschapel.org. Chapel open M-F 9am-3pm, Su 7am-3pm. Su Eucharist 8, 10am. Unwavering Spirit exhibit open M-Sa 10am-6pm, Su 9am-4pm. Free.)*

WOOLWORTH BUILDING. F.W. Woolworth supposedly paid $15.5 million to house the headquarters of his five-and-dime store empire in this elegant 1913 skyscraper, once known as the "Cathedral of Commerce." The skyscraper's fast-paced construction added an average of one and a half stories per week. Once finished, the 792 ft. building was the tallest in the world. In 1913, nearby 40 Wall St. surpassed it in height. The Woolworth Building's lobby, unfortunately closed to the public, has Gothic arches, glittering mosaics, gold painted mailboxes, imported marble designs, and carved caricatures. *(233 Broadway, between Barclay St. and Park Pl. Interior closed to public.)*

CITY HALL. The offices of New York City's mayor are in this elegant Neoclassical building, erected between 1803 and 1811. Press conferences and demonstrations are often held on its steps. In 1865, thousands of mourners paid their respects to the body of Abraham Lincoln under the hall's vaulted rotunda. Winding stairs lead to the **Governor's Room,** where portraits of American political heroes adorn the walls. City Hall sits in **City Hall Park,** which once held a jail, a public execution ground, and barracks for British soldiers. The park, a popular lunchtime spot, offers the best view of City Hall. The area along Park Row, now graced with a statue of journalist Horace Greeley, was once known as "Newspaper Row." Most of New York's papers were originally published near the one place in which they were guaranteed to find scandal. *(Broadway at Murray St., off Park Row. ☎212-788-6879. Closed to the public. Park open daily until dusk.)*

TWEED COURTHOUSE. Named after the infamous Boss Tweed of the Tammany Hall corruption scandals (p. 54), this courthouse took 10 years and $14 million—the equivalent of $166 million today—to build. Rumor has it that $10 million went to Tweed himself, setting off a public outcry that marked the beginning of the end for Tweed and his embezzling ways. In 2002, Mayor Michael Bloomberg moved the city's new Department of Education into the building. *(Chambers St., between Centre St. and Broadway, north of City Hall. Closed to the public.)*

SURROGATE'S COURT. Two sculpture groups—*New York in Its Infancy* and *New York in Revolutionary Times*—grace the Beaux Arts exterior of this overwhelming former Hall of Records (1907). In front of the building's Mansard roof stand eight statues of notable New Yorkers—you may want to cross the street to get a better view. *(31 Chambers St., near Centre St. ☎ 212-374-8244. Closed to the public.)*

AFRICAN BURIAL GROUND. In 1991, archaeologists discovered the remains of over 20,000 slaves buried 20 ft. underground as they were testing the terrain in preparation for the construction of a new office building. The site is today the largest excavated African cemetery in the world, encompassing five city blocks. The bodies, more than 40% of them children, were stacked on top of each other in unmarked graves until 1794; the site is evidence of New York's often unacknowledged participation in the slave trade. Congress has declared it a national landmark. An "Ancestral Libation Chamber" is currently being constructed on the site to commemorate the African people buried here. *(Corner of Duane and Elk St. Learn more at the Office of Public Education and Interpretation, 290 Broadway at Duane St. Open M-F 9am-4pm.)*

SOUTH STREET SEAPORT. The shipping industry thrived on this site for most of the 19th century, when New York was the most important port city in the US. In the 20th century, the industry gradually moved elsewhere and seedy bars, brothels, and crime took over. In the mid-1980s, the South Street Seaport Museum teamed up with the Rouse Corporation, which built Boston's Quincy Market, to create a 12-block "museum without walls." Unfortunately, the "museum" offers a great deal of unimaginative consumerism. **Pier 17** houses a three-story mall with the usual array of chain stores.

Still, kids and nautical history buffs may enjoy a visit to the seaport's piers. Nine historical ships are berthed here, and galleries showcase ship models, nautical designs, and paintings. The **Seaport Museum Visitors Center** provides detailed maps and sells passes to the galleries and ships. The **Peking**, built in 1911 by a Hamburg-based company is the second-largest sailing ship ever launched. She spent most of her career on the "nitrate run" to Chile, which passes through one of the world's most dangerous stretches of water. She also served as a floating boy's school in England for nearly 40 years. The ship was towed to its current location in 1975.

In addition to the *Peking*, there are seven other ships open to the public. Some are stationary, like the 325 ft. iron-hulled, full-rigged *Wavertree* and the *Ambrose*, a floating lighthouse built in 1908 to mark the entrance to New York Harbor. Others actually take to the open seas. The **Pioneer** (1885) offers 2hr. and 3hr. rides.

Back on land, the museum occupies a number of the area's early 19th-century buildings. **Bowne & Co.**, 211 Water St., is a re-creation of a 19th-century printing shop. It offers demonstrations of letterpress printing. On Fulton St., between South and Front St., is **Schermerhorn Row.** Constructed between 1811 and 1812, these Georgian-Federal buildings once housed shops that served the throngs exiting the Fulton Ferry. They now offer gallery space to rotating exhibits run by the museum, free with admission. *(Between FDR Dr. and Water St., and between Beekman and John St. S 2, 3, 4, 5, A, C, J, M, Z to Fulton St./Broadway/Nassau St. www.southstreetseaport-museum.com. VISITORS CENTER: 12 Fulton St. ☎ 212-748-8600. Open Apr.-Oct. Tu-Su 10am-6pm, Nov.-Mar. M and F-Su 10am-5pm. Ships and galleries $8, students and seniors $6, children under 12 free. M $3 off.)*

THE REAL DEAL: SOUTH STREET SEAPORT. Unless you have a hankering for suburban-style chain stores, the South Street Seaport will likely disappoint. Luckily, the scene changes entirely just a few blocks away. Wander the cobblestone streets just south of the Brooklyn Bridge for a more authentic seaport feel and some excellent dining options. —Amber Johnson

SOHO AND TRIBECA

SOHO

In the early part of the 20th century, SoHo was an industrial zone rife with factories, warehouses, and dark alleys. Artists began gravitating here in the 1940s, charmed by its low rents and spacious lofts. By the 60s, the trickle became a full-scale migration, and the art scene blossomed, led by Jean-Michel Basquiat, Keith Haring, and Kenny Scharf. Since then, the area has gentrified so much that few artists can actually afford to live there. Its streets today are a destination for gallery-goers, fashion shoppers, and tourists in search of the downtown coolness with which the name SoHo is synonymous. The neighborhood still boasts pockets of off-beat culture, high fashion, and meticulous design, and it's a celebrity magnet. Nicole Kidman, Lenny Kravitz, Leonardo DiCaprio, and Britney Spears have all had apartments here. The major fashion designers may have their flagship stores along Madison Ave., but they all have a chic, creative boutique here too.

Designated a historic district in 1973 by the Landmarks Preservation Commission, SoHo is filled with cast-iron warehouse buildings dating from the 19th century. Especially notable is the **Haughwout Building,** 488 Broadway, with its delicate facade of arched windows set between Corinthian columns. Built in 1857, the five-story Haughwout housed the world's first passenger elevator. Galleries abound on West Broadway and on a variety of the less populated streets, and street vendors neighbor name-brand boutiques on Houston, Spring, and Prince St. Walk west away from Broadway to see smaller shops and colorful restaurants. *(Bounded to the north by Houston St., to the south by Canal St., to the west by W Broadway, and to the east by Crosby St. [S] C, E to Spring St./Ave. of the Americas (6th Ave.); 6 to Spring St./Lafayette St.; N, R, W to Prince St.; 1 to W Houston St.; B, D, F, V to Broadway/Lafayette St.)*

TRIBECA

TriBeCa's story follows a classic Manhattan trajectory—it was once an industrial wasteland, but was made hip when a real estate developer dreamed up its acronym title ("Triangle Below Canal Street") in 1970. It's the address of many New York celebrities, most notably Robert DeNiro, who owns several local restaurants. One of the neighborhood's highlights is **Washington Market Park,** located in the triangle bounded by Greenwich, Chambers, and West St. The park hosts Thursday-evening concerts (late June to early Aug.) in its blue-and-white gazebo. *(Bounded by Canal St. to the north, the Hudson River to the west, Vesey St. to the south, and E Broadway to the east. [S] 1 to Canal St./Varick St.; A, C, E to Canal St./Ave. of the Americas (6th Ave.); 1 to Franklin St.; 1, 2, 3 to Chambers St./W Broadway; A, C to Chambers St./Church St.)*

CHINATOWN

Walk just a few blocks from stylish SoHo or buttoned-down Lower Manhattan, and the scene will suddenly change drastically before your eyes. Chinatown sidewalks are a frenetic, loud, and crowded jungle. English is no longer the dominant language in the streets (note those "Help Wanted: Must Speak Mandarin" signs in the shop windows), and the array of items for sale is dizzying. You'll see heaps of gorgeous Asian vegetables you've never imagined, enormous fresh fish chilling on ice, live turtles swimming in tubs, Juicy sunglasses in boutiques for a mere $300, and faux Louis Vuitton bags everywhere for $15. Merchants spread scarves, CDs, mini-Buddhas, bamboo hats, and I-Love-NY t-shirts on the sidewalk, and, if you're really lucky, you'll come across one hawking red-bean popsicles on a hot day. *([S] A, C, E to Canal St./6th Ave.; J, M, Z to Canal St./Centre St.; N, Q, R, W to Canal St./Broadway; 6 to Canal St./Lafayette St.; F to E Broadway; 6 to Spring St./Lafayette St.)*

FIRST SHEARITH ISRAEL GRAVEYARD. Long before Chinese immigrants called this neighborhood home, the area served as an enclave for a different immigrant community. This tiny cemetery served New York City's first Jewish congregation, the Spanish-Portuguese Shearith Israel Synagogue, founded in 1654. You can't walk through the cemetery, but by peering through the gates, you can see gravestones that date from as early as 1656, which make this the nation's oldest Jewish cemetery. *(South side of Chatham Sq., on St. James Pl., between James and Oliver St.* [S] *J, M, N, Q, R, W, Z, 6 to Canal St.)*

 MONEY UP. When spending the day in Chinatown, bring enough cash to buy the shopping and food items you'll want. Most Chinatown establishments only accept cash, and ATMs are much scarcer than elsewhere in Manhattan.

CHATHAM SQUARE AND KIMLAU SQUARE. In the center of Chatham Sq. stands the granite ceremonial gateway of Kimlau Sq., named after a Chinese-American bomber pilot who died in 1945 while serving in WWII. Also occupying the square is the 12 ft. statue of **Lin Ze Xu**. The inscription on the base describes him as a "pioneer" in the "war on drugs." Lin, a 19th-century Chinese commissioner in Canton, rounded up over two million tons of opium and destroyed it during the heyday of the East India Company. His actions are believed to have precipitated the 1839-42 Opium Wars. Even though the Chinese ultimately lost the Opium Wars and Lin Ze Xu lost his job, he is considered a national hero for his moral fortitude. *(At the intersection of Bowery and Doyers St., 3 blocks south of Canal St.* [S] *J, M, Z, to Chambers St.; 4, 5, 6 to Brooklyn Bridge/City Hall; 6, J, M, Z to Canal St.)*

MAHAYANA BUDDHIST TEMPLE. Just outside the temple's doors, long lines of travelers wait for the next Fung Wah Chinatown bus to Boston, and Canal St. traffic blares. But step inside, and you'll be soothed by the smell of incense, a profusion of golds and reds, and Chinese Buddhists praying, oblivious to the outside din. If you're used to thinking of Buddhism as practiced solely in musty monasteries in the mountains of Tibet, the large televisions, spotlights, and modern sound system in this space will surprise you. An enormous 20 ft. golden Buddha occupies the stage in the auditorium. Visitors are asked to wear modest clothes—shirts with sleeves, and either long pants or knee-length skirts. Services take place from 10am-noon on certain days each month, following the Chinese calendar (a schedule is posted inside the temple), and they are open to the public provided you arrive at least 10min. prior to start time. *(133 Canal St., near the Manhattan Bridge, between the Bowery and Chrystie St.* [S] *J, M, N, Q, R, W Z, 6 to Canal St.* ☎ *212-925-8787. Open daily 9am-6pm.)*

MANHATTAN BRIDGE. Walking northeast toward where the Bowery and E Broadway meet will bring you past the grand arch and flanking colonnades that mark the entrance to the Manhattan Bridge (1901). These were designed by Carrère and Hastings, the same firm that designed the New York Public Library (p. 180) and the Frick Mansion (p. 227). Though far less popular than the walkway on the Brooklyn Bridge, the south side's bike and pedestrian path affords incredible views of Lower Manhattan, not to mention the Brooklyn Bridge (p. 202). Due to safety concerns, the bike path is ramped and closed to pedestrians. It can be accessed from Canal/Forsythe St. Be particularly careful during rush hour, when the sheer volume of traffic makes the surrounding streets incredibly congested. *(Between Canal St. and the Bowery.* [S] *J, M, N, Q, R, W, Z, 6 to Canal St.)*

LOWER EAST SIDE

The Lower East Side was once the most densely settled area in New York, with 240,000 people crammed into a single square mile. The Irish, fleeing famine-stricken Ireland in the mid-1800s, were the first to arrive. From the 1880s until WWI, an influx of mainly Jewish Eastern Europeans arrived. After WWII, a wave of African-Americans and Puerto Ricans joined the mix, and over the last two decades, Latinos and Asians have moved in. Today, Chinatown is steadily creeping northward into the neighborhood.

While the Lower East Side's immigrant past remains visible in its many ethnic food stores and restaurants, perhaps the most obvious 21st-century influx consists of young hipsters, who patrol the neighborhood's community gardens and graffiti-marked streets. You'll find indie-rock and underground music clubs galore, and neighborhood shopping includes both vintage clothing stores and pricey independent boutiques. The **Lower East Side Visitor's Center,** 261 Broome St., provides maps, brochures, a free 90min. shopping tour of the area (Apr.-Dec. Su 11am; meet in front of Katz's Deli, p. 122), and a free discount card for shopping. (☎212-226-9010; www.lowereastsideny.com. Open daily 10am-4pm.) Sights are listed from north to south. *([S] F, V to Lower East Side/2nd Ave.; F to E Broadway; F, J, M, Z to Delancey St./Essex St.)*

CONGREGATION ANSHE CHESED. This red Gothic Revival building was built in 1849, making it the oldest Reform synagogue in New York. The building's understated but dramatically lit interior is open to the public. Though the synagogue hosts services twice a month (1st and 3rd F), the building is predominantly used by the Angel Orensanz Foundation's Center for the Arts. The foundation hosts classical music concerts, art exhibitions, and scholarly lectures. You can find a schedule of events on their website. *(172-176 Norfolk St., between E Houston and Stanton St. [S] F, V to 2nd Ave.; F, J, M, Z to Delancey St./Essex St. ☎212-529-7194; www.orensanz.com. Call in advance for admission.)*

SUNG TAK BUDDHIST ASSOCIATION. This Buddhist temple occupies a former synagogue. Look for the two imposing stone staircases on either side of a Chinese emporium, with a giant white Buddha at the top. The interior reflects the building's multicultural past in its juxtaposition of Middle Eastern and Asian architectural styles. Services are held daily. *(15 Pike St., between E Broadway and Henry St. [S] F to E Broadway. ☎212-587-5936. Open daily 9am-6pm. Free.)*

THE ELDRIDGE ST. SYNAGOGUE. This Moorish-style edifice, built in 1886 as the first synagogue for New York's Eastern Europeans, presides over a crowded, noisy block of what has now become Chinatown. The synagogue hosts community events almost every Sunday, including lectures, concerts, and festivals (free-$12). Call or check the website for upcoming events. *(12 Eldridge St., south of Canal St. [S] 6, N, R to Canal St. ☎212-219-0888; www.eldridgestreet.org. Tours Tu-Th and Su 11am-4pm. $5; students and seniors $3.)*

GREENWICH VILLAGE

Greenwich Village, also known as the West Village, layers artistry, gentrified grime, social activism, and counter-cultural subversiveness atop a tangle of wandering streets. In the mid-19th century, the neighborhood was a high-society playground that fostered literary invention. Henry James captured the Village's spirit in his 1880 novel, *Washington Square.* The list of writers and intellectuals who have lived here since then is stunning: Herman Melville, James Fenimore Cooper, Mark Twain, Willa Cather, John Steinbeck, John Dos Passos, and e.e. cummings, to name only the most prominent. The Beat movement crystallized in the area in the 1950s, and the 60s saw the growth of a vocal GLBT community around Christopher St. Violent clashes between police and openly gay residents resulted in the Stonewall Riots of 1969, one of the first insurrections in the struggle for gay rights. The 1970s saw the emergence of the punk scene, adding mohawked rockers to the already diverse cast of characters. In recent years, the neighborhood has become a fashionable and comfortable address for well-to-do New Yorkers with a bit more spunk than their uptown counterparts. The Village comes out in all of its counter-cultural glory for the wild Halloween Parade. Slap on your wig, strap on your appendage of choice, and join the crowd—no one will blink a rhinestoned eyelash. (S A, B, C, D, E, F, V to W 4th St.; A, C, E to 14th St./8th Ave.; 1, 2, 3, to 14th St./7th Ave.; F, V to 14th St./Ave. of the Americas (6th Ave.); L to 8th Ave., Ave. of the Americas (6th Ave.); 4, 5, 6, L, N, Q, R, W to 14th St./Union Sq.; 1 to Houston St., Christopher St.; N, R, W to 8th St./NYU; L to 6th Ave., 8th Ave.; 6 to Bleecker St.)

WASHINGTON SQUARE PARK AREA

Washington Square Park is at the center of Village life. Native Americans once inhabited the marshland here, but by the mid-17th century it was home to black slaves freed by the Dutch. The latter half of the 18th century saw the area pressed into service as a burial field for some 15,000 poor and unknown New Yorkers, and then as a hanging grounds during the Revolutionary War. In the 1820s, newly built residences made it the center of New York's social scene. On the north side of the park lies **the Row.** This stretch of tony, Federal-style brick residences, built in the 1830s, drew a sophisticated population of professionals, dandies, and novelists.

By the late 1970s and early 80s, Washington Square Park had become a hotbed for drug dealers and street crime. A noisy clean-up campaign has made the park fairly safe, although its drug traffic has not altogether vanished. Use caution here late at night. During the day, you'll find a motley mix of musicians, misunderstood teenagers, homeless people, and romping children in the park.

At the north end of the park stands the **Washington Memorial Arch,** built in 1889 to commemorate the centennial of George Washington's inauguration. Until 1964, Fifth Ave. actually ran through the arch. Residents complained of the noisy traffic, so the city cut the avenue short. (Washington Sq. Park between 4th St. and Washington Sq. Park N, MacDougal St. and Greene St. S A, B, C, D, E, F, V to W 4th St.)

NEW YORK UNIVERSITY. With 48,000 students in 14 schools, NYU is the country's largest private university. The school is known for its stellar communications and film departments, as well as some of the Village's least appealing modern architecture. Many buildings around Washington Sq. proudly fly the violet NYU flag.

Although the university sprawls throughout the city, its heart is Washington Square Park. When it was founded in 1831, NYU considered using the park as its central quad, but ultimately decided against it. Since 1976, NYU has held its commencement ceremonies here every May.

On the southeast side of the park looms the rust-colored **Elmer Holmes Bobst Library,** NYU's central library and one of the largest in the country. On the same block stands NYU's Reuben Nakian-designed **Loeb Student Center,** which is garnished with pieces of scrap metal, supposedly to represent birds in flight. Gould Plaza, which houses an aluminum sculpture by Dadaist Jean Arp, sits a few steps east on W Fourth St., in front of NYU's Stern School of Business and the Courant Institute of Mathematical Sciences.

From Gould Plaza you can walk north up Green St. to its intersection with Waverly Pl. Here sits NYU's **Brown Building,** the former site of the Triangle Shirtwaist Company, where a 1911 fire killed most of the primarily female staff, who had been locked inside to prevent them from taking too many breaks. The incident was pivotal in raising awareness of worker's rights. (NYU INFORMATION: 50 W 4th St. S 6 to Astor Pl.; N, R, W to 8th St./NYU; A, B, C, D, E, F, V to W 4th St.; 1 to Christopher St. ☎212-998-4636. Campus map posted throughout the Village.)

PICASSO. Proclaimed by *The New York Times* to be the city's ugliest piece of public art, this 36 ft., 60-ton structure made of Norwegian black stone and con-

A WALK THROUGH THE WEST VILLAGE

It's hard to think of a more perfect place for an afternoon stroll in New York than Greenwich Village. A paragon of cosmopolitan diversity, the Village truly has something for everyone. It was here that the national gay-rights movement got its start in the 1960s, owing to the courageous patrons of the Stonewall Inn. In the Village you'll also find sights dating from Revolutionary times and the hallowed stomping grounds of some of America's pre-eminent writers and artists.

TIME: 2-3 hr., preferably longer. Greenwich Village is built for wandering.

WHEN TO GO: Mid-afternoon. Time things right, and you'll end your tour during the early evening bustle, the perfect time to pick up dinner and drinks at one of the local restaurants and bars.

START: Washington Square Park. S A, B, C, D, E, F, V to W 4th St.; N, R, W to Broadway/E 8th St.

Amidst it all, you'll find countless cafes, restaurants, and bars, and some of the most vibrant street life anywhere in New York.

1 WASHINGTON SQUARE PARK. Start your walk at Washington Square Park, long the focal point of Greenwich Village life. The area served as a gallows during the Revolutionary War and as a burial ground for some 15,000 people, most of them poor and unidentified. From 1829-1833, elaborate brick houses, which came to be known as "The Row," were built along the park's northern edge. The rich and well-to-do moved in here, while poor immigrants lived in tenements on the park's southern edge. Artists and bohemians later came to populate the southern section, building a highly creative community. Today, the park is filled with chess players, kids, street musicians, and street-food vendors.

2 GRAY'S PAPAYA. Head north through the park's Washington Memorial Arch, built to commemorate the centennial of George Washington's inauguration, and continue north along Fifth Ave. Make a left on W Eighth St., and head west two blocks to Ave. of the Americas/Sixth Ave. Gray's Papaya New York's beloved "hot doggery" is on the northeast corner and serves up one of the city's cheapest meals. The "Recession Special" of two hot dogs and a fruit drink will set you back less than $3.

3 JEFFERSON MARKET LIBRARY. Turn right on Ave. of the Americas/Sixth Ave., and cross W Ninth St. to the north. Just up on your left, between W Ninth and 10th St., is the Jefferson Market Library. This architectural landmark served as both a women's prison and a courthouse before being converted to a public library. Its garden is lovely in good weather.

4 PATCHIN PLACE. Just north of the library, make a sharp left on W 10th St. Across the street from the library is the small gated alley called Patchin Place. Look for a street sign high up on the alley's wall. Marlon Brando, e.e. cummings, and Djuna Barnes all called this alley home at one time or another. It's still the site of private residences.

5 STONEWALL INN. Continue southwest on W 10th St. to Seventh Ave. S, and turn left. Walk south to the logic-defying intersection of Christopher St. and Seventh Ave. S. The modern gay-rights movement started just east of this intersection at 51-53 Christopher St., when gay patrons of the Stonewall Inn stood up to police who attempted to break up their party. The original establishment has closed, but you can still toast to the protesters at a new bar of the same name at the same address. On the first anniversary of the Stonewall Riots, New York's first gay-pride parade marched up Sixth Ave. from Christopher St. to Central Park.

6 PUFF & PAO. Cross to the western side of Seventh Ave. S, and walk southwest on Christopher St. The next few blocks, still a center of gay life, are filled with sex-toy shops that make for interesting window shopping. Indulge in New York's latest dessert trend by grabbing a cream puff at Puff & Pao, 105 Christopher St., near Bleecker St.

7 CHUMLEY'S. Turn left on Bedford St., and head southeast. One block down, at 86 Bedford St., between Grove and Barrow St., you'll pass Chumley's, a former speakeasy and literary hangout that retains its secret feel. There's no sign, but look for a cream building with two dark-brown doors. Push the one on the right, and you'll stumble into a timeless speakeasy,

WALKING TOUR

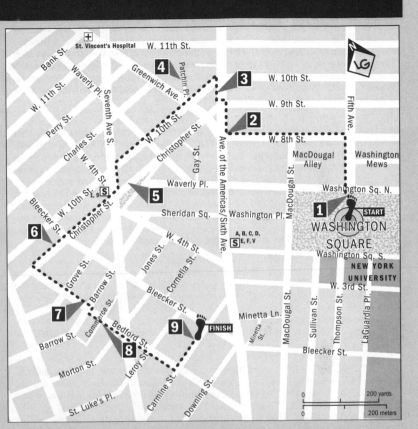

where Hemmingway, Faulkner, and Salinger all raised a glass. It's worth a visit whether or not you partake yourself.

8 75½ BEDFORD ST. Continue walking southeast on Bedford St. across Commerce St. Just past that intersection is 75½ Bedford St., the former home of writer Edna St. Vincent Millay and, later, anthropologist Margaret Mead. Measuring just 9½ ft. across, this is the Village's narrowest building.

9 THE NIGHT IS YOUNG. From here, wandering possibilities abound. If you return to Sixth Ave. and walk north to the W Fourth St. Basketball Courts, you'll find some serious pick-up basketball being played almost every afternoon. Or, head east on W Third St. to the heart of the NYU shopping and nightlife areas. Go south on MacDougal St. for a wide selection of restaurants and entertainment venues, or continue east on W Third St. to Thompson St. for boutique shopping and more quaint eateries. Challenge someone to chess at the Village Chess Shop, 230 Thompson St., or stop in at the Red Lion, 151 Bleecker St., at Thompson St., for live music and English football on TV.

crete is Norwegian artist Carl Nesjar's adaptation of a small sheet metal work by Picasso. (The original 24 in. sculpture was entitled *Bust of Sylvette.*) Nesjar's enormous version sits in a green square at the center of NYU's three 30-story Silver Towers (designed by I.M. Pei). The disastrous aesthetics of this concrete monolith have created one of the only quiet spaces in a frantic neighborhood. *(On Bleecker St., between LaGuardia Pl. and Mercer St., in the courtyard of the building complex on the south side of the street.* S *A, B, C, D, E, F, V to W 4th St.)*

THE NEW SCHOOL. In 1917 the founders of the New School envisioned a university that would be a center for political research, fostering a student body that would use its education as a tool for social change. During WWII, the New School rose to international fame when it opened the University in Exile, which offered teaching positions to European intellectuals forced to flee totalitarian regimes. The school continues its tradition of progressive-minded social and public policy research, and it has become one of the premier arts institutions in the US, housing the Parsons School of Design, the Actors Studio Drama School and undergraduate programs in classical, jazz, and contemporary music. Former Democratic politician Bob Kerrey is the university's president. *(66 W 12th St., between 6th and 5th Ave.* S *F, L, V to 14th St./Ave. of the Americas (6th Ave.). www.newschool.edu.)*

GRACE CHURCH. This Gothic church was constructed in 1845 using white marble mined by prisoners from the New York State prison, Sing Sing. Philanthropist Catharine Lorillard Wolfe funded many of the additions to the church, including the beautiful East Window. The dark, ornate interior hosts a lovely St. Matthew Passion at Easter. *(802 Broadway, at 10th St.* S *L, N, Q, R, W, 4, 5, 6 to 14th St./Union Sq.* ☎ *212-254-2000; www.gracechurchnyc.org. Open to the public Tu-Su noon-5pm. Services Sept.-June W 6pm, Su 9, 11am, and 6pm; July-Aug. W 6pm, Su 10am and 6pm. Free tours of the church Su at 1pm.)*

WEST OF SIXTH AVE.

75½ BEDFORD STREET. The narrowest building in the Village, measuring 9½ ft. across, this house was home to Edna St. Vincent Millay in the early 1920s. During this time she wrote the Pulitzer Prize-winning *Ballad of Harp Weaver* and founded the Cherry Lane Theater, around the corner at 38 Commerce St. (p. 261). Sandwiched between other private residences, the red-bricked facade of this building is easy to miss. Anthropologist Margaret Mead and actors Lionel Barrymore and Cary Grant each lived at 75½ Bedford after Millay's departure. *(Near the corner of Commerce St.* S *1 to Christopher St.)*

CHRISTOPHER PARK. The intersection of Seventh Ave., Christopher St. and W Fourth St. forms a green triangle home to one statue, two sculptures, and a few benches known (mistakenly) as Sheridan Square and (correctly) as Christopher Park. The park owes its common misidentification to the statue of General Sheridan that stands at the triangle's eastern tip. **Sheridan Square** is around the corner at the intersection of Washington Pl., W Fourth St., and Barrow St.

Protesters against the Civil War draft rioted here in 1863 in some of the bloodiest days in New York history. The park has been officially renamed Stonewall Pl. in homage to the **Stonewall Inn,** the site of the 60s police raid that sparked the gay rights movement (p. 299). In 1960s New York, it was illegal for bars to serve liquor to homosexuals or suspected homosexuals. The police would enter a bar, arrest the patrons they suspected of being homosexual, and fine the bar's owners. The names of the arrested men and women were often published in the papers the next day, subjecting them to the constant threat of losing their jobs and homes. When police attempted such a raid at the Stonewall Inn on June 27, 1969, the patrons resisted arrest, and the night ended in a standoff between hundreds of homosexual resisters and the police. The Stonewall Riots that followed are now regarded as having provided the catalyst for the gay rights movement. Each year, at the end of June, marches are held to commemorate the historic event. In Christopher Park, George Segal's sculpture, *Gay Liberation*, depicts two life-size same-sex couples locked in embrace. *(Intersection of 7th Ave., Christopher St., and W 4th St. [S] 1 to Christopher St.)*

CHURCH OF ST. LUKE IN THE FIELDS. At the western end of Grove St. is the Episcopal Church of St. Luke in the Fields. The third-oldest church in Manhattan, this severe brick building dates from 1821. The church is not open to the public for sightseeing, but it welcomes all for Sunday Eucharists. It also hosts a variety of community and cultural events, including art exhibits and dances. *(479-485 Hudson St., at Grove St. [S] 1 to Christopher St. ☎212-924-0562; www.stlukesinthefields.org. Services summer M-F 6:15pm, Su 8 and 10:30am; winter M-F 6:15pm, Su 8, 9:15, and 11:15am.)*

JEFFERSON MARKET LIBRARY. This beautiful building is one of New York's most eccentric and beloved landmarks. Built as a courthouse in 1877, it served for a period as a female detention facility before being slated for demolition in the early 60s. Instead, the building was restored in 1967 and converted into a public library. The Victorian Gothic design, with its detailed brickwork, stained-glass windows, and turreted clock tower, suggests a cross between a castle and a church. The library is open to the public. Just behind it, a small garden is maintained by the community. *(425 6th Ave., at the intersection of W 10th St. and 6th Ave. [S] 1 to Christopher St. ☎212-243-4334. Open M and W noon-8pm, Tu and Th noon-6pm, F 1-6pm, Sa 10am-5pm.)*

PATCHIN PLACE. These two modest, 145-year-old buildings were built as a boarding house for employees of a posh Fifth Ave. hotel, but since then they have housed writers e. e. cummings, Theodore Dreiser, and Djuna Barnes. Barnes was apparently so reclusive that her neighbor cummings would call her "just to see if she was still alive." Patchin Place has also housed Marlon Brando, John Masefield, Eugene O'Neill, and John Reed (who wrote the Russian Revolution chronicle *Ten Days that Shook the World* here). The buildings are still private residences. Look for a locked iron gate and a street sign that reads "Patchin Place," mounted high on the alley wall. The street is across from Jefferson Market Library on the south side of 10th St. *(Off 10th St., near 6th Ave. [S] 1 to Christopher St.)*

MEATPACKING DISTRICT. In the mid 19th century, New York was the beef processing capital of the United States. Fears of the health risks posed by unsanitary slaughtering practices, shockingly described in Upton Sinclair's 1906 *The Jungle*, drove the meat industry westward, but this district, bounded by W 15th St., Hudson St., Gansevoort St., and the Hudson River, survived for most of the 20th century as a gritty, often dangerous neighborhood of warehouses and processing plants. By the early 80s, the area was ridden with violent crime, drug dealing, and prostitution. When Giuliani's crime-fighting schemes succeeded in cleaning the neighborhood up, it experienced a tidal wave of gentrification that rages unabated to this day. Fashionable restaurants, bars, and clubs spring up seemingly daily in the district's old warehouses, factories, and stockyards. Top fashion designers, such as Stella McCartney and Alexander McQueen, have opened boutiques here. The nightly migration of the young and beautiful to the neighborhood's clubs has done much to diminish the neighborhood's sketchiness, but it's still best to exercise some caution on its less busy streets. *(South of West Chelsea, roughly from 17th St. to Little W 12th St. [S] A, C, E, L to 14th St./8th Ave.)*

EAST VILLAGE

The East Village, east of Broadway and north of E Houston St., was carved out of the Bowery and the Lower East Side in the early 1960s, as artists and writers moved to escape the high rents in Greenwich Village. In the East Village's heyday,

Jimi Hendrix and the Fugs played open-air shows for bright-eyed love children. Today you'll still find "deadbeatniks," anarchists, artists, and students hanging out in local cafes. Older Eastern European immigrants live alongside newer Latino and Asian arrivals, and punks, hippies, ravers, rastas, guppies, and goths are all mixed in to the fray. The neighborhood is one of the most diverse in Manhattan.

Recently, however, the area has found itself in the path of New York's wave of gentrification, evidenced by the increasing numbers of boutiques and chic eateries that have set up shop here. Many poorer residents of the East Village feel that wealthier newcomers are pushing them out by raising rents. Those tensions have made the East Village one of the most overtly politicized regions of New York City.

East of First Ave., south of 14th St., and north of Houston St., the avenues drop numbers and adopt letters. The **Alphabet City** area is generally safe during the day. At night the throngs of 20-somethings attracted to local bars on Ave. A and B ensure some protection, but use caution east of Ave. B. For information on current issues and events in Alphabet City, check the free local papers at St. Mark's Bookshop (p. 284) and other stores in the area. Neighborhood posters also advertise current happenings. Sights are listed from west to east. *([S] 6 to Astor Pl., Bleecker St.; L to 1st Ave., 3rd Ave.; F, V to Lower East Side/2nd Ave.)*

ST. MARK'S PLACE. In the 1960s, pot-smoking flower children and musicians filled this street. In the late 70s, they gave way to mohawked punks who hassled passersby from brownstone steps. The youths of the 60s and 70s now line the street as graying, but still tattooed, adults, who observe the stream of young locals with a mix of amusement and disdain.

Present-day St. Mark's Pl. is full of tiny ethnic eateries, street-level shops, and sidewalk vendors selling trinkets of all kinds—from plastic bug-eye sunglasses ($5) to belly rings ($8). In a way, St. Mark's resembles a small-town Main St.—but a small town with a bad-ass history. Unlike in most areas of the city, people here know one another by name and sometimes help each other out. Although some more-obscure-than-thou types now shun the increasingly commercialized and crowded areas of the street, St. Mark's remains a hub of East Village life. *(Where E 8th St. would be, between Cooper Sq. E and Ave. A. [S] 6 to Astor Pl.)*

ASTOR PLACE. A small road and a large cultural intersection, this western border of the East Village simmers with street life. Check out the ever-popular **Beaver Murals** at the Astor Pl. subway stop; they pay homage to John Jacob Astor's prolific fur trade. Upstairs from the murals, the cast-iron subway kiosk was built in 1985 as part of the station's reconstruction. A large black cube balances on its corner over Astor Pl. If you and your friends push it hard enough, the cube rotates, but you may disturb the various denizens of Astor Pl. who sit underneath it. **"The Cube"** (officially the *Alamo*, by Bernard Rosenthal) is a meeting point for countless rallies, marches, demonstrations, and impromptu performances. It also provides asphalt for hordes of skaters. *(At the junction of Lafayette Ave., 4th Ave., and E 8th St. [S] 6 to Astor Pl.)*

THE COOPER UNION FOUNDATION BUILDING. Despite having completed only one year of school, New York industrialist Peter Cooper invented the first transatlantic telephone cable, the first functioning steam engine, and, with the help of his wife Sarah, Jell-O. Cooper went on to found the Cooper Union for the Advancement of Science and Art in 1859 as a tuition-free technical and design school. Both the American Red Cross and the NAACP got their start in the Foundation Building. Cooper Union also stands as the oldest building in the US to incorporate steel beams, which are made of old railroad rails. The second-floor **Houghton Gallery** (☎212-353-4203; www.cooper.edu) hosts changing exhibits primarily by the talented student body. Augustus St-Gaudens's statue of the philanthropist stands in front of the building in Cooper Sq. *(7 E 7th St., at Cooper Sq., off Astor Pl. [S] 6 to Astor Pl.)*

ST. MARK'S CHURCH IN-THE-BOWERY. Erected in 1799, St. Mark's Church stands on the site where Peter Stuyvesant, the Dutch governor of the original New York colony, lies buried. Since the 19th century, the church has served the immigrant communities around Tompkins Sq. Park through religious services, political activism, and community art initiatives. In the 1960s, St. Mark's was a rallying place for civil rights and antiwar demonstrations. Sam Shepard staged his first plays here. Neighborhood teenagers and young adults rebuilt the church after a devastating fire almost destroyed it in 1978. Today, the church has a vibrant Hispanic ministry and offers a weekly Spanish Eucharist (Sa 5:30pm). The church hosts several community theater companies, including the **Ontological-Hysteric Theater,** producer of some of the better off-Broadway plays; the **Danspace Project;** and the **Poetry Project** (for an overview of all three projects, see p. 266). The **Reverend Billy and the Stop Shopping Gospel Choir** also calls this church home. *(131 E 10th St., between 2nd and 3rd Ave.* Ⓢ *6 to Astor Pl.* ☎ *212-674-6377; www.stmarkschurch-in-the-bowery.com. West Yard open Tu 3-5pm, W 3-6pm, Sa 10:30am-12:30pm, Su 11:30am-1pm. W Vespers 6pm 6:30pm, Su Eucharist 11am, Spanish Eucharist Sa at 5:30 in the Parish Hall.)*

COLONNADE ROW. Unfortunately, these four-columned houses are not open to the public. New York's most famous 19th-century millionaires—John Jacob Astor, Cornelius "Commodore" Vanderbilt, and members of the Roosevelt family—inhabited three of these 1833 structures. There used to be nine of them; the four remaining are, sadly, the worse for wear. *(428-434 Lafayette Ave., at 4th St.* Ⓢ *6 to Bleecker St.)*

THE SECOND AVENUE DELI. This famous Jewish landmark, founded by Abe Lebewohl, was all that remained of the "Yiddish Rialto"—the stretch of Second Ave. between Houston and 14th St. that contained the Yiddish theater district in the early part of the 20th century. Unfortunately, now even this establishment—at one time laying claim to the meanest pastrami sandwich in town—has closed its doors, rumored by some to soon be replaced by a bank. Stars of David in the sidewalk out front contain the names of actors and actresses who spent their lives entertaining Jewish immigrants. The community is no longer a Jewish enclave, so the closing of this historic deli symbolizes the end of an era. Across the street is **Abe Lebewohl Park,** built to commemorate the deli's founder, who was murdered in 1996. *(156 2nd Ave., at E 10th St.* Ⓢ *6 to Astor Pl.)*

NEW YORK MARBLE CEMETERIES. The New York Marble Cemeteries (so named for their 156 underground vaults made of solid white Tuckahoe marble) were the city's first two nonsectarian graveyards. Founded in 1830 and 1831, both cemeteries can be viewed through the iron fences that surround them. The Second St. cemetery has a better view. Descendents of the original 19th-century owners can still be buried here. *(2nd Ave., between E 2nd and 3rd St. and 52-74 E 2nd St., between 1st and 2nd Ave.* Ⓢ *F, V to Lower East Side/2nd Ave.)*

ST. GEORGE UKRAINIAN CATHOLIC CHURCH. Ukrainian-American life centers around E Seventh St.'s cafes and churches. The St. George Ukrainian Catholic Church is the most remarkable of the latter. The present-day building dates from 1978, when St. George's parishioners financed the new church, which is built in classical Ukrainian Byzantine style. The icons that ornament the outer doors are eclipsed by the inside artwork, which is only viewable Sunday after mass. The gold facade and domed ceiling are stunning. *(30 E 7th St., between 2nd and 3rd Ave.* Ⓢ *6 to Astor Pl.* ☎ *212-674-1615; www.brama.com/stgeorge. Su liturgy at 7, 8:30, 10am, and noon. See website for M-Sa schedule.)*

TOMPKINS SQUARE PARK. Tompkins Sq. Park has been the heart of the East Village since its construction in 1837. As the gathering place for a neighborhood of immigrants, low-income workers, and political activists, the park has played host to countless demonstrations and riots. In 1857, the city's poor gathered in Tompkins Sq. to protest rising unemployment. In 1967, arguments over the type of music that should be played in the park led to riots between local hippies and Latinos. In the late 1980s, the "Tompkins Square Riots" broke out over the issue of the neighborhood's growing gentrification. In the wake of the turmoil, police begin enforcing park curfews, resulting in the 1988 displacement of dozens of resident homeless. This, of course, inspired more riots.

Since its renovation in 1992 (in the wake of riots following the Rodney King verdict), the park has been markedly quieter. Locals still gather, but usually to take advantage of the basketball courts, playgrounds, and dog run. In the summer, local musicians perform here almost constantly. *(Between Ave. A and B and E 7th and 10th St.* Ⓢ *L to 1st Ave. Open daily 6am-midnight.)*

⅄CHELSEA

Chelsea is legendary for its art, which is shown everywhere from its gargantuan warehouses-turned-galleries to its sleek restaurants. The galleries around 10th-11th Ave. and 22nd St. are superb (p. 224). Chelsea is also New York's gay capital, with the highest concentration of GLBT nightlife in the city. The neighborhood is the center of Pride Weekend, generally held in late June, when exuberant parties and parades fill the local streets (☎212-807-7433; www.hopinc.org). Sights are listed from east to west. *(Ⓢ 1, 2, 3 to 14th St./7th Ave.; A, C, E, L to 14th St./8th Ave.; C, E to 23rd St./8th Ave.; 1 to 23rd St., 28th St./7th Ave.)*

HOTEL CHELSEA. This maze-like 400-room hotel (see **Accommodations,** p. 96) is hallowed ground for literati. Some 150 books have been penned here, including works by Arthur Miller, Mark Twain, Vladimir Nabokov, Thomas Wolfe, and O. Henry. Dylan Thomas drank himself to death here, and Joni Mitchell wrote the song "Chelsea Morning" in one of the rooms. In 1966, the building was designated the first New York Landmark for its architectural and historical value. Art fills the hotel from top to bottom—the lobby even has a sculpture hanging from the ceiling. Guests can get lost wandering the halls looking at all the paintings and photographs on display. *(222 W 23rd St., between 7th and 8th Ave. Ⓢ 1 to 23rd St./7th Ave.; C, E to 23rd St./8th Ave. ☎212-243-3700; www.hotelchelsea.com.)*

ST. PETER'S CHURCH. This Episcopal church is an interesting architectural mix, with a Greek Revival rectory and a Gothic Review sanctuary. The doors are usually locked, but stop by after services to peek at the Tiffany stained-glass windows. St. Peter's shares space with the non-denominational Chelsea Community Church. *(346 W 20th St., between 8th and 9th Ave. Ⓢ C, E to 23rd St./8th Ave. ☎212-929-2390. Eucharist W noon and Su 10am. Chelsea Community Church ☎212-886-5463; www.chelseachurch.org.)*

GENERAL THEOLOGICAL SEMINARY. Founded in 1817, GTS is the oldest Episcopal seminary in America. Hidden behind a rather unfortunate 1960s exterior is a compound of ivy-covered, Gothic Revival brick buildings, home to about 100 seminarians. The grounds are open to the public year-round, and visitors can spend a contemplative hour exploring the lawns, gardens, and chapel. An exhibit on the history of GTS hangs on a wall to the right of the building's entrance. If you're lucky, you may catch some aspiring priests playing tennis. *(175 9th Ave., between 20th and 21st St. Ⓢ C, E to 23rd St./8th Ave. ☎212-243-5150; www.gts.edu. Morning prayer M-F 8am, Sa 10:30am; Eucharist M and W-F 11:45am, Tu 6pm, Sa in Spanish 12:10pm, Su 6pm. For group tours, call ☎212-243-5150, ext. 306. Gardens open daily 11am-3pm.)*

CHELSEA MARKET. Nabisco's former cookie factory, in which the Oreo was produced in 1912, has been converted into a gourmet marketplace, retaining its turn-of-the-century industrial decor. The ground floor houses an array of markets and counter-service food shops, including a wholesale flower market, a Portico outlet, a fruit market, and a basket store. Stop by the bakery to see the decadent cupcakes adorned with huge icing flowers or listen to the occasional live music in the halls. Best of all, the **Chelsea Art Market Collective** hosts rotating art exhibits and the **Chelsea Wine Vault** offers free tastings (www.chelsea-winevault.com; F 4-7pm, Sa 1-5pm). *(75 9th Ave., between W 15th and W 16th St. $ A, C, E, L to 14th St./8th Ave. www.chelseamarket.com. Open M-F 8am-7pm, Sa-Su 10am-6pm.)*

CUSHMAN ROW. Named for builder Don Alonzo Cushman, a 19th-century dry-goods mogul, this terrace of brownstones is one of the city's finest examples of Greek Revival architecture. Admire the wrought-iron railings while enjoying the shade of the gingko trees in one of the most peaceful walkways in frenetic Chelsea. Next door is 404 20th St., the oldest building in Chelsea, built in 1830. *(406-418 W 20th St., between 9th and 10th Ave. $ C, E to 23rd St./8th Ave.)*

CHELSEA PIERS. This enormous, brightly colored complex provides space for just about every indoor sport you can think of. Outside, rollerbladers, skaters, and joggers monopolize the sidewalk. The Piers were once a major docking site for ocean liners—the Carpathia landed in Chelsea after rescuing survivors from the Titanic. The Piers were reincarnated in the 90s as a sports-entertainment complex with two ice rinks, a roller rink, bowling alley, high-tech sports center, skate park, driving range, and multiple restaurants. Sailing and boating companies run out of the marina, offering lessons and tours of the harbor. Check the website for detailed info. *(On the Hudson River, at the far west end of 20th St. $ C, E to 23rd St./8th Ave. ☎ 212-336-6666; www.chelseapiers.com. AMF CHELSEA PIERS LANES: ☎ 212-835-2695. Open daily 9am-5pm. Equipment rental $5; M-F $6 per person per game; Sa-Su $8 per person per game. Rates increase after 5pm. After 9pm those under 21 must be accompanied by someone 25 or older. SKATE PARK: ☎ 212-336-6200. Open summer M-Th 4-8pm, F 4-10pm, Sa-Su 10am-7pm; winter M-Th 3-7pm, F 3-9pm, Sa-Su 10am-7pm. $10 per 3hr. session. GOLF CLUB: ☎ 212-336-6400. Open daily Oct.-Mar. 6:30am-11pm, Apr.-Sept. 5am-midnight. 80-118 balls $20. Hours vary according to activity and season; call ahead.)*

UNION SQUARE, THE FLATIRON DISTRICT, AND MURRAY HILL

UNION SQUARE

Union Square is so named because it was a "union" of two main roads (the Bowery and Bloomingdale Rd., now Fourth Ave. and Broadway). Before the Civil War, aristocrats populated the square and the surrounding area. Early in the 20th century, the neighborhood became a center of New York's socialist movement; the masses held their popular May Day celebrations in the park. The 1970s were unkind to all of New York's parks, and Union Sq. was no exception. By the mid-80s, it was on the "do not visit" list of tourists and residents alike. Despite the danger and disrepair of the park, however, the surrounding neighborhood became the center of Manhattan's burgeoning hip-hop scene. After decades of renovations and shifting demographics, today's Union Sq. bears little resemblance to its earlier incarnations. Drug dealers have been replaced by bond traders, and aspiring MCs have given way to NYU undergrads.

At the nexus of a number of neighborhoods, Union Square has become the cross-roads of downtown. The scent of herbs and fresh bread wafts through the air four days a week, thanks to the ◙**Union Square Greenmarket** (p. 132). Farmers, fisherman, and bakers from all over the region come to sell fresh produce, jellies, and baked goods (year-round M, W, F-Sa 8am-6pm). In late November, the south end of the square is transformed into the **Union Square Holiday Market** (open M-F 11am-8pm, Sa 10am-8pm,

Su 11am-7pm). The square also offers free wireless Internet. *(Between Broadway and Park Ave. S, between 14th and 17th St.* Ⓢ *4, 5, 6, L, N, Q, R, W to 14th St./Union Sq.)*

> ⚡**TIP** **BEATING THE GREENMARKET CROWDS.** Early in the morning and afternoons between 2 and 4pm are the most tranquil times to visit the Union Square Greenmarket. Lunchtime is entertaining, but jam-packed.

UNION SQUARE SAVINGS BANK. Designed by Henry Bacon, architect of the Lincoln Memorial in Washington, D.C., this Neoclassical building features white granite and a Corinthian-temple facade. Formerly a bank, the site is now home to the **Daryl Roth Theatre,** which currently hosts the much talked about dance-rock-funk circus **De La Guarda** (for ticket information, see p. 245). *(20 Union Sq. E.* Ⓢ *4, 5, 6, L, N, Q, R, W to 14th St./Union Sq.)*

STUYVESANT SQUARE. This park, divided by Second Ave., is named after the Dutch colonial governor Peter Stuyvesant (p. 53), who donated his farm property to the city in the 17th century. The governor's statue, featuring his infamous peg leg, stands in the park's west side. It was created by Gertrude Vanderbilt Whitney, later the founder of the **Whitney Museum** (p. 230). On Rutherford Pl. is **St. George's Episcopal Church,** built in 1856 in the Romanesque Revival style, as well as a **Quaker Friends Meeting House,** built in Greek Revival style in 1860. Row houses dating from the 1850s and the more modern buildings of the Petrie Division of the Beth Israel Medical Center also surround the square. *(2nd Ave., between 15th and 17th St.* Ⓢ *L to 3rd Ave., 1st Ave.)*

GRAMERCY PARK. Gramercy Park endures today as the only private, key-protected park in New York City. In 1831 Samuel Ruggles, a developer fond of greenery, drained a 42 acre marsh and laid out 66 building lots around its perimeter. The land was known as Gramercy Seat, a name derived from the Dutch *krom moersaje* (crooked little swamp). Buyers of Ruggles's lots received keys to enter the park. For many years, the keys were made of solid gold.

More than 150 years later, little has changed. Gramercy, with its wide gravel paths, immaculately kept by its owners, is still rigorously exclusive. You can stare longingly through the eight-foot wrought-iron gates at the manicured garden to see what you're missing. The surrounding real estate—a charming mix of Greek Revival and Victorian Gothic-style townhouses—includes the National Arts Club, the Players Club, the School of Visual Arts, and some of the city's choicest residences. Past residents have included circus king John Ringling, actor John Barrymore, sculptor Daniel Chester France, and for a few months, an 11-year old John F. Kennedy. *(At south end of Lexington Ave., between 20th and 21st St.* Ⓢ *6 to 23rd St./Park Ave. S. Closed to the public.)*

NATIONAL ARTS CLUB. Founded in 1893 by art critic Charles de Kay, in an effort to create an American art scene independent of European inspiration, the National Arts Club boasts members like Martin Scorcese, Robert Redford, and Uma Thurman. The club, the first of its kind to admit both men and women, also welcomed non-artists, including former presidents Teddy Roosevelt, Woodrow Wilson, and Dwight D. Eisenhower. The club occupies the former mansion of Samuel Tilden. Tilden hired Calvert Vaux, famed co-designer of Central Park, to design the building's facade. While most of the portrait-filled club is restricted to members, a few galleries feature changing exhibits open to the public and free of charge. *(15 Gramercy Park S, at Irving Pl.* Ⓢ *6 to 23rd St./Park Ave. S. ☎212-475-3424; www.nationalartsclub.org. Gallery hours vary by exhibit; most are M-F 10am-5pm.)*

PLAYERS CLUB. Actor Edwin Booth (brother of Lincoln's assassin) established the Players Club in 1888 as an exclusive social club for actors. Booth died here in

1893. His bedroom has been left unchanged since that night, and his portrait hangs over the club's fireplace. Members have included Mark Twain, Sir Laurence Olivier, Frank Sinatra, and Richard Gere. The building, constructed in 1845, is one of the oldest brownstones in New York. Today, the club hosts an open run of productions by **Food For Thought,** which performs lunch-time and cocktail-hour readings of plays, followed by Q&As with well-known New York City actors. *(16 Gramercy Park S, at Irving Pl.* Ⓢ *6 to 23rd St./Park Ave. S.* ☎ *212-475-6116. Food for Thought Productions* ☎ *212-362-2560; www.foodforthoughtproductions.com. Tickets to lunchtime and cocktail-hour readings $58.)*

THE THEODORE ROOSEVELT BIRTHPLACE. Teddy Roosevelt, the only native New Yorker ever to be elected president, was born in this brownstone on October 27, 1858, and lived here until age 15. The original Gothic Revival townhouse was razed in 1916, but in 1923 the building was rebuilt as a museum. It now consists of five elegant period rooms, decorated by Roosevelt's wife and sister to appear as they would have during Teddy's childhood. The exhibit downstairs highlights events in the 26th president's life, displaying, among other things, the uniform Roosevelt wore as a Rough Rider during the Spanish-American War. *(28 E 20th St. between Broadway and Park Ave. S.* Ⓢ *N, R to 23rd St./Broadway.* ☎ *212-260-1616; www.nps.gov/thrb. Open Tu-Sa 9am-5pm. $3, children under 16 free. Guided tours leave on the hr. 10am-4pm.)*

MADISON SQUARE PARK. Madison Sq. Park offers wonderful views of surrounding skyscrapers like the Flatiron Building and the New York Life Insurance Building. Before the park's opening, this public space hosted a game known as "New York Ball," played by a group called the Knickerbockers. The sport evolved into America's favorite pastime—baseball. At the park's Broadway entrance, the statue of William Seward (former Governor of New York and US Secretary of State) welcomes visitors. Statues of famous 19th-century generals, as well as occasional exhibits of contemporary art, stand around the park. *(Southern end of Madison Ave., between 23rd and 26th St.* Ⓢ *N, R, W to 23rd St./Broadway; 6 to 23rd St./Park Ave. S.)*

▓ FLATIRON BUILDING. This building, designed by famed Chicago architect Daniel Burnham, was New York's first skyscraper to reach over 20 stories high, as well as one of the first buildings in which exterior walls were hung on a steel frame. Originally named the Fuller Building, it acquired its current name for its resemblance to the clothes-pressing device when viewed from the north (i.e., from Madison Sq. Park). The intersection of Broadway, Fifth Ave., and 23rd St. necessi-

LOCAL LEGEND

SEED OF THE BIG APPLE

New York City is also known, strangely enough, as the Big Apple. (Buenos Aires in Argentina goes by that nickname too, but we'll leave that story for another guide.) According to the New York Historical Society, the nickname originated in the 1920s, when John G. FitzGerald named his popular horseracing column "Around the Big Apple." FitzGerald said he overheard African-American stablehands in New Orleans speaking of traveling to Gotham as the big reward—the big "apple"—after years of serving on minor tracks. The term gained currency within the jazz community of Harlem, where the Big Apple Jazz Club adopted the name.

A less widely publicized story locates the nickname's origin in the city's more distant (and more salacious) past—in the city's 19th-century reputation for prostitutiion. A certain Evelyn de Saint-Evremond ran an infamous bordello in the city, and young men, it seems, began to refer to their amorous exploits as "having a taste of Eve's apples." Hence, the Big Apple as a name for a city where such exploits came easily.

Whatever the term's origin, its use didn't become widespread until Charles Gillett, president of the Convention and Visitors Bureau, popularized it with his Big Apple Campaign in 1971. This marketing blitz went a long way to reviving the city's then-flagging tourist economy.

tated its dramatic wedge shape (just 6 ft. wide at its narrowest point). When first constructed in 1902, the building's triangular shape produced wind currents that made women's skirts billow; police coined the term "23 skiddoo" to shoo gapers from the area. The building is now all commercial space. Among its tenants is ▧**St. Martin's Press,** the company that publishes this book. *(175 5th Ave., off the southwest corner of Madison Sq. Park.* Ⓢ *N, R, W to 23rd St./Broadway; 6 to 23rd St./Park Ave. S.)*

METROPOLITAN LIFE INSURANCE TOWER. This 700-foot-tall white tower was a 1909 addition to the 1893 edifice inspired by the bell-tower of San Marco in Venice. The tower made the building the world's tallest for the four years following its completion. The minute hands of the clocks on each of the building's four faces weigh 1000 lb. each. The annex on 24th St., connected by a walkway, has an eye-catching neo-Gothic facade. *(1 Madison Ave., at 23rd St.* Ⓢ *N, R, W to 23rd St./Broadway; 6 to 23rd St./Park Ave. S.)*

69TH REGIMENT ARMORY. A large structure in the Beaux Arts style, the armory hosted the famous 1913 International Exhibition of Modern Art that brought Picasso, Matisse, and Duchamp—a group Theodore Roosevelt called "a bunch of lunatics"—to America's shores. Now a recruiting facility for the Army National Guard, the Armory was thrown back into the spotlight after September 11, 2001, when it became the city's command center for family and friends seeking missing persons. *(68 Lexington Ave., at 26th St.* Ⓢ *6 to 28th St./Park Ave. S.* ☎ *212-532-6013. Closed to the public.)*

NEW YORK LIFE INSURANCE BUILDING. Built by Cass Gilbert (of **Woolworth Building** fame; p. 160) in 1928, this multi-tiered structure is topped by a golden, pyramid-shaped roof and a clock tower. The building is located on the former site of circus-meister P.T. Barnum's "Hippodrome," which was rebuilt by Stanford White and served as the original Madison Square Garden from 1890 to 1925. It soon became the premier spot for New York's trademark entertainment spectacles. White was fatally shot here in 1906 by the unstable husband of a former mistress. The story was fictionalized in E.L. Doctorow's *Ragtime.* Now the building houses commercial and office space and is closed to the public. *(51 Madison Ave., between 26th and 27th St.* Ⓢ *N, R, W to 28th St./Broadway; 6 to 28th St./Park Ave. S. Closed to the public.)*

CHURCH OF THE TRANSFIGURATION. In 1870, friends of Shakespearean actor George Holland sought a place to hold his funeral. They were turned away from fashionable churches—which deemed actors unworthy of their services—and were told there was "a little church around the corner where the matter might be arranged." Since then, this brick-and-brownstone church has maintained a special bond with lovers of the stage, and retained the epithet "The Little Church Around the Corner." The funerals of Edwin Booth, Richard Mansfield, and O. Henry were also held here. Today, this charming neo-Gothic cottage is home to the Episcopal Actors' Guild and features beautiful Lich Gate, peculiar green roofs, and a manicured garden with a bubbling fountain. Be sure to check out the stained-glass windows: they may look like biblical scenes, but at least one vignette is from *Hamlet.(1 E 29th St., between 5th and Madison Ave.* Ⓢ *N, R, W to 28th St./Broadway; 6 to 28th St./Park Ave.* ☎ *212-684-6770; www.littlechurch.org. Open daily 8am-6pm. Prayers M-F 8:40am and 5:10pm, Su 8:30am. Eucharist M-F 12:10pm; Su 8:30, 11am.)*

MURRAY HILL

Murray Hill is so named because Robert Murray, a rich man of Revolutionary times, made his country home close to the present-day intersection of 37th St. and Park Ave. The upper crust of the late 19th and early 20th centuries lived in warm brownstones and apartments on these sedate residential streets. The neighborhood remains one of the city's nicest residential areas.

On the neighborhood's southern border is one of America's premier acting schools—the **American Academy of Dramatic Arts**, 120 Madison Ave., between 30th and 31st St. A peek at the class photos hanging in the lobby reveals the fresh faces of Kirk Douglas, class of 1941; Grace Kelly, class of 1948-49; and Robert Redford, class of 1958-59. (For more info on studying here, see p. 73.) The highlight of Murray Hill is the recently expanded ⊠**Morgan Library and Museum**, 29 E 36th St., at Madison Ave. The original library building was designed by Charles McKim and completed in 1906. Built in the style of a Renaissance *palazzo*, the understated and elegant library is definitely worth a visit, both for architectural beauty and for its printed-word collection. (Ⓢ *6 to 33rd St.*)

MIDTOWN WEST

HERALD SQUARE AND THE GARMENT DISTRICT

The New York Herald used to publish its daily newspaper in a building at Broadway and Sixth Ave., between 34th and 35th St. The newspaper is long gone, but the triangular square survives. The area is a mid-range retail center—hundreds of chains compete for shoppers' attention, and tourists are everywhere. Move away from Broadway to find some peace and quiet during the day; move towards it to get near the nightlife hubbub at night. Sights are listed from east to west.

THE EMPIRE STATE BUILDING. Ever since King Kong first climbed the Empire State Building in 1933, this skyscraper has attracted scores of tourists. The observatories welcome nearly four million visitors every year. Built on the site of the original Waldorf-Astoria hotel and completed in 1931, the limestone, granite, and stainless-steel structure was among the first of the truly spectacular skyscrapers. It stretches 1454 ft. into the sky and contains two miles of elevator shafts containing 73 cars. When first completed, it included a docking platform for what was then thought to be the next frontier of modern transportation: the dirigible. Just one moored to the building before it was deemed too dangerous.

The lobby is a gleaming shrine to Art Deco, down to its stylized mail drops and elevator doors. It contains vaulted panels depicting the seven wonders of the ancient world. Follow the arrows on the wall to find the escalator to the concourse level, where you can purchase tickets to the observatory. Note the sign indicating the visibility level—a day with perfect visibility offers views for 80 mi. in any direction. Although the elevator shoots you up to the observation deck in less than a minute, prepare to wait up to two hours during peak visiting times in the summer to get on. If the view isn't exciting enough, the Empire State Building also offers the **New York Skyride**, a 22min. virtual reality ride that takes you over and through the city.

After the September 11 attacks destroyed the World Trade Center, the Empire State Building again became New York's tallest. The building has had its own share of disasters—in 1945, a B-25 bomber crashed into the 79th floor, killing 11 people. Security measures have been beefed up: all visitors and their bags must pass through metal detectors. Be prepared to show ID. *(350 5th Ave., at 34th St. Ⓢ B, D, F, N, Q, R, V, W to 34th St./Herald Sq. OBSERVATORY ☎ 212-736-3100. Open daily 8am-midnight; last elevator up at 11:15pm. $18, youth and seniors $16, children under 12 $12. Audio tour $6. SKYRIDE: ☎ 212-279-9777. Open daily 10am-10pm. $18, ages 12-17 $14, ages 4-11 and seniors $13. Combination Pass $36, seniors $24, youth $26, children $24. Hours are extended until 2am in the summer on Th-Sa nights.)*

MACY'S. Sprawling over 10 floors and housing two million sq. ft. of merchandise, from designer clothes to housewares, Macy's has come a long way from its first day of business in 1858. The oldest and largest Macy's in the world, this store retains some antique touches—check out the wooden escalators on the upper floors. Modern additions include a number of in-store eateries, like McDonald's in the children's department, Emack & Bolio's ice cream in the Juniors' department, and the Cellar Bar & Grill in the basement. The store sponsors the **Macy's Thanksgiving Day Parade,** a New York tradition buoyed by 10-story Snoopy balloons, marching bands, and floats. Other annual Macy-sponsored events (☎212-494-4455) include the **Fourth of July fireworks** extravaganza on the East River, and late-August's **Tap-A-Mania,** when hundreds of tap-dancers cut loose on the sidewalks of 34th St. *(151 W 34th St., Herald Sq., between Broadway and 7th Ave.* [S] *B, D, F, N, Q, R, V, W to 34th St./Herald Sq.; 1, 2, 3 to 34th St./Penn Station/7th Ave.* ☎*212-695-4400. Open M-F 10am-9pm, Sa 10am-10pm, Su 11am-8pm.)*

PENNSYLVANIA STATION. The original Penn Station was built in 1910. Modeled on the Roman baths of Caracalla, it featured a grand waiting room with a 150 ft. glass ceiling. In an act Lewis Mumford deemed "irresponsible public vandalism," the building was demolished in the 1960s in favor of a more practical space 50 ft. below ground. But the razing of the beautiful original station was not in vain: the public was so outraged by its destruction that the New York City Landmarks Preservation Committee was established to protect historical buildings shortly thereafter. The station now sits below entertainment center Madison Square Garden (p. 178), and greets visitors with a shopping mall of franchise restaurants and bookstores. More importantly, Penn Station also serves as one of the city's most central transportation hubs, allowing frazzled Manhattanites an escape route from the sweltering summer heat. *(Between 31st and 34th St., and between 7th and 8th Ave.* [S] *1, 2, 3 to 34th St./Penn Station/7th Ave.; A, C, E to 34th St./Penn Station/8th Ave.)*

MADISON SQUARE GARDEN. "The World's Most Famous Arena" sits triumphantly atop Penn Station. Madison Square Garden is home to the NBA's New York **Knicks,** the WNBA's New York **Liberty,** and the NHL's New York **Rangers.** It also hosts figure skating, boxing, and the annual Westminster Dog Show. The Garden also doubles as a concert venue. Tours depart from the box office lobby and include glimpses of the locker rooms, the arena and concert stage, backstage areas, and luxury boxes. *(Between 31st and 34th St., 7th and 8th Ave.* [S] *1, 2, 3 to 34th St./Penn Station/7th Ave.; A, C, E to 34th St./Penn Station/8th Ave.* ☎*212-465-5800, tours 212-465-5800; www.thegarden.com. Main entrance at 7th Ave. and 32nd St. Box office open daily 9am-6pm. Tours every 30min. on the hr., daily 11am-3pm. $17, children $12.)*

MAIN POST OFFICE (JAMES A. FARLEY BUILDING). New York's immense main post office overlooks Madison Square Garden with 53 ft. high Corinthian columns. The broad portico of this Neoclassical building was completed in 1913 and later named for a Postmaster General of the US. Climb up the grandiose stairs, step into the gorgeous vaulted hall, and send a postcard home.

The city is now beginning to convert the Post Office Building into a new Pennsylvania Station. Slated to open by 2008, the new terminus will bear the name of the late Senator Daniel Patrick Moynihan. *(421 8th Ave., between 31st and 33rd St.* [S] *A, C, E to 34th St./Penn Station/8th Ave. Open 24hr.)*

GARMENT DISTRICT. The Garment District was once a redlight district known as the Tenderloin. By the 1930s, its bordellos had given way to the largest concentration of apparel manufacturers in the world. Today, a small statue named *The Garment Worker,* depicting an aged man huddled over a sewing machine, sits near the corner of 39th St. and Seventh Ave. Walk along Broadway from the upper 20s to the lower 30s, and check out the latest fashions in wholesale and retail fabric, jewelry, clothing, perfume, accessories, and leather. Many of the stores are wholesale-only. Keep your eyes open for signs and handouts advertising sample sales. Seamstresses and sewers-for-hobby purchase yards of lush fabric to take home and fashion themselves. The **Fashion Institute of Technology** is on the corner of Seventh Ave. and 27th St. One block uptown you'll find the **Flower District,** 28th St., between Sixth and Seventh Ave. Wholesale distributors and buyers of flora congregate here each morning to stock the city's florists and garden centers year-round. In the summertime the scent of the flowers is especially strong. *(West 30s between Broadway and 8th Ave.* S *1, 2, 3 to 34th St./Penn Station/ 7th Ave.; A, C, E to 34th St./Penn Station/8th Ave.)*

HELL'S KITCHEN

HELL'S KITCHEN. Once one of the most dangerous neighborhoods in the country, gang-dominated Hell's Kitchen inspired Leonard Bernstein's 1957 *West Side Story* and the Marvel Comics crime-fighter Daredevil. It acquired its ominous name after one local policeman remarked to another after a particularly brutal night, "We truly are in Hell's Kitchen." The district is no longer particularly unsafe, and it's home to a slew of eccentric and affordable restaurants and bars (especially along 8th and 9th Ave.). The city attempted to speed the neighborhood's gentrification by re-christening it Clinton, but the name has not taken hold. *(Between 30th and 59th St., and between 8th Ave. and the Hudson River.* S *1, 2, 3 to 34th St./Penn Station/7th Ave.; A, C, E to 34th St./Penn Station/8th Ave.)*

JACOB K. JAVITS CONVENTION CENTER. This black-glass monstrosity covers five blocks and hosts some of the largest convention events in the world, including international boat, car, and motorcycle shows. The April International Auto Show (☎718-746-5300; www.autoshowny.com) draws the biggest crowds, but the center also hosts a toy fair, stationery expo, and fashion show. Check the website to see what's in town. *(55 W 34th St., at 11th Ave.* S *A, C, E to 34th St./Penn Station/8th Ave.* ☎212-216-2000; www.javitscenter.com.)

JOHN JAY COLLEGE OF CRIMINAL JUSTICE. Originally the College of Police Science (1965), John Jay now trains civil servants of all kinds. Renovations have given the 1903 neo-Victorian central building, once the DeWitt Clinton High School, a postmodern glass atrium and extension. You can peek at it from the front lobby. *(899 10th Ave. at 58th St.* S *1, A, B, C, D to 59th St./Columbus Circle.)*

TIMES SQUARE AND THE THEATER DISTRICT

At the intersection of 42nd St., Seventh Ave., and Broadway, Times Square is a non-stop, neon-lit, over-crowded, over-stimulating feast of excess. The Square was once the epicenter of New York seediness, chockablock with peep shows, prostitutes, and drug dens, but today the smut has been replaced by 30 ft.-tall video-screens, up-to-the-minute news crawls, and nearly 40 million tourists per year. This is technico-commercial postmodernity at its most apocalyptic. Stop by the **Times Square Information Center,** in the restored Embassy Movie Theatre on Seventh Ave., between 46th and 47th St. for free bathrooms, free Internet access, and a theater ticketing service. (☎212-869-1890; www.timessquarenyc.org. Open daily 8am-8pm.) *(*S *1, 2, 3, 7, N, Q, R, S, W to 42nd St./Times Sq.)*

 THE REAL DEAL. New Yorkers will go miles out of their way to avoid passing through hyper-congested **Times Square,** but for tourists, a walk through is a can't-miss. Still, avoid the area at rush hour when it's at its most feverish; later in the evening, its gaudy neon charm is easier to appreciate. —Amber Johnson

THEATER DISTRICT. New York's theater district, centered on Broadway just north of Times Square, is home to approximately 40 theaters, of which 22 have been declared historical landmarks. **Shubert Alley,** half a block west of Broadway, between 44th and 45th St., was originally built as a fire exit between the Booth and

Shubert Theaters, and is now a pedestrian zone, where theater groupies cluster after shows to get their playbills signed by their favorite actors. *(From 41st to 54th St., between 6th and 8th Ave.* Ⓢ *1, 2, 3, 7, N, Q, R, S, W to 42nd St./Times Sq. For info on specific theaters, see Entertainment, p. 258.)*

MIDTOWN EAST

■ **NEW YORK PUBLIC LIBRARY.** The main branch of the New York Public Library is a refreshing retreat from the bustle of Fifth Ave. A Beaux Arts facade—loosely modeled after the Louvre—adorns this house of knowledge. Featured in the film *Ghostbusters*, two marble lions representing Patience and Fortitude guard the library against illiteracy (and ghosts). Inside, the Main Reading Room is on the third floor. The famous "Cloud Scenes" ceiling—a stunning mass of copper- and gold-leaf coffering with inlaid frescoes depicting a cloudy sky—was recently cleaned and restored, and it is worth a look even if you aren't here to read. Galleries display rotating exhibits of art and rare books from the library's holdings, including a Gutenberg Bible and Thomas Jefferson's manuscript copy of the Declaration of Independence. To obtain a book from the stacks, pull up the call number from the library's online catalogue and give it to a librarian, who will retrieve the item for you to read on-site. *(42nd St. and 5th Ave.* Ⓢ *B, D, F, V to 42nd St./Ave. of the Americas (6th Ave.); 7 to 5th Ave./42nd St.* ☎ *212-869-8089; www.nypl.org. Open Tu-W 11am-7:30pm, Th-Sa 10am-6pm. Tours of Humanities and Sciences Library Tu-Sa at 11am and 2pm. Free; sign up at the information desk to the right of the 5th Ave. entrance. Tours of the exhibition Tu-Sa 12:30 and 2pm. Free.)*

BRYANT PARK. Bryant Park has a long and checkered history. The site first served as a 1776 battleground for George Washington's troops fleeing British forces. Since then, it has served as a pauper's graveyard; hosted the 1853 World's Fair's Crystal Palace; been destroyed by fire; provided drill grounds for the Union Army; and served as an open-air reading room for the New York Public Library. The area was renamed "Bryant Park" in 1884 to honor the memory of William Cullen Bryant (1794-1878)—editor, poet, and leading advocate of the creation of New York's Central Park (p. 186). The park continued to struggle until the Rockefeller brothers created the Bryant Park Restoration Corporation.

A century and a half after the glory days of the World's Fair, Bryant Park now hosts a stage that features free cultural events throughout the summer, including jazz concerts, classic film screenings, and amateur comedy. Be sure to get there early; it's a very popular venue. Films begin at dusk. Check the website or call for the schedule. You'll also find free wireless Internet in the park. *(6th Ave., between 40th and 42nd St., behind the New York Public Library.* Ⓢ *B, D, F, V to 42nd St./Ave. of the Americas (6th Ave.); 7 to 5th Ave./42nd St.* ☎ *212-768-4242; www.bryantpark.org. Open daily 7am-9pm; summer weekdays until 11pm. M film festival in summer. Free.)*

THE ALGONQUIN HOTEL. An old-New York setting that screams historical landmark, the Algonquin Hotel has a rich past connected to New York's arts and culture scenes. Alexander Woollcott's "Round Table," a regular gathering of 1920s authors and theatrical luminaries, made the hotel famous. Supposedly, *The New Yorker* magazine was conceived during one of these boozy luncheons. Faulkner wrote his Nobel Prize acceptance speech here, and Lerner and Loewe composed *My Fair Lady* in Loewe's suite. The Oak Room still serves tea every afternoon, and folks say that—for better or for worse—the restaurant's menu and wood-paneled decor have changed little in 50 years. A recent restoration preserved the hotel's intricate ironwork, dark walnut furnishings, and faint brush stroke paintings. If you're up for a splurge, rooms here start at $249 per night. The Blue Bar is a great place to soak up the hotel's clubby ambience. *(44th St., between 5th and 6th Ave.* Ⓢ *B, D, F, V to 42nd St./Ave. of the Americas (6th Ave.); 7 to 5th Ave./42nd St.* ☎ *212-840-6800; www.algonquinhotel.com.)*

ROCKEFELLER CENTER. Rockefeller Center got its start in the Roaring Twenties, when tycoon John D. Rockefeller, Jr. wanted to move the Metropolitan Opera to Midtown. The plans fell through when the Great Depression struck in 1929, so Rockefeller made the center a media hub instead. Built during the 30s in a classic Art Deco style, it became home to radio companies like RKO, RCA, and NBC. The center's many buildings cover seven million square feet of prime real estate.

The **Rockefeller Center Tour** is a worthwhile introduction to the highlights in and around the center. The main entrance is on Fifth Ave., between 49th and 50th St. Walking toward the entrance up Fifth Ave. from the park, you pass the **International Building** between 50th and 51st St. The large bronze sculpture of **Atlas** was initially not welcomed because of its purported resemblance to Italian dictator Benito Mussolini.

> **TIP**
> **RESERVE AHEAD.** Lines can be long for Rockefeller Center tours, and they sometimes sell out. Calling ahead or reserving online are easy ways to ensure you'll see all the historic complex has to offer.

To your right in the **Channel Gardens,** the main entrance is framed by the **Maison Francaise** on the left and the **British Empire Building** on the right. The gardens themselves feature numerous sculptures and fountains, as well as a variety of seasonal flowers, and are flanked on either side by rows of boutiques and sweet shops.

Tower Plaza is an elaborate sunken space at the foot of the gardens. It's topped by a gold-leafed statue of **Prometheus,** and surrounded by the flags of over 100 countries. In spring and summer, an **ice-skating rink** (p. 271) lies dormant beneath an overpriced cafe. The rink opens in winter, in time for the annual Christmas tree lighting, one of New York's greatest traditions. (Tree lighting the first W after Thanksgiving; call ☎212-332-6868 for info.)

Behind Tower Plaza is the **General Electric Building,** 30 Rockefeller Plaza. This 70-story tower, once home to RCA, is the jewel of the complex. The G.E. Building is notable not only for its scale but also for its artwork. Outside the building's main entrance is Lee Lawrie's limestone and glass frieze of *Wisdom.* On the inside, Jose Maria Sert's *American Progress* adorns the lobby's walls. NBC, which now makes its home here, offers a 1hr. **NBC Studio Tour** that traces the network's history, from its first radio broadcast in 1926 through the heyday of TV programming in the 1950s and 60s, up to today's sitcoms. The tour visits six studios, including the infamous 8H Studio, home of Saturday Night Live, and 6A Studio, home of Late Night with Conan O' Brien.

A block north, on the corner of Sixth Ave. and 51st St., is **Radio City Music Hall.** After narrowly escaping demolition in 1979, this Art Deco landmark received a complete interior restoration. Built in 1932, the 5874-seat theater remains the largest in the world. It functioned as a movie theater between 1933 and 1975, premiering films like *King Kong* and *Breakfast at Tiffany's.* Now it is used mostly for its original purpose, live performance. One of its main attractions is the **Rockettes,** a high-stepping, long-legged dance troupe, whose annual Christmas and Easter extravaganzas are legendary. The **Stage Door Tour** takes you through the Great Stage and various rehearsal halls and gives you the chance to meet one of the Rockettes. *(Between 48th and 51st St., 5th and 6th Ave.* Ⓢ *B, D, F, V to 47th-50th St./Rockefeller Center/ Ave. of the Americas (6th Ave.).* ☎*212-332-6868, tours 212-664-3700; www.rockefeller-center.com. NBC TOUR:* ☎*212-664-3700; www.shopnbc.com/nbcstore. Reservations recommended by phone or online. Departs every 30min. M-Th, every 15min. F-Su from the NBC Experience Store in the G.E. Building M-Sa 8:30am-5:30pm, Su 9:30am-4:30pm. No children under 6. $18.50, seniors and children ages 6-12 $15.50, groups over 10 or more $15.50. ROCKEFELLER CENTER TOUR:* ☎*212-664-3700. Departs every hr. from the G.E. Building. M-Sa 10am-*

5pm, Su 10am-4pm. Hours increase during summer or Christmas season. Children under 6 not admitted. $12, seniors and children ages 6-12 $10. Combo rate for NBC and Rockefeller Center Tours $23.45. RADIO CITY MUSIC HALL STAGE DOOR TOUR: ☎212-247-47777; www.radiocity.com. Departs every 30min. M-Su 11am-3pm. $17, seniors $14, children under 12 $10; group discounts available. Order by phone ☎212-307-7171. See p. 266 for Radio City Music Hall box office, p. 266 for ticket info about live TV shows taped at Rockefeller Center.)

ST. PATRICK'S CATHEDRAL. New York's most famous church and America's largest Catholic cathedral opened in 1879, 21 years after work on it began. The Civil War put construction on hold in the 1860s, and the cathedral's famed steeples had to be erected after its opening. Those twin spires flanking the Fifth Ave. facade are 330 ft. high, and have been captured in countless photos and postcards. The cathedral's Gothic exterior recalls similar European structures, but the interior's nave is more closely related to those of Westminster, Exeter, and other British cathedrals. Once inside, it is hard to miss the **Great Organ,** which commands attention with its nearly 8000 pipes, some of which are as long as 32 ft. It even has a mechanism to simulate the sound of a 64 ft. pipe by joining two of these together. The best way to hear the organ and choir is to come on a Sunday and attend the 10:15am High Mass. For a slightly more subdued worship experience, the Lady Chapel, by the South Transept, is hushed, delicate, and less overwhelmingly Gothic. *(Southeast corner of 5th Ave. and 51st St. [S] E, V to 5th Ave./53rd St. ☎212-753-2261. Open daily 7am-10pm. Mass Su 7, 8, 9, 10:15am, noon, 1, 4, 5:30pm. There is mass every day of the week. For the full schedule, go to the archdiocese website at www.archny.org.)*

UNIVERSITY CLUB. As its name suggests, this organization was among the first men's clubs to require its members to hold college degrees. The building was built in 1899 in the Palace style of the Italian Renaissance. The full-floor windows and heavy damask curtains hint at the swank interior, which mere mortals will never see—club entrance is for members and guests only. *(1 W 54th St., at 5th Ave. ☎212-247-2100. [S] E, V to 5th Ave./53rd St.)*

SONY PLAZA. The Sony Corporation recently bought and renamed Philip Johnson's postmodern masterwork, the former AT&T Building. It now features two superstores with interactive state-of-the-art products. Don't miss the **Sony Wonder Technology Lab** (p. 227). *(550 Madison Ave., between 55th and 56th St. [S] N, R, W to 5th Ave./59th St. ☎212-833-8830.)*

TRUMP TOWER. Finally, a building to match Donald Trump's ego—big, shiny, and utterly lacking in taste. Inside, stores like Cartier, Salvatore Ferragamo, and an Avon Spa cater to the big-spending crowd, but even the most frugal can splurge on a drink or some chocolate-covered fruit from Godiva. The 80-ft. indoor waterfall and sitting area provide free respite for weary Fifth Ave. shoppers. *(725 5th Ave., at 56th St. [S] N, R, W to 5th Ave./59th St. Open daily 8am-10pm.)*

GRAND CENTRAL TERMINAL. Completed in 1913, Grand Central is a train station of monumental proportions. On the classical facade on 42nd St., you'll find a beautiful sculpture of Mercury, Roman god of transportation. Inside, the Main Concourse is the terminal's central space. A $200 million, four-year renovation, has showcased the zodiac constellations painted on the ceiling. The info booth in the middle of the concourse is a popular meeting place.

In the past, the whirring masses departed from Grand Central to take voyages across the continent. Today, trains from the station only travel to Westchester and points north; longer distance trains arrive at Penn Station. For a pricey but delightful picnic, swing by the **Grand Central Market,** located on the main level. It boasts a dizzying array of chocolates, cheeses, breads, meats, and pastries. *(E 42nd St., between Madison and Lexington Ave., where Park Ave. should be. [S] 4, 5, 6, 7, S to 42nd St./*

Grand Central. Tours run by Municipal Arts Society (☎212-935-3960) W 12:30pm from info booth; run by the Grand Central Partnership (☎212-697-1245) F 12:30pm from Philip Morris/ Whitney Museum, on 42nd St. across the street from Grand Central. Grand Central Market open M-F 7am-9pm, Sa 10am-7pm, Su 11am-6pm. Free.)

MET LIFE BUILDING. The Met Life building (originally the Pan Am building) rises like a partly sheathed sword behind Grand Central Terminal. Constructed in 1963, it has frequently been criticized for blocking out most of the views from Park Ave. Visible from anywhere on the avenue, the building accommodates 2.4 million sq. ft. of corporate cubicles. *(200 Park Ave., at E 45th St.* Ⓢ *4, 5, 6, 7, S to 42nd St./Grand Central.)*

THE WALDORF-ASTORIA HOTEL. Ritzier than the Ritz, the Waldorf-Astoria is the *crème de la crème* of Park Ave. hotels. While not as impressive from the street as some of its peers, it has an opulent, Art Deco lobby leading to elegant curving staircases. Originally located on the site of the Empire State Building, the hotel was relocated farther uptown in 1931. Cole Porter's piano sits in the front lounge, and a huge nine-foot-tall, eight-sided clock decorated with pictures of Washington, Lincoln, Franklin, Queen Victoria, Cleveland, Harrison, Grant, and Jackson dominates the lobby. Every US President since Hoover has spent a night or two here. *(301 Park Ave., between 49th and 50th St.* Ⓢ *6 to 51st St.; E, V to Lexington Ave./53rd St.* ☎212-355-3000; www.waldorfastoria.com.)*

ST. BARTHOLOMEW'S CHURCH. This Byzantine-style Episcopal church (1918) is beautiful on the outside and contains an impressive mosaic of the Resurrection and a life-sized marble angel (in the devotional area left of the altar). St. Bart's hosts a free summer festival of classical music (Su 11am) as part of its weekly service. Just outside is Cafe St. Bart's, a lovely but expensive outdoor cafe with a small garden. *(109 E 50th St., at Park Ave.* Ⓢ *6 to 51st St.; E, V to Lexington Ave./53rd St.* ☎212-378-0200; www.stbarts.org. Services daily; check website for complete schedule. Eucharist M-F 12:05pm, Sa 10am, Su 9, 11am. Wheelchair accessible.)*

SEAGRAM BUILDING. This bronze and black skyscraper (1958) is the only building in the city designed by the architect **Ludwig Mies van der Rohe.** In 2000, *The New York Times* called it "the building of the millennium." The building blends Classical and Gothic architecture, innovatively using both color and glass. The flat plaza in front is a popular public sitting space, despite a lack of benches. People perch on the walls surrounding the plaza, rather than on benches, and sometimes venture into the reflecting pools in the summer to cool off. *(375 Park Ave., between 52nd and 53rd St.* Ⓢ *6 to 51st St.; E, V to Lexington Ave./53rd St.)*

CITIGROUP CENTER. Constructed in 1974, this aluminum and glass skyscraper is one of Midtown's more distinctive buildings. It hovers over St. Peter's Lutheran Church on 10-story stilts. The tower's base is cut away at the four corners; the enormous building stands dramatically on a cross-shaped foundation, which extends from the core to the center of each side. The atrium, open-air concourse, and office tower lobby were renovated in 1997. The 45-degree angled roof was intended to be a solar collector. Today the roof supports a high-tech gadget called a tuned mass dampener (TMD), which automatically sways against the movement of the building to keep it stable, reducing the number of vertical supports needed. *(The corner of 53rd St. and Lexington Ave.* Ⓢ *6 to 51st St.; E, V to Lexington Ave./53rd St.)*

TURTLE BAY AND UNITED NATIONS

Named after an 18th-century farm, the Turtle Bay neighborhood hosts the United Nations and its population of diplomats and bureaucrats. The area houses some of New York's more peaceful parks, which aren't in the perpetual shade of skyscrapers. Sights are listed from east to west.

SIGHTS

THE UNITED NATIONS. Founded just after WWII to serve as a "center for harmonizing the actions of nations," the United Nations fittingly makes its home in the world's most diverse city. Though located along what would be First Ave., the UN is international territory and not under US jurisdiction. The flags of the 191 member nations fly outside at equal height, in violation of American custom. The site consists of four main buildings: the **General Assembly Building,** the **Conference Building,** the 39-floor **Secretariat Building,** and the **Dag Hammarskjöld Library,** added in 1961 as a gift from the Ford Foundation. The complex was designed by an international team of 11 architects, led by Wallace K. Harrison from the US.

A prominent feature of the General Assembly lobby is a Foucault pendulum, given by the Netherlands to the UN in 1955. In the eastern side of the lobby is a stained-glass window designed by the French artist Marc Chagall. A Norman Rockwell mosaic, a Japanese Peace Bell, and a Chinese ivory carving are also exhibited in the building. The only way to view the enormous General Assembly and the council rooms is by guided tour. Outside, a rose garden and statuary park provide a lovely view of the East River and the industrial wastelands of west Queens. The UN garden has several sculptures and statues that have been donated by different countries. Note the Evgeniy Vuchetich statue called *Let Us Beat Swords into Plowshares*, a gift from the former USSR in 1959. The best way to learn about the building and the work done here is through one of the guided tours, which provide access to parts of the complex you can't visit on your own. *(1st Ave., between 42nd and 48th St. [S] 4, 5, 6, 7, S to 42nd St./Grand Central. ☎ 212-963-4475, tours 212-963-3242; www.un.org. 1hr. tours, available in 20 languages, depart from the UN visitor's entrance at 1st Ave. and 46th St. every 15min. M-F 9:15am-4:45pm, Sa-Su 9:30am-4:45pm. $12, seniors $8.50, students $8, children ages 5-14 $7. Reservations required for groups larger than 12. Children under 5 not admitted on tour.)*

THE CHRYSLER BUILDING. One of New York's most iconic buildings, and its second tallest, the Chrysler building is a monument to the car. The building's spire is meant to evoke a 1930 Chrysler car's radiator grille. Other motoring mementos on the facade include stylized lightning bolts symbolizing the energy of the new machine, and gargoyles styled after hood ornaments and hubcaps. While many consider it to be the most beautiful building in New York, it ruined architect William Van Alen's career; Walter Chrysler, unsatisfied with the final product, accused Van Alen of embezzlement and refused to pay him. Chrysler no longer has offices in the building.

The Art Deco lobby alone is worth a visit, with several different types of African marble, onyx, and amber set into the walls. The elevators are paneled with Japanese ash and oriental walnut. The ceiling fresco, titled *Transport and Human Endeavor*, was painted by Edward Trumbull, and depicts the Chrysler assembly line. *(405 Lexington Ave., at E 42nd St. [S] 4, 5, 6, 7, S to 42nd St./Grand Central.)*

CENTRAL PARK SOUTH, 57TH ST., AND VICINITY

Luxury hotels like the Essex House, the St. Moritz, and the Plaza overlook Central Park from Central Park S, between Fifth and Eighth Ave., where 59th St. should be. Two blocks south, on 57th St., galleries and stores surround Carnegie Hall. Sights are listed from west to east.

CARNEGIE HALL. Since hosting Tchaikovsky's American debut in 1891, Carnegie Hall has featured such classical artists as Caruso, Toscanini, and Bernstein; jazz greats like Dizzy Gillespie, Ella Fitzgerald, and Billie Holiday; and even rock-and-rollers such as The Beatles and The Rolling Stones. Performing here remains the mark of "making it" as an artist in North America.

Constructed in 1890 under Andrew Carnegie's patronage, this brick and brownstone Italian Renaissance structure was one of the last buildings of its size to be built without a steel frame. In the late 1950s, when an enormous red skyscraper threatened to replace Carnegie Hall, violinist Isaac Stern led a city-wide campaign to save the building. The City of New York purchased it for $5 million in 1960, and it was declared a historic landmark in 1962. Decades of patchwork maintenance and periodic face-lifts left the venue in various stages of disrepair until 1985, when a $60 million restoration and repair program returned the building to its earlier splendor. The small **Rose Museum** provides an exhibit on Carnegie Hall's history, as well as temporary displays of art memorabilia and photography. *(881 7th Ave., at W 57th St. [S] N, Q, R, W to 57th St.; B, D, E to 7th Ave./53rd St. ☎ 212-247-7800, tours 212-903-9765; www.carnegiehall.org. 1hr. tours M-F 11:30am, 2, 3pm. Purchase tour tickets at the box office. $9, students and seniors $6, children under 12 $3. Group tours available. ROSE MUSEUM: 154 W 57th St., 2nd fl. Open daily 11am-4:30pm and to concert ticketholders in the evenings. Museum, gift shop, and tours closed July to early Sept. See Entertainment, p. 250, for concert information.)*

CITY CENTER THEATER. City Center's unique neo-Moorish facade recalls the building's Masonic origins. It was built in 1923 as a meeting hall for the members of the Ancient Arabic Order of the Nobles of the Mystic Shrine. After reverting to city ownership in 1943, the building became Manhattan's first performing arts center, and the birthplace of both the New York City Opera and the New York City Ballet. Legendary artists Leonard Bernstein, Paul Robeson, and Tallulah Bankhead all performed here. Sickles and crescents still adorn each doorway, and four tiny windows on the limestone upper stories face Mecca (or at least the East Side). The theater will host the Eifman Ballet of St. Petersburg in 2007. *(130 W 55th St., between 6th and 7th Ave. [S] N, Q, R, W to 57th St.; B, D, E to 7th Ave./53rd St.; 57th St./Ave. of the Americas (6th Ave.). ☎ 212-581-1212 or 877-581-1212; www.citycenter.org. See p. 246 for box office info.)*

PLAZA HOTEL. A New York landmark, this hotel designed by Henry J. Hardenbergh dates from 1908. Its splendid carved marble fireplaces, gold leaf, and crystal chandeliers have entered New York lore through *Eloise* stories and films like *North by Northwest*, *The Way We Were*, *Plaza Suite*, and *Home Alone II*. Past guests have included Frank Lloyd Wright, The Beatles, Mark Twain, and F. Scott Fitzgerald. The Plaza was sold in 2005, and its hotel operation is being drastically scaled back, with most rooms being converted to private residences. *(758 5th Ave., at 59th St./Central Park S. [S] N, R, W to 5th Ave./59th St.)*

GRAND ARMY PLAZA. The dividing point between Midtown East and the Upper East Side, Grand Army Plaza sits across the street from the Plaza Hotel, and serves as an entrance to Central Park and the starting point for horse-drawn carriage rides. Karl Bitter's bronze statue of Pomona, the goddess of abundance, graces the plaza's southern half, atop the **Pulitzer Fountain.** On the other side of Central Park South sits St. Gaudens's 1903 gilt equestrian statue of Union General William Tecumseh Sherman led by a figure of victory. *(59th St. and 5th Ave. [S] N, R, W to 5th Ave./59th St.)*

CENTRAL PARK

Until the mid-1800s, the 843 acres that now make up Central Park were considered a social and geographical wasteland. The city's poorest residents, including Irish pig farmers, German gardeners, and the black Seneca Village population, squatted here in shantytowns, huts, and caves. Around 1850, some of the city's wealthiest citizens (including William Cullen Bryant, the editor of the *Evening Post*) began to advocate for the creation of a park in the style of the grand public spaces of London and Paris. In 1858, Frederick Law Olmsted collaborated with Calvert Vaux to design the Greensward Plan, inspired by the English Romantic tradition. To avoid an overly landscaped appearance, they preserved existing variations in terrain, and even created new ones. It took 15 years and over 20,000 workers to implement the design. The result is a delicate piece of man-made nature and a unique oasis of green in the midst of America's biggest city. With 58 mi. of pedestrian paths lined by 26,000 trees, it's a great place to escape Manhattan's traffic, pollution, and noise. Sights are listed from south to north. *(Between 59th St. and 110th St., between 5th Ave. and Central Park W. ☎ 212-310-6600 (M-F 9am-5pm); www.centralparknyc.org. The Central Park Conservancy, which runs the park and offers public programs, has 4 visitor centers offering brochures, calendars of events, and free park maps, at Belvedere Castle (☎ 212-772-0210), located mid-park at 79th St.; the Charles A. Dana Discovery Center (☎ 212-860-1370), at 110th St. between 5th and Lenox (6th) Ave., which features educational programs for all ages and rents fishing poles for nearby Harlem Meer; the North Meadow Recreation Center (☎ 212-348-4867); mid-park at 97th St., featuring indoor and outdoor climbing walls, basketball, and handball courts; and the Dairy, mid-park near 65th St. (☎ 212-794-6564), showcasing exhibits, books, and other historical items. Belvedere Castle, the Charles A. Dana Discovery Center, and the Dairy are open Tu-Su 10am-5pm. Call for the hours of the North Meadow Recreation Center. CARRIAGE TOURS: From Central Park S. ☎ 212-246-0520. $34 for 20min., $75 for 45-50min. CENTRAL PARK BICYCLE TOUR: From 2 Columbus Circle. ☎ 212-541-8759; www.centralparkbiketour.com. 10am, 1, 4pm. Additional tours 9 and 11am Sa-Su in summer. $40 for 2hr., children under 15 $20. NEW YORK SKATEOUT: From 72nd St. and Central Park W. ☎ 212-486-1919; www.nyskate.com. Inline skating tours Sa-Su 9am and 5pm. $25 for 1½hr.)*

THE CHILDREN'S DISTRICT. When Central Park was built, cholera outbreaks swept the more densely populated areas of the city. The **Dairy,** which looks like a slightly Gothic Swiss chalet, distributed food and pasteurized milk to poor families at risk for food poisoning. Restored in 1980, it's now one of the park's information centers, and it also lends out chess and checker sets for games at the nearby **Chess and Checkers House** (leave behind either a valid photo ID or a $20 deposit). East of the Dairy stand the 58 hand-carved horses of the Friedsam Memorial **Carousel,** the 1893 reconstruction of the 1870 original. Rides cost just $1. To the south is **Wollman Memorial Rink,** where New Yorkers ice-skate in the winter. In the summer, the rink is transformed into **Victorian Gardens,** a family amusement park complete with rides, games, and concessions. To the east is the **Central Park Wildlife Center,** a.k.a. **The Zoo,** which features polar bears and other mammals in their own simulated climates. The most popular attractions include the "Monkey Island" and the centrally located seal pool. Stop by during feeding time (11:30am, 2, or 4pm) to see the seals perform tricks for their meals. The **Tisch Children's Zoo,** a petting zoo built in 1997, stands to the north of the main zoo. You can pet and feed cows, sheep, and pot-bellied pigs. At the heart of the Children's Zoo is the "Enchanted Forest," a thickly forested aviary with turtles, frogs, and some of the park's 125 species of birds. *(Between 59th and 65th St. THE DAIRY: 65th St., mid-park. Open Tu-Su 10am-5pm. CAROUSEL: 64th St., mid-park (☎ 212-879-0244). Open Apr.-Oct. M-F 10am-6pm, Sa-Su 10am-7pm.; Nov.-Dec. daily 10am-dusk.; Jan. to mid-Mar. weekends and holidays only 10am-dusk. Weather permitting. Call for admission price and special events. WOLLMAN MEMORIAL RINK: East side between 62nd and 63rd St. For skating info, see p. 271. VICTORIAN GARDENS AMUSEMENT PARK: www.victoriangardensnyc.com. Open summer M-F 11am-7pm, Sa-Su 10am-8pm. $6.50; ride and game tickets $1, unlimited ride pass $12 M-F, $14 Sa-Su. Children under 36" free. CENTRAL PARK WILDLIFE CENTER AND CHILDREN'S ZOO: Between 63rd and 66th St., off 5th Ave. ☎ 212-439-6500. Open Apr.-Oct. M-F 10am-5pm, Sa-Su 10am-5:30pm; daily Nov.-Mar. 10am-4:30pm. Last entry 30min. before closing. $8, seniors $4, children ages 3-12 $3, children under 3 free.)*

■ **SHEEP MEADOW AND THE MALL.** Named for the sheep that grazed there until 1934 (when they were evicted to Brooklyn), the **Sheep Meadow** was a popular spot for love-ins and drug-fests in the 60s and 70s. Today, on summer days, it's a favorite sunbathing spot. The **Tavern on the Green** restaurant is located just west of the Sheep Meadow. Built in 1870, the Victorian Gothic structure originally housed sheep but was

THE BIG GREEN APPLE

When one thinks of parks and New York City, Central Park leaps to mind. This great urban park set a national standard for open space within cities. Yet New York City has 1700 other parks, playgrounds, and landscaped areas (247 in the borough of Manhattan). Many of these green spaces offer scenery, history, athletic fields, and other opportunities to refresh the body and spirit.

Even Central Park has neglected areas. The northern portion of the park, from 96th to 110th St., is its wildest and least traveled section. Near Central Park West and 102nd St., city water feeds a lovely pool. The overflow empties into a fast-running stream called the Loch. The water goes below the Lasker Swimming and Ice Skating Rink into Harlem Meer, which occupies the northeastern corner of the park.

North of Central Park is Morningside Park. In the 1960s, Columbia University tried to build a large gymnasium that would have bisected the park. The plan was abandoned after the 1968 riots, but Columbia had already blasted away a substantial portion of the rockface, turning a steep slope into a cliff. The City built a pool at its base.

St. Nicholas Park stretches to 141st St. The park has similar topography to Morningside. The school on the hill is the City College of New York, which was built at the turn of the last century. This northern area will be the third site for Alexander Hamilton's house.

Four blocks to the north, Jackie Robinson (formerly Colonial) Park separates Harlem from Sugar Hill. The name was changed almost 30 years ago after protests, to honor the great athlete and baseball pioneer. The 188-acre Highbridge Park runs north to Dyckman St. It formerly contained the ruins of a blockhouse named Fort George.

Far south, several beautiful parks are gathered near the Hudson River. Historic Battery Park contains Castle Clinton, where immigrants arrived before Ellis Island was built. Its concert hall became the New York City Aquarium until it was demolished by Robert Moses to clear a path for the Brooklyn Battery Tunnel. North of Battery Park is Robert F. Wagner, Jr. Park. Wagner Park has the best view of the Statue of Liberty. Nelson A. Rockefeller Park has animal sculptures by

Thomas Otterness, and a walkway to the Hudson's edge continued from Wagner Park.

If you're a biker or serious walker, visit the new Hudson River Park, which stretches 5 mi. north to 55th St. A number of recreational piers have been built, as well as a bikeway/pedestrian path that runs west of the West Side Hwy. Most construction still lies ahead.

Riverside Park South is at 68th St., with its 700 ft. long recreational pier (built by Donald Trump in exchange for city approval of Trump's construction). The eastern part was designed by Olmsted, and the western part was designed under Robert Moses. At 323 acres, Riverside is the second largest park in Manhattan. You can play softball, handball, or tennis, or eat at the Boat Basin Cafe, at 79th St.

Riverbank Park, between 138th and 145th St., was built over a billion-dollar sewage treatment plant about 20 years ago. The park, which cost over $110 million, has a soccer field, gymnasium, swimming pool, and ice-skating rink.

North of Riverbank, Riverside Park resumes, becoming Fort Washington Park (158 acres) 160th St., and stretching north past the George Washington Bridge (179th St.). There is a little red lighthouse under the great, gray bridge, made famous in a 1942 children's book by Geraldine Swift.

Fort Tryon Park contains the Cloisters. It has spectacular views of the Palisades in New Jersey. The Heather Garden is remarkable.

Inwood Hill (196 acres) is Manhattan's wilderness park. When you are in the midst of Inwood Hill Park, you cannot believe that you are on the island of Manhattan. Large tulip trees, some hundreds of years old, grow in the area. The Henry Hudson Parkway snakes its way along the west side of the park, moving toward the eponymous bridge that takes it, and its traffic, to Riverdale in the Bronx.

The waterfront parks of Manhattan don't surround the borough, but they cover most of the riverfronts. They have scenic, historical, and recreational value, and provide a beautiful circuit for visitors to hike or bike.

Henry J. Stern was New York City's Commissioner of Parks and Recreation for 15 years, serving under Mayors Ed Koch and Rudolph Giuliani.

launched as a restaurant in 1934. The food is not worth the prices, but the place is worth a visit for coffee or drinks in a beautiful setting ($10 cover).

Located to the east of the Sheep Meadow, **the Mall** is a peaceful walk lined by carefully trimmed hedges and rows of American elms. Statues of famous authors and artists border the walk, especially toward its southern end. The **Naumberg Bandshell** and **Rumsey Playfield,** the home of **SummerStage** (☎212-360-2756; www.summerstage.org), a series of free music, dance, film, and spoken word events, are toward the northern end. *(SHEEP MEADOW: From 66th-69th St., on the western side of Central Park, directly north of the Hecksher Ballfields. TAVERN ON THE GREEN: West of Sheep Meadow, between 66th and 67th St. ☎212-873-3200; www.tavernon-thegreen.com. Open M-Th noon-10:30pm, F noon-11:45pm, Sa-Su 10am-11:45pm, Su 11am-10:30pm. Lunch entrees $21-29, dinner entrees $26-38. THE MALL: Runs roughly on a north-south line, between 66th St. to 72nd St. BETHESDA TERRACE AND FOUNTAIN: At the end of the mall, about 72nd St., mid-park.)*

THE LAKE AND STRAWBERRY FIELDS. Would-be romantics steer rowboats awkwardly around the lake. You too can grab a boat at the **Loeb Boathouse,** mid-park at 75th St. (p. 270). To the west is **Strawberry Fields,** a memorial to John Lennon. It sits directly across from **The Dakota,** the apartment building in front of which he was shot (p. 192). Yoko Ono battled for this space against city-council members who had planned a Bing Crosby memorial on the same spot. On John Lennon's birthday, October 9th, thousands gather around the **"Imagine" mosaic.**

To the east of the terrace and the lake, hobbyists gather to race their model yachts on the **Conservatory Water.** Remote-control sailboats can be rented from nearby concession stands. A statue of **Alice in Wonderland** and her friends stands at 74th St., off Fifth Ave., at the north end of Conservatory Water. These are great fun to climb on; just ask the dozens of clambering kids. West of the Water sits a statue of **Hans Christian Andersen,** a gift from Copenhagen in 1956, depicting Anderson with his famous "Ugly Duckling." The NY Public Library sponsors summer storytelling at the Andersen statue. (Usually Sa 11am. Call ☎212-340-0849 for info.) North of the Lake is the **Ramble,** full of narrow trails that will make you forget you're in New York. Free hour-long walking tours depart most weekend afternoons in the summer from Belvedere Castle. Call ☎212-772-0210 for details. Stick to the pathways, and avoid rambling after dark. *(THE LAKE: Mid-park from 71st to 78th St. STRAWBERRY FIELDS: West side between 71st and 72nd St. at 72nd St. CONSERVATORY WATER: East side from 72nd to 75th. THE RAMBLE: 73rd to 79th St., mid-park.)*

THE GREAT LAWN AND TURTLE POND. The Great Lawn spreads across the park in the lower 80s. The New York Philharmonic and the Metropolitan Opera Company hold summer performances here (p. 254). Overlooking the lawn and neighboring Turtle Pond is **Belvedere Castle,** designed by Calvert Vaux in 1869. The castle, rising from Vista Rock, used to be a weather station. It has been renovated to include a nature observatory and conservation center. Fieldpacks containing binoculars and bird guide books can be borrowed here with picture ID. Belvedere Castle also hosts the "Woods and Water Exhibit," a hands-on look at the native flora and fauna of Central Park. (☎212-772-0210. Open Tu-Su 10am-5pm. Free.)

The **Delacorte Theater,** summer home of **Shakespeare in the Park** (p. 267), sits adjacent to Turtle Pond. The **Shakespeare Garden,** said to contain every plant, flower, and herb mentioned in the Bard's works, sits near the **Swedish Cottage Marionette Theater,** mid-park at 81st St. The former Swedish 19th-century schoolhouse hosts regular puppet shows year-round. *(GREAT LAWN: 79th to 85th St., mid-park. TURTLE POND: Between 79th and 80th St., mid-park. BELVEDERE CASTLE: Just off the 79th St. Transverse. Observatory open Tu-Su 10am-5pm. DELACORTE THEATER: Mid-park at 80th St. ☎212-539-8650. SWEDISH COTTAGE MARIONETTE THEATER: ☎212-988-9093. Reservations required. Shows usually Tu-F 10:30am and noon, Sa-Su 1pm. $6, children $5.)*

THE RESERVOIR AND POINTS NORTH. New Yorkers who jog around the **Reservoir's** 1.58 mi. are treated to wonderful views of the Central Park W skyline. To the northeast of the reservoir is **Conservatory Garden,** a romantic haven with ordered paths and colorful flowers that recall the European tradition of formal landscaping. The **Burnett Fountain,** in the middle of a large reflecting pool located in the center of the south (English) section, depicts Mary and Dickon from Frances Hodgson Burnett's classic novel *The Secret Garden.* Just above Conservatory Garden lies the southern tip of the **Harlem Meer,** an 11-acre body of water which helps support a transient waterfowl habitat, surrounded by cypress, beech, gingko, and oak trees. On the northern bank of the Meer, the **Charles A. Dana Discovery Center's** exhibitions and activities present Central Park as an environmental space to be explored by amateur and professional biologists alike. The center, which also leads tours, loans out free fishing rods and provides bait for use in the Meer; carp, largemouth bass, and chain pickerel abound, but a catch-and-release policy is in effect. The grounds of the center also hosts the **Harlem Meer Performance Festival** on Sundays from late May to early September. The **Lasker Rink and Pool** overlooking Harlem Meer is a popular stop for kids in both winter and summer. *(RESERVOIR: From 85th-96th St. CONSERVATORY GARDEN: East side from 104th-106th St. Enter at 5th Ave. and 105th or gate inside park at 106th St. ☎212-360-2766. Gates open daily spring-fall 8am-dusk. HARLEM MEER: East side from 106th-110th. ☎212-860-1370. Open Tu-Su Apr.-Oct. 10am-5pm; Nov.-Mar. 10am-4pm. LASKER POOL AND RINK: Mid-park between 106th and 110th St. (☎212-534-7639). Ice skating (☎917-492-3857) Nov.-Mar.; call for hours. Pool open daily July to Labor Day 11am-3pm and 4-7pm. Free.)*

> [TIP] **WATCH WHERE YOU'RE GOING!** Jogging around the Central Park Reservoir is serious business. Jog in a counter-clockwise direction, or you'll face a stampede of irritated runners.

UPPER EAST SIDE

Since the late 19th and early 20th centuries, the Upper East Side has been home to the city's most affluent residents. Though you probably can't share in the lifestyle of the old-moneyed gentry who live here, you can admire their dignified apartment buildings along **Park Avenue** or gawk at the fashion clothing sold in the boutiques that line **Madison Avenue** for a glimpse of what the high life must be like. The Upper East Side is also an art lover's paradise. Several of the elaborate mansions along **Fifth Avenue** have been turned into museums, such as the Frick Collection (p. 227) and the Cooper-Hewitt Museum (p. 231). **Museum Mile,** on Fifth Ave. from 82nd to 104th St., may boast the densest concentration of world-class museums anywhere in the world. The farther north and east you go, the less glamorous the Upper East Side becomes. Sights are listed from south to north.

PRIVATE SOCIAL CLUBS. These exclusive buildings are worth looking at, but don't even try to get in. The **Metropolitan Club** (whose first president was J. P. Morgan) was designed by Stanford White and built by David H. King Jr. in the Beaux Arts style favored by White's architectural firm. A group of distinguished gentlemen founded the Metropolitan in 1891 after the rejection of some of their friends from the very exclusive **Union Club.** Inversely, the **Knickerbocker Club** was founded in 1871 by Union men who believed that the club's admissions policies had become too lax and liberal. Its members included Hamilton, Eisenhower, and Roosevelt. *(Metropolitan Club, 1 E 60th St., at 5th Ave. [S] N, R, W to 5th Ave. Union Club, 101 E 69th St., between Park and Lexington Ave. [S] 6 to 68th St. Knickerbocker Club, 2 E 62nd St. [S] N, R, W to 5th Ave.)*

ARTS CLUBS. Again, these associations hardly welcome the plebian masses. The **Grolier Club,** an organization of book collectors founded in 1884, is named for Renaissance bibliophile Jean Grolier. Completed in 1917, this Georgian structure houses a collection of fine bookbindings, quarterly exhibitions (occasionally open to the public—check the website for dates), and a specialized research library open by appointment. The **Lotos Club,** a private organization of actors, musicians, and journalists, was founded in 1870 as an institution to nurture and promote the arts. Early members included Samuel L. Clemens (Mark Twain) and George M. Cohan. The building was designed by Richard Howland Hunt in the French Renaissance style. *(Grolier Club, 47 E 60th St., between Madison and Park Ave.* Ⓢ *N, R, W to 5th Ave.* ☎ *212-838-6690; www.grolierclub.org. Lotos Club, 5 E 66th St., between Madison and 5th Ave.* Ⓢ *6 to 68th St.)*

TEMPLE EMANU-EL. The largest synagogue in the world, Temple Emanu-El was completed in 1929 for its German-American congregation. Its 65th St. entrance features an intimidating Romanesque limestone facade trimmed with archways representing the 12 tribes of Israel. Tours are available after morning services and on Saturdays beginning at noon. Call the Temple for info. *(1 E 65th St., at 5th Ave.* Ⓢ *N, R, W to 5th Ave.* ☎ *212-744-1400; www.emanuelnyc.org. Open to the public daily 10am-5pm. Services M-Th and Su 5:30pm, call for F and Sa service schedule.)*

CHURCH OF ST. JEAN BAPTISTE. This massive, multi-domed Catholic church watches over the hustle and bustle of lengthy Lexington Ave. To get a better view of its paired towers and Corinthian porticoes, cross over to the northwest corner of Lexington Ave. and 76th St. The building's interior is rich, with high domes, intricate gold carvings, and paintings of biblical figures. The lively acoustics make it a wonderful place to hear music—a variety of classical and choral concerts are held here year round. Call the music office for details. *(Corner of Lexington Ave. and 76th St.* Ⓢ *6 to 77th St.* ☎ *212-472-2853, music office 212-570-2130. Service M-F 7:30am, 12:15, 5:30pm; Sa 9am, 12:15, 5:30pm; Su 9, 10:30am, noon, 5:30, 7:30pm.)*

CARL SCHURZ PARK AND GRACIE MANSION. Carl Schurz was a German immigrant who served as a Missouri senator, campaigned for President Lincoln, lobbied for universal suffrage, and edited *The New York Evening Post.* The 15-acre park named after him, built in 1896, overlooks the turbulent waters of the East River. **John Finley Walk** begins at E 82nd St. and borders the eastern side of the park. It's perfect for a run or a romantic evening stroll.

Gracie Mansion, at the northern end of the park (E 88th St.), was built in 1799. It housed the successful merchant Archibald Gracie until 1823, when Gracie's financial fortune took a turn for the worse. After changing hands, it temporarily served as the home of the Museum of the City of New York. It has been the official home of the mayor of New York City since 1942. Although Mayor Michael Bloomberg hosts numerous official meetings, receptions, press conferences, luncheons, and dinners at the house, he doesn't actually live in Gracie Mansion. Billionaire Bloomberg resides at 17 E 79th St., between Madison and Fifth Ave., in a five-story, 7500 sq. ft. limestone Beaux Arts mansion bought in 1986 for $3.5 million. Almost all of the objects in the recently restored Gracie Mansion were made in New York, and many of the paintings and prints depict scenes of the City. The privately funded Gracie Mansion Conservancy was established in 1981 to preserve, maintain, and enhance the mansion and its surroundings. Gracie Mansion's tradition of opening its doors to both tour and school groups is still honored. *(Between 84th and 90th St., along East End Ave.* Ⓢ *4, 5, 6 to 86th St. Park open dawn-1am. Gracie Mansion* ☎ *212-570-4751. 50min. tours of the mansion Mar. to mid-Nov. W at 10, 11am, 1, 2pm. By reservation only. $7, seniors $4, students free.)*

HENDERSON PLACE HISTORIC DISTRICT. Completed in 1882 and intended for "persons of moderate means," these private Queen Anne-style residences are notable for their ornately carved gables, dormers, mansards, and towers. *(Between York and East End Ave., 86th and 87th St.* Ⓢ *4, 5, 6, to 86th St.)*

THE CHURCH OF THE HOLY TRINITY. This French Gothic-influenced Episcopal church was built in 1899 to administer social services to the poorer residents of Yorkville. The interior contains an open-timbered oak ceiling and 17 spectacular stained-glass windows designed by Henry Holiday (1839-1927). Holiday had an eye for details and crafted lovely studies of human figures in opulent costumes. The stained-glass narratives provide a tour of biblical scenes from the Old and New Testaments. Holy Trinity is one of the few churches in the world in which all the windows were designed by one man. Set back from the street, the building graces the neighborhood with a lush front garden that bustles with children. *(316 E 88th St., between 1st and 2nd Ave.* Ⓢ *4, 5, 6 to 86th St.* ☎ *212-289-4100; www.holytrinity-nyc.org. Services W 6:30pm, Th 8:45am, and Su 8, 9, 11am, and 6pm.)*

ST. NICHOLAS RUSSIAN ORTHODOX CATHEDRAL. Five onion domes top this Russian Baroque-style cathedral. The building was designed by John Bergesen according to the characteristic Russian model, with seven domes above a dark red-brick facade trimmed with limestone and glazed tile in green, blue, and yellow. Czar Nicholas II made the first donation to the building fund in 1901. The church still attracts Russian immigrants, among many other visitors. *(15 E 97th St., between 5th and Madison Ave.* Ⓢ *6 to 96th St.* ☎ *212-289-1915. Open to the public daily 8am-5pm. Call for service schedule.)*

UPPER WEST SIDE

A certain type of New Yorker wouldn't dream of living anywhere else than the Upper West Side. With the cohesive sense of community that eludes much of Manhattan, the neighborhood is clean, quiet, and relatively safe, while still maintaining a lively restaurant and bar scene. Well-to-do families, young-professional social climbers, and aspiring intellectuals are proud to call the Upper West Side home. While Central Park West and Riverside Dr. are residential and quiet, Columbus Ave., Amsterdam Ave., and Broadway buzz with action. The farther north you go, the more diverse (and less yuppie-ish) the Upper West Side becomes. *(*Ⓢ *1, A, B (M-F only), C, D to 59th St./Columbus Circle; 1 to 66th St., 79th St., 86th St./Broadway; 1, 2, 3 to 72nd St./Broadway; B (M-F only), C to 72nd St., 81st St., 86th St., 96th St./Central Park W; 1, 2, 3 to 96th St./Broadway.)*

COLUMBUS CIRCLE. Here, Midtown ends and the Upper West Side begins. The Circle takes its name from the 1892 memorial to Columbus that stands at its center. Another statue, a 44-foot limestone pillar topped with a massive gold sculpture, commemorates those who died on the *USS Maine*. The black glass facade of Donald Trump's gargantuan Trump International Hotel and Towers stands at 1 Central Park W. Its shiny silver globe was supposedly designed by Trump's feng shui consultant to deflect the "bad energy" wafting up from Columbus Circle. Across the street is the controversial architecture of 2 Columbus Circle, the future home of the Museum of Arts and Design, slated to open in 2008. The glass behemoth next door is the Time Warner Center, a massive complex full of high-end stores and restaurants that also hosts Jazz at Lincoln Center (p. 254). The best view of the Circle is from the windows on the Time Warner Center's third floor. *(Intersection of Broadway, Eighth Ave., and Central Park S.* Ⓢ *1, 9, A, B, C, D to 59th St./Columbus Circle.)*

SIGHTS

LINCOLN CENTER. Inspired by John D. Rockefeller's belief that "the arts are not for the privileged few, but for the many," this 15-acre center for the performing arts is home to 12 facilities that can accommodate nearly 18,000 spectators in all. When Carnegie Hall (p. 184) and the Metropolitan Opera House near Times Square seemed fated for destruction in 1955, city planner **Robert Moses,** with the help of Rockefeller and Mayor Robert Wagner, spearheaded the design and fundraising for Lincoln Center. The center's construction, which lasted from 1959 until the late 1960s, forced the eviction of thousands and erased a major part of the Hell's Kitchen area (see p. 179). A re-interpretation of the public plazas in Rome and Venice, Lincoln Center was initially dismissed by *The New York Times* as "a hulking disgrace." Since then, its spare and spacious architecture—and the performances it hosts—have made Lincoln Center one of New York's beloved public spaces.

The Lincoln Center buildings center around the **Josie Robertson Plaza,** home to the popular summer 👍**Midsummer Night Swing** festivities (p. 247). Straight ahead is the Mondrian-inspired glass facade of Lincoln Center's centerpiece, the **Metropolitan Opera House.** The Met was designed in 1966 by Wallace K. Harrison, who also headed the team of architects that constructed the United Nations building. Two colorful Chagall murals, *Source of Music* and *Triumph of Music*, hang on either side of the lobby's grand staircase. They are visible from the plaza through the windows. Just north of the Met is the **New York Public Library for the Performing Arts,** featuring a large collection of dance, music, recorded sound, and theater resources available to the public.

To the left side of the plaza as you face the Opera House is the **New York State Theater,** home of the New York City Ballet (p. 245) and the New York City Opera (p. 255). **Damrosch Park,** the nondescript concrete square behind the theater, hosts frequent outdoor concerts and the perennially popular **Big Apple Circus** in the **Guggenheim Bandshell.** (Call for tour dates. ☎212-268-2500; www.bigapplecircus.org.)

On the right side of the plaza is **Avery Fisher Hall,** designed in 1962 by Max Abramovitz and home to the New York Philharmonic (p. 249). To the right of the Opera House are the **Vivian Beaumont Theater** and the **Mitzi E. Newhouse Theater,** both housed in an Eero Saarinen-designed glass box.

A footbridge across 65th St. leads to the prestigious **Juilliard School,** where the likes of violinist Itzhak Perlman and jazz legend Wynton Marsalis honed their skills and comedian Robin Williams tried out his first routines. Within the Juilliard complex, you'll find the intimate **Alice Tully Hall,** home to the Chamber Music Society of Lincoln Center (p. 249). Behind Juilliard, in the Samuel B. and David Rose Building, the **Walter E. Reade Theater** features foreign films and special festivals (p. 248). *(Columbus Ave., between 62nd and 66th St.* [S] *1 to 66th St.* ☎*212-721-6500; www.lincolncenter.org. Info booth near the Avery Fisher Hall entrance. 1hr.* 👍*tours of theaters and galleries meet at the concourse under the Met Opera House on the hour daily 10am-4pm; reservations* ☎*212-875-5350. $12.50, students and seniors $9, children $6. Backstage* 👍*tours of the Opera House most M-F at 3:30pm and Su 10:30am; reservations* ☎*212-769-7020. $15, students $5. For box office info, see p. 254.)*

DAKOTA APARTMENTS. Perhaps Manhattan's most famous apartment building, the Dakota counts Lauren Bacall, Leonard Bernstein, Roberta Flack, and Boris Karloff as former residents. The interior is closed to the public. The 200-square-foot, nine-story Dakota was designed by architect **Henry Hardenbergh** (who later designed the Plaza Hotel) and was built in 1884. It was so far removed from the rest of the city that someone remarked, "It might as well be in the Dakota Territory." Hardenbergh gave the building a frontier flair. Among the ornate railings, balustrades, and dormers are bas-relief Native American heads, corn stalks, and arrowheads. Oil lamps still burn on either side of the guarded front gate. The Dakota provided the eerie setting of Roman Polanski's New York horror classic,

Rosemary's Baby, and the sidewalk outside was the site of resident **John Lennon's** tragic assassination on December 8, 1980. *(1 W 72nd St., at the corner of Central Park W. [S] B, C to 72nd St./Central Park W.)*

THE ANSONIA APARTMENTS. This upscale condominium building, completed in 1904, was once the grande dame of Beaux Arts apartments. While the inside is closed to the public, the building's exterior—complete with weathered stone ornaments and rounded corner towers—is still worth a look. Soundproof walls and thick floors once enticed musically inclined tenants like Enrico Caruso, Arturo Toscanini, and Igor Stravinsky. These same features served the building well in the 1970s and 80s, when the Ansonia housed **Plato's Retreat**, an infamous sex club frequented by wealthy couples and celebrities. The Ansonia's developer, William Stokes, raised chickens, ducks, and a pet bear on the building's roof. *(2109 Broadway, between 73rd and 74th St. [S] 1, 2, 3 to 72nd St./Broadway.)*

RIVERSIDE PARK. Riverside Park stretches four miles along the Hudson River, from 72nd to 158th St. Here, Upper West Siders walk their pooches, jog, bike, and enjoy wonderful views of the river and the Palisades of New Jersey. Designed in 1875 by Frederick Law Olmsted (of Central Park fame), the park boasts a skate rink, a playground, a basketball court, and acres of tranquil riverside lawns. It's best to avoid the park at night; at the least, abide by the posted closing time of 1am. *(West of Riverside Dr., from 72nd St. to the George Washington Bridge/175th St. www.nycgovparks.org.)*

RIVERSIDE PARK FOR POCKET CHANGE. The **Riverside Park Fund** (www.riversideparkfund.org) organizes a host of (usually free) community-oriented activities in the park throughout the summer. Bird walks, stargazing, river kayaking, salsa lessons, yoga classes, bike rides, and outdoor concerts make an afternoon in this beautiful park a treat. There's some sort of organized activity almost every day in the summer; check the website for the schedule.

MORNINGSIDE HEIGHTS

Above 110th St. and below 125th, Morningside Heights, wedged between Harlem and the Upper West Side, is dominated by Barnard College and Columbia University. Broadway is the neighborhood's main thoroughfare. It's a quieter setting than Midtown, which increases its attractiveness for many residents. The neighborhood is home to several excellent parks. Sights are listed from south to north.

CATHEDRAL OF ST. JOHN THE DIVINE. The largest Gothic-style church in the world, the unfinished St. John the Divine cathedral has been under construction since 1892. This Episcopal church can house some 3000 worshippers at one time. Its many altars and bays commemorate those who suffered in tragedies such as 9/11, the AIDS epidemic, the Holocaust, the Bosnian crisis, and the Armenian genocide. The central nave contains a 100-million-year-old nautilus fossil; the world's second largest organ stop, which consists of some 8035 pipes; a "Poet's Corner" honoring writers such as Nathaniel Hawthorne and Edith Wharton; and an extraordinary tapestry by Raphael. With a poet and two dance companies in residence, the cathedral complements worship services through concerts, art exhibitions, poetry readings, lectures, theater, and dance events. For information and event schedule, call the box office or check online. The complex also contains a **Greek amphitheater** (still under construction), a peace fountain, and a beautiful "Biblical Garden." *(Amsterdam Ave., between 110th and 113th St. [S] 1 to Cathedral Pkwy. (110th St.)/Broadway. ☎212-316-7540, tours 212-932-7347; www.stjohndivine.org. Open daily M-Sa 7am-6pm, Su 7am-7pm. Tours Tu-Sa 11am, Su 1pm. $5, students and seniors $4. Parish* *box office ☎212-662-2133. Eucharists M-Sa 8:30am and 12:15pm; Su 8, 9, and 11am. Choral evensong and organ meditation Su 6pm.)*

COLUMBIA UNIVERSITY. This world-famous university was chartered in 1754 as King's College, but it lost its original name in the American Revolution. In 1897 President Seth Low, seeking a healthy academic environment for students and professors, moved the school from 49th St. and Madison Ave. to its current location, which was farmland at the time. The campus, designed by prominent New York architects, is urban—don't come looking for ivy and leafy quads. Its centerpiece, the majestic Roman-Classical **Low Library,** looms over **College Walk,** the school's central promenade, which bustles with academics, students, and quacks. The **Alma Mater Statue** in front of the building was a rallying point during the riots of 1968. Just to the east of Low Library stands **St. Paul's Chapel,** a small but beautiful space with magnificent acoustics, which holds free choral and chamber concerts Tuesday and Saturday (www.columbia.edu/cu/earl/stpauls.html). **Morningside Park,** where Meg Ryan discussed her sexual fantasies in *When Harry Met Sally,* is just east of the campus along Morningside Dr. (between 110th and 123rd St.). On Saturday nights in the summer, the park hosts free world music concerts. Bring a blanket or folding chair (☎212-865-3778; www.morningside-park.org). *(Morningside Dr. and Broadway, from 114th to 120th St. www.columbia.edu. [S] 1 to 116th St./Columbia University. Group tours for prospective students late fall through spring; no regularly scheduled public tours.)*

RIVERSIDE CHURCH. A majestic Gothic edifice financed by John D. Rockefeller Jr., this steel-frame church (completed in 1930) was constructed in only two years. Its central nave is intended to look like that of Chartres Cathedral in France. The congregation has been interdenominational since its inception, and it has been at the forefront of progressive Christian social activism for much of the 20th century. The tower observation deck looms 362 ft. above Riverside Dr. and commands an amazing view of both the bells in the tower and the Hudson River and Riverside Park below. Best heard from the parks around the church, The Laura Spelman Rockefeller Memorial Carillon contains 74 bronze bells given in memory of John's mother. It can generally be heard Sundays at 10:30am, 12:30, and 3pm. The church hosts interdenominational, interracial, and international services and activities. Check the website or call for the event schedule. *(490 Riverside Dr., at 120th St. [S] 1 to 116th St./Columbia University. ☎212-870-6792; www.theriversidechurchny.org. Su services 8:15, 10:45am. Open daily 7am-10pm. Tours Su 12:30pm, after services, and upon request. Free.)*

👍 **GENERAL GRANT NATIONAL MEMORIAL (GRANT'S TOMB).** This granite mausoleum is the largest of its kind in America. It rises to 150 ft. atop a hill overlooking the Hudson River. Once covered with graffiti, the monument to the Civil War general and 18th US President Ulysses S. Grant is now pristine. Bronze casts of other Union generals surround the tomb of Grant and his wife Julia. Grant's Civil War victories in the Battles of Vicksburg and Chattanooga, as well as Robert E. Lee's surrender at Appomattox, are depicted in mosaics, and the motto "Let Us Have Peace" adorns the top of the facade. Also highlighted is the effort of Richard T. Greener, the first black graduate of Harvard and secretary of the Grant Monument Association. On April 27, Grant's birthday, the tomb hosts a full cannon salute. Across the street, **Sakura Park,** in Riverside Park, features a statue of General Daniel Butterfield, who arranged the current setting of "Taps." The *sakura,* Japanese for "cherry blossoms," were a 1912 gift to the city. *(Near the intersection of Riverside Dr. and 122nd St. [S] 1 to 125th St./Broadway. ☎212-666-1640. Open daily 9am-5pm. Free. Informal ranger-guided tours depart every hr. 10am-4pm.)*

HARLEM

Manhattan's largest neighborhood, Harlem extends from 110th St. to the 150s, between the Hudson and East Rivers. In the 1870s, elevated trains brought the district within commuting distance from lower Manhattan. Upper middle-class German Jewish families settled in the area, building the ornate row houses for which Harlem is still famous. When these families began moving to more suburban locales early in the 20th century, Harlem became a largely African-American community. The prosperity of the 1920s, in conjunction with the Great Migration of African-Americans from the southern US and the Caribbean, gave rise to the artistic and literary boom of the **Harlem Renaissance.**

In the 1960s, the **Black Power** movement centered here. LeRoi Jones's Revolutionary Theater performed one-act plays in the streets, and Malcolm X, Stokely Carmichael, and H. Rap Brown spoke out against racism and injustice. Despite their activism, Harlem's economic welfare waned quickly. Today, pockets of Harlem are thriving again. Hoping to further this rebirth, the **Clinton Foundation** recently established an office on bustling 125th St.

Spanish Harlem, or **El Barrio,** sits on the East Side between 96th and 125th St. It supports a large Mexican and Puerto Rican population along its main artery of E 116th St. On the East Side, stark social and cultural stratification is apparent. Pockets of artistry do survive, however. Be sure to check out the **Graffiti Wall of Fame** at 106th St. and Park Ave. El Barrio struts its stuff with pride on Puerto Rican Constitution Day (July 25), when streets close off for festivities.

Harlem's parks provide some relief from Manhattan's asphalt: 12.8 acre **Jackie Robinson Park** (145th-152nd St., between Edgecombe and Bradhurst Ave.) includes a bronze statue of the baseball player and a public pool. **Marcus Garvey Park** (120th-124th St., between Fifth and Madison Ave.)—named after the prominent advocate of the "Back to Africa" movement— features huge canopy trees, sloping rocks, and unsurpassed views of the city.

Some major streets are known in the Harlem area by more than one name: note Frederick Douglass Blvd. (Eighth Ave.); Adam Clayton Powell Jr. Blvd. (Seventh Ave.); and Lenox Ave. (Sixth Ave. or Malcolm X Blvd.). Sights are listed from south to north. (Ⓢ *6 to 103rd St., Central Park N (110th St.), 116th St./Lexington Ave.; 4, 5, 6 to 125th St./Lexington Ave.; 2, 3 to Central Park N (110th St.), 116th St., 125th St., 135th St./ Lenox (6th) Ave.; 3 to 145th St./Lenox (6th) Ave., 148th St.; B, C to Cathedral Pkwy. (110th St.), 116th St., 135th St. at Central Park W; A, B, C, D to 125th St./Central Park W, 145th St./St. Nicholas Ave.; 1 to 125th St., 137th St., 145th St./Broadway.)*

■**CITY COLLEGE.** City College is the nation's first public college and the alma mater of Woody Allen, Colin Powell, Edward Koch, and Walter Mosley. Gothic buildings and sprawling green lawns grace the campus. Founded in 1847 by Townsend Harris to provide higher education for immigrants and the poor, the college settled on its hilltop site in 1909. Architect George Brown Post employed the Gothic style associated with prestigious Oxford and Cambridge Universities, but, seeking to identify the college as a "workingman's school," he insisted on rust-streaked and iron-spotted schist instead of marble or ivory. *(Offices at 138th St. and Convent Ave., campus from 130th to 140th St. Enter at 138th St. Ⓢ 1 to 137th St. ☎212-650-7000, campus tours through admissions ☎212-650-6977; www.ccny.cuny.edu.)*

■**THE SCHOMBURG CENTER FOR RESEARCH IN BLACK CULTURE.** This research branch of the **New York Public Library** (p. 180) houses the city's vast archives, manuscripts, and rare books on black history and culture. Scholar Arturo Schomburg collected some five million photographs, oral histories, and pieces of art. The Latimer/Edison Art Gallery shows rotating exhibits like *In Motion: The African-American Migration Experience* and *Lest We Forget:*

Harlem—likely the most famous African-American neighborhood in the United States—is a joy to discover on foot. Many traces of its vibrant cultural and artistic heritage endure, and though the neighborhood languished in poverty and crime in the decades after WWII, it seems today to be witnessing yet another rebirth. New shopping centers are opening, old landmarks are being renovated, and cultural institutions continue to serve as trendsetters in African-American culture.

TIME: 2-3 hr., longer with shopping and food breaks.

BEST TIMES: Early on a Sunday morning, in time to catch the 11am service at the Abyssinian Baptist Church or neighboring Mother Zion AME Church. Or, late afternoon, in time to end with a show at the Apollo Theater or Showman's Cafe.

START: The southwest corner of 135th St. and Adam Clayton Powell Jr. Blvd./7th Ave. Ⓢ 2, 3 to 135th St.; B, C to 135th St.

1 135TH ST. AND ADAM CLAYTON POWELL JR. BLVD./SEVENTH AVE. The intersection where this tour begins was, in the 1920s and 30s, the institutional hub of Harlem, housing the headquarters of the National Association of Colored People (NAACP), several major black newspapers, the National Urban League, and the Universal Negro Improvement Association. The New York City YMCA that was once reserved for "colored" visitors still stands to the east of here at 180 W 135th St. Legends like Langston Hughes, Richard Wright, and Ralph Ellison all called it home.

2 BIG APPLE RESTAURANT AND JAZZ CLUB. Cross to the northwest corner of the street, and glance at the "Big Apple" plaque on the side of 2300 Adam Clayton Powell Jr. Blvd./Seventh Ave. The plaque commemorates the now-defunct Big Apple Restaurant and Jazz Club, which was popular in the 1930s. Jazz musicians may have called New York City "The Big Apple" in recognition of its status as the world's jazz capital.

3 ST. NICHOLAS HISTORIC DISTRICT. Walk north along Powell, and turn left on 138th St. Head west toward Frederick Douglass Blvd./Eighth Ave., and you'll stroll through the heart of the St. Nicholas Historic District, which boasts beautifully preserved Georgian and Renaissance Revival houses. The area was nicknamed Striver's Row in the 1920s when an influx of African Americans striving to "make it" moved in.

4 SUGAR HILL. Head north on Douglass to 139th St., and stand on the southeast corner of the intersection. You're now at the edge of Sugar Hill, a more exclusive neighborhood than Striver's Row; it was for those who already had plenty of "sugar." In the late 1970s, the area was the birthplace of Sugar Hill Records, the rap label that spawned the Sugar Hill Gang. Glance west up the hill, and you'll see Shephard Hall, the main building of City College (CCNY). CCNY has graduated more Nobel Laureates than any other public college, along with notables like Upton Sinclair and Colin Powell.

5 ABYSSINIAN BAPTIST CHURCH. Head east on 139th St. and make a right on Powell. Walk one block south to 138th St., and turn left. Walk down the block, and you'll see the Abyssinian Baptist Church on your right. This Gothic Revival edifice, constructed in 1923, is home to one of the most famous gospel choirs in the country. The church became famous when civil-rights leader Adam Clayton Powell Jr. served as its pastor in the 1930s. On Sunday mornings, lines of visitors hoping to attend a gospel service snake around the block. If you're wearing your Sunday best, join them.

6 MISS MAUDE'S SPOONBREAD TOO. Assuming you've worked up an appetite, continue walking west to Malcom X. Blvd./Lenox Ave., and turn right. Stop for a delicious soul-food meal (or just a lemonade) at Miss Maude's Spoonbread Too, 547 Lenox Ave.

7 SCHOMBURG CENTER. Take a right out of Miss Maude's, and continue south on Lenox. History buffs could get lost for hours at the Schomburg Center for Research in Black Culture on the northwest corner of 135th St. and Lenox Ave. The center is named after a black Puerto Rican whom contemporaries dubbed "The Sherlock Holmes of Black History" for his unflagging commitment to documenting it. It is now a branch of the New York Public Library and is filled with

WALKING TOUR

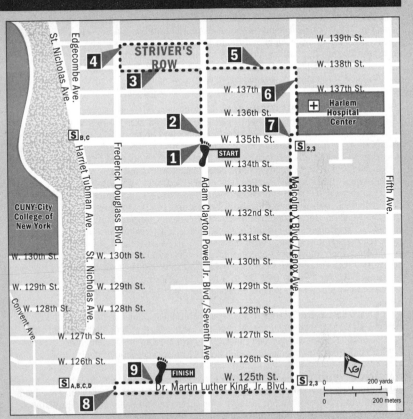

manuscripts, recordings, and photographs by African American artists. The ashes of poet Langston Hughes are also stored here.

8 HARLEM SHOPPING. Head down Lenox to 125th St. The headquarters of the Clinton Foundation are just to your left, at 55 W 125th St. If you turn right, however, you'll find yourself in the commercial hub of Harlem today and the site of substantial new development. Walk along the crowded street and bargain for wares with the many street vendors, or pop your head in the discount shops. The Harlem USA Mall, owned by Magic Johnson, stands at the southwest corner of 125th St. and Frederick Douglass Blvd./Eighth Ave. For excellent African-American book browsing, head left on Eighth Ave., and cross the street to Hue-Man Books, 2319 Frederick Douglass Blvd.

9 APOLLO THEATER. Back on 125th St., you have two excellent options for evening entertainment. The Apollo Theater, 253 W 125th St., which opened in 1914 as Hurtig and Seamon's New Burlesque Theatre, originally did not admit blacks. When new management took it over in the 30s, the theater's Amateur Night helped launch the careers of African-American music greats like Ella Fitzgerald, James Brown, the Jackson Five, and Stevie Wonder. The tradition continues today, and it's still good fun. Most prominent contemporary African-American performers have graced the Apollo's stage. If you can't score tickets, live jazz at Showman's Cafe will still take you back to Harlem's heyday.

The Triumph Over Slavery. The large and impressive research library contains a year-round exhibit featuring biographies of 100 notable black New Yorkers. The center also houses the **American Negro Theater,** famous during the 1940s, and the **Langston Hughes Auditorium.** Concerts are held here occasionally. *(515 Lenox (6th) Ave., at 135th St. [S] 2, 3 to 135th St./Lenox (6th) Ave. ☎212-491-2200; www.schomburgcenter.org. General Research and Reference open Tu-W noon-8pm, Th-F noon-6pm, Sa 10am-6pm. Exhibition house open Tu-Sa 10am-6pm. Wheelchair accessible.)*

THE ABYSSINIAN BAPTIST CHURCH. In 1808, several wealthy black traders from Abyssinia (now Ethiopia) sought to attend a Baptist service and were forced to watch it from the slave loft. In response, the traders began a boycott that led to the foundation of the Abyssinian Baptist Church a year later. Settled in its present location since 1923, the church become known for its contributions to the community as well as its famous preachers. Adam Clayton Powell Sr., credited with catalyzing black migration to Harlem, once presided over the pulpit. His son, Adam Clayton Powell Jr. (after whom Harlem's Seventh Ave. is named), succeeded his father in 1937 before becoming New York's first black Congressman. Today, the eloquent Calvin Butts preaches to the 5000-strong congregation every Sunday. A well-known choir also belts out gospel. This is a a popular Sunday morning stop with tourists. If you want to attend a service, arrive early and stand in the visitors line. Often, the church can't accommodate everyone, but a slew of other churches along W 116th St. tend to be less crowded. *(132 W 138th St./Odell Clark Pl., between Lenox (6th) Ave. and Powell Blvd. [S] 2, 3 to 135th St./Lenox (6th) Ave. ☎212-862-7474; www.abyssinian.org. Services W 6pm, Su 9 and 11am; W prayer service 6pm.)*

[TIP] **GOSPEL BACKUP.** If the Abyssinian Baptist Church is packed to the limit on Sunday morning, a nearby alternative is the **Mother AME Zion Church,** 140-146 W 137th St., between Lenox (Sixth) Ave. and Adam Clayton Powell Jr. Blvd. Head there for the music-filled Sunday 11am service, without the big crowds.

HAMILTON HEIGHTS. Between Convent and St. Nicholas Ave., this brownstone-filled residential neighborhood is home to the **Riverbank State Park** along the Hudson. Built over a sewage plant in 1993, it features ice and roller rinks, a pool, tennis courts, tracks, baseball diamonds, and picnic fields. *(Between St. Nicholas and Amsterdam Ave., and between 140th and 145th St. RIVERBANK STATE PARK: Off the West Side Hwy.; enter at 135th St. [S] 1 to 145th St./Broadway. ☎212-694-3600. Open F-Su 9am-5pm. Free.)*

STRIVER'S ROW. Created as a "model housing project" for middle-class whites, Striver's Row acquired its nickname from Harlemites who felt their neighbors were striving too hard to attain middle-class status. The buildings, designed by David H. King Jr., were only opened to African Americans in 1919, when they attracted the likes of composer W.C. Handy (232 W 139th St.) and surgeon Dr. Louis T. Wright (218 W 138th St.). Now part of the St. Nicholas Historic District, the impressive 1891 brownstones are featured in Spike Lee's *Jungle Fever.* The tan brick buildings, ranging in style from Neocolonial to Italian Renaissance, sport wrought-iron railings and inviting stoops. *(138th and 139th St., between Powell and Frederick Douglass Blvd. (8th Ave.). [S] B, C to 135th St./St. Nicholas Ave.)*

SUGAR HILL. African Americans with "sugar" (that is, money) moved here in the 1920s and 30s. Musical legends Duke Ellington and W.C. Handy lived in the neighborhood, while leaders W.E.B. DuBois and Thurgood Marshall inhabited 409 Edgecombe Ave. Some of the city's most notable gangsters also operated here—Wesley Snipes starred as one in the film *Sugar Hill.* The area is also the birthplace of Sugarhill Records, the rap label that created the Sugarhill Gang. Their 1979 "Rapper's Delight" became the first hip-hop song to enter the Top 40. Today, skyrocketing real estate prices in Manhattan have made Sugar Hill's brownstones prized possessions once more. *(145th to 155th St., between St. Nicholas and Edgecombe Ave. $\boxed{S}$ A, B, C, D to 145th St./St. Nicholas Ave.)*

WASHINGTON HEIGHTS

Even hillier than Brooklyn's Park Slope, Washington Heights and its several parks form one of the greenest neighborhoods in the five boroughs. Some buildings peer down hundreds of feet at their next-door neighbors. Once predominantly Irish, Washington Heights's collection of Dominican, African-American, Greek, Armenian, and Jewish communities make it one of upper Manhattan's most diverse neighborhoods. North of Washington Heights, suburban-feeling Inwood (formerly "Tubby Hook") is one-third parkland. Sights are listed from south to north. *($\boxed{S}$ C to 155th St./St. Nicholas Ave., 163rd St.; 1, A, C to 168th St./Broadway; A to 175th St., 181st St., 190th St.; 1 to 181st St./St. Nicholas Ave., 191st St.)*

MORRIS-JUMEL MANSION. The Morris-Jumel Mansion is Manhattan's oldest free-standing house, built in 1765, and it has a colorful history. When the Revolutionary War began, Loyalist owner Roger Morris abandoned it and fled to England. In 1776, George Washington stayed here while devising his battle plan for the Battle of Harlem Heights. Stephen Jumel purchased the house in 1810 for his wife Eliza, a former prostitute. Just a year after Stephen died, in 1832, Eliza married Aaron Burr (Vice President under Thomas Jefferson) in the front room. The house has famous bedrooms, Napoleonic ornaments, and regal furniture. The slightly unkempt gardens afford a great view of the Harlem River. Ring the doorbell for admission, even if the museum looks closed. The small gift shop sells copies of Eliza's obituary ($1), colonial currency ($2.75), mugs ($6.25), and t-shirts ($15). Across the street on Sylvan Terr., French colonial houses stretch down the narrow, cobbled street. *(65 Jumel Terr., between 160th and 162nd St. $\boxed{S}$ C to 163rd St. Follow 160th or 162nd St. east to the mansion. ☎ 212-923-8008; www.morrisjumel.org. Open W-Su 10am-4pm. $3, seniors and students $2, accompanied children under 12 free. Guided tours daily by appointment. 1hr. tour of building $3.50, under 12 $2.50; 90min. tour of building, grounds, and history of neighborhood $7. Free rotating-focus tours every Sa at noon; reservations recommended.)*

AUDUBON BALLROOM. On February 21, 1965, black leader Malcolm X was assassinated on the grounds of this building. Most of the ballroom has been swallowed by commercial space, but a memorial statue of Malcolm X stands in the main lobby. Unfortunately, the lobby is now closed to the public; visitors can only peer inside through the building's glass doors. Formerly one of Harlem's great theaters, the Audubon was built by William Fox (of 20th-Century Fox fame). The Marx Brothers appeared on its stage. The Audubon, partly rededicated in 1997 as a memorial to Malcolm X, also houses a medical research center. *(3940 Broadway, between 165th and 166th St. $\boxed{S}$ C to 163rd St.)*

GEORGE WASHINGTON BRIDGE. The construction of this 14-lane, 3500 ft. suspension bridge coincided with the beginning of the Great Depression. Purse-tightening left the bridge's two towers without the granite sheathing designer Othmar Amman had intended. During the long construction, neighborhood children would use the structural supports of the George Washington Bridge as diving boards into the Hudson River. Le Corbusier, who proclaimed it "the most beautiful bridge in the world," was struck by the naked steelwork's modernist aesthetic. The north sidewalk is for pedestrians only and the south sidewalk (reached via a steep ramp on the Manhattan side) is shared with bicycles. *(Best views from the corner of 181st St. and Riverside Dr. and from Fort Tryon Park. $\boxed{S}$ A to 181st St./Washington Ave. Great views of Manhattan from the walking path on the bridge itself; north entrance located at 179th St. and Cabrini Blvd., south entrance at 178th St. and Cabrini Blvd. Toll NJ to NY $6, NY to NJ free.)*

SIGHTS

JEFFREY'S HOOK LIGHTHOUSE. Originally constructed in 1921 to steer barges away from Jeffrey's Hook, this tiny lighthouse is featured in Hildegarde Hoyt Swift's book *The Little Red Lighthouse and the Great Grey Bridge*. When the lighthouse was decommissioned in 1947, Swift's book played a major role in saving it from demolition. Millions of children spoke out when the US Coast Guard wanted to dismantle and sell the structure. The trail to the lighthouse is a tad confusing and rather steep, but it's manageable. To the south of the lighthouse are tennis courts and some lovely grass areas with picnic tables. At some places you can get down to the water's edge. *(Fort Washington Park, 178th St. and Hudson River.* Ⓢ *A to 181st St./Washington Ave. From Lafayette Pl. at W 181st St., take the footbridge over the highway, down to the park and south to the lighthouse.* ☎ *212-304-2365; www.nyc.gov/parks. Tours available spring-fall; call for details.)*

YESHIVA UNIVERSITY. The 7000-student Yeshiva University traces its beginnings to 1886 on the Lower East Side. In 1929, the university moved its main campus to these pallid institutional buildings in the middle of a bustling Hispanic neighborhood. The rabbinical and men's undergraduate programs are conducted here. The recently renamed David H. Zysman Hall is the campus's Gothic centerpiece, featuring Romanesque windows and colorful minarets. *(Amsterdam Ave., from 182nd to 186th St.* Ⓢ *1 to 181st St./St. Nicholas Ave. Administrative offices at 500 185th St. Administrative offices* ☎ *212-960-5400, admissions and tours* ☎ *212-960-5277; www.yu.edu.)*

FORT TRYON PARK. Frederick Law Olmsted, Jr., son of the famed Central Park co-designer, landscaped this lovely park. In 1935, John D. Rockefeller Jr. donated the park to the city in exchange for permission to construct Rockefeller University. This is one of the most majestic and beautiful landscapes in the city. Inside are the crumbling remains of Fort Tryon, a Revolutionary War bulwark captured by the British in 1776, and the well-tended Heather Garden. Proceeds from the gourmet New Leaf Cafe (p. 143; 1 Margaret Corbin Dr.) support ongoing restoration work in the park. Outside are sensational views of the George Washington Bridge and the Palisades. The Cloisters (p. 228), the Met's palatial sanctuary for medieval art, overlooks the park from its northern perch. *(Bounded by Broadway to the east, the Hudson River to the west, Riverside Dr. to the north, and Overlook Terr. to the south.* Ⓢ *1 to 191st St./St. Nicholas Ave.; A to 190th St./Fort Washington Ave. Garden walking tours, concerts, fitness activities, and other events; see www.nyc.gov/parks.)*

ROOSEVELT ISLAND

Just off the east coast of Manhattan, this 147-acre island in the East River is home to only 9500 residents. In 1969, during Mayor John Lindsay's term, the New York State Urban Development Corporation signed a 99-year lease with New York City to develop the island into a mixed-income residential community with a largely traffic-free environment. The island was renamed Roosevelt Island in 1973, and the first residential complex opened in 1975.

Don't miss the bright red tram shuttle to the East River, one of the few publicly operated commuter cable cars in the world. The ride provides a grand view of the East Side as you rise to 250 ft. above the United Nations complex. Once on the island, walk north or take the mini-bus ($0.25) up Main St. and roam around a bit. A walking/skating path encircles the island. **Lighthouse Park,** at the northernmost tip of the island, is a landscaped park with views of the East River. More interesting is Southpoint, a public space at the foot of the island, with an incredible panorama of both Manhattan and Long Island City. Set in the restored ruins of an old mental asylum, the land is mostly uncultivated, and is a lovely spot for a picnic, though rumor has it that new residences are soon to be built in the area. Shopping options are limited on the island, so you might want to hit a deli on the mainland first. Southpoint can be reached by the mini-bus, and is open in the summer 8am-9:30pm, in the fall and spring

8am-8:30pm, and in the winter 8am-6:30pm. *([S] F to Roosevelt Island, Lexington Ave./63rd St.; 4, 5, 6, N, R, W to 59th St./Lexington Ave. Walk 2 blocks east from 59th St. and Lexington to 2nd Ave. and hop on the tram. ☎ 718-832-4555. Tram every 15min. M-Th and Su 6am-2am, F-Sa 6am-3:30am; twice as frequently at rush hr. One-way $2. MetroCards accepted. 4min. each way.)*

BROOKLYN

Until 1898, Brooklyn was its own metropolis—and second only to New York (i.e., Manhattan) as the country's most populated city. When it voted, by the narrowest of margins, to unite with New York City in 1898, it laid the foundation for the modern-day, five-borough municipal structure. Brooklyn is New York's most populated borough today, and on its own it would be the fourth-most populated city in the United States. Home to a huge variety of neighborhoods, many of them immigrant in character, Brooklyn has also become a magnet for 20- and 30-somethings, who first came in search of low rents but now gravitate to the area's thriving art communities, innovative restaurant scene, and hip nightlife.

WILLIAMSBURG AND GREENPOINT

Two decades ago, Williamsburg was mired in grim industrial decay—economically depressed and culturally impoverished. Though the community's industrial past is still visible, a warehouse here now is likely to function as an art gallery, and graffiti is likely to be of a political and artistic bent. The area's young residents wear their piercings and tattoos proudly, ride the local streets on their refurbished bicycles, and take full advantage of the offbeat dining and nightlife scenes. **Bedford Avenue** and **Berry Street** are the neighborhood centers, though each year sees further development. Three free community publications, *11211*, *Block*, and *The Brooklyn Rail* report on arts, local news, and special events.

A Hasidic Jewish community thrives on the south side of town along Broadway, Heyward St., Wythe St., and Bedford Ave. North of Broadway is a predominantly Latino area. Greenpoint, bounded by Java St. to the north, Meserole St. to the south, and Franklin St. to the west, is Brooklyn's northernmost region and borders Queens. Home to a large Polish population, it is also the birthplace of Mae West. Italianate and Grecian houses, built during the 1850s shipbuilding boom, grace the neighborhood.

RUSSIAN ORTHODOX CATHEDRAL OF THE TRANSFIGURATION. Five copper-covered, onion-shaped domes carry you off to Mother Russia. Built between 1916 and 1921, the cathedral's gorgeous stained-glass windows and triple-slashed crosses are only a hint of the beauty within. Doors are locked during the week; for a peek inside, stop by after Sunday mass. *(228 N 12th St., at Driggs Ave. [S] L to Bedford Ave.; G to Nassau Ave. Vespers Sa 6pm, mass Su 9am.)*

ST. ANTHONY-ST. ALPHONSUS CHURCH. Built in 1873 by Brooklynite Patrick Keeley, this Roman Catholic church features some of the best stained-glass windows in New York. The "flamboyant Gothic" architecture includes a clock in the steeple and a Columbus organ from 1892. Old nautical maps of the area use the steeple as a landmark; it was once the highest point in Brooklyn. The lower chapel is open daily, but the main church opens its doors only for mass, held on Saturday and Sunday in both English and Spanish. *(862 Manhattan Ave., at Milton St. [S] G to Greenpoint Ave. ☎ 718-383-3339. Lower chapel open daily 7am-5pm. Masses M-F 8:15am; Sa 8:15am and 5:30pm; Su 9:30, in Spanish 11am, 12:30pm.)*

BROOKLYN BREWERY. In the days when beer was the primary safe alternative to unsanitary drinking water, enterprising immigrants began a century-long Brooklyn brewing tradition. Slow sales in the 1960s brought the beer boom to an end, but the Brooklyn Brewery, established in 1987, still makes Brooklyn Lager and Brooklyn Brown Ale. The brewery is a busy factory during the week and a lively gathering spot on weekends. Friday nights and Saturday afternoons, the brewery opens its taps and serves $3 beers (2 for $5). It also offers free 30min. tours on Saturdays, with complimentary beer at the end. A small store sells t-shirts, hats, and glassware with the Brooklyn Brewery insignia. *(79 N 11th St., at Wythe Ave.* S *L to Bedford Ave.; G to Nassau Ave.* ☎ *718-486-7422; www.brooklynbrewery.com. Free tours and tasting Sa 1-5pm on the hour. Company store and tap room open F 6-10pm, Sa noon-5pm.)*

BROOKLYN HEIGHTS AND DOWNTOWN

FULTON LANDING AND DUMBO

Brooklyn owes most of its development to Robert Fulton. After inventing the steamboat, Fulton chartered a ferry route across the East River, and Brooklyn grew from a village of 2000 in 1816 to a city of half a million in less than 40 years. Fulton Landing hasn't been a ferry dock since 1924, but in recent years a high-speed water taxi has taken up the former ferry route from Fulton St. in Brooklyn to Fulton St. in Manhattan. DUMBO, which stands for Down Under Manhattan Bridge Overpass, is a funky neighborhood with a thriving arts scene, a growing residential community, and numerous parks, bars, and stores.

■**BROOKLYN BRIDGE.** The walk across the Brooklyn Bridge at sunrise or sunset is one of the most beautiful in New York City. The bridge spans from Lower Manhattan's cluster of skyscrapers to Brooklyn's own surprisingly tall skyline. South St. Seaport and Fulton Ferry make pleasant bookends.

The bridge is the product of elegant calculation, careful design, and strenuous human exertion. When chief architect John Augustus Roebling crushed his foot in a surveying accident and died of gangrene, his son, Washington Roebling, took over the project. Washington himself died of the bends, and his wife Emily Warren inherited the bridge. Plaques at either end of the walkway commemorate the Roeblings and the workers who died in underwater chambers during the bridge's construction. The bridge was finished in just 13 years, opening in 1883. Georgia O'Keeffe and Joseph Stella immortalized it on canvas, and Hart Crane paid tribute to it in verse. *(Entrance from Brooklyn at the end of Adams St., at Tillary St.* S *A, C to High St. Entrance from Manhattan at Park Row.* S *J, M, Z, 4, 5, 6 to Brooklyn Bridge/City Hall.)*

FULTON FERRY. This section of faded buildings is named for the ferry that ran from here to Manhattan from 1642 to 1924. The ferry pier has a beautiful view of Lower Manhattan and the Brooklyn Bridge. The new **New York Water Taxi** (☎212-742-1969; www.nywatertaxi.com) stops at Fulton Ferry Landing, bringing commuters and sightseers to South St. Seaport, Wall St., Battery Park, the World Financial Center, Greenwich Village, Chelsea, and the W 44th St. Piers in Manhattan; Hunters Point, Brooklyn Army Tunnel, and Red Hook in Brooklyn; and Jersey City in New Jersey. (One-way from $4.50; 10-trip passes from $28; monthly passes from $138.50, depending on destination and day of the week.) Water taxis leave Fulton Ferry daily 7-10am and 4:30-8pm. Call or check website for exact schedule and route map. *(At the East River end of Old Fulton St.* S *A, C to High St.)*

DOWN UNDER MANHATTAN BRIDGE OVERPASS (DUMBO). The area just under the Manhattan Bridge overpass is a paper recycling station, but the surrounding blocks are home to some famous Brooklyn restaurants and shops and a number of old warehouses that have been transformed into galleries and theaters. The **Empire Fulton Ferry** and **Brooklyn Bridge State Parks,** which span the waterfront between the Manhattan and Brooklyn Bridges, make lovely spots for a picnic. During the summer, movies are shown for free in the park. Check the website (www.brooklynbridgepark.org) for details. *(The area between the Brooklyn and Manhattan Bridges.* S *F to York St.; A, C to High St. Parks open daily 8am-8pm.)*

BROOKLYN HEIGHTS

Brooklyn Heights sprang up in 1814 with the development of steamboat transportation between Brooklyn and Manhattan. Its rows of Greek Revival and Italianate houses became New York's first suburb. Montague St., the neighborhood's main drag, has stores, cafes, and mid-priced restaurants. Arthur Miller and W.H. Auden called the area home in the 1940s and 50s. Today, young and upwardly mobile types live here, most of whom commute into Manhattan to work. Atlantic Ave. has a thriving Middle Eastern community. Downtown is the location of Brooklyn's Civic Center, and contains several grand municipal buildings. Sights are listed from north to south. *(Ⓢ M, R, 2, 3, 4, 5 to Court St./Borough Hall.)*

🔲THE BROOKLYN HEIGHTS PROMENADE. The view of the lower Manhattan skyline and the Brooklyn Bridge from this bench-lined waterfront walkway is lovely—even if the walkway doubles as the roof of the toxic Brooklyn-Queens Expressway (BQE). To the left, Lady Liberty peeps from behind Governor's Island. In fair weather, you can see Ellis Island (to the left of the tip of Manhattan) and Staten Island (to the left of Governor's Island), along with the Chrysler Building, the Empire State Building, and the Brooklyn Bridge. *(By the East River, between Remsen and Orange St. Ⓢ 2, 3 to Clark St.)*

PLYMOUTH CHURCH OF PILGRIMS. Before the Civil War, this simple red-brick church was a stop on the Underground Railroad, playing a part so large that it become known as "Grand Central Depot." Its courageous first minister was Henry Ward Beecher, brother of *Uncle Tom's Cabin* author Harriet Beecher Stowe. Abraham Lincoln came to worship here on several occasions. A section of Plymouth Rock was added to the adjoining arcade in 1934. In summer (June-Aug.), the church offices and reception room are usually open during the day. In winter (Sept.-June), you can call ahead for a free tour of the historic sanctuary. *(75 Hicks St., on the corner of Hicks St. and Orange St. ☎ 718-624-4743; www.plymouthchurch.org. Ⓢ 2, 3 to Clark St. Services Sept.-June Su 11am in the sanctuary; June-Aug. Su 10am in the reception room. Sept.-June call for tours of the sanctuary.)*

WILLOW STREET. Willow St. buildings numbering 155-159 are among the oldest preserved Federal-style row houses of the early 19th century (c. 1830). Dormer windows punctuate the sloping roofs. A window in the sidewalk near the gate for number 157 once lit an underground tunnel leading from number 159 to a nearby stable. *(Willow St., between Clark and Pierrepont St. Ⓢ 2, 3 to Clark St.)*

ST. ANN'S AND THE HOLY TRINITY EPISCOPAL CHURCH. One of the more impressive landmarks on Montague St., St. Ann's contains over 4000 sq. ft. of stained glass. **Saint Ann's School,** an esteemed private school (alums include Jennifer Connelly, Mike D of the Beastie Boys, and Emily Parker) was founded on the church grounds and is now located in the old Crescent Athletic Club, up the block on Pierrepont St. The church hosts arts events, including the One World Symphony, which performs here during the summer. *(☎ 718-462-7270; www.oneworldsymphony.org. Concerts $30, students and seniors $20; open rehearsals $5.) (Montague St., on the corner of Clinton St. Ⓢ 2, 3, 4, 5, M, R to Court St./Borough Hall; A, C to High St. ☎ 718-875-6960. Services Su 11am. Open for prayer daily noon-2pm. Free organ concert W 1:10pm.)*

BOROUGH HALL. Completed in 1851, this building was once the city hall of an independent Brooklyn. It now houses the Borough President's office and a fantastic tourism center, where visitors can find free maps and advice. Locals congregate outside to read, sun, and nap. *(209 Joralemon St., at the southern end of Fulton St.*

Mall. [S] 2, 3, 4, 5, M, R to Court St./Borough Hall; A, C to High St. Tours Tu 1pm. Free. Tourist center ☎ 718-802-3846; www.brooklyn-usa.org. Open M-F 10am-6pm.)

CARROLL GARDENS AND RED HOOK

Just south of Atlantic Ave. lies Cobble Hill, whose brownstone-lined side streets merge into Carroll Gardens. **Smith Street** is lined with some of the city's best new restaurants and bars. Red Hook, on the waterfront, was separated from the other two neighborhoods by the construction of the Brooklyn-Queens Expressway. Today one of Brooklyn's up-and-coming neighborhoods, Red Hook's industrial heritage remains visible. *(Bounded by the water to the south and west, Hoyt St. to the east, and Atlantic Ave. to the north. [S] F, G to Bergen St./Smith St., Carroll St., Smith St./9th St.)*

PARK SLOPE AND PROSPECT PARK

A neighborhood of lovely brownstones, Park Slope is politically progressive with a strong sense of community. Young urbanites flock to the neighborhood's **Fifth Avenue** to enjoy its boutiques, cafes, restaurants, and bars.

PROSPECT PARK. Central Park designers Frederick Law Olmsted and Calvert Vaux also designed Brooklyn's Prospect Park. While Manhattan's park incorporated existing swamps and bluffs, Prospect Park's "nature" was constructed entirely from scratch. Supposedly, the two designers liked Prospect Park better.

The 80 ft. tall **Soldiers and Sailors Arch,** in the middle of **Grand Army Plaza,** was built in the 1890s to commemorate the North's Civil War victory. The bronze Victory Quadriga atop the arch, sporting a central female flanked by two winged figures, symbolizes the victorious Union. "Celebrate Brooklyn!" summer concerts are held at the **Prospect Park Bandshell,** in the park's northwestern corner (enter at Prospect Park W and 9th St.).

Sunbathers and ballplayers congregate on the **Long Meadow.** South of the meadow, **Prospect Lake** and **Lookout Hill** both offer views of still pools. Athletes can play tennis at the **Prospect Park Tennis Center,** ride at **Kensington Stables,** and hop in a pedal boat (in summer) or skate (in winter) at **Wollman Rink.**

The park is also home to a children's museum and a zoo. **Leffert's Homestead,** a preserved Dutch-style farmhouse, built between 1777 and 1783 and moved here from its original location in 1918, houses the tiny **Children's Historic House Museum.** Nearby is the **Carousel,** where rides cost $1. The **Prospect Park Wildlife Center's** exotic fauna include a pair of capybaras, a red panda, and a cotton-top tamarin. The sea lions get fed at 11:30am, 2, and 4pm. *(Bounded by Prospect Park W, Flatbush Ave., Ocean Ave., Parkside Ave., and Prospect Park SW. [S] 2, 3 to Grand Army Plaza; F to 15th St./Prospect Park; B, Q, S to Prospect Park. ☎ 718-965-8951, information and events 718-965-8999; www.prospectpark.org. TENNIS CENTER: Parkside and Coney Island Ave., at the Parade Grounds. ☎ 718-436-2500. Open daily 7am-dusk. KENSINGTON STABLES: E 8th St. and Caton Pl. ☎ 718-972-4588. Stables open daily 10am-sunset. Rides $25 per hr.; lessons $25 per 30min., $45 per hr. WOLLMAN RINK: Parkside/Ocean Ave. ☎ 718-287-6431. Open Nov.-Mar. for ice skating. $5, children under 14 and seniors $3. Skate rental $5. Open May-Oct. for pedal boating, Th-Su noon-5pm. $15 per hr.; $10 deposit. CAROUSEL: Flatbush Ave. and Empire Blvd. ☎ 718-282-7789. Open Apr.-June and Sept.-Oct. Th-Su and holidays noon-5pm; July to Labor Day Th-Su and holidays noon-6pm. ZOO: Flatbush Ave., at Empire Blvd. ☎ 718-399-7339; www.prospectpark-zoo.com. Open Apr.-Oct. M-F 10am-5pm, Sa-Su 10am-5:30pm; Nov.-Mar. daily 10am-4:30pm. $3, children 3-12 $3, seniors $4. No bikes or in-line skates. Wheelchair accessible.)*

BROOKLYN BOTANIC GARDEN. This 52-acre oasis was founded in 1910 by the Brooklyn Institute of Arts and Sciences on a reclaimed waste dump. The artificial scenery is so convincing that water birds flock to the site. Favorite spots include the Discovery Garden; the discovery center in the Steinhardt Conservatory; the Fragrant

Garden with mint, lemon, violet, and other aromas; and the Japanese Hill-and-Pond Garden. The more formal **Cranford Rose Garden** (closed Nov.-Mar.) crams in over 1200 blooming varieties of roses into archways, bushes, and shrubbery. Every spring, visitors can take part in the **Sakura Matsuri** (Japanese cherry blossom festival), when over 40 varieties of oriental flowering cherry trees bloom on the Cherry Walk and Cherry Esplanade. The **Shakespeare Garden** displays 80 plants that are mentioned in the Bard's works. The various pavilions of the **Steinhardt Conservatory** are climate-controlled to simulate desert, tropical, and other environments. Just outside the conservatory, 100 varieties of tropical water lilies and sacred loti grace the **Lily Pool Terrace** (in summer). The **Annual Border's** rainbow assortment of flowering annuals blooms nearby. Free guided tours of the grounds are given Saturday and Sunday at 1pm. *(1000 Washington Ave.; other entrances on Eastern Pkwy. and on Flatbush Ave.* [S] *S to Botanic Garden; B, Q, S to Prospect Park; 2, 3 to Eastern Pkwy./Brooklyn Museum.* ☎ *718-623-7000, visitor services 718-398-2400; www.bbg.org. Open Apr.-Sept. Tu-F 8am-6pm, Sa-Su 10am-6pm; Oct.-Mar. Tu-F 8am-4:30pm, Sa-Su 10am-4:30pm. $5, students with ID and seniors $3, under 16 free, school groups free. Tu and Sa 10am-noon free, F seniors free.)*

[TIP] **LOST IN PARK SLOPE?** Many street names change at the intersection with 5th Ave., so you might not be as far off as you think.

BROOKLYN PUBLIC LIBRARY. The striking Art Deco main branch of the Brooklyn Public Library stands majestically on Grand Army Pl. Its front doors are flanked by two great pillars with gold engravings and the words "Here are enshrined the longings of great hearts." The library has spawned 53 branches and contains 1,600,000 volumes. Changing exhibitions are on the second floor. A renovation project will bring an outdoor plaza and auditorium to the library in the next few years. *(Corner of Eastern Pkwy. and Flatbush Ave.* [S] *2, 3 to Grand Army Plaza.* ☎ *718-230-2100; www.brooklynpubliclibrary.org. Open M and F 9am-6pm, Tu-Th 9am–9pm, Sa 10am-6pm.)*

BEDFORD-STUYVESANT

Although less well-known than Harlem, "Bed-Stuy" is New York City's oldest and largest African-American community. It's not a heavily touristed part of town, in part because it's not always safe after dark, in part because it's mainly residential. If you walk its streets during the day, however, you will be treated to some of the city's finest brownstones, especially in the southernmost part of the neighborhood, on Macon, MacDonough, Decatur, Bainbridge, and Chauncey St. *(Bounded by Bedford Ave. to the west, Atlantic Ave. to the south, Broadway to the east, and Flushing Ave. to the north.* [S] *G to Bedford/Nostrand Ave.; C, S to Franklin Ave.; A, C to Nostrand Ave.; C to Kingston/Throop Ave.)*

FLATBUSH

Transformed by the introduction of the trolley in the late 19th century, Flatbush grew from a small town into a stomping ground for the well-to-do. You can wander around Argyle St. and Ditmas Ave. to see some of their old mansions, or go on the annual house tour (☎ 718-859-4868) in April. In the first half of the 20th century, the neighborhood was home to the beloved **Brooklyn Dodgers,** who played in Ebbets Field. The stadium was demolished in 1957 when owner Walter O'Malley moved the club to Los Angeles. A housing complex now stands in its place. The neighborhood is home to **Erasmus Hall Academy,** 911 Flatbush Ave., at Church Ave., the second-oldest high school in North America. Alumni include Neil Diamond, Barbara Streisand, and Barry Manilow. It was constructed in 1787 with the participation of Aaron Burr, John Jay, and Alexander Hamilton. Its charter stipulates that no brick can be moved from the school's central building, or a neighboring Dutch Reform Church will repossess it.

Once a predominantly Jewish immigrant neighborhood, Flatbush now contains significant Jamaican and West Indian populations. On summer days, reggae music and exotic fruit stands fill major thoroughfares like Nostrand and Church Ave. **Brooklyn College,** the first public co-ed liberal arts college in New York City, lies to the south, as does the **Brooklyn Center for the Performing Arts** (p. 264). *(Bounded by Coney Island Ave. to the west, Ave. H to the south, Nostrand Ave. to the east, and Parkside Ave. to the north. [S] B, Q to Church Ave./E 18th St., Newkirk Ave.; 2, 5 to Church Ave./Nostrand Ave., Flatbush Ave./Brooklyn College.)*

SUNSET PARK AND GREEN-WOOD CEMETERY

Home to sizable Chinese and Latino populations, Sunset Park embodies the New York melting pot. Lunch trucks sell Mexican food in the heart of Brooklyn's Chinatown. The area's **Fifth Avenue** is lined with discount stores and hybrid restaurants. Just to the northeast of the neighborhood is **Green-Wood Cemetery,** at Fifth Ave. and 25th St. With lakes, a chapel, and hills (some of which offer views to Manhattan and beyond), Green-Wood is as peaceful as its name suggests. On a clear day, the Statue of Liberty is visible from the Gothic Revival entrance on 25th St. This 478-acre expanse of mausoleums and tombstones makes for a pleasant walk.

More than 200 baseball pioneers are buried in Green-Wood, including Charles Ebbets (owner of the Brooklyn Dodgers), James Creighton Jr. (1860s star of the now-defunct Excelsior Club team), and Henry Chadwick (baseball journalist who invented the batting average and the box score). Other celebrities buried here include Samuel Morse, Louis Comfort Tiffany, F.A.O. Schwarz, the Brooks Brothers, Horace Greeley, William "Boss" Tweed, Leonard Bernstein, and Mae West. There are historic, bird-watching, and baseball-themed walking tours (free-$10) most Saturdays and Sundays. Call or check the website for hours. *(Bounded by the water to the west, 65th St. to the south, 8th Ave. and Green-Wood Cemetery to the east, and the Prospect Expwy. to the north. [S] M, R to 25th St.; D, M, N, R to 36th St.; R to 45th St., 53rd St., 59th St. GREEN-WOOD CEMETERY: ☎718-768-7300; www.green-wood.com. [S] M, R to 25th St. Open daily 8am-4pm; call for extended summer hours.)*

BENSONHURST AND BOROUGH PARK

The setting for the *Honeymooners* and *Jungle Fever*, Bensonhurst is one of the most famous neighborhoods of Brooklyn. Alternating between Italian pizzerias, Chinese restaurants, and bridal stores, 18th Ave. traverses southern Brooklyn, and shoppers will find extremely cheap clothes in the area's discount stores. The area around **Stillwell** and **Park Avenues** has seen an influx of Russians from Brighton Beach, and, far from the skyscrapers of Manhattan, it has the feel of an ethnically diverse suburb. Borough Park is the largest Hasidic Jewish neighborhood in Brooklyn. In contrast to more visible Crown Heights Lubavitchers, the Bobovers of Borough Park prefer to maintain an insular community. As in the other Hasidic areas of Brooklyn, visitors feel more welcome when dressed conservatively. One of the coolest experiences Bensonhurst and Borough Park have to offer is the view from the **D train** between the Fort Hamilton Pkwy. and 50th St. subway stops. *(Bensonhurst is bounded by 26th St. to the southeast, 61st St. to the northeast, 14th Ave. to the northwest, and Gravesend Bay to the southwest. [S] N to 18th Ave./64th St.; D, M to 62nd St., 71st St., 79th St., 18th Ave. Borough Park is north of Bensonhurst.)*

BAY RIDGE

Bay Ridge, scene of John Travolta's strutting in *Saturday Night Fever*, is full of Italian bakeries, pizza joints, rowdy youth, and discount stores. The neighborhood centers on **86th Street.** Nearby **Shore Road** is lined with mansions overlooking New York Harbor. The majestic, 4260 ft. long **Verrazano-Narrows Bridge** is the only way to connect to Staten Island by automobile. When it opened in 1964, it was the world's longest suspension bridge, and it is still greatly admired as an engineering feat. *(Bounded by Belt Pkwy. to the west, 101st St. to the south, Fort Hamilton Pkwy. to the east, 65th St. to the north.* Ⓢ *R to Bay Ridge Ave., 77th St., 86th St., Bay Ridge/95th St.)*

CONEY ISLAND AND BRIGHTON BEACH

Coney Island is Brooklyn straight out of the 1940s and 50s. Rides like the Parachute Jump, the Wonder Wheel, and the Cyclone are legendary in these parts. It's a ridiculously popular place on the weekends, though you'll definitely want to avoid it after night falls. Beyond Ocean Pkwy., east of Coney Island, lies Brighton Beach, an area of Eastern European immigrants, and great delis and grocery stores. At night, Russian music, from disco to folk, livens up the streets. Manhattan Beach lies on the island's east coast. *(*Ⓢ *D, F, Q to Coney Island/Stillwell Ave.; F, Q to W 8th St./NY Aquarium; Q to Ocean Pkwy., Brighton Beach.)*

▨ **CONEY ISLAND.** Coney Island is both a theme park and a slice of unadulterated Americana. Over a century old, the island has undergone several transformations. When the first mechanical thrill rides appeared here in the early 20th century, attendance averaged a whopping 90,000 people per day. Coney Island barely survived the Great Depression, however, and it entered a serious decline in the 1940s. Today, the amusement park is alive and well, and it retains its early-20th-century charm. The **Coney Island Museum** provides an ever-growing collection of memorabilia and photographs. (1208 Surf Ave., at 12th St. ☎718-372-5101. Open F-Sa noon-5pm. $1.)

Coney Island is a great place to take kids if they're tired of looking at brownstones. Take a rickety whirl on the legendary **Cyclone,** built in 1927. The National Register has designated it a Historic Place; couples have been married on it ($6 per ride, $4 per re-ride). The **Wonder Wheel,** at 150 ft., was the world's tallest when it was built (in Deno's, on Surf Ave., $5). **The Ghost Hall** is about as unscary as *The Munsters,* but it's pure Coney Island camp. (12th St., off Bowery. $5.) For the extra small, **Deno's,** right next to Astroland, has kiddie-sized rides like the Sea Serpent roller coaster ($2.50 per ride, $20 for 10). Find Coney Island's real spirit at the **Coney Island Circus Sideshow,** housed in the original 1917 building. It still features sword swallowers, snake charmers, jugglers, and "freaks." (1208 Surf Ave., at 12th St. Open F 2-8pm, Sa-Su 1-11pm $4, children under 12 $3.) Don't miss June's **Mermaid Parade,** which includes risqué floats and

THE CYCLONE

Coney Island is home to what is almost certainly the world's most famous roller coaster, the Cyclone. Built in 1927, this classic wooden roller coaster may not have the gravity-defying loops or super high speeds of contemporary steel coasters, but for character and vintage feel, it can't be beat. And the Cyclone is no slouch in the thrills department. It boasts 12 drops, the first more than 80 ft. at a 60° angle; six 180° turns; and a top speed of 60 mph. Charles Lindbergh said that a ride on the Cyclone was more exciting than his historic first solo flight across the Atlantic. The Cyclone made headlines in 1948 when Emilio Franco, a mute, reportedly regained his voice after riding it. His first words? "I feel sick."

The historic Cyclone sits on a site previously occupied by an even older roller coaster—the world's first, called the Switchback Railway. Built in 1884, this early thrill ride reached a top speed of 7 mph and had to be pushed up a small hill at the end of each ride. When the Cyclone opened, it immediately drew huge crowds to Coney Island, and it was soon copied closely in amusement parks around the country. Today, it's a National Historic Landmark, owned by the City of New York and operated by the Department of Parks and Recreation. A ride on the Cyclone is still an awesome one minute and 50 seconds.

antique cars. *(Entrance at 834 Surf Ave., at W 10th St. ☎ 718-372-5159; www.coneyisland-usa.com. Open mid-June to Sept. daily noon-midnight; Easter to mid-June F-Su noon-midnight. Admission is free, rides at the 2 separate amusement centers $2.50-5. Play-all-day pass $23 ($18 without the Cyclone). Free F shuttle from* S *Coney Island.)*

■**NEW YORK AQUARIUM.** Home to the first beluga whale born in captivity, the aquarium's marine inhabitants range from penguins and piranhas to sharks and jellyfish. An outdoor theater features wonderful performances by California sea lions. You can also participate in guided feedings of sharks, sea otters, walruses, and penguins. Feeding times are posted at the aquarium's front entrance. There's also a 3D deep-sea ride ($6). *(At Surf and W 8th St.* S *F, Q to W 8th St./NY Aquarium. ☎ 718-265-3474; www.nyaquarium.com. Open May-Oct. M-F 10am-6pm, Sa-Su and holidays 10am-7pm; Nov.-Apr. daily 10am-4:30pm. $12, seniors and children ages 2-12 $8. Last tickets sold 45min. before closing. No bikes, in-line skates, or pets allowed. Wheelchair accessible.)*

KEYSPAN PARK. After 43 years, baseball is back in Brooklyn. Newly erected Key-span Park is a 7500-seat stadium for the minor-league Cyclones (the Class A affili-ate of the Mets), which Brooklynites have whole-heartedly embraced. Ruins of Coney Island rides recall the days when the carnival grounds extended farther west. One can still see some half-sunk, rusted cars from the defunct Thunderbolt coaster and the tall, worn skeleton of the Parachute Jump. The scenery fits per-fectly with a night at the park. *(On the south side of Surf Ave., between W 17th and 19th St.* S *D, F, Q to Coney Island/Stillwell Ave. ☎ 718-449-TIXS/8497. Tickets $5-12.)*

QUEENS

Primarily residential Queens is home to a diverse array of distinct ethnic commu-nities. Unlike Brooklyn, which has many neighborhoods but remains united as a whole, Queens is more a collection of independent enclaves. According to the 2004 Census, Queens County is the most ethnically diverse county in the United States. Jackson Heights is its most diverse neighborhood.

The organization of Queens's streets derives from a mixed bag of urban planning techniques whose success, in retrospect, was hit-or-miss. The grid follows a logical but extremely complex system; whatever you do, bring a map. Streets generally run north-south and are numbered from west to east, from First St. in Astoria to 271st St. in Glen Oaks. Avenues run perpendicular to Streets and are numbered from north to south, from Second Ave. to 165th Ave. The address of an establishment or residence often tells you the closest cross-street; for example, 45-07 32nd Ave. is near the inter-section with 45th St. There are also a number of Drives, Roads, and Places—just to keep things interesting. Sights are listed from west to east.

ASTORIA AND LONG ISLAND CITY

Astoria is home to the largest Greek population in the US, and if you spend time here, you're certain to hear Greek spoken on the streets and to have the opportu-nity to eat as much lamb and baklava as you can stomach. Thirtieth Ave. is the major thoroughfare, while the blocks surrounding the Ditmars Blvd. subway stop are known as **"Little Athens."** Ditmars Blvd. has restaurants on every corner for about five blocks from 31st St. Industrial-looking Long Island City has recently experienced a resurgence as Queens's artistic center—a revival anchored by P.S.1 (p. 238) and an infusion of expats from Manhattan and Brooklyn. Vernon Blvd. has pleasant boardwalks along the water that end near the Socrates Sculpture Park. *(Astoria is in the northwestern corner of Queens, across the river from Manhattan. Long Island City is southwest of Astoria, and can be reached by walking south on 21st or 31st St.* S *All N, W stops between 36th Ave. and Astoria Ditmars Blvd. G, R, V to 36th or Steinway St.)*

THE STEINWAY PIANO FACTORY. The Steinway company has manufactured world-famous pianos here ever since it moved from its original Varick St. location in the Village during the 1860s. The area in Long Island City that it moved to became known as "Steinway Village"—a company town complete with parks and post offices for employees. The 12,000 parts of a typical Steinway piano, which weighs anywhere from 750-1365 lb., include a 340 lb. plate of cast iron and tiny bits of Brazilian deer skin. Over 95% of piano performances in the US are played on Steinway grands. If you're interested in visiting the factory, plan in advance to take the tour, which takes you through the process of construction. *(1 Steinway Pl., at 19th Rd. and 77th St.* §️ *N, W to Ditmars Blvd.* ☎ *718-721-2600; www.steinway.com/factory. Free tours every other Th; call ahead for info.)*

THE SOCRATES SCULPTURE PARK. In 1986, a coalition of local artists and residents transformed an abandoned landfill into an open-air studio, exhibition space, and neighborhood park. You can participate in the arts scene by taking a free workshop with local artists or stopping by the annual **Summer Solstice Celebration.** This outdoor film festival, on Wednesday evenings in August, screens a variety of independent and foreign films, all free, beginning at sunset. The adjacent waterfront has a great view of the Midtown skyline. Though the park is pleasant, safety in the neighborhood is still spotty after dark. Know where you're going, and don't travel alone. Call or check the website for upcoming events and exhibitions. *(At the end of Broadway, across the Vernon Blvd. intersection.* §️ *N, W to Broadway.* ☎ *718-956-1819; www.socratessculpturepark.org. Open daily 10am-dusk. Free.)*

KAUFMAN-ASTORIA STUDIOS. The largest American film studio outside of Los Angeles, the Kaufman Astoria Studios occupy a 14-acre plot with eight sound stages. Paramount Pictures used these facilities to make such films as *Scent of a Woman* and *The Secret of My Success.* Television's *The Cosby Show* and *Sesame Street* were taped here as well. The studios, opened in 1920, are also home to Lifetime Television for Women and a 14-screen movie theater. The studios are closed to the public entirely, but the **American Museum of the Moving Image** (p. 237) is next door. *(34-12 36th St., corner of 35th St. and 35th Ave.* §️ *G, R, V to 36th St.* ☎ *718-392-5600; www.kaufmanastoria.com.)*

CITICORP BUILDING. This 48-story blue-glass office building is the tallest structure in Queens and in all of New York outside Manhattan. Bankers and other office bees mill around the plaza at lunchtime, appearing somewhat out of place in this neighborhood of warehouses. *(1 Court Sq., at Jackson Ave.* §️ *E, V to 23 St./Ely Ave.; G to 21st St. Not open to tourists.)*

ELMHURST, CORONA, AND FLUSHING
ELMHURST AND CORONA

Elmhurst is home to immigrants from over 100 countries. The corner of Broadway and Whitney Ave. has tons of great ethnic restaurants. Corona, which is now mostly Hispanic, was the site of Archie Bunker's house in All in the Family. Malcolm X lived at 23-11 97th St., in nearby East Elmhurst, from 1954 until his death in 1965. *(ELMHURST:* §️ *G, R, V to Elmhurst Ave., Grand Ave./Newtown. CORONA:* §️ *7 to 103rd St./Corona Plaza, 111th St.)*

> ▌ ❗ Be cautious and travel in groups in Corona; the area is best avoided at night.

LOUIS ARMSTRONG HOUSE. Jazz legend Louis Armstrong and his wife Lucille lived in this two-story Corona home from 1943 to the end of their lives. Don't miss the first-floor bathroom, completely paneled in mirrors, or the original manuscripts and papers in Louis's den. Check the website for a schedule of occasional performances in the house. *(34-56 107th St.* §️ *7 to 103rd St./Corona Plaza.* ☎ *718-478-8274;*

www.satchmo.net. Open Tu-F 10am-5pm, Sa-Su noon-5pm. Guided tours of the house leave every hr. on the hr. from front hall; last tour 4pm. Tours $8; students, children, and seniors $6.)

FLUSHING

Flushing—whose name is a corruption of Vlissingen, the Dutch name for the village—was founded in 1654. Today, it's the Chinatown of Queens—and, for many New Yorkers, a more authentic experience than can be found on Mott St. in Manhattan. You'll find plenty of Korean- and Chinese-lettered signs and store windows filled with Asian pastries and heaps of exotic produce. **Main Street** and **Roosevelt Avenue** are the area's commercial hubs. *([S] 7 to Flushing/Main St.)*

THE KINGSLAND HOMESTEAD. Built in 1775 and moved to its current location in 1968, the Kingsland Homestead was designed in the Long Island half-house form. It holds a permanent collection of antique china and memorabilia that belonged to early trader Captain Joseph King, as well as a collection of antique dolls. A fully furnished "Victorian Room," on the second floor, depicts the middle-class furnishings of the time and holds diaries and notebooks kept by former residents. Home of the **Queens Historical Society,** the homestead annually displays three or four exhibits focusing on aspects of the borough's history. *(143-35 37th Ave. [S] 7 to Flushing/Main St. ☎718-939-0647; www.preserve.org/queens/kingsland. Open Tu and Sa-Su 2:30-4:30pm. $3, students and seniors $2. Historical Society open by appointment M-F 9:30am-5pm.)*

QUEENS BOTANICAL GARDEN. Created for exhibition at the 1939 World's Fair in nearby Flushing Meadows-Corona Park (p. 210), this garden had to be moved when the park was redesigned for the 1964 World's Fair. At its present site, it boasts a rose garden of 5000 bushes, a 23-acre arboretum, and more than nine acres of "theme gardens," including a bird garden, an herb garden, and a garden tended by children. Check out the plant shop, which sells potted plants, fresh honey, and gardening books. *(43-50 Main St., between Cherry and Dahlia Ave. [S] 7 to Flushing/Main St. Walk 10min. south from the Flushing/Main St. station or take the Q44 bus toward Jamaica. ☎718-886-3800; www.queensbotanical.org. Open Apr.-Sept. Tu-F 8am-6pm, Sa-Su 8am-7pm; Oct.-Mar. Tu-Su 8am-4:30pm. Free, but donations welcomed. Wheelchair accessible.)*

FLUSHING TOWN HALL. This 1862 building now functions as a gallery, a performance space, and the home of the Flushing Council of Culture and the Arts. Local art and historical exhibits await inside. A small permanent exhibit on jazz in Queens includes original postcards and letters written by Louis Armstrong. Pick up the free **Queens Jazz Trail** map for details on how to get to the former homes of Dizzy Gillespie, Ella Fitzgerald, Billie Holiday, Lena Horne, Cannonball Adderly, and ol' Satchmo himself. Live jazz and classical concerts take place on occasional Friday nights and Sunday afternoons—call or check the website for a schedule. *(137-35 Northern Blvd. [S] 7 to Flushing/Main St. ☎718-463-7700; www.flushingtownhall.org. Concert tickets start around $25, students and seniors $15. Free, though some exhibits have an entrance fee.)*

FLUSHING MEADOWS-CORONA PARK

From the Van Wyck Expwy., motorists gaze on rusting towers and dilapidated buildings, punctuated by the serene trees of Flushing Meadows-Corona Park. Formerly a 1255-acre swamp, nestled between Corona and Flushing, the park's site was a huge rubbish dump until city planners decided to turn the area into fairgrounds. The site hosted the 1939 and 1964 World's Fairs. Unfortunately, the remnants from the first are long gone, and the monuments from the second are fast deteriorating. The park is not particularly well-maintained, and parents should keep an eye on their kids. The park does have several gardens, however, and one or two well-kept monuments, including old steel and concrete dinosaurs from the 1964 festivities. The park also has 17 baseball diamonds, public tennis courts, soccer and cricket fields, and vast stretches of open grass dotted with pushcarts sell-

ing Asian delicacies. The park is full of life during the day, as picnickers, couples, families, and children play or get ready to go to Mets' games, but it's best to avoid the park after dark. *([S] 7 to 111th St. or Willets Point/Shea Stadium.)*

SHEA STADIUM. When the Brooklyn Dodgers were looking for new digs, Robert Moses offered team owner Walter O'Malley a chance to build a new stadium on marshland in northeastern Queens. O'Malley turned him down, and eventually moved the team to Los Angeles in 1957. When Manhattan's New York Giants left for the West Coast that same year, New York was stuck with the boringly successful Yankees as its sole team. Five years later, **William Shea** united the blue of the Dodgers and the orange of the Giants to create the **New York Mets.** Although the 1962 Mets set new standards for futility—finishing the season with a 40-120 record—the team captured the hearts of New Yorkers from all five boroughs. In 1964, the Mets moved to Shea Stadium, which in later years would host Jets games, Beatles concerts, and papal masses. In 1969, the "Miracle Mets" won their first world championship. Due to its location near LaGuardia Airport, Shea Stadium is officially the noisiest ballpark in the major leagues, but it's still a fun place to take in a game. *([S] 7 to Willets Point/Shea Stadium. ☎718-507-8499.)*

THE UNISPHERE. This huge, stainless-steel globe tilts over an outdoor fountain in retro-futuristic glory. You may remember it from the cover of the Beastie Boys' album, *Licensed to Ill.* The 700-ton Unisphere was constructed by the steel industry for the 1964 World's Fair. The globe's three rings represent the orbits of the first communications satellite and the first American and Russian astronauts. When the fountain isn't running, it functions as a halfpipe for toddlers on tricycles. *(In front of the Arthur Ashe Stadium. [S] 7 to Willets Point/Shea Stadium.)*

NEW YORK STATE PAVILION. A true eyesore, this stadium is encircled by a mass of concrete fins and stringy wire. The two adjacent towers, by architect Philip Johnson, formed the original center of the 1964 World's Fair. Part of the pavilion is now the **Queens Theater in the Park** (p. 268). South of the pavilion, across the expressway overpass, and behind the Planet of the Apes Fountain, a restored Coney Island carousel pipes out manic Chipmunks tunes. Remnants of the Pavilion's World's Fair heyday include a huge map of New York on the ground (now overgrown with weeds). Proposals for the pavilion's future include a possible air and space museum, but, for now, no consensus has been reached and the pavilion continues to decay. *(In Flushing Meadows Park. [S] 7 to Willets Point/Shea Stadium.)*

OTHER SIGHTS. While in the park, you can try your hand at a par-three pitch 'n' put **golf course.** (☎718-271-8182. Open daily 9am-10pm. Greens fee Sa-Su $9-13.50, M-F $10-12.50. $1 per club rental.) To the south, **Meadow Lake** offers paddle- and row-boating, as well as a track for running, biking, and walking. The **Willow Lake Nature Area** (☎718-699-4204) offers free tours. Nearby, the **USTA National Tennis Center** and **Arthur Ashe Stadium** (☎718-760-6200) host the US Open every August.

The Queens Wildlife Center/Zoo, 53-51 111th St., near 53rd Ave., features animals from North America and beyond. Don't miss the bison and sea lions. Sheep, goats, cows, and other cuddly creatures frolic in the petting zoo. (☎718-271-1500; www.wcs.org. Open M-F 10am-5pm, Sa-Su 10am-5:30pm. $8, seniors $4, children $3, under 3 free.) The **Queens Museum of Art** (☎718-592-9700; www.queensmuseum.org) is in the north wing of the New York City Building, next to the Unisphere. It contains the *Panorama of the City of New York*, the world's largest scale model of an urban area; one inch corresponds to 100 ft. of New York. The one-hour tour gives an interesting history of the city and its major landmarks. (Open June-Sept. W-Su 1-8pm; Sept.-June W-F 10am-5pm, Sa-Su noon-5pm. Suggested donation $5, students and seniors $2.50, children under 5 free.)

FOREST HILLS AND FOREST PARK

Forest Hills is an upscale residential part of town, with private streets and suburban-style houses. There aren't many tourist attractions, but the area is pleasant to walk around in. To the south stands Forest Park, a densely wooded area with miles of park trails, a bandshell, a golf course, a carousel ($1), baseball diamonds, tennis courts, and horseback riding (p. 271). *([S] E, F, G, R, V to Forest Hills/71st Ave. FOREST PARK: [S] J, Z to Woodhaven Blvd. ☎718-235-4100, events info 718-520-5941, golf 718-296-0999. Open daily 6am-9pm.*

JAMAICA AND THE ROCKAWAYS

JAMAICA

Jamaica's main strip is the section of **Jamaica Avenue** stretching from 150th to 168th St. Though the area is not particularly tourist friendly, it offers succulent Jamaican beef patties, African clothing and braids, and a brick-lined pedestrian mall on 165th St. great for bargain hunting. Saint Albans is best explored with a walk down **Linden Boulevard.** West Indian culture proliferates on both sides of **Hillside Avenue** in the area's eastern part. *([S] E, J, Z to Jamaica Center.)*

> **!** Be cautious and travel in groups in Jamaica; the area is best avoided at night.

KING MANOR MUSEUM. Built in 1750, **King Manor Museum** was the 1805-27 residence of Rufus King—an early abolitionist, framer and signer of the Constitution, New York Senator, presidential candidate, and ambassador to Great Britain. Now it's the oldest house in Jamaica. Set in 11-acre **King Park,** it combines Georgian and Federal architectural styles. The period rooms downstairs give a glimpse of 19th-century life, and the surrounding park is bustling with people. *(At Jamaica Ave. and 153rd St. ☎718-206-0545; www.kingmanor.org. Open Feb.-Dec. Th-F noon-2pm, Sa-Su 1-5pm. Admission with guided tour: $5, students and seniors $3.)*

OTHER SIGHTS. Grace Church, 155-03 Jamaica Ave., is one of Queens's oldest churches. Its stone exterior is beautiful, and Rufus King is buried in the graveyard. (☎718-291-4901. Open daily 11am-1pm. Services Su 8 and 10am.) The elaborate Spanish-style facade of the **Tabernacle of Prayer,** 165-11 Jamaica Ave., makes clear the building's past—but today it's a Loews movie theater seating 3500.

THE ROCKAWAYS

JAMAICA BAY WILDLIFE REFUGE. At 9155 acres, the Jamaica Bay Wildlife Refuge is roughly the size of Manhattan—10 times larger than Flushing Meadows-Corona Park. The refuge harbors more than 325 species of birds and small animals, including the American oyster-catcher and the black-bellied plover. Slide shows and ranger-led walks are held on weekends; these fill up quickly, so call ahead to reserve a spot. Visits in spring offer a great opportunity to spot the first songbirds returning north, and in late March, bird-fanciers can hear the evening mating rituals of the American Woodcock. Those who arrive in the late summer and the fall can view the southward migration of shorebirds, hawks, waterfowl, and songbirds. If you don't feel like getting knee-deep in the marsh, the A train runs above ground through the park, providing a scenic route to Rockaway Beach. *(On Broad Channel, Jamaica Bay. [S] A, S to Broad Channel. You can also take the Triboro Q53 bus (☎718-335-1000); $1-1.50, MetroCards accepted. ☎718-318-4340. Park open daily dawn-dusk. Visitors/Nature Center open daily 8:30am-5pm. Free; pick up map and permit at Visitors Center. Wear long pants with socks to avoid ticks, and be prepared to get damp.)*

ROCKAWAY BEACH. Immortalized by the Ramones in their pop-punk anthem "Rockaway Beach," this 10 mi. long public beach is lined by a boardwalk. It's often pleasantly free of crowds, is well-maintained, and there are no souvenir stalls. Birds from the nearby refuge like to nest here—stay out of their way. *(From Beach 3rd St. in Far Rockaway to Beach 149th St. in the west. Ⓢ A (marked "Far Rock-away") to all stops between Beach 36th St. and Beach 67th St. or A (marked "Rockaways") or A, S to all stops between Beach 90 St. and Rockaway Park/Beach 116 St. ☎ 718-318-4000. Life-guards Memorial Day-Labor Day 10am-6pm; swimming allowed only when they are on duty.)*

 TAKING THE A TRAIN. The A train is the only line that services the Rock-aways, and service can be slow. Exercise caution when waiting in subway sta-tions alone. On the other hand, since tracks here are above ground, you'll be treated to beautiful city and waterfront views once you're on board.

FIRST PRESBYTERIAN CHURCH. Railroad tycoon Russell Sage donated the money to build this Gothic Revival church, noted for its enormous Louis Tiffany stained-glass window and huge cemetery. It was a church of some social prominence in the first quarter of the century, and it has been recently restored. *(1324 Beach 12th St., at Cen-tral Ave. Ⓢ A to Far Rockaway/Mott Ave. ☎ 718-327-2440. Open daily 10am-6pm.)*

JACOB RIIS PARK. Part of the 26,000-acre Gateway National Recreation Area that extends into Brooklyn, Staten Island, and New Jersey, this park was named for photojournalist Jacob Riis. In the early 1900s, Riis persuaded the city to turn the then-overgrown beach into a public park. Today, in addition to a lovely beach and boardwalk, there's an area cordoned off for swimming, basketball and hand-ball courts, and a golf course. West of the park entrance, nature trails run through the remnants of **Fort Tilden,** a former US Army base. Families spread their blankets toward the center of the beach. A former nude beach is at the eastern end; in the 1980s the beach decided to "clean up its act" and now allows only topless sunbath-ing. *(Just west of Rockaway Beach, separated from it by a huge chain-link fence. Ⓢ A (marked "Rockaways") or S; stop at Rockaway Park/Beach 116th St., then transfer to Green Bus Lines Q22 (☎ 718-995-4700) westward; $1-1.50, MetroCards accepted. ☎ 718-318-4300. Open 6am-midnight; swimming permitted weekdays 9am-6pm, weekends 9am-7pm.)*

THE BRONX

The Bronx is not a traditional tourist destination by any means. The poverty, racial tension, and crime long associated with the borough keep crowds away. Certain pockets in the area are gradually improving, but caution is still in order when visit-ing. Destinations like the New York Botanical Gardens, City Island, and Belmont's "Little Italy" make the journey from Manhattan worthwhile.

SOUTH BRONX

During the 1970s, landlords in this troubled neighborhood torched buildings to collect insurance, and tenants burned down their own houses to collect welfare. When Ronald Reagan visited, he compared the South Bronx to a bombed-out London after the Battle of Britain. Thanks to a huge influx of government funds and a stronger econ-omy, the South Bronx and the borough as a whole have taken steps forward. Still, aside from the immediate vicinity of Yankee stadium, the South Bronx is a not a safe place for a tourist to walk around.

YANKEE STADIUM. "The House That Ruth Built" opened in 1923, and it remains one of the Bronx's main attractions. Yankee Stadium was the first baseball complex to be called a "stadium" rather than a field or park. It underwent an extensive (and, in retro-spect, highly unfortunate) renovation in the mid-70s, which forced the Yankees to share Shea Stadium with the Mets for the 1974-75 seasons. A new Yankee Stadium is currently under construction on the nearby site previously occupied by Macombs Dam Park, so catch a game in this historic shrine while you can. Stick close to the sta-

IN RECENT NEWS

BASEBALL GETS A FACELIFT IN NEW YORK

In both the Bronx and Queens, new baseball stadiums are rising to replace the current homes of the Yankees and the Mets. The two stadiums, both set to open for the 2009 season, are each being constructed next door to their team's current site, promising new fan comforts and designs that evoke classic features of earlier parks. The new Yankee Stadium will replicate the original's characteristic limestone facade and bronze frieze and will reinstate original features obscured by the park's 1976 renovation. The new Mets park will incorporate design elements from Ebbets Field and Tiger Stadium.

Still, construction of the two stadiums has not been without controversy. The new Yankee Stadium is being built on Macombs Dam Park, valuable green space for Bronx residents. The Yankees are replacing the acres they use with an equal number of new park acres around the borough, but they can't replicate a single expanse as big. On the other hand, local Little Leaguers will soon get to play on the field of the original Yankee Stadium.

Construction of the new Mets park was hastily agreed to in 2005 in hopes of attracting the 2012 Summer Olympics to New York, but this honor went to London instead. Community members are disappointed, no doubt, but most welcome the replacement of now-dilapidated Shea.

dium area; the neighborhood gets really bad, really fast. *(E 161st St., at River Ave. [S] 4, B, D to 161st St./Yankee Stadium. Station right outside stadium. ☎718-579-4531; www.yankees.com. 1hr. tours, generally available M-F or daily when the team is on the road, start at noon; no tours on game days. $14, students and seniors $7; groups of 10 or more receive $2 per person discount. More extensive (and expensive) tours available. Call or check online for details.)*

BRONX PARK

👍 **BRONX ZOO.** The Bronx Zoo/Wildlife Conservation Park is the largest urban zoo in the US. It houses over 4000 animals in a 265-acre expanse of recreated natural habitats. Grab a free map at the entrance. The **World of Reptiles** is home to a poison dart frog, timber rattlesnake, and Samantha the python, the largest snake in the US. More benign beasts wander free in the park's "protected sanctuary," allowing for interactions between inhabitants and visitors. Indian elephants frolic in **Wild Asia,** which can be toured by monorail ($2 per ride; May-Oct.). White-cheeked gibbons tree-hop in **Jungle World.** More apes can be seen at the **Congo Gorilla Forest,** a 6.5-acre African rain forest habitat featuring 400 animals of 55 different species. The forest has a separate entrance. The **Himalayan Highlands** are near the **World of Darkness,** which houses a collection of nocturnal animals in dimly lit rooms. At **Tiger Mountain,** six Siberian cats prowl around three acres of recreated natural habitat. Don't miss the "enrichment sessions" (11:30am, 1:30, and 3:30pm), when the keepers feed and play with the tigers. The new **African Wild Dogs** exhibit draws serious crowds. Kids imitate animals at the **Children's Zoo,** where they can climb a spider's web or try on a turtle shell. If you tire of the kids, the crocodiles are fed Mondays and Thursdays at 2pm; the sea lions are fed daily at 11am and 3pm. All ages enjoy the daily primate training sessions at the **Monkey House** (Apr.-Oct. 3:30pm; Nov.-Mar. 2:30pm). To beat the crowds, the park recommends visiting on a non-holiday weekend or a weekday afternoon. *(Entrances on Bronx Park S, Southern Blvd., E Fordham Rd., and the Bronx River Pkwy. [S] 2, 5 to West Farms Sq./E Tremont Ave. Follow Boston Rd. for 3 blocks until the Bronx Park S gate. Buses: Bx9, Bx12, Bx19, Bx22, and Q44 pass various entrances to the zoo. The BXM11 Express Bus leaves from Madison Ave. in Midtown for the Bronxdale entrance to the zoo, and picks up at 26th, 32nd, 39th, 47th, 54th, 63rd, 70th, 84th, and 99th St. ($4 each way, MetroCards accepted). Zoo ☎718-367-1010 or 718-220-5100, disabled access 718-220-5188; www.bronxzoo.com. Open daily M-F 10am-5pm, Sa-Su and holidays 10am-5:30pm. Parts of the zoo closed Nov.-Apr. $12, seniors and ages 2-12 $9. W free; donation suggested. Congo Gorilla Forest $3; Children's Zoo $3; some rotating exhibits also have* *additional charges. Full pass (not for camel rides) $20, seniors and children $16. Children under 17 must be accompanied by an adult.)*

■ **NEW YORK BOTANICAL GARDEN.** Across from the zoo, the 250-acre New York Botanical Garden, created in 1891, serves as a research laboratory and plant museum, with rare specimens like the Japanese pagoda tree, the Kobus magnolia, and the Daybreak Yoshino cherry. The 50-acre **native forest** is the last of the woodlands that once covered the city. The **Rockefeller Rose Garden** is an elaborate herb garden, and the **Rock Garden** has a waterfall. Although it costs a few extra dollars to enter, the **Enid A. Haupt Conservatory** also deserves a visit. The gorgeous domed greenhouse, the largest in North America, contains several different ecosystems of exquisite plant life. The **Everett Children's Adventure Garden** is equally inviting. If you go exploring by yourself, get a garden map. The crowded 30min. **tram ride** ($2, free with combo ticket) lets you glimpse most of the major sights. **The LuEsther T. Mertz Library** features a rotating exhibit and an orchid terrarium in the lobby. An ongoing **Plants and Fungi** exhibit in the **Britton Science Rotunda and Gallery** is also a popular stop. The **Visitors Center Pavilion,** which offers maps, brochures, a plant shop, a cafe, and an orientation center, is a recent addition. *(Dr. Theodore Kazimiroff Blvd. S 4 to Bedford Park Blvd./Lehman College; B, D to Bedford Park Blvd. Walk 8 blocks east or take the Bx26 bus. Bus: Bx19 or Bx26. Train: Metro-North Harlem line goes from Grand Central Terminal to Botanical Garden station, which is right outside the Moshalu gate. Conservatory gate on Kazimiroff Blvd., a bit north of Fordham Rd. ☎ 212-532-4900 for Metro-North line info. BOTANICAL GARDEN ☎ 718-817-8700; www.nybg.org. Open Apr.-Oct. Tu-Su 10am-6pm; Nov.-Mar. Tu-Su 10am-5pm. Grounds-only admission $6, students with ID $2, seniors $3, children 2-12 $1. Free W and Sa 10am-noon. Certain exhibits throughout the garden, including the Conservatory and the Children's Adventure Garden, cost extra; combination tickets ($13, students and seniors $11, children 5-12 $5) allow you to see all exhibits. Various tours depart daily; inquire at the Visitor Center.)*

! Subway stations in the Bronx can be deserted at night and feel unsafe even during daylight hours. To assure that you're not isolated, pick an entrance manned by station personnel and stand in the designated off-peak-hours waiting areas.

FORDHAM AND BELMONT

Fordham University is the Bronx's largest college. Its peaceful grounds offer refuge from its fast-paced surroundings. Belmont is the Bronx's fun Little Italy—and it puts Manhattan's kitschy Mulberry St. to shame.

FORDHAM UNIVERSITY. Opened in 1841 by John Hughes as St. John's College, 80-acre Fordham has matured into one of the nation's foremost Jesuit schools. Robert S. Riley built the campus in classic collegiate Gothic style in 1936. Part of *The Exorcist* was filmed here. *(441 E Fordham Rd., between Webster Ave. and Dr. Theodore Kazimiroff Blvd. S B, D to Fordham Rd./Grand Concourse. ☎ 718-817-1000, admissions 718-817-4000. Arrange campus tours through the admissions office.)*

■ **BELMONT.** This uptown Little Italy offers some of the best Italian food west of Naples. The main road is **Arthur Avenue,** where boisterous crowds devour pasta at **Dominick's** (see Food), between 186th and 187th St. To get a sense of the area in one concentrated locale, stop into **Arthur Avenue Retail Market,** 2334 Arthur Ave., between 186th and Crescent St. The indoor market has a cafe, butcher, grocer, cheese shop, and deli. The **Church of Our Lady of Mt. Carmel** is located at 627 187th St., at Belmont Ave. (☎ 718-295-3770; Su mass at 8:30, 9:30, 11am in Italian, 12:30, and 7:30pm). Signs of a recent Kosovar influx mark the area—the red Kosovar flag graces the windows of many stores and eateries. *(Centering on Arthur Ave. and E 187th St., near the Southern Blvd. entrance to the Bronx Zoo. S B, D to Fordham Rd./Grand Concourse. Walk 11 blocks east (or take Bx12) to Arthur Ave. and head south.)*

> **!** When riding the Bx12 bus, be sure to verify that it goes all the way to Orchard Beach; the bus travels different routes from the same departure point.

EDGAR ALLAN POE COTTAGE. Poe lived in this cottage from 1846 to 1849 with his tubercular cousin and wife, Virginia. The writer married her when he was 26 and she only 13. Here, Poe wrote "Annabel Lee," "Eureka," and "The Bells," which refers to the bells of nearby Fordham University. The museum, a small clapboard structure, displays a slew of Poe's manuscripts and macabre effects, including the bed in which his young bride died. *(E Kingsbridge Rd. and Grand Concourse, 5 blocks west of Fordham University.* [S] *4 to Kingsbridge Rd./Jerome Ave. or B, D to Kingsbridge Rd./Grand Concourse.* ☎ *718-881-8900. Open Sa 10am-4pm, Su 1-5pm, weekdays for pre-scheduled group tours only. $3, students and seniors $2.)*

RIVERDALE AND VAN CORTLANDT PARK

In stark contrast with the rest of the Bronx, Riverdale features some extremely wealthy residences and a triumvirate of esteemed private schools: **Fieldston School,** Fieldston Rd., at Manhattan College Pkwy.; **Horace Mann School,** 231 W 246th St.; and **Riverdale Country School,** 5250 Fieldston Rd. The **Riverdale Historic District** is on Sycamore Ave., between W 252nd and W 254th St. The shady suburbs here seem light-years away from Manhattan.

VAN CORTLANDT PARK. Van Cortlandt Park spreads across 1146 acres of the northwest Bronx and is the third-largest park in the city. Apart from soccer, football, and cricket fields, the park also has tennis courts, baseball diamonds, a kiddie recreation area, two golf courses, a large swimming pool, and barbecue facilities. Hikers and mountain bikers have plenty of options: the **Cass Gallagher Nature Trail,** in the park's northwestern section, leads to rock outcroppings amid the most untamed wilderness in the city. The area is also known as a birdwatcher's paradise. The **Old Putnam Railroad Track,** once the city's first rail link to Boston, now leads past the quarry that supplied marble for Grand Central Terminal. Ballplayers have a choice between the baseball and softball diamonds of the **Parade Grounds** and the **Indian Field recreation area** (located atop the burial grounds of the Stockbridge Indians, who were massacred by British troops during the Revolutionary War). Horseback riders of all abilities are welcome at the **Riverdale Equestrian Center.** For those who would rather see the park by foot, there are racing tracks, cross-country courses, and well-maintained hiking trails. *(Sprawling east of Broadway and north of Van Cortlandt Park S, all the way to the Westchester border.* [S] *1 to Van Cortlandt Park/242nd St.* ☎ *718-601-1460, programs office* ☎ *718-601-1553; www.vancortlandt.org. The park's programs office has info about the many concerts and sports activities that take place during the warmer months. Park closes at 10pm.)*

VAN CORTLANDT HOUSE. This national landmark, built in 1748 by the prominent political clan of the same name, is the oldest building in the Bronx. It is located near the southwest corner of Van Cortlandt Park. George Washington held his 1781 meeting with Rochambeau in this building, determining Revolutionary War strategy. He also began his triumphal march into New York City from here in 1783. The stone house, operated by the National Society of Colonial Dames in the State of New York, features various rooms decorated in period styles. These include an 18th-century kitchen, the nation's oldest dollhouse, and a colonial-era garden and sundial. *(Broadway, at W 246th St.* [S] *1 to Van Cortlandt Park/242nd St.* ☎ *718-543-3344; www.vancortlandthouse.org. Open Tu-F 10am-3pm, Sa-Su 11am-4pm. $5, seniors and students $3, on W and under 12 free. Self-guided tour booklet free.)*

MANHATTAN COLLEGE. As you walk up 242nd St., you'll see the red-brick buildings and chapel of this 140-year-old private liberal arts institution. The campus sprawls over stairs, squares, and plateaux. Hardy souls who ascend the campus's peaks can take in a cinemascopic view of the Bronx. The college was originally located at 131st St. and Broadway in Manhattan. The Manhattan College Jaspers are named after their first baseball coach, Brother Jasper of Mary, who may have invented the seventh-inning stretch. *(From the corner of Broadway and 242nd St., take 242nd St. to the top of the hill. S 1 to 242nd St. ☎ 718-862-8000; www.manhattan.edu. Campus tours arranged through the admissions office; available M-F 10am-3:30pm.)*

■ **WAVE HILL.** This 28-acre garden and cultural center commands a broad view of the Hudson River and the Palisades. Samuel Langhorne Clemens (a.k.a. Mark Twain), conductor Arturo Toscanini, and Teddy Roosevelt all resided in the original Wave Hill House, built in 1843. The current building, a Georgian revival structure known as Glyndor House, was erected in the 1920s, after the original was destroyed by fire. Horticultural enthusiasts will enjoy the greenhouses and formal gardens, which showcase rare trees and seasonal flowers. The **Wild Garden's** hillside garden and gazebo date from 1915. The garden was inspired by the informally planted English wild garden and is one of the most popular wedding locations in the state. The **T.H. Everett Alpine House** features a collection of high-altitude rock garden plants. Glyndor House and the Wave Hill House both feature contemporary art exhibits (June-July M-Tu 10am-4:30pm, W 10am-8pm, Th-Su 10am-4:30pm). The estate is bordered by 10 acres of woodlands, which can be explored via a cedar trail. *(Independence Ave., at W 249th St. S 1 to 231st St., then bus Bx7 or Bx10 to 252nd St. ☎ 718-549-3200; www.wavehill.org. Walk across the Henry Hudson Pkwy. and turn left; walk to 249th St., turn right and walk to Wave Hill Gate. Open Apr. 15-Oct. 14 Tu-Su 9am-5:30pm; June-July W until 9pm. Oct. 15-Apr. 14 Tu-Su 9am-4:30pm. $4, students $2, seniors free. Sa 9am-noon, Tu, and Dec.-Feb. free. Greenhouses open 10am-noon and 1-4pm. Galleries open 10am-4:30pm; June-July W until 8pm. Free garden and greenhouse tours depart the conservatory Su at 2:15pm. Wheelchair accessible.)*

WOODLAWN AND WOODLAWN CEMETERY

Huge, bucolic Woodlawn Cemetery contains the grave sites of many prominent Americans, such as composer Oscar Hammerstein, New York mayor Fiorello LaGuardia, and novelist Herman Melville. Music lovers visit the resting places of jazz legends Miles Davis, Duke Ellington, and Lionel Hampton. Woodlawn, to the north, is a neighborhood filled with Irish immigrants. The park is filled with winding asphalt paths that curl around the ornate gravemarkers alongside a few rare weeping beech trees. *(East of Van Cortlandt Park. S 4 to Woodlawn. Main entrance at Webster Ave. and E 233rd St. ☎ 718-920-0500; www.thewoodlawncemetery.org. Open daily 8:30am-5pm; check website for holiday hours.)*

PELHAM BAY PARK

New York City's largest park, 2700-acre **Pelham Bay Park** boasts playing fields, tennis courts, basketball courts, well-paved biking trails, golf courses, wildlife sanctuaries, **Orchard Beach** (p. 272), and training grounds for the city's mounted police force. The knowledgeable **park rangers** lead a variety of history- and nature-oriented walks. From the **Pelham Bay Stables,** you can take a guided ride around the park on horseback. The Empire/Greek Revival **Bartow-Pell Mansion Museum** sits within a formal English garden landscaped in 1915. The house's wonders include a freestanding spiral staircase and a pond, complete with goldfish and a spouting cherub. *(In the northeast corner of the Bronx. S 6 to Pelham Bay Park. ☎ 718-430-1890; www.nycgovparks.org. Open dawn to dusk. STABLES: Shore Rd. at City Island Dr. Take Bx29 from the Pelham Bay Park station. ☎ 718-885-0551; www.nychorse.com. Open daily 9am-dusk. $30 per hr. 30min. lesson $40; reserve ahead. BARTOW-PELL MANSION MUSEUM: 895 Shore Rd., opposite the golf courses. ☎ 718-885-1461; www.bartowpellmansionmuseum.org. Open W and Sa-Su noon-4pm. $5, students and seniors $3, under 6 free.)*

SIGHTS

CITY ISLAND

The self-proclaimed "seaport of the Bronx," this salty maritime village was once a ship- and submarine-building hub. Nautical ventures today are more recreational than commercial. Plenty of diving shops, tackle stores, and seafood shacks line City Island Ave., the neighborhood's major thoroughfare. Proud residents sometimes refer to themselves as "clam diggers"; outsiders are mere "mussel suckers." Rent a fishing boat, take a sunset cruise, or dine at one of the many waterfront restaurants for a distinct change of pace from downtown New York City. *([S] 6 to Pelham Bay Park; board bus Bx29 outside the station. Bus drops off at various points along City Island Ave., the main drag. www.cityisland.com.)*

STATEN ISLAND

Staten Island has a limited tourist infrastructure and is quite difficult to get around without a car. Cabs are rare and bus service is infrequent. Despite some quirky and worthwhile sights, the borough is almost entirely residential. Its many parks are vast and lush, and you'll find a number of historical sights. The **Staten Island Ferry** is almost certainly the most-visited tourist sight in the borough. Because of the hills, the distances, and some dangerous neighborhoods in between sights, it's a bad idea to try to get around the borough by walking. If you don't have access to a car, plan your excursion in advance with the bus schedule in mind; the lag between buses can be over an hour. You can pick one up from the VISIT booth on the Manhattan side of the ferry, or from the Staten Island Chamber of Commerce, 130 Bay St. Bear left from the ferry station onto Bay St. (☎718-727-1900; www.sichamber.com. Open M-F 9am-5pm.) The Chamber sells street maps ($2).

NEW YORK HARBOR FOR POCKET CHANGE. The view of the Statue of Liberty and the Lower Manhattan skyline is unbeatable from the Staten Island ferry. Best of all, it's free. You can ride round-trip without ever getting off. [S] N, R to Whitehall St. or 1 to South Ferry. Departures every 30-60min.

SNUG HARBOR CULTURAL CENTER. Founded in 1801, Sailors' Snug Harbor served as a home for retired sailors for 175 years. The iron fence kept old mariners from quenching their thirst at nearby bars. Purchased by the city and opened in 1976 as a cultural center, this national landmark now includes 28 historic buildings scattered over 83 acres of placid, unpopulated parkland. Hours and admission prices for the various on-site museums vary widely. Admission is free to the **Staten Island Botanical Garden's** 20 formal gardens, but a well-spent $5 gets you into both the **New York Chinese Scholar's Garden** and **The Connie Gretz Secret Garden.** The former is a one-acre walled garden home to a collection of 18th- and 19th-century Ming furniture and set amid a traditional Chinese landscape; the latter is a maze-like garden beneath a turreted entrance. In the restored Main Hall, one of the Center's most breathtaking buildings, the **Newhouse Center for Contemporary Art** shows revolving exhibits. Nearby, the **John A. Noble Maritime Collection** houses local artist Noble's artwork on a working waterfront. The museum includes Noble's transplanted houseboat studio. The **Children's Museum** features interactive exhibits, including a theater with costumes and props, an exhibit on bugs with a larger-than-life ant home, and a climbable fire truck. Snug Harbor also offers an array of cultural programs to Staten Islanders, and often hosts festivals and exhibitions on the grounds. *(CULTURAL CENTER: 1000 Richmond Terr. Bus S40. ☎718-448-2500; www.snug-harbor.org. Free tours of the grounds offered Apr.-Nov. Sa-Su 2pm, starting at the Visitors Center. BOTANICAL GARDEN: ☎718-273-8200; www.sibg.org. Open daily dawn-dusk. CHINESE SCHOLAR'S GARDEN: open Apr.-Oct. Tu-Su 10am-5pm; Nov.-Mar. W-Su 10am-4pm. $5; seniors, students, and children under 12 $4. Tours W, Sa-Su on the hour noon-3pm. NEWHOUSE*

CENTER: ☎ 718-448-2500, ext. 508. Open Tu-Su; hours vary with exhibit. $3, seniors and children under 12 $2. NOBLE COLLECTION: ☎ 718-447-6490. Open Th-Su 1-5pm and for groups by appointment. CHILDREN'S MUSEUM: ☎ 718-273-260. Open July-Labor Day Tu-Su 10am-8pm; Labor Day-June Tu-F noon-5pm, Sa-Su 10am-5pm. $5. Free parking.)

HISTORIC RICHMOND TOWN. This 25-acre, recreated village documents three centuries of Staten Island culture and history. Historic Richmond Town's reconstructed 17th- to 19th-century dwellings feature artifacts from the Staten Island Historical Society's collection that reflect the Victorian era. Authentic "inhabitants" (costumed craftspeople and their apprentices) give well-informed tours of the grounds from September to June (W-F 1 tour per day, Sa-Su 2 tours per day; call or check online for times). During July and August, visitors can roam the village, meeting "villagers" in the farmhouses, carpenter shop, and general store. Especially noteworthy is **Voorlezer's House,** built in 1695, the oldest surviving elementary school on its original site in the US. On the weekends the village often hosts festivals, fairs, and harvests, including Revolutionary War Weekend in September; call or check the website for upcoming events. *(441 Clarke Ave. Bus S74 to Richmond Rd. and St. Patrick's Pl. 40min. ☎ 718-351-1611; www.historicrichmondtown.org. Open Sept.-June W-Su 1-5pm; July-Aug. W-Sa 10am-5pm, Su 1-5pm. $5, seniors $4, children 5-17 and students with ID $3.50, children under 5 free.)*

MORAVIAN CEMETERY. The 113-acre non-sectarian cemetery (est. 1740) is a serene spot with manicured grounds, an ocean view, and natural knolls. It contains graves dating back 250 years with the remains of everyone from Eberhard Faber (the pencil guy) to famous mobsters. For a map of the grounds and a searchable database of graves, stop by the information booth in the cemetery's office behind the Moravian Church. *(2205 Richmond Rd., at Todt Hill Rd., in Dongan Hills. Bus S74 to Todt Hill Rd. ☎ 718-351-0136. Gates open daily 8am. Richmond Rd. gates close 4:30pm, Todt Hill gates 6:30pm. Office open M-F 9am-4pm. Information booth open same hours as cemetery.)*

RICHMOND COUNTY BANK BALLPARK AT ST. GEORGE. A newly acquired minor-league Yankees farm team recently relocated to Staten Island, and at its ballpark, you can watch home runs soar into the Atlantic Ocean. Games are played three to five days per week from June to early September. The grounds are often open during afternoon practices. *(75 Richmond Terr., take a right out of the Ferry station. ☎ 718-720-9265; www.siyanks.com. Call or check website for schedule and ticket information. Box office open M-F 9am-5pm, Sa 10am-3pm and during games. Tickets $5-11.)*

THE LOCAL STORY

UNSUCCESSFUL SECESSION

In November 1993, Staten Island, tired of being New York's "forgotten borough," decided it no longer wanted to be a borough at all. Its residents voted two-to-one to secede from New York City. The attempt was ultimately unsuccessful, but it drew attention to the lingering malaise in the city's smallest borough, which can still be felt today. The island's fraught association with New York City really shouldn't come as a surprise. Suburban, even rural, in parts, ethnically homogenous, difficult to access via public transportation, often politically conservative, Staten Island seems far removed from the rest of New York City.

The most irksome source of Staten Island's resentment, however, has likely been the presence of the Fresh Kills Landfill on its shores. For more than 50 years, this landfill disposed of the majority of New York City's trash. It was the largest landfill in the United States, and it grew into the largest manmade hill on the East Coast.

Since 2001, though, the Fresh Kills Landfill has been permanently closed, and the site has the potential to foster rosier relations between Staten Island and New York City. The New York City Department of Parks and Recreation is working to turn it into a scenic wetland estuary, including a mixed-use public park three times the size of Central Park.

MUSEUMS AND GALLERIES

New York City's blockbuster museums are the Met, the MoMA, and the Museum of Natural History—and they are indeed world-class. But don't limit yourself to these three; the city is home to an almost embarrassing number of high-quality museums, many of which would, in most places, be considered peerless. The Frick, the Guggenheim, the Morgan Library and Museum, and the Brooklyn Museum are all world-class. But the city's more idiosyncratic museums are often your best bet for a straight-up good time. Check out the New York Transit Museum (p. 236), the Lower East Side Tenement Museum (p. 223), the Museum of Television and Radio (p. 226), and the Museum of the City of New York (p. 230) when you tire of obligatory masterworks.

During the annual **Museum Mile Festival** (☎ 212-606-2296) in mid-June, Fifth Ave. museums keep their doors open until late at night, staging engaging interactive exhibits and filling the streets with music. Many sponsor film series and live concerts throughout the year (see **Entertainment,** p. 245). Be aware that several major museums, including the Met, the Cloisters, the Frick, and the Whitney, are closed on Monday. The MoMA is closed Tuesday and Wednesday.

New York's galleries are trendsetters in the art world, and they don't charge for admission. Pick up a free copy of *The Gallery Guide* (www.galleryguideonline.com) at any major museum or gallery. Published every two to three months, it lists the addresses, phone numbers, and hours of virtually every showplace in the city. Gallery info can also be found in the "Choices" listings of the *Village Voice*, the Art section of *New York Magazine*, and the "Goings On About Town" section of *The New Yorker*. Most galleries are open Tuesday to Saturday, from 10 or 11am to 5 or 6pm. Galleries tend to be open only on weekend afternoons in the summer, and many close altogether from late July to early September.

MUSEUMS DIRECTORY

MUSEUMS (side tab)

MUSEUMS BY NEIGHBORHOOD

LOWER MANHATTAN

MUSEUM OF JEWISH HERITAGE. This sleekly modern building, completed in 1997, is a living memorial to both the vitality of the Jewish people and its tragic history. The building's six sides recall at once the Star of David and the six million victims of the Holocaust. The collection consists of personal artifacts and hours of poignant recorded first-person narratives, which seek to educate visitors about the broad tapestry of Jewish life in the 20th century, before, during, and after the Holocaust. *(36 Battery Pl. at Battery Park City.* S *4, 5 to Bowling Green; R, W to Whitehall St.; J, M, Z to Broad St.; R, W, 1 to South Ferry.* ☎ *646-437-4200; www.mjhnyc.org. Open M-W and Su 10am-8pm, Th 10am-5:45pm, F and eve of Jewish holidays 10am-5pm. Closed on Jewish holidays. $10, seniors $7, students $5, children under 12 free.)*

NATIONAL MUSEUM OF THE AMERICAN INDIAN. Housed in the architecturally stunning Custom House, this excellent museum showcases some of the Smithsonian's vast collection of Native American artifacts, most on loan from the Washington, D.C. headquarters. The rotating exhibits are all conceived and designed by Native American artists and craftsmen. Recent shows include *Born of Clay*, an overview of Native American ceramics, and *Autoimmune Response*, which presents a counter-narrative to the romantic vision of Indians living in a changeless past. *(1 Bowling Green.* S *4, 5 to Bowling Green; 1 to South Ferry.* ☎ *212-514-3700; www.si.edu/nmai. Open M-W and F-Su 10am-5pm, Th 10am-8pm. Free.)*

NEW YORK CITY POLICE MUSEUM. The police museum houses an extensive collection of badges, guns, criminal profiles, and other police memorabilia. The *Vintage Weapons and Notorious Criminals* exhibit features the machine gun used by Al Capone's gang to assassinate Frankie Yale. One wing is dedicated to the officers who lost their lives on September 11. The rotating exhibits change frequently. *(100 Old Slip, between Water and South St.* S *4, 5 to Bowling Green; 2, 3 to Wall St./William St.; R, W to Whitehall St.* ☎ *212-480-3100; www.nycpolicemuseum.org. Open M-Sa 10am-5pm. Wheelchair accessible. $5, seniors $3, children ages 6-18 $2, under 6 and NYPD free.)*

SKYSCRAPER MUSEUM. This small museum, housed in the Ritz Carlton building, is worth a visit if you're interested in modern architecture and the history of New York's skyline. A fascinating display of photographs of the Lower Manhattan skyline tracks the impact of the construction and destruction of the World Trade Center on the cityscape. Rotating exhibits focus on the history of New York architecture and the technology and construction techniques that underlie it. *(39*

Battery Pl. 🅂 *4, 5 to Bowling Green; R, W to Whitehall St.; 1 to South Ferry.* ☎ *212-968-1961; www.skyscraper.org. Open W-Su noon-6pm. $5, students and seniors $2.50.)*

SOHO AND TRIBECA

NEW YORK CITY FIRE MUSEUM. Housed in a renovated 1904 stone firehouse, the museum displays impressive fire-fighting memorabilia, like a hand-pulled truck from the era when George Washington was a volunteer New York City firefighter. Other exhibits feature a variety of old-fashioned hoses and pumps. The permanent exhibit on September 11, *If They Could Speak*, displays photos and artifacts from Ground Zero and has a searchable database of the city firefighters and police officers killed during the attacks. Guided group and children's tours are available by reservation; call ahead for information. *(278 Spring St., between Varick and Hudson St.* 🅂 *1 to Houston St.* ☎ *212-691-1303; www.nycfiremuseum.org. Open Tu-Sa 10am-5pm, Su 10am-4pm. Suggested donation $5, students and seniors $2, children under 12 $1.)*

CHINATOWN

MUSEUM OF THE CHINESE IN THE AMERICAS. The first museum to be dedicated to the history of the Chinese and their descendants in the Western hemisphere, this museum has artistic, historical, and architectural exhibits. Though located behind an unassuming door and an uninviting staircase, it is home to a number of interesting exhibits, many of which are works in progress, such as *Many True Stories: Life in Chinatown On and After September 11th*, as well as *Where is Home?—Chinese in the Americas*. For the 2007-2008 season, the museum is planning an exhibit on *qui paos*, traditional Chinese dresses. One of the many unique aspects of the museum is that it collects ideas and artifacts for its exhibits from the surrounding inhabitants of Chinatown. The gift shop sells Chinese books, prints, and trinkets. *(70 Mulberry St., 2nd floor, on the corner of Bayard and Mulberry St.* 🅂 *6, J, M, N, Q, R, W, Z to Canal St.* ☎ *212-619-4785; www.moca-nyc.org. Open Tu-Th noon-6pm, F noon-7pm, Sa-Su noon-6pm. $3, students and seniors $1, children under 12 free. F free admission.)*

LOWER EAST SIDE

■ **LOWER EAST SIDE TENEMENT MUSEUM.** This museum, dedicated to the experience of New York's immigrants in the early 20th century, offers one of the most personal and fascinating approaches to New York City history around. Before it became a museum, this tenement building languished empty and in disrepair for over 50 years. You can only visit it by guided tour, and it's best to reserve ahead. One tour focuses on the lives of a pair of Depression-era families, one German-Jewish, another Sicilian-Catholic. A second focuses on the hardships of turn-of-the-century garment workers, and a third, led by costumed guides, presents the life of a sephardic Jewish family. One-hour neighborhood walking tours focus on historic buildings throughout the Lower East Side. *(108 Orchard St., between Broome and Delancey St.* 🅂 *F, J, M, Z to Delancey St./Essex St.* ☎ *212-431-0233, tickets 866-811-4111; www.tenement.org. Visitor center and gift shop open M 11am-5:30pm, Tu-F 11am-6pm, Sa-Su 10:45am-6pm. Tours are limited to 15, and spots fill up quickly. Buy tickets at least 24hr. in advance by phone or online. Limited same-day tickets go on sale when the shop opens. $15, students and seniors $11.)*

GREENWICH VILLAGE

FORBES MAGAZINE GALLERIES. Located in the *Forbes Magazine* headquarters, this small museum contains the eclectic possessions of the late Malcolm S.

Forbes, Sr. The multi-millionaire financier had a penchant for the offbeat. The collection includes 500 model boats, 12,000 toy soldiers, and several troves of former US Presidents' personal papers. Of particular note is a room tracing the history of the game *Monopoly*—check out the "Oligopoly" version made just for Forbes, using properties he actually owned. The Forbes Museum also has the world's largest collection of Fabergé objets d'art, including 12 of the famous eggs. Even the Kremlin has only 10, while Queen Elizabeth lags behind at two. The galleries host an array of changing exhibits; call for details. *(62 5th Ave., at 12th St. S N, R, W to 8th St./NYU; 4, 5, 6, L, N, Q, R, W to 14th St./Union Sq. ☎212-206-5548. Open Tu-Sa 10am-4pm; Th reserved for groups with advance reservations. Free.)*

PARSONS EXHIBITION CENTER. Parsons's ever-changing exhibits of student and faculty work include photography, computer art, painting, and sculpture. Check the Parsons School of Design website for upcoming shows and gallery hours. *(2 W 13th St., at Parsons School of Design on 5th Ave. S 4, 5, 6, L, N, Q, R, W to 14th St./Union Sq. ☎212-229-8987; www.parsons.edu/events. Hours vary with exhibitions. Free.)*

EAST VILLAGE

MERCHANT'S HOUSE MUSEUM. This three-floor museum, located in the townhouse of well-off 19th-century merchant Seabury Tredwell, showcases furniture, clothing, and other belongings of the Tredwell family. It's the city's only family home preserved intact, inside and out, from the 19th century. Rumor has it that the house is haunted. Peek at the outdoor garden in good weather. *(29 E 4th St., between Lafayette Ave. and the Bowery. S N, R to 8th St.; 6 to Astor Pl. ☎212-777-1089; www.merchantshouse.com. Open M and Th-Su noon-5pm. Ring to be let in. $8, students and seniors $6, children under 12 free. Free tours Sa-Su at 1pm.)*

CHELSEA

THE MUSEUM AT THE FASHION INSTITUTE OF TECHNOLOGY. This small museum is a fascinating place for both fashion buffs and people who can't tell the difference between satin and lace. Rotating exhibits feature photography, fabric, sculpture, and mannequin displays. Previous exhibits have included *Love and War: The Weaponized Woman*, an in-depth look at the evolution of lingerie and the effect of weaponry on fashion design. Student work from the Fashion Institute of Technology is also shown. *(7th Ave. at 27th St. 1 to 18th St./7th Ave. ☎212-217-5800; www.fitnyc.edu/museum. Open Tu-F noon-8pm, Sa 10am-5pm.)*

DIA CENTER FOR THE ARTS. This arts center's four floors of long-term exhibits cover a range of media and styles, rewarding repeat visits. The rooftop holds an ongoing video installation, *Rooftop Urban Park Project*, as well as a cafe with a decent view. Poetry readings and lectures are held occasionally; call for schedule. *(548 W 22nd St., between 10th and 11th Ave. S C, E to 23rd St./8th Ave. ☎212-989-5566; www.diacenter.org. Open in summer M and Th-Su 11am-6pm; in winter M and F-Su 11am-4pm. Bookstore open W-Su 11am-6pm. $10, students and seniors $7, children under 12 free.)*

UNION SQUARE, THE FLATIRON DISTRICT, AND MURRAY HILL

■ THE MORGAN LIBRARY AND MUSEUM. The Morgan Library houses the personal collection of the illustrious turn-of-the-century financier Pierpont Morgan, and it is a fascinating and diverse trove of ancient, old, and otherwise valuable documents, books, manuscripts, and artwork. The library is based in Morgan's former home, and the complex recently underwent an extensive expansion and renovation, led by Italian architect Renzo Piano. The complex is now a mix of subdued modern lines and splendidly ornate turn-of-the-century stylings. The rooms that once served as Morgan's personal library and study are particularly magnificent. The collection ranges widely and claims to "encompass the entire history of the printed word." Among the riches, you'll find the most complete known set of medieval tarot cards in existence, illuminated medieval manuscripts, three Gutenberg Bibles, handwritten drafts by Mozart and Thoreau, handwritten letters by Hemingway and Pound, and a huge collection of Rembrandt etchings. *(225 Madison Ave., at 36th St.* $\boxed{S}$ *6 to 33rd St.* ☎ *212-685-0008; www.themorgan.org. Open Tu-Th 10:30am-5pm, F 10:30am-9pm, Sa 10am-6pm, Su 11am-6pm. $12; students, seniors, and children under 16 $8; children under $12 free. Themed tours are available daily; call for schedule.)*

MUSEUM OF SEX. This museum opened its doors in 2002 with the exhibit *How New York City Changed Sex in America.* Since then, it's hosted rotating exhibits exploring the history, evolution, and cultural significance of human sexuality. The permanent collection addresses the themes of sex in art, law, public morality, advertising, and more. Recent temporary exhibits have included *Peeping, Probing, and Porn: Four Centuries of Graphic Sex in Japan* and *Stags, Smokers, and Blue Movies: The Origins of American Pornographic Film.* Check out the gift shop for home accents, clothing, and sex toys. *(233 5th Ave., at 27th St.* ☎ *212-689-6337; www.museumofsex.com.* $\boxed{S}$ *N, R, W to 28th St./Broadway; 6 to 28th St./Park Ave S. $14.50, student and seniors $13.50. 18+. Open M-F and Su 11am-6:30pm, Sa 11am-8pm; last entrance 45min. before closing. Advance tickets available with a $1.50 service charge per ticket at* ☎ *866-MOSETIX.)*

MIDTOWN WEST

■ **MUSEUM OF MODERN ART (MOMA).** In the 1920s, when the conservative Met Museum refused to display modernist work, scholar Alfred Barr responded by holding the first exhibit of what would become the MoMA, featuring Cézanne, Gauguin, Seurat, and van Gogh in a Fifth Ave. office building. As the ground-breaking works of the 20th century have gone from shockers to masterpieces, the contemporary MoMA has shifted from revolution to institution. Still, it's one of the world's best. With over 100,000 paintings, 2000 videos, and 25,000 photographs, MoMA owns much more 20th-century art than it will ever have space to display.

The most stunning aspect of the MoMA today may well be its newly renovated building. In 2002, the museum relocated to a temporary space in Queens for three years. Its main complex, one of the first examples of the International School, underwent a $650-million expansion and renovation, designed by Japanese architect Yoshio Taniguchi, which nearly doubled its size. The new building's clean lines, soaring spaces, and city views have breathed new life into the museum and cast many previously neglected works in an exciting new light. The **Abby Aldrich Rockefeller Sculpture Garden,** a beautiful, canyon-like outdoor space surrounded by midtown skyscrapers, is a must-see. The MoMA's renovation brought with it the sticker shock of a $20 admission fee, but the museum is worth the steep price (and it's free F 4-8pm).

First-time visitors to the museum will likely want to spend most of their time on the fourth and fifth floors, which house the museum's departments of Painting and Sculpture. A walk through these galleries is like a walk through the art-history textbook you used in school. You'll find van Gogh's *Starry Night*, Cézanne's *The Bather*, Picasso's *Les Demoiselles d'Avignon*, Matisse's *The Dance*, Miro's *The Birth of the World*, Pollock's *One (Number 31, 1950)*, Malevich's *White on White*, and Warhol's signature *Marilyn Monroe* and *Campbell Soup Cans.* The museum rewards those who venture off the star-strewn path, however. It's home to world-class departments of Architecture and Design, Drawings, Film and Media, Photography, and Prints and Illustrated Books. One of the best ways to get to know the collection is with a free docent-led gallery talk (available M and W-Su 11:30am and 1:30pm; check website for rotating topics). *(11 W 53rd St., between 5th and 6th Ave. [S] E, V to 5th Ave./53rd St.; B, D, F to 47-50 St./Rockefeller Ctr. ☎ 212-708-9400, TTY 247-1230; www.moma.org. Open M, W-Th, and Sa-Su 10:30am-5:30pm, F 10:30am-8pm. Free jazz and classical concerts in Sculpture Garden early July to mid-Aug. Audio tour free with ID; audio tour available for download on website. $20, seniors $16, students $12, children 16 and under free. F 4-8pm free.))*

> TIP **TAKE ME ON AN AUDIO TOUR.** Virtually all major museums in New York offer handheld audio tours, which enable you to punch in a number listed at major exhibits to hear a recorded explanation. They're almost always worth the few dollars they cost (and they're sometimes free). You'll be able to visit the museum at your own pace but learn far more than you could soak up on your own. At the Met, the tour is narrated by the museum's long-time director, Phillipe de Montebello himself.

MUSEUM OF TELEVISION AND RADIO. Though modern life is a flood of television images and radio sounds, these media tend to be transitory. On archive here are over 200,000 TV and radio programs donated by the major networks and accessible through a vast catalogue. You can watch "I Love Lucy" episodes, listen to the original announcement of the Pearl Harbor attacks, or wonder at the popularity of the "Newlywed Game." Most shows arrive with their original commercials intact.

Each day the museum also screens several retrospectives on everything from superheroes to the depiction of sex in 1950s sitcoms, as well as particularly excellent pilot episodes and Emmy-winning documentaries. Pick up a daily schedule at the front counter, or check online. *(25 W 52nd St., between 5th and 6th Ave. [S] B, D, F, V to 47th-50th St./Rockefeller Ctr./6th Ave. or E, V to 5th Ave./53rd St. ☎ 212-621-6600, daily schedule 212-621-6800; www.mtr.org. Open Tu-W and F-Su noon-6pm, Th noon-8pm. $10, students and seniors $8, children under 14 $5. Inquire about guided tours at the front desk. Check online for schedule of seminars with critics and performers.)*

INTERNATIONAL CENTER OF PHOTOGRAPHY. Housed in a Midtown skyscraper, ICP is the city's only photography museum. It showcases historical and contemporary works from fine art to photojournalism. The two floors rotate exhibits every three months. *(1133 Ave. of the Americas (6th Ave.), at 43rd St. [S] B, D, F, V, to 42nd St./Ave. of the Americas (6th Ave.). ☎ 212-857-0000; www.icp.org. Open Tu-Th 10am-5pm, F 10am-8pm, Sa-Su 10am-6pm. $10, students and seniors $7, children under 12 free. F 5-8pm voluntary contribution. Wheelchairs available upon request.)*

INTREPID SEA-AIR-SPACE MUSEUM. Currently closed for renovations and scheduled to re-open in May 2008, this museum is housed in the *Intrepid*, a WWII and Vietnam aircraft carrier, which has a 900 ft. flight deck holding old and new warplanes. Check out the declassified CIA A-12 Blackbird, the world's fastest spy plane. Don't miss the Vietnam War destroyer *Edson* and the only publicly displayed guided-missile submarine, the *Growler*. Pioneer's Hall displays models, antiques, and film shorts of flying devices from 1900 to the 30s. It also holds a tribute to the victims and survivors of the 9/11 attacks. Iraqi tanks captured in the Gulf War are parked near the gift shop. The museum recently acquired a British Airways Concorde. Tough visitors should check out the two flight-zone simulators, which shake you into a greater appreciation for the work of military personnel. *(Pier 86, at 46th St. and 12th Ave. [S] A, C, E to 42nd St./Port Authority. Take the M42 west to*

42nd St. and Hudson River (12th Ave.). Walk north to the museum. ☎ *212-245-0072; www.intrepidmuseum.com. Open Apr.-Sept. M-F 10am-5pm, Sa-Su 10am-6pm; Oct.-Mar. Tu-Su 10am-5pm. Last admission 1hr. before closing. $16; seniors, children ages 12-17, veterans $12.50; children ages 6-11 $9.50, ages 2-5 $4.50; active-duty servicemen and children under 2 free; wheelchair-bound patrons half-price.)*

MIDTOWN EAST

SONY WONDER TECHNOLOGY LAB. This free children-oriented museum combines the history of communications with cutting-edge technology. After entering the lab as a "Media Trainee," you progress at your own speed through exhibits that allow you to edit movies, mix songs, play new video games on massive consoles, learn how television works, and interact with robots. At each checkpoint, your card is swiped to document your new knowledge. Make sure to pick up your personalized graduation certificate on the way out the door. Be warned: this place is often swarmed by school groups, birthday parties, and crowds of children trying to get their hands on the interactive exhibits. Try to get there as close to opening as possible, preferably on a Sunday. *(550 Madison Ave., between 55th and 56th St. Enter at 56th St.* Ⓢ *N, R, W to 5th Ave./59th St.* ☎ *212-833-8100; www.sonywondertechlab.com. Open Tu-Sa 10am-6pm, Th until 8pm, Su noon-6pm. Last admission 30min. before closing. Free.)*

JAPAN SOCIETY. Junzo Yoshimura's building design—a plain, Western facade with an entirely Asian interior—embodies the society's mission to unite the peoples of Japan and the US. An interior garden on the first floor, complete with stones, a reflecting pool, and bamboo trees, evokes the spirit of a traditional Japanese home. The second-floor gallery exhibits traditional and contemporary Japanese art, including photography and video installations. The society screens a variety of documentaries and short films ($10, students and senior $5) and hosts lectures on topics ranging from the intricacies of *kabuki* to Japanese politics (adults $25, students and seniors $10). *(333 E 47th St., at 1st Ave.* Ⓢ *E, V, 6 to 51st St.* ☎ *212-832-1155; www.japansociety.org. Gallery open Tu-Th 11am-6pm, F 11am-9pm, Sa-Su 11am-5pm. Tours Tu and Th 12:30pm. $5, students and seniors $3.)*

MUSEUM OF ARTS AND DESIGN. This museum has three phenomenal floors of ceramic, glass, metal, wood, and origami by contemporary artists. Previous exhibits have included the first American retrospective of Rita Duckworth's sculpture and an overview of the evolution of glassware. *(40 W 53rd St., between 5th and 6th Ave.* Ⓢ *B, D, F, V to 47th-50th St./Rockefeller Center; E, V to 5th Ave./53rd St.* ☎ *212-956-3535; www.madmuseum.org. Open daily 10am-6pm. $9, students and seniors $7, children under 12 free; Th 6-8pm "pay what you wish." Wheelchair accessible.)*

UPPER EAST SIDE

■ **FRICK COLLECTION.** Built in the style of an 18th-century mansion, the magnificent former residence of industrialist **Henry Clay Frick** was transformed into a museum in 1935. Frick was a self-made millionaire, operating H.C. Frick and Co., a business that turned coal into coke (a substance required for the production of steel) and sold it to the steel company of fellow industrialist titan Andrew Carnegie. Reaching millionaire status at the age of 30, Frick became an avid art collector, using his personal wealth to purchase many famous paintings and to have others commissioned. The current Frick collection, two-thirds of which belonged to Frick himself, includes impressive Western masterpieces from the early Renaissance through the late 19th century. Paintings by numerous Old Masters are displayed, in addition to vases, 18th-century French sculptures, Renaissance bronzes, and porcelain. The list of artists on view includes Renoir, van Eyck, Constable, Turner, Goya, Whistler, El Greco, and Titian. Frick's favorite organ music sometimes plays in the relaxing Garden Court. Upcoming special exhibits include "Rococo Exotic: French Mounted Porcelain and the Taste for the East" (Feb.-May 2007), and "Gabriel de Saint-Aubin" (Oct. 2007-Jan. 2008).

HIGHLIGHTS IN A HURRY: THE FRICK COLLECTION. Though the Frick residence is stunning in itself, don't miss seeing Giovanni Bellini's austere **St. Francis in the Desert** in the Living Hall, Gilbert Stuart's iconic image of **George Washington** in the Library, and the West Gallery's stately self-portrait of **Rembrandt** and three paintings by **Vermeer** (only 36-40 survive worldwide).

The Frick Collection also operates an **art reference library,** at 10 E 71st St. (☎212-288-8700), which is one of the leading institutions for research in the history of art. *(1 E 70th St., at 5th Ave.* [S] *6 to 68th St.* ☎*212-288-0700; www.frick.org. Open Tu-Sa 10am-6pm, Su 11am-5pm. Wheelchair accessible. Group visits by appointment only. Free audio tour. Guidebooks $1. Slide show on the history of the collection and the grounds runs every hour on the half-hour. $15, seniors $10, students $5; Su 11am-1pm, admission is "pay what you wish." Children under 10 not admitted; children under 16 must be accompanied by an adult.)*

GUGGENHEIM MUSEUM. The Guggenheim's biggest draw is its actual building, an inverted, white, multi-ridged shell designed by **Frank Lloyd Wright.** The gallery spaces form a spiral design around a central rotunda. Though critics once feared that the design would overshadow the art housed within, frequent acquisitions and spectacular minimalist exhibits have put those concerns to rest.

The founders, philanthropist Solomon R. Guggenheim and artist-advisor Hilla Rebay, insisted on acquiring a new kind of art to accompany this revolutionary space. The Museum of Non-Objective Painting, as the Guggenheim was first known, originally focused on the radical new forms being developed by Modernist artists like Kandinsky, Klee, and Mondrian. The Guggenheim's large collection of modern and postmodern paintings includes significant works in Impressionism, Cubism, Surrealism, American Minimalism, and Abstract Expressionism. Each arc of the museum's spiral holds one sequence or exhibit, featuring art drawn from the permanent holdings. Beginning with Impressionist works by giants such as Manet, van Gogh, Gauguin, Matisse, and Cézanne, the collection proceeds to more contemporary highlights by the likes of Mondrian, Alber, and Kaminsky. The Guggenheim has a particularly strong selection of sculpture and geometric art, including pieces by Albers, Brancusi, Degas, and de Kooning.

HIGHLIGHTS IN A HURRY: THE GUGGENHEIM. The Guggenheim's permanent **Thannhauser Collection** on the second level, jammed with paintings you probably learned about in school, should be the focus of any time-pressed visit. Still, be sure to check out the Guggenheim's unique collection of paintings by the Russian pioneer of abstraction **Wassily Kaminsky.**

In 1992, under the leadership of director Thomas Krens, the Guggenheim significantly expanded its operations, embarking on an ambitious program of international expansion (subsequently scaled back due to financial constraints). The New York building received a thorough restoration and a new tower, adding exhibition space while preserving the splendor of Wright's original rotunda. *(1071 5th Ave., at 89th St.* [S] *4, 5, 6 to 86th St./Lexington Ave.* ☎*212-423-3500, wheelchair-access info 212-423-*

3539; www.guggenheim.org. Open M-W and Sa-Su 10am-5:45pm, F 10am-8pm. $18, students and seniors $15, children under 12 free; F 6-8pm "pay what you wish.")

✗■**METROPOLITAN MUSEUM OF ART.** Founded in 1870 by a group of distinguished philanthropists and artists, the Met is today the largest museum in the Western Hemisphere. It holds more than two million works of art spanning 5000 years of art history; you could camp out here for a month and still not see everything the museum has to offer. The free floor plan, audio tour, and guided tours make a visit more manageable.

Egyptian Art lies immediately to the right of the main entrance. This massive display (36,000 objects) spans from the Paleolithic Era (300,000 BC) to the Roman Period (AD 400). It includes beautiful vestiges of ancient Egyptian culture: Middle and New Kingdom jewelry, mummies in their wrappings, and the Old Kingdom tomb of Pernab. Most impressive is the fully intact **Temple of Dendur,** given to the US by Egypt in 1965 and installed in the Sackler Wing in 1978.

The southern wing of the first floor showcases the arts of Africa, Oceania, and the Americas. Beautifully carved wooden sculptures from sub-Saharan Africa and the Pacific Islands depict lineages, everyday customs, and seasonal celebrations. The gold, silver, copper, and ivory artifacts date from the second millennium BC.

The **European Paintings** collection is perhaps the world's greatest of its kind, with a whopping 2500 works. The entrance is centrally located at the top of the main staircase on the second floor. Jacques-Louis David's larger-than-life portrait of the French chemist Lavoisier and his wife hangs on the first chamber's western wall. Farther ahead are familiar masterpieces by van Gogh, Cézanne, Vermeer, and Monet, not to mention seminal works such as van Eyck's *The Crucifixion* and *The Last Judgement;* El Greco's luminous *View of Toledo;* Botticelli's *The Last Communion of Saint Jerome;* and Brueghel's starkly realistic *The Harvesters.*

HIGHLIGHTS IN A HURRY: THE MET. Art lovers could happily spend months in the Met, but if you're in a hurry, be sure not to miss the first floor's Greek and Egyptian antiquities, including the reconstructed **Temple of Dendur.** In the American wing, check out the famous paintings by Leutze and Cassat, and be sure to visit the **Frank Lloyd Wright** room, reconstructed from a summer home he designed in Minnesota. The second floor's **European Paintings** gallery boasts can't-miss works by Giotto, Raphael, Titian, Rubens, and Rembrand. Don't leave without taking the elevator from the first floor to the **Roof Garden** for spectacular city views.

Directly above the northern wing and the Egyptian galleries stands the largest and most comprehensive collection of **Asian Art** in the West. Buddhist sculptures and statuettes stand near a serene recreation of a Ming scholar's garden. On the same floor, huge winged icons guard a passageway in the **Ancient Near Eastern Art** gallery. They originally guarded Ashurnasirpal's palace at Nimrud in the 9th century BC. Unique bas-reliefs of the Assyrian kings adorn the walls.

Another highlight is the world-renowned **Costume Institute,** at the north end of the museum's ground floor. The Institute is home to some 75,000 costumes and accessories, spanning five continents and five centuries, and it hosts a variety of lively and entertaining temporary exhibits.

The **American Art** wing includes such classics as Sargent's *Madame X,* and others by Gilbert Stuart, Mary Cassatt, and James McNeill Whistler. Here you'll find one of the most famous canvases in all of American art: the 1851 painting *Washington Crossing the Delaware,* by Emanuel Gottlieb Leutze. The neighboring department of **Greek and Roman Art** combines ancient marble torsos and heads with wall paintings from Roman villas, painted urns, and glass- and silverware.

Many of the artifacts in the department of **Musical Instruments** are still played for occasional recordings, concerts, and lectures. One historic American pipe organ is used in a recital on the first Wednesday of each month, from October to May. Another noteworthy seasonal display is the annual **Christmas tree** that goes up at the end of November on the first floor, covered with the Met's stunning collection of papier-mâché angels and accompanied by a Neapolitan nativity crêche. *(1000 5th Ave., at 82nd St. $\boxed{S}$ 4, 5, 6 to 86th St./Lexington Ave. ☎ 212-879-5500, recorded info 212-535-7710, upcoming concerts and lectures 212-570-3949, wheelchair-access info ☎ 212-570-3764, TTY 570-3828; www.metmuseum.org. Foreign Visitors Desk (☎ 212-570-3583) has maps, brochures, and assistance in numerous languages. Free daily gallery tours in 10 different languages, as well as lectures. Inquire at the main info desk for schedules, topics, and meeting places. Audio tour $6; discounted for groups. Open Tu-Th and Su 9:30am-5:30pm, F-Sa 9:30am-9pm. Suggested donation $20, students and seniors $10, children under 12 free. Wheelchairs available at the coat check; enter through the 81st St. entrance.*

 MET MUSEUM FOR POCKET CHANGE. The Met caused quite a stir recently when it raised its "suggested donation" to $20. The museum doesn't take pains to advertise the voluntary nature of the fee, but if you're strapped for cash, remember that the price is flexible. You'll be granted entry for as little as a penny—just be ready to endure a less-than-pleased look from the guard.

■ **MUSEUM OF THE CITY OF NEW YORK.** This fascinating museum recounts the Big Apple's history through a vast 1.5 million-object collection. Highlights include an extensive photography exhibit documenting New York's evolution in the first half of the 20th century, a display explaining the 1898 consolidation of the five boroughs, a toy gallery, a fascinating theater exhibit, and a collection of 19th-century vehicles used by the Police and Fire Departments. Rotating exhibits like "Global New York: The Lower East Side," "Subway Centennial," and "On the Couch: Cartoons from The New Yorker," which traces the history of psychoanalysis in New York through the magazine's cartoons. Don't miss the reconstructed rooms from the Rockefeller mansion on the fifth floor. *(1220 Fifth Ave., at 103rd St. $\boxed{S}$ 6 to 103rd St./Lexington Ave. ☎ 212-534-1672; www.mcny.org. Open Tu-Su 10am-5pm. Suggested donation $9; seniors, students, and children $5, families $20, children under 12 free.)*

WHITNEY MUSEUM OF AMERICAN ART. In 1929, the Metropolitan Museum declined a donation of over 500 works from the Greenwich Village sculptor and collector **Gertrude Vanderbilt Whitney.** The wealthy patron founded her own museum instead. In 1966, the collection settled into its present-day digs—a futuristic, fortress-style building designed by Marcel Breuer.

This museum, unique in its aim to champion the works of living American artists, has assembled a 12,000-object collection of 20th- and 21st-century American art, the largest in the world. Even the skeptic of modern art will be impressed by Jasper John's *Three Flags,* Joseph Stella's *Brooklyn Bridge,* Ad Reinhardt's *Abstract Painting, Number 33,* a magnificent array of Edward Hoppers, and flower paintings by Georgia O'Keefe. The mezzanine-level galleries, accessible from the top floor, host Alexander Calder's *Circus* collection. Rotating exhibitions showcase selections from the permanent collection. *(945 Madison Ave., at 75th St. $\boxed{S}$ 6 to 77th St. ☎ 800-944-8639 or 212-570-3676, tours 212-570-3676; www.whitney.org. Wheelchair accessible. Open W-Th and Sa 11am-6pm, F 1-9pm, Su 11am-6pm. Free audio tour and guided tours . $15, students and seniors $10, children under 12 free; F 6-9pm "pay what you wish." Second branch at 120 Park Ave., at 42nd St. ☎ 917-663-2453. Open M-W and F 11am-6pm, Th 11am-7:30pm. Free sculpture court open M-Sa 7:30am-9:30pm, Su 11am-7pm.)*

MUSEUM MILE FOR POCKET CHANGE. Though Upper East Side museums are world-class, they charge the steep admissions fees (or strongly "suggested" donations) to match. Many, however, have at least a couple of hours a week when admission is **"pay what you wish."** At the Frick those budget-friendly hours are Su 11am-1pm, at the Guggenheim F 6-8:30pm, at the Whitney F 6-9pm, and at the Jewish Museum Th 5-9pm.

THE ASIA SOCIETY. The Asia Society, housed in a sleek, recently renovated space, exhibits Asian art from places as diverse as Iran, Japan, Yemen, and Mongolia. It also hosts films, public lectures, and works by Asian-American artists. Rotating exhibits feature work in a variety of media—computer imaging, video, photography, paint, and watercolor. *(725 Park Ave., at 70th St. Ⓢ 6 to 68th St. ☎212-288-6400; www.asiasociety.org. Wheelchair accessible. Open Tu-Su 11am-6pm, F 11am-9pm. Free tours M-Th and Su noon-2pm, F noon-2pm and 6-9pm, Sa 12:30pm. Free audio tour. $10, seniors $7, students $5, children under 16 free.)*

COOPER-HEWITT NATIONAL DESIGN MUSEUM. Founded in 1897 by the Hewitt sisters, the National Design Museum was the first, and remains the only, museum in the US devoted exclusively to design. It displays everything from teapots to rugs, furniture, and flatware. Housed in the splendid Carnegie Mansion since 1967, the museum contains over 250,000 objects. Unfortunately, the vast majority of the permanent collection is never on display to the public. Tourists with a preternatural fascination with 19th-century pottery should make an appointment to explore these archives privately. Public exhibitions are small but engaging and unusual. The building itself, with intricate wood paneling and a stunning staircase, makes a visit worthwhile. *(2 E 91st St., at 5th Ave. Ⓢ 4, 5, 6 to 86th St./Lexington Ave.; 6 to 96th St./Lexington Ave. ☎212-849-8400 library 212-849-8330; www.cooperhewitt.org. Wheelchair accessible. Open Tu-Th 10am-5pm, F 10am-9pm, Sa 10am-6pm, Su noon-6pm. Library open daily by appointment until 5:30pm. Museum $12, students and seniors $7, under 12 free.)*

EL MUSEO DEL BARRIO. This bilingual museum and expansive Latino cultural institution, founded in 1969 by Puerto Rican artists and activists, features art and culture from throughout the Caribbean and Latin America. The permanent collection includes works by Santos de Palo, hand-crafted wooden saint figures from Latin America, and a vast exhibit, *Voyagers of the Caribbean*, on pre-Columbian and Taino art, with ceramics dating back to AD 1200. Artistic treasures such as the colorful Chicano prints and Haitian *Vodun* flags complement contemporary exhibits celebrating Latin American culture's past and present. Temporary exhibitions tend toward the avant garde. *(1230 5th Ave., at 104th St. Ⓢ 6 to 103rd St./Lexington Ave. ☎212-831-7272; www.elmuseo.org. Open W-Su 11am-5pm. Suggested donation $6, students and seniors $4, children under 12 free; Th seniors free.)*

THE JEWISH MUSEUM. The museum's permanent exhibition spans two floors and 4000 years of Jewish art, beginning with ancient biblical artifacts and ceremonial objects and moving to contemporary masterpieces by Marc Chagall, Frank Stella, and George Segal. Culminating in post-modernity, the museum includes a deconstructivist *mezuzah* and an interactive Talmud exhibit. Rotating exhibits emphasize art interpretation through the lens of social history. *(1109 5th Ave., at 92nd St. Ⓢ 6 to 96th St. ☎212-423-3200, wheelchair-access info 212-423-3225; www.jewish-museum.org. Open M-W and Su 11am-5:45pm, Th 11am–9pm, F 11am-5pm. Closed on Jewish holidays. Free gallery talks usually M-Th at 12:15, 2:15, 4:15pm; inquire at admissions desk. Free audio guides on 4th fl. $10, students and seniors $7.50, children under 12 free; Th 5-9pm "pay what you wish.")*

MOUNT VERNON HOTEL MUSEUM AND GARDEN. From 1826 to 1833, the Mount Vernon Hotel served as a country retreat for overheated city dwellers; at the time, Manhattan extended no farther north than 14th St. This careful reconstruction, owned and operated by an organization called "The Colonial Dames of America," portrays early 19th-century hotel life through exhibits, lectures, and concerts. Summer Garden Evenings offer games and music from the period for both adults and children, as well as an open bar. *(421 E 61st St., between York and First Ave.* S *4, 5, 6, N, R, W to 59th St./Lexington Ave.; F to Lexington Ave./63rd St.* ☎ *212-838-6878; www.mvhm.org. Open Tu-Su 11am-4pm. $8, students and seniors $7, children under 12 free. Summer Garden Evenings June-July Tu 6-9pm; $12, children $7.)*

MUSEUM OF AMERICAN ILLUSTRATION. Established in 1981 by the Society of Illustrators, this museum contains over 1500 illustrations by artists like Rockwell, Pyle, and Wyeth. The museum holds an annual juried exhibition, showcasing the works of over 400 artists, who compete for the prize of best illustration for the year. Though large portions of the museum are open only to members, the quality and accessibility of the works on public display make it a fun visit for all. *(128 E 63rd St., between Lexington and Park Ave.* S *4, 5, 6, N, R, W to 59th St./Lexington Ave.; F to Lexington Ave./63rd St.* ☎ *212-838-2560; www.societyillustrators.org. Open Tu 10am-8pm, W-F 10am-5pm, Sa noon-4pm. Free.)*

NATIONAL ACADEMY OF DESIGN MUSEUM. Founded in 1825 to "promote the fine arts through exhibition and instruction," the Academy trains young artists and hosts exhibits. Past and present members include Jasper Johns, I.M. Pei, and Frank Gehry. The permanent collection, which showcases over 5000 pieces of 19th- and 20th-century American art, features the work of Reginald Marsh, Winslow Homer, John Singer Sargent, Augustus Saint-Gaudens, and others. *(1083 5th Ave., between 89th and 90th St.* S *4, 5, 6 to 86th St./Lexington Ave.* ☎ *212-369-4880; www.nationalacademy.org. Wheelchair accessible. Open W-Th noon-5pm, F-Su 11am-6pm. $10; seniors, students, and children under 16 $5.)*

UPPER WEST SIDE

AMERICAN MUSEUM OF NATURAL HISTORY. Generations of New York schoolchildren and curious New Yorkers of all ages have come to the Natural History Museum to marvel at its huge dinosaur skeletons, ogle its priceless jewels, stargaze at its planetarium, and buy mineral slabs and rubber snakes from the gift shop. Sprawling over several city blocks, this is one of the largest science museums in the world. The undisputed champions of its many exhibits are the ▨**dinosaur halls,** which display actual fossils (rather than mere plaster casts) in 85% of the exhibits. The mounted skeletons of T. Rex, Triceratops, and the rest of the gang are stunning. The Brontosaurus mount is the world's tallest free-standing dinosaur exhibit. The newly renovated Halls of Vertebrate Origins display the largest and most diverse array of vertebrate fossils in the world. Visitors follow a giant "family tree" of vertebrates that covers over 500 million years of evolution.

HIGHLIGHTS IN A HURRY: MUSEUM OF NATURAL HISTORY. The towering **Saurischian and Ornithiscian Dinosaurs** are the highlight of any visit; head straight for the fourth floor to see how you size up. Then check out some slightly smaller beasts in the **Akeley Hall of African Mammals** on the third and second floors. Dip down to the first floor for a peek at the bling in the **Morgan Memorial Hall of Gems,** but be sure to head back up to the second for a glimpse of the suspended blue whale in the **Milstein Hall of Ocean Life.**

"MINDBENDING"
—Daily News

"JOLT OF ADRENALINE"
—The New York Times

CÒSMIC COLLISIONS

AN ALL-NEW SPACE SHOW
NARRATED BY ROBERT REDFORD

The Hayden Planetarium
at the Rose Center
for Earth and Space

AMERICAN MUSEUM OF NATURAL HISTORY

OPEN DAILY • CENTRAL PARK WEST AT 79TH STREET • 212-769-5100 • VISIT AMNH.ORG

On the first floor, check out the 90-foot blue whale suspended from the ceiling and see if you can find its bellybutton (stand directly beneath it, and scan your eyes backward along its central axis until you see a little "x"). The first floor also houses the popular **IMAX,** one of New York's largest movie screens—four stories high and 66 feet wide. Recent shows have included *Bugs!* and *Amazing Caves.* The nearby **Rose Center for Earth and Space** houses the 87-foot sphere of the 🖾**Hay-den Planetarium,** which opened its doors in 2000. From the outside at night, the planetarium resembles a floating globe in a glass and steel box. The new 🖾**Cosmic Collisions** Space Show details our solar system's explosive past through real images from space. Don't miss the **Morgan Memorial Hall of Gems,** home to the Star of India, a 563 karat sapphire, and a ruby second only in size to the Crown Jewels.

Make sure to grab a map by the entrance—this place could keep you wandering for weeks. Call ahead or visit the website for a listing of current exhibits. *(Central Park W, between 77th and 81st St.* Ⓢ *B, C to 81st St. Entrances at Columbus Ave., Central Park W, and 81st St.* ☎ *212-769-5100; www.amnh.org. Open daily 10am-5:45pm. Rose Center same hours except 1st F of month 10am-8:45pm, when open for* 🖾 *live jazz and tapas (sets 6-7pm and 7:30-8:30pm). Discovery Room for children ages 5-12 open M-F 1:30-5:15pm, Sa-Su 10:30am-1:30pm and 2:15-5:15pm. Wheelchair accessible. Highlights tours 6 per day from 10:15am-3:15pm, usually leaving 15min. past the hr.; ask at the 2nd-floor info desk. Free. Museum $14, students with ID and seniors $10.50, children ages 2-12 $8. Museum and IMAX combo ticket $21, students and seniors $16, children ages 2-12 $12. Museum and Rose Center Space Show combo ticket $22, students and seniors $16.50, children ages 2-12 $13.)*

🖾**NEW YORK HISTORICAL SOCIETY.** Founded in 1804, this block-long Neoclassi-cal building houses a library and New York's oldest continuously operating museum. The society's extensive, six million-object collection, displayed in the **Henry Luce Center for the Study of American Culture** on the fourth floor, includes 132 Tiffany lamps, an array of children's toys, George Washington's bed, Napoleon's chair, 435 Audubon watercolors, and a small 9/11 display. The Hudson River School landscapes on the second floor present varied depictions of US terrain. Since explanations throughout the museum are scarce, it's important to pick up the floor plan and the free audio tour, both available at the downstairs ticket desk. The lower floors host rotating exhibits drawn from the society's holdings, and fre-quent lectures and book readings. Check the website for details. *(170 Central Park West at 77th St.* Ⓢ *1, B, C to 81st St.* ☎ *212-873-3400; www.nyhistory.org. Museum open Tu-Su 10am-6pm. Wheelchair accessible. Library open Memorial Day to Labor Day Tu-F 10am-5pm; Labor Day to Memorial Day Tu-Sa 10am-5pm. 45min. gallery tours at 1 and 3pm. $10, students and seniors $5, children free.)*

THE CHILDREN'S MUSEUM OF MANHATTAN. Founded in 1973 by Harlem and Upper West Side artists and educators in response to the elimination of music and cultural programs in public schools, this colorful, hands-on museum is full of inter-active exhibits for kids, particularly those ages eight and younger. Rotating exhib-its run from children's artwork to Dr. Seuss, and the permanent programming includes both a media center and the popular "Creativity Lab." Summer programs for kids available; check the website for details. *(212 W 83rd St., off Amsterdam Ave.* Ⓢ *1, 9 to 79th St., 86th St./Broadway.* ☎ *212-721-1234; www.cmom.org. Open July-Sept. Tu-Su 10am-5pm; Sept.-June W-Su 10am-5pm. Wheelchair accessible. $8, seniors $5, children under 1 free. All strollers must be folded and checked.)*

HARLEM

🖾**THE CLOISTERS.** Crowning a hilltop at the northern tip of Manhattan, this tran-quil branch of the Metropolitan Museum of Art focuses on the art and architecture of medieval Europe. Fragments of five 12th- and 13th-century French monasteries are incorporated into the building's own medievalist architecture; the building is as much of an attraction as the artwork it houses. John D. Rockefeller Jr. donated the site and much of the Cloisters' rich collection, which includes frescoes, panel paintings, and stained glass. Hymns are played in the serene Cuxa and St. Guilhem Cloisters daily at 3:30pm. Other highlights include the sublimely detailed **Unicorn Tapestries,** which portray the hunt for a magic unicorn; the Treasury, where the museum's most fragile offerings are found; and the Robert Campin 1425 altarpiece, one of the first known oil paintings. The museum's terraces boast spectacular views of the Hudson River, the George Washington Bridge, and Fort Tryon Park. One terrace holds a flower and herb garden that includes more than 250 plants grown in medieval times. The museum offers "Gallery Talks" and workshops for families in the summertime on Saturday afternoons at noon and 2pm; call or check the website for details. *(Fort Tryon Park in Washington Heights. [S] A to 190th St., and follow Margaret Corbin Dr. or transfer to M4 bus one stop to Cloisters. ☎212-923-3700; www.metmuseum.org. Open Mar.-Oct. Tu-Su 9:30am-5:15pm; Nov.-Feb. Tu-Su 9:30am-4:45pm. Tours Mar.-Oct. Tu-F 3pm, Su noon. Free garden tours May-June and Sept.-Oct. Tu-Su. Adult programming every Sa at 2pm. Suggested admission $20, students and seniors $10, children under 12 free. Audio tour $6. Includes same-day admission to the Met on 5th Ave. Limited access for people with disabilities.)*

HISPANIC SOCIETY OF AMERICA. Once part of John James Audubon's estate and game preserve, this regal Beaux-Arts terrace was once home to five museums; today, only one remains. Facing an impressive sculpture of *El Cid* by Anna Hyatt Huntington (wife of the society's founder), the society's museum includes mosaics, ceramics, and paintings by El Greco, Velázquez, and Goya. Students of Spanish and Portuguese arts and culture will enjoy the library's collection of 15,000 books printed before 1701, including rare editions of *Tirant Lo Blanc* and *Don Quixote*. The collection includes works from Spain, Portugal, Latin America, and the Philippines. *(613 W 155th St. Enter from plaza on Broadway between W 155th and 156th St. [S] 1 to 157th St. ☎212-926-2234; www.hispanicsociety.org. Open Tu-Sa 10am-4:30pm, Su museum only open 1-4pm. Library closed in Aug. Free. Limited access for people with disabilities.)*

STUDIO MUSEUM. Founded in 1967 at the height of the Civil Rights Movement, this museum is dedicated to the works of contemporary black artists. It features four exhibits per year of multimedia works, paintings, sculptures, and photographs. The museum's calendar is full of special programs, from architectural tours of Harlem ($20), to poetry and fiction readings (free), to jazz performances ($15). Check the website for upcoming events. *(144 W 125th St., between Adam Clayton Powell Jr. Blvd. (7th Ave.) and Lenox (6th) Ave. [S] 2, 3 to 125th St./Lenox (6th) Ave. ☎212-864-4500; www.studiomuseum.org. Open W-F and Su noon-6pm, Sa 10am-6pm. Gallery talks and tours Sa 1pm. Outdoor music and dancing 1 F each month in summer. Suggested donation $7, seniors and students with ID $3, members and children under 12 free. 1st Sa of month free.)*

BROOKLYN

BROOKLYN MUSEUM OF ART. In most other US cities, the Brooklyn Museum would have the largest and most impressive art collection in town. Even when compared to the giants of Manhattan's Museum Mile, the Brooklyn Museum of Art stands out as one of the city's finest cultural destinations.

Art at the museum comes from all over the world. The central two-story space on the first floor is devoted to the art of Africa, the Pacific, and the Americas—the towering totem poles couldn't fit anywhere else. When it opened in 1923, the **African collection** was the first of its kind in a US museum. Also on the first floor is the

Learning Center, which provides computer work stations, Internet access to art-related sites, and art history lesson plans.

The third floor holds the ancient **Egyptian galleries.** Only London's British Museum and Cairo's Egyptian Museum have larger collections. Also on this floor is European art from the **early Renaissance** to **post-Impressionist** periods. Crafts, textiles, and period rooms on the fourth floor tell the story of American upper-class interiors from the 17th to the 19th centuries. Be sure to visit the **Moorish Room,** a lush bit of exotica from John D. Rockefeller's Manhattan townhouse. John Singer Sargent and the Hudson River School grace the fifth floor. Galleries downstairs host temporary exhibits and weekend talks.

In 1999, the Brooklyn Museum found itself at the center of a worldwide debate on censorship when Mayor Giuliani attempted to suppress a show of controversial modern art that included a portrait of the Virgin Mary clumped with elephant dung. After a number of courts ruled against the mayor's efforts to cut off the BMA's funding, the show went on and was met with critical acclaim and lines snaking down Eastern Pkwy. The BMA continues to host ground-breaking exhibits, such as a 2004 retrospective of the controversial African-American clothing designer Patrick Kelly.

Free tours of the museum are offered most weekends around 1:30pm, but call or check the website for times. In addition to offering a wide selection of educational programs, the museum hosts a free night of lectures, films, storytelling, and dancing on the first Saturday of each month. *(200 Eastern Pkwy., at Washington Ave.* S *2, 3 to Eastern Pkwy./Brooklyn Museum.* ☎ *718-638-5000; www.brooklynart.org. Open W-F 10am-5pm, Sa-Su 11am-6pm; 1st Sa of the month open 11am-11pm. Audio tours $3. $8, students with ID and seniors $4, children under 12 free; 1st Sa of each month after 5pm free. LEARNING CENTER: 1st floor in Education Gallery.* ☎ *718-501-6464. Open Oct.-July Sa-Su noon-6pm.)*

■ **BROOKLYN CHILDREN'S MUSEUM.** Founded in 1899, the Brooklyn Children's Museum is the oldest American museum of its kind. The interactive exhibits tackle subjects ranging from culture and history to the natural sciences. The *Together in the City* exhibit focuses on the communal life of New Yorkers, while the animal corner has live turtles, spiders, and a Burmese python. Children can dress up and stage impromptu performances in the "Main Stage Theater," or spend quiet time in the library. There's a special "Totally Tots" area for toddlers. Check the website for special events like family stepping classes, puppet concerts, rooftop jams, and GLBT family days. *(145 Brooklyn Ave., at St. Mark's Pl.* S *3 to Kingston Ave.; C to Kingston/Throop Ave.; A to Nostrand Ave.* ☎ *718-735-4400; www.brooklynkids.org. Open Sept.-June W-Th noon-6pm, F noon-6:30pm, Sa-Su 11am-6pm; July-Aug. Tu-Th noon-6pm, F noon-6:30pm, Sa-Su 11am-6pm. $4, children under 1 free; Sa-Su before noon and first Th of every month free.)*

■ **NEW YORK TRANSIT MUSEUM.** Embrace your inner subway nerd. This museum, housed in the now-defunct Court St. subway station (yes, the entrance is, in fact, a subway stop), portrays the birth and evolution of New York's mass transit system. Exhibits include old subway maps, turnstiles, and even restored trains as well as an in-depth look at how the subway was constructed. The museum is also home to one of the best tourist shops in New York—souvenirs include subway-emblem-emblazoned socks ($6.50) and t-shirts ($20), and Metro-Card playing cards ($4.50). *(Corner of Schermerhorn St. and Boerum Pl.* S *2, 3, 4, 5, M, R to Court St./Borough Hall; A, C, G, to Hoyt-Schermerhorn; A, C, F to Jay St./Borough Hall.* ☎ *718-694-1600; www.mta.info/museum. Open Tu-F 10am-4pm, Sa-Su noon-5pm. $5, children and senior citizens $3, W seniors free.)*

BROOKLYN HISTORICAL SOCIETY. This striking 1881 building, lined with busts of Shakespeare, Beethoven, and others, contains a museum devoted to Brooklyn's past and present. Recent exhibits include *Dodgers Do It!: Celebrating Brooklyn's*

1955 Big Win and *Brooklyn Works: 400 Years of Making a Living in Brooklyn.* In addition to overseeing the museum, the Historical Society hosts themed walks in Brooklyn neighborhoods, including tours ($15) of Historic Williamsburg and Brewer's Row, Walt Whitman's Brooklyn, and other interesting areas; see the online calendar for specific dates, times, and prices. *(128 Pierrepont St., at Clinton St.* Ⓢ *2, 3, 4, 5, M, R to Court St./Borough Hall; A, C to High St. ☎ 718-222-4111; www.brooklynhistory.org. Open W-Su noon-5pm. $6, seniors and students with ID $4, children under 12 free.)*

QUEENS

■ **AMERICAN MUSEUM OF THE MOVING IMAGE.** This museum, dedicated to the art of film and television production, features fascinating and fun exhibits explaining television and film production, along with a cool collection of movie memorabilia. Check out the Yoda puppet from *The Empire Strikes Back*, the chariot from *Ben Hur*, and the jowl-enhancing mouthpiece worn by Marlon Brando in *The Godfather.* Start on the top floor and work your way down; the exhibits on behind-the-scenes editing and production here are some of the most fun in the museum. On the third floor, you can create your own animated film sequence, dub your voice into scenes from *My Fair Lady* or the *Wizard of Oz* (there's nothing like hearing your own voice come out of Judy Garland's mouth), or alter sound effects from movies like *Terminator 2* and *Jurassic Park.* Be sure to check out the section on how live television is edited—you'll never watch a ballgame the same way again. There's also an extensive collection of costumes from movies and TV shows like the recent remake of *Chicago* and The Cosby Show, which was taped next door in Kaufman-Astoria Studios. The museum's **Riklis Theater** hosts almost-daily screenings of independent and foreign films. *(35th Ave., at 36th St., Astoria.* Ⓢ *G, R, V to Steinway St. Walk 1 block down Steinway St., turn right onto 35th Ave. ☎ 718-784-0077; www.movingimage.us. Open W-Th 11am-5pm, F noon-8pm, Sa-Su 11am-6:30pm. $10, students and seniors $7.50, children ages 5-18 $5, under 4 free; F after 4pm free. Admission includes screening tickets.)*

■ **ISAMU NOGUCHI GARDEN MUSEUM.** The stunning, recently restored home of the Noguchi Museum showcases over 240 pieces by the celebrated sculptor Isamu Noguchi, whose works probe the relationship between the natural and the manmade. Works include a variety of stone, wood, clay, and metal installations. The building, a converted factory, encircles a climate-controlled garden. Not on exhibit

THE LOCAL STORY

UNDERGROUND MOVEMENT

In any three-year time span, New York City's subway cars cover a distance equivalent to that traveled by all of the world's population put together. The subway is truly integral to the city's life; like the neighborhood a New Yorker calls home, the subway line she rides every day is a defining characteristic of who she is.

Before the first subway opened on October 27, 1904, New York's population was densely concentrated in neighborhoods like the Lower East Side. It was only after the first subway line opened that the city began to expand to its current size. It took less than 20 years for the formerly unpopulated Bronx to reach a population of 1 million in 1923.

Though most New York subway stations are plain and utilitarian, many contain works of art—from mosaics of dinosaurs at the 81st St. B, C station, to a light-sculpture by Nancy Holy at the Fulton St./Broadway St. A station. The website www.nycsubway.org has a searchable database of more than 125 permanent works of art beneath New York City's streets.

The subway system continues to evolve every year, with the most noticeable change in recent memory being the disappearance of the subway token in favor of a MetroCard-only system in 2003. In 2005, the subway hit a 50-year record in total ridership, with 23 million more riders than just one year before.

at the museum, but highly indicative of the artist's vision, is Noguchi's *Sculpture to Be Seen From Mars*, a two-mile long face carved in the dirt next to Newark Liberty International Airport. *(32-37 Vernon Blvd., at 10th St. and 33rd Rd., in Long Island City.* Ⓢ *N, W to Broadway.* ☎ *718-204-7088; www.noguchi.org. Open W-F 10am-5pm, Sa-Su 11am-6pm. $10, students and seniors $5.)*

■ **P.S.1 CONTEMPORARY ART CENTER.** P.S.1, the first public school in then-independent Long Island City, was converted into an art space in 1971. Even the staircase landings are used as display areas. Rotating exhibits, including large-scale video installations and group shows, keep up the museum's avant-garde reputation. Be aware that many works include extremely graphic content; bring a strong stomach and maybe not young children. The fourth floor offers a spectacular view of Manhattan and the surrounding area. In the summer, P.S.1 holds **Warm Up,** a Saturday afternoon festival of visual arts and music, with local and international DJs and bands performing in the outdoor galleries. *(22-25 Jackson Ave., at 46th Ave.* Ⓢ *7 to 45th Rd./Courthouse Sq.; E, V to 23rd St.-Ely Ave.; G to 21st St./Jackson Ave.* ☎ *718-784-2084; www.ps1.org. Open W-Su noon-6pm. Wheelchair accessible. Suggested donation $5, students and seniors $2. Warm Up runs for 10 weeks, beginning in early July Sa 3-9pm. $10; season pass $100. Check online for details.)*

NEW YORK HALL OF SCIENCE. This concrete hall, built in 1964, was recently refurbished and offers an array of state-of-the-art scientific exhibits. The museum is largely oriented toward children, but its 225 hands-on displays will keep parents and chaperones occupied as well. Exhibits include *Marvelous Molecules*, *CSI: Crime Scene Insects*, and *Physics in Sports*. The staff does scientific demonstrations throughout the day. Call or check the website for upcoming events. *(47-01 111th St., at 48th Ave.* Ⓢ *7 to 111th St.* ☎ *718-699-0005; www.nyhallsci.org. Open July-Aug. Tu-Su 9:30am-5pm; Sept.-June Tu-W 9:30am-2pm, Th-Su 9:30am-5pm. $9; seniors, students, and children ages 5-17 $6; ages 2-4 $2.50; under 2 free. Free Sept.-June and F 2-5pm.)*

THE BRONX

THE BRONX MUSEUM OF THE ARTS. Located in the rotunda of the Bronx Courthouse, the museum's two small galleries exhibit provocative works by contemporary and local artists, with a focus on Latino, African-American, and Asian talents. The museum seeks to showcase artists who have lived or worked in the Bronx, or whose work addresses Bronx-related themes. Past exhibits have included *Urban Mythologies: The Bronx Represented Since the 1960s* and *One Planet Under a Groove: Hip Hop and Contemporary Art*. The museum encourages the community to create textual and visual responses to the permanent collection and mounts the (often nutty) viewer feedback alongside the original work. *(1040 Grand Concourse, at 165th St.* Ⓢ *4 to 161st St./Yankee Stadium, then walk east 3 blocks to Grand Concourse; B, D to 167th St., exit at rear of station and walk south 2 blocks on Grand Concourse.* ☎ *718-681-6000; www.bronxmuseum.org. Open W noon-9pm, Th-Su noon-6pm. $5, students and seniors $3, children under 12 free. W free.)*

STATEN ISLAND

ALICE AUSTEN HOUSE MUSEUM. This 18th-century cottage "Clear Comfort" was the home of photographer Alice Austen, who took more than 8000 photographs of her upper-middle-class family, as well as turn-of-the-century street life in Manhattan and Staten Island. After the 1929 stock market crash, Austen languished in the poorhouse until the Staten Island Historical Society discovered her work and published it in *Life* months before her death. Clear Comfort, Austen's home for over 80 years, is now a National Historic Landmark. The museum within displays a small collection of Austen's photos, plus a changing exhibit of modern photography. The house's waterfront lawn has great views of the Verrazano-Narrows Bridge. The museum also hosts a variety of events, such as antique shows, dance performances, and field trips to other sights. Check website for details. *(2 Hylan Blvd., on north end of Staten Island. Bus S51 to Hylan Blvd. Walk 1 block east toward the water. ☎718-816-4506; www.aliceausten.org. Open Mar.-Dec. Th-Su noon-5pm; grounds open daily until dusk. Suggested donation $2.)*

JACQUES MARCHAIS MUSEUM OF TIBETAN ART. This hilltop museum's Tibetan bronzes, paintings, and sculptures make up one of the largest private collections of Tibetan art in the West. Its centerpiece is a Buddhist altar, consecrated by the Dalai Lama in 1991 and currently used by monks for traditional ceremonies. The terraced sculpture gardens look down on the distant Lower Bay. The museum hosts a variety of programs, including lectures on feng shui, opportunities to meet and chant with Buddhist monks, and guided meditation. A small but well-stocked gift shop offers jewelry (from $15), pashminas ($70), and CDs ($20). Many of the items are made by Tibetans living in exile. *(338 Lighthouse Ave., at Nugent St., Staten Island. Bus S74 to Richmond Rd. and Lighthouse Ave. (30min.). Turn right and walk up the very steep Lighthouse Ave. ☎718-987-3500; www.tibetanmuseum.org. Open W-Su 1-5pm. $5, seniors and students $3, children under 6 free.)*

GALLERIES

SOHO AND TRIBECA

The most cutting-edge galleries are often on the second or third floors of gallery-packed buildings. The buildings at 560-594 Broadway, between W Houston and Prince St., are known as the **Broadway Gallery Buildings,** and are filled with numerous small shops. *(Ⓢ C, E to Spring St./Ave. of the Americas (6th Ave.); 6 to Spring St./Lafayette St.; N, R, W to Prince St.; 1 to Houston St.; B, D, F, V to Broadway/Lafayette St.)*

▨ **Artists Space,** 38 Greene St. (☎212-226-3970; www.artistsspace.org), 3rd floor, at Grand St. Ⓢ 1 to Canal St./Varick St.; A, C, E to Canal St./Ave. of the Americas (6th Ave.). A non-profit gallery founded in 1972, which champions work by emerging and unaffiliated artists. The multi-room space is often used for several small exhibits at once. While the gallery presents works in all media, architecture, performance, and design are specialties. The Irving Sandler Artists File—containing slides and digitized images of works by more than 3000 unaffiliated artists—is open to critics, curators, and the public. Open Sept.-July Tu-Sa 11am-6pm. Slide file open by appointment F-Sa.

▨ **The Drawing Center,** 35 Wooster St. (☎212-219-2166; www.drawingcenter.org), between Grand and Broome St. Ⓢ 1 to Canal St./Varick St.; A, C, E to Canal St./Ave. of the Americas (6th Ave.). Specializing in original works on paper, this nonprofit space sets up reliably high-quality exhibits that strive to reveal the creative process behind the development of the final product. Works from Picasso to Kara Walker on rotation. Open Sept.-June Tu-F 10am-6pm, Sa 11am-6pm. Suggested donation $3. More space at the **Drawing Room,** 40 Wooster St.

Deitch Projects, 76 Grand St. (☎212-343-7300; www.deitch.com), between Greene and Wooster St. Ⓢ 1 to Canal St./Varick St.; A, C, E to Canal St./Ave. of the Americas (6th Ave.). A red-and-black arch frames the entrance of this 3-room exhibition space. More avant garde than the average gallery, it often features video and digital media. Open Tu-Sa noon-6pm. Also at 18 Wooster St., between Canal and Grand St.

Dia Center for the Arts, 141 Wooster St. (☎212-473-8072; www.earthroom.org), between W Houston and Prince St. Ⓢ N, R, W to Prince St. Since 1971 this extension of the Chelsea gallery of the same name has been showing Walter De Maria's *New York Earth Room,* a

280,000 lb. interior earth sculpture that uses 250 cubic yards of earth. There are only 2 others like it in the world. Open Sept. to mid-June W-Sa noon–3pm and 3:30-6pm.

Moss, 146 Greene St. (☎212-204-7100; www.mossonline), between Prince and W Houston St. [S] B, D, F, V to Broadway/Lafayette St.; N, R, W to Prince St. A furniture and design gallery and store that treads the line between aesthetic aspiration and functional use. Open M-Sa 11am-7pm, Su noon-6pm.

Ronald Feldman Fine Arts, 31 Mercer St. (☎212-226-3232; www.feldmangallery.com), between Canal and Grand St. [S] N, R, W to Prince St. This well-known, well-respected gallery offers works by equally well-known, well-respected artists, mostly mid-career. Even though the gallery has one of the best reputations in the area, the staff are still friendly, and the gallery is open and inviting. Open Sept.-June Tu-Sa 10am-6pm; July-Aug. M-Th 10am-6pm, F 10am-3pm.

The Painting Center, 52 Greene St. (☎212-343-1060; www.thepaintingcenter.com), 2nd fl., at Broome St. [S] 6 to Spring St./Lafayette St.; C, E to Spring St./Ave. of the Americas (6th Ave.). Founded in 1993 by artists who felt that SoHo needed more gallery space devoted to painting, this center features both famous and obscure painters and has gained recognition for its openness to schools of all types. Open Tu-Sa 11am-6pm.

Phyllis Kind Gallery, 136 Greene St. (☎212-925-1200; www.phylliskindgallery.com), between Prince and Houston St. [S] 6 to Spring St. Distinguished by its focus on artists outside the mainstream art world, specifically those without any formal training. Exhibits often include folk art and *art brut,* along with occasional works by contemporary international artists. Open Tu-Sa 10am-6pm.

Pop International Galleries, Inc., 473 W Broadway (☎212-533-4262; www.popinternational.com), between Prince and W Houston St. [S] 6 to Spring St./Lafayette St.; C, E to Spring St./Ave. of the Americas (6th Ave.); N, R, W to Prince St. This established gallery offers works by pop art icons like Warhol, Lichtenstein, and Haring, along with neo-pop sensations like Britto, Burton Morris, and Marco. It also has a large selection of Beatles, Eric Clapton, and Associated Press photos. The sports-lovers exhibit features paintings of boxing great Muhammed Ali. Open M-Sa 10am-7pm, Su 11am-6pm.

Staley-Wise, 560 Broadway (☎212-966-6223; www.staleywise.com), 3rd fl. room 305, at Prince St. [S] N, R, W to Prince St. Overlooking busy Broadway, this space focuses on fashion photography, especially by greats like Louise Dahl-Wolfe, Man Ray, and David LaChapelle. Open Sept.-June Tu-Sa 11am-5pm; July-Aug. M-F 11am-5pm.

> [TIP] **GALLERY HOPPING ON THE LOWER EAST SIDE.** On the last Sunday of every month, art studios and galleries on the Lower East Side open their doors for free guided (and self-guided) tours. Formal walking tours leave from the Lower East Side Visitors Center, 261 Broome St. between Allen and Orchard St., at 1pm. Or, just print out a gallery map online and scavenge for yourself anytime between 1 and 7pm. For details, visit www.elsles.org.

CHELSEA

Cheaper rents and beautiful spaces have lured many of the original SoHo galleries to Chelsea's converted warehouses. The area west of Ninth Ave., between 17th and 26th St., is full of display spaces holding all kinds of art from sculpture and installation to abstract paintings. One could easily spend an entire day wandering the streets and stopping in galleries. Don't worry, if you enter a gallery, there's no onus on you to buy a piece of art. The area enclosed by Fifth and Sixth Ave. and 17th and 21st St. is known as the Photography District for its many professional photo labs. *([S] A, C, E, L to 14th St./8th Ave.; C, E to 23rd St./8th Ave.)*

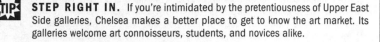

> **TIP** **STEP RIGHT IN.** If you're intimidated by the pretentiousness of Upper East Side galleries, Chelsea makes a better place to get to know the art market. Its galleries welcome art connoisseurs, students, and novices alike.

529 W 20th St., between 10th and 11th Ave. This 11-floor colossus houses over 20 contemporary art galleries, including the **ACA Galleries** (☎212-206-8080; www.acagalleries.com), and the **Dorfman Projects** (☎212-352-2272; www.dorfmanprojects.com).

Sonnabend, 536 W 22nd St. (☎212-627-1018; www.artnet.com/sonnabend.html), between 10th and 11th Ave. Originally located in SoHo, this famous gallery has shown works by well-known American and European contemporary artists for 40 years, without losing its edge. Painting, sculpture, and photography have all found their way inside the doors of the Sonnabend. Recent exhibits have included works by Ashley Bickerton, Jeff Koons, and Matthew Weinstein. Open Tu-Sa 10am-6pm; call to verify summer hours.

Matthew Marks Gallery, 522 W 22nd St. (☎212-243-0200; www.matthewmarks.com), between 10th and 11th Ave. A leader of the Chelsea gallery scene, with exhibits by major modern and contemporary artists (Willem de Kooning, Ellsworth Kelly, Nan Goldin) in 2 large spaces. Open Tu-Sa 11am-6pm. Additional location at 523 W 24th St., between 10th and 11th Ave.

525 W 22nd St., between 10th and 11th Ave. A handful of excellent, petite galleries of contemporary art in one space, including the **303 Gallery** (☎212-255-1121; www.303gallery.com; open Tu-Sa 10am-6pm, call for summer hours), which focuses on photography. Many galleries cater to an art-student clientele.

Andrea Rosen, 525 W 24th St. (☎212-627-6000; www.andrearosengallery.com), between 10th and 11th Ave. Features a fantastic mix of photography, sculpture, and painting, including works by Wolfgang Tillmans, Matthew Ritchie, John Coplans, and John Currins. The space underwent renovation in the summer of 2006. Open Tu-Sa 10am-6pm.

Anton Kern, 532 W 20th St. (☎212-367-9663; www.antonkerngallery.com), between 10th and 11th Ave. Cutting-edge installations, often featuring three-dimensional works. Works by Kai Althoff, Monica Bonvicini, and Alessandro Pessoli have all been shown here. Open Tu-Sa 10am-6pm.

Cheim & Read, 547 W 25th St. (☎212-242-7727; www.cheimread.com), between 10th and 11th Ave. A well-respected gallery that emphasizes photography and highly conceptual art, sometimes with a political bent. Diane Arbus, Michael Hurson, Pat Steir, and Lynda Benglis have been featured. Open Tu-Sa 10am-6pm; summer Tu-F only.

Kashya Hildebrand, 531 W 25th St. (☎212-366-5757; www.kashyahildebrand.org), between 10th and 11th Ave. A well-curated space with an emphasis on photography. Kate Dineen, Farhad Moshiri, and Thierry Feuz have been featured. Open Tu-Sa 10am-6pm.

Max Protetch, 511 W 22nd St. (☎212-633-6999; www.maxprotetch.com), between 10th and 11th Ave. Started as an exhibition space for architectural drawings, Protetch now hosts impressive, intelligent shows of painting, sculpture, and all things in between. Open Sept.-June Tu-Sa 10am-6pm; July-Aug. M-F 10am-6pm.

Gagosian, 555 W 24th St. (☎212-741-1111; www.gagosian.com), between 10th and 11th Ave. This massive downtown branch of the Gagosian offers exciting video art, space for installations, and works by both established masters and hot rising stars. Recent displays have showcased the work of Damien Hirst, Ed Ruscha, and Richard Serra. Open Tu-Sa 10am-6pm.

MIDTOWN EAST

Christie's, 20 Rockefeller Plaza (☎212-636-2000; www.christies.com), at 49th St. [S] B, D, F, V to 47th-50th St./Rockefeller Center. This branch of the famous international auction house flaunts an impressive collection of valuables, ranging from a Giovanni painting to Eric Clapton's guitar to a dress worn by Marilyn Monroe to a model of the Star Trek Voyager. The galleries and auctions are open to the public. There are 2-3 sales per week during the height of the season; summer months are almost dead. Call ahead for a schedule, or check online. Open M-F 9:30am-5:30pm.

Leo Kaplan Modern (☎212-872-1616; www.lkmodern.com), in the Fuller Building, 7th fl. Ⓢ 4, 5, 6 to 59th St.; N, R, W to 5th Ave./59th St. Contemporary glass art and furniture design, including the work of Dan Daily, Richard Jolley, Gary Knox Bennett, and Tommy Simpson. Many pieces are quite unusual. Open Sept.-May M-Sa 10am-5:30pm; June-Aug. M-F only.

Pace Gallery, 32 E 57th St. (4th fl. Pace Prints and Primitive ☎212-421-3237, 9th fl. Pace-MacGill 212-759-7999, 2nd fl. Pace Wildenstein 212-421-3292; www.paceprints.com), between Park and Madison Ave. Ⓢ 4, 5, 6 to 59th St.; N, R, W to 5th Ave./59th St. Four floors spread over this 10-story building are dedicated to the promotion of disparate forms of art, from West African sculpture to American contemporary painting and photography. The 3rd floor is home to the Pace Master Prints, featuring works by well-known artists such as Picasso, Miró, Matisse, and Cézanne. It's best to call for hours; most rooms are open M-Sa 9:30am-5:30pm.

Peter Findlay Galleries (☎212-644-4433; www.findlay.com), in the Fuller Building, 8th floor. Ⓢ 4, 5, 6 to 59th St.; N, R, W to 5th Ave./59th St. This small space showcases 19th- to 20th-century European and American art, with works by Miro, Picasso, Cézanne, and Degas, and more contemporary figures like Guy Dill and Steve Perrault. Open Sept.-May Tu-Sa 10am-6pm, June-Aug. M-F 10am-5pm.

UPPER EAST SIDE

The Upper East Side's galleries provide a venue for contemporary artists to have their shot at becoming the next master venerated by New York's art cognoscenti. Madison Ave., between E 63rd and E 81st St., boasts numerous ritzy showplaces, whose primary goal is to get work off the gallery walls and onto those of a Park Ave. socialite. A number of slightly less opulent galleries sit on 57th St., between Madison and Park Ave.

Acquavella, 18 E 79th St. (☎212-734-6300; www.acquavellagalleries.com), between Madison and 5th Ave. Ⓢ 6 to 77th St. This majestic 5-story townhouse displays Impressionist, post-Impressionist, and postwar contemporary paintings, drawings, and sculpture. Picasso, Chagall, Dali, Lucian Freud, Degas, Cézanne, Giacometti, Monet, and Pollack all turn up at this high-end showcase. Open Sept.-June M-F 10am-5pm. Call for hours July-Aug.

Gagosian Gallery, 980 Madison Ave. (☎212-744-2313; www.gagosian.com), between 76th and 77th St. Ⓢ 6 to 77th St. This sprawling and well-established gallery features the work of modern and contemporary artists. Exhibits have included drawings by Ed Ruscha, Picasso's sculpture, Roy Lichtenstein's early black-and-white work, and Frank Stella's "Exotic Birds" paintings. Open Tu-Sa 10am-6pm; call for summer hours.

Sotheby's, 1334 York Ave. (☎212-606-7000, ticket office 212-606-7171; www.sothebys.com), at 72nd St. Ⓢ 6 to 68th St. This headquarters of the international Sotheby's conglomerate is one of the city's oldest and most respected auction houses. Visitors are welcome to peruse materials soon to go up for auction—which range from Disney artifacts, to Degas paintings, to the personal effects of Martin Luther King Jr. Most auctions are open to the public, though some of the most popular ones require a ticket. Galleries open M-Sa 10am-5pm, Su 1-5pm.

Hirschl and Adler Galleries, 21 E 70th St. (☎212-535-8810; www.hirschlandadler.com), between Madison and 5th Ave. Ⓢ 6 to 68th St. Two floors of rotating exhibitions show a variety of 18th- and 19th-century European and American art, along with modern and contemporary pieces. Featured artists have included Gauguin, Cassatt, O'Keefe, Monet, and Pissaro. Open late Sept. to Memorial Day Tu-F 9:30am-5:15pm; Memorial Day to late Sept. M-F 9:30am-4:45pm.

Leo Castelli, 18 E 77th St., Apartment 3A (☎212-249-4470; www.castelligallery.com), between Madison and 5th Ave. [S] 6 to 77th St. Leo Castelli, a highly influential art dealer known for showcasing the early efforts of Frank Stella and Andy Warhol, founded this legendary gallery in 1957, which shows a selection of established and up-and-coming artists. Open mid-Aug. to late June Tu-Sa 10am-6pm.

M. Knoedler & Co., Inc., 19 E 70th St. (☎212-794-0550; www.knoedlergallery.com), between Madison and 5th Ave. [S] 6 to 68th St. Established in 1846, this gallery is one of New York's oldest and most respected, specializing in postwar and contemporary art with an emphasis on the artists of the New York School. Recent exhibits have featured the work of James Castle, Walker Evans, and John Walker. Open Labor Day to Memorial Day M-Sa 9:30am-5pm; Memorial Day to Labor Day Tu-Sa 9:30am-5pm.

BROOKLYN

WILLIAMSBURG

The Bohemian pilgrims that moved into Williamsburg in the 80s quickly made it a magnet for up-and-coming artists. The neighborhood now boasts over 30 galleries, and new ones spring up constantly. Young artists who have yet to break into the commercialized world of Manhattan exhibit here. As a result, local art is vital and fresh. Many galleries cluster around **Bedford Avenue** and **Grand Street** but smaller gems are tucked deeper into Williamsburg.

[TIP] **CALL AHEAD.** Most Park Slope galleries keep irregular hours, often opening only on the weekends and closing for weeks at a time between exhibitions and in the summer. Be sure to call ahead before visiting.

👍 **Brooklyn Bridge Anchorage,** Cadman Plaza W (☎212-206-6674; www.creativetime.org), on the corner of Hicks and Old Fulton St. [S] A, C to High St. A gallery and performance space housed in the cavernous suspension-cable storage chambers of the Brooklyn Bridge. Cutting-edge multimedia installations make spectacular use of the vaulted 80 ft. ceilings. Open mid-May to mid-Oct. M-Tu and Th-Su noon-8pm, W noon-7pm.

👍 **Parker's Box,** 193 Grand St. (☎718-388-2882; www.parkersbox.com), between Bedford and Driggs Ave. [S] L to Bedford Ave. Showcases a variety of international contemporary artists, in both solo and group installations. Features short films, sculpture, painting, and explorations of emerging media. Recent exhibits have included work by Caroline McCarthy, Bruno Peinado, and Samuel Rousseau. Open M and F-Su 1-7pm.

👍 **Pierogi,** 177 N 9th St. (☎718-599-2144; www.pierogi2000.com), between Bedford and Driggs Ave. [S] L to Bedford Ave. Hosts 2 solo shows per month by artists like Gene Oldfield, Andrea Way, and Lawrence Weiner. Monthly openings feature free pierogis and vodka. Flip through the legendary "flatfiles" of bundled art; most of these pieces can be purchased for under $200. Open M and Th-Su 11am-6pm; Aug. by appointment only.

Figureworks, 168 N 6th St. (☎718-486-7021; www.figureworks.com), between Bedford and Driggs Ave. [S] L to Bedford Ave. Contemporary sculpture, painting, pencil drawings, and stained glass, focusing on the human form. Artists include Howard Eisman and Bonnie Faulkner. Open F-Su 1-6pm.

The Williamsburg Art and Historical Center, 135 Broadway (☎718-486-7372; www.wahcenter.net), at Bedford Ave. [S] J, M, Z to Marcy Ave.; L to Bedford Ave. The epicenter of the Williamsburg arts scene. Beautiful 2nd-floor gallery in a historic building. Local and international artists. A monthly musical performance, annual dance festival, and biannual international show keep it bustling with artists of all kinds. Theater and music events. Periodic auctions and rummage sales. Open Sa-Su noon-6pm.

ENTERTAINMENT

This section provides for your nights on the town, and your days getting ready for them. With coverage of dance, film, music, theater, and sports, we hope you'll never be able to say that you're bored.

THE PERFORMING ARTS

On any given night in New York, you can choose between seeing Broadway block-busters, avant-garde modern dance, stand-up comedy, grand opera, and just about everything in between. Check local sources to get the scoop on current offerings. Look through publications like *Village Voice, New York Magazine,* and *The New York Times* (particularly the Sunday edition) for the most up-to-date listings. The monthly *Free Time* calendar ($2) lists free cultural events throughout Manhattan. Call the NYC Parks Department's 24hr. entertainment hotline (☎212-360-3456) for special events in parks throughout the city.

DANCE

COMPANIES

▧ **Alvin Ailey American Dance Theater** (☎212-767-0590; www.alvinailey.org). Founded in 1958 by modern dance pioneer Alvin Ailey, AAADT is now run by artistic director Judith Jamison. It is internationally known for its powerful dancers and moving performances. Repertory regularly features famous Ailey masterpieces such as *Revelations, Escapades,* and *Memoria.* Works by other choreographers include Ohad Naharin's *Black Milk* and Dwight Roden's celebrated *New Rhoden.* Open classes in ballet, modern, jazz, and Horton technique available at the Ailey School (405 W 55th St).

▧ **American Ballet Theatre** (☎212-477-3030, box office 212-362-6000; www.abt.org), at the Metropolitan Opera House, Lincoln Center. See p. 192 for directions. This 64-year-old company (once headed by Mikhail Baryshnikov, now under the direction of Kevin McKenzie) puts on full-length ballet classics like *Swan Lake, Romeo and Juliet,* and *Don Quixote,* starring some of the world's best dancers. It also performs more contemporary works by choreographers like Twyla Tharp and George Balanchine. The ballet also performs at City Center (p. 246). Tickets from $25. Box office open June-Aug. M-F 10am-6pm; Sept.-May M-Sa 10am-8pm, Su noon-6pm.

Martha Graham Center of Contemporary Dance, 316 E 63rd St. (☎212-838-5886; www.marthagrahamdance.org), is home to the **Martha Graham Dance Company** and eponymous school. Led by artistic directors Terese Capucilli and Christine Dakin, the company is dedicated to preserving Graham's revolutionary modern dance technique through performances of her work. Beginning in spring 2005, the company began presenting new works by guest choreographers and cross-disciplinary collaborations.

New York City Ballet (☎212-870-5570; www.nycballet.com), at the New York State Theater, Lincoln Center. Founded by George Balanchine and now headed by former *premier danseur* Peter Martins, the company tours both domestically and internationally. It has put on critically acclaimed performances of Balanchine's most famous works like *Serenade* and *Apollo.* It is most well-known in the city, however, for Balanchine's staging of the *Nutcracker* (late Nov. to early Jan.)—a New York Christmas tradition. Every spring brings the Balanchine production of *A Midsummer Night's Dream.* Reserve early for both classics, or be forced to sit in the uppermost tier of the State Theater. Tickets (from $30 depending on the performance) can be purchased at the NY State Theater. $12 student rush tickets available online or in person for certain shows; arrive at the box office on the day of performance with student ID and proof-of-age for pick up. Call the Student Rush Ticket Hotline (☎212-870-7766) for details. Box office open M 10am-7:30pm, Tu-Sa 10am-8:30pm, Su 11:30am-7:30pm.

The Parsons Dance Company, 229 W 42nd St. (☎212-869-9275; www.parsons-dance.org). This company is dedicated to performing newly commissioned works by modern dance choreographer David Parsons, known for such celebrated work as *Kind of Blue*, a tribute to Miles Davis. The company tours extensively throughout the US, and performs at a variety of New York City venues and festivals. Call or check the website for a schedule of their open classes held at the 42nd St. studios.

VENUES

City Center, 130 W 55th St. (☎212-581-1212, from outside New York 877-581-1212; www.nycitycenter.org), between 6th and 7th Ave. Ⓢ N, R, Q, W to 57th St./7th Ave.; B, D, E to 7th Ave./53rd St. or 57th St./Ave. of the Americas (6th Ave.). Manhattan's first performing arts center. Many companies perform here annually, including the Alvin Ailey Dance Company, Paul Taylor Dance Company, and American Ballet Theatre. Long-time home of the Manhattan Theatre Club (see p. 261), with its full season of plays and "Writers in Performance" series on Stage I and Stage II. The *Encores!* series features popular revivals like *Bye Bye Birdie.* Box office open M-Sa noon-8pm, Su noon-6pm.

Dance Theater Workshop, 219 W 19th St. (☎212-924-0077; www.dtw.org), between 7th and 8th Ave. Ⓢ 1 to 18th St./7th Ave. Innovative contemporary dance performances throughout the year that often focus on political and social causes. Call the box office for possible discounts and promotions. Box office open M-Sa 10am-6pm.

Joyce Theater, 175 8th Ave. (☎212-242-0800; www.joyce.org), between 18th and 19th St. Ⓢ 1 to 18th St./7th Ave. The place to go for modern dance. Also classical ballet, jazz, tap, and contemporary. Such companies as the Parsons, the Sydney Dance Company, and Pilobolus regularly perform here. You can also catch the dancers of tomorrow when American Ballet Theatre's studio company comes to the Joyce. Tickets $25-40. Student rush tickets go on sale 1hr. before showtime; $15 with student ID (call for availability). Box office open daily noon to 1hr. before first show (usually 7pm).

Mark Morris Dance Center, 3 Lafayette Ave. (☎718-624-8400; www.mmdg.org), at Reade St., Downtown Brooklyn. Ⓢ B, M, Q, R to Dekalb Ave. Brooklyn-born Mark Morris leads one of America's foremost dance troupes. The Mark Morris Dance Company has the distinction of being the only modern company in America to feature live music at every performance. Morris, the company's director has choreographed for dozens of the world's best dance companies and has become a modern dance icon. His center offers dance classes for all ages. Adult classes in ballet, jazz, modern, West African, as well as pilates and yoga, are offered throughout the week. $12 per class; $110 for 10 classes. Check the website for class times.

Thalia Spanish Theater, 41-17 Greenpoint Ave. (☎718-729-3880; www.thaliatheatre.org), Sunnyside, Queens. Ⓢ 7 to 40th St./Bowery St. Dedicated to the arts of Spanish-speaking cultures, the theater was showcasing exquisite dance performances long before Latin dance forms became popular with the mainstream public. Thalia heats it up year-round with tango, flamenco, and theater performances. Dance performances F-Sa 8pm, Su 4pm. Tickets $25-30. Check website for further details.

FESTIVALS

Dances for Wave Hill, W 249th St. and Independence Ave. (☎718-549-3200), Wave Hill, Bronx. Ⓢ 1 to 231st St. then Bx7 or Bx10 to 252nd St. June-July W outdoor performances, featuring choreography inspired by the Wave Hill landscape. $4, students and seniors $2, children under 6 and members free.

PARTICIPATORY EVENTS

■ **Midsummer Night Swing,** outdoors in Josie Robertson Plaza (☎212-875-5766; www.lincolncenter.org), at Lincoln Center, Columbus and 63rd St. See p. 192 for directions. For the past 2 decades, some of the best names in jazz, big band, swing, Latin, and even line dancing have been coming to play at this exuberant month-long festival (mid-June to July). Past performers have included Big Bad Voodoo Daddy (of *Swingers* fame), the Harry James Orchestra, and Wynton Marsalis. Come with or without a partner to dance the night away, watch the other couples, or merely take in the ambience at the gorgeous Lincoln Center plaza. If access to the dance floor is sold out, you can strut your stuff anywhere in the surrounding area (the formal dance floor only takes up a small area). Tickets go on sale at 5:45pm, but the line often begins at 4:30pm. Dancing 7:30-10pm; free lessons 6:30pm. Bags are discouraged, and can be checked at Avery Fisher Hall. Tickets $15 (cash only); 6-night pass $78; season pass $225.

Dancing on the Plaza (☎212-860-1370), at the Dag Hammarskjold Plaza, E 47th between 1st and 2nd Ave. See p. 184 for directions. Free dancing under the stars to the sounds of salsa, classic disco, swing, soul, and R&B.

FILM

Movie theaters showing big box office hits are easy to find in the city. Just look in any paper. The following listings are for theaters where you may find something special, like foreign, independent, and documentary features.

Angelika Film Center, 18 W Houston St. (☎212-995-2000, box office 212-995-2570; www.angelikafilmcenter.com), at Mercer St. Ⓢ B, D, F, V to Broadway/Lafayette St.; N, R, W to Prince St.; 6 to Bleecker St.; C, E to Spring St./Ave. of the Americas (6th Ave.). Six screens of alternative, independent, and foreign cinema located underground. Also lower-radar mainstream films. Wheelchair access. Showtimes start around noon and end around 10:30pm. Tickets $10.75, seniors and children under 12 $7. Box office opens at 10:30am.

Anthology Film Archives, 32 Second Ave. (☎212-505-5181; www.anthologyfilmarchives.org), at E 2nd St. Ⓢ F, V to Lower East Side/Second Ave.; 6 to Bleecker St. Housed in what used to be the Second Ave. Courthouse, this forum for independent films focuses on the contemporary, offbeat, and avant-garde US and foreign productions. The AFA hosts numerous film festivals, including the annual **New York Underground Film Festival** (Mar.). Tickets $8, students and seniors $5. Tickets available day of show only, at the box office. Box office opens 30min. before 1st show of the day. Check the website for the film schedule. Cash only.

■ **BAMRose Cinemas,** at the Brooklyn Academy of Music, 30 Lafayette Ave. (☎718-636-4100, tickets 718-777-FILM; www.bam.org), Brooklyn. Ⓢ 2, 4, 5, Q to Atlantic Ave.; or M, N, R, W to Pacific St. New York's newest independent theater might also be its best. A great selection of films, a gorgeous space, and an array of special programs, including abundant opportunities to meet and hear filmmakers and actors. $10; M-Th seniors, students with ID, and children $7.

Cinema Classics, 332 E 11th St. (☎212-677-5368; www.cinemaclassics.com), between First and Second Ave. Ⓢ 6 to Astor Pl. By day it may seem like your standard East Village cafe, but by night the screenings of classic, cult, foreign and independent films attract cineastes from all over. (Screenings around 8pm, 9pm and/or 10pm; $6). The bar serves beer $4, mixed drinks $5, coffee $2 daily 6:30pm-2am. Also an attached video store (☎212-677-6309; open M-F 11:30am-7:30pm, Sa noon-6pm).

Film Forum, 209 W Houston St. (☎212-727-8110; www.filmforum.com), between Ave. of the Americas (6th Ave.) and Varick St. [S] 1 to Houston St.; E to Spring St./Ave. of the Americas (6th Ave.). A nonprofit cinema founded in 1970, with 3 screens showing classics, foreign films, and documentaries, many from the 50s and 60s (*Seven Year Itch*, anyone?). $10, children under 12 $5, seniors and members M-F before 5pm $5. Tickets can be purchased 7 days in advance online or day-of-show at the box office. Box office opens 12:30pm; showtimes roughly 1-10:30pm. Cash only at the box office.

Landmark's Sunshine Cinema, 143 E Houston St. (☎212-330-8182, tickets ☎212-777-FILM, ext. 687; www.landmarktheatres.com, tickets www.moviefone.com), between Forsyth and Eldridge St. [S] F, V to Lower East Side/2nd Ave. An independent movie house in a restored Yiddish theater. Stadium seating and air conditioning make for a comfy experience. Mostly features artsy new releases. F and Sa midnight shows reserved for classics like *Jaws, Sixteen Candles,* and *The Big Lebowski.* $10.75, seniors $7.

Millennium Film Workshop, 66 E 4th St. (☎212-673-0090; www.millenniumfilm.org), between the Bowery and 2nd Ave. [S] F, V to Lower East Side/2nd Ave. In addition to F and Sa night experimental film screenings, this media arts center offers classes and workshops ($75-195) on basic filmmaking, digital filmmaking, and optic printing. Equipment available for rental. Tickets $8. Most shows begin at 8pm.

Walter Reade Theater, 165 W 65th St. (☎212-875-5600 or 212-496-3809; www.filmlinc.com), at Lincoln Center. See p. 192 for directions. Foreign and independent films dominate at this cinema next to the Juilliard School. Annual home of the acclaimed ✎ **Human Rights Watch International Film Festival** in June. Tickets $10, students with ID $7, seniors at weekday matinees $5, children 5-12 with adult $5. Bi-monthly "Independents Night" showcases American documentaries, often with directorial commentary. Children allowed only to "Movies for Kids" and "Reel to Real" screenings. Box office open M-F 12:30-6pm or 15min. after start of last show, Sa-Su open 30min. before start of 1st film to 15min. after start of last film. Online booking for $1.25 fee.

Ziegfeld, 141 W 54th St. (☎212-765-7600; www.clearviewcinemas.com), between 6th and 7th Ave. [S] B, D, F, V to Rockefeller Center; N, Q, R, W to 57th St. An old-school, throw-back of a cinema, this red-velvet palace was the original home of the "Ziegfeld Follies" and it still boasts one of the largest screens in America. A popular venue for film premieres. $10.75, seniors and children under 11 $7.50.

FILM FESTIVALS

Bryant Park Film Festival, at Bryant Park (☎212-512-5700; www.bryantpark.org), between 40th-42nd St. and 6th Ave. [S] B, D, F, V to 42nd St./Ave. of the Americas (6th Ave.); 7 to 5th Ave./42nd St. From mid-June to mid-Aug., this free outdoor venue screens classics like *American Graffiti, The Big Sleep, On the Town, Bye Bye Birdie,* and *Young Frankenstein.* Check online for schedule. Movies begin M at sunset; rain date Tu night. Bring blankets—no chairs permitted.

New York Video Festival, at Walter Reade Theater in Lincoln Center (☎212-496-3809; www.filmlinc.com). See p. 192 for directions. This edgy, experimental indie fest runs in mid-July, in conjunction with the Lincoln Center Festival. Animated shorts, music videos, and documentaries dominate. $9.50, seniors $4.50 for weekday matinees, children ages 5-12 $5. Prices may vary for special events. Call for ticket info.

MUSIC

Music is woven into the very fabric of New York City. Whether you're looking for sweet vibrations or killer beats, New York is an unbeatable place to catch the best tunes. Nearly every performer who comes to the States plays here, and thousands of local bands and DJs compete for audiences. Venues range from stadiums to concert halls to back-alley sound-systems. Every day of the year, clubs and bars host everything from open-mic folk singers to DJ-ed electronica. Seasonal festivals abound, with off-beat fusions of classical music, theater, and performance art.

CLASSICAL MUSIC

Musicians advertise themselves vigorously in New York City, so you should have no trouble spotting good listening opportunities. Free recitals are common, especially in smaller spaces; just look in publications like *The Village Voice*, *The New Yorker*, and *The New York Times* for countless event listings.

LINCOLN CENTER

Lincoln Center, between Columbus and Amsterdam Ave. and W 62nd and 66th St. (see p. 192 for directions and background info), remains the center for New York's classical music (☎212-875-5456; www.lincolncenter.org). Regular tickets are pricey, but student and rush rates exist for select performances. You can buy all Lincoln Center tickets through **CenterCharge** (☎212-721-6500; open M-Sa 10am-8pm, Su noon-8pm), online (www.lincolncenter.org), or at the box office. (**Alice Tully Hall** box office ☎212-875-5050; see p. 192 for directions. Open M-Sa 11am-6pm, Su noon-6pm. **Avery Fisher Hall** box office ☎212-875-5030; see p. 192 for directions. Open M-Sa 10am-6pm, Su noon-6pm.)

▨ **New York Philharmonic** (☎212-875-5656; www.newyorkphilharmonic.org), at Avery Fisher Hall. Likely the country's best orchestra. Previous Philharmonic directors include Leonard Bernstein, Arturo Toscanini, and Leopold Stokowski. The current director is Lorin Maazel. Season Sept.-June. Tickets $20-80. A limited number of rush tickets ($10) is available to students, senior citizens, and disabled persons on the day of the performance at the Avery Fisher Hall box office. ID required. Limit 2 tickets per person. Call ahead.

Chamber Music Society (☎212-875-5788; www.chambermusicsociety.org), at Alice Tully Hall. The Chamber Music Society is composed of 18 world-class musicians, who are frequently joined by guest artists and visiting conductors. Tickets $27.50-37.50; some half-price student tickets can be purchased in advance. Student rush tickets ($10) available at box office 1hr. before performance.

Great Performers Series (☎212-875-5456; www.lincolncenter.org), at Alice Tully and Avery Fisher Halls, and some other locations. A series that features quality classical music, films, and world premieres. Tickets $20-60. Advance student tickets ($20) available through Avery Fisher Hall or Alice Tully Hall box offices; must be purchased at box office.

Mostly Mozart (☎212-875-5456; www.lincolncenter.org), at Walter Reade Theater, NY State Theater, Alice Tully, and Avery Fisher Halls. This summer festival, which runs from late July to late Aug., features Mozart (along with some Schubert, Beethoven, and Haydn) performed by the Mostly Mozart Festival Orchestra, the Freiburg Baroque Orchestra, the Orchestra of the Age of Enlightenment, and the Mark Morris Dance Group. Tickets $25-70. 25% discount for Fleet or Bank of America customers. A few free events. Advance student tickets ($20) available through Avery Fisher Hall or Alice Tully Hall box offices.

National Chorale, at Avery Fisher Hall (☎212-333-5333; www.nationalchorale.org). New York's preeminent choral ensemble. Season runs Nov.-May. During the Christmas season, the Chorale puts on both the original Handel's Messiah (Dec. 15) and a Messiah sing-in, featuring audience participation (Dec. 21st). Tickets $27-88. Limited number of tickets may be available at Avery Fisher Hall box office to students with ID up to 3 days before performance. Limit 2 tickets per person.

ENTERTAINMENT

VENUES ELSEWHERE

▨ **Carnegie Hall,** 7th Ave. (☎212-247-7800; www.carnegiehall.org), at 57th St. See p. 184 for directions. The New York Philharmonic's original home is still the favorite coming-out location for musical debutantes. Top soloists and chamber groups are booked regularly. Some shows have rush tickets for students and seniors for as little as $10—call for info. Box office open M-Sa 11am-6pm, Su noon-6pm.

Frick Collection, 1 E 70th St. (☎212-288-0700; www.frick.org), at 5th Ave. See p. 227 for directions. The Frick Collection hosts free classical concerts twice a month Sept-May on Su 5pm and Th at 6pm. Limit 2 tickets per person; children under 10 not admitted. Secure tickets online well in advance, or arrive 30min. early and try to take the seats of no-shows. Call the museum or check the website for a schedule.

Metropolitan Museum of Art, 1000 5th Ave. (☎212-570-3949 or 212-535-7710; www.metmuseum.org), at 82nd St. See p. 229 for directions. The Met hosts a schedule of performances covering the spectrum from traditional Japanese music and Russian balalaika to all-star classical arts like Arthur Rubenstein, Yo-Yo Ma, and Kathleen Battle, Sept.-June in the Grace Rainey Rogers Auditorium. $35-60. Call for info. Chamber music in balcony above main hall on F evenings; free with museum admission.

FESTIVALS

Concerts in the Park (☎212-875-5709; www.newyorkphilharmonic.org). See p. 185 for directions. The Philharmonic plays magnificent outdoor concerts in parks throughout the 5 boroughs July-Aug. Concerts 8pm, followed by fireworks.

Cooper-Hewitt Museum, 2 E 91st St. (☎212-849-8400; http://ndm.si.edu), at 5th Ave. See p. 231 for directions. Free Cross-Currents concert series brings everything from classical to hip-hop to the museum's garden late June-July Tu 6:30-8pm. DJ dance parties July-Aug. F 6-9pm. Call ahead or check website for schedule.

Bryant Park (☎212-708-9491; www.bryantpark.org). See p. 180 for directions. "Summergarden," a contemporary classical music series, features Juilliard students performing behind the New York Public Library (p. 180). Sponsored by MoMA, this series used to be held in its sculpture garden. July-Aug. F-Sa at 6pm. Free.

MUSIC SCHOOLS

Music schools promise low-cost, high-quality music—a gift for a weary budget traveler. Except for opera and ballet productions ($5-12), concerts at the following schools are free and frequent, especially during the school year (Sept.-May).

Juilliard School of Music (☎212-769-7406; www.juilliard.edu), at Lincoln Center. See p. 192 for directions. New York's most prestigious music school. **Paul Recital Hall** hosts free student recitals almost daily Sept.-May. **Alice Tully Hall** (p. 192) holds larger student recitals (also free) Sept.-May W 1pm. Orchestral recitals and faculty performances as well as chamber music, dance, and theater events, never cost more than $10. These frequently showcase visiting conductors, celebrity guests, and alumni. Check the website for all events.

Manhattan School of Music, 122 Broadway (☎212-749-2802, box office 917-493-4428; www.msmnyc.edu), at Thames St. Ⓢ 1 to 116th St. Presents a small number of critically acclaimed musical productions every year. Tickets $10-20.

Mannes College of Music, 150 W 85th St. (☎212-580-0210; www.mannes.edu), between Columbus and Amsterdam Ave. Ⓢ 1 to 86th St./Broadway. Over 400 free performances a year, running Sept.-May, showcasing performances by student ensembles, faculty, alumni, and visiting artists-in-residence. Check website or call for schedules. Most events require no advance ticketing; all are free.

JAZZ

Since its beginnings, jazz has played a central role in New York's music scene. During the 1950s, Charlie Parker, Dizzy Gillespie, and Thelonious Monk overthrew traditional swing, jamming together uptown at Minton's. Today, New York remains the jazz capital of the world. Its multitude of genres range from Big Band orchestras to free, fusion, and avant-garde artists. Downtown's sound and crowds are more young, funky, and commercialized; uptown in Harlem, you'll find more intimate jazz settings. Check out one of the many hazy dens that bred lingo like "cat" and "hip" (a "hippie" was originally someone on the fringes of jazz culture who talked the talk but was never really in the know). More formal shows take place at Lincoln Center. Summer brings open-air (often free) sets in parks and plazas. Check the papers to find listings of jazz venues around the city.

JAZZ CLUBS

You can expect high covers and drink minimums at the legendary jazz spots, but a few bars supply reliable up-and-comers free of charge. Major credit cards accepted unless otherwise specified; call ahead to see which ones. Bring cash just in case.

■ **Birdland,** 315 W 44th St. (☎212-581-3080; www.birdlandjazz.com), between 8th and 9th Ave. Ⓢ 1, 2, 3, 7, N, Q, R, S, W to 42nd St./Times Sq. This dinner-and-jazz club serves up Cajun food and splendid jazz in a candlelit, 40s-era setting. The Creole seafood gumbo ($21) and the Cajun popcorn shrimp ($13) are as famous as the club itself. Live music cover $25-35; includes a drink if you sit at the bar. Additional $10 food/drink min. for tables—reservations recommended. M Broadway series. W Dixieland early show 5:30pm. F big band 5:30pm. Check the website or call for schedule of performers. Open daily 5pm-1am. 1st set 9pm, 2nd 11pm.

■ **Detour,** 349 E 13th St. (☎212-533-6212; www.jazzatdetour.com), between 1st and 2nd Ave. Ⓢ L to 1st Ave. Acclaimed nightly jazz and no cover on weeknights—a perfect mix. The impressive nightly lineup makes this more than just the local hole-in-the-wall. 2-drink min. F-Sa cover $5. Mixed drinks $6. Bottled beer $5-6. Wine $6-8. Happy hour daily 4-7pm; $3 drinks. 21+. Open M-Th and Su 4pm-2am, F-Sa 4pm-4am.

■ **Smalls,** 183 W 10th St. (☎212-675-7369), between 7th Ave. and W 14th St. Ⓢ 1 to Christopher St. One of the best cheaper jazz clubs in the city, catering to an in-the-know crowd. The atmosphere is divey, and the musicians are top-notch. Cover $20; includes 2 drinks. Open M-Th 9:30pm-2am, F-Sa 8pm-4am, Su 9pm-2am.

■ **Smoke,** 2751 Broadway (☎212-864-6662; www.smokejazz.com), between 105th and 106th St. Ⓢ 1 to 103rd St./Broadway. Smoke may no longer be a den of fumes, but fantastic music keeps this 70-seat restaurant and jazz venue sultry. Surprise guests have included legends like Dr. Lonnie Smith, George Benson, and Ronnie Cuber. The regular lineup includes Cedar Walton, Larry Willis, and George Coleman. Executive chef Patricia Williams (of Nobu fame) designed the New American dinner menu. 21+. No cover M-Th and Su, but $15-drink min. per person per set. Cover F-Sa $25, with $10-drink min. per person per set. Sets usually M-Th and Su 6:30, 7:45, 9, 11pm, and 12:30am; F-Sa 8 (dinner seating), 10, 11:30pm, and 1am. Jazz vocalist sets Su 6:30 and 7:45pm. Jazz brunch Sa-Su 11am-4pm. Open daily 5pm-4am.

■ **Joe's Pub,** 425 Lafayette St. (☎212-539-8777, tickets ☎212-239-6200; www.joes-pub.com, tickets www.telecharge.com), between Astor Pl. and E 4th St. Ⓢ 6 to Astor Pl. Located at the Joseph Papp Public Theater. Events at this music club and cabaret range from Norwegian acid-folk bands, to classical chamber music performances, to dance contests. It's a popular, intimate venue for both big names and up-and-coming musical acts. Guests can watch performances from small cafe tables, but sold-out sets mean that nearly everyone stands. 2-3 bands perform each night; set times around 7, 9, and 11pm.

AMATEUR NIGHT AT THE APOLLO

The Apollo Theater is a world-famous landmark—and the club where legends like James Brown, Ella Fitzgerald, and Aretha Franklin all got their start. Shows here can often be pricey, but you can save money—and see the promising talent of tomorrow—by going to Amateur Night, which has been an Apollo tradition since 1934. This contest for up-and-coming artists packs the theater every Wednesday night. Audiences vote by applause for their favorite singing, dancing, comedy, and hip-hop acts. Winners are invited back for monthly "show off" nights every two months. The stakes are high—a victory at the Apollo can be a ticket to national recognition.

Not all acts make it big, though. Booing is permitted, even encouraged, during performances that don't immediately grab the raucous crowd's attention. If the boos last more than a few seconds, the "Executioner" appears, sending the dejected artist offstage. "Getting executed" is a right of passage that many big names have endured. Luther Vandross performed here six times before completing a song. Ella Fitzgerald planned to dance during her first appearance, but decided to sing instead after getting intimidated by the crowd. *(First-time contestant shows $18-24; show-off nights $17-34. Student tickets $15 with valid ID.)*

Late-night DJs spin hip-hop, rock, and 80s hits for a packed dancing crowd. Call ahead for dinner and show reservations to ensure you'll get a seat during performances. Box office open daily 6-10pm; tickets also sold at Public Theater box office at 425 Lafayette St. M and Su 1-6pm and Tu-Sa 1-7:30pm. Open daily 6pm-4am.

✎ **Zinc Bar,** 90 W Houston St. (☎212-477-8337; www.zincbar.com), at LaGuardia Pl. (W Broadway). [S] 1, 2, 3 to Houston St. A downstairs jazz hole serving up avant-garde jazz, Brazilian, Cuban, and African music. All shows cost $5, with a 2-drink min. most nights. Usually 3-4 sets per night. Times vary, starting as early as 9pm and as late as 2am; check the website for the schedule. Open daily 6pm-3:30am.

Apollo Theater, 253 W 125th St. (☎212-531-5301, box office 212-531-5305, backstage tours 212-531-5337; www.apollotheater.com), between Frederick Douglass and Adam Clayton Powell Blvd. [S] A, B, C, D to 125th St./St. Nicholas Ave. This Harlem landmark has heard Duke Ellington, Count Basie, Ella Fitzgerald, and Billie Holliday. A young Malcolm X shined shoes here. The Apollo's legendary and often-televised Amateur Night W at 7:30pm ($16-24; $15 with student ID) is a big draw, and the audience isn't shy. Lauryn Hill, Mo'Nique, Michael Jackson, Stevie Wonder, and James Brown all ran the Amateur Night gauntlet. Some shows have age restrictions, but there are many family shows. Order tickets through Ticketmaster (☎212-307-7171) or at the box office. Open M-Tu and Th-F 10am-6pm, W 10am-8:30pm, Sa noon-6pm.

Arthur's Tavern, 57 Grove St. (☎212-675-6879; www.arthurstavernnyc.com), between Bleecker St. and 7th Ave. S. [S] 1 to Christopher St. Live jazz and blues where Al Bundy jammed and Charlie Parker stomped. The dark cavern glitters with hanging Christmas lights and a local crowd that's always on its feet. A popular late-night hangout. Light continental menu. Drinks $7-8. No cover, but 2-drink min. Check the website for specific performers. First performer 7-10pm, second 10pm-3am. Open Tu-Sa 6:30pm-4am, Su-M 8pm-4am. Cash only.

Blue Note, 131 W 3rd St. (☎212-475-8592; www.bluenote.net/newyork), near 6th Ave. [S] A, B, C, D, E, F, V to W 4th St. This legendary jazz club was home to Ray Charles, Dizzy Gillespie, and Natalie Cole among others. It still brings in all-stars, but at a definitely premium price and in a commercialized atmosphere. Music charge per set per person $25 at table, $15 at bar. M (lesser acts) $10; students half-off cover M-Th 10:30pm set only. $5 food/drink min. Set times 8 and 10:30pm. Brunch ($19.95) is the most affordable option; served Su 11:30am-4pm with sets at 12:30 and 2:30pm. Price includes food, 1 drink, and jazz. Open M-Th and Su 7pm-1am, F-Sa 7pm-3am.

Cotton Club, 656 W 125th St. (☎212-663-7980 or 800-640-7980; www.cottonclub-newyork.com), at Riverside Dr. [S] 1, 9 to 125th St./Broadway. This jazz hall, home to legends like Lena Horne, Ethel Waters, and Calloway, has been around since 1923. Now it's often clogged with tourists. M evening Swing Dance Big Band. Th-Sa evenings buffet dinner and jazz show. M and Th-Sa evenings 21+; call for age restrictions at other events. Su brunch $30 (Gospel shows noon, 2:30pm). Jazz shows $38; dinner included. Call ahead (2 weeks is standard) for reservations and schedule.

Iridium, 1650 Broadway (☎212-582-2121; www.iridiumjazzclub.com), at 51st St. [S] C, E, 1 to 50th St.; N, R, W to 49th St. This jazz venue caters to tourists and locals alike. Jazz greats, like Les Paul, take the stage every night. 2-3 sets per night, starting 8-11:30pm. $10 drink min. Tickets available online, via phone, or at the box office. Student half-price admission on last sets Tu-Sa. The jazz brunch Su 11am-3pm features an all-you-can-eat buffet ($22); sets begin at 11am and 1pm but arrive anytime. M sets at 8 and 10pm. Tu-Th and Su sets 8:30 and 10:30pm, F-Sa additional midnight set. Open M 6pm-midnight, Tu-Th 7pm-midnight, F-Sa 7pm-1am, Su 7pm-midnight.

ENTERTAINMENT

Lenox Lounge, 288 Lenox (6th) Ave. (☎212-427-0253; www.lenoxlounge.com), between 124th and 125th St. [S] 2, 3 to 125th St./Lenox (6th) Ave. This lounge and its famous Zebra Room are quintessential Harlem—intimate, offbeat, and filled with great jazz. Still sporting its original 1939 Art Deco decor, with smooth red booths and tiled floors. M Patience Higgins & the Sugar Hill Quartet 9:30pm and 2:30am. Tu Latin Night. W Nathan and Max Lucas Organ Trio 6:30pm-midnight. Th blues and R&B sets 8, 9:30, 11pm. F-Sa jazz 9, 10:30pm, midnight. Su jazz vocalist jam session with Lafayette Harris Trio 7-11pm. 21+. Cover free-$15 with 1-2 drink min. Check the website or call for upcoming shows. Open daily 11am-4am.

Showman's Cafe, 375 W 125th St. (☎212-864-8941), between St. Nicholas and Morningside Ave. [S] A, B, C, D to 125th St./St. Nicholas Ave. This cozy, low-key jazz club attracts a largely local crowd for nightly shows and friendly company. Showtimes Tu-Th 8:30, 10, 11:30pm; F-Sa 9:30, 11:30pm, 1:30am. 21+. No cover, but 2-drink min. per person per show. Open M noon-1am, Tu-W noon-2am, Th noon-3am, F-Sa noon-4am.

St. Nick's Pub, 773 St. Nicholas Ave. (☎212-283-9728; www.stnicksjazzpub.com), at 149th St. [S] A, B, C, D to 145th St./St. Nicholas Ave. The oldest continuously operating jazz club in Harlem, once owned by Duke Ellington's piano player. A small, haphazardly decorated space that fills up with a dedicated crowd. Many young musicians prove themselves here before advancing to other venues. M jam sessions. Tu new and known talent. Th-Su more established artists. Beer $4. Mixed drinks $7. No cover, but 2-drink min. Call for schedule. Shows start at 10pm. Bar open daily noon-2am.

Swing 46 Jazz and Supper Club, 349 W 46th St. (☎212-262-9554; www.swing46.com), between 8th and 9th Ave. This jazz and supper club has jumped on the big band wagon. The schedule changes monthly, but Su always draws a crowd with Buster Brown's Crazy Tap Jam. Dinner ($14-26) served daily 5pm-midnight. Entrees include a mean sesame salmon filet with sweet-and-sour teriyaki marinade and wild rice ($19). 21+, 18 with parent. Cover includes swing lessons at 9:15pm on M, 8pm on Tu, and 9pm F-Sa. $10 music charge in main room M-Th and Su, $5 in bar. F-Sa $10 music charge with dinner, $12 with drinks only. Happy hour daily 5-8pm; 2-for-1 drinks. Sets M-Th and Su 8:30-11:30pm, F-Sa 9:30pm-1am. Open daily 5pm-2am.

Village Vanguard, 178 7th Ave. (☎212-255-4037; www.villagevanguard.net), between W 11th and Perry St. [S] 1, 2, 3 to 14th St./7th Ave. This old-school jazz club serves its music straight up—no food, and no talking during sets. The club is in a windowless, wedge-shaped basement 70-years-thick with the memories of John Coltrane, Lenny Bruce, Leadbelly, Miles Davis, and Sonny Rollins. Every M, the Vanguard Orchestra unleashes its Big Band sound at 9 and 11pm. All ages welcome. Cover M-Th and Su $20, F-Sa $25. $10 drink min. Sets M-Th and Su 9 and 11pm; F-

Sa 9, 11pm, and sometimes 12:30am. $10 discount with student ID for M-Th and Su 11pm set. Reservations recommended.

OTHER JAZZ VENUES

Jazz at Lincoln Center (☎212-258-9830; www.jalc.org) Frederick P. Rose Hall in the Time Warner Center, Columbus Circle. See p. 192 for directions. This year-round festival celebrating one of America's great music forms is led by Artistic Director Wynton Marsalis. The new $128 million, 100,000 sq. ft. jazz-specific performance space features guests like Tony Bennett, Branford Marsalis, and the Boys Choir of Harlem, plus a slew of dance performances and traveling festivals. Tickets $30-150. Call the box office for student and senior rush ticket availability.

Saint Peter's Lutheran Church, 619 Lexington Ave. (☎212-935-2200; www.stpeters.org), at 52nd St., at the Citicorp Center. [S] E, V, 6 to 51st St./Lexington Ave. This church sets itself apart with unique modern architecture and an excellent schedule of regular jazz concerts. Jazz vespers Su 5pm. One night in Oct. is set aside for the annual All Night Soul session (5pm-5am). Call ahead for current schedule of St. Peter's performances. Services M-F 12:15pm; W 6pm; Su 8:45am, 11am, in Spanish 1:30pm.

SUMMER JAZZ AND FESTIVALS

The **JVC Jazz Festival** comes into the city from June to July. All-star performers of past series have included Elvin Jones, Ray Charles, Tito Puente, and Mel Torme. Tickets go on sale in early May, but many events take place outdoors in the parks and are free. Check the newspaper for listings. **Damrosch Park** at Lincoln Center, Columbus Ave., between 62nd and 66th St., hosts a large number of these concerts; so does **Bryant Park,** Sixth Ave., between 40th and 42nd St., which also hosts events throughout the summer (info ☎212-501-1390 or 212-496-9000; www.festivalproductions.net). For directions to Damrosch Park, see p. 192; for directions to Bryant Park, see p. 180.

Central Park Summerstage, at 72nd St. in Central Park (☎212-360-2777; www.summerstage.org), features many performing arts, including jazz. See p. 185 for directions. Call ahead, or pick up Central Park's calendar of events, available at the Dairy in Central Park (p. 185). The free concerts run from mid-June to early August.

The **World Financial Center Plaza** (☎212-945-0505 or 646-772-6835), occasionally hosts free concerts between June and September as part of the **Hudson River Festival.** See p. 159 for directions. The festival features such jazz performers as Little Jimmy Scott and the Kit McClure Big Band, an all-female jazz orchestra. The **South Street Seaport** (☎212-732-7678; www.southstseaport.org) sponsors a series of outdoor concerts from July to early September at Pier 17, Ambrose Stage, and the Atrium. See p. 161 for directions.

OPERA

The Metropolitan Opera Company (☎212-362-6000; www.metopera.org), at the Lincoln Center's Metropolitan Opera House. See p. 192 for directions. North America's premier opera, the Met performs on a stage as big as a football field. Artistic director James Levine conducts the likes of Placido Domingo and Deborah Voigt in new productions and favorite repertory classics. Tickets can be as much as $195; the upper balcony is a good deal at around $65, but the cheapest seats have an obstructed view. You can stand in the orchestra with the real opera buffs for $20 or sit in the fourth-tier Family Circle ($15, cash only, arrive at box office early Sa morning for tickets for the upcoming week). M-Th performances are cheaper than Sa-Su. Student rush tickets M-Th $25, F-Sa $35. Season Sept.-May M-Sa. Box office open Aug. 25 to late May M-Sa 10am-8pm, Su noon-6pm.

The New York City Opera (☎212-870-5630; tickets 212-496-0600; www.nycopera.com), at Lincoln Center's New York State Theater. See p. 192 for directions. It may not be the juggernaut that the Met Opera is, but this smaller opera company has gained a reputation for inventive programming under the direction of Paul Kellogg. City now has a split season (Sept. 8 to Nov. 21 and Mar. 4 to April 24), and it keeps its ticket prices low year-round ($12-105). Limited number of rush tickets ($10) are available to students and seniors with valid ID; these can be purchased only at the New York State Theater box office on the day of performance. Box office open M 10am-7:30pm, Tu-Sa 10am-8:30pm, Su 11:30am-7:30pm.

Dicapo Opera Company, at the Dicapo Opera Theater, 184 E 76th St. (☎212-288-9438; www.dicapo.com), between 3rd and Lexington Ave. Ⓢ 6 to 77th St. This East Side opera company has been earning critical acclaim and standing ovations at every performance. It's easy to understand why tickets go very quickly (usually around $40; senior discounts available). Recent highlights have included Puccini's *Madame Butterfly* and *La Boheme,* Carlyle Floyd's *Susanna,* Mozart's *Magic Flute,* and Gounod's *Faust.* Showtimes Th-Sa 8pm and Su 4pm.

ROCK, POP, PUNK, FUNK

Hundreds of small venues grace the city with stages that hosted famous artists when they were but up-and-comers. Nothing beats catching the latest in indie in a dark, crowded room while sipping a PBR. If arena rock is more your style, check out **Madison Square Garden** (☎212-465-6000; www.thegarden.com), perhaps America's most famous mass-scale entertainment facility. See p. 178 for directions. The Garden hosts over 600 events and nearly 6,000,000 spectators every year. New Jersey's **Meadowlands** (☎201-935-3900; www.meadowlands.com) and the **Nassau Coliseum** (☎516-888-9000; www.nassaucoliseum.com) also stage high-priced performances. From June to early September, the **Coca-Cola Concert Series** (☎516-221-1000; www.jonesbeach.com) brings rock, jazz, and reggae concerts to Jones Beach. (Tickets $15-40. See **Long Island,** p. 313, for transportation info.)

Music festivals are hot tickets and provide the opportunity to see multiple bands at the same time. The **CMJ Music Marathon** (☎917-606-1908; www.cmj.com) runs for four nights in the fall and includes over 400 bands and workshops on alternative music culture and college radio production. **The Digital Club Festival** (☎212-677-3530), a newly reconfigured indie-fest, visits New York in late July. For more electronic experimental sounds, check out Creative Time's **Music in the Anchorage** (☎212-206-6674; www.creativetime.org), a June concert series that takes place in the cavernous stone chambers at the base of the Brooklyn Bridge. See p. 202 for directions.

▦ **Mercury Lounge,** 217 E Houston St. (☎212-260-4700; www.mercuryloungenyc.com, advance tickets www.ticketweb.com), between Essex and Ludlow St. Ⓢ F to Delancey St. This lounge with a tombstone embedded in its bar has attracted an amazing range of local and big-name acts to its 250-person back room. Indie rock and punk rule the day here, but all types of music are featured. Past standouts include spoken-word artist Maggie Estep, Joan Jett, and Lou Reed. The club set out to build the area's best sound system, and it did. 21+. Cover varies. Box office open M-Sa noon-7pm. Cash only.

▦ **SOBs (Sounds of Brazil),** 204 Varick St. (☎212-243-4940; www.sobs.com), at W Houston St. Ⓢ 1 to Houston St. This dinner-dance club has some of New York's best live music, featuring alternative, African, Latin, salsa, urban, and (of course) Brazilian. The club attracts some of hip-hop's best talent, including Talib Kweli, Blackalicious, and Black Eyed Peas. The Brazilian food is good (lobster empanadas $10, calypso chicken $18, crabcakes $22). M nights begin with a 1hr. Latin dance class ($5) at 7pm; Latin bands play at 9pm. F night early sets feature emerging artists; the late night French-

ENTERTAINMENT

Caribbean dance party ($15-30) starts at midnight. Sa Samba ($20) 6:30pm-4am. Usually 21+, sometimes 18+. Box office (located next door at 200 Varick St.) open M-F 11am-6pm. Opens M-Sa at 6:30pm. Cash only.

■ **Southpaw,** 125 Fifth Ave. (☎718-230-0236; www.spsounds.com), between Sterling and St. John's Pl., Brooklyn. Ⓢ M, N, R, to Union St.; Q to Seventh Ave.; 2, 3 to Bergen St. One of the hottest music venues in all of New York, this former 99¢ store now hosts DJs, local musicians, and plenty of well-known talent. The past two years have seen performances from Ben Lee, the late Elliot Smith, and members of Wu-Tang Clan. Most shows 18+. Cover $7-20. Call or check the website for upcoming shows. Doors usually open around 8pm.

Arlene's Grocery, 95 Stanton St. (☎212-995-1652; www.arlenesgrocery.net), between Ludlow and Orchard St. Ⓢ F, V to Lower East Side/2nd Ave. Hosts at least 3 bands every night. Old grocery store signs and votive candles decorate the performance space and bar. Mostly local indie acts, but big names like Sheryl Crow have also played this intimate space. Bob Dylan once stopped by, but only to use the bathroom. Popular punk-rock karaoke M 10pm. 21+. Cover Tu-Su $7. Most shows start at 7 or 8pm.

The Bitter End, 147 Bleecker St. (☎212-673-7030; www.bitterend.com), between Thompson and LaGuardia Pl. Ⓢ A, B, C, D, E, F, V to W 4th St.; B, D, F, V to Broadway/Lafayette St.; 6 to Bleecker St. A small, mellow space, hosting folk, blues, and roots acts. Claims that artists like Billy Joel, Blues Traveler, Woody Allen, Tori Amos, and James Taylor performed here as unknowns. Look for the famous faces of other former performers on the gaudily painted mural behind the bar. Features prominently in Ethan Hawke's debut novel, *The Hottest State.* Usually 21+, sometimes 18+. Cover $5-15. Call or check website for show times.

Bowery Ballroom, 6 Delancey St. (☎212-533-2111, tickets ☎866-468-7619; www.boweryballroom.com, tickets www.ticketweb.com), between Chrystie St. and the Bowery. Ⓢ J, M, Z to the Bowery. This medium-sized club retains many 20s Beaux-Arts details. One of the city's best venues for indie rock, with a 550-person capacity and good sight lines all around. A popular stop for big-name bands making small-club appearances. Its stage has recently been graced by Modest Mouse, Ziggy Marley, and the Yeah Yeah Yeahs. Tickets $10-20. Box office at **Mercury Lounge** (p. 255).

Cafe Wha?, 115 MacDougal St. (☎212-254-3706; www.cafewha.com), between Bleecker and W 3rd St. Ⓢ A, B, C, D, E, F, V to W 4th St. In the 60s, this "beat/rock" club was famous both for its regular customers (Allen Ginsberg, Abbie Hoffman, and Bob Dylan) and its musical and comedy performers (Jimi Hendrix, Bruce Springsteen, Kool and the Gang, Bill Cosby, and Richard Pryor). Mary Travers (of Peter, Paul, and Mary fame) was a waitress here. Live music nightly. Beer $4.50. Mixed drinks $5.50-6.50. M Brazooka band (Brazilian), Tu Too Low Funk Band (vintage funk and R&B), W-Su house Cafe Wha Band (rock, R&B, funk, reggae). 18+. Cover M and F-Sa $10, Tu $7, Th $5, W and Su free. Open M-Th and Su 8:30pm-2:30am, F-Sa 8:30pm-3am.

CBGB/OMFUG (CBGB's), 315 Bowery (☎212-982-4052; www.cbgb.com), at Bleecker St. Ⓢ F, V to Lower East Side/2nd Ave.; 6 to Bleecker St. The initials stand for "Country, BlueGrass, Blues, and Other Music for Uplifting Gourmandizers." Since its opening in 1973, this music club has become synonymous with punk, hosting the likes of the New York Dolls, Television, the Ramones, Patti Smith, and the Talking Heads. Music here remains loud, raw, and hungry. 16+. Cover usually $10-25. Check online for schedule and showtimes. Next door, the **313 Gallery,** 313 Bowery (☎212-677-0455), has changing free art exhibits open to the public daily noon-7pm.

Continental, 25 3rd Ave. (☎212-529-6924; www.continentalnyc.com), at Stuyvesant St. Ⓢ 6 to Astor Pl. This dark club hosts a loud set nightly. Come for authentic local noise, hardcore rock, and punk. Bigger names like Iggy Pop, Debbie Harry, and Patti Smith stop by for the occasional surprise performance, but you're more likely to hear some homegrown New York City rock. Check the website for the schedule. Rock 'n roll happy hour daily 4-7pm; half-price drinks and $2 shots. Usually 21+. Cover up to $10. Open daily 4pm-2am.

Irving Plaza, 17 Irving Pl. (☎212-777-6800, concert info 212-777-1224; www.irving-plaza.com), at 15th St. Ⓢ 4, 5, 6, L, N, Q, R, W to 14th St./Union Sq.; L to 3rd Ave. A mid-sized club decorated in an opulent chinoiserie style. Primarily musical acts. National bands come here to play to an intimate crowd. Excellent sightlines all around. Under 16 must come with parent or guardian. Cover $15-50. Doors open at 8pm. Box office open M-F noon-6:30pm, Sa 1-4pm.

Lion's Den, 214 Sullivan St. (☎212-477-2782; www.ceg.com/lionsden), between Bleecker and W 3rd St. Ⓢ A, B, C, D, E, F, V to W 4th St. Wash down some good old college rock with $5 beers and cocktails in this chill, mostly standing-room venue. Guster, Howie Day, and Ben Folds have all played here; they typify the sound of the Lion Den's less-famous performers. M night comedy is free. 18+. Cover $8-10. Doors open M 9pm, W-Sa around 7pm.

✕ **The Living Room,** 154 Ludlow St. (☎212-533-7235; www.livingroomny.com), between Stanton and Rivington St. Ⓢ F, V to Lower East Side/2nd Ave.; F, J, M, Z to Delancey St./Essex St. The "music room" has votives on the tables and Christmas lights on the walls. Couches line the upstairs—it's like listening to the singer-songwriters in their own homes. Norah Jones and Jesse Harris have graced The Living Room's folk-rock stage. Drinks $6. Most shows no cover, but a 1-drink min. and a $5 suggested tip-jar donation in the wait-service music room. Happy hour Sa-Su 2-7pm; $3 drafts. Check the website for the performance schedule. Bar open M-Th and Su 6:30pm-2am, F-Sa 6:30pm-4am.

Pianos, 158 Ludlow St. (☎212-505-3733; www.pianosnyc.com), at Stanton St. Ⓢ F, V to Lower East Side/2nd Ave.; F, J, M, Z to Delancey St./Essex St. The old piano-store sign above the door marks the tropical bar inside. The front room and upstairs lounge offer vegetable dumplings ($8), tuna steak ($14), and fruit-infused vodka drinks ($10), while the back room has a huge array of music, from hip-hop to folk. PJ Harvey, Beth Orton, and Carnegie Hall concert musicians have all played here recently. Popular Tu "cross pollination" acoustic night. Happy hour daily 3-7pm; beer and well drinks $3, wine $4, burgers $5. Cover $7-12 for back room; entrance to bar free. Check the website for the performance schedule. Open M-Sa 3pm-4am, Su 3pm-2am.

Roseland Ballroom, 239 W 52nd St. (☎212-777-6800; www.roselandballroom.com), between Broadway and 8th Ave. Ⓢ 1 to 50th St./Broadway; C, E to 50th St./8th Ave. A swing-dance hall in the 40s, the ballroom is now a concert club featuring major-label alt-rock and hip-hop. Massive Attack, the Pretenders, Beck, Jamiroquai, and many others have played this newly renovated space. Also hosts boxing matches and film premieres. Tickets $15-50. Check website for schedule. Box office open only on the day of a concert. Tickets at www.livenation.com or via TicketMaster (☎212-307-7171).

Sin-é, 150 Attorney St. (☎212-388-0077; www.sin-e.com), at Stanton St. Ⓢ F, V to Lower East Side/2nd Ave.; F, J, M, Z to Delancey St./Essex St. In the early 90s, this venue (at a prior location) helped launch the careers of David Gray and Jeff Buckley. Pretend like you belong and pronounce it right: "sha-nay." Beer specials $3. Mixed drinks $5-8. Cover $7-15. Usually 21+; occasionally 18+. Doors open around 7pm; 3-4 shows each night. Check the website for schedule.

Tonic, 107 Norfolk St. (☎212-358-7501, tickets ☎866-468-7619; www.tonicnyc.com, tickets www.ticketweb.com), between Delancey and Rivington St. Ⓢ F to Delancey St. This converted winery hosts a small performance space for avant-garde and experimental musicians. No hipsters or bar gimmicks; just people who take their music seriously. In Subtonic, the cave-like downstairs lounge, enormous wine barrels have been split open and filled with chairs and couches for seating. Upstairs cover $6-12; 18+. Downstairs lounge with DJ no cover; 21+. Evening performance times vary. Upstairs open M-Tu 8pm-midnight, W-Sa 8pm-2am. Downstairs open M-W 9pm-2am, Th-Sa 9pm-4am.

THEATER

Broadway warhorses like *The Phantom of the Opera* and *Les Misérables* continue to pack armies of tourists into Broadway theaters nightly. But New York's theater and entertainment scenes are hardly limited to blockbusters; the arts thrive in off-Broadway and off-off-Broadway productions and in dance and studio spaces, museums, parks, and even parking lots

Broadway tickets are pricey, starting around $40-50, but many money-saving schemes exist. **TKTS**, in Duffy Sq., at 47th St., sells tickets for many Broadway and some larger off-Broadway shows at a 25-50% discount on the day of the performance. There is a second TKTS location at the corner of Front and John St. in the South St. Seaport. The lines at both locations begin to form an hour or more before the booths open, but they move fairly quickly. More tickets become available as showtime approaches, so you may find fewer possibilities if you go too early. There is a $3 service charge per ticket. (Tickets sold at Times Square location M-Sa 3-8pm for 8pm performances, W and Sa 10am-2pm for matinees, Su 11am-3pm for matinees and 3-8pm for Su evening performances. Tickets at South St. Seaport location sold M-F 11am-6pm for 8pm performances, Sa 11am-7pm for Sa evening performances. Tickets for Tu, W, and Su matinees available the day before only. Cash and traveler's checks only.)

> **THINK OUTSIDE TIMES SQUARE.** The South Street Seaport TKTS booth, at the corner of Front and John St., is a welcome alternative to the mob scene at the Times Square location. By noon, the wait for tickets there is often less than five minutes.

The **Theatre Development Fund** (☎212-221-0885; www.tdf.org) offers discount vouchers for off- and off-off-Broadway productions, and for other events sponsored by small, independent production companies. Those eligible include students, teachers, performing-arts professionals, nonprofit employees, retirees, union and armed forces members, and clergy. You must first join the TDF mailing list by sending an application and $25. Once you are a member (6-8 weeks after you turn in the application), you can purchase four vouchers for $28. These are redeemable at the box office of any participating production, as well as online.

To discover which individual theaters are currently offering rush, student rush, or otherwise discounted tickets, ask at the **Times Square Visitors Center** (p. 179), which posts all such deals at their main information desk. Many theaters will sell standing-room-only tickets during sold-out shows. See www.bigapplevisitors-center.com/ept.htm for information about buying discounted tickets directly from the box office.

> **CASH IS KEY.** If you're planning to take advantage of student-rush, standing-room, and lottery theater tickets, be sure to bring plenty of cash, since that is usually the only acceptable form of payment for these offers.

 You may reserve full-price tickets over the phone and pay by credit card using **Tele-Charge** (☎212-239-6200, outside NYC 800-432-7250; www.tele-charge.com) for Broadway shows; **Ticket Central** (☎212-279-4200; www.ticket-central.org) for off-Broadway shows; **Ticketmaster** (☎212-307-4100; www.ticketmaster.com) for all shows. All three services have a per-ticket service charge. You can avoid these fees if you buy tickets directly from the box office.

BROADWAY

Most Broadway theaters are north of Times Square, between Eighth Ave. and Broadway. Below is a list of current blockbusters in the city. For more info, consult www.nytheatre.com. (S C, E to 50th St./8th Ave.; 1 to 50th St./Broadway; N, R, W to 49th St./7th Ave.; A, C, E to 42nd St./Port Authority; 1, 2, 3, 7, N, Q, R, S, W to 42nd St./Times Sq.)

Avenue Q, Golden Theater, 252 W 45th St. (www.avenueq.com), between Broadway and 8th Ave. The underdog winner of 3 Tony awards in 2004, this popular new comedy tells the story of puppets and their human friends struggling to figure out what to do with their post-college lives. Tickets $47-101. M-F day-of-show lottery for $21 tickets. Front-row tickets held at 6pm for 8pm shows, noon for Sa matinee, 12:30pm for Su matinee, 5:30pm for Su 7pm show.

Beauty and the Beast, Lunt-Fontanne Theatre, 205 W 46th St. (www.disney.go.com/disneytheatrical), between 8th and Broadway. Based on the Disney movie. Tickets $40-110. Standing-room tickets, available for sold-out shows, $25.

Chicago, Ambassador Theater, 219 W 49th St. (www.chicagothemusical.com). An excellent revival with stunning choreography by Anne Reinking. Tickets $59-111. Student rush tickets $27.

The Color Purple, Broadway Theatre, 1681 Broadway (www.colorpurple.com), at 53rd St. A moving interpretation of Alice Walker's classic book. Tickets $26-111.

Dirty Rotten Scoundrels, Imperial Theatre, 249 W 45th (www.dirtyrottenscoundrelsthemusical.com), between Broadway and 8th Ave. A hilarious adaptation of the Steve Martin and Michael Cane movie. Tickets $41-111. Lottery 2hr. before performances for $26 front-row tickets. Limit 2 tickets per winner; cash only.

 TOO GOOD TO BE TRUE. Think twice before buying cheap theater tickets on the street; fakes are common. Bargain tickets from the TKTS booth or rush tickets directly from the theater box office are safer ways to save money.

The Drowsy Chaperone, Marquis Theatre, 1535 Broadway (www.drowsychaperone.com), at the Marriot Marquis Hotel. This comic musical-inside-a-musical won 5 Tony awards in 2006. Tickets $25-110. Lottery for $25 tickets 1hr. before performances. Limit 2 tickets per winner; cash only.

Hairspray, Neil Simon Theater, 250 W 52nd St. (www.hairsprayonbroadway.com), between Broadway and 8th Ave. A high-school dancer uses big hair to fight racism. Tickets $25-100. Lottery for $25 rush tickets 3hr. before performances. Limit 2 tickets per person; cash only. Standing-room tickets, available during sold-out shows, $20.

Jersey Boys, August Wilson Theatre, 245 W 52nd St. (www.jerseyboysbroadway.com), between Broadway and 8th Ave. Based on the life story of Frankie Valli and the Four Seasons. Tickets $26-111. Student-rush tickets $26.

The Lion King, Minskoff Theatre, 1515 Broadway (www.go.disney.com/disneytheatrical), at 45th St. Lavish costumes make this award-winning show an aesthetic masterpiece. Tickets $51-111. Tickets available in the event of cancellations 2hr. before performance; call ☎212-869-0550 for info. Limit 1 cancellation ticket per person. Standing-room tickets, available during sold-out shows, $15-20.

Mamma Mia! Cadillac Winter Garden Theatre, 1634 Broadway at 50th St. (www.mammamia.com). Wedding drama, disco, and ABBA songs. Tickets $56-100. W 2pm show all seats $5 off. Standing-room tickets, available during sold-out shows, $21.

Phantom of the Opera, Majestic Theater, 247 W 44th St. (www.thephantomoftheopera.com), between Broadway and 8th Ave. This classic still packs them in every time. Tickets $20-100. Standing-room tickets, available during sold-out shows, $21.

The Producers, St. James Theater, 246 W 44th St. (www.producersonbroadway.com), between Broadway and 8th Ave. This Mel Brooks musical won a record 12 Tony Awards in 2001. Based on the 1967 movie. Tickets $31-111. Rush tickets $25; stop by box office for information.

Rent, Nederlander Theater, 208 W 41st St. (www.siteforrent.com), at 8th Ave. A modern version of La Bohème set in New York's Alphabet City in the wake of the AIDS epidemic. Tickets $40-95. Lottery for $20 tickets 2hr. before performances. Arrive 30min. before drawing; limit 2 per person; cash only.

Spamalot, Shubert Theatre, 225 W 44th St. (www.montypythonspamalot.com), between Broadway and 8th Ave. Tony winner for Best Musical in 2005. "Lovingly ripped off" from the motion picture Monty Python and the Holy Grail. Tickets $36-111. Standing-room tickets, available during sold-out shows, $26.

Tarzan, Richard Rodgers Theatre, 226 W 46th St. (www.disney.go.com/disneytheatrical), between Broadway and 8th Ave. Based on the Disney musical and featuring music by Phil Collins. Tickets $51-101. Student-rush tickets, sold 2hr. before performance, $20. Limit 2 tickets per person; cash only.

The Wedding Singer, Al Hirschfield Theatre, 302 W 45th St. (www.theweddingsingerthemusical.com), at 8th Ave. Based on the Adam Sandler movie. Tickets $56-111.

Wicked, Gershwin Theatre, 222 W 51st St. (www.wickedthemusical.com), between Broadway and 8th Ave. The Blockbuster prequel to "The Wizard of Oz." Tickets $50-110. Limited view orchestra seats $55. Lottery for $25 front-row seats held 2hr. before performances. Arrive 30min. before drawing; limit 2 tickets per person; cash only.

[TIP] **KNOW WHEN YOU'RE ON BROADWAY.** Contrary to popular belief, whether a theater is "on-Broadway" or not has nothing to do with its street address. Instead, according to official definitions used in Actors' Equity contracts, a Broadway theater is any New York theater with 500 or more seats. An "off-Broadway" theater has 100-499 seats, while an "off-off Broadway" theater has less than 100. Of course, many of those 500-or-more-seat theaters just happen to be, geographically speaking, on Broadway.

OFF-BROADWAY

Off-Broadway theaters tend to feature less mainstream, and often more creative, production than their Broadway counterparts. Runs are generally short; nonetheless, shows occasionally jump to Broadway houses (as in the case of *Rent*). Many of the best off-Broadway houses are in the Sheridan Sq. area of the West Village. Others are located to the west of Times Square. Off-Broadway tickets usually cost $15-45. You may see shows for free by arranging to usher; this usually entails dressing neatly and showing up at the theater around 45min. ahead of curtain, helping to seat ticket-holders, and then staying after the performance to clean up. Speak with the house manager far in advance. Check publications like *New York* magazine, the *New York Press*, and the *New Yorker* for up-to-date theater listings.

Actors Playhouse, 100 7th Ave. S (☎212-463-0060), between Christopher and Bleecker St. [S] 1 to Christopher St. This small playhouse hosted Naked Boys Singing for 5 years; more recently it featured Irish comedian Tommy Tiernan. Call or stop by the box office for current productions. Tickets $35-55. Box office open Tu-F 3-8pm, Sa 2-8pm, Su 1-8pm.

Astor Place Theater, 434 Lafayette St. (☎800-258-3626; www.blueman.com), between E 4th St. and Astor Pl. [S] 6 to Astor Pl.; R, W to 8th St./NYU. Home to the Blue Man Group: mimed humor, blueface, and rocking PVC pipes. Shows Tu-Th 8pm; F 7 and 10pm; Sa 4, 7, and 10pm; Su 2, 5, and 8pm. Tickets $59-69. Student rush tickets available 1hr. before all but F-Sa 7pm performances; $25. Limit 1 per person.

Charlie Pineapple Theater, 248 N 8th St. (☎718-907-0577; www.charliepineapple.com), at Driggs Ave., Brooklyn. [S] L to Bedford Ave. A small independent theater. Featured Lyle Kessler's *Orphans* in 2006. Tickets $15; reservations recommended. Call or check website for showtimes.

Cherry Lane Theatre, 38 Commerce St. (☎212-989-2020; cherrylanetheatre.com), at Bedford St. [S] 1 to Christopher St., Houston St. New York's oldest continuously running off-broadway theater. This converted box-factory and tobacco warehouse has hosted a slew of plays by famous playwrights such as Beckett, Albee, O'Neill, Shepard, and others. Tickets $35-55. An alternative theater in the same building hosts more experimental productions. Box office open 2hr. before showtime. Tickets $12.

Joseph Papp Public Theater, 425 Lafayette St. (☎212-539-8750; www.publictheater.org), between E 4th St. and Astor Pl. [S] 6 to Astor Pl.; N, R, W to 8th St./NYU. Built as a library by J.J. Astor, it now houses 6 venues, which present a wide variety of productions, many exploring political themes. **Shakespeare in the Park** (p. 267) tickets handed out free at the box office 1-3pm during summer. People generally start lining up by 8 or 9am. Limit 2 tickets per person for that night's show only. Advance tickets available for purchase. Box office open M and Su 1-6pm, Tu-Sa 1-7:30pm. Tickets for regular performances $20-50. Student tickets $25. Student rush tickets, available 1hr. before curtain, $20. Limit 2 per person.

Lamb's, 130 W 44th St. (☎212-575-0300, ext. 21; www.lambstheatre.org), between 6th and 7th Ave. [S] 1, 2, 3, 7, 9, N, Q, R, S, W to 42nd St./Times Sq.; B, D, F, V to 42nd St./Ave. of the Americas (6th Ave.). Family-oriented plays and musicals in 2 theaters, 349-seat and 29-seat. Recently featured the hit *A Jew Grows in Brooklyn.* Call or check the website for schedule of events. Tickets $25-35.

Manhattan Theatre Club, at City Center, 131 W 55th St. (☎212-581-1212; www.mtc-nyc.org), between Broadway and 7th Ave. [S] N, Q, R, W to 57th St./7th Ave.; F to 57th St./Ave. of the Americas (6th Ave.); B, D, E to 7th Ave./53rd St. Also hosts productions at Biltmore Theatre, 261 W 47th between Broadway and 8th Ave. A popular venue for new and often critically acclaimed plays. *A Rabbit Hold* starring Cynthia Nixon of *Sex and the City* recently played here. Call or check website for schedule of events. Tickets $45-60.

New York Theatre Workshop, 79 E 4th St. (☎212-460-5475; www.nytw.org), between the Bowery and 2nd Ave. [S] 6 to Astor Pl.; F, V to Lower East Side/2nd Ave.; B, D, F, V to Broadway/Lafayette St. Small 150-seat theater featuring new works and works in progress. Many are pertinent to current politics and world affairs. Tickets $50-60, students $15, seniors $28. Su 7pm show $20; buy in advance on day of show; cash only. Ushers may attend performance for free; call ☎212-780-9037. Wheelchair accessible. Box office open Tu-Su 1-6pm.

Orpheum, 126 2nd Ave. (☎212-477-2477; www.stomponline.com), between E 7th St. and St. Mark's Pl. [S] 6 to Astor Pl. Now playing *Stomp,* a percussive extravaganza using household items for instruments. Shows Tu-F 8pm, Sa 7 and 10:30pm, Su 3 and 7pm. Tickets $35-60. Box office open M 1-6pm, Tu-F 1-7pm, Sa-Su 1-6pm.

Primary Stages, 354 W 45th St. (☎212-840-9705; www.primarystages.com), between 8th and 9th Ave. [S] A, C, E to 42nd St./Port Authority. This theater, opening its 22nd season, features new American plays. Additional performance spaces at 59 E 59th St. and in the Phil Bosakowski Theatre, 354 W 45th St. Box office open M noon-6pm, Tu-Sa noon-8pm, Su noon-3pm.

SoHo Think Tank Ohio Theater, 66 Wooster St. (☎212-966-4844; www.sohothink-tank.org), between Spring and Broome St. S 1 to Canal St./Varick St.; A, C, E to Canal St./6th Ave.; N, Q, R, W to Canal St./Broadway. Provocative pieces combining theater, performance art, dancing, and sketch comedy. Obie Award-winning summer Ice Factory festival offers an array of challenging (and entertaining) works. $15, students and seniors $10. Tickets available from SmartTix (☎212-868-4444; www.smarttix.com). Shows usually W-Sa at 7pm.

Theater for the New City, 155 1st Ave. (☎212-254-1109; www.theaterforthe-newcity.net), between E 9th and 10th St. S 6 to Astor Pl. This prolific cultural center produces 30-40 new American plays per year, many by emerging playwrights. It dispatches a roving theater troupe throughout the city for its Annual Summer Street Theater Tour, which stops primarily in low-income neighborhoods throughout the 5 boroughs; free. Houses an admirably irreverent leftist bookstore. Tickets around $10. Call or check the website for upcoming events and showtimes.

Union Square Theatre, 100 E 17th St. (☎212-505-0700), between Park Ave. and Irving Pl. S 4, 5, 6, L, N, Q, R, W to 14th St./Union Sq. A respectable off-Broadway theater with small capacity and a penchant for off-beat productions. Box office open Tu-Su 1-6pm. Tickets $25-60.

Vineyard Theater Company's Dimson Theatre, 108 E 15th St. (☎212-353-0303; www.vineyardtheatre.org), between 4th Ave. and Irving Pl. S 4, 5, 6, L, N, Q, R, W to 14th St./Union Sq. Vineyard produces bold and idiosyncratic new plays and musicals aimed at a 20-something audience. The original home of Avenue Q, now a popular Broadway hit. The 2006-2007 season includes *The Internationalist*, about living abroad as an American, and *The Agony*. Usher opportunities available. Box office open M-F 1-6pm.

COMEDY CLUBS

Comic Strip Live, 1568 2nd Ave. (☎212-861-9386; www.comicstriplive.com), between 81st and 82nd St. S 4, 5, 6 to 86th St./Lexington Ave. The lobby wall is covered in autographed headshots of all of the comics who have paid their dues at this club. Look for those of Jerry Seinfeld, Eddie Murphy, Paul Reiser, Adam Sandler, and Chris Rock. The batch of jokesters that currently calls this club home includes Tony Rock (Chris's brother), Vanessa Hollingshead, and Mike Britt. 2-drink min. per person per show. New Talent Night Th 6-8pm. 18+. Cover M-Th and Su $15, F-Sa $20. Regular shows M-Th 8:30pm; F 8:30, 10:30pm, and 12:30am; Sa 8, 10:15pm, and 12:30am, Su 8pm. Try to make reservations on M at noon, especially for weekend shows.

Dangerfield's, 1118 1st Ave. (☎212-593-1650; www.dangerfields.com), between 61st and 62nd St. S 4, 5, 6, N, R, W to Lexington Ave./59th St. Rodney's comic-launching pad has been the setting for HBO specials featuring Chris Rock and Jerry Seinfeld. Be prepared for a surprise in the closing act—the lineup is only available the day of the show, and unannounced guest comedians like Dennis Miller and Darrell Hammond frequently drop by to finish the show. Cover M-Th and Su $12.50, F-Sa $15, Sa after 10:30pm $20. Shows M-Th and Su 8:45pm; F 8:30 and 10:30pm; Sa 8, 10:30pm, and 12:30am. Doors open 1hr. before 1st show.

Gotham Comedy Club, 208 W 23rd St. (☎212-367-9000; www.gothamcomedy-club.com), between 7th and 8th Ave. S F, V to 23rd St./Ave. of the Americas (6th Ave.); N, R to 23rd St./Broadway. Upscale comedy club, hosting late-night television regulars and the occasional superstar. Jerry Seinfeld and Roseanne Barr have both made recent appearances. Cover $12-20 with 2-drink min. New talent showcase F 6:30pm and Sa 6pm. Shows M-Th and Su 8:30pm; F 8:30 and 10:30pm; Sa 8, 10, and 11:45pm. 8-week stand-up comedy classes $375.

Stand-Up New York, 236 W 78th St. (☎212-595-0850; www.standupny.com), between Amsterdam Ave. and Broadway. S 1 to 79th St. This stand-up club boasts a star-studded lineup, including current SNL writers. Neighborhood man Jerry Seinfeld got his start here and still does occasional drop-ins, as do Robin Williams and Chris Rock. 18+. Reservations recommended. 2-drink min. ($3.50-11 each). Cover M-Th and Su $15, F-Sa $20. Shows M-Th and Su 9pm; F-Sa 8, 10pm, and midnight. Call about free early shows on some weekend nights.

Rififi, 332 E 11th St. (☎212-677-5368; www.rififinyc.com), between 1st and 2nd Ave. Ⓢ 6 to Astor Pl. This former movie house now hosts a variety of comedy, improv, and burlesque acts with occasional film screenings. All are attended by neighborhood hipsters. Film screenings M at 10pm; admission $6. Comedy daily at 10pm; admission generally $5 or 1-drink min. W is especially popular. Burlesque shows Su and Th at 10pm; $5. DJs spin F and Sa at 10pm. The bar serves beer ($4), mixed drinks ($5), and coffee ($2). Open M-Th and Su 6pm-2am, F-Sa noon-4am.

Upright Citizens Brigade Theatre, 307 W 26th St. (☎212-366-9176; www.ucbtheatre.com), between 8th and 9th Ave. Ⓢ 1 to 23rd St./7th Ave.; F, V to 23rd St./Ave. of the Americas (6th Ave.). Offbeat sketch and improv comedy, as seen on Comedy Central. The original gang shows up for Su performances. 3-4 shows (free-$8) per night (usually 8, 9:30, 11pm). Call or check the website for performance schedule and prices. Reservations recommended for some shows. Also offers improv classes ($325), taught by UCBT veterans, typically running 3hr. per week for 8 weeks.

GENERAL ENTERTAINMENT VENUES

Brooklyn Academy of Music, 30 Lafayette Ave. (☎718-636-4100; www.bam.org), between St. Felix St. and Ashland Pl. Ⓢ 2, 4, 5, Q to Atlantic Ave.; M, N, R, W to Pacific St. Oldest performing arts center in the country, with a colorful history of magnificent performances. Pavlova danced, Caruso sang, and Sarah Bernhardt played here. The venue now focuses on new, non-traditional, multicultural programs, with the occasional classical music performance. Jazz, blues, performance art, opera, film, and dance available. Annual Next Wave Festival (Oct.-Dec.) features contemporary experimental music, dance, theater, and performance art. The Brooklyn Philharmonic performs here Nov.-May. Some opera performances as well; call for schedule. Tickets $20-50. Manhattan Express Bus ("BAM bus") departs from 120 Park Ave., at 42nd St., 1hr. before performances (☎718-636-4100 for info and reservations; round trip $10).

The Kitchen, 512 W 19th St. (☎212-255-5793; www.thekitchen.org), between 10th and 11th Ave. Ⓢ C, E to 23rd St./8th Ave. A world-renowned arts showcase in an unassuming Meatpacking District location. The center features experimental and avant-garde film and video, as well as concerts, dance performances, art exhibits, public lectures, and poetry readings. The Kitchen prides itself on its support of budding or underrepresented artists who are willing to take risks. Ticket prices vary by event. Box office open Tu-Sa 2-6pm.

92nd Street Y, 1395 Lexington Ave. (☎212-996-1100; www.92y.org), at 92nd St. Ⓢ 6 to 96th St. Upper East Side cultural center. The Y's Kaufmann Concert Hall seats only 916 people and offers an intimate setting unmatched by New York's larger halls. Notable series include Jazz in July, Chamber Music at the Y (T and W nights), and Lyrics and Lyricists (M and Sa-Su nights). Also hosts ongoing series of literary readings at the Poetry Center and some of the most engaging lectures in New York—Tony Kushner, Al Franken, E.L. Doctorow, and Anna Quindlen have spoken here. $15-100 for tickets to all events. Visit the website for updated schedules.

ABC No Rio, 156 Rivington St. (☎212-254-3697; www.abcnorio.org), between Clinton and Suffolk St. Ⓢ F, J, M, Z to Delancey St./Essex St. A nonprofit, community-run art space with a vibrant mural marking its entrance. Offers print-making studio, darkrooms, computer labs, and a library. Volunteer-taught classes available most weeknights. Center is open to the public and hosts many community events, from art exhibitions to poetry readings to Sa afternoon hardcore punk matinees. No alcohol or beverages served. Cover $2-5. Call for changing schedule.

Beacon Theatre, 2124 Broadway (☎212-496-7070, tickets ☎212-307-7171 or www.ticketmaster.com), at 74th St. [S] 1, 2, 3 to 72nd St./Broadway. Attached to the Beacon Hotel, this mid-sized venue hosts a variety of music acts, plus performances and plays—everything from the Foo Fighters to His Holiness the Dalai Lama. Call or check website for schedule. Tickets from $35. Box office open M-F 11am-7pm, Sa noon-6pm.

The Bowery Poetry Club, 308 Bowery (☎212-614-0505; www.bowerypoetry.com), between Houston and Bleecker St. [S] F, V to Lower East Side/2nd Ave.; 6 to Bleecker St. Poetry for the people, and we mean all people—everything from an Emily Dickinson Marathon to a Beatbox Summit. During the day, readings and workshops are complemented with cupcakes ($3), sandwiches ($7-8), and coffee ($1.50) from the cafe. At night, the poetry gets increasingly opaque as you indulge in beers at the bar ($4-6). 3-5 events per day. Cover free-$10. Check the website for the schedule. Open M-F 9am until the last show ends, Sa-Su 11am until the last show ends.

Brooklyn Center for Performing Arts, 2900 Campus Rd. and Hillel Place (☎718-951-4500 or 718-951-4600; www.brooklyncenter.com), 1 block west of the junction of Flatbush and Nostrand Ave., on the campus of Brooklyn College. [S] 2, 5 to Flatbush Ave./Brooklyn College. Ray Charles, Luciano Pavarotti, and Harry Belafonte have performed at this neighborhood favorite, founded in 1954. A wide range of projects grace the Art Deco Walt Whitman Stage every year, including Su Broadway shows, ballets, Caribbean dance, and performances by Brooklyn College's theater and music departments. Season Oct.-May. Wheelchair accessible. Tickets usually $15-40. 3-event subscriptions ($60-144) available for the Broadway, Dance, Celebrities, Virtuoso, and Caribbean Celebration series. Less expensive student rush tickets are also available. Box office open Tu-Sa 1-6pm and 1hr. before performances.

Cathedral of St. John the Divine (☎212-662-2133). See p. 193 for directions. This beautiful church offers an array of concerts, exhibits, lectures, plays, movies, and dance events. The NY Philharmonic performs here on occasion. Saxophonist Paul Winter gives annual Summer and Winter Solstice concerts. Prices vary. Box office open M-F 10am-2pm, Sa-Su 9am-5pm.

Cultural Institutes: These cultural centers are valuable for their libraries, small but interesting exhibits, classes, and lectures. Some services are only open to members, but all the institutes have useful lists of cultural events throughout the city.

French Institute Alliance Française, Florence Gould Hall, 22 E 60th St. (☎212-355-6160 or 212-307-4100; www.fiaf.org), between Park and Madison Ave. [S] 4, 5, 6 to 59th St.; N, R, W to 5th Ave. This cultural arm of the French Embassy offers lectures, classes, programs, and films. Admission varies according to event, but most are inexpensive and give discounts to members. Film tickets available day of screening at box office from 11am. Doors open 20min. before screening. Box office open Tu-F 11am-7pm, Sa-Su 11am-3pm.

Americas Society, 680 Park Ave. (☎212-628-8950; www.americas-society.org/as), between 68th and 69th St. [S] 6 to 68th St./Hunter College. Concerts and visual arts exhibitions showcasing North and South American photographers, experimental art, and famous names in music. Other educational programs also offered. Gallery admission free. Exhibits rotate bimonthly. Concerts are sometimes free, and almost always inexpensive. Gallery open Tu-Su noon-6pm; call for event schedule.

Asia Society (p. 231) Shows films from or about Asia. Call for schedule and ticket info.

China Institute, 125 E 65th St. (☎212-744-8181; www.chinainstitute.org), between Park and Lexington Ave. [S] 6 to 68th St./Hunter College. Promotes the understanding of Chinese culture and history through classes (including calligraphy, painting, and language), lectures, performances, and film series. Gallery showcases a broad spectrum of Chinese art and architecture from the Neolithic period to the present. Gallery open M, W, F-Sa 10am-5pm; Tu and Th 10am-8pm. Closed major holidays and between exhibitions. $5, students and seniors $3, children under 12 free; Tu and Th 6-8pm free. Call ahead or visit website for present schedules.

Goethe-Institut, 1014 5th Ave. (☎212-439-8700; www.goethe.de), between 82nd and 83rd St. Ⓢ 6 to 77th St.; 4, 5, 6 to 86th St. Imports Germanic culture via films, concerts, classes, and lectures. Many events and exhibits free. Closed much of July-Aug. Office open M-Th 9am-5:30pm, F 9am-4:15pm. Library open Tu and Th noon-7pm, W and F-Sa noon-5pm. Gallery hours depend on current exhibition.

Italian Cultural Institute, 686 Park Ave. (☎212-879-4242; www.iicnewyork.esteri.it), between 68th and 69th St. Ⓢ 6 to 68th St./Hunter College. Library open M-F 1-4pm. Reading room and institute open M-F 9am-1pm and 2-4pm.

Spanish Institute, 684 Park Ave. (☎212-628-0420; www.spanishinstitute.org), between 68th and 69th St. Ⓢ 6 to 68th St./Hunter College. Housed in a 1927 landmark townhouse, the institute was founded in 1954 to promote Spanish culture through lectures, symposia, language, and translation. Most events and lectures free; check the website for the schedule. Open M-F 10am-6pm, Sa 10am-5pm.

Knitting Factory, 74 Leonard St. (☎212-219-3006; www.knittingfactory.com), between Broadway and Church St. Ⓢ 1 to Franklin St. This multi-level performance space features several shows each night, ranging from avant-garde and indie rock to jazz and hip-hop. There are 2 shows nightly—one at the bar, one on the main stage. Cover $5-25. Tickets are available online, by phone, or at the box office (most from $8). Box office open M-Sa 10am-2am, Su 2pm-2am. Bar open 6pm-4am.

Merkin Concert Hall, 129 W 67th St. (☎212-501-3330; www.merkinconcerthall.org), between Broadway and Amsterdam Ave. Ⓢ 1 to 66th St. An intimate theater known as "the little hall with the big sound," this division of the Elaine Kaufman Cultural Center features an eclectic mix of blues, jazz, classical, and world music along with the occasional play or book reading. Season Sept.-June. Tickets usually $10-35. Advance student tickets available at the discretion of individual programs, generally on a half-price basis. Half-price rush tickets for full-time students also available 30min. before most performances; cash only. Box office open Jan.-Oct. M-Th and Su noon-7pm, F noon-4pm; Nov.-Dec. M-Th and Su noon-7pm, F 3pm-close.

The Point, 940 Garrison Ave. (☎718-542-4139; www.thepoint.org), at the corner of Manida St., the Bronx. Ⓢ 6 to Hunts Point Ave. This venue houses a growing artistic community and is home to dancer/choreographer Arthur Aviles. Unfortunately, it sits on the border of one of NY's poorest neighborhoods. Monthly Latin jazz and hip-hop performances; studio facilities; a theater; summer programs for neighborhood youth; and art classes. Community-based efforts like the annual South Bronx Film and Video Festival. Call or check online for events. Films generally $12. Open M-F 8:30am-7pm, Sa 10am-5pm.

HOT TIME, SUMMER IN THE CITY

When temperatures soar, many New Yorkers flee the concrete jungle for the sea breezes of Long Island. But even though summer in New York can be sweltering, it's still an excellent time to visit. Free cultural events abound, and museums and sights stay open late to accommodate the crowds. Here are some favorite summertime diversions:

1. Shakespeare in the Park. Morgan Freeman, Meryl Streep, Natalie Portman, and Denzel Washington have all headlined these free performances in Central Park's Delacorte Theater. The Public Theater stages two productions each summer, each running for three to four weeks (p. 267).

2. Bryant Park Film Festival. From late June to late August, HBO sponsors this free Monday-night film festival (p. 248). Picnickers lounge in front of a big screen showing classics like *Rocky*, *M*A*S*H*, and *The Birds*.

3. Midsummer Night Swing. Every night from late June to late July, Lincoln Center hosts outdoor dance parties at the Josie Robertson Plaza. Live bands play everything from salsa to swing to funk; group dance lessons begin at 6:15pm and live music and dancing run from 7:30-10pm.

4. Philharmonic Concerts in the Parks. Over the course of a week in mid-July, the New York Philharmonic offers a series of free concerts in parks throughout the five boroughs (p. 250).

Radio City Music Hall, 1260 6th Ave. (☎212-307-7171; www.radiocity.com), at 50th St. [S] B, D, F, V 47th-50th St./Rockefeller Center. See p. 181 for directions. The list of entertainers who have performed here reads like an invitation to the Music Hall of Fame: Ella Fitzgerald, Frank Sinatra, Ringo Starr, and Elton John, among others. The auditorium also hosts readings by the likes of Stephen King, J.K. Rowling, and John Irving. Tickets generally start around $35. Box office open M-Sa 10am-8pm, Su 11am-8pm; in summer M-Sa 11:30am-6pm.

St. Ann's Warehouse, 38 Water St. (☎718-254-8779; www.artsatstanns.org, tickets www.ticketweb.com), near Dock St. [S] A, C to High St.; F to York St. In 2001, Arts at St. Ann's moved from the Church of St. Ann and the Holy Trinity in Brooklyn Heights to its current warehouse in DUMBO, transforming this venue into a full-out theater and performance space. The theater is home to the renowned "Puppet Lab" that holds the annual spring Labapalooza! showcasing new projects and interdisciplinary collaborations. Volunteer ushers see shows for free; call ☎718-254-9601 or email housemanager@artsatanns.org for info. Check website for upcoming performances and prices. Main office at 70 Washington St. (☎718-834-8794, ext. 10). Box office open Tu-Sa 1-7pm and from 1pm until 1hr. before performances on show days.

St. Mark's Church in-the-Bowery, 131 E 10th St. (☎212-674-6377; www.stmarks-church-in-the-bowery.com), between 2nd and 3rd Ave. [S] 6 to Astor Pl. Home to the **Ontological-Hysteric Theater** (☎212-420-1916; www.ontological.com), **Danspace Project** (☎212-674-8112; www.danspaceproject.org), and **Poetry Project** (☎212-674-0910; www.poetryproject.com). While the Ontological Theater pioneered the wackiness of playwright Richard Foreman, Danspace has provided a venue for emerging dancers and experimental styles of movement since the 1920s. Isadora Duncan and Martha Graham danced here. Poetry Project stages regular evening readings Sept.-May. For info on upcoming events, call, check the websites, or look for notices outside the church. Tickets for Danspace usually $15; Poetry Project $8, students and seniors $7.

Symphony Space, 2537 Broadway (☎212-864-5400; www.symphonyspace.org), at W 95th St. [S] 1, 2, 3 to 96th St./Broadway. This diverse performing arts venue showcases film festivals, world music ensembles, classical orchestras, modern dance, and readings by authors such as David Sedaris and Walter Mosley. Before and after performances, check out the Barocco at the Thalia Cafe, chow on Mediterranean sandwiches, and mingle with performers. Most movies $10, seniors $8. Other events $15-32. Student/senior discounts often available—call ahead for individual performances. Tickets available online. Box office open Tu-Su noon-7pm.

World Financial Center (☎212-417-7000; www.worldfinancialcenter.com), in Battery Park City. See p. 159 for directions. A variety of festivals are held here year-round in the Winter Garden and in Rockefeller Park, but they are more common during the summer. Free concerts by big-name performers like Lyle Lovett. Check online for schedule.

FESTIVALS

👍 **Central Park Summerstage,** at the Rumsey Playfield (☎212-360-2777; www.summerstage.org), at 72nd St., near 5th Ave., in Central Park. See p. 185 for directions. Mid-June to mid-Sept., Summerstage hosts free concerts, dance performances, and spoken word events. Past performers have included Ben Folds, Courtney Love, Rufus Wainwright, Damien Rice, and The Strokes. Big names from all genres, but also an outstanding selection of up-and-coming performers.

👍 **Lincoln Center Festival** (☎212-875-5928; www.lincolncenter.org), box office at Avery Fisher Hall, Lincoln Center. See p. 192 for directions. Cutting-edge dance, theater, opera, and music events throughout the Lincoln Center complex in July. Tickets vary in price depending on the performance; $30-200. Students can buy up to 2 advance tickets for $20 at the Avery Fisher Hall or Alice Tulley Hall box offices.

Lincoln Center Out-of-Doors (☎212-875-5108; www.lincolncenter.org). See p. 192 for directions. For 3 weeks in Aug., Lincoln Center sponsors a completely free performance arts festival, with an emphasis on jazz and activities for the kids. Performances run the gamut from Brazilian dance to Chinese opera.

LIVE TELEVISION

For free tickets to live tapings of your favorite television shows, go to www.tvtickets.com—or check with the relevant network via telephone or the Internet.

👍 **The Daily Show (Comedy Central),** 513 W 54th St. (www.comedycentral.com), at 10th Ave. [S] 1, A, B, C, D to 59th St./Columbus Circle. To request tickets, email requesttickets@thedailyshow.com. Last-minute tickets are available by calling ☎212-586-2477 F 11-11:30am the week before desired show. Show tapes M-Th. 18+, ID required. Doors open 5pm.

👍 **The Colbert Report (Comedy Central),** 513 W 54th St. (www.comedycentral.com). [S] 1, A, B, C, D to 59th St./Columbus Circle. Check website for instructions. 18+, ID required. Standby tickets sometimes available; arrive early.

Late Night with Conan O'Brien (NBC) (☎212-664-3056), [S] B, D, F, V to Rockefeller Center, in the G.E. Building at Rockefeller Center. See p. 181 for directions. For reservations, call the NBC ticket office several months ahead of time. Advance reservations limited to 4 tickets per group. For standby tickets, arrive no later than 9am on the morning of the taping, under the "NBC Studios" marquee at the 49th St. entrance of 30 Rockefeller Pl. 1 ticket per person. Standby tickets do not guarantee admission. 16+, ID required. No large bags.

Late Show with David Letterman (CBS), Ed Sullivan Theater, 1697 Broadway (☎212-975-1003; www.cbs.com/latenight), at 53rd St. [S] E to 7th Ave./53rd St. Tickets can be requested in person at the CBS lobby M-F 9:30am-12:30pm, Sa-Su 10am-6pm. Lining up prior to 9am not permitted. Tickets can be requested online; recipients will be notified by phone. Waiting time may be over 9 months. Tapings M-Th. Stand-by tickets available on the day of the show by calling ☎212-247-6497 at 11am. Phones will be answered until allocation is gone. Only 2 tickets will be issued per caller; the recipient must have ID to match the name given when calling. 18+. Ticketing may be subject to answering a trivia question about The Late Show. If you do get tickets, bring a sweater–the studio is notoriously cold.

Live with Regis and Kelly (ABC), W 67th St. and Columbus Ave. (☎212-456-7777). [S] 1 to 66th St. This is one of the only shows that still distributes tickets by mail. Send a postcard with your name, address, phone number, approximate date of the show you'd like to attend, and your request for up to 4 tickets to: "Live with Regis and Kelly" Tickets, Ansonia Station, P.O. Box 230-777, New York, NY 10023-0777. Wait may be up to 12 months. For standby tickets, arrive no later than 6:30am on the day of the show at W 67th St. and Columbus Ave. (7 Lincoln Sq.).

Saturday Night Live (NBC) (☎212-664-3056). [S] B, D, F, V to Rockefeller Center, in the G.E. Building at Rockefeller Center. See p. 181 for directions. SNL on hiatus June-Aug. Enter ticket lottery by sending an email to snltickets@nbcuni.com in Aug. If selected, you will get 2 tickets to a random week's show. Limit 2 tickets per household. For standby tickets, arrive no later than 7am on the morning of the taping, under the "NBC Studios" marquee at the 49th St. entrance of 30 Rockefeller Pl. You may choose a standby ticket for either the 8pm dress rehearsal or the 11:30pm live show. Only 1 ticket per person. Standby tickets do not guarantee admission. 16+.

OUTDOOR THEATERS

👍 **Shakespeare in the Park** (☎212-539-8750; www.publictheater.org). See p. 185 for directions. This renowned series is a New York summer tradition, presenting one Shakespeare play each summer from mid-June to early Aug. at the outdoor Delacorte amphitheater in Central Park. Past stars have included Sean Patrick Thomas, Sam Waterson, Jeff Goldblum, Morgan Freeman, Natalie Portman, Christopher Walken, Denzel Washington, Meryl Streep, Patrick Stewart, and the late Sir John Gielgud. Tickets available 1pm the day of performance at the Delacorte and 1-3pm at the Public Theatre at 425 Lafayette St.; try to get there by 9am at the latest. Standby line forms at 6pm. Limit 2 tickets per person. Doors open Tu-Su 7:30pm; shows at 8pm.

Queens Theatre in the Park (☎ 718-760-0064; www.queenstheatre.org), in the New York State Pavilion in Flushing Meadows/Corona Park. See p. 211 for directions. Film and performing arts center that hosts the annual Latino Cultural Festival (late July to mid-Aug.), among other events. Call for dance and theater listings. Box office open Tu-Sa noon-6pm. Tickets also available online.

SPORTS

SPECTATOR SPORTS

BASEBALL

Founded in 1903, the **New York Yankees**—the team of Joe DiMaggio, Whitey Ford, Mickey Mantle, Babe Ruth, and Lou Gehrig— are baseball's most storied franchise. Possessing 26 world championships and 36 American League pennants, the Bronx Bombers have won more titles than any other team in American sports. The team plays ball at **Yankee Stadium** in the Bronx. See p. 213 for directions to stadium. (☎ 718-293-4300. Tickets $12-115 usually available day of game; you can also find them on the web at www.ticketmaster.com.)

Created in 1962 to replace the much-mourned Dodgers (who had moved to California after the 1957 season), the **New York Mets** (short for "Metropolitans") set the still-unbroken major league record for losses in a season during their first year. Seven years later, however, the "Miracle Mets" captured the World Series. See p. 211 for information about the Mets' home, **Shea Stadium** (☎ 718-507-6387; tickets $5-70).

BASKETBALL

The **New York Knicks** do their regular season dribbling at **Madison Square Garden** (☎ 212-465-5867; see p. 178) from early November to late April. Tickets start at $10 and are nearly impossible to come by unless you order well in advance. The Garden plays host to Big East Conference contender **St. John's Red Storm** during the winter and the **NIT** and **Big East** tournaments in March. Also playing at the Garden are the **New York Liberty** (☎ 212-564-9622) of the WNBA. The season runs from June to August; tickets start at $10.

FOOTBALL

Both the New York **Giants** and **Jets** teams play across the Hudson at **Giants Stadium** (☎ 201-935-3900) in East Rutherford, New Jersey. Tickets are nigh impossible to get—season ticket holders have booked them all for the next 40 years, and the waiting list holds over 15,000 people. Befriend a fan, or view the action from a local sports bar.

HOCKEY

The **New York Rangers** hit the ice at Madison Square Garden. (MSG ☎ 212-465-6741, Rangers ☎ 212-308-6977. See p. 178 for directions. Season Oct.-Apr. Tickets, on sale Aug., start at $25; reserve well in advance.) The **New York Islanders** hang their skates at the Nassau Coliseum in Uniondale, Long Island. (☎ 516-794-9300. Season Oct.-Apr. Tickets $27-70.)

HORSE RACING

Fans seeking equine excitement can watch the stallions at **Belmont Park.** (☎718-641-4700; www.nyra.com/belmont. See p. 215 for directions. Races May-July and Sept. to mid-Oct. W-Su. Tickets $2-5.) The **Belmont Stakes,** run the first Saturday in June, is one leg in the Triple Crown. (The "Belmont Special" train leaves Penn Station twice per day. $11 round-trip, $15 if bought onboard.) The **Aqueduct Racetrack** (www.nyra.com/aqueduct), near JFK Airport, has races from late October to early May. (☎718-641-4700. [S] A to Aqueduct. Races W-Su. Tickets $1-2.)

SOCCER

Soccer's recent rise in popularity has culminated in the birth of **Major League Soccer.** New Yorkers turn out to see the **New York Red Bulls** play at **Giants Stadium,** 50 Rte. 120, East Rutherford, NJ. (Tickets ☎888-4-METROTIX or 888-463-8768. Season late Mar. to early Sept. $20-38.) The Port Authority Bus Terminal in Manhattan, at Eighth Ave. and 41st St., offers bus service (20min.) to Giants Stadium. (1st bus from New York leaves 2hr. in advance of the game; last one departs 30min. after event begins. Return service to New York begins immediately after game ends and continues to operate for up to 30min. after the event. Round-trip $6.50. For more information, contact New Jersey Transit ☎800-772-2222.)

TENNIS

Tennis enthusiasts who get their tickets three months in advance can attend the prestigious **US Open,** one of tennis's four Grand Slam events, held in late August and early September at the United States Tennis Association (USTA) Tennis Center in Flushing Meadows Park, Queens. See p. 210 for directions. (☎718-760-6200. On sale by early June; call ☎866-673-6849. Tickets from $22.)

LEISURE SPORTS AND ACTIVITIES

Although space in much of the city is at a premium, the **City of New York Parks and Recreation Department** (☎800-201-PARK/7275 for a recording of park events) manages to maintain numerous parks in all boroughs, for everything from baseball and basketball to croquet and shuffleboard. Activities are listed in alphabetical order.

BASKETBALL

Basketball is one of New York's favorite pastimes. Courts can be found in parks and playgrounds all over the city, and are frequently occupied. Pickup basketball games can be found throughout the city, each with its own rituals, rules, and degree of intensity. **The Cage,** at W Fourth and Sixth Ave., is home to some of the city's best amateur players: rumor has it that scouts for college and pro teams occasionally drop by incognito to ferret out new talent. Other pickup spots worth checking out include Central Park, 96th and Lexington Ave., Tompkins Sq. Park, and 76th and Columbus Ave.

BEACHES

Manhattan Beach (¼ mi. long), on the Atlantic Ocean. Ocean Ave. to Mackenzie St. in Brooklyn (☎718-946-1373). [S] D to Brighton Beach; then bus B1.

Orchard Beach and Promenade, in the Bronx's Pelham Bay Park (☎718-885-2275). [S] 6 to Pelham Bay Park; then bus Bx5 (summer weekends only) or Bx12 (summer only) to Orchard Beach. Despite being manmade, this is a pretty 1¼ mi. sandy stretch facing Long Island Sound. Mobbed by snack stands and sun-seekers on hot summer days. 26 courts for basketball, volleyball, and handball available for pickup games. Lifeguards keep watch Memorial Day to Labor Day daily 10am-6pm. Excellent picnic area with grills in the grassy area behind beach.

Rockaway Beach and Boardwalk (7½ mi. long), on the Atlantic Ocean (☎ 718-318-4000). See p. 212 for directions. Lifeguards Memorial Day-Labor Day daily 10am-6pm. **Staten Island: South Beach, Midland Beach,** and **Franklin D. Roosevelt Boardwalk** (2½ mi.), on Lower New York Bay. Bus S51 from the ferry terminal (20min.). Touted as one of NYC's best beaches, South Beach offers spectacular views of the Narrows. Due to possible pollution, swimming after heavy rainfall is not recommended.

BICYCLING

Packs of cyclists navigate the wide roads of **Park Drive,** a six-mile circular loop in Central Park. The road is car-free Monday-Thursday 10am-3pm and 7-10pm, Friday 10am-3pm, and Friday 7pm until Monday 6am. Up the west side of Manhattan, the Hudson River bike trail beginning in Battery Park is another popular ride. Other excellent places to cycle on the weekends include the well-paved paths of **Pelham Bay Park** in the Bronx and the unadorned roads of Brooklyn's **Prospect Park.** If you must leave your bike unattended, use a strong "U" lock. Thieves laugh at (and then cut through) chain locks. Don't leave quick-release items unattended; you will find them very quickly released. If you're in the area, don't miss the **Five Borough Bike Ride** sponsored by **Bike New York** (☎ 212-932-2453; www.bikenewyork.org) in May. This bike ride through all five boroughs on traffic-free roads, alongside 28,000 other cyclists, is a two-decade springtime tradition. Visit www.transalt.org for maps and suggested bicycle routes throughout the city.

Metro Bicycle Stores (☎ 212-427-4450; www.metrobicycles.com), on Lexington Ave. at 88th St. Seven convenient locations throughout the city, including Canal Street Bicycles at 417 Canal St. and Midtown Bicycles at 360 W 47th St. Entry-level mountain bikes and hybrids. $7 per hr., $35 per day, $45 overnight. Helmet rental $2.50 per bike. Daily rentals due back 30min. before store closes; overnight rentals next day at 10am. Credit card and valid ID required. All stores have different hours; consult website. Lexington Ave. location open spring/summer M-Sa 9:30am-6:30pm (Th until 7pm), Su 9:30am-6pm. Consult website for low-season hours.

Pedal Pushers, 1306 2nd Ave. (☎ 212-288-5592; www.pedalpusherbikeshop.com), at E 69th St. Ⓢ 6 to 68th St. All bikes $6 per hr., $25 per day. Helmet an extra $4 per day, or free with online coupon. Central Park audio tours ($10) with CD or cassette player. Rentals require a major credit card. Open M and W-Su 10am-6pm.

BOATING

You can rent rowboats at the Loeb Boathouse in **Central Park.** See p. 185 for directions. (☎ 212-517-2233. $10 for the first hr., $2.50 for each additional 15min.; refundable $30 deposit. Up to 5 people per boat. Open daily Mar.-Oct., 10am-5pm, weather permitting.) "Authentic Venetian gondola rides" are also available from the Loeb Boathouse during the summer months, weather permitting. (☎ 212-517-2233. $30 for 30min. M-F 5-9pm, Sa-Su 9am-4:30pm.)

BOWLING

Bowlmor Lanes, 110 University Pl. (☎ 212-255-8188; www.bowlmor.com), between 12th and 13th St. Ⓢ 4, 5, 6, L, N, R, Q, W to 14th St.-Union Sq. Bowling, music, food, and alcohol all in one place. Watch your game deteriorate as you knock a couple back with the NYU crowd. On M nights $20 gets you shoes, DJ-ed music, glow-in-the dark pins, and all-you-can-bowl. $8 per game M-Th, F $9, Sa $9.25, and Su $9. Shoe rental $5. Imported beer $7, domestic $5.25. Wraps and salads $7-9. 21+ after 5pm. Open M 11am-3am, Tu-W 11am-1am, Th 11am-2am, F-Sa 11am-4am, Su 11am-midnight.

CLIMBING

ExtraVertical Climbing Center, The Harmony Atrium on Broadway (☎212-586-5718; www.extravertical.com), on the left side of the street between 62nd and 63rd St. ⓢ A, B, C, D, 1 to Columbus Circle. Let out your frustrations on 3000 sq. ft. of climbing area in the heart of Manhattan. Locker rooms, gear rental, and assistance available. Day pass $20, $15 with student ID. Special $10 days for women, men, and couples listed on website. Harness rental for day pass holders $4. One-time climb with staff assistance and harness $9, additional climbs $5. Longer packages and group rates available. Open M-F 3-10pm, Sa-Su noon-8pm.

North Meadow Recreation Center (☎212-348-4867), at 97th St. in Central Park. See p. 185 for directions. 4-week courses (every Sa 10am-1pm) $200 per person. Call for reservations. For ages 8-17, the 4-week course is just $25, and allows free climbing during youth open climbing hours (Su 11am-1pm) and the use of equipment. Adults who have completed their course are permitted to climb free during adult open sessions (Th 5:30pm-closing, Su 1-4:30pm) for a one-time $50 fee. Day pass $5. Call ☎212-348-4687x10 for details.

GOLF

There are 13 well-manicured city golf courses. Most are found in the Bronx or Queens, such as **Pelham Bay Park** (☎718-885-1258; see p. 217), **Van Cortlandt Park** (☎718-543-4595; see p. 216), and **Forest Park** (☎718-296-0999; see p. 212). Greens fees are approximately $12-29 for NYC residents and $17-35 for non-NYC residents, depending on time of day and week. Reserve at least one week in advance for summer weekends. Long Island is home to some of the country's best public courses; **Bethpage** (☎516-249-7000) also features five top-notch ones. The Black course hosted the 2002 U.S. Open won by Tiger Woods. On the eastern tip of Long Island is **Montauk Downs** (☎631-668-5000), which is among the country's top 50 public courses.

HORSEBACK RIDING

Central Park horseback riding, for those well-versed in English equitation, operates out of **Claremont Stables,** 175 W 89th St., between Columbus and Amsterdam Ave. (☎212-724-5100. $50 per hr. Make reservations. Open daily 1hr. after sunrise to 1hr. before sunset.) **Lynne's Riding School,** 88-03 70th Rd. offers guided trail rides in Forest Park. (☎718-261-7679. ⓢ J, Z to Woodhaven Blvd. $25 per hr. Open M-F 9am-4:30pm, Sa-Su 9am-6pm. Call and make an appointment.)

ICE-SKATING

Each of the rinks in the city has its own character. Nearly all have lockers, skate rentals, and a snack bar.

Skating Rink, Rockefeller Center (☎212-332-7654; www.therinkatrockcenter.com). ⓢ B, D, F, V to 47th-50th St./Rockefeller Center/Ave. of the Americas (6th Ave.). One of the best first-date options in a city full of romantic possibilities. Skate rental $7. Admission M-Th $9, children and seniors $7; F-Su and holidays $13/8). Private lessons available from $30 per person per 30min. Especially beautiful in the holiday season, when the Christmas tree is lit in the plaza. Open Oct.-Apr.

Sky Rink at Chelsea Piers (☎212-336-6100), at W 21st St. and the Hudson River. See p. 173 for directions. Learn to skate or practice on 1 of the 2 full-sized indoor Olympic ice rinks. Adults $11, children under 13 and seniors $8.50; free June Su 1-3:50pm. Skate rentals $6, helmet $3.25. Open mid-June to Aug. M, W, F 12:30-2:20pm, Sa-Su noon-3:50pm; Sept. to mid-June M-W and F 1:30-5:20pm, Th 1:30-4:50pm, Sa-Su 1-3:50pm.

ENTERTAINMENT

Trump Wollman Rink (☎212-439-6900; www.wollmanskatingrink.com). See p. 185 for directions. Located in a particularly scenic section of Central Park, near 64th St. M-F $8.50, Sa-Su $11; children $4.25/4.50. Skate rental $4.75. Open late Oct.-Apr.

IN-LINE SKATING

There are many in-line skate rental locations throughout the city. For low prices and convenience, **Blades** (☎212-996-1644) has three stores in the Metropolitan area. (Flat rate $20; includes all protective gear. $200 deposit or credit is required. Open M-Sa 11am-8pm, Su 11am-6pm.) Blades also has various sister stores that feature the same prices and conditions—**Peck and Goodie Skates,** 917 Eighth Ave., between 54th and 55th St. (☎212-246-6123), will also hold your shoes while you whiz past your favorite New York sights. They also offer private lessons for a fee of $40 per hr. (Open M-Sa 10am-8pm, Su 10am-6pm.) Good places to skate in the city include Battery Park, West St. between Christopher to Horatio St., Chelsea Piers, and East River Promenade between 60th and 81st St. Central Park has several roller zones including the Outer Loop, a slalom course near Tavern on the Green.

RUNNING

When running in **Central Park** during no-traffic hours (see **Bicycling,** above), stay in the right-hand runners' lane to avoid being mowed down by reckless pedal-pushers. Stay in populated areas and stay out of the park after dark. Recommended courses include the 1½ mi. soft-surface track around the **Jacqueline Kennedy Onassis Reservoir** (between 84th and 96th St.) and a picturesque 1¾ mi. route along West Dr., starting at Tavern on the Green, heading south to East Dr., and circling back west on 72nd St. Another beautiful place to run is **Riverside Park,** which stretches along the Hudson River bank from 72nd to 116th St.; don't stray too far north. A six-mile jog along the East River from 63rd St. to 125th St. will take you past Gracie Mansion, fishermen, and river-view highrises. For information on running clubs, clinics, and racing events around the city, call the **New York Roadrunner's Club,** 9 E 89th St. (☎212-860-4455; www.nyrr.org), between Madison and Fifth Ave. They host races in Central Park on summer weekends. If you're serious about running, don't miss the **New York City Marathon.** On the first Sunday in November, spectators line rooftops, sidewalks, and promenades to cheer 22,000 runners (16,000 racers actually finish). The November 3 race begins on the Verrazano Bridge and ends at Central Park's Tavern on the Green. Call the **NY Roadrunner's Club** (contact info above) for info on signing up.

SWIMMING

Two of the city's nicer pools include **John Jay Pool**, east of York Ave. at 77th St. (☎212-794-6566), and **Asser Levy Pool** at E 23rd St. and Asser Levy Pl. (☎212-447-2020), next to the East River. Ⓢ to John Jay Pool: 6 to 77th St. Pool is four blocks east from station. Ⓢ to Asser Levy Pool: 6 to 23rd St./Lexington Ave. Walk five blocks east from station. Both pools listed above are safe, clean and free but you must bring your own lock and a proper bathing suit, although Asser Levy's heated indoor pool is open only to members. All outdoor pools are open early July through Labor Day, 11am or noon to 7pm, depending on the weather. Call ☎800-201-7275 for other locations. Indoor pools can be somewhat safer than outdoor pools, but most require some sort of annual membership fee ($10 or more).

FITNESS

Membership at most of New York City's swank gyms is high-priced. Cheaper alternatives include public fitness centers and YMCA/YWCAs. **Public fitness centers,** or recreation centers, are run by the city government and feature most of the amenities, classes, and equipment of the brand-name gyms. Membership is an astounding $10-75 per *year* and there are over 30 branches throughout the city.

MANHATTAN

92nd Street Y, 1395 Lexington Ave. (☎212-415-5729; www.92y.org), at 92nd St. Ⓢ 6 to 96th St. The Y offers spinning, dance aerobics, weight training, acquacise, Pilates, yoga, kickboxing, Tai Chi, swimming, racquetball, and self-defense. Most classes $100-200 for 10 sessions. Call or check online for schedule.

Asphalt Green, 555 E 90th St. (☎212-369-8890; www.asphaltgreen.org), at York Ave. Ⓢ 4, 5, 6 to 86th St. A massive multi-story fitness facility offering over 50 exercise classes weekly, including belly dancing, cycling, yoga, kickboxing, Pilates, Tai Chai, and strength training. Also includes a state-of-the-art fitness center and Olympic-sized swimming pool as well as a new outdoor pool. Call for membership rates and information. Open M-F 5:30am-10pm, Sa-Su 8am-8pm.

Bikram Yoga, 182 5th Ave. (☎212-206-9400; www.bikramyoganyc.com), 3rd floor. between 22nd and 23rd St. Bikram (hot) yoga studio offers 3-5 classes daily, starting as early as 6:45am, and as late as 8pm. For yogis of all levels. Single class $20; 5 classes $90; 1-month unlimited pass $175; 3-month $500. Mat rental $5. Additional locations at 173 E 83rd), 208 W 72nd St. and 797 8th Avenue.

Crunch Gym, 1109 2nd Ave. (☎212-758-3434; www.crunch.com), at 59th St. Ⓢ 4, 5, 6, N, R, W to 59th/Lexington Ave. The largest branch of the popular fitness chain, this outpost of Crunch Gyms offers a full range of cardio and strength-training machines, as well as a staggering number of classes. You can try cardio tai box, capoeira, belly dancing, ballet pilates, bikini bootcamp, "cardio striptease," and African dance, amidst a host of others. Day pass $24; or bring your hotel or hostel keys and pay only $16. $1 towel deposit, bring your own lock. Open M-Th 5am-11pm, F 5am-10pm, Sa-Su 8am-9pm. 18+.

Dance Forum, 20 E 17th St. (☎212-633-7202; www.danceforum.org), 2nd floor, between 5th and 6th Ave. Nonprofit dance studio and performance space. Offers BodiBalance classes, designed to condition the bodies of performance artists and dancers. Single class $15, 10 classes $140. Space also available for rent. Call or check the website for a calendar of class types and times.

Equinox Fitness Clubs, 2465 Broadway (☎212-799-1818; www.equinoxfitness.com), at 92nd St. Ⓢ 1, 2, 3 to 96th St. This souped-up branch of the popular fitness facility boasts a health cafe, childcare, yoga, Pilates, the full range of Precor machines, massages, dance classes, and a juice bar. A $25-35 day pass gives you full use of the gym, admission to all classes, and use of the locker room. Open M-Th 5:30am-11pm, F 5:30am-10pm, Sa-Su 8am-9pm. See website for schedules and other locations.

Harlem YMCA, 180 W 135th St. (☎212-281-4100; www.ymcanyc.org), between Lenox (Sixth) Ave. and Adam Clayton Powell, Jr. Blvd. Opened in 1932 under the YMCA's official segregation policy (which didn't end until 1946), this "colored Men's Branch" is steeped in history. Famous African Americans from Jackie Robinson to Sidney Poitier to Malcolm X have been involved in the YMCA. A designated landmark, the center now boasts impressive fitness resources, including a cardiovascular center, boxing studio, free-weight room, steam room, sauna and two heated pools. African dance, mambo, salsa, yoga, tai-chi, karate and belly-dancing classes are offered, as well as more traditional step and aerobics. Day pass $12; annual membership around $400. Rooms are also available; from $50 per night. Open M-F 6am-11pm, Sa 6am-8pm, Su 10am-4pm.

Integral Yoga Institute, 227 W 13th St. (☎212-229-0586; www.integralyogany.org), between 7th and 8th Ave. Ⓢ 1, 2, 3 to 14th St./Seventh Ave.; A, C, E, L to 14th St./Eighth Ave. Drop-in Hatha yoga classes at introductory, intermediate, and advanced levels, as well as special prenatal, postpartum, Spanish-language, and HIV/AIDS classes. Classes last 60-105 min. and are offered daily 7:15am-8:30pm; call or check the website for times. Single class $15 (includes mat); 5-class pass $70; 10-class pass $130; 20-class pass $220. $50 cards gets all-you-can-yoga for 7 days. HIV classes $7 or by donation. Seniors receive 50% discount.

J. Hood Wright, 351 Ft. Washington Ave. (☎212-927-1563), at 174th St. [S] A to 174th St. A small NYC-run fitness center with a fitness room, 2 basketball courts, 2 athletic fields and 2 handball courts. Membership only available for full-year ($50). Open M-Th 9am-10pm, F 9am-6pm, Sa 9am-5pm.

Manhattan Motion Dance Studios, 215 W 76th St. (☎212-724-1673; www.manhattanmotion.com), between Broadway and Amsterdam. [S] 1 to Broadway and 79th St. Lively, low-pressure dance studio offers drop-in classes in several disciplines, including jazz, tap, hip-hop, ballet, salsa, and bellydancing. Special student deal: 3 drop-in classes $40. Regular single class $16; 10 classes $130. Call or check online for class schedule.

Namaste, 371 Amsterdam (☎212-580-1778; www.lifeinmotion.com), between 77th and 78th St. [S] 1 to Broadway/79th St. This quiet, attractive yoga and Pilates studio offers 140 classes a week, with under 14 participants per class. Exceptionally friendly leaders. Some dance and meditation classes meet as well. A one-time first drop-in class is $10, subsequent single classes are $15 and a package of 10 is $135. Mat rental available ($1). Check website or call for times.

New York Sports Clubs, 125 Seventh Ave. (☎212-206-1560; www.nysc.com), at 10th St. [S] 1 to Christopher St. In addition to cardio and weightlifting, offers spinning, step, kickboxing, yoga, and Pilates classes daily (reservations required). Check website for schedules. Babysitting, massage, and towel service available. Day passes $15. Apply online for free 1 week trial. Call or check online for membership rates. Members can use any NYSC location. Open 24hr. M at 6am-Sa 10pm, Su 8am-10pm.

North Meadow Recreation Center, mid-park at 97th St in Central Park. (☎212-348-4867; www.centralparknyc.org). Set in the 23 acres of the North Meadow (Central Park's largest open space), the Center features 12 playing fields (baseball, soccer, basketball, and football), indoor and outdoor climbing walls (see p. 185 for details), Tai Chi (Sa 10am-11:30am, 18+, $5), and Hatha Yoga (Sa noon-1:30pm, 18+, $5). If you leave a photo ID, you can borrow a free "Field Day Kit," complete with balls, bats, hula-hoops, frisbees, and jump ropes. Open May-Sept. M-F 10am-8pm, Sa-Su 10am-6pm; Sept.-Oct. M-F 10am-7pm, Sa-Su 10am-6pm; Oct.-Mar. M-F 10am-6pm, Sa-Su 10am-4:30pm; Mar.-May M-F 10am-7pm, Sa-Su 10am-6pm.

Tiger Schulmann's Karate, 39 W 19th St. (☎212-727-0773; www.tsk.com), between 5th and 6th Ave. The Manhattan location of Northeast Karate gym chain. 8-15 classes daily, including Core, Kickboxing, Grappling, Bag Training and Close Range Defense for adults and children. Check the website for class times. Classes $13-25, call for details on memberships and discounted rates. Classes M-F 7am-8:30pm, Sa 10am-1pm, Su noon-4pm.

YMCA-Vanderbilt, 224 E 47th St. (☎212-756-9600; fax 752-0210), between 2nd and 3rd Ave. [S] 6 to 51st St.; E, V to Lexington Ave./53rd St. Boasts a six-lane pool, the full range of Precor fitness machines, and a variety of exercise and dance classes. Bring a shower cap and your own lock. $2530 day pass. Membership desk open M-F 6am-9pm, Sa-Su 8am-5pm.

BROOKLYN

Body Elite, 348 Court St. (☎718-935-0088; www.bodyelitegym.com), at Union St. [S] F, G to Carroll St. Cardio machines, weightlifting equipment, group classes (like step and yoga), and tanning bed. Day pass $15; 3-month $279; 6-month $425; 12-month

$789. Babysitting (by appointment) $4 per hr. Open M-Th 5:30am-11pm, F 5:30am-10pm, Sa-Su 8am-8pm.

Eastern Athletic, 43 Clark St. (☎ 718-625-0500; www.easternathleticclubs.com), at Hicks St. Ⓢ 2, 3 to Clark St. 75,000 sq. ft. gym with a pool. Many class options. Yoga, tai chi, pilates, and step classes are complimentary; boxing, ballet, karate, swimming and fencing require extra fee ($60-150 per 7 sessions). Racquetball and squash court rentals ($18 peak, $6 off-peak per hr.). Day pass $25. Membership fees vary. Open M-F 6:30am-11:30pm, Sa-Su 9am-7:30pm.

Gleason's Gym, 83 Front St. (☎ 718-797-2872; www.gleasonsgym.net), between Adams and Washington St. Ⓢ A, C to High St. Oldest boxing gym in the US. Has trained more than 120 world boxing champions, including Tyson and Ali. But don't be intimidated: around 60% of their clientele are businessmen. Lessons start at $20 per hr. Day pass $15; $80 per month. Open M-F 6am-10pm, Sa 8am-6pm.

Go Yoga, 218 Bedford Ave. (☎ 718-486-5602), at N 5th St., in the Girdle Factory, in Williamsburg. Ⓢ L to Bedford Ave. 6-7 classes per day, beginning as early as 10am and as late as 8:15pm. Basic, mixed-level, and intermediate/advanced vinyasa yoga classes offered, as well as pilates. Mother/child and pre-natal classes are also offered. Single classes $15, some discounted to $10; 5-class card $70; 10-class $130; 1-month unlimited $175.

Metropolitan Pool and Fitness Center, 261 Bedford Ave. (☎ 718-599-5707; www.nycgovparks.org), at Metropolitan Ave. Ⓢ L to Bedford Ave. Designed by Henry Bacon, architect of Washington's Lincoln Memorial, this pool and fitness center is run by the city. Membership only available for full-year ($75). Check the website or call for details on programs for children and adults. Building open M-F 7am-10pm, Sa 7am-6pm; pool M-F 7am-9:30pm, Sa 7am-5:30pm; fitness room M-F 9am-9:30pm, Sa 9am-5:30pm.

Park Slope Sports Club, 330 Flatbush Ave. (☎ 718-783-5152; www.fitnessventures.net), between Sterling and Park Pl. Ⓢ 2, 3 to Grand Army Plaza. Fitness club offers cardio equipment, strength training, and group exercise classes. 7-8 classes daily, including dance fitness, spinning, and hatha yoga. Day pass $20; membership fees vary. Check the website or call for details. Open M-Th 5:30am-11pm, F 5:30am-10pm, Sa-Su 7am-7pm.

The Yoga Lab, 388 Atlantic Ave. (☎ 718-858-3265; www.theyogalab.com), between Bond and Hoyt St. Ⓢ A, C, G to Hoyt-Schermerhorn. Hatha yoga classes offered at beginner, intermediate, and advanced levels. Ashtanga (power), core strength, and pre-natal classes offered. In the summer, some classes are held on the rooftop. 4hr. weekend fundamental classes ($55) offered monthly. Single class $15 (2nd class free); 5 classes $70, 10 $130. Yoga mat included. 3-5 classes per day, beginning as early as 8am and as late as 8pm; call or check website for the schedule.

QUEENS

The Rock Health and Fitness Club, 22-15 31st St. (☎ 718-204-1400; www.therockhealthandfitness.com), Astoria. Ⓢ N, W to Astoria Blvd. Full-service workout facility boasts a comprehensive range of cardio and weight machines, 30 ft. climbing wall, and boxing ring. Classes, including martial arts, yoga, and belly dancing; free 1-day trial guest pass. 6-month membership $500. Year-long membership $850. Open M-F 24hr., Sa 7am-11pm, Su 7am-10pm.

SHOPPING

From the world's (former) largest department store to the hottest designer boutiques, New York has everything you could possibly want for sale, and much you didn't know you wanted until now. Whether you're actually looking to buy or you're mainly out for a stroll, New York is a shopper's paradise. You'll find everything from strictly vintage wares to the highest high-end merchandise.

SHOPPING BY TYPE

ACCESSORIES

Lord of Design (290)	UWS
Tiffany & Co. (287)	ME
Ugly Luggage (292)	BR
Venture Stationers (289)	UES
Xukuma (291)	H

ANTIQUES AND COLLECTIBLES

■ Las Venus Lounge (281)	LES
Hell's Kitchen Flea Market (286)	MW
Love Saves the Day (284)	EV
William LeRoy Antiques (284)	EV

BEAUTY AND HAIR

New York Adorned (284)	EV
■ Astor Place Hairstylist (283)	EV
Sephora(279)	SoT

BOOKSTORES

Argosy Bookstore (289)	UES
Biography Bookstore (282)	GV
Bluestockings (281)	LES
Books of Wonder (285)	CHE
The Complete Traveller (287)	MW
The Drama Book Shop (286)	MW
■ Gotham Book Mart (286)	MW
Hue-Man Bookstore and Cafe (291)	H
Murder Ink/Ivy's (290)	UWS
Oscar Wilde (282)	GV
Revolution Books (285)	UFM
Shakespeare and Co. (282)	GV
■ St. Mark's Bookshop (284)	EV
Strand Annex (278)	LM
■ Strand Bookstore (282)	GV

CLOTHING, GENERAL

■ Allan and Suzi (289)	UWS
Bird (293)	BR
Chill on Broadway (279)	SoT

SHOES

Shoegasm	UPM
Soula Shoes	BR

DEPARTMENT STORES CON'T

Century 21 (278)	LM
Lord and Taylor (288)	ME
Macy's (287)	MW
Pearl River (279)	CLI, SoT
Saks Fifth Avenue (288)	ME

ELECTRONICS

Apple Store (287)	ME
Hammacher Schlemmer (288)	ME
Rita Ford Music Boxes (289)	UES

MALLS

Girdle Company (291)	BR
Fulton Street Mall (292)	BR
Shops at Columbus Circle (286)	MW

MUSIC

Academy Records and CDs (285)	CHE
■ Beat Street (292)	BR
■ Disc-O-Rama (282)	GV
Downtown Music Gallery (284)	EV
Generation Records (283)	GV
■ Halycon (292)	BR
Jammyland (284)	EV
■ Kim's Video and Audio (283)	EV
■ Other Music (283)	EV
Rock and Soul (286)	UFM
Westider Records (290)	UWS

SEX (AND SEXY) SHOPS

Condomania (283)	GV
La Petite Coquette (283)	GV
The Leather Man (283)	GV
■ Toys in Babeland (279)	SoT, LES

Dirty Jane (279)	SoT	**SEX (AND SEXY) SHOPS**	
Exstaza (279)	SoT	Condomania (283)	GV
�belleFlirt (292)	BR	La Petite Coquette (283)	GV
H&M (286)	MW	The Leather Man (283)	GV
Lucky Brand Jeans (279)	SoT	✤Toys in Babeland (279)	SoT, LES
Something Else (292)	BR		
✤Sude (290)	UWS	**SPECIALTY STORES**	
		The Barking Zoo (285)	CHE
CLOTHING, VINTAGE		Harlemade (291)	H
17@17 (285)	CHE	La Brea (290)	UWS
✤Beacon's Closet (291)	BR	Malcolm Shabazz Harlem Market (291)	H
Bobby 2000 (284)	EV	Maxilla & Mandible (290)	UWS
Encore (289)	UES	Reminiscence (285)	UFM
✤FAB208 (283)	EV	Tender Buttons (289)	UES
Find Outlet (281)	CLI	Universal News and Cafe Corp. (281)	SoT
Tokyo 7 Consignment (284)	EV		
Tokyo Joe (284)	EV	**SPORTING GOODS**	
Union Max (292)	BR	KCDC (291)	BR
		Paragon Sports (285)	UFM
DEPARTMENT STORES			
✤Barney's New York (288)	UES	**TOYS AND GAMES**	
Bergdorff-Goodman (288)	ME	FAO Schwarz (288)	ME
✤Bloomingdale's (288)	UES	Toys "R" Us (286)	MW
		✤Village Chess Shop (281)	GV

BR Brooklyn; **BX** Bronx; **CHE,** Chelsea; **CLI**, Little Italy; **EV** East Village; **GV** Greenwich Village; **H** Harlem; **LES** Lower East Side; **LM** Lower Manhattan; **MW** Midtown West; **ME** Midtown East; **MH** Morningside Heights; **QU** Queens; **SI** Staten Island; **SoT** SoHo, TriBeCa; **UFM**, Union Sq., Flatiron District, and Murray Hill; **UES** Upper East Side; **UWS** Upper West Side.

SHOPPING BY NEIGHBORHOOD

LOWER MANHATTAN

Lower Manhattan isn't the sort of neighborhood you come to with the primary purpose of shopping in mind, but it nonetheless has plenty of stores catering to all those office workers.

Century 21, 22 Cortlandt St. (☎212-227-9092), between Broadway and Church St. Ⓢ 2, 3, 4, 5, A, C, J, M, Z to Fulton St./Nassau St. This discount department store sells designer clothes to hordes of bargain-hunters. You'll find Diesel jeans ($60) and tons of Chanel, Prada, and Miu Miu apparel (40-70% off). The housewares department has some remarkable finds as well. Show up early in the morning to avoid the crowds. Open M-W 7:45am-8pm, Th-F 7:45am-8:30pm, Sa 10am-8pm, Su 11am-7pm.

Strand Annex, 95 Fulton St. (☎212-732-6070), between William and Gold St. Ⓢ 2, 3, 4, 5, A, C, J, M, Z to Fulton St./Nassau St. The younger, less crowded, and more manageable sibling of the behemoth landmark bookstore. Great remaindered-books section with a strong supply of used books (from $1). Pick up a trendy Strand tote bag or t-shirt (from $6). Open M-F 9:30am-9pm, Sa-Su 11am-8pm.

SOHO AND TRIBECA

SoHo's shopping is decidedly upscale, but you can still find some deals at the district's used clothing stores and street-side stands. Prince, Spring, and Greene St. house the SoHo branches of the world's best fashion brands. The spaces themselves are often works of art. Many a credit rating has suffered a sad demise at the hands of the salespeople here. The farther south you head toward Canal St., the cheaper the clothes generally get. Check out the daily "fair" that sets up shop on the southwest corner of Wooster and Spring St.

Toys in Babeland, 43 Mercer St. (☎212-966-2120; www.babeland.com), between Broome and Grand St. Ⓢ A, C, E to Canal St.; 6 to Canal St. A toystore of the adult variety, this shop sells vibrators (from $12), sex books of every stripe (from $12), massage oils (from $3), and a huge array of dildos. The pristine, yellow-walled space is as unintimidating as it gets, and the friendly staff is happy to offer advice. If you're unsure how to use the cockrings ($15), or you just want to improve your technique, "Babeland University" offers evening workshops ($30) like "G-Spotting," "S&M 101," and "Oral Ambitions." Advance reservations suggested. 18+. Open M-Sa noon-9pm, Su noon-7pm. Second location at 94 Rivington St. (☎212-375-1701), at Ludlow St.

Chill on Broadway, 427 Broadway (☎212-343-2709), at Howard St. Ⓢ J, M, N, Q, R, W, Z, 6 to Canal St. Just the right mix of Canal Street discount and SoHo style, this shop sells everything from clubwear, to everyday clothing, to shoes and accessories. Blouses $20. Dresses $30. Shoes from $20-$50.

Lucky Brand Jeans, 38 Greene St. (☎212-625-0707; www.luckybrandjeans.com), at Grand St. Ⓢ J, M, N, Q, R, W, Z, 6 to Canal St. Designer denim is all over SoHo, and Lucky Brand is one of the extortionists selling $200 slacks. What sets this store apart, however, is that its sales are serious—jean prices drop to as low as $40. Open M-Sa 11am-8pm, Su noon-6pm.

Dirty Jane, between Broome and Grand St. Ⓢ J, M, N, Q, R, W, Z, 6 to Canal St. Punkish skater-style clothes at reasonable prices. Buy a Hummel jacket ($100), and get the matching pants free. Lots of cargo and camouflage. Open daily 10am-9pm.

Exstaza, 491 Broadway (☎212-925-8193), at Broome St. N, R, W to Prince St. A nice but cheap store that carries the trendy stuff you saw in SoHo's boutiques at a fraction of the price. Not always designer labels, but stylish nonetheless. Shirts $20. Dresses $30. Denim $45. Open M-Sa 10am-9pm, Su 10am-8pm.

Pearl River, 477 Broadway (☎212-431-4770; www.pearlriver.com), between Greene and Mercer St. Ⓢ J, M, N, Q, R, W, Z, 6 to Canal St. This Chinese-run department store has outgrown its original Chinatown location and moved up into this spacious SoHo site. You'll find dozens of gorgeous Mandarin dresses ($31.50) and other Chinese products for fabulously low prices. Brocade satin purses 2 for $20. Shoes $14.50. I Love NY t-shirts (in Chinese) $10. Tea sets $42.50. Open daily 10am-7:20pm.

Sephora, 555 Broadway (☎212-625-1309; www.sephora.com), between Spring and Prince St. Ⓢ C, E to Spring St./Ave. of the Americas (6th Ave.); 6 to Spring St.; N, R, W to Prince St. As ubiquitous in New York as McDonald's, this store offers a huge selection of cosmetics, including perfumes, powders, haircare products, and makeup from top brands like Chanel, Stila, Clinique, Dior, and Clarins. There's everything from bargain-bin deals to $50 Chanel foundation. Knowledgeable staff. Also sells men's fragrances and skincare products. Open M-Sa 10am-8pm, Su 11am-7pm.

SHOPPING

SOHO SHOPPING, HIGH- AND LOW-BROW

TIME: 2-3 hr. You could spend (much) longer, but for your budget's sake, a self-imposed time limit is a good idea.

START: Broadway and Prince St. S N, R, W to Prince St.

TIME OF DAY: Optimal shopping time is mid-afternoon on a weekday, when self-respecting people are at work.

SoHo shopping is the epitome of downtown chic. Can you afford a spree in these boutiques? Probably not. Is it fun to dream here (and maybe brainstorm which knockoffs you want to look for on Canal St.)? You bet.

1 PRADA. On the northwest corner of Prince St. and Broadway, the Prada store is a stunning must-see. If you think it looks like a museum, well, it used to be one; the site housed the now-defunct Guggenheim SoHo. Famed Dutch architect Rem Koolhaas executed the building's renovation and conversion to retail use. The soaring, two-story space is dominated by a serpentine wave made of zebrawood, which traverses the store from top to bottom. Check out the translucent dressing rooms—the walls only become opaque when you push a button. In addition to a fabulous selection of women's bags and shoes, Prada also has an unusually extensive menswear collection.

2 LOUIS VUITTON. Continue down Prince St., and make a left on Green St., where you'll see the Louis Vuitton store. To work in the Financial District as a female, it seems, you've got to come armed with one of these LV-tattooed bags on your shoulder.

3 LONGCHAMP. Continue down Greene St., and take a right at Spring St. On your left, you'll see the dramatically sculpted Longchamp boutique. The classic Le Pliage bags start under $100, but more leather quickly escalates the price.

4 CHANEL. Across the street from Longchamp, at the corner of Wooster and Spring St. you'll find the Chanel store, whose clothes and accessories define classic, timeless style. It's worth stopping in just to marvel at how impeccably groomed the salespeople are.

5 KATE SPADE. Head south down Wooster, and hang a left at Broome St. At the corner of Mercer and Broome St., you'll see the Kate Spade store, which features simple accessories in a nostalgic 50s and 60s style.

6 YOHJI YAMAMOTO. At the corner of Mercer and Grand St., you'll find Yohji Yamamoto, another gallery-like space, this time truly avant-garde in character. Within this minimalist setting, you'll find garments that can look more like sculpture than clothes—all exposed hems, reconstructed seams, and asymmetrical lines.

7 CANAL STREET. Continue down Mercer to Canal St. for a reprise of today's highlights. Look! More Louis Vuitton bags, more Longchamp wallets, more Kate Spade sunglasses—all spread before you on the sidewalk and suddenly well within your budget. Just don't look too close. The L and V don't fit together perfectly on those handbags. The leather detailing on the "Prada" purses isn't as impeccable as on the ones in the Broadway shrine. Then again, you can make a few purchases here and still be able to pay for dinner.

WALKING TOUR

Universal News and Cafe Corp., 484 Broadway (☎212-965-9042), between Broome and Grand St. [S] C, E to Spring St./Ave. of the Americas (6th Ave.); 6 to Spring St./ Lafayette St. Over 7000 foreign and domestic magazine titles, covering everything from fashion to politics. The cafe provides decent fare and spacious seating. Muffins $1.50. Sandwiches $5-6. Bagels from $0.60. Computers are available for Internet use ($2 per 10min, $5 per 30min.) Open daily 6am-11pm.

CHINATOWN

So long as authenticity doesn't concern you, Chinatown is the perfect place to bargain hunt. You can find Asian imports, $5 burned CDs, and a convincing copy of that Chloe bag you've been eyeing. If you're really lucky, you might even find legitimate designer goods discounted to a fraction of their original price. The shopper with a meticulous eye will have a heyday along Canal St.

Find Outlet, 229 Mott St. (☎212-226-5167; www.findoutlet.com), between Prince and Spring St. [S] 6 to Spring St. This outlet sells wares from Nolita boutiques at a discount—often 50-80% off the original. Designer jeans $55, down from $225. Open daily noon-7pm, sometimes until 11pm in summer. Second location at 361 W 17th St. (☎212-243-3177).

Pearl River, 277 Canal St. (☎212-431-4770), at Broadway. [S] J, M, N, Q, R, W, Z, 6 to Canal St. This Chinese department store sells all the basic necessities, along with a few hard-to-find luxuries: satin slippers ($20), Mandarin-style dresses ($50), and fancy bamboo birdcages ($75). Open daily 10am-7:30pm.

LOWER EAST SIDE

Shopping on the Lower East Side is becoming an expensive venture. Trendy boutiques abound on Stanton and Ludlow St., displaying their cutting edge, often handmade wares in spaces that look like museums. For a mix of thrift stores and high fashion, head to Orchard St., between Houston and Delancey St.

👍 **Las Venus Lounge 20th Century Pop Culture,** 163 Ludlow St. (☎212-982-0608), at Stanton St. [S] F, J, M, Z to Delancey St./Essex St. A wild vintage store selling everything from giant retro floor lamps (from $400) to 1960s porn magazines ($20). Scenesters stroll into this hotspot on the weekend, kick back on the pleather couches, and transform it into a spontaneous party. M-Sa noon-9pm, Su noon-8pm.

Toys in Babeland, 94 Rivington St. (☎212-982-0608; www.babeland.com), between Orchard and Ludlow St. [S] F, J, M, Z to Delancey St./Essex St. Though smaller than the SoHo location (p. 279), this women-run sex emporium is still a haven of sexual empowerment and good advice. 18+. Open M-W and Su noon-10pm, Th-Sa noon-11pm.

Bluestockings, 172 Allen St. (☎212-777-6028; www.bluestockings.com), between Rivington and Stanton St. [S] F, J, M, Z to Delancey St./Essex St. A progressive bookstore and fair trade cafe that "promotes empowerment...through words, art, and activism." The store doubles as a space for lectures, readings, poetry jams, and workshops. Website lists the nightly events. Open daily 11am-11pm.

GREENWICH VILLAGE

Greenwich Village shopping is quirky, unique, and fun. The best stores here tend to be highly specialized, with extraordinarily knowledgeable and helpful staffs.

👍 **Village Chess Shop,** 230 Thompson St. (☎212-475-9580), between Bleecker and W 3rd St. [S] A, B, C, D, E, F, V to W 4th St. In this dusty little chess shop, the Village's

S H O P P I N G

keenest intellects face off in strategic combat while sipping coffee ($1) and juice ($1.50). Play is $1, or $1.50 for clocked play per hr. per person. There are a variety of chess sets for sale, including breathtaking antique pieces. Prices range from $5-10,000. Open daily noon-midnight.

■ **Strand Bookstore,** 828 Broadway (☎212-473-1452), at E 12th St. Ⓢ 4, 5, 6, L, N, Q, R, W to 14th St./Union Sq. The world's largest used bookstore, the Strand is a must-see, with 8 mi. of shelf space and nearly 2 million books in stock, including rare titles and 1st editions. Check the outdoor carts for $1 specials. 50% off review copies and paperbacks. Vast collection of art books. Call with the bibliographic information of the title you'd like, and the store will call you back within 3hr. to let you know if it's available. Open M-Sa 9:30am-10:30pm, Su 11am-10:30pm.

■ **Disc-o-Rama,** 186 W 4th St. (☎212-206-8417; www.discorama.com), between Mac-Dougal St. and 6th Ave. Ⓢ A, B, C, D, E, F, V to W 4th St. Although they won't always have everything you want, Disc-o-Rama rarely charges more than $11 for a new CD. Such ridiculous bargains, together with an impressive used CD selection, makes Disc-o-Rama a must-visit destination. Second location at 44 W 8th St. Open M-Th 10:30am-10:30pm, F 10:30am-11:30pm, Sa 10am-12:30am, Su 11:30am-8pm.

Oscar Wilde Gay and Lesbian Bookshop, 15 Christopher St. (☎212-255-8097; www.oscarwildebooks.com), at 6th Ave./Gay St. Ⓢ 1 to Christopher St. Founded in SoHo in 1967, this cozy shop claims to be the world's first gay and lesbian bookstore. In addition to a small selection of rare and 1st edition books, the store stocks a multitude of DVDs, travel guides, fiction, and magazines. Open daily 11am-7pm.

La Petite Coquette, 51 University Pl. (☎212-473-2478; www.thelittleflirt.com), between 9th and 10th St. Ⓢ N, R, W to 8th St./NYU. According to Rebecca, the owner of this lingerie store, "A good bra is like a good man—supportive, good looking, and will never let you down." If this is true, then the saleswomen here are the best matchmakers in town. The prices are high (bras from $40, silk slips from $100), but you'll leave with perfectly fitted and lovely lingerie. Come for the post-Valentine's Day sale; most items are 40% off. Open M-W 11am-7pm, Th 11am-8pm, F-Sa 11am-7pm, Su noon-6pm.

Condomania, 351 Bleecker St. (☎212-691-9442; www.condomania.com), at W 10th St. Ⓢ 1 to Christopher St. "America's first condom store" stocks over 150 types of prophylactics ($0.75-1.50 each) in every imaginable color, fit, texture, and shape. Custom-fit condoms 3 for $12. The X-rated fortune cookies, penis-shaped cake pan ($15), nipple balloons ($5), and pecker sipping straws ($0.75 each) are popular bachelorette party gifts. The friendly staff answers all your questions and gives safe-sex tips. Check the website for coupons. Open M-Th and Su 11am-11pm, F-Sa 11am-midnight.

Shakespeare and Company, 716 Broadway (☎212-529-1330; www.shakespearean-dco.com), at Washington Pl. Ⓢ N, R, W to 8th St./NYU. Carries high-quality literature, high-brow journals, and a great selection of vintage crime, art, and theater books that won't cost you a pound of flesh. Hardbacks always 10% off; staff-selected "buyer's pick" 20% off. Other branches: 939 Lexington Ave. (☎212-570-0201), between 68th and 69th St.; 137 E 23rd St. (☎212-505-2021), near Lexington Ave.; 14 Hillel Pl. (☎718-434-5326) in Brooklyn; and 1 Whitehall St. (☎212-742-7025), near South Ferry. Open M-Th 10am-11pm, F-Sa 10am-midnight, Su 11am-9pm.

Biography Bookstore, 400 Bleecker St. (☎212-807-8655), at W 11th St. Ⓢ 1 to Christopher St. *The New York Times* once listed this biography-oriented bookstore as the "best place to pick someone up"—referring, presumably, to the biographies. The store also has good travel, history, fiction, drama, and GLBT sections. Hardcovers are always

20% off. Outside tables hold remainders up to 50% off; they keep the best ones in the shelves under the register. Open M-Th 11am-10pm, F-Sa 11am-11pm, Su 11am-10pm.

Generation Records, 210 Thompson St. (☎212-254-1100), between Bleecker and 3rd St. Ⓢ A, B, C, D, E, F, V to W 4th St. All kinds of alternative, metal, and underground rock on CD and vinyl. The hard-core and industrial/experimental selections are especially impressive. Fairly low prices (CDs $12-15) and an impressive assortment of hard-to-find imports and concert DVDs. Great deals on used merchandise downstairs (CDs and vinyl $6-8). Open M-Th 11am-10pm, F-Sa 11am-1am, Su noon-10pm.

The Leather Man, 111 Christopher St. (☎212-243-5339; www.theleatherman.com), between Bleecker and Hudson St. Ⓢ 1 to Christopher St. The dim upstairs of this rather freaky S&M shop is dominated by rows of leather erotic apparel, handcuffs (from $10), and bondage equipment (from $30). Braving the spiral staircase takes you to a whole other level of kink. The store specializes in custom apparel made on the premises: pants and chaps (from $395), vests (from $100), boots (from $140). Must be 21+ to enter. Open M-Sa noon-10pm, Su noon-8pm.

EAST VILLAGE

If you're looking for brand names you'd be better off in SoHo, but if you're searching for vintage goods, you can't do better than the East Village. St. Mark's Pl. shops sell a fantastic assortment of silver jewelry and odd trinkets. Record stores line both sides of St. Mark's Pl., between Third Ave. and Ave. A.; the barely organized shelves can keep you browsing for hours. Boutiques along Ninth St., off Ave. A, sell fashionable one-of-a-kinds.

▨ **Astor Place Hairstylist,** 2 Astor Pl. (☎212-475-9854), at Broadway. Ⓢ 6 to Astor Pl.; N, R, W to 8th St./NYU. The world's largest hair-cutting establishment, famed for its low-priced approach to style. It's also the king of New York City flavor. DMC, Adam Sandler, and Joan Rivers are some of the celeb clientele whose photos adorn the windows. Over 75 stylists work in the basement salon. Haircuts $12-35; Su $1 extra. Open daily M-Sa 8am-8pm, Su 9am-6pm.

▨ **Kim's Video and Audio,** 6 St. Mark's Pl. (☎212-598-9985; www.mondokims.com), between 2nd and 3rd Ave. Ⓢ 6 to Astor Pl. Three floors of hip entertainment selections. The ground floor has a strong selection of independent and import CDs, with beats ranging from 1970s Jamaican dub to avant-jazz. The "establishment" section offers more popular fare. The 2nd floor holds new and used vinyl, a collection of music and film books, and a video selection specializing in independent and foreign films. The third floor has video rentals. Open daily 9am-midnight; video store opens at 10am.

▨ **FAB208,** 75 E 7th St. (☎212-673-7581), between 1st and 2nd Ave. Ⓢ 6 to Astor Pl. This family-operated shop, run by a tattooed-and-mohawked mom and pop, sells vintage and new clothing. Jo will help you find the perfect necklace to match that denim skirt with silk trim ($69). Earrings from $15. Open Tu-Sa noon-7:45pm, Su 2-6pm.

▨ **Other Music,** 15 E 4th St. (☎212-477-8150; www.othermusic.com), between Lafayette St. and Broadway. Ⓢ 6 to Bleecker St. Alternative and avant-garde music in a clean, well-ordered setting. A bit of everything, from electronic to indie to experimental to underground. If you can't find it anywhere else, you'll find it here. Avoid steep import prices by shopping the sizable used-CD ($5-10) section. The white boards above the register keep clientele updated on where to see their favorite performers. Knowledgeable staff. Open M-F noon-9pm, Sa noon-8pm, Su noon-7pm.

👍 **St. Mark's Bookshop,** 31 3rd Ave. (☎212-260-7853; www.stmarksbookshop.com), at E 9th St. [S] 6 to Astor Pl. The ultimate East Village bookstore, with an excellent selection in the fields of literary theory and criticism, philosophy, film, fiction, and poetry. They also have a good selection of mainstream and avant-garde magazines ($4-20) and a small collection of self-published 'zines on consignment ($2-5). Staff is helpful. Open M-Sa 10am-midnight, Su 11am-midnight.

New York Adorned, 47 2nd Ave. (☎212-473-0007; www.newyorkadorned.com), between E 2nd and 3rd St. [S] F, V to Lower East Side/2nd Ave. A comfortable, safe, and friendly piercing and tattoo parlor that seeks to make you look "beautiful, not mutilated." Some of the best piercing artists in the city work here. Nose $15. Navel $20. There's a wide variety of jewelry for sale ($35-3800). Traditional henna work from $20. Tattoos $150 per hr.; $75 minimum. Open M-Th and Su 1-9pm, F-Sa 1-10pm. Cash only for tattoos.

Downtown Music Gallery, 342 Bowery (☎212-473-0043; www.downtownmusicgallery.com), between 2nd and 3rd St. [S] F, V to Lower East Side/2nd Ave. Diverse selection of CDs and records, sure to please non-mainstream music enthusiasts. Knowledgeable and helpful staff. Genres include jazz, folk, classical, and electronic. Used CDs and vinyl from $7; new from $13. Open M-Th and Su noon-9pm, F-Sa noon-11pm.

Jammyland, 60 E 3rd St. (☎212-614-0185; www.jammyland.com), between 1st and 2nd Ave. [S] F, V to Lower East Side/2nd Ave. All Jamaican music—featuring reggae, dub, dance hall, and ska. Friendly staff. CDs $12-16. LPs $10-12. Open M-Th and Su noon-8pm, F-Sa noon-10pm.

Love Saves the Day, 119 2nd Ave. (☎212-228-3802), at E 7th St. [S] 6 to Astor Pl. Costumey vintage clothing ($8-25 shirts), random collectibles, and toys and games since 1966. *I Love Lucy* metal lunchboxes $20. Smurf pez dispenser sets $45. Star Wars figurines from $12. Open daily noon or 1pm until 8 or 9pm.

William LeRoy Antiques and Props, 76 E Houston St. (☎917-576-6980), between Elizabeth St. and the Bowery. [S] B, D, F, V to Broadway/Lafayette. This small warehouse is filled with oversized antiques and collectibles you won't find anywhere else, from neon signs to carnival games. Most pieces are under $1000: a working 1948 TV is $200. Amish workbench $500. Stop signs ($40) and trucker hats ($15) are about the least expensive items you'll find. Pieces are often rented for film and photo shoots. Open daily 1-8pm weather permitting.

Bobby 2000, 104 E 7th St. (☎212-674-7649), between 1st Ave. and Ave. A. [S] 6 to Astor Pl.; N, R, W to 8th St. A tiny vintage shop of Adidas, Puma, and Lacoste men's wear ($19-34). Good selection of men's shirts, jeans, and sport coats. Small women's section. Choose carefully; there are no returns or refunds. Open daily 1-8pm.

Tokyo 7 Consignment Store, 64 E 7th St. (☎212-353-8443), between 1st and 2nd Ave. [S] 6 to Astor Pl. A small space selling used designer clothes. Recent finds include Versace trousers ($40), Louis Vuitton pumps ($100), and a Juicy Couture shirt ($50). Sunglasses ($40-60) by the register. Bring in your used clothes—if they sell you get 50% of the profits. No refunds or exchanges. Open M-Sa noon-8:30pm, Su noon-8pm.

Tokyo Joe, 334 E 11th St. (☎212-473-0724), between 1st and 2nd Ave. [S] 6 to Astor Pl.; L to 1st Ave. Consignment store with well-priced brand-name women's clothing, plus hard-to-find Japanese brands like Pluto Cat on the Earth. Purple silk Cynthia Rowley dress $42, J. Crew miniskirt $12. Open daily noon-9pm.

CHELSEA

Chelsea tends not to be a shopping destination in its own right, its focus fixed primarily on art and nightlife. Still, there are a number of fun shops to enjoy.

17 @ 17 Thrift Shop, 17 W 17th St. (☎212-727-7516), between 5th and 6th Ave. Ⓢ 1 to 18th St. This nonprofit thrift shop sells secondhand goods and clothing in a serene setting. The vintage Emilio Pucci clothing sold at silent auction might cost you $400, but a paperback book costs only $0.50. Glorious finds have included a Dolce and Gabbana calf-length jean skirt for $25 and an Oscar de la Renta white jacket for $90. They sell furniture too—check out the re-upholstered couches and old restaurant-style booths ($300). Open M-Sa 11am-6pm.

Academy Records and CDs, 12 W 18th St. (☎212-242-3000; www.academy-records.com), between 5th and 6th Ave. Ⓢ 1 to 18th St.; F, L, V to 14th St. A small, well-stocked store of classical, jazz, and pop vinyls and CDs (most $8-15) that is a neighborhood favorite. The helpful staff will be happy to point you in the right direction or recommend a favorite. Albums can also be ordered online; the website is updated daily. Open M-Sa 11:30am-8pm, Su 11am-7pm. The 77 E 10th St. location (☎212-780-9166) stocks more jazz and pop.

The Barking Zoo, 172 9th Ave. (☎212-255-0658; www.thebarkingzoo.com), between 20th and 21st St. Ⓢ 1 to 18th St. This adorable pet store sells quirky, premium goods for extra-special dogs and cats. Dress your feline or canine friend to the nines with polo shirts (from $28) and running shoes ($55). Leashes of all shapes and sizes from $20. Shea Butter Shampoo $17. M-F 11am-8pm, Sa 10am-6pm, Su noon-5pm.

Books of Wonder, 18 W 18th St. (☎212-989-3270; www.booksofwonder.net), between 5th and 6th Ave. Ⓢ F, V to 23rd St./Ave. of the Americas (6th Ave.). A large selection of current children's books, topped off with a collection of vintage reads. A 1952 edition of *Nancy Drew and The Mystery of the Lilac Inn* sells for $50. Original artwork for well-known children's books hangs on the walls (for sale for up to $30,000). Hosts a variety of programs related to children's books. Open M-Sa 11am-7pm, Su noon-6pm.

UNION SQUARE, THE FLATIRON DISTRICT, AND MURRAY HILL

If you know where to look, you'll discover some excellent specialty stores and discount boutiques in these lower Midtown neighborhoods.

Paragon Sports, 867 Broadway (☎212-255-8036; www.paragonsports.com), at 18th St. Ⓢ N, R, W to 23rd St./Broadway. This 3-floor sporting goods distributor has everything you could possibly need for sports ranging from kayaking to squash. Puma bags $35-40. Lacoste tennis shirts $80. Patagonia, North Face, and Gregory backpacks $35-150. Open M-Sa 10am-8pm, Su 11:30am-7pm.

Reminiscence, 50 W 23rd St. (☎212-243-2292; www.reminiscence.com), between 5th and 6th Ave. Ⓢ N, R, W to 23rd St./Broadway. Happily stuck in a 70s groove, this Japan-based store features a wide selection of campy gifts. Revisit childhood with an Etch-a-Sketch ($23), or hit Central Park with one of their pocket kites ($5). The back has a large selection of clothing. Open M-Sa 11am-7:30pm, Su noon-7pm.

Revolution Books, 9 W 19th St. (☎212-691-3345), between 5th and 6th Ave. Ⓢ F, V to 23rd St./Ave. of the Americas (6th Ave.); 4, 5, 6, L, N, Q, R, W to 14th St./Union Sq. America's largest revolutionary bookstore is nonprofit and staffed mostly by volunteers.

Large collection of works on Marx, Mao, and Malcolm X. Wares ($2-12) range from polit-
ical science volumes to manifestos, from posters to 'zines. Meaty selection of anti-war
and anti-Bush paraphernalia and literature. Significant number of Spanish-language
works. Open M-Sa noon-7pm, Su noon-5pm.

Rock and Soul, 462 7th Ave. (☎212-695-3953; www.rockandsoul.com), between 35th
and 36th St. Ⓢ 1, 2, 3 to 34th St./Penn Station/7th Ave. Head past the bling-bling
jewelry and DJ equipment up front, and you'll find a pathway to full crates of vinyls. Old-
school classics and new releases in house, R&B, reggae, or hip-hop. Most LPs around
$15. Used CDs from $7. Open M-Sa 9:30am-7pm.

Shoegasm, 20 W 23rd St. (☎212-741-3288), between 5th and 6th Ave. Ⓢ F, V to 23rd
St./Ave. of the Americas (6th Ave.); 4, 5, 6, L, N, Q, R, W to 14th St./Union Sq. They
may not be designer, but Shoegasm's shoes look good, and come at budget-friendly
prices. Frequent sales on Steve Madden, N.Y.L.A., Franco Sarto, and Chinese Laundry
footwear. A limited selection of men's shoes. Open M-Sa 10am-8pm, Su 11am-6pm.

MIDTOWN WEST

Chain stores predominate in Midtown, though you'll find some delightful exceptions to that rule. And even some of the chain stores here are worth the trip.

▨ **Gotham Book Mart,** 16 E 46th St. (☎212-719-4448), between Madison and 5th Ave.
Ⓢ B, D, F, V to 50th St./Rockefeller Ctr. The sign outside reads "Wise men fish here,"
and bookworms have been doing just that since 1920. Gotham's legendary selection of
new and used 20th-century writing made it a favorite of Jacqueline Onassis and
Katherine Hepburn. Novelist John Updike has described it as his favorite bookstore in
North America. The little store once smuggled in censored copies of works by Joyce,
Lawrence, and Miller. LeRoi Jones, Tennessee Williams, and Allen Ginsberg all worked
here as clerks. Open M-F 9:30am-6:30pm, Sa 9:30am-6pm.

The Drama Book Shop, 250 W 40th St. (☎212-944-0595), between 7th and 8th Ave.
Ⓢ 1, 2, 3, 7, N, Q, R, S, W to 42nd St./Times Sq.; A, C, E to 42nd St./Port Authority. If
it has appeared on-stage, you can probably find it here in print. A necessary stop for
any theater, film, or performing-arts buff. An intimate 50-seat on-site theater is used for
occasional signings and free lectures. Check online for upcoming events. Open M-Sa
10am-8pm, Su noon-6pm.

Hell's Kitchen Flea Market, 39th St. (www.hellskitchenfleamarket.com), between 9th
and 10th Ave. An outdoor flea market with an unusually high-quality selection, this is a
destination of choice for discerning shoppers looking for vintage clothing, jewelry, and
furniture. Open Sa-Su 10am-6pm.

Toys "R" Us, 1514 Broadway (☎800-869-7787), at 44th St. Ⓢ 1, 2, 3, 7, N, Q, R, S, W
to 42nd St./Times Sq. The flagship branch of this popular chain is way more fun than the
outpost at your local strip mall. There's a working 60ft. ferris wheel (rides $3), a 20ft. ani-
matronic T-Rex, a mixed candy bar ($8.36 per lb.), and a 2-story Barbie Doll House. Try to
beat the post-school rush. Open M-Th 10am-10pm, F-Sa 10am-11pm, Su 11am-9pm.

The Shops at Columbus Circle, 10 Columbus Circle (☎212-823-6300). Ⓢ A, B, C, D to
59th St./Columbus Circle. A large high-end shopping mall, home to the usual list of
suspects—Borders Books, Brooks Brothers, Coach, J. Crew, Williams-Sonoma, etc. This
relatively new complex also hosts a number of gourmet restaurants, an Inside CNN tour,
and Jazz at Lincoln Center (p. 254). When it's hot outside, the excellent A/C here is reason enough to stop in.

H&M, 1328 Broadway (☎212-473-1165), at 34th St. Ⓢ B, D, F, N, Q, R, V, W to 34th
St./Herald Sq. This popular Swedish chain offers ridiculously cheap but surprisingly styl-

ish clothing. A 3-floor behemoth of a store, with a great selection of men's and women's clothing, as well as an excellent selection of accessories. Open M-Sa 10am-10pm, Su 10am-9pm. Additional locations at 640 5th Ave., at 51st St. (M-F 10am-8pm, Sa 10am-9pm, Su 11am-7pm); 558 Broadway, between Prince and Spring St. (M-Sa 10am-9pm, Su 11am-5pm); 125 W 125th St., between Lenox and 7th Ave. (M-Sa 10am-8pm, Su 11am-7pm); 435 7th Ave., at 34th St. (M-Sa 10am-9pm, Su 11am-7pm).

The Complete Traveller Bookstore, 199 Madison Ave. (☎212-685-9007), at 35th St. Ⓢ 6 to 33rd St. Arnold and Harriet Greenberg stock a wide selection of antique travel guides ($10-10,000) about distant lands. The store is strictly vintage, so don't come looking for the latest edition of *Let's Go.* Still, old travel guides can be entertaining; apparently a horse-drawn cab from Grand Central terminal once cost $0.35. Open Sept.-May M-F 10am-6:30pm, Sa 10am-6pm, Su noon-5pm; June-Aug. M-F 10am-7pm, Sa 10am-6pm, Su by appointment.

Macy's, 151 W 34th St. (☎212-695-4400; www.macys.com), between Broadway and 7th Ave. Ⓢ B, D, F, N, Q, R, V, W to 34th St./Herald Sq. This New York institution alternately provides thrills and frustration. Don't get in the way of crazed shoppers on sale days (almost every W and Sa). In this ultimate one-stop shop, you can purchase a book, grab a snack, get a facial, have your jewelry appraised, exchange currency, and purchase theater tickets. Open M-Sa 10am-9pm, Su 11am-8pm. (See also p. 177.)

MIDTOWN EAST

High-priced boutiques and enormous chain stores line Fifth Ave. south of Central Park. Whether or not you're planning on buying anything, these franchise flagships and one-of-a-kind emporiums provide highly entertaining shopping experiences that don't cost a cent to enjoy.

Apple Store, 767 5th Ave. (☎212-336-1440; www.apple.com), at 58th St. Ⓢ N, R, W to 5th Ave./59th St. The store isn't just a supply depot for Apple lovers; it's a sleek, always-open shrine to all things Apple. Above ground, it's just an enormous glass cube with a giant glowing apple and an elevator inside. Below, you'll find row upon row of iPods (a must-have for New Yorkers) and all the other Apple gear. Plus, there's free Internet on all the display models. Open 24hr.

Tiffany & Co., 727 5th Ave. (☎212-755-8000), at 57th St. Ⓢ N, R, W to 5th Ave./59th St. Like Holly Golightly, you may not be able to afford the precious gems at this

THE HIDDEN DEAL

SURVIVING A SAMPLE SALE

Sample sales are what enable so many New Yorkers to look so stylish all the time, despite their high cost of living and through-the-roof rents. At the end of a season, cutting-edge designers often put a sample of their line on sale at ridiculously low prices—as much as 90% off. Serious shoppers live by the sample-sale schedule.

Some ultra-exclusive brands reserve their sample sales for invite-only guest lists. Most sales, however, are open to anyone; you just have to know how to hear about them. Websites like www.dailycandy.com and www.nymag.com are good sources. If you're willing to brave the chaotic and cut-throat crowds, sample sales can save you serious money. Here are some tips for surviving them:

1. Avoid lunch hour at all cost. This is when fashion-hungry shoppers escape their office prisons and descend upon the sales *en masse.* Arrive early in the morning on the first day of the sale for the best selection. If the best bargains are what you're after, go late in the sale, when discounts can become truly outlandish.

2. Be prepared to bare it all. Many sales don't offer dressing rooms, or, if they do, they're communal. Wear bike shorts or slim layers under your clothes to try on potential purchases with ease.

3. Come prepared to pay cash, and examine items closely; sample sales are usually final.

sparkling jewelry sanctuary, but the library-like 5-story emporium is worth seeing none-theless. For the ultimate in vicarious living, go be blinded by the engagement rocks on the 2nd floor. Open M-F 10am-7pm, Sa 10am-6pm, Su noon-5pm.

Bergdorff-Goodman, 754 5th Ave. (☎212-872-3000), at 58th St. Ⓢ N, R, W to 5th Ave./59th St. This marble- and chandelier- bedecked haven of clothing and pomp is a favorite of celebrity shoppers. The men's store is across the street. Open M-W 10am-7pm, Th 10am-8pm, F-Sa 10am-7pm, Su noon-6pm.

FAO Schwarz, 767 5th Ave. (☎212-644-9400; www.fao.com), at 58th St. Ⓢ N, R, W to 5th Ave./59th St. A kid's paradise and a respite for adults tired of having to act like grown-ups. Toy soldiers guard the doors to this famous toy store filled with everything from old-fashioned marbles ($0.50 each) to an enormous playable piano, seen in the movie *Big* (just $250,000). Open M-Sa 10am-7pm, Su 11am-6pm.

Saks Fifth Avenue, 611 5th Ave. (☎212-753-4000), between 49th and 50th St. Ⓢ N, R, W to 5th Ave./59th St. This chic institution has aged well, continuing to combine inflated prices with smooth, solicitous courtesy. Keep an eye out for end-of-season sales. Open M-W and F-Sa 10am-7pm, Th 10am-8pm, Su noon-6pm.

Hammacher Schlemmer, 147 E 57th St. (☎212-421-9000; www.hammacher.com), between 3rd and Lexington Ave. Ⓢ 4, 5, 6, N, R, W to Lexington Ave./59th St. Selling "the best, the only, and the unexpected" since 1848, Hammacher Schlemmer was the first to carry such items as the steam iron, the electric razor, the microwave, and the cordless telephone. Today it sells tomorrow's innovations, like a transparent kayak ($1460) and a 7-person "conference bike" ($19,000). Open M-Sa 10am-6pm.

Lord and Taylor, 424-434 5th Ave. (☎212-391-3344), between 38th and 39th St. Ⓢ B, D, F, V to 42nd St./Ave. of the Americas (6th Ave.); 7 to 5th Ave./42nd St. This classic department store was the first in the world to feature elaborate window displays at Christmastime. It inaugurated this holiday tradition by filling its windows with mock bliz-zards during an unusually balmy winter in 1905. Today, the hectic store features 10 floors of fashion frenzy, caring service, and free early-morning coffee (by the 5th Ave. entrance). Open M and W-F 10am-8:30pm, Tu and Sa 10am-7pm, Su 11am-7pm.

UPPER EAST SIDE

You don't come to the Upper East Side to shop for life's basic necessities. This is where fashion and culinary creation become art forms, and where prices correlate to aesthetic beauty and international cachet rather than function. Whether you buy anything or not, shopping here is a cultural experience you shouldn't miss. You'll also find a number of quirky, one-of-a-kind stores dotting the neighborhood.

▓ **Bloomingdale's,** 1000 3rd Ave. (☎212-705-2000; www.bloomingdales.com), at 59th St. Ⓢ 4, 5, 6, to 59th St. Founded in 1872 by two brothers, Bloomie's is "not just a store, it's a destination." This huge high-end emporium—occupying 9 floors, 2 subfloors (with an entrance in the 59th St. station), and a full city block—invented the designer shopping bag ("big brown bag," anyone?) in 1961. It turned Ralph Lauren, Donna Karan, and Fendi into household names. If you can survive the mobs of dazed tourists and shoppers, you'll love getting lost here. Personal shoppers are available for the financially endowed and the stylistically challenged. A cafe on the metro level offers a wildly popular frozen yogurt for $3.75. Open M-F 10am-8:30pm, Sa-Su 10am-7pm.

▓ **Barneys New York,** 660 Madison Ave. (☎212-826-8900; www.barneys.com), at 61st St. Ⓢ 4, 5, 6, to 59th St.; N, R, W to 5th Ave./59th St. An exclusive department store known for finding relative unknowns and turning them into cutting-edge designers.

Armani suits, Balenciaga bags, Prada galore—you get the idea. Barney's is hardly for the frugal shopper, though sales and markdowns do happen, and sample sales are frequent enough to tempt even the most frugal. Displays, done in a stark, minimalist aesthetic are practically works of art. Did we mention they have a spa too? Open M-F 10am-8pm, Sa 10am-7pm, Su 11am-6pm.

Encore, 1132 Madison Ave. (☎212-879-2850), at 84th St., 2nd fl. S 4, 5, 6 to 86th St. This magnet for discerning shoppers has been selling new and gently used designer clothing for 50 years. These are still not cheap clothes, but you might find a new $3000 Armani suit selling for $700, or a pair of Manolos for $100. Chanel suits from around $300, and designer denim from $14 (yes, $14). Open M-W and F 10:30am-6:30pm, Th 10:30am-7:30pm, Sa 10:30am-6pm, Su noon-6pm; July to mid-Aug. closed Su.

Venture Stationers, 1156 Madison Ave. (☎212-288-7235; www.ventureonmadison.com), near 86th St. S 4, 5, 6, to 86th St. Are you pining after a handbag you keep seeing on fashionable New Yorkers' shoulders, but you have no idea who makes it or where to go to buy it yourself? Then head to Venture Stationers, where, in addition to the full slate of high-quality stationary supplies, you'll find a thorough selection of big-name designer bags, often on sale. Longchamp, Vera Bradley, Hervé Chapelier, and Kate Spade—all in one place. Open M-F 8am-7pm, Sa 9am-7pm, Su 11am-6pm.

Rita Ford Music Boxes, 19 E 65th St. (☎212-535-6717; www.ritafordmusicboxes.com), between Madison and 5th Ave. S 6 to 68th St. The first, and only, store in the US to service, repair, and sell both antique and contemporary music boxes. Rita Ford has been designing boxes since 1947 for such customers as the White House, the State Department, and overseas royalty. Though you have to have some serious cash to make a purchase here, the shop is a spectator's paradise. Choose a song from the store's wide selections. Popular choices include "Lara's Theme" from Dr. Zhivago, and Eric Clapton's "Wonderful Tonight." Open M-Sa 9am-5pm.

Argosy Bookstore, 116 E 59th St. (☎212-753-4455; www.argosybooks.com), between Lexington and Park Ave. S 4, 5, 6, to 59th St. This 6-floor bookstore, established in 1921, specializes in old, rare, and out-of-print books. You'll also find autographed editions, original letters by authors, Americana, book covers, bookends, and antique maps and prints (from $3). Racks of $1 books outside. Open Sept.-May M-F 10am-6pm, Sa 10am-5pm; June-Aug. M-F only.

Tender Buttons, 143 E 62nd St. (☎212-758-7004), between 3rd and Lexington Ave. S 4, 5, 6, to 59th St.; N, R, W to 5th Ave. For over 40 years, Tender Buttons has provided Upper East Siders with millions of... buttons. Alice in Wonderland buttons, mini-cigarette pack buttons, and, yes, even plain white buttons. If you carelessly lost the button on your favorite Renaissance doublet, you will find a replacement here. The store is tiny and narrow; walking in is like falling down a rabbit hole. Cufflinks also available. Open M-F 10:30am-6pm, Sa 10:30am-5:30pm.

UPPER WEST SIDE

Though locals are quick to bemoan the Upper West Side's inundation with chain stores, the area still boasts many independent boutiques.

Allan and Suzi, 416 Amsterdam Ave. (☎212-724-7445), at 80th St. S 1 to 79th St.; B, C to 81st St. From 70% off new Gaultier wear to vintage cocktail dresses and fabulous Jimmy Choo shoes, this store's discounted haute couture will have you dressing for the nightclubs without breaking the bank. For fashion tips, seek the advice of the owners, former hosts of "At Home with Allan and Suzi" on the Home Shopping Network. A large selection of 50s pumps, 60s platforms, and feather boas. Men's clothing includes Gucci, D&G, and Hugo Boss suits. Madonna, Courtney Love, and Tommy Hilfiger have been spotted shopping here. Dresses $20-1000, shoes $40-400. Haggling is worth the effort; prices are not set. Open M-Sa noon-7pm, Su noon-6.

■ **Sude,** 2470 Broadway (☎212-721-5721), between 91st and 92nd St. S 1,2,3 to 96th St. This reasonably priced women's clothing boutique carries the latest looks from 7 for All Mankind, Free People, To the Max, AG, Ella Moss, Splendid, Goldhawk, and 12 Street. The friendly owners and manageable space make this an enjoyable place to shop. You'll even have some money leftover for shoes. Open M-Sa noon-8pm, Su noon-6:30pm.

Westsider Records, 233 W 72nd St. (☎212-874-1588), between Broadway and West End Ave. S 1, 2, 3 to 72nd St. A relaxed place with wall-to-wall shelves of classical, Broadway, and jazz LPs, many hard to find. Hundreds of $1 records and books, with a particularly great selection on music and theater. Knowledgeable staff. Open daily 11am-8pm.

Lord of Design, 2142 Broadway (☎212-875-8815), between 75th and 76th St. S 1 to 79th St. Fun skirts ($25-70), chunky bracelets ($10-50), and a great staff make this independent boutique the place to come if you want to look cutting edge on a limited budget. It's small, but you could browse here for hours. Open M-Sa 11am-8:30pm, Su 11am-7:30pm.

Maxilla and Mandible, 451 Columbus Ave. (☎212-724-6173; www.maxillaandmandible.com), between 81st and 82nd St. S 1 to 79th St.; B, C to 81st St. Selling fossils, skulls, and other assorted scientific oddities, this old and cluttered store is truly one of a kind. Look for the 350 million-year-old trilobite fossil ($58), the 100 million-year-old dinosaur tooth ($170), and, for the kiddies, real shark teeth ($5). Touching the items is discouraged. Beyond the gallery lies the real business, where paleontologists and artists create traveling museum exhibits. Open M-Sa 11am-7pm, Su 1-5pm. Call before visiting; hours can be erratic.

Murder Ink/Ivy's, 2486 Broadway (☎212-362-8905; www.murderink.com), between 92nd and 93rd St. S 1, 2, 3 to 96th St. Murder Ink claims to carry every mystery in print. Next door is Ivy's, a less mysterious independent bookstore with some first editions and out-of-print finds. Ask to see their first edition of *Catcher in the Rye*, but please don't touch (it's valued in the 5 digits). Open M-Sa 10am-9pm, Su 11am-7pm.

La Brea, 2130 Broadway (☎212-873-7850; www.labrea.com), at 74th St. S 1, 2, 3, to 72nd St. Need a gift in a pinch? Look no further than this quirky boutique with a huge selection of gifts, from classy to comic. For the practically minded, there are silver picture frames, candles, and gift books. For the jokesters, there are Jesus bobbleheads and Freud action figures. For the lewd, there's a range of bachelorette party gift ideas. You'll also find greeting cards, party supplies, and t-shirts. Open M-Th 9am-11pm, F-Sa 8am-midnight, Su 10am-10:30pm.

HARLEM

Harlem is the place to come for discount clothing and an eclectic mix of records, African handicrafts, and street vendor knick-knacks. Wallet-friendly stores line 125th St. between St. Nicholas and Fifth Ave. A recent influx of upscale boutiques has made the neighborhood's shopping more diverse. Head to Lenox and Seventh Ave. between 114th and 135th St. to browse the slew of new, high-end retail stores, many with a focus on African-American designers.

Harlemade, 174 Lenox (6th) Ave. (☎212-987-2500; www.harlemade.com), between 118th and 119th St. Ⓢ 2, 3 to 116th St./Lenox (6th) Ave. For those looking to take a little piece of Harlem back home, Harlemade is the place to go. The small store sells t-shirts ($18), bags ($30-35), and books (from $12) that celebrate Harlem and its African-American community. New products are introduced monthly. Also hosts occasional readings. Call or check the website for details. Open Tu-Sa 11:30am-7:30pm, Su noon-5pm.

Hue-Man Bookstore and Cafe, 2319 Frederick Douglass Blvd. (8th Ave.) (☎212-665-7400; www.huemanbookstore.com), between 124th and 125th St. Ⓢ A, B, C, D to 125th St. One of the largest and most well-known African-American bookstores in the country. Maya Angelou, Toni Morrison, Alicia Keys, and President Bill Clinton have all made appearances here. Frequent open-mic nights, readings, and book discussions. Open M-Sa 10am-8pm, Su 11am-7pm.

Xukuma, 183 Lenox (6th) Ave. (☎212-222-0490; www.xukuma.com), between 119th and 120th St. Ⓢ 2, 3 to 116th St. This new boutique, pronounced "zoo-koo-ma," sells one-of-a-kind accessories, housewares, and women's apparel. There's also a selection of men's accessories and stationary. Show your Harlem pride with a popular Soul-Sista brand t-shirt. Open Tu-Sa noon-7pm, Su noon-6pm.

Malcolm Shabazz Harlem Market, 52 W 116th St. (☎212-987-8131), near Malcolm X Blvd./Lenox (6th) Ave. Ⓢ 2, 3 to 116th St. This covered market, packed with stalls run primarily by Senegalese merchants, offers African clothing, crafts, masks, instruments, incense, and fake designer purses. Open daily 10am-8pm.

BROOKLYN

WILLIAMSBURG AND GREENPOINT

Williamsburg is home to some of the best vintage shopping in the city. Come here to furnish your Bohemian apartment or to add to your hipster wardrobe.

🖾 **Beacon's Closet,** 88 N 11th St. (☎718-486-0816). Ⓢ L to Bedford Ave. A warehouse-like space with an enormous selection of vintage clothing. Almost everything is less than $20. Shirts $7-15. Shoes $12-20. Belts $5-10. The huge selection of women's clothing includes some designer labels. Good men's selection. Green-tag specials are 50% off. Open M-F noon-9pm, Sa-Su 11am-8pm. The Park Slope location at 220 5th Ave. is a more manageable size.

Girdle Company, 218 Bedford Ave., at N 5th St. Ⓢ L to Bedford Ave. A cavernous collective of small retail spaces, including **Verb Cafe** (☎718-599-0977); **Hello, Beautiful Salon** (☎718-387-4732); and **Earwax,** a music store (☎718-486-3771). The fantastic **Spoonbill Sugartown Bookstore** (☎718-387-7322; www.spoonbillbooks.com) holds readings and book parties about once a month. **Internet Garage** (☎718-486-0059) charges $0.15 per min. for Internet access.

KCDC, 90 N 11th St. (☎718-387-9006; www.kcdcskateshop.com), between Berry St. and Wythe Ave. Ⓢ L to Bedford Ave. At first glance, this resembles a typical skate shop, selling t-shirts ($15-25), shoes ($40-150), and videos ($10-30). Then you notice the skater art gallery (free exhibitions change every other month) and the half pipe on the premises. To use the half pipe, you must be over 18 and a member of Skate Parks of America (annual membership $30; join at KCDC). Open M-Sa noon-8pm, Su noon-7pm.

Ugly Luggage, 214 Bedford Ave. (☎718-384-0724), at N 5th St. Ⓢ L to Bedford Ave. A tiny vintage furniture store that's full of retro accessories, like old black-and-white photos ($1), brass belt buckles ($15), and 70s pitcher and glasses sets ($40). There's always a working typewriter in stock. Open M-F 1-8pm, Sa-Su 1-6pm.

BROOKLYN HEIGHTS AND DOWNTOWN

Though it can't quite match Williamsburg for coolness, Downtown Brooklyn none-theless has a number of good shopping opportunities.

🔲 **Beat Street,** 494 Fulton St. (☎718-624-6400; www.beatstreet.com), at Duffield St., in Fort Greene. Ⓢ 2, 3, 4, 5 to Nevins St.; A, C, G to Hoyt St./Schermerhorn. The largest record store in Brooklyn, Beat Street offers lots of hip-hop and an unparalleled vinyl col-lection. 45s $3. Mix CDs $8-10. LPs from $12. Open M-W 10am-7pm, Th-Sa 10am-7:30pm, Su 10am-6pm.

🔲 **Halcyon,** 57 Pearl St. (☎718-260-9299; www.halcyonline.com), at Water St. Ⓢ A, C to High St. Once merely an apartment where local music-lovers gathered, Halcyon is now a hip record store with a rock-garden floor, new-age lounge chairs, and DJs spinning while you shop. The store offers a wonderland of vinyl (from $8), CDs (from $15), DVDs (from $20) and art books (from $15). Open Tu and Th-F noon-9pm; W and Sa noon-8pm, Su noon-6pm.

Fulton Street Mall, Fulton St. (☎718-858-5118), from Adams St. to Flatbush Ave. Info center located near Bond St. Ⓢ M, R, 2, 3, 4, 5 to Borough Hall/Court St. This 7-block strip of over 200 stores is one of the country's largest outdoor shopping malls, filled mostly with fast-food chains and discount clothing shops. Hours vary by store.

CARROLL GARDENS AND RED HOOK

Carroll Gardens is home to tons of independent designer boutiques. They're not cheap, but many offer superior deals to those you'll find in Manhattan.

🔲 **Flirt,** 252 Smith St. (☎718-858-7931; www.flirtbrooklyn.com), between Douglass and Degraw St. Ⓢ F, G to Carroll St. An independent women's clothing store with off-beat apparel at affordable prices. Friendly service. Open Tu-Sa noon-8pm, Su noon-6pm. Additional location in Park Slope, 93 5th Ave. (☎718-783-0364), between Baltic and Warren St.

Soula Shoes, 185 Smith St. (☎718-834-8423; www.soulashoes.com), between Warren and Wyckoff St. Ⓢ F, G to Bergen St. A huge selection of designer sneakers and dress shoes. Prices match the trendy labels, but deals are good during sales. Open Tu-Sa 11am-7pm, Su noon-6pm.

Union Max, 110 Union St. (☎718-222-1785), at Columbia St. Ⓢ F, G to Carroll St. A one-woman operation specializing in vintage beaded necklaces (strands $3-40). Assorted housewares, clothing, and knick-knacks are also on hand. Open F-Su 1-7pm, but call if you'd like to visit at another time.

PARK SLOPE AND PROSPECT PARK

Park Slope is a stroller's heaven, whether or not you want to pay its sometimes-elevated designer prices.

Something Else, 208 5th Ave. (☎718-230-4063), at Union St. Ⓢ M,R to Union St. An excellent selection of both designer items and quirky, affordable finds. The emphasis is on jeans and shoes. Open daily noon-8pm.

Beacon's Closet, 220 5th Ave. (☎718-230-1630), between President and Union St. This vintage clothing mecca, with a second location in Williamsburg, is a budget shopper's dream. Smaller than the Williamsburg site, this store provides a more manageable shopping experience. Open M-F noon-9pm and Sa-Su 11am-8pm.

Bird, 430 7th Ave. (☎718-768-4940), between 14th and 15th St. Ⓢ F to 7th Ave. A fashionable women's boutique, selling designer shirts (from $100), jeans (from $120), earrings (from $36), and bags (from $100) to keep the local hipsters supplied. For those looking to spend less, try the end-of-season sales in late July and early Aug. and Jan. for discounts (20-70% off). Open M-Sa 11:30am-7:30pm, Su noon-6pm.

SHOPPING

NIGHTLIFE

New York nightlife scarcely needs an introduction; its legend precedes it. Whether you prefer a candlelit Nolita wine bar, a rocking Harlem jazz club, a post-industrial Williamsburg boîte, or an A-list Meatpacking District lounge, New York offers an always-evolving cornucopia of nightlife. To keep up on the latest openings and parties, watch publications like *Village Voice* and *New York Magazine*, keep your eyes out for flyers, and pay attention to word-of-mouth. This last source is probably the most important; often the best parties stay underground.

While you can find a fun place to imbibe at virtually any hour of the day or night in New York, bear in mind that nightlife here generally gets going late. A hot bar might be dead until 11pm or so on the weekend; many clubs don't even start to get going until 1 or 2am. Dress well, or you'll appear gauche; leave your drab, conventional duds, especially your sneakers, at home. Remember that New York nightlife, like virtually everything else here, is pricey. Pre-partying before going out is a good way to save money. As the crowds of chimneys outside every New York nightspot can attest, the city is now non-smoking in all in-door public spaces.

GLBT options of every stripe can be found throughout Manhattan, but they're most concentrated in Chelsea and Greenwich Village. Many gay and lesbian bars are proud of their mixed crowds, though some frown on admitting members of one or the other gender. The Lower East Side, the East Village, and Williamsburg, in Brooklyn, are all sure bets for awesome nightlife, but gems often lurk in unexpected places. Discovering them is one of the best part of going out here.

LOWER MANHATTAN

Catering mainly to buttoned-up types looking to loosen their ties at happy hour, Lower Manhattan isn't much of a nightlife destination in its own right. It's home to a lovely splurge, though, if you want to treat yourself after a visit to the Statue of Liberty, Wall Street, or Ground Zero.

🍸 **Rise Bar,** 2 West St. (☎212-344-0800), on the 14th floor of the Ritz Carlton hotel. [S] 4, 5 to Bowling Green. This elegant hotel bar offers dramatic panoramas of the Statue of Liberty and New York Harbor. Unbeatable at sunset, it's a romantic destination that makes a wonderful stop after a long day of sightseeing. Open M-Th 4pm-midnight, F-Sa 4pm-2am, Su 5:30pm-midnight.

SOHO

Artsy types, hipsters, and the professionals striving to pass for them rub shoulders in SoHo. The scene is stylish but slightly less frenetic than that of the Meatpacking District or Chelsea. Rather than clubs, you'll mostly find bars and lounges, which are often excellent restaurants before they give themselves over to drinking.

🍸 **Lucky Strike,** 59 Grand St. (☎212-941-0772), at W Broadway. [S] 1 to Canal St./Varick St.; A, C, E to Canal St./Ave. of the Americas (6th Ave.). France meets the Wild West at this stylishly worn hangout. At meal times it serves tasty and unpretentious food (most entrees $12-18), and it's a great place for a late-night drink. Wine and mixed drinks from $7. Lucky Strike martini $9.50. Open M-W and Su noon-1am, Th noon-2am, F-Sa noon-2:30am.

🍸 **Grand Bar and Lounge,** 310 W Broadway (☎212-963-3588), 2nd fl. of the SoHo Grand Hotel. [S] 1 to Canal St.; A, C, E to Canal St. If you want a full dose of Downtown cool in one single location, pony up some serious cash for a drink at this über-hip hotel bar.

The mixed drinks ($12) here are outstanding; try the Honeysuckle (Cruzan rum and maraschino liqueur) or the Perfect 10 (Stoli vanilla, pineapple, lemon, and lime). Grand margarita $18. Open M-Th and Su 6pm-3am, F-Sa 6pm-4am.

👍 **Milady's,** 160 Prince St. (☎212-226-9069), at Thompson St. [S] C, E to Spring St./Ave. of the Americas (6th Ave.). Down-to-earth decor, friendly staff, low prices, and Manhattanites drunk enough to leave their scowls at home make Milady's a welcome break from the SoHo scene. Beer $3.50-5. No mixed drinks over $7. Open daily 11am-4am.

MercBar, 151 Mercer St. (☎212-966-2727), between Prince and W Houston St. [S] N, R, W to Prince St. A stylish crowd frequents this bar with an enigmatically rustic decor. It's a subdued spot for conversation early, but it becomes a rowdier scene late. Beer $6. Mixed drinks from $12. Open M-Tu 5pm-1:30am, W 5pm-2am, Th 5pm-2:30am, F-Sa 5pm-3:30am, Su 5pm-1:30am.

Bar 89, 89 Mercer St. (☎212-274-0989; www.bar89.com), between Spring and Broome St. [S] N, R, W to Prince St. An upscale bar and restaurant serving haute American fare to a stylish crowd in a minimalist space. The unisex bathroom features glass doors that only become opaque when latched closed. Extremely popular with the early 30s set. Open daily noon-1am.

Raoul's, 180 Prince St. (☎212-966-3518; www.raouls.com), between Thompson and Sullivan St. [S] N, R, W to Prince St. Sexy French charm is the order of the day at this expensive and well-known restaurant with a cool late-night bar scene. Mixed drinks $8-12. Tiny enclosed garden open year-round. Open daily 5pm-1am.

Canal Room, 285 W Broadway (☎212-941-8100; www.canalroom.com), at Canal St. [S] 1 to Canal St. A big, black-and-white lounge that is a good bet if you're in the mood for a celebrity sighting or two. Keep your eye on the glass-enclosed VIP section, but don't even think of going up there yourself. Beer $6. Mixed drinks $9-12. Th 11pm-4am, F-Sa 10pm-4am.

X-R Bar, 128 W Houston St. (☎212-674-4080), at Sullivan St. [S] 1 to Houston St. This comfortable but lively bar caters to an unpretentious crowd that lives in the area. Snack on complimentary ruffled potato chips in the cozy window seats. Beer $3.50-5. Mixed drinks $6-9. M-Tu live music 10pm; Th-Sa DJ spins rock, hip-hop, and soul from 9:30pm. Happy hour daily 4-7pm. Open daily 3pm-4am.

Circa Tabac, 32 Watts St. (☎212-941-1781), between 6th Ave. and Thompson St. [S] C, E to Spring St./Ave. of the Americas (6th Ave.). Despite Bloomberg's ban, this lounge is a specially licensed smoker's haven. The jazz soundtrack, heavy curtains, suede seats, and Art Deco furniture give it a speakeasy feel. 180 kinds of cigarettes are on offer, with a large cigar selection too. Mixed drinks $8-12. Open daily 4pm-4am.

LOWER EAST SIDE

Lower East Side nightlife defines the word "hipster." Packs of 20-somethings roam the streets in designer sneakers, designer jeans, and thrift-store t-shirts. New bars and clubs open constantly, one-upping each other in underground coolness. The neighborhood is also an unbeatable destination for live music. Many New Yorkers consider Lower East Side nightlife to be among Manhattan's best.

👍 **The Back Room,** 102 Norfolk St. (☎212-228-5098), between Rivington and Delancey St. [S] F, J, M, Z to Delancey St./Essex St. This faithful rendition of a Prohibition-era speakeasy, housed in an ordinary-looking apartment building, is appropriately difficult to find. Go through the iron gate by the "Lower East Side Toy Company" sign; there's a bouncer posted there on the weekends. Head to the back of the courtyard, and go up the stairs to your right. You'll find yourself in a classy parlor-like space, where 20- and 30-somethings drink hard-liquor concoctions out of teacups and beer from bottles wrapped in paper bags. A sliding bookcase gives way to a "secret" 2nd bar. A fireplace blazes in the winter. Large groups, especially of men, could have trouble at the door. Open Tu-Sa 7:30pm-2am.

👍 **Happy Ending,** 302 Broome St. (☎212-334-9676; www.happyendinglounge.com), between Eldridge and Forsyth St. [S] F, J, M, Z to Delancey St./Essex St. This bar and lounge was converted from a massage parlor (yes, *that* kind). Mirrors etched with naked women remain, and the saunas have become semi-private booths, their waist-high shower heads left intact. Popular W 8pm reading series; the 3rd W of each month is erotica-themed. Th 10pm "Something Tight" gay dance party. There's a DJ every night downstairs. The canopy outside still reads "Xie He Health Club"; you're in the right place. Beer $3-6. Mixed drinks $6-10. Open Tu-Sa 10pm-4am, Su 7pm-4am.

👍 **Lotus Lounge,** 35 Clinton St. (☎212-253-1144), at Stanton St. [S] F, J, M, Z to Delancey St./Essex St. During the day, Lotus Lounge is a lovely, low-key cafe where locals discuss community politics or tap away on laptops, sipping coffee and eating sandwiches. At night, the lights go down, the taverns are lit, and DJs start spinning around 10pm. Happy hour daily 4-8pm; $2 Buds, $3 drafts. Open M-Sa 8am-4am, Su 8am-2am.

The Delancey, 168 Delancey St. (☎212-254-9920; www.thedelancey.com), between Clinton and Attorney St. [S] F, J, M, Z to Delancey St./Essex St. This 3-level bar and music club draws big crowds. The all-season rooftop bar, complete with palm trees and an aquarium, offers beautiful views of the Williamsburg Bridge. A good lineup of local bands plays in the basement performance space nearly every night; cover $5-10. Open daily 5pm-4am.

Whiskey Ward, 121 Essex St. (☎212-477-2998; www.thewhiskeyward.com), between Rivington and Delancey St. [S] F, J, M, Z to Delancey St./Essex St. Back when New York City was divided into wards, the Lower East Side became known as the Whiskey Ward for its high concentration of neighborhood saloons and willing patrons. This Western-style bar keeps the tradition going with a long list of single-malt bourbons and scotches. Happy hour M-Sa 5-8pm and M-Tu midnight-3am; half-price drafts and well drinks. Try a Knock Out Drop ($6), a shot of tequila and whiskey that will make the next morning rough. Open daily 5pm-4am.

The Slipper Room, 167 Orchard St. (☎212-253-7246; www.slipperroom.com), at Stanton St. [S] F, V to Lower East Side/2nd Ave. Inspired by the Vaudeville variety acts that thrived on the Lower East Side from 1870 to 1930, this converted sneaker store provides a slightly racy assortment of vaudeville and burlesque. Nightly performances range from sketch comedy to go-go dancers. The bachelorette-heavy crowd spills onto Orchard St. Check the website for performance schedules. Th-Sa cover $5; occasionally for other performers as well. Open Tu 8pm-2am, W-Sa 8pm-4am.

> [TIP] **LATE NIGHT MUNCHIES?** A favorite of famished Lower East Side bar-hoppers, **Bereket Turkish Kebab House,** 187 E Houston St. serves up tasty lamb and chicken *shawarma* and falafel. (At Orchard St. [S] F, V to 2nd Ave. ☎212-475-7700. Open 24hr.)

Cake Shop, 152 Ludlow St. (☎212-253-0036; www.cake-shop.com), between Stanton and Rivington St. [S] F, J, M, Z to Delancey St./Essex St. A one-stop shop that houses a daytime cafe serving fresh baked goods, a backroom used-record store, and a beer and wine bar downstairs. Live local bands play most nights; cover free-$8. Happy hour daily 5-8pm; 2-for-1 drinks. Open mic "anti-slam" W at 8pm; $3 cover. Cafe open from 8am. Record store open noon-2am. Bar open 5am-2am.

Welcome to the Johnson's, 123 Rivington St. (☎212-420-9911), between Essex and Norfolk St. [S] F, V to Lower East Side/2nd Ave. A 70s-style living room, complete with puke-green bar stools, shag carpeting, and old trophies on display. There's a pool table in the back, a plastic tree in the corner, and plenty of locals on the couches. Use the graffiti-covered bathrooms at your own risk. PBR $2. Bud $3. Open daily 11am-5pm and 6pm-4am. Cash only.

'inoteca, 98 Rivington St. (☎212-614-0478; www.inotecanyc.com), at Ludlow St. Ⓢ F, J, M, Z to Delancey St. The younger sibling of tiny 'ino, a popular wine bar in the West Village, this Lower East Side outpost improved on the original by adding a menu of Italian snacking plates. But the affordable and extensive wine list is still the biggest draw, and it attracts casual crowds every night. Big wooden tables are group-friendly. The downstairs wine cellar is the best place for subdued conversations. Brunch Sa-Su 10am-4pm. Open daily noon-3am.

Local 138, 138 Ludlow St. (☎212-477-0280), between Stanton and Rivington St. Ⓢ F, J, M, Z to Delancey/Essex St. A neighborhood bar with nary a decoration in sight—just simple wooden tables, a bar, and booths. A terrific spot to lay low and grab a beer ($5), watch a game, or make friends. Happy hour daily 4-9pm; $3 drafts and wine. Open daily 4pm-4am.

Max Fish, 178 Ludlow St. (☎212-529-3959), at Houston St. Ⓢ F, V to Lower East Side/2nd Ave. A great divey hangout with colorful striped and polka-dot walls and one of the best jukeboxes in town. Huge crowds pack in on the weekends. Beer $5. Open daily 6pm-4am.

GREENWICH VILLAGE

Greenwich Village presents an unbeatable variety of outstanding nightlife options. Because of the neighborhood's large student population, many are quite affordable and cater to a youthful crowd. As one of New York's GLBT centers, the Village is home to a wide array of gay and lesbian bars and clubs. As a rule, their clientele tends to be less exclusively of one gender or orientation than that of Chelsea nightspots. The neighborhood is well integrated, and the local scene is truly mixed. Given the Village's illustrious literary history, many of its bars are still haunted by the ghosts of patrons past, perhaps still hungover from their days of hard living and visionary inspiration.

🏆 **Employees Only,** 510 Hudson St., between W 10th St. and Christopher St. Ⓢ 1 to Christopher St. In this classy bar with a 20s feel, skilled bartenders in white chef's uniforms—all with handlebar moustaches—mix up some of the best vintage cocktails in the city. The name derives from the establishment's goal of mixing drinks so good that other bars' employees come here for their own libations. There's no sign other than the neon "Psychic" in the window; one is often on hand. Open daily 6pm-4am.

🏆 **Henrietta Hudson,** 438 Hudson St. (☎212-924-3347; www.henriettahudsons.com), between Morton and Barrow St. Ⓢ 1 to Christopher St. A young, clean-cut lesbian crowd, along with an assortment of gay and straight males, frequents this friendly Greenwich Village institution. Happy hour M-F 5-7pm; $3 beers. Different music every night: M old school, Tu requests, W karaoke, Th world, F house, Sa pop, Su Latin. Cover Sa-Su $7-10. Open M-F 4pm-4am, Sa 1pm-4am, Su 3pm-4am.

🏆 **Chi Chiz,** 135 Christopher St. (☎212-462-0027), at Hudson St. Ⓢ 1 to Christopher St. A hot spot for attractive, well-groomed African-American and Latino gay men, along with an increasing crowd of lesbians on the weekends. Pool table in back. Happy hour daily 5-9pm; 2-for-1 drinks. Open daily 4pm-4am.

The White Horse Tavern, 567 Hudson St. (☎212-989-3956), at W 11th St. Ⓢ 1 to Christopher St. A historic pub that served and over-served the likes of Dylan Thomas and Jack Kerouac, the White Horse today hosts locals who reminisce about its $0.20 beers, a smattering of tourists, and a rowdy singles scene. Outdoor patio. Beer $4-5. Open M-Th and Su 11am-2am, F-Sa 11am-4am.

Chumley's, 86 Bedford St. (☎212-675-4449), between Grove and Barrow St. Ⓢ 1 to Christopher St. Once the epicenter of Greenwich Village literary culture, this bar and restaurant became a speakeasy in Prohibition days. Hundreds of authors, including the Johns Dos Passos, William Faulkner, Ernest Hemingway, J.D. Salinger, and John Steinbeck have raised a glass here. Jackets from their books adorn the walls of this dimly lit hideaway. The fascinating building–complete with original trap doors, secret elevators, and hidden escape routes–has survived 4 fires. The site is worth a visit even if you don't order a drink. Perhaps in homage to its clandestine history, no sign indicates that this cream-colored building with a brown door is a bar. Open M-Th 4pm-midnight, F-Sa noon-1:30am, Su 3pm-midnight.

Red Lion, 151 Bleeker St. (☎212-260-9797; www.redlion-nyc.com), at Thompson St. [S] A, B, C D, E, F, V to W 4th St./Washington Sq. A cool neighborhood bar that hosts 3 bands every night of the week (7, 10pm, 1am). The music is everything from R&B to rock, and there's a wide variety of European and American sports on the TV. If you find yourself here red-eyed in the early afternoon, they have the ultimate hangover cure–a Bloody Mary with bacon bits and a Guiness head ($9). Open daily 11:30am-4am.

The Cubbyhole, 281 W 12th St. (☎212-243-9041), at W 4th St. [S] A, C, E, L to 14th St./8th Ave. Hanging fish, seaweed, and kites put this friendly bar somewhere between a magic underwater garden and a kindergarten classroom. Though predominantly lesbian, the crowd is truly mixed, with straight and gay men warmly welcomed. Happy hour M-F 4-7pm, Sa 2-7pm, Su 2-10pm. Open M-F 4pm-3am, Sa-Su 2pm-3am.

The Duplex, 61 Christopher St. (☎212-255-5438; www.theduplex.com), at 7th Ave. S. [S] 1 to Christopher St. With a talented performing waitstaff, this renowned piano bar is New York's oldest continuing cabaret. Famous alumni include Woody Allen and Joan Rivers. The mixed gay and straight crowd, filled with thespians who can recite every lyric from *On the Twentieth Century,* mingles on the colorful outdoor patio from Memorial Day through Halloween. Cabaret performance room and game room upstairs. Happy hour M-F 4-8pm. Most drinks $6. Cabaret room cover $5-25, depending on event. 2-drink min. per set. Call or check the website for the schedule. Performances start at 9pm M-F, 4pm Sa-Su. Bar open daily 4pm-4am.

Stonewall Bar, 53 Christopher St. (☎212-463-0950), at 7th Ave. S. [S] 1 to Christopher St. Entrance at 113th/7th Ave S. The site of the legendary 1969 Stonewall Riots (p. 55), the Stonewall is still a lively gay bar, though it encounters far less resistance from law enforcement today than it did in 1969. M hip-hop. W and Sa Latin. Th pop and a younger crowd. Enter the Su night male amateur strip contest (appropriately named "Meatpacking"), and win $200. Happy hour M-F 3-9pm; 2-for-1 drinks. Free *hors d'oeuvres* served nightly. M, W, and Sa-Su cover $6. Open daily 3pm-4am

TIP **BEEN A ROUGH NIGHT?** If you're craving grease in the West Village when the bars close at 4am, head to **Mamoun's,** 119 MacDougal St., between W 4th and 3rd St., for great falafel ($2) and *shawarma* ($4), along with baklava, grape leaves, and other Middle Eastern delectables. (☎212-674-8685. [S] A, B, C, D, E, F, V to W 4th St. Open daily 11am-5am.)

Lips, 2 Bank St. (☎212-675-7710; www.lipsnyc.com), at Greenwich Ave. [S] A, C, E, L to 14th St./8th Ave.; 1, 2, 3 to 14th St./7th Ave. A drag-queen cabaret serving Italian and American food and good laughs nightly. You're likely to be surrounded by bachelorette parties, especially on F nights. M salsa fever with $2 margaritas, Tu Trailer Trash karaoke, W popular Bitchy Bingo, Th-Sa dinner with the divas, F late "dirty show" and all-male revue, Su All-you-can-drink champagne brunch 11:30am-4pm and All Beef Patty's Big Fat Juicy Dinners. Cover $7 at tables for show. Open M-Th 5:30pm-midnight, F-Sa 5:30pm-1:30am, Su 11:30am-4pm and 5:30-11pm. Reservations recommended. ❸

NIGHTLIFE

Tortilla Flats, 767 Washington St. (☎212-243-1053), at W 12th St. Ⓢ A, C, E to 14th St. Though close to the Meatpacking District geographically, this fun-loving restaurant and bar couldn't be farther away in spirit. Filled with Christmas lights, fake cacti, and sombreros, it draws a rowdy singles crowd. The chimichangas ($10), chicken mole ($12), and enchiladas ($11) are good if you're hungry, but the margaritas (from $7) are the real draw. M-Tu bingo, W raucous hula hoops contest, Su trivia at 8pm. Happy hour M-F 4-7pm and F-Sa 1-4am; 2-for-1 Rolling Rocks and PBR, $5 off pitchers of margaritas. Sa-Su brunch noon-3:30pm. Open M-Th and Su noon-2am, F-Sa noon-4am.

When traveling home from the Meatpacking District late at night, remember that streets get more deserted the further west you travel. It's best to avoid dark areas west of 10th Ave. in the wee hours of the morning.

MEATPACKING DISTRICT

The Meatpacking District is an orgy of jet-set pretty young things, see-and-be-seen clubs, stone-faced bouncers, pointy shoes, fake boobs, and $16 cocktails. Haughtiness and high prices are to be expected here, but Meatpacking District nightspots are celebrity-filled and often undeniably cool.

■ **Cielo,** 18 Little W 12th St. (☎917-312-8892), between Washington and Greenwich St. A proudly exclusive and surprisingly intimate dance club, centered on a sunken dance floor. High-caliber DJs spin electronica, nu jazz, future soul, and deep house every night. The clientele is stylish and the door is tightly guarded; plan your outfit well. Cover $10-20. Extremely expensive bottle service only at tables. Open W-Sa 10pm-4am.

■ **Plunge,** 18 9th Ave. (☎212-206-6700; www.hotelgansevoort.com). Ⓢ B, D, F, N, Q, R, W to 34th St. The view from the rooftop bar of the swanky Hotel Gansevoort, which overlooks the Hudson River, may be the most scenic in New York City. Luxurious contemporary furniture, candlelight, and a retractable roof provide the perfect setting for the beginning or the end of the evening. The dress code is business casual—don't show up in jeans or sneakers. Mixed drinks from $14. Open daily 11am-4am.

TIRED OF REJECTION? Clubs in the Meatpacking District are notorious for their brutally exclusive doors. The buzz surrounding a club is sometimes as much about the despair in the rope line as it is about the vibe inside. If you're desperate to join the A-list crowd, eating dinner at the club's restaurant is a sure-fire way to ensure that you're part of the party later on. But never lose sight of the prices you're paying; mediocre food never cost so much.

Gaslight, 400 W 14th St. (☎212-807-8444; www.gaslightnyc.com), at 9th Ave. Ⓢ B, D, F, N, Q, R, W to 34th St. A young crowd fills this funky parlor-like space. For once in the Meatpacking District, the atmosphere is unpretentious, drinks are cheap, and there's never a cover charge. Open daily 1pm-4am.

APT, 419 W 13th St. (☎212-414-4245; www.aptwebsite.com), between 9th and Washington St. Ⓢ A, C, E, L to 14th St./8th Ave. Yes, you found it. Though APT doesn't have the bouncer or the rope line you'd expect (and only a small, inconspicuous square sign), push open that unpromising door. On the main floor is a pricey restaurant that's best skipped; downstairs is a starkly hip bar and club that gets going late. Open 10pm-4am.

Lotus, 409 W 14th St. (212-243-4420; lotusnewyork.com), at 9th Ave. Ⓢ A, C, E, L to 14th St./8th Ave. Lotus is the prototype of the Meatpacking District nightclub. Upstairs, it's an over-priced Asian-fusion bistro. Downstairs, when the night gets late, it's full of well-dressed young professionals dancing up a storm. The door here isn't as merciless as elsewhere, and the DJs are top-notch. Cover $20. Open Tu-Su 10pm-4am.

EAST VILLAGE

East Village nightlife runs the gamut from grungy dive bars, to drag-queen cabarets, to artsy underground music venues, to late-night dance clubs, to sedate wine bars. Whether you're visiting New York for the first time or you live here, you can't do much better than the East Village as a nightlife destination.

👍 **Angel's Share,** 8 Stuyvesant St., between 9th St. and St. Mark's Pl. [S] 6 to Astor Pl. Hidden behind an unmarked door in the back of a bustling Korean restaurant, this secluded nightspot with soft jazz playing in the background is a great choice for a romantic night out. The house rules here are strictly enforced: no parties larger than 4, no shouting, and no standing. The potential inconvenience pays off; you'll find a genuinely serene atmosphere, in addition to a heavenly menu of cocktails. Try the Lady in Satin (sake, violet liqueur, and vodka; $10) or the Sophisticated Lady (plum wine, compari, and grapefruit juice; $10). Excellent selection of whiskeys and brandies. 1-drink min. Mixed drinks $8-12. Open 6pm-2:30am.

👍 **d.b.a.,** 41 1st Ave. (☎212-475-5097; www.drinkgoodstuff.com), between E 2nd and 3rd St. [S] F, V to Lower East Side/2nd Ave. A sophisticated choice for your inner alcohol connoisseur, this bar has 19 always-changing premium beers on tap, well over 100 bottled imports and microbrews, 50 kinds of bourbon, 130 single-malt whiskeys, and 45 different tequilas. Classic rock, grunge, and 90s tunes play from the jukebox, and conversations fill the air. Outdoor beer garden open until 10pm; space heaters keep it toasty even on cold winter nights. Happy hour 5-7pm; $4 drinks. Open daily 1pm-4am.

👍 **Tribe,** 132 1st Ave. (☎212-979-8965; www.tribebar.com), at St. Mark's Pl. [S] 6 to Astor Pl. A glamorous dark-wood-and-leather bar with colorful but subtle backlighting. Comfortable lounge areas offer just enough room for a late-night DJ-ed dance party. Management requested that *Let's Go* note that ladies should remove their shoes before dancing on the leather furniture. Late 20s crowd. Beer $4-6. Mixed drinks $7-11. DJ nightly from 9pm: lots of hip-hop, rock, 80s, and pop. Tu 7-10pm live funk, rock, and indie music. Happy hour daily 5-9pm; $3 domestic beers and $5 well drinks. Open daily 5pm-4am.

👍 **McSorley's Old Ale House,** 15 E 7th St. (☎212-473-9148), at 3rd Ave. [S] 6 to Astor Pl. McSorley's motto is, "We were here before you were born," and unless you're 152 years old, they're right. The historic bar has hosted luminaries such as Abraham Lincoln, Teddy and Franklin Roosevelt, and John Kennedy, and little seems to have changed inside since they drank here. Women weren't allowed in until 1970, and the bar still caters to a primarily male crowd. Only 2 beers—light and dark—are served by the surly Irish bartenders. Double-fisters take note: mugs come cheaper 2 at a time ($2.50 for 1, $4 for 2). Go on a weeknight to avoid a line. Open M-Sa 11am-1am, Su 1pm-1am. Cash only.

Lucky Cheng's, 24 1st Ave. (☎212-995-5500; www.planetluckychengs.com), between E 1st and 2nd St. [S] F, V to Lower East Side/2nd Ave. One of New York City's best-known drag clubs. The upstairs restaurant and downstairs bar are decorated in over-the-top Asian kitsch and are serviced by gorgeous "girls." Karaoke runs M-Th and Su 9pm-2am and F-Sa 9pm-4am. Bachelorette parties, cut-throat banana eating contests, and dinner drag shows every night. Cocktails with names like Ruby's Boobies and Trampy Toratini $9. Pan-Asian cuisine served M-Th and Su 6-11pm, F-Sa 5:30pm-midnight. 3-course fixed-price meal $32. Bar open M-Th and Su 5pm-2am, F-Sa 5pm-4am.

Niagara, 112 Ave. A (☎212-420-9517), at corner of E 7th St. [S] 6 to Astor Pl.; L to 1st Ave. Across from Thompson Park, this spacious corner bar dominates the Ave. A scene. After-midnight crowds flock to its dark-wood tables, booths, and bars. Downstairs Lei Lounge is open M-Sa for dancing. Th 3 bands play here with no cover, $3 beers, and a free art show. DJs M-Sa 10pm. Beers $5-6. Mixed drinks $6-10. Open daily 4pm-4am.

FROM THE ROAD

CHELSEA (EARLY) MORNING

I spent the day snooping through Chelsea hotels, ducking in galleries, and eating at every falafel stand, fashion cafe, and new-new American bistro that might possibly be worthy of *Let's Go*. Then I walked back to my apartment in the East Village. But I won't be resting my feet for long. I'm about to head back to Chelsea for nightlife research.

It's 3:30am. I'm in my bathroom, not quite sure how I got here. I'm drunk. My feet are swollen. I'm crying. What happened?

The answer, I now realize, is four straight days of nightlife research in and around Chelsea. Luckily, I had my friend Ray to serve as my local guide. I fell head-over-heels for the classy setting and vintage cocktails at the **Flatiron Lounge** (p. 305). Then I fell in love all over again at stylish **Plunge,** in the Hotel Gansevoort (p. 300). At **Barracuda** (p. 304), I befriended Arthur, the bouncer. He told me that he was quadralingual—and that, no, that did not mean something sexual, like cunnilingus. I received a full-frontal flashing from a go-go dancer at **Splash** (p. 303). I screamed.

Now that the end of the summer is approaching, I've practically got carpal tunnel from all this typing, and the outline of my flip flops is burned into my feet. But still, most of the time—when it's not 3:30am and stiflingly hot in my bathroom—I love my job.

—Kate Penner

Sing Sing Karaoke, 81 Ave. A (☎212-674-0700), between 5th and 6th St. This Asian-style karaoke bar has 15 sound-proofed private chambers where you can sing your heart out for the benefit of only your closest friends. Once the liquid courage kicks in, however, head out to the bar area and belt out your ditty for the world. Or just chill at the bar and watch others embarrass themselves. Beer $5-6. Mixed drinks $8-9. Deluxe shot sampler sure to make you think you're Pavarotti $32. Open M-Th 3pm-3am, F-Sa 2pm-4am, Su 2pm-3am.

Nuyorican Poets Cafe, 236 E 3rd St. (☎212-505-8183; www.nuyorican.org), between Ave. B and C. [S] F, V to Lower East Side/2nd Ave. New York City's leading venue for poetry slams (check out F night slam at 10pm) and spoken-word performances. Several regulars have been featured on MTV. Shows are a mixed bag of doggerel, with occasional gems to be discovered. If you don't like the poets, don't worry—there's likely to be a heckler in the house. Also features music, hip-hop, film and video, and theater. W night is open mic slam; sign up in advance. Cover $7-12. Check the website or call for upcoming performances and hours. Usually shows at 8, 9 and/or 10pm; some Sa and Su afternoon events too.

KGB, 85 E 4th St. (☎212-505-3360; www.kgbbar.com), at 2nd Ave. [S] F, V to Lower East Side/2nd Ave. Formerly a meeting place for the Ukrainian Communist Party; today a hangout for literati and Slavophiles. Many well-known authors and poets do readings here; recent appearances by Michael Cunningham and Jhumpa Lahiri. The bar retains its original Soviet furnishings, including a Lenin propaganda banner and candle-illuminated photos of factories, and serves over 20 kinds of Stoli shots ($3). Poetry readings M nights. Fiction readings Su nights. Frequent literary events Tu-Th as well; call or check the website for details. Open daily 7pm-4am.

Lakeside Lounge, 162 Ave. B (☎212-529-8463; www.lakesidelounge.com), between E 10th and 11th St. [S] L to First Ave.; 6 to Astor Pl. A divey, lively, hillbilly bar, always filled with a local crowd. Lots of boating-inspired stuff on the walls. Photo booth ($4) lets you immortalize just how bad your beer goggles were. Nightly live rock music (mostly local bands paid in beer) starts M-Th and Su 9:30pm, F-Sa 11pm. Happy hour 4-8pm; 2-for-1 drinks. Open 4pm-4am daily.

Lit, 93 2nd Ave. (☎212-777-7987), at E 6th St. [S] 6 to Astor Pl.; F, V to Lower East Side/2nd Ave. A hipster-rocker bar, with live music downstairs Tu-Sa and DJs upstairs every night. Mostly populated by "artists of the industry." Most drinks $4-8. A glass-walled art gallery in the back hosts changing exhibits of acrylic and oil paintings by local and international artists. "Dirty Down" electronic music every other F; no cover. Karaoke every Su at 10:30pm. Happy hour daily 5-9pm; $2 off most drinks. Gallery open Tu-Sa 2-7pm. Bar open M-Sa 5pm-4am, Su 8pm-4am.

Swift Hibernian Lounge, 34 E 4th St. (☎212-227-9438), between Bowery and Lafayette St. [S] 6 to Bleecker St.; N, R, W to 8th St. This resolutely Irish pub is dotted with references to Jonathan Swift and his *Gulliver's Travels.* A curving bar leads into the back room, filled with wooden booths and communal tables. 23 drafts and 65 bottles make for an unbeatable beer selection. Tu live traditional Irish music. Happy hour noon-5pm; $0.50 off all beers. Open daily noon-4am.

Decibel, 240 E 9th St. (☎212-979-2733), between Stuyvesant St. and 2nd Ave. [S] 6 to Astor Pl. The entrance to this somewhat hidden bar is down a flight of stairs; look for the wooden archway just above them. At Decibel, Japanese charm meets the aggressive funk of a Village basement. It's a tiny and fantastic place for sake bombs. Killer sakes $4-6 per glass. Also serves an assortment of Japanese finger foods. Steamed soybeans $3. Pickled garlic with soy sauce $3. Seafood and vegetable pancake $7. $8 min. per person during busy weekend hours. Open M-Sa 8pm-3am, Su 8pm-1am.

St. Dymphna's, 118 St. Mark's Pl. (☎212-254-6636; www.stdymphnas.com), between First Ave. and Ave. A. [S] 6 to Astor Pl. This bright and cozy Irish pub, named after the patron saint of the mentally ill, is an excellent low-key option for a relaxed night out. Kick back with a local crowd, a pint ($5), and a great homemade burger ($9). If you're looking to tame a hangover rather than create one, go for the Irish breakfast, with eggs, potatoes, beans, mushrooms, and an assortment of meats ($11). Free wireless. Kitchen open daily 11am-midnight. Bar open M-W 10am-3am, Th-Su 10am-4am.

7B, 108 Ave. B (☎212-473-8840), at 7th St. [S] F, V to Lower East Side/2nd Ave; L to 1st Ave. A rowdy, unaffected college bar, with pinball machines, a photo booth, video bowling, and a Big Buck Hunter video game. Happy hour daily noon-7pm; $3.50 drafts. Open daily noon-4am.

TIP **STAY FUELED FOR A LONG NIGHT.** When you're taking advantage of all East Village nightlife has to offer, you'll want some sustenance to keep you going. Tonight is your lucky night—the East Village has tons of awesome (and cheap) late-night options. Try fries from **Pommes Frites** (p. 127), *pierogis* at **Veselka** (p. 128), or a "schawafel" at **Chickpea** (p. 129).

Webster Hall, 125 E 11th St. (☎212-353-1600; www.websterhall.com), between 3rd and 4th Ave. [S] 4, 5, 6, L, N, Q, R, W to 14th St./Union Sq. You'll find a trendier scene elsewhere, but Webster Hall can boast 4 floors, each with its own DJ-ed music, along with a sports bar and coffee bar to boot. The array of weekly activities is out-of-control. Th hunks' male revue $15 online, $20 at the door; includes open bar 9:30-11:30pm; show at 10pm. Th free cover for women. Everything from bikini contests to music by resident DJs F night; check website for schedule. Website has guest passes that get you $10-15 off. Open Th-Sa 10pm-5am.

CHELSEA

The unquestioned capital of New York's GLBT scene, Chelsea is an intense extravaganza of fog, mood lights, constantly thumping music, and beautiful gay men. Though nightlife in the area is definitely gay-driven, many spots, particularly where the neighborhood bleeds into the Meatpacking District and the West Village, welcome a mixed crowd.

SBNY, 50 W 17th St. (☎212-691-0073; www.splashbar.com), between 5th and 6th Ave. [S] 1 to 18th St./7th Ave.; F, V to 23rd St./Ave. of the Americas (6th Ave.). One of the most popular gay mega-bars, the newly renamed and renovated Splash Bar New York (formerly

NIGHTLIFE

known simply as Splash) is an enormous 2-floor complex. Industrial decor provides a sleek backdrop for a crowded scene. Nightly theme parties. Happy hour M-Sa 4-9pm; 2-for-1 beer and mixed drinks. Cover after 11pm M-W $5, Th $10, F $20; cover often increases after midnight. Open M-Th and Su 4pm-4am, F-Sa 4pm-5am, Su 3pm-4am.

 g, 223 W 19th St. (☎212-929-1085; www.glounge.com), between 7th and 8th Ave. Ⓢ 1 to 18th St./7th Ave. A brightly colored, oval-shaped bar popular with pumped-up and pretty Chelsea men cruising to the sounds of DJ-ed house. Shirtless bartenders serve famous frozen cosmos ($7). Happy hour M-F 4-9pm. Open daily 4pm-4am. Cash only.

■ **Barracuda,** 275 W 22nd St. (☎212-645-8613), between 7th and 8th Ave. Ⓢ C, E to 23rd St./8th Ave. Classic movies play on TVs above the bar, and dramatic red lighting directs patrons to a plush back lounge of armchairs, booths and sofas at this gay-friendly hangout that draws a mixed crowd. Frequent live music. Drinks from $6. Happy hour M-F 4-9pm; 2-for-1 drinks. Open daily 4pm-4am. Cash only.

TIP: DRESS TO IMPRESS. Chelsea nightspots place a definite premium on looking good. Now's the time to give your ratty jeans and sneakers a rest and break out your fabulous-looking duds.

Heaven, 579 Ave. of the Americas (6th Ave.) (☎212-243-6100), between 16th and 17th St. Ⓢ 1, 2, 3 to 14th St./7th Ave.; F, L, V to 14th St./Ave. of the Americas (6th Ave.). A fun-loving gay club that attracts a youngish crowd and doesn't take itself too seriously. The white-on-white, intensely mirrored chamber on the ground floor is called Heaven, a small lounge in back is called Purgatory, and the top floor, by far the most fun, is called Hell. Women are always welcome. Th Latin music. F lesbian night. Sa gay college party. Open daily 5pm-4am.

The Roxy, 515 W 18th St. (☎212-645-5156; www.roxynyc.com), at 10th Ave. Ⓢ A, C, E, L to 14th St./8th Ave. Catering to both gay and straight crowds, The Roxy boasts a series of gigantic and luxurious spaces for drinking and dancing. Downstairs, you'll find high ceilings, a beautiful dance floor, and pounding techno and house. Upstairs is a more intimate setting, where the DJ focuses on pop and hip-hop. Beer $5. Mixed drinks from $6. W indoor Roller Disco (cover $25) attracts a mixed gay and straight crowd; free roller skating classes W 6:30-7:45pm. F straight night. Sa gay night. Open W 8pm-2am, F 11pm-4am, Sa 11pm-6am.

View, 232 8th Ave. (☎212-929-2243), at W 22nd St. Ⓢ C, E to 23rd St./8th Ave. One of Chelsea's most fashionable see-and-be-seen gay lounges. A different theme and crowd every night. W martini and jazz, F Drag Queen Puppet Bingo, Su steam room with $3 beers if you take off your shirt, and occasional live oil wrestling. Happy hour M-F 4-8pm. Open M-F 4pm-4am, Sa 3pm-2am, Su 1pm-4am.

TIP: BRING CASH. Most bars in Chelsea accept credit cards, but clubs often have a sizable minimum credit-card charge. Unless you're planning on running up a serious tab, hit the ATM first so you don't have to leave the party.

The Big Apple Ranch, 39 W 19th St., 5th fl. (☎212-358-5752; www.bigappler-anch.com), at Dance Manhattan, between 5th and 6th Ave. Ⓢ F, V to 23rd St./Ave. of the Americas (6th Ave.); N, R to 23rd St./Broadway. A friendly crowd of urban cowboys and cowgirls welcomes all to a romping evening of gay and lesbian two-stepping on Sa nights. The club was founded in order to provide a dance venue for same-sex partners in the New York community. Cover $10, includes lesson. Sa only 8pm-1am: beginner's two-step lesson 8pm, line dancing lesson 8:30pm, open dance starts at 9pm. Call or check the website for upcoming themes and events.

Rawhide, 212 8th Ave. (☎212-242-9332), at W 21st St. Ⓢ C, E to 23rd St./8th Ave. The name says it all; Rawhide is a one-room haven for leather daddies. Popular with an after-work and after-hours crowd. W-Su go-go boys at 8pm. Beer $5. Happy hour 10am-10pm; domestic beers $3. Open M-Sa 10am-4am, Su noon-4am.

UNION SQUARE, THE FLATIRON DISTRICT, AND MURRAY HILL

Nightlife to the east of lower Midtown is a mixed bag. While the Flatiron District is becoming a trendy, upscale center, much of the area caters mainly to tourist and after-work crowds. There are some gems in the neighborhood, but it's not jam-packed with cool nightspots.

👍 **Flatiron Lounge,** 37 W 19th St. (☎212-727-7741; www.flatironlounge.com), between 5th Ave. and Ave. of the Americas (6th Ave.). [S] 1, 6, F, N, R, V to 23rd St. Candlelight, tinkling jazz, and a vintage atmosphere provide respite from this neighborhood's busy pace. The 30 ft. mahogany bar was salvaged from The Ballroom, which hosted the likes of Frank Sinatra. Today, it provides the setting for a 30s-inflected menu of classic cocktails. Try the NY Sour (rye whiskey, fresh lemon juice, a dash of orange, and a float of dry red wine; $12) or the Corpse Reviver #2 (Gin, Cointreau, Lillet Blanc, and lemon; $12). Open M-W and Su 5pm-2am, Th-Sa 5pm-4am.

Pete's Tavern, 129 E 18th St. (☎212-473-7676), at Irving Pl. [S] 4, 5, 6, L, N, Q, R, W to 14th St./Union Sq. This famous and popular nightspot claims to be "New York's oldest original bar"—it's been serving alcohol since 1864. Photos on the wall document the days of prohibition, and legend has it that O. Henry wrote *The Gift of the Magi* in the 1st booth as you enter. On warm nights, you can take your beer outside to the sidewalk tables. Open daily 11am-2:30am.

Heartland Brewery, 35 Union Sq. W (☎212-645-3400), at 17th St. [S] 4, 5, 6, L, N, Q, R, W to 14th St./Union Sq. A popular (though slightly touristy) after-work hangout. Six types of home brews on tap, along with handcrafted black cherry soda and root beer. Open M-F 11am-11pm, Sa-Su 11am-midnight.

Old Town Bar and Grill, 45 E 18th St. (☎212-529-6732), between Park Ave. S and Broadway. [S] 4, 5, 6, L, N, Q, R, W to 14th St./Union Sq. A dark, 105-year-old hideaway with wood and brass furniture. Beer on tap $4. Open M-F 11:30am-1am, Sa noon-1am, Su noon-10pm.

UPPER EAST SIDE

The Upper East Side is not a nightlife destination in its own right, but if you're in the area, there's no shortage of places to drink and party. In between neighborhood's staid and elegant hotel bars, there's a preponderance of sports bars catering to a young and preppy crowd.

👍 **Metropolitan Museum Roof Garden,** 1000 5th Ave. (☎212-535-7710). [S] 4, 5, 6 to 86th St. On the 5th fl. of the Met, this lovely patio bar (open only in the summer) affords spectacular views of Central Park and the Manhattan skyline. It's an ideal place to start the evening with a glass of wine ($9), a beer ($7), or a martini ($10). Enter at the main entrance and take the elevator from the first floor. Open May-Oct., weather permitting. Tu-Th 10am-4:30pm, F-Sa 10am-8:15pm, Su 10am-4:30pm.

The Big Easy, 1768 2nd Ave. (☎212-348-0879; www.bigeasynyc.com), at 92nd St. [S] 6 to 96th St. A post-grad hangout for those who miss their college years, with 4 beirut tables in the back and a Skee-Ball machine up front. Happy hour every night 5-8pm. Karaoke W. $2 Bud drafts 11pm-midnight. A good spot for cheap, strong drinks before a long New York City night. Open M-F 5pm-4am, Sa-Su noon-4am.

Merchants NY, 1125 1st Ave. (☎212-832-1551; www.merchantsny.com), at 62nd St. [S] N, R, W, 4, 5, 6 to 59th St. Though the food (and drinks) at this candlelit nightspot are pricey, the ambiance is classy and—with funky-colored couches and red-shaded lamps—not at all stuffy. Downstairs, Merchant's boasts a cigar and brandy bar, fireplace, and live jazz midweek (Tu and W 9pm-1am). The sour apple martini ($10) is worth the price. Live DJ Th-Sat 11:30pm-1:30am. Open daily 11:30am-4:30am.

American Spirits, 1744 2nd Ave. (☎212-289-7510; www.americanspiritsbar.net), between 90th and 91st St. [S] 4, 5, 6 to 86th St./Lexington Ave. In a neighborhood of seemingly indistinguishable sports bars, two things separate this one from the rest: $7 pitchers of beer and Sa 11pm karaoke. Beer $4-5. Mixed drinks $4-8. Nightly drink specials vary—look out for $15 buckets of PBR and $3 frozen margaritas in summer. F once a month has live music, with a tendency toward rock and singer-songwriters. Th night trivia. Pool league M-Tu and Su. Happy hour M-F 4-8pm. Open daily 4pm-4am.

Dorrian's Red Hand, 1616 2nd Ave. (☎212-772-6660), at 84th St. [S] 4, 5, 6 to 86th St. This old-fashioned and preppy sports bar is rumored to be a favorite hangout of Yankees players. The bar opens right onto 2nd Ave. and hosts a popular karaoke night on Tu. Open M-Th and Su 11:30am-1am, F-Sa 11:30am-2am.

Mo's Caribbean Bar and Mexican Grill, 1454 2nd Ave. (☎212-650-0561), at 76th St. [S] 6 to 77th St. With fake palm trees, huge TVs, 50 kinds of margaritas, 6 kinds of scorpion bowls, and 7 nights of drink specials, Mo's is one merry place. It's a good spot to satisfy a Mexican food craving (nachos $7; enchiladas from $10; fajitas from $12). Happy hour 4-7pm; entire bar half-price. Open M-F 4pm-4am, Sa-Su 11:30am-4am.

Ship of Fools, 1590 2nd Ave. (☎212-570-2651; www.shipoffoolsnyc.com), between 82nd and 83rd St. [S] 4, 5, 6 to 86th St. One of the most popular sports bars in Manhattan, Ship of Fools has great buffalo wings and 40 TVs to let you catch everything from baseball to rugby. If you'd rather not be a spectator, head to the back rooms for a game of pool ($1.50) or darts ($10 deposit at the bar). Mixed drinks $4. Bottled beers $16 for a bucket of 5. Happy hour M-F 4-7pm; $2 pints of Miller and $4 frozen margaritas. Th nights are Retro Island nights, featuring 80s and 90s videos with tropical drinks and giveaways. Open M-Th 3pm-4am, F-Su 11:30am-4am.

UPPER WEST SIDE

Nightlife on the Upper West Side tends to be split between dive-bar playgrounds for 20-somethings and classier watering holes to which these young professionals eventually graduate. Though it can't claim the cutting-edge sophistication of downtown, Upper West Side nightlife is relaxed and plentiful.

👍 **Dive 75,** 101 W 75th St. (☎212-362-7518), between Columbus and Amsterdam Ave. [S] 1, 2, 3 to 72nd St. This cozy bar offers all the joys of your favorite dive without the unusable bathroom. Locals lounge on comfy couches—watching TV, enjoying the pop-rock jukebox, and pondering the eerily glowing fish tank. A stack of board games sits in the corner. W night bingo with the "Dive Bar Divas" 9-11pm. Happy hour 5-7pm; Buds $2.50, mixed drinks $4. Open M-Th 5pm-4am, F 2:30pm-4am, Sa-Su noon-4am.

👍 **Shalel Lounge**, 65½ W 70th St. (☎212-873-2300), between Central Park West and Columbus Ave. [S] B, C to 72nd St.; 1, 2, 3 to 72nd St. This subterranean jewel, beneath eatery Metsovo, oozes romance. Bead-draped nooks, lightly tinkling waterfalls, dim votive lighting, and a chic international crowd create a definite mystique. On weekends, a Moroccan band plays softly in the background. Wines $9. Martinis $10. Malt liquors $12. Open M-Th and Su 6pm-2am, F-Sa 6pm-3am.

👍 **The Dead Poet,** 450 Amsterdam Ave. (☎212-595-5670), at 81st St. [S] 1 to W 79th St. Photos, quotes, and books from some of history's most well-known wordsmiths line the walls of this cozy, dimly lit tavern. You can even sign out books to take home. Thankfully, the place doesn't take itself too seriously, and the diversions aren't all highbrow: pool, darts, and sports on TV keep the laid-back crowd entertained. Drink 500 pints of Guinness and you get your own plaque on the wall. Happy hour M-F 4-8pm with $3 pints. Open M-Sa 8am-4am, Su noon-4am. Less than $15 cash only.

West 79th Street Boat Basin Cafe, W 79th St. (☎212-496-5542; www.boatbasincafe.com) at the Hudson River. [S] 1 at 79th St. Follow 79th St. to a rotunda near the water's edge, and climb downstairs. Only open in the summer, and then only when the weather's nice, this relaxed and friendly outdoor bar has the feel of a block party or family picnic. Frequented by neighborhood softball teams and locals with their dogs, this bar is the perfect place to eat a burger, drink a beer, and watch the sun set over the Hudson River. Burgers and sandwiches $8-14. Beer and wine $5-7. Brunch served Sa-Su 11am-3pm. Open M-F noon-11pm, Sa 11am-11pm, Su 11am-10pm. If the weather is uncertain, call ahead to see if they're open.

Citrus Bar and Grill, 320 Amsterdam Ave. (☎212-595-0500; www.josiesnyc.com), at 75th St. Ⓢ 1, 2, 3 to 72nd St. This upscale restaurant and bar, lit in a host of citrus hues, promises "Latin fare, Asian flair" and caters to an upscale under-30 crowd. The food (shrimp dumplings $8.75; coriander and three-pepper crusted yellowfin tuna $23) is delicious if pricey, the margaritas made with fresh purees of exotic fruits ($9) are enticing, and the vast tequila selection will satisfy even the most snobbish shot taker. Streetside outdoor seating in warm weather. Open M 5:30-11pm, Tu-Th 5:30pm-midnight, F-Sa 5:30pm-1am, Su 11:30am-11pm.

 LATE NIGHT MUNCHIES? The greasy food at 24hr. Upper West Side classics like **Gray's Papaya** (p. 140) and **Big Nick's Burger Joint** (p. 139) tastes best at 3am.

Yogi's, 2156 Broadway (☎212-873-9852), between 76th and 75th St. Ⓢ 1 to 79th St. Midriff-baring bartenders pour seriously cheap alcohol (mugs of beer $1.25-2.25, pitchers $5-7, shots from $2.50) at this neighborhood dive, where bras and a giant picture of Elvis hang from the bar. Crowds of 20-somethings enjoy the constant stream of country twanging from the stereo. Open daily 11:30am-4am.

Bin 71, 237 Columbus Ave. (☎212-362-5446), at 71st St. Ⓢ 1, 2, 3, B, C to 72nd St. This tiny wine bar draws after-work crowds that spill onto the sidewalk every night. Wear comfy shoes as you'll probably be standing. Over 100 wines are available by the bottle ($23-300); most glasses cost around $10. The beer selection is decent, and the Mediterranean and Spanish tapas offerings, like polenta with prosciutto and lobster salad with avocado ($6-15), are excellent. Open M-Tu 4:30pm-1:30am, W-Su noon-2am.

The Evelyn Lounge, 380 Columbus Ave. (☎212-724-2363), at 78th St. Ⓢ B, C to 81st St. Blazing fireplaces illumine exposed brick walls and leather furniture, creating a romantic and slightly macabre atmosphere. Popular with after-work and late-night sets. The lounge downstairs is open on weekends, with 5 more rooms and 2 more bars. Patrons dance to DJ-spun hip-hop. Cultured locals sip martinis ($11) and beer ($6). Collared shirts for men are required, and no sneakers or baggy jeans are allowed. Open M-Th and Su 5pm-2:30am, F-Sa 5pm-4am. Lounge open Th-Sa 8pm-4am.

BROOKLYN

The secret is out: Brooklyn nightlife is hot. It's prompted many a hipster to relocate here, and it even draws died-in-the-wool Manhattanites across the East River for the night. Here, candlelight and over-priced cosmos give way to refurbished industrial decor, microbrews, and indie-rock jukeboxes. Once you get to know the scene, you may wonder why you've been throwing away money downtown.

WILLIAMSBURG AND GREENPOINT

The capital of the new Brooklyn's nightlife is Williamsburg. Every night of the week, young locals crowd the neighborhood's eclectic bars, each of which seems to be trying to best the others for the title of strangest past incarnation.

Galapagos, 70 N 6th St. (☎718-384-4586; www.galapagosartspace.com), between Kent and Wythe St., in Williamsburg. Ⓢ L to Bedford Ave. Once a mayonnaise factory, this space is now one of the coolest nightspots in the city. The industrial decor centers on a giant reflecting pool—formerly the mayonnaise tank. Wild, slightly scandalous theme nights virtually every night. M 8pm Smut, a provocative readings series (free); M 10pm burlesque show ($5). Tu-W live rock bands ($6-7). F Evolve theater series ($10). Sa after 10pm DJs and theme parties (no cover). Check the website for an up-to-date calendar of shows, DJs, and theme nights. Happy hour M-Sa 6-8pm. Open M-Th and Su 6:30pm-2am, F-Sa 6pm-4:30am.

Pete's Candy Store, 709 Lorimer St. (☎718-302-3770; www.petescandystore.com), between Frost and Richardson St. [S] L to Lorimer St. This soda-shop-turned-bar hosts live music every night at 9pm and a quirky assortment of activities beforehand. M 7:30pm alternates between spelling bees and stand-up comedy. Tu 7-9pm bingo night. W 7:30pm quiz-off. Every other Th 7:30pm prose and poetry readings. Sa 5-8pm partners Scrabble. Su in summer 5-9pm barbecue in the backyard. Pomegranate margaritas $8. Open M-Tu and Su 5pm-2am, W-Sa 5pm-4am.

Union Pool, 484 Union Ave. (☎718-609-0484), off Skillman Ave. [S] L to Bedford Ave. Converted from an old swimming pool supply depot, this bar hosts a variety of whimsical events, from circus performances to film festivals. Barbecues are frequent in the recently renovated backyard. Live DJ or music nearly every night, usually at 9pm; cover $5-10. Beer $4-5. Mixed drinks $6-7. Happy hour daily 5-8pm; Bud with a shot of Jim Bean $6. Photo booth $3. Open M-Sa 5pm-4am, Su 5pm-2am; open later in summer.

Artland, 609 Grand St. (☎718-599-9706). [S] L to Lorimer St. Filled with Persian rugs, and overstuffed chairs, Artland has plenty of books to read and board games and pinball machines to play. The bar has an unusually good selection of high-quality liquors. M free pool (normally $1) and happy hour prices all night long. Su 8pm open mic, followed by performances by local folk musicians. Happy hour daily until 9pm; $1 off mixed drinks and 2-for-1 beers. Open M-F 5pm-4am, Sa-Su 4pm-4am.

Brooklyn Ale House, 103 Berry St. (☎718-302-9811), at N 8th St. [S] L to Bedford Ave. Less self-consciously hip than the rest of the Williamsburg scene, this is a laid-back hangout with a great beer (draft $4-5, bottle $3) and whiskey ($5-8) selection. Happy hour M-F 3-7pm; domestic beer $2, imports $3. Open daily 3pm-4am.

BROOKLYN HEIGHTS AND DOWNTOWN

Though Brooklyn Heights can't claim to be quite as much a nightlife mecca as other Brooklyn neighborhoods, it still offers a number of friendly hangouts.

Water Street Restaurant and Bar, 66 Water St. (☎718-625-9352; www.waterstreetrestaurant.com), on the corner of Main St. [S] A, C to High St.; F to York St. An upscale pub with art on the walls, jazz on the stereo, and great food. Beer $4-5. Wine $7-8. Creole salad with blackened salmon $9. Grilled cheese with wilted arugula and bacon $10. Downstairs "Underwater" Lounge with F and Sa bands. Open M-Th 11:30am-2am, F-Sa 11:30am-4am, Su 10:30am-2am.

Last Exit, 136 Atlantic Ave. (☎718-222-9198; www.lastexitbar.com), between Henry and Clinton St. [S] 2, 3, 4, 5, M, R to Court St./Borough Hall. This neighborhood bar has mod couches, lots of 20-somethings, and live funk and rock music (Th-Sa 10pm). Super popular on the 1st and 3rd M of the month for its quiz night. Beer $2-4. Honey-apple martini $8. Happy hour 4-7pm; $3 pints, $10 "bucket o'" 6 PBRs. Open daily 4pm-4am.

Waterfront Ale House, 155 Atlantic Ave. (☎718-522-3794; www.waterfrontalehouse.com), between Henry and Clinton St. [S] 2, 3, 4, 5, M, R to Court St./Borough Hall. Though it's not actually on the water, this local hangout is still worth a trip. The food menu draws on every ethnic cuisine around. Santa Fe chicken wrap $9. Steamed vegetable dumplings $6. Tandoori veggie burger $9. The 15 beers on tap change seasonally; try to get a pint of Brooklyn Brown. Live jazz Sa 11pm-2am. Happy hour M-F 4-7pm; pints $3. Open daily noon-4am.

CARROLL GARDENS AND RED HOOK

The emerging Carroll Gardens nightlife scene, centered on **Smith Street,** is relaxed, unpretentious, and fun, providing a refreshing breather from Brooklynite hipdom.

👍 **Gowanus Yacht Club,** 323 Smith St. (☎718-246-1321), at President St. [S] F, G to Carroll St. A friendly outdoor patio with the feel of a rowdy neighborhood barbecue. 10 kinds of hot dogs (including a vegan "Not Dog"), juicy cheeseburgers, and nothing costing more than $4. Open daily 4pm-2am.

Quench, 282 Smith St. (☎718-875-1500), at Sackett St. [S] F, G to Bergen St. A small space with half-moon booths and a blue swirl-patterned wall, this bar fills up late and becomes a definitive pick-up joint. Beer $4. Pomegranate, coconut, and raspberry mojitos $9. Sa before 8pm mojitos $5. Su before 8pm margaritas $5. Open daily 5pm-4am.

Moonshine, 317 Columbia St. (☎718-422-0563), between Woodhull and Hamilton St. [S] F, G to Carroll St. You've heard of restaurants that are BYOB. This bar is BYOM—Bring Your Own Meat. They'll grill for you and furnish all the condiments you need. You'll also find a selection of board games, an upright piano for public use, and plenty of free peanuts, the shells of which litter the floor. Cans of beer $1.50-2. Bottles of beer $3. Draft beers $4. Open daily 4pm-2am, later on busy nights.

PARK SLOPE AND PROSPECT PARK

Slightly more mainstream than Williamsburg, Park Slope has a mellow but still very cool nightlife scene.

👍 **The Gate,** 321 5th Ave. (☎718-768-4329), at 3rd St. [S] M, R to Union St. A few short years ago, Park Slope was a nightlife wasteland. The Gate's welcoming atmosphere and 24 beers on tap ($4-7) paved the way for the 5th Ave. renaissance. The large patio fills quickly when the weather is warm. Happy hour M-Th 4-8pm, F 3-7pm; $1 off drafts and mixed drinks. Open M-Th 4pm-4am, F 3pm-4am, Sa-Su 1pm-4am.

👍 **Buttermilk Bar,** 577 5th Ave. (☎718-788-6297), at 16th St. [S] F to 7th Ave. Packed nightly with a young and devoted clientele, Buttermilk boasts an excellent beer selection, a hip minimalist ambience, frequent live music, and regular Candyland and Trivial Pursuit tournaments. Open daily 6pm-4am.

Commonwealth, 497 5th Ave. (☎718-768-2040), at 12th St. A clean decor of hardwood floors, exposed bricks, and candlelight makes for a chill setting. There's a comfortable back patio where smoking is permitted. A bulletin board provides space for "brutally honest personal ads," which are hilarious, whether or not they achieve their intended purpose. Excellent indie jukebox. Open M-Th 6pm-4am, F 3pm-4am, Sa-Su 3pm-4am.

Loki Lounge, 304 5th Ave. (☎718-965-9600), at 2nd St. [S] M, R to Union St. A sky-lit lounge that looks like a 40s living room, with worn rose-patterned sofas and chaises partitioned by red velvet curtains. There's also a pool table and a huge fireplace. Beer $5. Mixed drinks $5.50. Wine $6. Open M-F 3pm-4am, Sa-Su 1pm-4am.

QUEENS

Few would consider Queens nightlife worth traveling to for its own sake, but if you find yourself in Astoria or Long Island City, you'll have a number of good options. The best of the bunch is an old-school standby.

Beer Garden at Bohemian Hall, 29-19 24th Ave. (☎718-274-4925; www.bohemianhall.com), in Astoria. [S] N, W to 30th Ave. Operated by the Bohemian Citizens' Benevolent Society, this rowdy Czech restaurant and 900-seat outdoor beer garden is packed every night with a fun-loving, heavy drinking, heavy smoking crowd. If you're hungry, try Bohemian staples like fried cheese with french fries ($8) and crunchy pork schnitzel ($10.50). Open M-Th 5pm-2am, F 5pm-3am, Sa-Su noon-3am.

DAYTRIPS

DESTINATION	HIGHLIGHTS	TRAVEL TIME
Atlantic City, NJ	Casinos	2½-3hr.
Bear Mountain State Park	Hiking	2½-3hr.
Fire Island	Beaches	1½-2hr.
The Hamptons and Montauk	Beaches, celebrities	2-3hr.
Jones Beach	Waves, sand, sunbathers	1hr.
Oyster Bay, LI	Historic town, sun, beaches	45min.-1hr.
Tarrytown and Sleepy Hollow	Historic states	45min.-1hr.
West Point	Boot camp	1-1½hr.

Many daytrips are possible from New York City. While most short-term visitors to the city will see little reason to leave it, once you've been here a while you'll relish your opportunities for a change of pace. If you tire of skyscrapers and screeching traffic, head off to the Catskills or Long Island. If you'd rather gamble away your earnings, the casinos of Atlantic City are just a few hours away. Whatever your craving, here's how—and where—to get away from it all.

LONG ISLAND

Long Island, 120 mi. long, is the largest island in the US, and it's a land of multiple personalities. To the west, its strip malls, congested roads, and homogenous housing leave no doubt that you're in suburbia. In fact, Levittown, one of the first planned mega-suburbs in post-WWII America, sits smack in the middle of its western end. Nonetheless, to the north, you'll find the legendary Gold Coast, a ritzy and exclusive enclave since the Roaring Twenties. As you travel east, the island begins to feel more like a holiday escape. The Hamptons, on the south fork of the island's eastern tip, are the weekend vacation spot of choice for legions of well-to-do Manhattanites. Blissfully undeveloped Fire Island, just to the south, provides true natural serenity—and hosts a pair of gay communities with some of the wildest nightlife anywhere. The bucolic North Fork of the island is home to an emerging crop of charming wineries.

TRANSPORTATION

Trains: Long Island Railroad, LIRR (☎718-217-5477, TDD 718-558-3022; www.mta.info). Trains leave from Penn Station in Manhattan (34th St. at 7th Ave.; [S] 1, 2, 3 to 34th St./Penn Station/7th Ave.; A, C, E to 34th St./Penn Station/8th Ave.) and connect in Jamaica, Queens ([S] E, J, Z to Jamaica Center/Parsons/Archer) for the journey eastbound to the North Shore, North Fork, South Shore, and the Hamptons. LIRR also connects in Queens via the 7 line to Vernon Blvd./Jackson Ave. (Long Island City), Hunters Pt. Ave., and Flushing/Main St. stations, as well as to Brooklyn's Flatbush Ave. station ([S] 2, 4, 5, Q to Atlantic Ave.; M, N, R to Pacific St.). Fares vary daily and by zone. Rush-hour peak tickets (Manhattan-bound 5-9am, outbound 4-8pm) cost $1.50-4 more than off-peak fares. Tickets can be purchased, with cash only, aboard trains, but you will be surcharged $4.75-5.50. Purchase tickets online for 5% discount.

Buses:

MTA Long Island Bus (☎516-228-4000; www.mta.info). Daytime bus service in eastern Queens, Nassau, and western Suffolk. The bus runs along major streets, but routes are complex—confirm your destination with the driver. Some buses run every 15min., others every hr. Fare $2 (Metrocard or exact change only); transfers $0.25, free with MetroCard. Disabled travelers and senior citizens with proper ID pay half-fare. Serves Jones Beach daily late June to early Sept.; 20-25min., every 20-40min. from the LIRR station in Freeport. Also serves neighboring Long Beach.

Suffolk Transit (☎631-852-5200, TTY 631-853-5658; www.sct-bus.org). Runs from Lindenhurst to the eastern end of Long Island. The 10a, 10b, and 10c lines make frequent stops along the South Fork. Buses run in summer from the LIRR station in Babylon to Robert Moses State Park on Fire Island, every hour M-F and every 30min. Sa-Su. Fare $1.50, students with ID ages 14-22 $1, seniors and disabled travelers $0.50, children under 5 free; transfers $0.25.

Hampton Jitney (☎631-283-4600 or 800-327-0732; www.hamptonjitney.com). A luxury bus serving the Hamptons via Montauk and Westhampton lines. Also serves the North Fork. Expensive, but more comfortable and comprehensive than other bus services. Departs from various Manhattan locales and Queens airports. One-way $29, round trip $51. Some fares $5-7 less Tu-Th and for riders under 12 and 60+. Reservations advisable; book online or call in advance, especially on weekends.

WESTERN LONG ISLAND

Though western Long Island is home to some interesting sights and miles of popular beaches, few of its towns are tourist destinations in their own right. Jones Beach State Park, along with nearby Robert Moses State Park, is a good choice if you're looking for a quick escape from Manhattan. Sagamore Hill and the Planting Fields Arboretum are quirky and worthwhile sights to visit on the North Shore.

NORTH SHORE

By car, take Long Island Expwy. to Rte. 106N; follow the signs to Oyster Bay. LIRR trains travel from Penn Station to Oyster Bay with a connection at Jamaica; check schedule online. One-way fare $12-14 on train, $4-5 cheaper online or at station. For a taxi, call ☎516-921-2141.

The nation's wealthiest families have been building palatial homes on Long Island's North Shore for over a century. Often referred to as Long Island's "Gold Coast," the area provided the glittering setting for Fitzgerald's *The Great Gatsby*. **Oyster Bay,** a North Shore town with many lovely estates, makes a picturesque stop. The town got its name either for the plentiful oysters located in the offshore waters or for its harbor's oyster-like shape. Nearby **⬛Sagamore Hill,** on Sagamore Hill Rd., off Cove Neck Rd., is a Queen Anne-style house that once belonged to President Theodore Roosevelt. During his presidency, he used it as the "summer" White House. It's stuffed with hunting trophies, including a polar bear rug and a rhinoceros-foot inkwell, from Roosevelt's many exotic vacations. In 1905, Roosevelt met here with envoys from Japan and Russia, arranging talks for the treaty that ended the Russo-Japanese War. He won the Nobel Peace Prize for his part in the negotiations. To get to the estate from the Long Island Expwy., take Rte. 106N to Rte. 25A. Turn right, drive 2½ mi., and turn left on Cove Rd. After 1½ mi., follow the sign to Sagamore Hill. Sagamore Hill is a $10 taxi ride from the Oyster Bay LIRR station. (☎516-922-4788; www.nps.gov/sahi. Visitors center open daily 9am-5pm. 50min. tours, required to view the house, leave every hour 10am-4pm. $5, children under 15 free. Grounds free. Park open dawn-dusk.)

Also nearby is the **Planting Fields Arboretum,** 1395 Planting Fields Rd., a 409-acre estate with two greenhouses, a rhododendron park, and other quirky highlights. Don't miss the "synoptic garden" of plants alphabetized according to their Latin names. The flowers bloom during the unlikely months of December, January, and February, when most city-dwellers have begun to forget what greenery looks like. In the center of the estate is **Coe Hall,** constructed in 1921. The mansion has rows of 12th-century stained-glass windows. (☎516-922-9210. Tours Apr.-Sept. noon-3:30pm. $5, students with ID and seniors $3.50, ages 7-12 $1.) The arboretum hosts many family events, including a summer jazz festival and concert series. (☎516-922-8600; www.plantingfields.org. Concert series info ☎516-922-0061; www.fotapresents.org. Arboretum open daily 9am-5pm. Main greenhouse open daily 10am-4:30pm. Parking May-Oct. and weekends $6. Entrance free.)

The tourist population of Oyster Bay swells during the **October Oysterfest.** This two-day festival is Long Island's largest street and waterfront fair, with oysters prepared every way Bubba Gump could imagine. The LIRR offers a one-day getaway package to the festival, which includes round-trip fair from Manhattan and a voucher for three oysters on the half shell (www.mta.nyc.ny.us/lirr/getaways; $14, children ages 5-11 $2.50). For quality seafood throughout the year, try the **Oyster Bay Fish and Clam Bar ❸**, 103 Rte. 106/Pine Hollow Rd. (☎516-922-5522. 12 steamed clams $13. 12 oysters $18. Shrimp, clams, and scallops in white sauce $19. Open Apr.-Oct. M-Th 3-11pm, F-Sa 11am-midnight, Su 11am-11pm. Cash only.)

JONES BEACH

By car, take Long Island Expwy. E or Grand Central Pkwy. E, to Northern State Pkwy. E, to Wantagh Pkwy. S, to Jones Beach State Park (about 33 mi.). Parking Lot 4 is open until midnight; all others are open until sundown ($8). To get to the beach by train, take LIRR to Freeport, and the shuttle bus to Jones Beach (summer package deal from Manhattan $11).

Jones Beach comprises 6½ mi. of public beaches, popular with a diverse, urban crowd. When New York State Parks Commissioner Robert Moses (p. 58) set to work on the beach in 1921, it was a barren strip of land off the Atlantic shore of Nassau County. Within 10 years he had bought up the surrounding land, imported tons of sand, planted beach grass to preserve the new dunes, and completed dozens of buildings. The wealth of attractions at Jones Beach State Park and the close proximity of its sand and surf to Manhattan attract huge numbers of beachgoers every day. There are nearly 2500 acres of beachfront with eight different public beaches on the rough Atlantic Ocean and the calmer Zachs Bay. Along the 1½ mi. **boardwalk** you'll find two Olympic-size pools, softball fields, roller-skating, mini-golf, a fitness course, basketball, and nightly dancing. The **Nikon at Jones Beach Theater,** inside the park, hosts big-name concerts. (☎516-221-1000; www.ticketmaster.com. Box office open Tu-Sa 10am-6pm, Su noon-6pm; night of shows until 9pm.)

⚡TIP⚡ **JONES BEACH TOO CROWDED?** Tobay beach, just to the east, almost always has more room. The surfing isn't quite as good there, but you'll have more space to spread out in.

THE HAMPTONS AND MONTAUK

The Hamptons, located on the southern fork of eastern Long Island, are a curious mix of the serene, the sexy, and the overpriced. Huge crowds of well-to-do Manhattanites make the area a hotbed of conspicuous consumption in the summer. A prized vacation-home location, the Hamptons are best visited when its flowers are in bloom and beachgoers are enjoying the ocean waves. You can visit the Hamptons in a single day if you set out early in the morning, but you'll likely feel rushed. Most

THE BIG SPLURGE

WINE CAMP

If you associate the East End of Long Island primarily with the Hamptons' summertime crowd of baked and bejeweled visitors, the burgeoning wine industry on Long Island's North Fork will come as a pleasant surprise. For more than 30 years a small but dedicated group of wine-growers has used fields that formerly nurtured only potato vines to produce some surprisingly good wines.

You can, of course, visit these North Fork wineries at any time, but one of the most fun—and educational— ways to visit is through a four-day, three-night program known as Wine Camp, which is organized every few months. The experience is a far cry from the bunk beds, mosquitoes, and ghost stories of the camps of your youth. Wine Campers stay in their choice of five participating B&Bs, and the price also includes a sumptuous breakfast every day, two gourmet dinners, a case of local wine to take home, and valuable educational opportunities—from instruction in working the fields, to classes on Long Island *terroir* and pairing food with wines, to guided tastings. Wine Camp is definitely not cheap, but considering the knowledge (and the official certificate) you'll take home with you, it might just be a good investment. It's one your future dining companions will appreciate for sure. (*$749 per person, based on double occupancy.* ☎ *631-495-9744; www.winecamp.org.*)

inns and guesthouses in the Hamptons are pricey, especially in the summer. If you want to stay the night, camping or staying in one of Montauk's motels are your most realistic options. It's imperative to call ahead. To see the area without breaking the bank, try visiting in the warm low-season weeks after Labor Day. The LIRR train from Penn Station serves all towns except Sag Harbor, but to move freely and take advantage of the cheaper hotel prices off the main drag, you'll need a car.

SOUTHAMPTON

From the Southampton LIRR station, head right out of the parking lot along Railroad Plaza to N Main St.; turn left onto N Main St. and walk to the stop sign; bear left and keep walking as N Main St. becomes Main St., taking you to the center of town (about ½ mi. altogether). For a taxi, call ☎ 631-283-1900 or 631-283-1900.

Founded in 1640 as the first English colony in future New York State, Southampton is home to beautiful, expansive houses. On Dune Rd., by the ocean, enormous gates and rows of hedges guard beachfront mansions. Most **beaches** require resident parking permits, but lots at the end of Beach Rd. D, off Meadow Lane, offer free parking. For more info, pick up a pamphlet at the **Chamber of Commerce,** 76 Main St. (☎ 631-283-0402; www.southamptonchamber.com. Open M-F 10am-4pm, Sa-Su 11am-4pm.) **Cooper's Beach** is the main public beach (parking $25).

In town, the **Southampton Historical Museum,** 17 Meeting House Ln., replicates an 1800s Main St. with a schoolhouse, carpenter, cobbler, apothecary, and blacksmith. (☎ 631-283-2494; www.southamptonhistoricalmuseum.org. Open Tu-Sa 11am-5pm, Su 1-5pm. $4, seniors $3, students $2.) The Venetian-style **Parrish Art Museum,** 25 Job's Ln., on the other side of Main St., houses a contemporary art collection focused on American artists like William Merritt Chase and Fairfield Porter. The Parrish is surrounded by a garden that showcases reproduced Roman busts. (Open June to mid-Sept. M-Sa 11am-5pm, Su 1-5pm; late Sept. to May M and Th-Sa 11am-5pm, Su 1-5pm. $10, seniors and students with ID $5, children under 18 free. Wheelchair accessible.)

EAST HAMPTON AND AMAGANSETT

Both towns are directly off Rte. 27. If you arrive at the East Hampton train station, walk along Newtown Ln. into town. From the Amagansett train station, walk along Main St./Montauk Hwy. into town. For a taxi, call ☎ 631-324-0077.

The center of East Hampton is home to art galleries, clothing stores, and colonial memorabilia outlets. The town is great for strolling, window-shopping, and whiling away the hours. Many artists, most prominently Jackson Pollack, have found inspiration here. Main Beach, along Ocean Ave. at the southern edge of town, is a gorgeous stretch of sand with a view of some large mansions. Parking is $15 and no nonresident permits are given on weekends.

Nearby Amagansett offers little outside its tiny Main St. If you want to glimpse some of the area's large houses, head south of the highway to Further Ln. and size up the estates from the street. Back in town, the **Farmer's Market**, 367 Rte. 27 (Main St.) attracts locals and tourists alike. (☎ 631-267-3894. Open daily Memorial Day to Labor Day 7am-9pm; Labor Day to Memorial Day 6am-6pm.) Although the Hamptons' beaches try to keep ordinary folk out by requiring parking permits, the **Atlantic Avenue Beach** is walkable from the center of town (approx. 1 mi.). Amagansett features some great live music in the evenings. The **Stephen Talkhouse**, 161 Main St., hosts a wide range of performers. (☎ 631-267-3117; www.stephentalk-house.com. Tickets $10-165.) For a cheap bite to eat in East Hampton, head to **Rowdy Hall ❷**, 10 Main St. Famous burgers, excellent French onion soup, and hand-cut fries are the staples at this much-loved local hangout. (☎ 631-324-8555. Open June-Aug. M-Th and Su noon-3:30pm and 5-11pm, F-Sa noon-3:30pm and 5pm-midnight; Sept.-May daily noon-3:30pm and 5-11pm.)

SAG HARBOR

The LIRR does not stop at Sag Harbor, but the town is accessible via Bridgehampton. For a taxi, call ☎ 631-537-7400.

Sag Harbor sits on the north shore of the South Fork. Founded in 1707, the port used to be more important than New York Harbor. At its peak, the village was the world's fourth-largest whaling port. James Fenimore Cooper began his first novel, *Precaution*, in a Sag Harbor hotel in 1824. During Prohibition, the harbor served as a major meeting place for rum-runners from the Caribbean.

An increasing number of tourists frequent the tree-lined streets of salt-box cottages and Greek Revival mansions. Sag Harbor's former grandeur survives in the second-largest US collection of colonial buildings. Check out the **Sag Harbor Whaling Museum**, 200 Main St. A huge whale rib arches over the front door. Note the antique washing machine, made locally in 1864, and the excellent scrimshaw collection. (☎ 631-725-0770; www.sagharborwhalingmuseum.org. Open May-Nov. M-Sa 10am-5pm, Su 1-5pm; Oct.-Dec. Sa-Su noon-4pm. Tours for groups of 10 or more by appointment year-round. $5, seniors and students $3, children under 12 free.) The equally intriguing **Custom House**, Main and Garden St., an authentic 18th-century home across from the museum, features an extensive collection of period furniture and keepsakes. (☎ 631-725-0250; www.splia.org. Open June-Sept. Sa-Su 10am-5pm; July-Aug. daily 10am-5pm. $3, children ages 7-14 and seniors $2.) Less than a mile from the wharf is **Haven's Beach** (parking $10). The local chamber of commerce is housed in a large windmill at the center of town. (☎ 631-725-0011; www.sagharborchamber.com. Open May-Oct. daily 10am-4pm.)

MONTAUK

By car, take the Long Island Expwy. east to Exit 70 (Manorville). Go south to Rte. 27 (a.k.a. Sunset Hwy. or Montauk Hwy.), and head east to Montauk (about 50 mi.). Towns are located near the highway. LIRR runs to Montauk; head to the right out of the train station along the 2-lane Edgemere Rd., which leads straight to the village green (15-20min.). The Hampton Jitney makes more than a dozen trips daily.

As the easternmost point of the South Fork, Montauk offers an unobstructed view of the Atlantic Ocean. Despite the commercialized tourist and hotel areas and the three-hour drive required to get here from New York, the peaceful salt air is worth the effort. The 110 ft. **Montauk Point Lighthouse,** at the end of Rte. 27 in Montauk State Park, was built in 1796 by special order of President George Washington. The first public-works project in the newly formed United States, the lighthouse guided many ships into the harbor, including the schooner *La Amistad.* If your lungs are willing, climb the 137 spiraling steps to the top for a view across the Long Island Sound to Connecticut and Rhode Island. (☎631-688-2544; www.montauklighthouse.com. Open June-Sept. M-F and Su 10:30am-6pm, Sa 10:30am-7pm. $7, seniors $6, children under 12 $3. Parking daily 8am-4pm $6.) If you want to catch your dinner, **Viking** (☎631-668-5700; www.vikingfleet.com) and **Lazybones** (☎631-668-5671; www.montauksportfishing.com/lazybones) offer half- and full-day fishing excursions. Surfers head to **Ditch Plains** beach; windsurfers favor **Fort Pond Bay. Gin Beach** on Montauk's northeastern corner is popular with locals for swimming and sunbathing. For more info on things to do and see in Montauk, stop at the **Chamber of Commerce,** 742 Montauk Hwy., in the center of town. (☎631-668-2428; www.montaukchamber.com. Open M-Sa daily 10am-5pm, Su 10am-4pm.)

If you're looking for an affordable seafood meal, take Rte. 77 to the ocean, where you'll find **Gosman's Clam Bar ❷,** on West Lake Dr./Rte. 77. This takeaway seafood shack serves up excellent fare near a harborside outdoor patio. Dependable standards like filet of swordfish ($9) and crab cakes with salad and fries ($9) make good choices. (☎631-668-5330. Open late Apr. to mid-Oct. 11am-9pm daily.) If you'd like to camp, **Hither Hills State Park ❶,** located four miles west of Montauk along Old Montauk Hwy., offers campsites near lovely beaches, swimming, and picnicking spots. (☎631-668-2554. Park open daily 8am-dusk. Camping available early Apr. to mid-Nov. Reservations required; make them through Reserve America at ☎800-456-CAMP/2267. Mid-June to mid-Sept. reservations only available by the week. The campsite books up months in advance, but last-minute cancellations are common. Show up early in the day and ask to be placed on the wait list; chances are good that you'll have a spot by 3pm, especially on weekdays. M-Th and Su $24 per campsite per night, F-Sa $27; prices are double for out-of-state visitors.) A more traditional choice is **Gosman's Culloden House Motel ❸,** 540 West Lake Dr., accessible via the summer-only S-94 bus to Montauk Dock. Close to Block Island Sound, this motel has large and clean rooms, friendly staff, and basic, somewhat dated decor. (☎631-668-9293. Lawn area with chairs and BBQ. Free beach passes for guests with $40 deposit. A/C, cable, and fridges. 2- to 3-night min. stay during summer and all weekends. Economy rooms with 2 twin beds $70-120; large rooms with king or 2 double beds $80-150.)

FIRE ISLAND

Fire Island feels more distant from New York City than anywhere on Long Island. Its pristine villages and laid-back attitude contrast sharply with the commercialism and status-consciousness of the nearby Hamptons. Most areas on Fire Island are designated as either state parks or federal wilderness areas. The lack of infrastructure ensures both tranquility and inconvenience; visitors must often take water taxis to shuttle between towns. Fire Island's 17 communities, generally inhabited only in summer, have distinct identities—middle-class residential clusters, gay-only hangouts, and pockets of vacationing Hollywood stars.

TRANSPORTATION AND ORIENTATION. On the island, only Smith Point County State Park (☎ 631-854-4949) and Robert Moses State Park are accessible by **car.** You can walk from the parking lots to the Fire Island Lighthouse and the Fire Island Wilderness Visitors Center. To get to the island by **train,** take the LIRR to Sayville ($9.50-13), and then take a taxi to the port. **Ferries** from Sayville (☎ 631-589-0810; sayvilleferry.com) go to Sailors' Haven (round-trip $12), Cherry Grove, and Fire Island Pines (round-trip $14, children under 11 $5). You can also take the LIRR to Bay Shore ($11-13), whose port is within walking distance of the train station down Maple Ave. **Ferries** from Bay Shore (☎ 631-665-3600; www.fireislandferries.com) go to Kismet, Saltaire, Fair Harbor, Atlantique, Dunewood, Ocean Beach, Seaview, and Ocean Bay Park (round-trip $14, children under 12 $6.50). Bicycles are not allowed on the ferries. For a **water taxi** between towns on the island, call ☎ 631-665-8885 (Ocean Beach to Watch Hill $16 per person).

SIGHTS. The **Fire Island National Seashore** is the official name of the island's sandy coastline (☎ 631-289-4810). The beaches are great for fishing, clamming, and guided nature walks. The 19th-century **Fire Island Lighthouse** in Kismet, at the western end of the National Seashore, has served as a major landmark for transatlantic ships and is still functional today. (☎ 631-661-4876; www.fireislandlighthouse.com. Small museum open daily 9:30am-5:30pm.) **Sailor's Haven,** just west of the Cherry Grove community, is home to a marina, a nature trail, and a famous beach. (Visitors center ☎ 631-597-6183.) There are similar facilities and a gorgeous beach at **Watch Hill.** (Visitors center ☎ 631-289-9336; www.watchhillfi.com.) The **Sunken Forest,** named for its location behind the dunes, is one of the island's natural wonders. Located directly west of Sailor's Haven, its soil supports an unusual and attractive combination of gnarled holly, sassafras, and poison ivy. Some of the forest's specimens are over 200 years old. From atop the dunes, you can see the forest's trees laced together in a hulking, unbroken mesh.

Ocean Beach is the largest community on Fire Island and provides the starting point for many tourists. Its main street is lined with gray-shingled buildings, restaurants, small groceries, and beach-wear shops. Take any side street perpendicular to the main drag across the island, and you'll arrive at miles and miles of coastline. Homes grow larger as you travel either way down the beach, with the most impressive located about two miles west of Ocean Beach in posh **Saltaire** (an entirely residential community), followed closely by up-and-coming **Fair Harbor.** If you walk just over 2½ mi. east, you will reach two predominantly gay and lesbian villages. The private bungalows and raised boardwalks of **Cherry Grove** are home to a sizable lesbian community, and the colossal homes of **Fire Island Pines** are inhabited primarily by gay men (see below for more).

ACCOMMODATIONS. Prices on Fire Island vary drastically depending on the season and day of the week. While weekends and holidays can be prohibitively expensive, if you can visit midweek, accommodations on the island become much more affordable. **Clegg's Hotel ❸,** 478 Bayberry Walk, a five-minute walk from the ocean, has clean rooms with country blue decor and a knowledgeable staff. (☎ 631-583-5399; www.cleggshotel.com. May-Oct. doubles with shared bath midweek $110, weekend $320; triples with shared bath $165/480, studios with kitchen $210/420.) **Watch Hill,** across Great South Bay from Patchogue, is home to a beautiful **campsite ❶,** a short walk from an excel-

DAYTRIPS

lent beach. Running water, grills, showers, and bathrooms are all available. (☎631-567-6664; www.watchhillfi.com/campsites.html. Camping mid-May to mid-Oct. Reservation request form online; reservations for upcoming season processed in the order received beginning Jan. 1. Max 5 adults and 3 children under 21 per site; 1 21+ group member required. 2-night min. stay. $40, each additional night $20.) If you're coming to Fire Island for its gay nightlife, the **Cherry Grove Beach Hotel** [5], 41 River Rd., is a good bet close to the action. (☎631-597-6600; www.grovehotel.com. Open May-Oct. All rooms have private bath. Singles and doubles $40-500, depending on the time of week.)

FIRE ISLAND FOR POCKET CHANGE. For a free night's stay on Watch Hill, get a backcountry pass from the Visitor Center on the ferry dock. You can then pitch a tent anywhere behind the dunes in the Otis Pike Wilderness Area, about a mile away. Use of the nearby campground showers is permitted.

GAY NIGHTLIFE. Though a sizable lesbian population inhabits Cherry Grove, the nightlife scene in both Cherry Grove and Fire Island Pines caters exclusively to gay men. In these communities, crowded "streets"—really just wooden pathways—border spectacular Atlantic Ocean beaches, and parties rage late into the night. Gay nightlife on the island has an established rhythm that may be confusing to newcomers. To find out what's happening, it's best just to ask around at hotels and restaurants. The undeveloped stretch of beach and dunes between the Pines and the Grove is a loosely bounded area that those in the know call the **Meat Rack.** Things go down amid the myriad walkways—Gay Men's Health Crisis (GMHC, p. 49) actually puts condoms in the trees to keep everyone safe. Another similar cruising location, sometimes called the **Dick Dock,** has sprung up on Harbor Walk, between Fire Island Blvd. and Ocean Walk.

Cherry Grove, with raised boardwalks leading to small, shingled houses, is a bit more commercial than the nearby Pines. A night in Cherry Grove usually begins at the **Ice Palace,** attached to the Cherry Grove Beach Hotel (see above), where you can sing karaoke, gawk at drag queens, and dance until dawn. (☎631-597-6600; www.grovehotel.com. Open July-Aug. daily noon-4am; Sept.-June noon-10pm.) **Fire Island Pines** (www.thepinesfireisland.com; www.fipines.com) is a 10min. walk up the beach from Cherry Grove. Houses here are spacious and often stunningly modern, with huge windows and an asymmetric aesthetic. Boardwalks are often poorly lit; you may want to bring a flashlight. The Pines' active and upscale scene has a secret club feel—you need to be in the know or look like you know the program. "Tea Dance" (a.k.a. "Low Tea") takes place at the **Blue Whale,** from 5-8pm (☎631-597-6500, ext. 27). "High Tea" happens from 8-10pm on the balcony above **The Pavillion,** the premier disco in the Pines (☎631-597-6500, ext. 31). Stay there to dance the night away.

HUDSON VALLEY

TARRYTOWN AND SLEEPY HOLLOW

To get to Tarrytown by car, take the New York State Thrwy. (I-87) to Exit 9 (Tarrytown). Turn left on Rte 119W. Go to first traffic light, and turn left on Rte. 9 S. Metro-North Hudson Line trains run from Grand Central Station. Trains depart 5:45am-1:50am, with the last

*return at 1:12am. (☎212-532-4900; www.mta.info. 50min. local, 30min. express. $7.25-
9.75.) From the station, cross the parking lot, and walk uphill on the other side of
the police station to Main St. A taxi (☎201-659-9191, 201-792-7100 or 201-420-
1480) is the easiest way into town.*

Less than 30 mi. north of the city, the rural towns of Tarrytown and Sleepy Hollow represent the landscape and legends of 19th-century American Romanti-
cism with their historic mansions, estates, farms, and churches. The
Tarrytown area provided the inspiration for 19th-century author Washington
Irving's tales—most famously, *The Legend of Sleepy Hollow.* An amateur
landscape artist with an interest in architecture, Irving transformed a two-
story Dutch cottage into his magnificent estate, **Sunnyside,** on W Sunnyside Ln.
To get there, walk two miles up Main St. to Rte. 9, and then head south. The
house offers a fascinating glimpse into Irving's life; the manicured grounds
alone are worth the visit. Summer and special events include jazz festivals and
candlelit tours. (☎914-591-8763. $10, seniors $9, children ages 5-17 $5, under 5
free. Grounds open Mar.-Dec. daily 10am-5pm; mansion open M and W-Su
10am-5pm. Tours depart 10:30am-4pm.)

A few miles north along Rte. 9 lies **Lyndhursts,** 635 S Broadway, just off Rte. 9, a
Gothic Revival palace acquired by railroad tycoon Jay Gould in 1880. The stately
grounds surrounding the 19th-century mansion sport rose and fern gardens, a carriage house, and the remains of a private conservatory. The gardens are the main
draw. (☎914-631-4481; www.lyndhurst.org. Open mid-Apr. to Oct. Tu-Su 10am-
5pm; Nov.-Mar. Sa-Su 10am-4pm. $10, seniors $9, children ages 12-17 $4, children
under 12 free; grounds alone $4.) Approximately 10 mi. north of Tarrytown is
Sleepy Hollow's **Union Church of Pocantico Hills,** 555 Bedford Rd., three miles down
Rte. 114 off Rte. 9. The walls are adorned with nine stained-glass windows by Marc
Chagall. Henri Matisse's last completed work, *Rose Window*, hangs above the
altar. (☎914-631-2069. Open Apr.-Dec. M and W-F 11am-5pm, Sa 10am-5pm, Su 2-
5pm. Services Su 8:30 and 10am. $5, discounted for Kykuit visitors.) About two
miles north along Rte. 9 lies **Phillipsburg Manor,** a 17th-century farm and living-his-
tory venue with rare breeds of cattle and sheep, costumed guides, and a working
mill wheel. A variety of tours ($19-36) run out of Phillipsburg Manor to the Rock-
efeller Estate. (☎914-631-3992. Open Mar. Sa-Su 10am-4pm, last tour 3pm; Apr.-
Oct. M and W-Su 10am-5pm, last tour 4pm; Nov.-Dec. M and W-Su 10am-4pm, last
tour 3pm. $10, seniors $9, ages 5-17 $6, children under 5 free.)

WEST POINT

*To get to West Point by car, take I-87 to Palisades Interstate Pkwy., heading north. Follow
signs for Rte. 9W north, and travel along it until the West Point exit. Short Line Bus
(☎800-631-8405) runs from the Port Authority (roundtrip with tour $41). Check www.coa-
chusa.com for schedule.*

America's oldest and most famous service academy, West Point is carved into
the cliffs of the Hudson Highlands, the foothills of the Catskills. Its list of illustrious graduates include Ulysses S. Grant, Robert E. Lee, and Dwight D. Eisenhower. The expansive campus holds Revolutionary War sights, imposing
Gothic buildings, and majestic vistas. The Visitors Center, located just below
Thayer Gate and across from a tourist-oriented "Main Street," with shops and
food, is a good starting place. The center provides pamphlets and walking- and
driving- tour maps. It also shows a brief video, army memorabilia, and a replica
of a cadet's room. (☎845-938-2638. Open daily 9am-4:45pm.) Just behind the
Visitors Center lies the **West Point Museum.** The Gothic building houses one of

the nation's largest and oldest collections of military memorabilia, with weapons and uniforms dating to colonial times. (☎ 845-938-2203 or 938-3590. Open daily 10:30am-4:15pm.) The campus itself features two Revolutionary War sites—**Fort Clinton** and **Fort Putnam,** the latter originally under the command of George Washington. Also of interest is the assortment of war monuments, particularly **Trophy Point,** the storehouse for many intriguing US war relics, and the **Battle Monument,** purportedly the largest polished granite shaft in the Western Hemisphere. Other popular sights include the **Cadet Chapel,** which contains the world's largest organ, and **The Plain,** the famous West Point parade ground. One- and two-hour tours leave from the Visitors Center throughout the day. (1-hour tour $9, children ages 2-11 $6, children under 2 free; 2hr. tour $11/9. Photo ID required for all visitors over 16.)

THE CATSKILLS

BEAR MOUNTAIN STATE PARK

The park is located about 50 mi. north of the city, at the intersection of the Palisades Pkwy. and Rte. 9W. Short Line Buses (☎ 800-631-8405; www.coachusa.com/shortline) run from Port Authority to the park and take about 1½hr. (round-trip $25). Metro-North runs trains to Peekskill and Garrison. From there, you can take a $25 cab to the park. Park open daily 8am-dusk.

Bear Mountain State Park's 80 sq. mi. of wilderness and 140 mi. of trails include some of the taller Catskill Mountains, the expansive and sparkling Hessian Lake, a section of the Hudson River, and a giant swimming pool. The other main attraction, the **Trailside Museums and Zoo,** is the oldest of its kind in the US. Visitors can view injured and rehabilitated wildlife, which includes a bobcat and two black bears. The museum's focus is on the park's history, local geology, and nature study. A statue of an "afoot and lighthearted" **Walt Whitman** stands next to one of the zoo's shaded paths. The park also contains the earliest part of the Appalachian Trail, and it stars in a Bob Dylan song about a picnic gone horribly wrong ("Talking Bear Mountain Picnic Massacre Blues"). **Paddleboats** can be used on Hessian Lake. (Apr.-June Sa-Su 11am-5pm; June-Sept. M-F 11am-4pm, Sa-Su 11am-5pm. $5, with $20 deposit.) Other diversions include an outdoor ice-skating rink (open late Oct. to mid-Mar.), lake and river fishing, swimming, hiking, biking, and cross-country skiing. The park features a ski jump and a swimming pool. For further park information, call the **Park Visitors Center.** (☎ 845-786-5003. Open Apr.-Oct. 8am-6pm; Nov.-Mar. 8am-5pm.) The chalet-style **Bear Mountain Inn ❸,** overlooking Hessian Lake, stands in the center of the park. Although the standard rooms are not very large, they're relatively cheap; the inn also provides quieter, more remote lodges. (☎ 845-786-2731; www.bearmountaininn.com. Doubles with queen-size bed and bath $100, with 2 twin beds $110. Book at least 1 month in advance on weekends.)

ATLANTIC CITY

Atlantic City is halfway down New Jersey's eastern seashore, accessible via the Garden State Pkwy. and the Atlantic City Expwy., and easily reached by train. Greyhound buses travel between the Port Authority and most major casinos. (☎ 800-231-2222; www.greyhound.com. 2½-3hr., 30-40 per day, round-trip from $36.) New Jersey Transit offers hourly service from the Atlantic Ave. station, between Michigan *and Ohio St., to New York. (☎215-569-3752 or 800-582-5946; www.njtransit.com. 2½hr. One-way $26, seniors $11.75; roundtrip $46, seniors $21.) Inquire at casinos about shuttle services; many offer cheaper rates. In Atlantic City, individually owned Atlantic City Jitneys (www.jitneys.net) run around the clock and cover 4 different routes (one-way $2).*

In the early years of the 20th century, Atlantic City was an elegant seaside resort town. From the late 20s onward and for much of the 20th century, however, it languished in a seedy cocktail of vice, depression, and crime. Gambling wasn't legalized here until 1977, and this change gave birth to the Atlantic City of today—a city of 30,000 slot machines, flashy casino-hotels, cheesy carnival games, and a certain gaudy charm. You'll probably recognize the street names from your *Monopoly* board, whose setup is based on turn-of-the-century Atlantic City geography. The opulence of the original Boardwalk and Park Place have long since faded, but the town is still popular with gamblers who'd rather not fly to Las Vegas, professionals looking for fast times and a quick tan, and bachelor parties blitzing down the Boardwalk. Though AC was for many years the host of the Miss America pageant, the show decamped to Vegas in 2006.

SIGHTS

The five-mile **Boardwalk** is lined with carnival-game arcades, including **Central Pier Arcade and Speedway** (☎609-345-5219), at Tennessee Ave. That teddy bear in the window is a lot easier to win than the convertible on display at Caesar's. The historic 1898 **Steel Pier** (☎609-898-7645 or 866-386-6659; www.steelpier.com), at Virginia Ave., has a roller coaster, carousel, and "games of skill" aplenty. Its ferris wheel juts out over the water. (Open M-F 3pm-midnight, Sa-Su noon-1am; for winter hours call the Taj Mahal. Rides vary in price; booklet of 35 tickets $25, unlimited day pass $35.) When you tire of spending money, check out the historic **Atlantic City Beach.** The **Morey's Piers and Raging Waters Waterparks,** on the Boardwalk at 25th, Schellenger, and Spencer Ave., are always a sure bet for a good time (☎609-522-3900 or 888-667-3971; www.moreyspiers.com). Just west of Atlantic City, **Ventnor City** offers more tranquil shores.

CASINOS

All the casinos on the Boardwalk fall within a dice toss of one another, and all are open 24hr. Unlike in Vegas, where casinos have become playground-like destinations fun even for families, there's little to do here besides gamble. Gaming rooms are crowded with bleary-eyed patrons hunched and squinting at their slot machines. The casinos furnish players with a steady supply of food and drinks so they never have to leave the table; they'd put catheters in them if they could.

Atlantic City Hilton (☎609-347-7111 or 800-257-8677; www.hiltonac.com), at Boston Ave. and the Boardwalk, between Providence and Boston Ave. The farthest casino south and one of the more tasteful. It features a 1200-person theater that hosts big-name shows.

The Borgata, 1 Borgata Way (☎866-692-6742; www.theborgata.com). The newest casino in town, featuring a well-reputed spa.

Caesar's Boardwalk Resort and Casino, 2100 Pacific Ave. (☎609-348-4411; www.caesarsatlantcity.com), at Arkansas Ave. All glitz and glamor, host to some big-name shows.

DAYTRIPS

The Sands (☎ 609-441-4000; www.acsands.com), at Indiana Ave.

Showboat, 801 Boardwalk (☎ 609-343-4000 or 800-621-0200; www.harrahs.com), at Delaware Ave. and Boardwalk. Home of a popular Family Feud live stage show.

Trump Marina (☎ 609-441-2000; www.trumpmarina.com), on Huron Blvd. at the Marina. In summer, energetic partiers go to "rock the dock" at Trump *Marina*'s enormous indoor/outdoor bar/restaurant, **The Deck** (☎ 877-477-4697).

Trump Taj Mahal Hotel and Casino, 1000 Boardwalk (☎ 609-449-1000; www.trumptaj.com), at Virginia Ave. Too ostentatious to be missed. It looks like the castle from *Aladdin*, but without the subtlety.

FOOD

Although not recommended by nutritionists, Atlantic City's food is cheap and plentiful. Hot dogs and pizza slices are everywhere. So are vendors selling bags of salt-water taffy, which was "discovered" in Atlantic City after a storm flooded a candy store on the Boardwalk. Most of the casinos have all-you-can-eat buffets, great if you've got a hollow leg to fill. Slightly better food can be found off the seashore.

Inn of the Irish Pub, 164 St. James Pl. (☎ 609-344-9063; www.theirishpub.com). The atmosphere is convivial and the food is greasy and good. The daily lunch special (11:30am-2pm; $2) includes a sandwich and a cup of soup. Prices are cheap enough for even the most deflated gambler. Bacon burger $4.50. BLTs $2.40. Domestic drafts $1.90. Open 24hr. Cash only. ❶

Sundae Ice Cream, on the Boardwalk (☎ 609-347-8424), between South Carolina and Ocean Ave. Over 20 flavors of ice cream and frozen yogurt ($3). The chocolate chip cookie dough is terrific. Banana splits $6. Open M-Th and Su 10am-midnight, F-Sa 10am-3am. Cash only. ❶

Tun Tavern, 2 Miss America Way (☎ 609-347-7800; www.tuntavern.com), attached to the Sheraton Hotel, across from the Atlantic City Convention Center. A pricier option than most, this restaurant maintains its AC sense of class, hosting bikini contests regularly. Live music nightly in a casual atmosphere. Pasta with lump crab meat $23. Filet mignon $28. W $7 pitchers and $0.25 chicken wings after 10pm. Th ladies night. F dance floor opens 5:30pm. Open daily 11am-2am. ❹

Tony's Baltimore Grille, 2800 Atlantic Ave. (☎ 609-345-5766; www.baltimoregrill.com), between Pacific and Baltic, at Iowa Ave. A loyal neighborhood crew joins tourists for standard American fare. Spaghetti from $6. Pizza from $8. Beer from $1.25. Open daily 11am-3am. Bar open 24hr. Cash only. ❷

White House Sub Shop, 2301 Arctic Ave. (☎ 609-345-8599, pickup 609-345-1564), at Mississippi Ave. Sinatra was rumored to have had subs from here flown to him. The line is often out the door. Sandwiches $5. Open M-Th and Su 10am-10pm, F-Sa 10am-11pm. Cash only. ❷

SHOPPING

The Walk, Atlantic City Outlets, 1931 Atlantic Ave. (☎ 609-872-7002; www.acoutlets.com) between Arkansas and Ohio Ave. and Baltic and Atlantic Ave. This enormous outlet mall, famous throughout the surrounding region, offers designer goods at bargain prices. Brands include COACH, Polo Ralph Lauren, Gap, Banana Republic, Guess, Tommy Hilfiger, and H&M. Open M-Sa 10am-9pm, Su 10am-7pm.

DAYTRIPS

ACCOMMODATIONS

Inn of the Irish Pub, 164 St. James Pl. (☎609-344-9063; www.theirishpub.com), between New York Ave. and Tennessee, near the Ramada Tower. A flashback to vintage AC, this antique-filled inn offers spacious, clean rooms and a fantastic staff. There are no TVs, phones, or A/C, and the elevator is manually operated. Enjoy the rocking chairs and Atlantic breeze on the porch. The downstairs bar offers lively entertainment and a friendly atmosphere. Key deposit $5. Weekdays doubles $40, with bath $55; weekend doubles $45/80. ❸

Comfort Inn, 154 S Kentucky Ave. (☎609-348-4000; www.comfortinn.com), between Martin Luther King Blvd. and New York Ave., near the Sands (p. 321). Basic rooms with king-size or queen-size beds and—true to Atlantic City's style of swank—jacuzzis. Breakfast, free parking, and heated pool. Rooms with ocean views $20 extra, but with fridge, microwave, and a larger jacuzzi. Reserve well in advance for weekends and holidays. Prices vary drastically depending on the time of year; rooms from $80. ❹

MAP APPENDIX

MAP APPENDIX

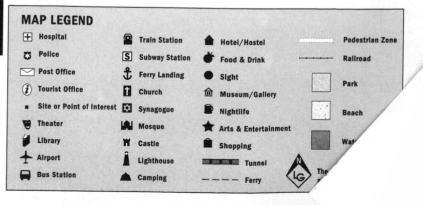

MAP LEGEND

Hospital	Train Station	Hotel/Hostel	Pedestrian Zone
Police	Subway Station	Food & Drink	Railroad
Post Office	Ferry Landing	Sight	Park
Tourist Office	Church	Museum/Gallery	
Site or Point of Interest	Synagogue	Nightlife	Beach
Theater	Mosque	Arts & Entertainment	
Library	Castle	Shopping	Wat
Airport	Lighthouse	Tunnel	The
Bus Station	Camping	Ferry	

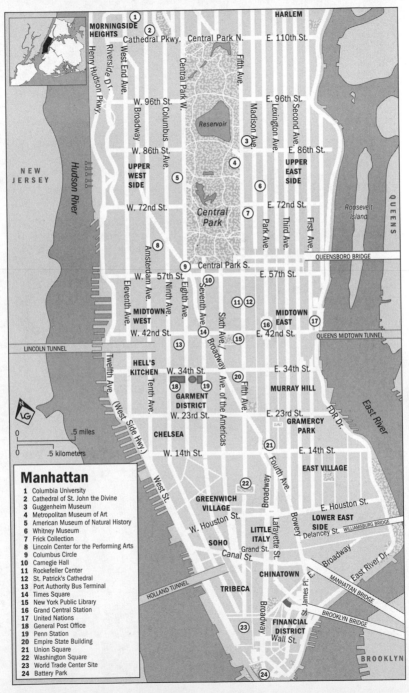

Manhattan

1 Columbia University
2 Cathedral of St. John the Divine
3 Guggenheim Museum
4 Metropolitan Museum of Art
5 American Museum of Natural History
6 Whitney Museum
7 Frick Collection
8 Lincoln Center for the Performing Arts
9 Columbus Circle
10 Carnegie Hall
11 Rockefeller Center
12 St. Patrick's Cathedral
13 Port Authority Bus Terminal
14 Times Square
15 New York Public Library
16 Grand Central Station
17 United Nations
18 General Post Office
19 Penn Station
20 Empire State Building
21 Union Square
22 Washington Square
23 World Trade Center Site
24 Battery Park

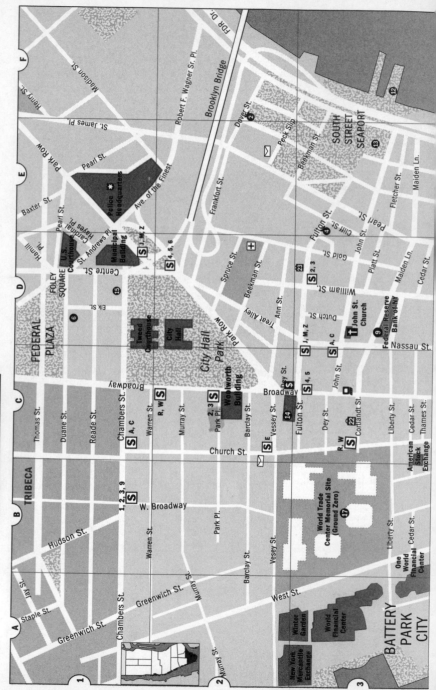

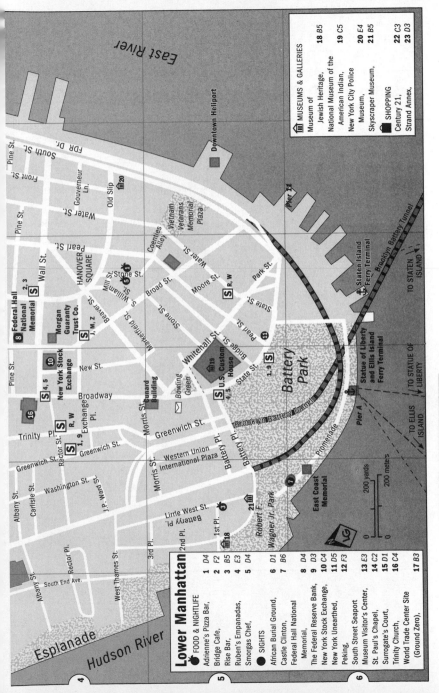

East River

Pine St.
South St.
FDR Dr.
Front St.
Old Slip

Downtown Heliport

🏛20

Pine St.

Gouverneur Ln.

Water St.

Vietnam Veterans Memorial Plaza

Pier 11

Coenties Alley

Pearl St.

Wall St.

Water St.

Stone St.

HANOVER SQUARE

🍴9

Federal Hall National Memorial 2, 3
🏛8

S

William St.

Broad St.

Moore St.

Park St.

S R, W

Staten Island Ferry Terminal

Brooklyn Battery Tunnel

Pine St.

Morgan Guaranty Trust Co.
1, M, z

Beaver St.

Stone St.

State St.

TO STATEN ISLAND

New St.

New York Stock Exchange
🏙10

S 4, 5

Maidenfield St.

Whitehall St.

Bridge St.

Pearl St.

State St.

🏛19
U.S. Custom House

S 4, 5

🏛11

Statue of Liberty and Ellis Island Ferry Terminal

Broadway

Trinity Pl.

16

S R, W
1, 9

Exchange Pl.

Morris St.

Standard Building

Bowling Green

S 1, 9

Battery Park

TO STATUE OF LIBERTY

Rector St.

Greenwich St.

Greenwich St.

Greenwich St.

Western Union International Plaza

Battery Pl.

Battery Pl.

Brooklyn Battery Tunnel

Promenade

Pier A

TO ELLIS ISLAND

Albany St.

Carlisle St.

Washington St.

Morris St.

J.P. Ward St.

East Coast Memorial

🍴7

200 yards

200 meters

Little West St.

Battery Pl.

1st Pl.

🍴3

🏛21
Robert F. Wagner Jr. Park

🏛18
2nd Pl.

0   0

Rector Pl.

West St.

3rd Pl.

South End Ave.

West Thames St.

Albany St.

Esplanade

Hudson River

Lower Manhattan

🍴 FOOD & NIGHTLIFE

Adrienne's Pizza Bar,	**1** *D4*
Bridge Cafe,	**2** *F2*
Rise Bar,	**3** *B5*
Ruben's Empanadas,	**4** *E3*
Smorgas Chef,	**5** *D4*

● SIGHTS

African Burial Ground,	**6** *D1*
Castle Clinton,	**7** *B6*
Federal Hall National Memorial,	**8** *D4*
The Federal Reserve Bank,	**9** *D3*
New York Stock Exchange,	**10** *C4*
New York Unearthed,	**11** *D5*
Peking,	**12** *F3*
South Street Seaport,	
Museum Visitor's Center,	**13** *E3*
St. Paul's Chapel,	**14** *C2*
Surrogate's Court,	**15** *D1*
Trinity Church,	**16** *C4*
World Trade Center Site (Ground Zero),	**17** *B3*

🏛 MUSEUMS & GALLERIES

Museum of Jewish Heritage,	**18** *B5*
National Museum of the American Indian,	**19** *C5*
New York City Police Museum,	**20** *E4*
Skyscraper Museum,	**21** *B5*

🛍 SHOPPING

Century 21,	**22** *C3*
Strand Annex,	**23** *D3*

4

5

6

SoHo and TriBeCa
see map p. 329

🍎 FOOD

Antique Garage,	**1**	*D3*
Bubby's,	**2**	*B6*
Cafe Bari,	**3**	*D2*
Cubana Café,	**4**	*C2*
Dean and Deluca,	**5**	*D2*
HQ,	**6**	*C5*
Jerry's,	**7**	*D2*
Kelley and Ping Asian Grocery and Noodle Shop,	**8**	*C1*
Lupe's East L.A. Kitchen,	**9**	*B3*
Miro Cafe,	**10**	*D3*
Pakistan Tea House,	**11**	*C7*
Ruben's Empanadas,	**12**	*C3*
Salaam Bombay,	**13**	*B7*

☕ NIGHTLIFE

Bar 89,	**14**	*D3*
Canal Room,	**15**	*C4*
Circa Tabac,	**16**	*B3*
Grand Bar & Lounge,	**17**	*C4*
Jane Restaurant and Bar,	**18**	*C1*
Lucky Strike,	**19**	*C4*
MercBar,	**20**	*D1*
Milady's,	**21**	*C2*
Raoul's,	**22**	*B2*
X-R Bar,	**23**	*B1*

🏛 MUSEUMS & GALLERIES

Artists Space,	**24**	*C3*
Deitch Projects,	**25**	*C4*
Dia Center for the Arts,	**26**	*C1*
Drawing Center,	**27**	*C3*
Moss,	**28**	*D1*
New York City Fire Museum,	**29**	*A3*
The Painting Center,	**30**	*C3*
Phyllis Kind Gallery,	**31**	*D1*
POP International Galleries, Inc.,	**32**	*C1*
Ronald Feldman Fine Arts,	**33**	*D4*
Staley-Wise,	**34**	*D2*

🛍 SHOPPING

Chill On Broadway,	**35**	*D4*
Dirty Jane,	**36**	*D3*
Exstaza,	**37**	*D3*
Lucky Brand Jeans,	**38**	*C4*
Pearl River,	**39**	*D3*
Sephora,	**40**	*D2*
Toys in Babeland,	**41**	*D3*
Universal News and Cafe Corp.,	**42**	*D3*

⭐ ARTS & ENTERTAINMENT

Angelika Film Center,	**43**	*D1*
Film Forum,	**44**	*A1*
Knitting Factory,	**45**	*C6*
SoHo Think Tank Ohio Theater,	**46**	*C3*

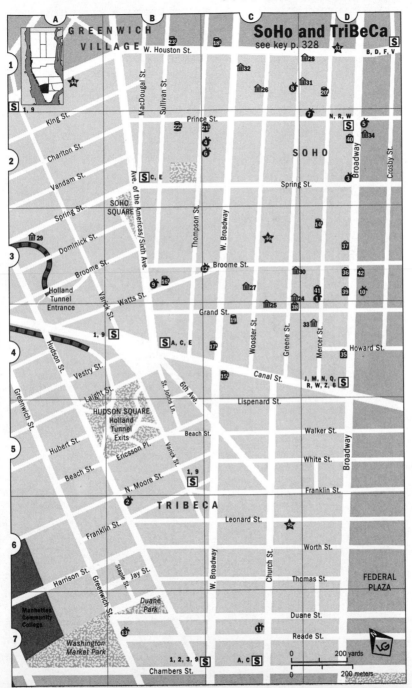

GREENWICH VILLAGE

W. Houston St.

SoHo and TriBeCa
see key p. 328

B, D, F, V

SOHO

King St.

Charlton St.

Prince St.

Vandam St.

Ave. of the Americas/Sixth Ave.

Spring St.

SOHO SQUARE

Spring St.

Dominick St.

Broome St.

Holland Tunnel Entrance

Watts St.

Broome St.

Grand St.

Wooster St.

Greene St.

Mercer St.

Howard St.

Canal St.

Vestry St.

Laight St.

HUDSON SQUARE
Holland Tunnel Exits

Beach St.

Ericsson Pl.

Lispenard St.

Walker St.

White St.

Franklin St.

N. Moore St.

TRIBECA

Franklin St.

Leonard St.

Worth St.

Harrison St.

Jay St.

Thomas St.

FEDERAL PLAZA

Manhattan Community College

Duane Park

Duane St.

Washington Market Park

Reade St.

1, 2, 3, 9

A, C

Chambers St.

0   200 yards

0   200 meters

MacDougal St.

Sullivan St.

Thompson St.

W. Broadway

Broadway

Crosby St.

Hudson St.

Greenwich St.

St. Johns Ln.

6th Ave.

Varick St.

Hubert St.

Beach St.

W. Broadway

Church St.

Broadway

N, R, W

J, M, N, Q, R, W, Z, 6

1, 9

1, 9

MAP APPENDIX

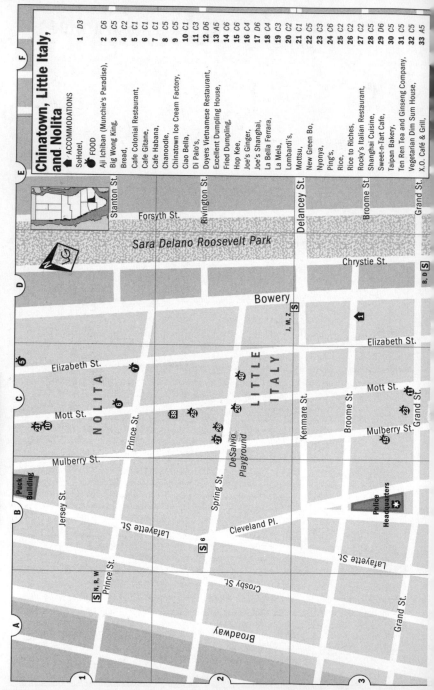

MAP APPENDIX

Chinatown, Little Italy, and Nolita

ACCOMMODATIONS		
SoHotel,	1	D3
● FOOD		
Aji Ichiban (Munchie's Paradise),	2	C6
Big Wong King,	3	C5
Bread,	4	C2
Cafe Colonial Restaurant,	5	C1
Cafe Gitane,	6	C1
Cafe Habana,	7	C1
Chanoodle,	8	C5
Chinatown Ice Cream Factory,	9	C5
Ciao Bella,	10	C1
Di Palo's,	11	C3
Doyers Vietnamese Restaurant,	12	D6
Excellent Dumpling House,	13	A5
Fried Dumpling,	14	C6
Hop Kee,	15	C6
Joe's Ginger,	16	C4
Joe's Shanghai,	17	D6
La Bella Ferrara,	18	C4
La Mela,	19	C3
Lombardi's,	20	C2
Mottsu,	21	C1
New Green Bo,	22	C5
Nyonya,	23	C3
Ping's,	24	C6
Rice,	25	C2
Rice to Riches,	26	C2
Rocky's Italian Restaurant,	27	C2
Shanghai Cuisine,	28	C5
Sweet-n-Tart Cafe,	29	D6
Taipan Bakery,	30	C5
Ten Ren Tea and Ginseng Company,	31	C5
Vegetarian Dim Sum House,	32	C5
X.O. Café & Grill,	33	A5

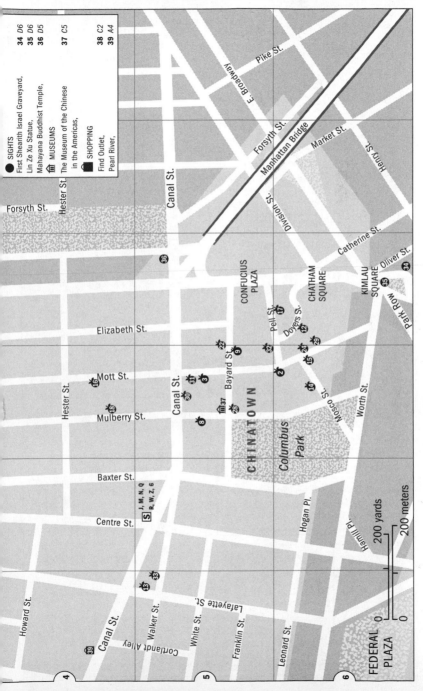

● SIGHTS
First Shearith Israel Graveyard,   34 D6
Lin Ze Xu Statue,   35 D6
Mahayana Buddhist Temple,   36 D5

🏛 MUSEUMS
The Museum of the Chinese   37 C5
in the Americas,

🛍 SHOPPING
Find Outlet,   38 C2
Pearl River,   39 A4

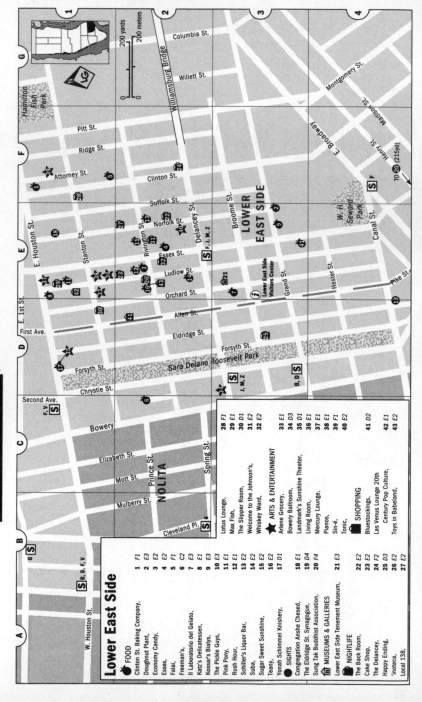

MAP APPENDIX

Lower East Side

FOOD

Clinton St. Baking Company,	1 F1
Doughnut Plant,	2 E3
Economy Candy,	3 E2
Essex,	4 E2
Falai,	5 F1
Freeman's,	6 C2
Il Laboratorio del Gelato,	7 E3
Katz's Delicatessen,	8 E2
Kossar's Bialys,	9 E3
The Pickle Guys,	10 E3
Pink Pony,	11 E1
Rush Hour,	12 E1
Schiller's Liquor Bar,	13 E2
Suba,	14 E2
Sugar Sweet Sunshine,	15 E2
Teany,	16 E2
Yonah Schimmel Knishery,	17 D1

SIGHTS

Congregation Anshe Chesed,	18 E1
The Eldridge St. Synagogue,	19 D4
Sung Tak Buddhist Association,	20 F4

MUSEUMS & GALLERIES

Lower East Side Tenement Museum,	21 E3

NIGHTLIFE

The Back Room,	22 E2
Cake Shop,	23 E2
The Delancey,	24 F2
Happy Ending,	25 D3
'inoteca,	26 E2
Local 138,	27 E2
Lotus Lounge,	28 F1
Max Fish,	29 E1
The Slipper Room,	30 D1
Welcome to the Johnson's,	31 E2
Whiskey Ward,	32 E2

ARTS & ENTERTAINMENT

Arlene Grocery,	33 E1
Bowery Ballroom,	34 D3
Landmark's Sunshine Theater,	35 D1
Living Room,	36 E1
Mercury Lounge,	37 E1
Pianos,	38 E1
Sin-é,	39 F1
Tonic,	40 E2

SHOPPING

Bluestockings,	41 D2
Las Venus Lounge 20th Century Pop Culture,	42 E1
Toys in Babeland,	43 E2

Greenwich Village and the Meatpacking District
see map pp. 334-335

🏠 ACCOMMODATIONS

Larchmont Hotel,	1	D2
Washington Square Hotel,	2	D4

🍎 FOOD

Arturo's Pizza,	3	E5
Caffe Dante,	4	D5
Caffe Pane e Cioccolato,	5	F4
Chez Brigitte,	6	B3
Esperanto Cafe,	7	D5
The Grey Dog,	8	C5
The Magnolia Bakery,	9	A3
Mamoun's,	10	D5
Markt,	11	A1
Moustache,	12	B4
Pastis,	13	A1
Peanut Butter & Co.,	14	D4
Pink Tea Cup,	15	B4
Restaurant Florent,	16	A1
Sacred Chow,	17	D5
Soy Luck Club,	18	B2
Spice Market,	19	A1
Tartine,	20	B3
Tomoe Sushi,	21	E5

● SIGHTS

75½ Bedford Street,	22	B5
Christopher Park,	23	B4
Church of St. Luke's in the Fields,	24	A5
Grace Church,	25	F3
Jefferson Market Library,	26	C3
The New School,	27	D2
Patchin Place,	28	C3
Picasso,	29	E5
Sheridan Square,	30	B4
West 4th St. Basketball Courts,	31	D4

🏛 MUSEUMS & GALLERIES

Forbes Magazine Galleries,	32	E2
Parsons Exhibition Center,	33	E2

🍺 NIGHTLIFE

APT,	34	A1
Chi Chiz,	35	A4
Chumley's,	36	B4
Cielo,	37	A1
The Cubbyhole,	38	A3
The Duplex,	39	B4
Employees Only,	40	A4
Gaslight,	41	A1
Henrietta Hudson,	42	B5
Lips,	43	B2
Lotus,	44	A1
Plunge,	45	A1
Red Lion,	46	E5
El Rey de los Caridad,	47	A3
New Leaf Café,	48	A2
Stonewall Bar,	49	B4
Tortilla Flats,	50	A3

⭐ ARTS & ENTERTAINMENT

Actors Playhouse,	51	B4
Angelika Film Center,	52	F5
Arthur's Tavern,	53	B4
The Bitter End,	54	E5
Blue Note,	55	D4
Bowlmor Lanes,	56	E2
Cherry Lane Theatre,	57	B5
Smalls,	58	B3
Village Vanguard,	59	B3

🛍 SHOPPING

Biography Bookstore,	60	A3
Condomania,	61	B4
Disc-o-Rama,	62	D4
Forbidden Planet,	63	F2
Generation Records,	64	E5
La Petite Coquette,	65	F3
The Leather Man,	66	B4
Oscar Wilde Bookstore,	67	C3
Shakespeare and Company,	68	F4
Strand Bookstore,	69	F2
Village Chess Shop,	70	E5

MAP APPENDIX

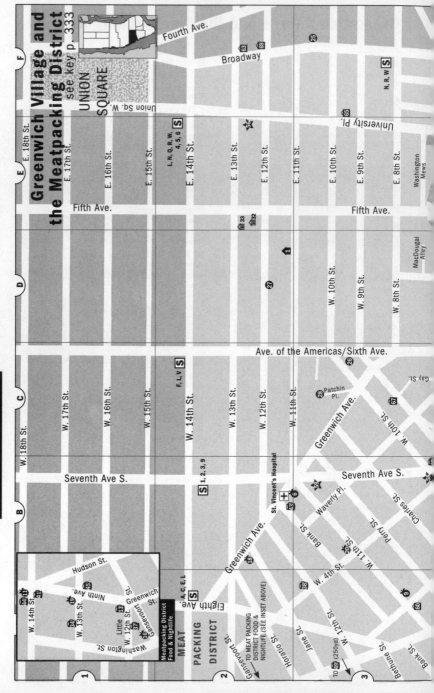

Greenwich Village and
the Meatpacking District
see key p. 333

UNION SQUARE

Fourth Ave.
Broadway
Union Sq. W.

Fifth Ave.
Fifth Ave.

Ave. of the Americas/Sixth Ave.

E. 18th St.
E. 17th St.
E. 16th St.
E. 15th St.
E. 14th St.
E. 13th St.
E. 12th St.
E. 11th St.
E. 10th St.
E. 9th St.
E. 8th St.

University Pl.
Washington Mews
MacDougal Alley

W. 18th St.
W. 17th St.
W. 16th St.
W. 15th St.
W. 14th St.
W. 13th St.
W. 12th St.
W. 11th St.
W. 10th St.
W. 9th St.
W. 8th St.

Seventh Ave S.
Seventh Ave S.

Greenwich Ave.
Patchin Pl.
Gay St.
W. 10th St.
Waverly Pl.
Charles St.
Perry St.
Bank St.
W. 11th St.
W. 4th St.
Bethune St.
Bank St.
Jane St.
W. 12th St.
Horatio St.
Greenwich Ave.
St. Vincent's Hospital

Hudson St.
Ninth Ave.
Greenwich St.
Washington St.
Little W. 12th St.
Gansevoort St.
W. 13th St.
W. 14th St.

Eighth Ave.

MEAT PACKING DISTRICT

Meatpacking District
Food & Nightlife

Gansevoort St.

Gas to MEAT PACKING
DISTRICT FOOD &
NIGHTLIFE (SEE INSET ABOVE)

TO 49 (250yd)

N, R, W S

L, N, Q, R, W, 4, 5, 6 S

F, L, V S

S 1, 2, 3, 9

A, C, E, L S

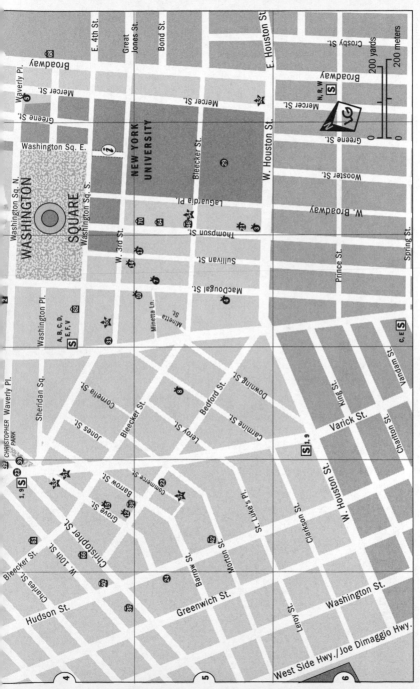

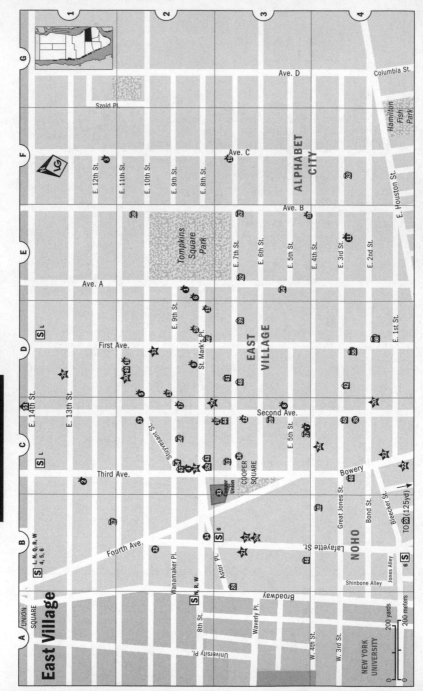

East Village

East Village

🍴 FOOD

Alt.Coffee,	1 E2
Blue 9 Burger,	2 C1
Cafecito,	3 F1
Chickpea,	4 C2
Chikalicious Dessert Bar,	5 D2
Crif Dogs,	6 D2
Cucina di Pesce,	7 C3
Frank,	8 C3
Jules,	9 D2
Kate's Joint,	10 E3
Mama's Food Shop,	11 E4
Moishe's Bake Shop,	12 C3
Mudspot,	13 D2
Pomme Frites,	14 C3
St. Dymphna's,	15 E2
Veniero's,	16 D2
Veselka,	17 C2
Yaffa Cafe,	18 D2
Zum Schneider,	19 F3

★ ARTS & ENTERTAINMENT

Anthology Film Archives,	20 C4
Astor Place Theater,	21 B3
The Bowery Poetry Club,	22 C4
CBGB,	23 C4
Continental,	24 C2
Detour,	25 D1
Joe's Pub,	26 B3
The Joseph Papp Public Theater,	27 B3
Millennium Film Workshop,	28 C4
Orpheum,	29 C2
Rififi,	30 D2
Theater for the New City,	31 D2

● SIGHTS

Colonnade Row,	32 B2
The Cooper Union Foundation Building,	33 C3
The Cube,	34 B2
New York Marble Cemeteries,	35 C4
St. George Ukrainian Catholic Church,	36 C3
St. Mark's Church in-the-Bowery,	37 C2

🛍 SHOPPING

Astor Place Hairstylist,	38 B3
Bobby 2000,	39 D3
Downtown Music Gallery,	40 C4
FAB208,	41 D3
Jammyland,	42 D4
Kim's Video and Audio,	43 C2
Love Saves the Day,	44 C3
New York Adorned,	45 C4
Other Music,	46 B3
St. Mark's Bookshop,	47 C2
Tokyo 7 Consignment Store,	48 D3
Tokyo Joe,	49 D2
William LeRoy Antiques & Props,	50 B4

ACCOMMODATIONS

Jazz on the Town,	51 C1
St. Mark's Hotel,	52 C2

🏠 NIGHTLIFE

7B,	53 E3
Angel's Share,	54 C2
d.b.a.,	55 D4
Decibel,	56 C2
KGB,	57 C3
Lakeside Lounge,	58 E2
Lit,	59 C3
Lucky Cheng's,	60 D4
McSorley's Old Ale House,	61 C2
Niagara,	62 E3
Nuyorican Poets Cafe,	63 F4
Sing Sing,	64 E3
Swift Hibernian Lounge,	65 B4
Tribe,	66 D2
Webster Hall,	67 B1

MAP APPENDIX

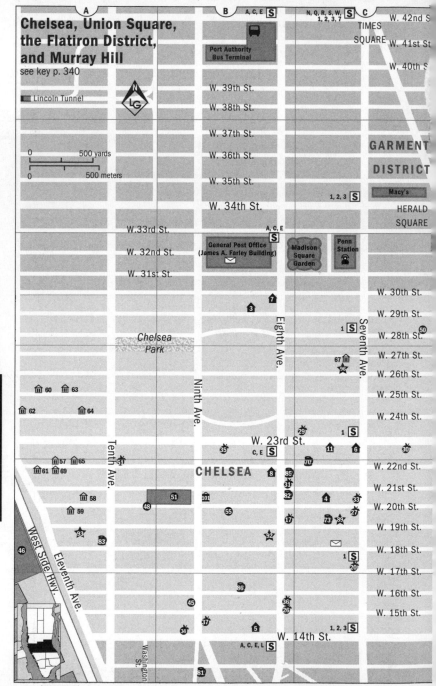

Chelsea, Union Square, the Flatiron District, and Murray Hill

see key p. 340

■ Lincoln Tunnel

0   500 yards
0   500 meters

A, C, E

N, Q, R, S, W,
1, 2, 3, 7

TIMES SQUARE

W. 42nd St
W. 41st St
W. 40th St
W. 39th St.
W. 38th St.
W. 37th St.
W. 36th St.
W. 35th St.

GARMENT
DISTRICT

Macy's

1, 2, 3

W. 34th St.

HERALD SQUARE

W.33rd St.

A, C, E

Port Authority
Bus Terminal

General Post Office
(James A. Farley Building)

Madison
Square
Garden

Penn
Station

W. 32nd St.
W. 31st St.

W. 30th St.
W. 29th St.

Eighth Ave.

Seventh Ave.

1

W. 28th St.

Chelsea
Park

67
96

W. 27th St.
W. 26th St.

Ninth Ave.

60   63

62   64

W. 25th St.
W. 24th St.

29

1

W. 23rd St.

35

C, E

11   6

30

Tenth Ave.

57   65

61   69

51

70

CHELSEA

8

85
31
32

W. 22nd St.

W. 21st St.

58

51

48

101

4

33
27

W. 20th St.

59

55

17

73

W. 19th St.

99

83

92

W. 18th St.

46

West Side Hwy.

1

20

W. 17th St.

86

W. 16th St.

45

36
26

W. 15th St.

Eleventh Ave.

34

37

5

1, 2, 3

W. 14th St.

Washington St.

A, C, E, L

81

Chelsea, Union Square, the Flatiron District, and Murray Hill
see map pp. 338-339

🏠 ACCOMMODATIONS

American Dream Hostel,	1	F4
Carlton Arms Hotel,	2	F4
Chelsea Center Hostel,	3	B3
Chelsea International Hostel,	4	C5
Chelsea Pines Inn,	5	B6
Chelsea Savoy Hotel,	6	C4
Chelsea Star Hotel,	7	B3
Colonial House Inn,	8	B5
Gershwin Hotel,	9	D4
Hotel 17,	10	F5
Hotel Chelsea,	11	C4
Hotel Grand Union,	12	E3
The Marcel,	13	F4
Murray Hill Inn,	14	F3
ThirtyThirty,	15	E3

🍎 FOOD

Artisanal Fromagerie and Bistro,	16	E3
Better Burger,	17	B5
Blue Smoke,	18	E4
Bread Bar at Tabla,	19	E4
Cafeteria,	20	C5
Chat 'n' Chew,	21	D6
Chef & Co.,	22	D5
Chocolat,	23	E5
The City Bakery,	24	D5
Craftbar,	25	E5
Diner 24,	26	B6
elmo,	27	C5
Empire Diner,	28	A5
F & B,	29	C4
Garden of Eden Gourmet Marketplace,	30	C4
Kitchen/Market,	31	B5
Kitchen 22,	32	E5
Le Zie,	33	C5
Little Pie Co.,	34	B6
Negril,	35	B4
Pad Thai Noodle Lounge,	36	B6
Pop Burger,	37	B6
Rainbow Falafel and Shawarma,	38	E6
Republic,	39	E6
Rosa Mexicana,	40	D5
Shake Shack,	41	E4
Sunburst Espresso Bar,	42	F5
Zen Palate,	43	E6

⬤ SIGHTS

American Academy of Dramatic Arts,	44	E3
Chelsea Market,	45	B6
Chelsea Piers,	46	A5
Church of the Transfiguration,	47	D3
Cushman Row,	48	A5
Flatiron Building,	49	D4
Flower District,	50	C3
General Theological Seminary,	51	B5
Metropolitan Life Insurance Tower,	52	E4
National Arts Club,	53	E5
New York Life Insurance Building,	54	E4
St. Peter's Episcopal Church,	55	B5
The Theodore Roosevelt Birthplace,	56	E5

🏛 MUSEUMS & GALLERIES

525 W. 22nd St.,	57	A5
529 W. 20th St.,	58	A5
Anton Kern Gallery,	59	A5
Cheim & Read,	60	A4
Dia Center for the Arts,	61	A5
Gagosian,	62	A4
Kashya Hildebrand Gallery,	63	A4
Matthew Marks,	64	A5
Max Protetch,	65	A5
Morgan Library,	66	E2
The Museum at Fashion Institute of Technology,	67	C4
Museum of Sex,	68	D4
Sonnabend,	69	A5

🎵 NIGHTLIFE

Barracuda,	70	C5
Big Apple Ranch,	71	D5
Flatiron Lounge,	72	D5
g,	73	C5
Heartland Brewery,	74	E6
Heaven,	75	D6
Old Town Bar and Grill,	76	E5
Park Bar,	77	D6
Pete's Tavern,	78	E5
Pipa,	79	E5
Player's Club,	80	E5
Plunge,	81	B6
Rawhide,	82	B5
The Roxy,	83	A5
SBNY,	84	D6
View,	85	B5
XL,	86	B6

⭐ ARTS & ENTERTAINMENT

Bikram Yoga,	87	D4
Dance Forum,	88	D6
Dance Theater Workshop,	89	C5
Daryl Roth Theater,	89	E6
Gotham Comedy Club,	90	D5
Irving Plaza,	91	E6
Joyce Theater,	92	B5
The Kitchen,	93	A5
Tiger Schulmann's Karate Fitness,	94	D5
Union Square Theatre,	95	E6
Upright Citizens Brigade Theater,	96	C4
Vineyard Theater Company's Dimson Theater,	97	E6

🛍 SHOPPING

17@17 Thrift Shop,	98	D5
ABC Carpet & Home,	99	E5
Academy Records and CDs,	100	D5
The Barking Zoo,	101	B5
Books of Wonder,	102	D5
Paragon Sports,	103	E5
Reminiscence,	104	D4
Revolution Books,	105	D5
Shoegasm,	106	D4
Side,	107	F5

Midtown

see map pp. 342-343

ACCOMMODATIONS

Americana Inn,	**1**	*D5*
Big Apple Hostel,	**2**	*C4*
Broadway Inn,	**3**	*C4*
Herald Square Hotel,	**4**	*D6*
Hotel Pickwick Arms,	**5**	*F3*
Hotel Stanford,	**6**	*D6*
Hotel Wolcott,	**7**	*D6*
Novotel,	**8**	*C3*
YMCA-Vanderbilt,	**9**	*F3*

FOOD

Becco,	**10**	*B4*
Chola,	**11**	*F2*
Empanada Mama,	**12**	*A3*
Ess-a-Bagel,	**13**	*E3*
Fresco by Scotto,	**14**	*E3*
Fresco by Scotto On The Go,	**15**	*E3*
Heartland Brewery,	**16**	*D6*
Hourglass Tavern,	**17**	*B4*
Island Burgers & Shakes,	**18**	*B3*
Kangsuh Korean Restaurant,	**19**	*D6*
Kum Gang San,	**20**	*D6*
Mangia,	**21**	*D3*
Minar,	**22**	*D6*
Sapporo,	**23**	*C3*
Say Cheese!,	**24**	*B4*
Teuscher Chocolatier,	**25**	*D3*
Wolf & Lamb,	**26**	*D3*

SIGHTS

The Algonquin Hotel,	**27**	*D4*
Bryant Park,	**28**	*D5*
Carnegie Hall,	**29**	*D3*
Chrysler Building,	**30**	*E4*
Citigroup Center/Saint Peter's,	**31**	*E2*
City Center Theater,	**32**	*C2*
The Empire State Building,	**33**	*D6*
General Electric Building,	**34**	*D3*
General Post Office,	**35**	*B6*
Grand Central Station,	**36**	*E4*
Jacob K. Javits Convention Center,	**37**	*A5*
Macy's,	**38**	*C6*
Madsion Square Garden,	**39**	*C6*
Met Life Building,	**40**	*E4*
New York Public Library,	**41**	*D5*
Penn Station,	**42**	*C6*
Plaza Hotel,	**43**	*D2*
Radio City Music Hall,	**44**	*D3*
Rockefeller Center,	**45**	*D3*
Seagram Building,	**46**	*E3*
Sony Plaza,	**47**	*D2*
St. Bartholomew's Church,	**48**	*E3*
St. Patrick's Cathedral,	**49**	*D3*
Times Square,	**50**	*C4*
Trump International Hotel,	**51**	*B1*
Trump Tower,	**52**	*D2*
United Nations,	**53**	*F4*
University Club,	**54**	*D2*
Waldorf Astoria Hotel,	**55**	*E3*

ARTS & ENTERTAINMENT

Birdland,	**56**	*B4*
Carnegie Hall,	**57**	*C2*
City Center,	**58**	*C2*
Crunch Gym,	**59**	*F1*
The Daily Show,	**60**	*A2*
Lamb's,	**61**	*C4*
Late Show with David Letterman,	**62**	*C2*
Majestic Theater,	**63**	*C4*
Manhattan Theater Club,	**64**	*C2*
NBC Studios,	**65**	*D3*
Nederlander Theater,	**66**	*B5*
Neil Simon Theater,	**67**	*C3*
New Amsterdam Theater,	**68**	*B4*
Peck and Goodie Skates,	**69**	*B2*
Primary Stages,	**70**	*B4*
Roseland Ballroom,	**71**	*C3*
Samuel Beckett Theater,	**72**	*B4*
St. James Theater,	**73**	*C4*
Swing 46,	**74**	*B4*
TKTS,	**75**	*C4*
Ziegfeld,	**76**	*C2*

SHOPPING

Apple Store,	**77**	*D1*
Bergdorff-Goodman,	**78**	*D2*
The Complete Traveller Bookstore,	**79**	*E6*
The Drama Book Shop,	**80**	*C5*
Gotham Book Mart,	**81**	*D4*
H & M,	**82, 83**	*D3, D6*
Hammacher Schlemmer,	**84**	*E2*
Hell's Kitchen Flea Market,	**85**	*B5*
Lord and Taylor,	**86**	*D5*
Macy's,	**87**	*C6*
Rock and Soul,	**88**	*C6*
Saks Fifth Avenue,	**89**	*D3*
Shops at Columbus Circle,	**90**	*B1*
Tiffany & Co.,	**91**	*D2*
Toys 'R' Us,	**92**	*C4*

MUSEUMS & GALLERIES

Christie's,	**93**	*D3*
International Center of Photography,	**94**	*C4*
Intrepid Sea-Air-Space Museum,	**95**	*A4*
Japan Society,	**96**	*F3*
Leo Kaplan Modern,	**97**	*E2*
Museum of Arts and Design,	**98**	*D3*
Museum of Modern Art,	**99**	*D2*
Museum of Television and Radio,	**100**	*D3*
Pace Gallery,	**101**	*E2*
Peter Findlay Galleries,	**102**	*E2*
Sony Wonder Technology Lab,	**103**	*D2*

Midtown
see key p. 341

Lincoln Center

Central Park

W. 62nd St.
W. 61st St.
W. 60th St.
W. 59th St.
W. 58th St.
W. 57th St.
W. 56th St.
W. 55th St.
W. 54th St.
W. 53rd St.
W. 52nd St.
W. 51st St.
W. 50th St.
W. 49th St.
W. 48th St.
W. 47th St.
W. 46th St.
W. 45th St.
W. 44th St.
W. 43rd St.
W. 42nd St.
W. 41st St.
W. 40th St.
W. 39th St.
W. 38th St.
W. 37th St.
W. 36th St.
W. 35th St.
W. 34th St.
W. 33rd St.
W. 32nd St.
W. 31st St.
W. 30th St.

COLUMBUS CIRCLE
Central Park S.

Eleventh Ave.
Tenth Ave.
Ninth Ave.
Eighth Ave.
Seventh Ave.
Broadway

HELL'S KITCHEN

THEATER DISTRICT

RESTAURANT ROW

DUFFY SQUARE

TIMES SQUARE

Equitable Life

THEATER ROW

Port Authority Bus Terminal

Dyer Ave.

Lincoln Tunnel

Jacob K. Javits Convention Center

TO 🏛 (150yd)

Madison Square Garden

Penn Station

Macy's

General Post Office
(James A. Farley Building)

GARMENT DISTRICT

A, B, C, D, 1, 9

N, Q, R, W

B, D, E

C, E

1, 9

N, R, W

B, D, F, V

A, C, E

N, Q, R, S, W, 1, 2, 3, 7, 9

1, 2, 3, 9

A, C, E

D   E   S F   F

E. 63rd St.
E. 62nd St.
E. 61st St.
E. 60th St.

Queensboro
Bridge

GRAND
ARMY
PLAZA   S N, R, W

N, R, W,
4, 5, 6 S   Bloomingdale's   59

Plaza
Hotel 43   77

E. 59th St.

E. 58th St.   11

78

97   102   102

84   NY Computer
Cafe

E. 57th St.

S F
Carnegie
Hall
29

91

52   103 47

E. 56th St.
E. 55th St.
E. 54th St.

54

31   E. 53rd St.

99 S
E, V

98   100

AXA
Financial
Center
82

44

46 Seagram
Building

S E, V, 6

Fifth Ave.

Madison Ave.

E. 52nd St.

14 15

Second Ave.

First Ave.

Sutton Pl.

E. 51st St.
49 St. Patrick's
Cathedral

48

Rockefeller
Center 45   25
65 34   89
93

26 21
DIAMOND ROW   E. 47th St.

LITTLE BRAZIL ST.

27

81

55 Waldorf-
Astoria

13 E. 50th St.

E. 49th St.

E. 48th St.

9

Park Ave.

Lexington Ave.

Third Ave.

5

Beekman Pl.

96   United
Nations

E. 46th St.
E. 45th St.
E. 44th St.

MetLife
Building

Grand
Central
Terminal

40

36

i

Chrysler
Building
30

S B, D, F, V, 7

Vanderbilt Ave.

E. 43rd St.

E. 42nd St.

S 4, 5, 6, 7 S

(VEHICULAR TUNNEL BELOW STREET)

First Ave.

53

United
Nations

Bryant
Park 28   41

New York
Public Library

E. 41st St.
E. 40th St.

Tudor City Pl.

Ave. of the Americas/Sixth Ave.

Madison Ave.

(VEHICULAR TUNNEL BELOW STREET)

Park Ave.

E. 39th St.

MURRAY
HILL

Queens
Midtown
Tunnel

FDR Dr.

American
Standard
Building
86

Fifth Ave.

E. 38th St.

E. 37th St.

Pierpont
Morgan
Library

Lexington Ave.

E. 36th St.

Tunnel Entrance St.

B, D, F, N,
Q, R, V, W
S 83   Empire State
Building 33

16

79

E. 35th St.

E. 34th St.

HERALD
SQUARE
i
20
19

6

22

S 6

E. 33rd St.

E. 32nd St.

0   300 yards

VG

7

E. 31st St.

0   300 meters

E. 30th St.

1

2

3

4

5

6

MAP APPENDIX

Upper West Side

Upper West Side

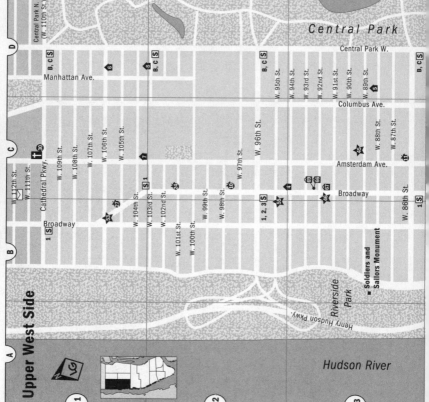

Citrus Bar and Grill,	37 C5
Dead Poet,	38 C4
Dive 75,	39 C5
The Evelyn Lounge,	40 C4
Shalel Lounge,	41 D5
West 79th Street Boat Basin Cafe,	42 A4
Yogi's,	43 C5

★ **ARTS & ENTERTAINMENT**

Beacon Theatre,	44 C5
Claremont Riding School,	45 C3
Equinox Fitness Clubs,	46 C3
ExtraVertical Climbing Center,	47 D6
Live with Regis and Kelly (WABC),	48 D6
Manhattan Motion Dance Studio,	49 C4
Mannes College of Music,	50 C4
Merkin Concert Hall,	51 C2
Namaste,	52 C4
Smoke,	53 B1
Stand-Up New York,	54 C4
Symphony Space,	55 B2
The View,	56 B6
at Lincoln Center:	
Alice Tully Hall,	57 C6
Avery Fisher Hall,	58 C6
Metropolitan Opera House,	59 C6
New York Public Library for	
the Performing Arts,	60 C6
New York State Theater,	61 C6
Vivian Beaumont Theater and Mitzi E.	
Newhouse Theater,	62 C6
Walter Reade Theater,	63 C6

■ **SHOPPING**

Allan and Suzi,	64 C4
La Brea,	65 C5
Lord of Designs,	66 C3
Süde,	67 C3
Maxilla & Mandible,	68 C4
Murder Ink/Ivy's,	69 C3
Westsides Records,	70 C5

MAP APPENDIX

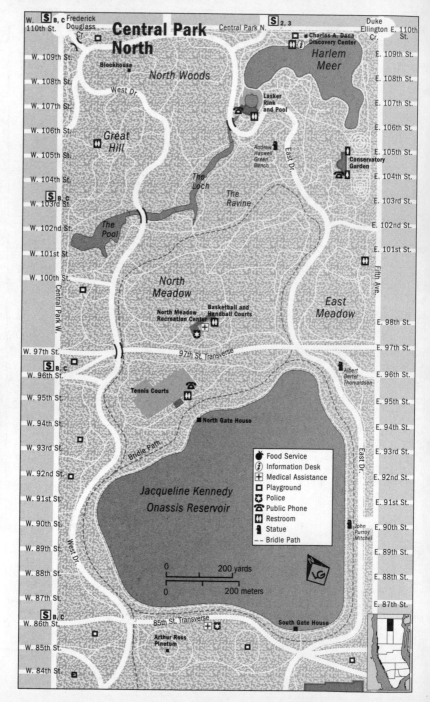

Central Park North

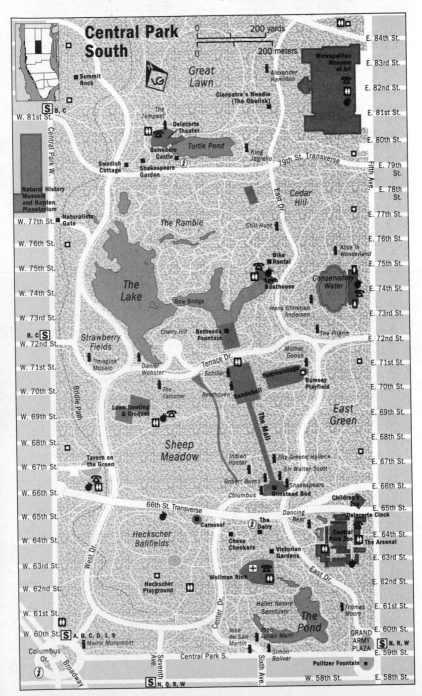

Central Park
South

0   200 yards

0   200 meters

Summit Rock

Great Lawn

Alexander Hamilton

Metropolitan Museum of Art

E. 84th St.

E. 83rd St.

E. 82nd St.

Cleopatra's Needle (The Obelisk)

S B, C

W. 81st St.

Central Park W.

The Tempest

Delacorte Theater

E. 81st St.

E. 80th St.

Belvedere Castle

Turtle Pond

King Jagiello

79th St. Transverse

Fifth Ave.

E. 79th St.

Swedish Cottage

Shakespeare Garden

Natural History Museum and Hayden Planetarium

Cedar Hill

E. 78th St.

Naturalists Gate

The Ramble

East Dr.

E. 77th St.

W. 77th St.

Still Hunt

W. 76th St.

Alice in Wonderland

E. 76th St.

W. 75th St.

Bike Rental

E. 75th St.

Loeb Boathouse

Conservatory Water

W. 74th St.

The Lake

E. 74th St.

W. 73rd St.

Bow Bridge

Hans Christian Andersen

E. 73rd St.

B, C S

W. 72nd St.

Cherry Hill

Bethesda Fountain

Strawberry Fields

The Pilgrim

E. 72nd St.

"Imagine" Mosaic

Daniel Webster

Terrace Dr.

Mother Goose

E. 71st St.

W. 71st St.

Schiller

Summerstage

Rumsey Playfield

East Green

E. 70th St.

W. 70th St.

The Falconer

Beethoven

Bandshell

Bridle Path

Lawn Bowling & Croquet

E. 69th St.

W. 69th St.

Sheep Meadow

The Mall

E. 68th St.

W. 68th St.

Tavern on the Green

Indian Hunter

Fitz-Greene Halleck

E. 67th St.

W. 67th St.

Sir Walter Scott

Robert Burns

Shakespeare

E. 66th St.

W. 66th St.

Columbus

Olmstead Bed

66th St. Transverse

Children's Zoo

Delacorte Clock

E. 65th St.

W. 65th St.

Dancing Bear

Carousel

The Dairy

W. 64th St.

Heckscher Ballfields

Chess & Checkers

Central Park Zoo

The Arsenal

E. 64th St.

West Dr.

Victorian Gardens

E. 63rd St.

W. 63rd St.

Heckscher Playground

Wollman Rink

East Dr.

E. 62nd St.

W. 62nd St.

Center Dr.

Hallet Nature Sanctuary

The Pond

Thomas Moore

E. 61st St.

W. 61st St.

José de San Martín

José Julian Martí

E. 60th St.

W. 60th St.

S A, B, C, D, 1, 9

Maine Monument

Simón Bolívar

GRAND ARMY PLAZA

S N, R, W

E. 59th St.

Columbus Cr.

Broadway

Seventh Ave.

Central Park S.

Sixth Ave.

Pulitzer Fountain

S N, Q, R, W

W. 58th St.

E. 58th St.

MAP APPENDIX

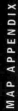

MAP APPENDIX

Upper East Side

Thomas Jefferson Park

Wards Island Park

Footbridge

Metropolitan Hospital Center

Mt. Sinai Hospital

CARNEGIE HILL

0   300 yards
0   300 meters

Second Ave.
Park Ave.
Madison Ave.
Lexington Ave.
Madison Ave.

E. 13th St.
E. 112th St.
E. 111th St.
E. 110th St.
E. 109th St.
E. 108th St.
E. 107th St.
E. 106th St.
E. 105th St.
E. 104th St.
E. 103rd St.
E. 102nd St.
E. 101st St.
E. 100th St.
E. 99th St.
E. 98th St.
E. 97th St.
E. 96th St.
E. 95th St.
E. 94th St.
E. 93rd St.
E. 92nd St.
E. 91st St.
E. 90th St.
E. 89th St.
E. 88th St.
E. 87th St.

▲ ACCOMMODATIONS
De Hirsch Residence, 1 B3

● FOOD
Barking Dog Luncheonette,	2	B3
Brother Jimmy's BBQ,	3	B4
Candle Cafe,	4	B5
DT.UT,	5	C4
Dylan's Candy Bar,	6	B6
EJ's Luncheonette,	7	B5
Grace's Marketplace,	8	B5
Il Vagabondo,	9	C6
Jackson Hole,	10	B6
La Maison du Chocolat,	11	A4
Le Pain Quotidien,	12	A4
Merchants NY,	13	C6
Mon Petit Cafe,	14	B6
Payard,	15	B5
Serendipity 3,	16	B6
Shanghai Pavilion,	17	B4
Vermicelli,	18	C4

● SIGHTS
The Church of Holy Trinity,	19	C3
Church of St. Jean Baptiste,	20	B5
Gracie Mansion,	21	D3
Grolier Club,	22	B6
Henderson Place Historic District,	23	C4
Knickerbocker Club,	24	A6
Lotos Club,	25	B5
Metropolitan Club,	26	A6
Roosevelt Island,	27	D5
St. Nicholas Russian Orthodox Cathedral,	28	A2
Temple Emanu-El,	29	A6
Union Club,	30	A6

▥ MUSEUMS & GALLERIES
Acquavella Gallery,	31	A4
The Asia Society,	32	B5
Cooper-Hewitt National Design Museum,	33	A3
El Museo del Barrio,	34	A2
Frick Collection,	35	A5
Gagosian Gallery,	36	A5
Guggenheim Museum,	37	A3
Hirschl & Adler Galleries,	38	A5
The Jewish Museum,	39	A3

40 A5
41 A5
42 A4
43 C6
44 B6
45 A2
46 A3
47 C5
48 A5

Leo Castelli,
M. Knoedler & Co., Inc,
Metropolitan Museum of Art,
Mt. Vernon Hotel Museum and Garden,
Museum of American Illustration,
Museum of the City of New York,
National Academy of Design Museum,
Sotheby's,
Whitney Museum of American Art,

NIGHTLIFE

49 C3
50 C3
51 C4
52 C6
53 A4
54 C5
55 C4

American Spirits,
The Big Easy,
Dorian's Red Hand,
Merchants NY,
Metropolitan Museum Roof Garden,
Mo's Caribbean Bar and Grille,
Ship of Fools,

ARTS & ENTERTAINMENT

56 B3
57 B5
58 C4
59 C6
60 B5
61 C4
62 B3
63 C5

92nd Street Y,
The Asia Society,
Comic Strip Live,
Dangerfield's,
Dicapo Opera Theater,
John Jay Pool,
Metro Bicycle Stores,
Pedal Pushers,
Cultural Institutes:

64 B6
65 B5
66 B6
67 A4
68 B5
69 B5

Alliance Francaise,
Americas Society,
China Institute,
Goethe-Institute,
Italian Cultural Institute,
Spanish Institute,

SHOPPING

70 B6
71 A6
72 B6
73 A4
74 C6
75 A6
76 B6
77 A4

Argosy Bookstore,
Barneys New York,
Bloomingdale's,
Encore,
Merchants NY,
Rita Ford Music Boxes,
Tender Buttons,
Venture Stationers,

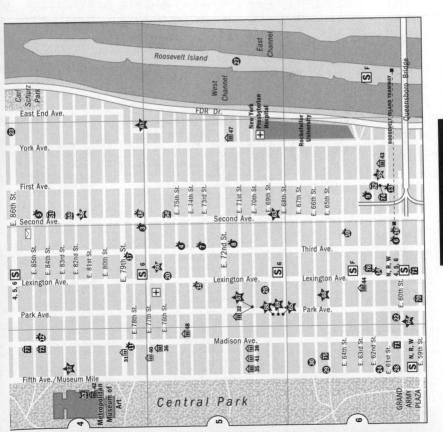

MAP APPENDIX

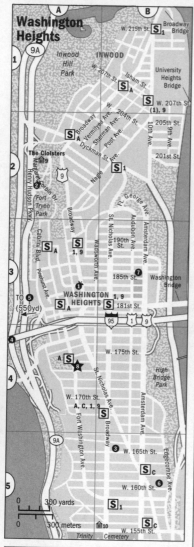

Morningside Heights, Harlem, and Washington Heights

Washington Heights

🍴 FOOD
El Rey de los Caridad,	1	A3
New Leaf Café,	2	A2

⬤ SIGHTS
Audubon Ballroom,	3	B5
The George Washington Bridge,	4	A4
Little Red Lighthouse,	5	A3
Morris-Jumel Mansion,	6	B5
Yeshiva University,	7	B3

★ ARTS & ENTERTAINMENT
J. Hood Wright,	8	A4

🏛 MUSEUMS & GALLERIES
Cloisters,	9	A2
Hispanic Society of America,	10	B5

Harlem and Morningside Heights

🛏 ACCOMMODATIONS
Harlem YMCA Claude McKay Residence	1	C5
Jazz on Harlem	2	C5

🍴 FOOD
Amir's Falafel,	3	A6
Bistro Itzocan,	4	D7
Charles' Southern Style Kitchen,	5	B3
Dinosaur BBQ,	6	A5
Fairway,	7	A5
The Hungarian Pastry Shop,	8	B7
La Fonda Boricua,	9	D7
La Marmite,	10	B6
Manna's Soul Food Restaurant,	11	C5
Massawa,	12	B6
Milano Market,	13	A7
Miss Maude's Spoonbread Too,	14	C4
Nussbaum & Wu,	15	A7
Settepani,	16	C6
Sylvia's,	17	C5
Symposium,	18	A7
Toast,	19	A5
Tom's Restaurant,	20	A7
Wimp's Southern Style Bakery,	21	C5

⬤ SIGHTS
The Abyssinian Baptist Church,	22	C4
Cathedral of St. John the Divine,	23	B7
City College,	24	B4
Columbia University,	25	A6
General Grant National Memorial,	26	A6
Hamilton Grange,	27	B4
Riverside Church,	28	A6
The Schomburg Center for Research in Black Culture,	29	C4

🏛 MUSEUMS & GALLERIES
El Museo del Barrio,	30	C7
Museum of the City of New York,	31	C7
Studio Museum,	32	C5

🛍 SHOPPING
Harlemade,	33	C6
Hue-Man Bookstore,	34	B5
Malcom Shabazz Harlem Market,	35	C6
Xukuma,	36	C6

★ ARTS & ENTERTAINMENT
Apollo Theater,	37	B5
Cotton Club,	38	A5
Harlem YMCA/Claude McKay Residence,	39	C5
Lenox Lounge,	40	C2
Showman's Cafe,	41	B5
St. Nick's Pub,	42	B3

MAP APPENDIX

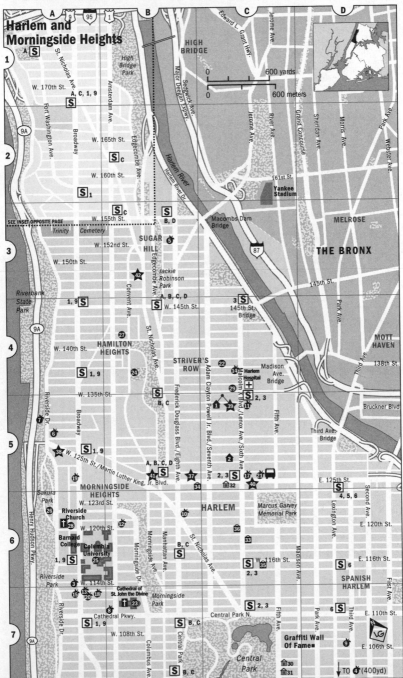

Harlem and Morningside Heights

Downtown Bus Routes

— North-South routes

— East-West routes

15 All numbers are Manhattan lines, which carry M-prefix on bus display.

Q B X "Q" are Queens lines; "B" are Brooklyn lines "X" are express lines

MAP APPENDIX

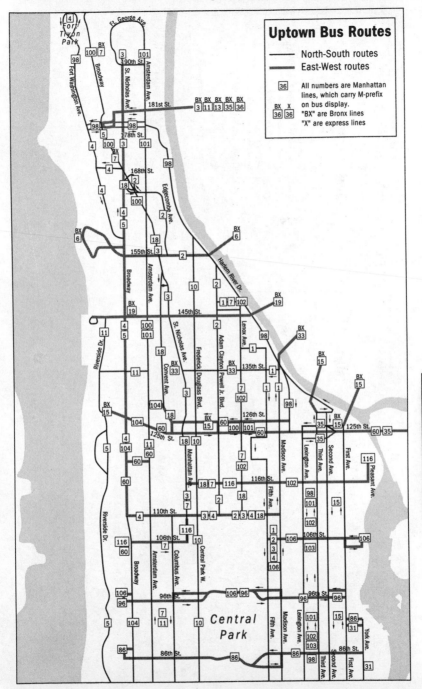

Uptown Bus Routes

— North-South routes

━ East-West routes

36 All numbers are Manhattan lines, which carry M-prefix on bus display.

BX 36 X 36 "BX" are Bronx lines
"X" are express lines

MAP APPENDIX

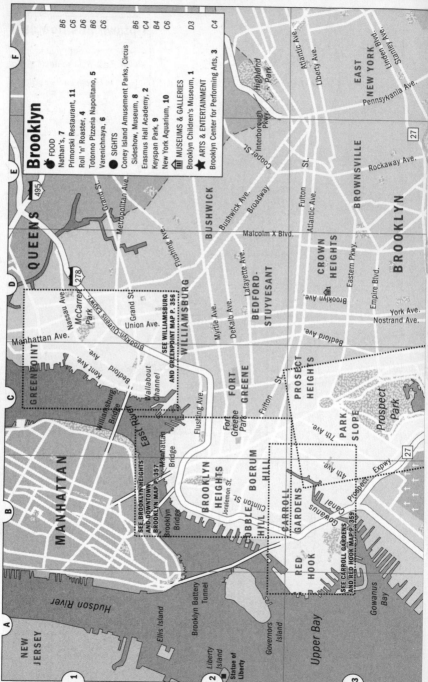

Brooklyn

FOOD
Nathan's, 7	B6
Primorski Restaurant, 11	C6
Roll 'n' Roaster, 4	D6
Totonno Pizzeria Napolitano, 5	B6
Varenichnaya, 6	C6

SIGHTS
Coney Island Amusement Parks, Circus Sideshow, Museum, 8	B6
Erasmus Hall Academy, 2	C4
Keyspan Park, 9	B4
New York Aquarium, 10	C6

MUSEUMS & GALLERIES
Brooklyn Children's Museum, 1	D3

ARTS & ENTERTAINMENT
Brooklyn Center for Performing Arts, 3	C4

MAP APPENDIX

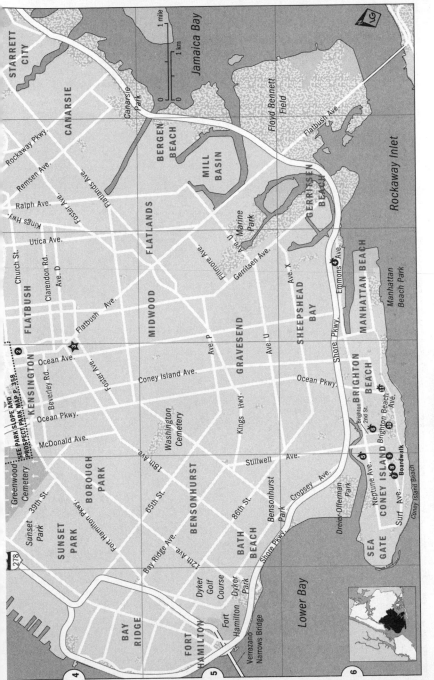

Jamaica Bay

STARRETT CITY

CANARSIE

Rockaway Pkwy.

Remsen Ave.

Ralph Ave.

Utica Ave.

Kings Hwy.

Foster Ave.

Flatlands Ave.

Church St.

FLATBUSH

Clarendon Rd.

Ave. D

Flatbush Ave.

Ocean Ave.

Beverley Rd.

Foster Ave.

Ocean Pkwy.

McDonald Ave.

KENSINGTON

Greenwood Cemetery

SEE PARK SLOPE AND PROSPECT PARK, MAP 7, 358

BERGEN BEACH

MILL BASIN

FLATLANDS

Marine Park

Fillmore Ave.

Gerritsen Ave.

MIDWOOD

GRAVESEND

Ave. P

Ave. U

Kings Hwy.

Washington Cemetery

18th Ave.

Stillwell Ave.

Floyd Bennett Field

Flatbush Ave.

GERRITSEN BEACH

SHEEPSHEAD BAY

Ave. X

Emmons Ave.

Shore Pkwy.

Ocean Pkwy.

Rockaway Inlet

MANHATTAN BEACH

Manhattan Beach Park

BRIGHTON BEACH

Brighton 2nd St.

Brighton Beach Ave.

Neptune Ave.

CONEY ISLAND

SEA GATE

Surf Ave.

Boardwalk

Coney Island Beach

Dreier-Offerman Park

Cropsey Ave.

BENSONHURST

BATH BEACH

Bensonhurst Park

Shore Pkwy.

86th St.

65th St.

BOROUGH PARK

SUNSET PARK

Sunset Park

39th St.

Fort Hamilton Pkwy.

278

BAY RIDGE

FORT HAMILTON

Fort Hamilton

Dyker Golf Course

Dyker Park

Bay Ridge Ave.

12th Ave.

Verrazano Narrows Bridge

Lower Bay

Canarsie Park

1 mile

1 km

0

0

Williamsburg and Greenpoint

🏛 MUSEUMS & GALLERIES
Figureworks, **1** *C3*
Parker's Box, **2** *C3*
Pierogi, **3** *C3*
The Williamsburg Art and Historical Center, **4** *B4*

🌙 NIGHTLIFE
Artland, **5** *D3*
Brooklyn Ale House, **6** *C2*
Galapagos, **7** *B2*

Pete's Candy Store, **8** *D3*
Union Pool, **9** *D3*

🍴 FOOD
Bliss, **10** *C3*
Bonita, **11** *B3*
Chai, **12** *C3*
Diner, **13** *B4*
DuMont Restaurant, **14** *D3*
Sea, **15** *C3*

● SIGHTS
Brooklyn Brewery, **16** *C2*
Russian Orthodox Cathedral, **17** *C2*
St. Anthony - St. Alphonsus Church, **18** *C1*

★ ARTS & ENTERTAINMENT
Brick Theater, **19** *D3*
Charlie Pineapple Theater, **20** *C3*

Go Yoga, **21** *C3*
Metropolitan Pool and Fitness Center, **22** *C3*

🛍 SHOPPING
Beacon's Closet, **23** *C2*
Girdle Company, **24** *C3*
KCDC, **25** *C3*
Ugly Luggage, **26** *C3*
Vice Versa, **27** *C3*

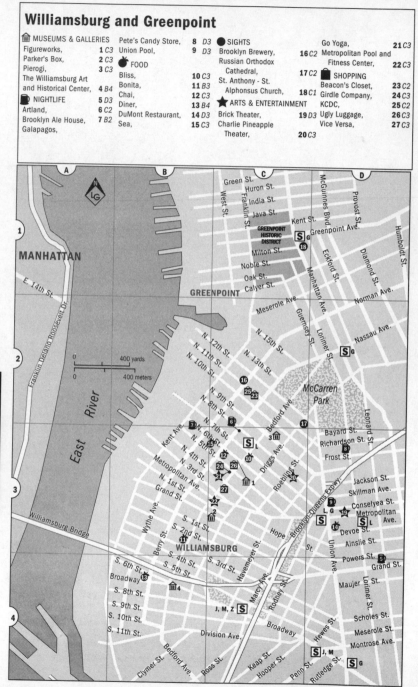

MANHATTAN

E. 14th St.

East River

Franklin Delano Roosevelt Dr.

MAP APPENDIX

Green St.
Huron St.
India St.
Java St.
West St.
Franklin St.
Kent St.
Greenpoint Ave.
McGuinness Blvd.
Provost St.
Humboldt St.

GREENPOINT HISTORIC DISTRICT **18**

Milton St.
Noble St.
Oak St.
Calyer St.

GREENPOINT

Meserole Ave.
Eckford St.
Diamond St.
Norman Ave.

Manhattan Ave.
Guernsey St.
Lorimer St.
Nassau Ave.
Leonard St.

N. 15th St.
N. 13th St.
N. 12th St.
N. 11th St.
N. 10th St.
N. 9th St.
N. 8th St.
N. 7th St.
N. 6th St.
N. 5th St.
N. 4th St.
N. 3rd St.

McCarren Park

Bayard St.
Richardson St.
Frost St. **8**

Bedford Ave.
Driggs Ave.
Roebling St.

16
25 **23**
7
5
6
3 🏛
17
12
10
24 **26**
27
1
20

Kent Ave.
Metropolitan Ave.
N. 1st St.
Grand St.

Williamsburg Bridge

Wythe Ave.
Berry St.

WILLIAMSBURG

S. 1st St.
S. 2nd St.
S. 3rd St.
S. 4th St.
S. 5th St.
S. 6th St.
Broadway **13**
S. 8th St.
S. 9th St.
S. 10th St.
S. 11th St.

Havemeyer St.
Hope St.
Marcy Ave.
Rodney St.
Brooklyn-Queens Expwy.
Union Ave.

Jackson St.
Skillman Ave.
Conselyea St.
Metropolitan Ave.
Devoe St.
Ainslie St.
Powers St.
Grand St.
Maujer St.
Lorimer St.
Scholes St.
Meserole St.
Montrose St.

9
19

2
17
4 🏛

Bedford Ave.
Clymer St.
Ross St.
Keap St.
Hooper St.
Penn St.
Rutledge St.

Division Ave.
Broadway

J, M, Z **S**
J, M **S**
S G

0   400 yards
0   400 meters

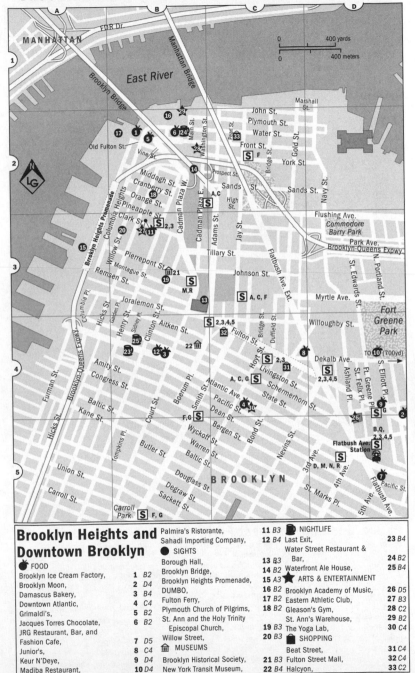

Brooklyn Heights and Downtown Brooklyn

🍎 FOOD

Brooklyn Ice Cream Factory,	1	B2
Brooklyn Moon,	2	D4
Damascus Bakery,	3	B4
Downtown Atlantic,	4	C4
Grimaldi's,	5	B2
Jacques Torres Chocolate,	6	B2
JRG Restaurant, Bar, and Fashion Cafe,	7	D5
Junior's,	8	C4
Keur N'Deye,	9	D4
Madiba Restaurant,	10	D4

Palmira's Ristorante,
Sahadi Importing Company,

● SIGHTS

Borough Hall,
Brooklyn Bridge,
Brooklyn Heights Promenade,
DUMBO,
Fulton Ferry,
Plymouth Church of Pilgrims,
St. Ann and the Holy Trinity
  Episcopal Church,
Willow Street,

🏛 MUSEUMS

Brooklyn Historical Society,
New York Transit Museum,

	11	B3
	12	B4
	13	B3
	14	B2
	15	A3
	16	B2
	17	B2
	18	B2
	19	B3
	20	B3
	21	B3
	22	B4

🍷 NIGHTLIFE

Last Exit,
Water Street Restaurant &
  Bar,
Waterfront Ale House,

★ ARTS & ENTERTAINMENT

Brooklyn Academy of Music,
Eastern Athletic Club,
Gleason's Gym,
St. Ann's Warehouse,
The Yoga Lab,

🛍 SHOPPING

Beat Street,
Fulton Street Mall,
Halcyon,

	23	B4
	24	B2
	25	B4
	26	D5
	27	B3
	28	C2
	29	B2
	30	C4
	31	C4
	32	C4
	33	C2

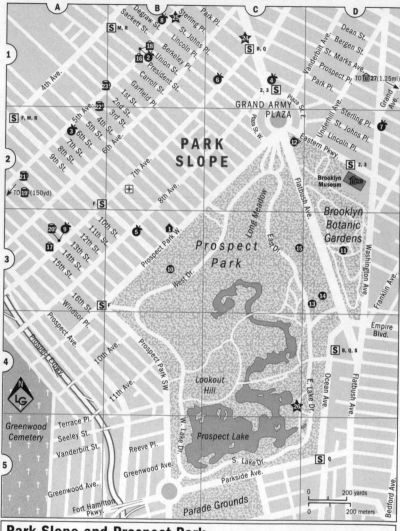

Park Slope and Prospect Park

🏠 ACCOMMODATIONS
Bed & Breakfast on the Park,   1 B3

🍴 FOOD
Beso,   2 B1
Chip & Curry Shop,   3 A2
Christie's Bakery,   4 C1
Dizzy's,   5 B3
Santa Fe Grille,   6 C1
Tom's Restaurant,   7 D2
V-Spot,   8 B1
Watana Siam,   9 A3

🍎 SIGHTS
Bandshell,   10 B3
Brooklyn Botanic Gardens,   11 D3
Brooklyn Public Library,   12 C2
Carousel,   13 D4
Leffert's Homestead,   14 D3
Prospect Park Wildlife
  Center/Zoo,   15 C3

🛍 SHOPPING
Beacon's Closet,   16 B2
Bird,   17 A3
Something Else,   18 B2

🍸 NIGHTLIFE
Buttermilk Bar,   19 A2
Cafe Steinhoff,   20 A3
Commonwealth,   21 A2
The Gate,   22 A1
Loki Lounge,   23 A1

★ ARTS & ENTERTAINMENT
Park Slope Sports Club,   24 C1
Sampaw,   25 B2
Wollman Rink,   26 C4

🏛 MUSEUMS
Brooklyn Children's Museum,   27 D1
Brooklyn Museum of Art,   28 D2

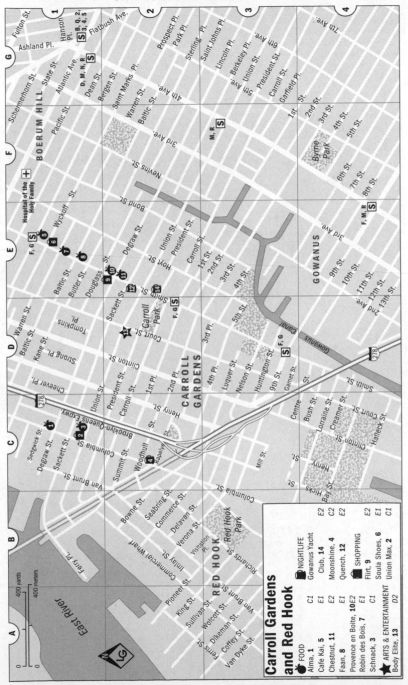

Carroll Gardens and Red Hook

🍴 FOOD
Alma, 1	C1
Cafe Kai, 5	E1
Chestnut, 11	E2
Faan, 8	E1
Provence en Boite, 10	E2
Robin des Bois, 7	E1
Schnack, 3	C1

⭐ ARTS & ENTERTAINMENT
Body Elite, 13	D2

🍸 NIGHTLIFE
Gowanus Yacht Club, 14	E2
Moonshine, 4	C2
Quench, 12	E2

🛍 SHOPPING
Flirt, 9	E2
Soula Shoes, 6	E1
Union Max, 2	C1

MANHATTAN

Little Neck Bay

Throgs Neck Bridge

BAYSIDE

Bell Blvd.

BAY TERRACE

Clearview Expwy.

Alley Park

Lewis Blvd.

Bay Island Pkwy.

Cross Island Pkwy.

Francis

Northern Blvd.

46th Ave.

Cunningham Park

JAMAICA ESTATES

HOLLIS

ST. ALBANS

Linden Blvd.

Merrick Blvd.

Hillside Ave.

Jamaica Ave.

Guy Brewer Ave.

FRESH MEADOWS

UTOPIA

164th St.

HILLCREST

JAMAICA

SOUTH JAMAICA

Rockaway Blvd.

Bronx-Whitestone Bridge

WHITESTONE

AUBURNDALE

Kissena Park

Main St.

Willow Lake Nature Area

Van-Wyck-Expwy.

Lefferts Blvd.

Flushing Bay

East River

Rikers Island

COLLEGE POINT

FLUSHING

Flushing Meadow Corona Park

Meadow Lake

Grand Central Pkwy.

KEW GARDENS

RICHMOND HILL

LaGuardia International Airport

CORONA

Flushing

SEE ELMHURST, CORONA, AND FLUSHING MAP P. 363

Junction Blvd.

ELMHURST

Queens Blvd.

Forest Park

Myrtle Ave.

Woodhaven Blvd.

WOODHAVEN

OZONE PARK

Conduit Ave.

EAST ELMHURST

Astoria Blvd.

Northern Blvd.

JACKSON HEIGHTS

Roosevelt Ave.

Broadway

REGO PARK

Metropolitan Ave.

FOREST HILLS

Jackie Robinson Interboro Pkwy.

Jamaica Ave.

Ditmars Blvd.

ASTORIA

Grand Central Pkwy.

21st St.

31st St.

WOODSIDE

SUNNYSIDE

Long Island Expwy.

Queens Blvd.

MIDDLE VILLAGE

MASPETH

RIDGEWOOD

GLENDALE

Triborough Bridge

LONG ISLAND CITY

HUNTER POINT

Queensboro Bridge

FDR Dr.

SEE ASTORIA AND LONG ISLAND CITY MAP P. 362

Queens Midtown Tunnel

Brooklyn

Manhattan Bridge

Atlantic Ave.

QUEENS

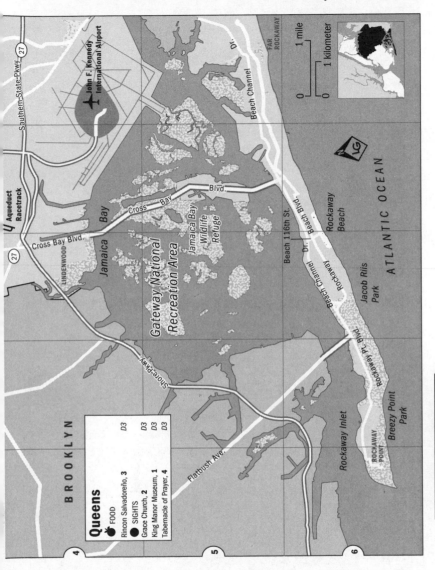

BROOKLYN

Queens

🍴 FOOD
Rincon Salvadoreño, 3   D3

● SIGHTS
Grace Church, 2   D3
King Manor Museum, 1   D3
Tabernacle of Prayer, 4   D3

Southern State Pkwy

John F. Kennedy
International Airport

Aqueduct
Racetrack

Cross Bay Blvd.

LINDENWOOD

Jamaica
Bay

Cross Bay Blvd.

Gateway National
Recreation Area

Jamaica Bay
Wildlife
Refuge

Shore Pkwy.

Flatbush Ave.

Rockaway Inlet

ROCKAWAY
POINT

Breezy Point
Park

Jacob Riis
Park

Rockaway Pt. Blvd.

Beach Channel Dr.

Rockaway

Beach 116th St

Beach Blvd.

Rockaway
Beach

Beach Channel

FAR
ROCKAWAY

ATLANTIC OCEAN

1 mile

1 kilometer

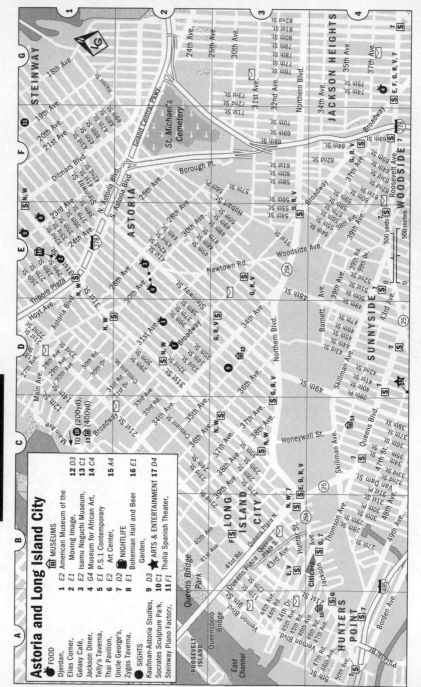

Astoria and Long Island City

🍴 **FOOD**
Djerdan, 1 E2
Elias Corner, 2 E1
Galaxy Café, 3 E2
Jackson Diner, 4 G4
Telly's Taverna, 5 E1
Thai Pavilion, 6 E2
Uncle George's, 7 D2
Zygos Taverna, 8 E1

● **SIGHTS**
Kaufman-Astoria Studios, 9 D3
Socrates Sculpture Park, 10 C1
Steinway Piano Factory, 11 F1

🏛 **MUSEUMS**
American Museum of the Moving Image, 12 D3
Isamu Noguchi Museum, 13 C1
Museum for African Art, 14 C4
P.S.1 Contemporary Art Center, 15 A4

🎭 **NIGHTLIFE**
Bohemian Hall and Beer Garden, 16 E1

★ **ARTS & ENTERTAINMENT**
Thalia Spanish Theater, 17 D4

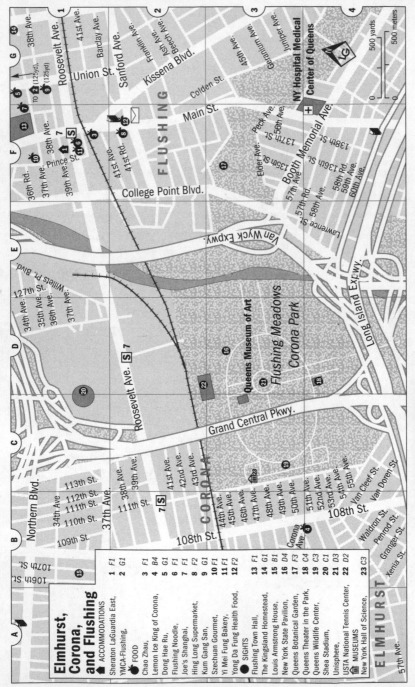

MAP APPENDIX

Elmhurst, Corona, and Flushing

▲ ACCOMMODATIONS

Sheraton LaGuardia East,	1 F1
YMCA-Flushing,	2 G1

● FOOD

Chao Zhau,	3 F1
Lemon Ice King of Corona,	4 B4
Dong Hae Ru,	5 G1
Flushing Noodle,	6 F1
Joe's Shanghai,	7 F1
Hing Long Supermarket,	8 F2
Kum Gang San,	9 G1
Szechuan Gourmet,	10 F1
Yi Mei Fung Bakery,	11 F1
Yong Da Fung Health Food,	12 F2

● SIGHTS

Flushing Town Hall,	13 F1
The Kingsland Homestead,	14 G1
Louis Armstrong House,	15 B1
New York State Pavilion,	16 D4
Queens Botanical Garden,	17 F3
Queens Theater in the Park,	18 C4
Queens Wildlife Center,	19 C3
Shea Stadium,	20 C1
Unisphere,	21 D3
USTA National Tennis Center,	22 D2

🏛 MUSEUMS

New York Hall of Science,	23 C3

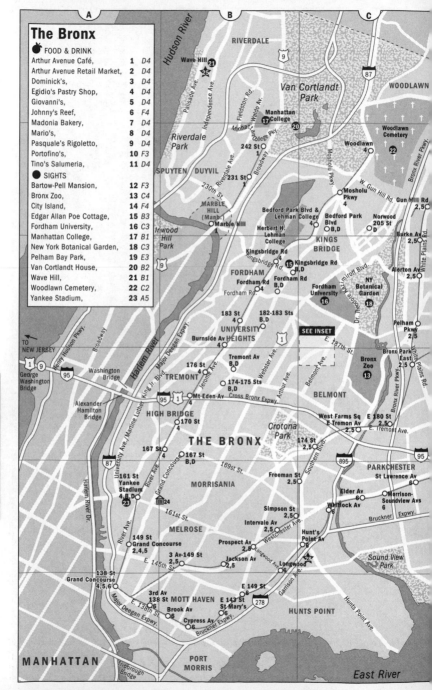

The Bronx

🍎 FOOD & DRINK

Arthur Avenue Café,	1	D4
Arthur Avenue Retail Market,	2	D4
Dominick's,	3	D4
Egidio's Pastry Shop,	4	D4
Giovanni's,	5	D4
Johnny's Reef,	6	F4
Madonia Bakery,	7	D4
Mario's,	8	D4
Pasquale's Rigoletto,	9	D4
Portofino's,	10	F3
Tino's Salumeria,	11	D4

● SIGHTS

Bartow-Pell Mansion,	12	F3
Bronx Zoo,	13	C4
City Island,	14	F4
Edgar Allan Poe Cottage,	15	B3
Fordham University,	16	C3
Manhattan College,	17	B1
New York Botanical Garden,	18	C3
Pelham Bay Park,	19	E3
Van Cortlandt House,	20	B2
Wave Hill,	21	B1
Woodlawn Cemetery,	22	C2
Yankee Stadium,	23	A5

D

Wakefield
241 St
2,5

WESTCHESTER
COUNTY

Nereid Av
2,5

Nereid Av.

E

233rd St.

233 St
2,5

EDENWALD

Baychester Ave.

Eastchester
Dyre Av
5

225 St
2,5

219 St
2,5

222nd St.

EASTCHESTER

WILLIAMS
BRIDGE

Baychester
Av
5

95

1

E. Gun Hill Rd.

Eastchester Rd.

Boston Rd.

Gun Hill Rd
5

Allerton Ave.

Williamsbridge Rd.

Pelham
Parkway
6

Bronx and Pelham Pkwy.

WESTCHESTER
HEIGHTS

Morris
Park
5

Hutchinson River Pkwy.

Pelham Bay
Park
6

Pelham Bay
Park

19

12

Pelham Bay Park

Orchard
Beach

Shore Rd.

City Island Rd.

Bridge St.

City Island Rd.

Eastchester Bay

Terrace St.

Minnieford
City Island Av.

10

**Belmont
Inset**

E. 187th St.

Church of
Our Lady
of Mt.
Carmel

11

Hoffman St.

Arthur Ave.

4

Hughes Ave.

E. 186th St.

Belmont Ave.

Belmont
Ave.

Crescent Ave.

5

3 7

1 2 8

9

Third Ave.

400 yards

0

0   400 meters

Buhre Av
6

Middletown Rd
6

95

E. Trenton Ave.

695

Fordham St.

14

City Island Av.

CITY
ISLAND

4

6

N

LG

0   1 mile

0   1 kilometer

5

278

95

SOUNDVIEW

White Plains Rd.

THROGS NECK

295

CLASON POINT

Ferry Point
Park

678

Cross Bronx Expwy. Ext.

Bronx-Whitestone Bridge

TO QUEENS AND
LONG ISLAND

Throgs Neck Bridge

TO QUEENS AND
LONG ISLAND

6

1

F

🏛 MUSEUMS
The Bronx Museum
of the Arts,   **24** *B5*
★ ARTS & ENTERTAINMENT
Dances for Wave Hill, **25** *B1*
The Point,   **26** *C5*

1

2

3

4

5

6

MAP APPENDIX

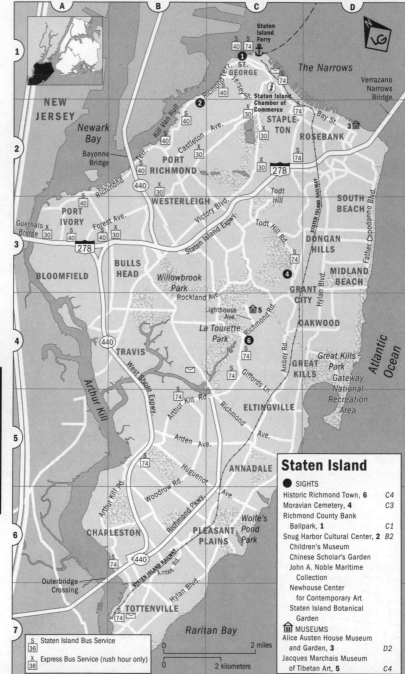

NEW JERSEY

Newark Bay

The Narrows

Staten Island Ferry

Verrazano Narrows Bridge

Bayonne Bridge

Kill Van Kull

ST. GEORGE

Staten Island Chamber of Commerce

STAPLE-TON

ROSEBANK

Castleton Ave.

PORT RICHMOND

278

SOUTH BEACH

WESTERLEIGH

Victory Blvd.

Todt Hill

DONGAN HILLS

MIDLAND BEACH

Staten Island Railway

Father Capodanno Blvd.

PORT IVORY

Forest Ave.

Goethals Bridge

Richmond

Staten Island Expwy.

278

BLOOMFIELD

BULLS HEAD

Willowbrook Park

Rockland Ave.

Lighthouse Ave.

La Tourette Park

GRANT CITY

OAKWOOD

Hylan Blvd.

TRAVIS

West Shore Expwy.

Arthur Kill

Richmond Rd.

Amboy Rd.

GREAT KILLS

Great Kills Park Gateway National Recreation Area

Atlantic Ocean

Giffords Ln.

ELTINGVILLE

Arthur Kill Rd.

Richmond

Ave.

Arden Ave.

Huguenot

ANNADALE

Woodrow Rd.

Richmond Pkwy.

Ave.

Wolfe's Pond Park

CHARLESTON

PLEASANT PLAINS

440

STATEN ISLAND RAILWAY

Amboy

Hylan Blvd.

Outerbridge Crossing

TOTTENVILLE

Raritan Bay

0   2 miles

0   2 kilometers

Staten Island

● SIGHTS

Historic Richmond Town, **6**	C4
Moravian Cemetery, **4**	C3
Richmond County Bank	
Ballpark, **1**	C1
Snug Harbor Cultural Center, **2**	B2
Children's Museum	
Chinese Scholar's Garden	
John A. Noble Maritime	
Collection	
Newhouse Center	
for Contemporary Art	
Staten Island Botanical	
Garden	

🏛 MUSEUMS

Alice Austen House Museum	
and Garden, **3**	D2
Jacques Marchais Museum	
of Tibetan Art, **5**	C4

S   Staten Island Bus Service
36

X   Express Bus Service (rush hour only)
36

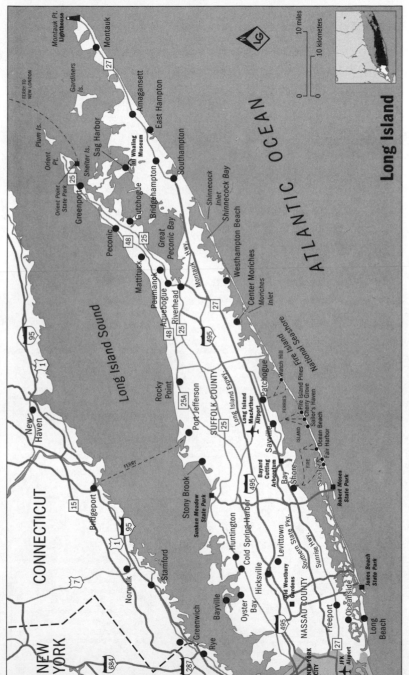

MAP APPENDIX

Long Island

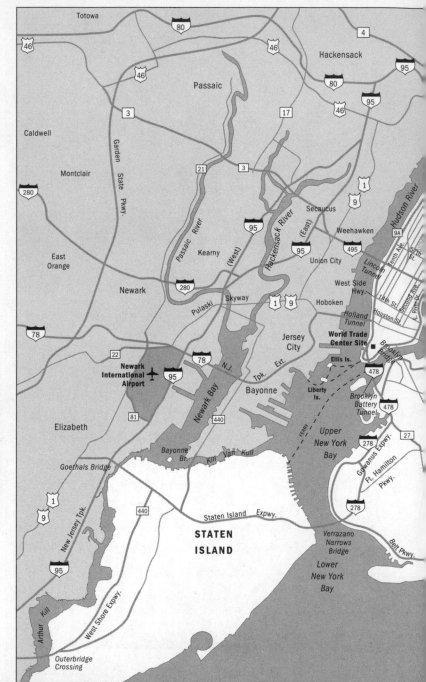

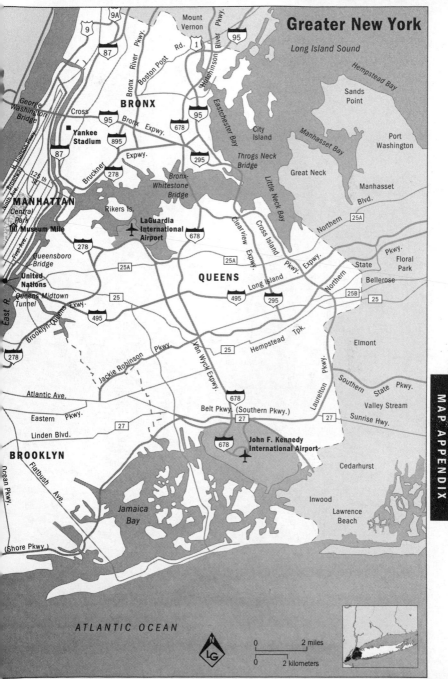

Greater New York

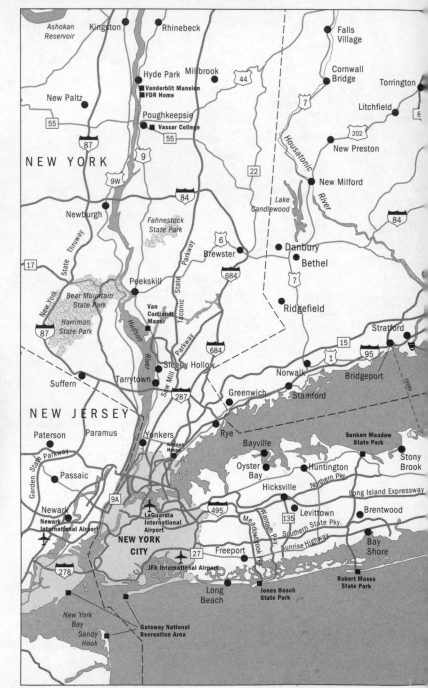

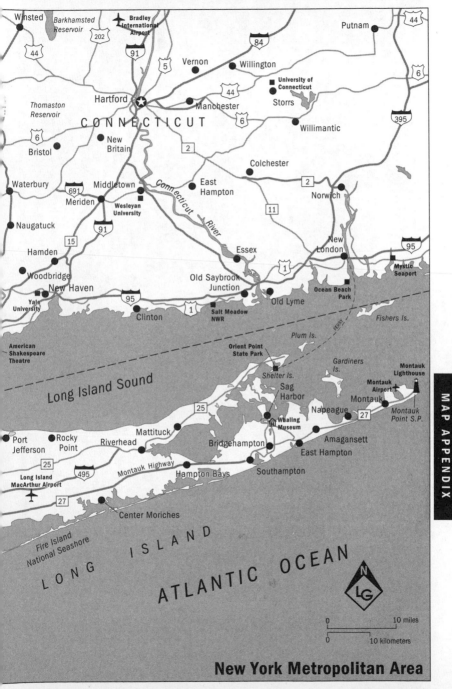

New York Metropolitan Area

Atlantic City

ACCOMMODATIONS
Comfort Inn, **7**
Inn of the Irish Pub, **8**

● **FOOD**
AC Diner, **3**
Evo, **5**
Inn of the Irish Pub, **9**
Sundae Ice Cream, **4**

Tony's Baltimore Grille, **2**
Tun Tavern, **6**
White House Sub Shop, **1**

INDEX

INDEX

INDEX

INDEX